C# 7.0

ALL-IN-ONE

C# 7.0

ALL-IN-ONE

by John Paul Mueller,
Bill Sempf, and Chuck Sphar

for
dummies®
A Wiley Brand

C# 7.0 All-in-One For Dummies®

Published by: **John Wiley & Sons, Inc.,** 111 River Street, Hoboken, NJ 07030-5774, www.wiley.com

Copyright © 2018 by John Wiley & Sons, Inc., Hoboken, New Jersey

Media and software compilation copyright © 2018 by John Wiley & Sons, Inc. All rights reserved.

Published simultaneously in Canada

No part of this publication may be reproduced, stored in a retrieval system or transmitted in any form or by any means, electronic, mechanical, photocopying, recording, scanning or otherwise, except as permitted under Sections 107 or 108 of the 1976 United States Copyright Act, without the prior written permission of the Publisher. Requests to the Publisher for permission should be addressed to the Permissions Department, John Wiley & Sons, Inc., 111 River Street, Hoboken, NJ 07030, (201) 748-6011, fax (201) 748-6008, or online at http://www.wiley.com/go/permissions.

Trademarks: Wiley, For Dummies, the Dummies Man logo, Dummies.com, Making Everything Easier, and related trade dress are trademarks or registered trademarks of John Wiley & Sons, Inc. and may not be used without written permission. All other trademarks are the property of their respective owners. John Wiley & Sons, Inc. is not associated with any product or vendor mentioned in this book.

LIMIT OF LIABILITY/DISCLAIMER OF WARRANTY: THE PUBLISHER AND THE AUTHOR MAKE NO REPRESENTATIONS OR WARRANTIES WITH RESPECT TO THE ACCURACY OR COMPLETENESS OF THE CONTENTS OF THIS WORK AND SPECIFICALLY DISCLAIM ALL WARRANTIES, INCLUDING WITHOUT LIMITATION WARRANTIES OF FITNESS FOR A PARTICULAR PURPOSE. NO WARRANTY MAY BE CREATED OR EXTENDED BY SALES OR PROMOTIONAL MATERIALS. THE ADVICE AND STRATEGIES CONTAINED HEREIN MAY NOT BE SUITABLE FOR EVERY SITUATION. THIS WORK IS SOLD WITH THE UNDERSTANDING THAT THE PUBLISHER IS NOT ENGAGED IN RENDERING LEGAL, ACCOUNTING, OR OTHER PROFESSIONAL SERVICES. IF PROFESSIONAL ASSISTANCE IS REQUIRED, THE SERVICES OF A COMPETENT PROFESSIONAL PERSON SHOULD BE SOUGHT. NEITHER THE PUBLISHER NOR THE AUTHOR SHALL BE LIABLE FOR DAMAGES ARISING HEREFROM. THE FACT THAT AN ORGANIZATION OR WEBSITE IS REFERRED TO IN THIS WORK AS A CITATION AND/OR A POTENTIAL SOURCE OF FURTHER INFORMATION DOES NOT MEAN THAT THE AUTHOR OR THE PUBLISHER ENDORSES THE INFORMATION THE ORGANIZATION OR WEBSITE MAY PROVIDE OR RECOMMENDATIONS IT MAY MAKE. FURTHER, READERS SHOULD BE AWARE THAT INTERNET WEBSITES LISTED IN THIS WORK MAY HAVE CHANGED OR DISAPPEARED BETWEEN WHEN THIS WORK WAS WRITTEN AND WHEN IT IS READ.

For general information on our other products and services, please contact our Customer Care Department within the U.S. at 877-762-2974, outside the U.S. at 317-572-3993, or fax 317-572-4002. For technical support, please visit https://hub.wiley.com/community/support/dummies.

Wiley publishes in a variety of print and electronic formats and by print-on-demand. Some material included with standard print versions of this book may not be included in e-books or in print-on-demand. If this book refers to media such as a CD or DVD that is not included in the version you purchased, you may download this material at http://booksupport.wiley.com. For more information about Wiley products, visit www.wiley.com.

Library of Congress Control Number: 2017958295

ISBN: 978-111-9-42811-4; ISBN 978-111-9-42810-7 (ebk); ISBN ePDF 978-111-9-42812-1 (ebk)

Manufactured in the United States of America

33614080509341

10 9 8 7 6 5 4 3 2 1

Contents at a Glance

Table of Contents

Introduction

C# is an amazing language! You can use this single language to do everything from desktop development to creating web applications and even web-based application programming interfaces (APIs). While other developers have to overcome deficiencies in their languages to create even a subset of the application types that C# supports with aplomb, you can be coding your application, testing, and then sitting on the beach enjoying the fruits of your efforts. Of course, any language that does this much requires a bit of explanation, and *C# 7.0 All-in-One For Dummies* is your doorway to this new adventure in development.

So, why do you need *C# 7.0 All-in-One For Dummies* specifically? This book stresses learning the basics of the C# language before you do anything else. With this in mind, the book begins with all the C# basics in Books 1 through 3, helps you get Visual Studio 2017 installed in Book 4, and then takes you through more advanced development tasks, including basic web development, in Books 5 through 6. Using this book helps you get the most you can from C# 7.0 in the least possible time.

About This Book

Even if you have past experience with C#, the new features in C# 7.0 will have you producing feature-rich applications in an even shorter time than you may have before. *C# 7.0 All-in-One For Dummies* introduces you to all these new features. For example, you discover the new pattern-matching techniques that C# 7.0 provides. You also discover the wonders of using tuples and local functions. Even the use of literals has improved, but you'll have to look inside to find out how. This particular book is designed to make using C# 7.0 fast and easy; it removes the complexity that you may have experienced when trying to learn about these topics online.

To help you absorb the concepts, this book uses the following conventions:

» Text that you're meant to type just as it appears in the book is in **bold**. The exception is when you're working through a step list: Because each step is bold, the text to type is not bold.

>> Words for you to type that are also in *italics* are meant as placeholders; you need to replace them with something that works for you. For example, if you see "Type **Your Name** and press Enter," you need to replace *Your Name* with your actual name.

>> I also use *italics* for terms I define. This means that you don't have to rely on other sources to provide the definitions you need.

>> Web addresses and programming code appear in `monofont`. If you're reading a digital version of this book on a device connected to the Internet, you can click the live link to visit a website, like this: `www.dummies.com`.

>> When you need to click command sequences, you see them separated by a special arrow, like this: File⇨New File, which tells you to click File and then click New File.

Foolish Assumptions

You might have a hard time believing that I've assumed anything about you — after all, I haven't even met you yet! Although most assumptions are indeed foolish, I made certain assumptions to provide a starting point for the book.

The most important assumption is that you know how to use Windows, have a copy of Windows properly installed, and are familiar with using Windows applications. If installing an application is still a mystery to you, you might find this book a bit hard to use. While reading this book, you need to install applications, discover how to use them, and create simple applications of your own.

You also need to know how to work with the Internet to some degree. Many of the materials, including the downloadable source, appear online, and you need to download them in order to get the maximum value from the book. In addition, Book 6 assumes that you have a certain knowledge of the Internet when working through web-based applications and web-based services.

Icons Used in This Book

As you read this book, you encounter icons in the margins that indicate material of special interest (or not, as the case may be!). Here's what the icons mean:

Tips are nice because they help you save time or perform some task without a lot of extra work. The tips in this book are timesaving techniques or pointers to resources that you should try so that you can get the maximum benefit when performing C#-related tasks.

I don't want to sound like an angry parent or some kind of maniac, but you should avoid doing anything that's marked with a Warning icon. Otherwise, you might find that your configuration fails to work as expected, you get incorrect results from seemingly bulletproof processes, or (in the worst-case scenario) you lose data.

Whenever you see this icon, think advanced tip or technique. You might find these tidbits of useful information just too boring for words, or they could contain the solution you need to get a C# application running. Skip these bits of information whenever you like.

If you don't get anything else out of a particular chapter or section, remember the material marked by this icon. This text usually contains an essential process or a bit of information that you must know to work with C#.

Beyond the Book

This book isn't the end of your C# learning experience — it's really just the beginning. John Mueller provides online content to make this book more flexible and better able to meet your needs. Also, you can send John email. He'll address your book-specific questions and tell you how updates to C# or its associated add-ons affect book content through blog posts. Here are some cool online additions to this book:

>> **Cheat sheet:** You remember using crib notes in school to make a better mark on a test, don't you? You do? Well, a cheat sheet is sort of like that. It provides you with some special notes about tasks that you can do with C# that not every other person knows. To find the cheat sheet for this book, go to www.dummies.com and search for *C# 7.0 All-in-One For Dummies Cheat Sheet*. It contains really neat information such as how to figure out which template you want to use.

>> **Updates:** Sometimes changes happen. For example, I might not have seen an upcoming change when I looked into my crystal ball during the writing of this book. In the past, this possibility simply meant that the book became outdated and less useful, but you can now find updates to the book at www.dummies.com.

In addition to these updates, check out the blog posts with answers to reader questions and demonstrations of useful book-related techniques at http://blog.johnmuellerbooks.com/.

» **Companion files:** Hey! Who really wants to type all the code in the book manually? Most readers prefer to spend their time actually working with C#, creating amazing new applications that change the world, and seeing the interesting things they can do, rather than typing. Fortunately for you, the examples used in the book are available for download, so all you need to do is read the book to learn C# development techniques. You can find these files at www.dummies.com. You can also download Online Chapters 1–7. To find the source code and online chapters, search this book's title at www.dummies.com and locate the Downloads tab on the page that appears.

Where to Go from Here

Anyone who is unfamiliar with C# should start with Book 1, Chapter 1 and move from there to the end of the book. This book is designed to make it easy for you to discover the benefits of using C# from the outset. Later, after you've seen enough C# code, you can install Visual Studio and then try the programming examples found in the first three minibooks.

This book assumes that you want to see C# code from the outset. However, if you want to interact with that code, you really need to have a copy of Visual Studio 2017 installed. (Some examples will not work at all with older Visual Studio versions.) With this in mind, you may want to skip right to Book 4 to discover how to get your own copy of Visual Studio 2017. To help ensure that everyone can participate, this book focuses on the features offered by Visual Studio 2017 Community Edition, which is a free download. That's right, you can discover the wonders of C# 7.0 without paying a dime!

The more you know about C#, the further you can start in the book. If all you're really interested in is an update of your existing skills, check out Book 1, Chapter 1 to discover the changes in C#. Then, scan the first three minibooks looking for points of interest. Install C# by using the instructions in Book 4, Chapter 1, and then move on toward the advanced techniques found in later chapters.

1

The Basics of C# Programming

Contents at a Glance

Chapter **1**

Creating Your First C# Console Application

This chapter explains a little bit about computers, computer languages — including the computer language C# (pronounced "see sharp") — and Visual Studio 2017. You then create a simple program written in C#.

Getting a Handle on Computer Languages, C#, and .NET

A computer is an amazingly fast but incredibly stupid servant. Computers will do anything you ask them to (within reason); they do it extremely fast — and they're getting faster all the time.

Unfortunately, computers don't understand anything that resembles a human language. Oh, you may come back at me and say something like, "Hey, my telephone lets me dial my friend by just speaking his name." Yes, a tiny computer runs your telephone. So that computer speaks English. But that's a computer *program* that understands English, not the computer itself.

The language that computers truly understand is *machine language.* It's possible, but extremely difficult and error prone, for humans to write machine language.

Humans and computers have decided to meet somewhere in the middle. Programmers create programs in a language that isn't nearly as free as human speech, but it's a lot more flexible and easier to use than machine language. The languages occupying this middle ground — C#, for example — are *high-level* computer languages. (*High* is a relative term here.)

What's a program?

What is a program? In a practical sense, a Windows program is an executable file that you can run by double-clicking its icon. For example, Microsoft Word, the editor used to write this book, is a program. You call that an *executable program,* or *executable* for short. The names of executable program files generally end with the extension `.exe`. Word, for example, is `Winword.exe`.

But a program is something else as well. An executable program consists of one or more *source files.* A C# *source file,* for instance, is a text file that contains a sequence of C# commands, which fit together according to the laws of C# grammar. This file is known as a *source file,* probably because it's a source of frustration and anxiety.

Uh, grammar? There's going to be grammar? Just the C# kind, which is much easier than the kind most people struggled with in junior high school.

What's C#?

The C# programming language is one of those intermediate languages that programmers use to create executable programs. C# combines the range of the powerful but complicated C++ (pronounced "see plus plus") with the ease of use of the friendly but more verbose Visual Basic. (Visual Basic's newer .NET incarnation is almost on par with C# in most respects. As the flagship language of .NET, C# tends to introduce most new features first.) A C# program file carries the extension `.cs`.

Some people have pointed out that C sharp and D flat are the same note, but you shouldn't refer to this new language as "D flat" within earshot of Redmond, Washington.

C# is

>> **Flexible:** C# programs can execute on the current machine, or they can be transmitted over the web and executed on some distant computer.

>> **Powerful:** C# has essentially the same command set as C++ but with the rough edges filed smooth.

>> **Easier to use:** C# error-proofs the commands responsible for most C++ errors, so you spend far less time chasing down those errors.

>> **Visually oriented:** The .NET code library that C# uses for many of its capabilities provides the help needed to readily create complicated display frames with drop-down lists, tabbed windows, grouped buttons, scroll bars, and background images, to name just a few.

TIP

.NET is pronounced "dot net."

>> **Internet-friendly:** C# plays a pivotal role in the .NET Framework, Microsoft's current approach to programming for Windows, the Internet, and beyond.

>> **Secure:** Any language intended for use on the Internet must include serious security to protect against malevolent hackers.

Finally, C# is an integral part of .NET.

REMEMBER

This book is primarily about the C# language. If your primary goal is to use Visual Studio, program Windows 8 or 10 apps, or ASP.NET, the *For Dummies* books on those topics go well with this book. You can find a good amount of information later in this book on how to use C# to write Windows, web, and service applications.

What's .NET?

.NET began several years ago as Microsoft's strategy to open the web to mere mortals like you and me. Today, it's bigger than that, encompassing everything Microsoft does. In particular, it's the new way to program for Windows. It also gives a C-based language, C#, the simple, visual tools that made Visual Basic so popular.

A little background helps you see the roots of C# and .NET. Internet programming was traditionally very difficult in older languages such as C and C++. Sun Microsystems responded to that problem by creating the Java programming language. To create Java, Sun took the grammar of C++, made it a lot more user friendly, and centered it around distributed development.

REMEMBER

When programmers say "distributed," they're describing geographically dispersed computers running programs that talk to each other — via the Internet in many cases.

When Microsoft licensed Java some years ago, it ran into legal difficulties with Sun over changes it wanted to make to the language. As a result, Microsoft more or less gave up on Java and started looking for ways to compete with it.

Being forced out of Java was just as well because Java has a serious problem: Although Java is a capable language, you pretty much have to write your entire program *in* Java to get the full benefit. Microsoft had too many developers and too many millions of lines of existing source code, so Microsoft had to come up with some way to support multiple languages. Enter .NET.

.NET is a framework, in many ways similar to Java's libraries — and the C# language is highly similar to the Java language. Just as Java is both the language itself and its extensive code library, C# is really much more than just the keywords and syntax of the C# language. It's those things empowered by a well-organized library containing thousands of code elements that simplify doing about any kind of programming you can imagine, from web-based databases to cryptography to the humble Windows dialog box.

Microsoft would claim that .NET is much superior to Sun's suite of web tools based on Java, but that's not the point. Unlike Java, .NET doesn't require you to rewrite existing programs. A Visual Basic programmer can add just a few lines to make an existing program *web-knowledgeable* (meaning that it knows how to get data off the Internet). .NET supports all the common Microsoft languages — and hundreds of other languages written by third-party vendors. However, C# is the flagship language of the .NET fleet. C# is always the first language to access every new feature of .NET.

What is Visual Studio 2017? What about Visual C#?

(You sure ask lots of questions.) The first "Visual" language from Microsoft was Visual Basic. The first popular C-based language from Microsoft was Visual C++. Like Visual Basic, it had Visual in its name because it had a built-in graphical user interface (GUI — pronounced "GOO-ee"). This GUI included everything you needed to develop nifty-gifty C++ programs.

Eventually, Microsoft rolled all its languages into a single environment — Visual Studio. As Visual Studio 6.0 started getting a little long in the tooth, developers anxiously awaited version 7. Shortly before its release, however, Microsoft decided to rename it Visual Studio .NET to highlight this new environment's relationship to .NET.

That sounded like a marketing ploy to a lot of people — until they started delving into it. Visual Studio .NET differed quite a bit from its predecessors — enough to warrant a new name. Visual Studio 2017 is the ninth-generation successor to the original Visual Studio .NET. (Book 4 is full of Visual Studio goodness, including instructions for customizing it. You may want to use the instructions in Book 4, Chapter 1 to install a copy of Visual Studio before you get to the example later in this chapter. If you're completely unfamiliar with Visual Studio, then reviewing all of Book 4 is helpful.)

Microsoft calls its implementation of the language Visual C#. In reality, Visual C# is nothing more than the C# component of Visual Studio. C# is C#, with or without Visual Studio. Theoretically, you could write C# programs by using any text editor and a few special tools, but using Visual Studio is so much easier that you wouldn't want to try.

Okay, that's it. No more questions. (For now, anyway.)

Creating Your First Console Application

Visual Studio 2017 includes an Application Wizard that builds template programs and saves you a lot of the dirty work you'd have to do if you did everything from scratch. (The from-scratch approach is error prone, to say the least.)

Typically, starter programs don't really do anything — at least, not anything useful. However, they do get you beyond that initial hurdle of getting started. Some starter programs are reasonably sophisticated. In fact, you'll be amazed at how much capability the App Wizard can build on its own, especially for graphical programs.

This starter program isn't even a graphical program, though. A *console* application is one that runs in the "console" within Windows, usually referred to as the DOS prompt or command window. If you press Ctrl+R and then type cmd, you see a command window. It's the console where the application will run.

The following instructions are for Visual Studio. If you use anything other than Visual Studio, you have to refer to the documentation that came with your environment. Alternatively, you can just type the source code directly into your C# environment.

Creating the source program

To start Visual Studio, press the Windows button on your keyboard and type **Visual Studio**. Visual Studio 2017 appears as one of the available options. You can access the example code for this chapter in the \CSAIO4D\BK01\CH01 folder in the down-loadable source, as explained in the Introduction.

Complete these steps to create your C# console app:

1. **Open Visual Studio 2017 and click the Create New Project link, shown in Figure 1-1.**

FIGURE 1-1:
Creating a new project starts you down the road to a better Windows application.

Visual Studio presents you with lots of icons representing the different types of applications you can create, as shown in Figure 1-2.

2. **In this New Project window, click the Console App (.NET Framework) icon.**

WARNING

Make sure that you select Visual C# — and under it, Windows — in the Project Types pane; otherwise Visual Studio may create something awful like a Visual Basic or Visual C++ application. Then click the Console App (.NET Framework) icon in the Templates pane.

REMEMBER

Visual Studio requires you to create a project before you can start entering your C# program. A *project* is a folder into which you throw all the files that go into making your program. It has a set of configuration files that help the compiler do its work. When you tell your compiler to build (*compile*) the program, it sorts through the project to find the files it needs in order to re-create the executable program.

FIGURE 1-2:
The Visual Studio
App Wizard is
eager to create
a new program
for you.

TECHNICAL STUFF

Visual Studio 2017 provides support for both .NET Framework and .NET Core applications. A .NET Framework application is the same as the C# applications supported in previous versions of Windows; it runs only in Windows and isn't open source. A .NET Core application can run in Windows, Linux, and Mac environments and relies on an open source setup. Although using .NET Core may seem ideal, the .NET Core applications also support only a subset of the .NET Framework features, and you can't add a GUI to them. Microsoft created the .NET Core for these uses:

- Cross platform development

- Microservices

- Docker containers

- High performance and scalable applications

- Side-by-side .NET application support

3. **The default name for your first application is** App1, **but change it this time to** Program1 **by typing in the Name field.**

TIP

The default place to store this file is somewhere deep in your Documents directory. For most developers, it's a lot better to place the files where you can actually find them and interact with them as needed, not necessarily where Visual Studio wants them.

4. **Type** C:\CSAIO4D\BK01\CH01 **Location field to change the location of this project.**

5. **Click the OK button.**

   After a bit of disk whirring and chattering, Visual Studio generates a file named Program.cs. (If you look in the window labeled Solution Explorer, shown in Figure 1-3, you see some other files; ignore them for now. If Solution Explorer isn't visible, choose View ⇨ Solution Explorer.)

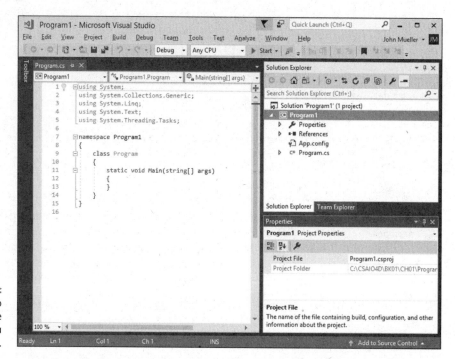

FIGURE 1-3:
Visual Studio displays the project you just created.

C# source files carry the extension .cs. The name Program is the default name assigned for the program file.

The contents of your first console app appear this way (as shown in Figure 1-3):

```
using System;
using System.Collections.Generic;
using System.Linq;
using System.Text;
using System.Threading.Tasks;
```

```
namespace Program1
{
    class Program
    {
        static void Main(string[] args)
        {
        }
    }
}
```

TIP

You can manually change the location of the project with every project. However, you have a simpler way to go. When working with this book, you can change the default program location. To make that happen, follow these steps after you finish creating the project:

1. **Choose Tools ⇨ Options.**

   The Options dialog box opens. You may have to select the Show All Options box.

2. **Choose Projects and Solutions ⇨ General.**

3. **Select the new location in the Projects Location field and click OK.**

   (The examples assume that you have used C:\CSAIO4D for this book.)

You can see the Options dialog box in Figure 1-4. Leave the other fields in the project settings alone for now. Read more about customizing Visual Studio in Book 4 and in Online Chapter 2, which you find by going to www.dummies.com, searching this book's title, and locating the Downloads tab on the page that appears.

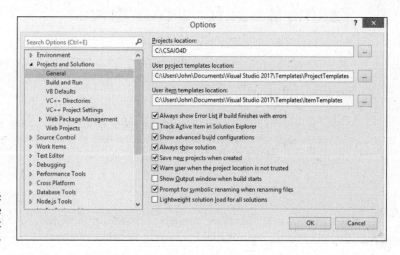

FIGURE 1-4: Changing the default project location.

REMEMBER

Along the left edge of the code window, you see several small plus (+) and minus (−) signs in boxes. Click the + sign next to using .... This expands a *code region*, a handy Visual Studio feature that minimizes clutter. Here are the directives that appear when you expand the region in the default console app:

```
using System;
using System.Collections.Generic;
using System.Linq;
using System.Text;
```

Regions help you focus on the code you're working on by hiding code that you aren't. Certain blocks of code — such as the namespace block, class block, methods, and other code items — get a +/− automatically without a #region directive. You can add your own collapsible regions, if you like, by typing #region above a code section and #endregion after it. It helps to supply a name for the region, such as Public methods. This code section looks like this:

```
#region Public methods
... your code
#endregion Public methods
```

REMEMBER

This name can include spaces. Also, you can nest one region inside another, but regions can't overlap.

For now, using System; is the only using directive you really need. You can delete the others; the compiler lets you know whether you're missing one.

Taking it out for a test drive

Before you try to create your application, open the Output window (if it isn't already open) by choosing View➪Output. To convert your C# program into an executable program, choose Build➪Build Program1. Visual Studio responds with the following message:

```
------ Build started: Project: Program1, Configuration: Debug Any CPU ------
Program1 -> C:\CSAIO4D\BK01\CH01\Program1\Program1\bin\Debug\Program1.exe
========== Build: 1 succeeded, 0 failed, 0 up-to-date, 0 skipped ==========
```

The key point here is the 1 succeeded part on the last line.

TIP

As a general rule of programming, succeeded is good; failed is bad. The bad — the exceptions — is covered in Chapter 9 of this minibook.

To execute the program, choose Debug⇨Start. The program brings up a black console window and terminates immediately. (If you have a fast computer, the appearance of this window is just a flash on the screen.) The program has seemingly done nothing. In fact, this is the case. The template is nothing but an empty shell.

TIP

An alternative command, Debug⇨Start Without Debugging, behaves a bit better at this point. Try it out.

Making Your Console App Do Something

Edit the `Program.cs` template file until it appears this way:

```
using System;

namespace Program1
{
  public class Program
  {
    // This is where your program starts.
    static void Main(string[] args)
    {
      // Prompt user to enter a name.
      Console.WriteLine("Enter your name, please:");

      // Now read the name entered.
      string name = Console.ReadLine();

      // Greet the user with the name that was entered.
      Console.WriteLine("Hello, " + name);

      // Wait for user to acknowledge the results.
      Console.WriteLine("Press Enter to terminate...");
      Console.Read();
    }
  }
}
```

TIP

Don't sweat the stuff following the double or triple slashes (// or ///) and don't worry about whether to enter one or two spaces or one or two new lines. However, do pay attention to capitalization.

Choose Build⇨Build Program1 to convert this new version of `Program.cs` into the `Program1.exe` **program.**

From within Visual Studio 2017, choose Debug⇨Start Without Debugging. The black console window appears and prompts you for your name. (You may need to activate the console window by clicking it.) Then the window shows Hello, followed by the name entered, and displays Press Enter to terminate .... Pressing Enter closes the window.

You can also execute the program from the DOS command line. To do so, open a Command Prompt window and enter the following:

```
CD \C#Programs\Program1\bin\Debug
```

Now enter **Program1** to execute the program. The output should be identical to what you saw earlier. You can also navigate to the \C#Programs\Program1\bin\ Debug folder in Windows Explorer and then double-click the Program1.exe file.

To open a Command Prompt window, try choosing Tools⇨Command Prompt. If that command isn't available on your Visual Studio Tools menu, open a copy of Windows Explorer, locate the folder containing the executable as shown in Figure 1-5, and then choose File⇨Open Command Prompt. You see a command prompt where you can execute the program.

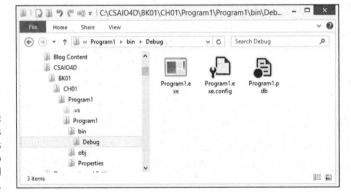

FIGURE 1-5:
Windows Explorer provides a quick way to open a command prompt.

Reviewing Your Console Application

In the following sections, you take this first C# console app apart one section at a time to understand how it works.

The program framework

The basic framework for all console applications starts as the following:

```
using System;
using System.Collections.Generic;
using System.Linq;
using System.Text;

namespace Program1
{
  public class Program
  {
    // This is where your program starts.
    public static void Main(string[] args)
    {
        // Your code goes here.
    }
  }
}
```

The program starts executing right after the statement containing `Main()` and ends at the closed curly brace (}) following `Main()`. (You find the explanation for these statements in due course. Just know that they work as they should for now.)

REMEMBER

The list of `using` directives can come immediately before or immediately after the phrase `namespace Program1 {`. The order doesn't matter. You can apply `using` to lots of things in .NET. You find an explanation for namespaces and `using` in the object-oriented programming chapters in Book 2.

Comments

The template already has lots of lines, and the example code adds several other lines, such as the following (in boldface):

```
// This is where your program starts.
public static void Main(string[] args)
```

C# ignores the first line in this example. This line is known as a *comment.*

TIP

Any line that begins with // or /// is free text, and C# ignores it. Consider // and /// to be equivalent for now.

Why include lines if the computer ignores them? Because comments explain your C# statements. A program, even in C#, isn't easy to understand. Remember that a programming language is a compromise between what computers understand and what humans understand. These comments are useful while you write the code, and they're especially helpful to the poor sap — possibly you — who tries to re-create your logic a year later. Comments make the job much easier.

Comment early and often.

The meat of the program

The real core of this program is embedded within the block of code marked with Main(), like this:

```
// Prompt user to enter a name.
Console.WriteLine("Enter your name, please:");

// Now read the name entered.
string name = Console.ReadLine();

// Greet the user with the name that was entered.
Console.WriteLine("Hello, " + name);
```

Save a ton of routine typing with the C# Code Snippets feature. Snippets are great for common statements like Console.WriteLine. Press Ctrl+K,X to see a pop-up menu of snippets. (You may need to press Tab once or twice to open the Visual C# folder or other folders on that menu.) Scroll down the menu to cw and press Enter. Visual Studio inserts the body of a Console.WriteLine() statement with the insertion point between the parentheses, ready to go. When you have a few of the shortcuts, such as cw, for, and if, memorized, use the even quicker technique: Type **cw** and press Tab twice. (Also try selecting some lines of code, pressing Ctrl+K, and then pressing Ctrl+S. Choose something like if. An if statement *surrounds* the selected code lines.)

The program begins executing with the first C# statement: Console.WriteLine. This command writes the character string Enter your name, please: to the console.

The next statement reads in the user's answer and stores it in a *variable* (a kind of workbox) named name. (See Chapter 2 of this minibook for more on these storage locations.) The last line combines the string Hello, with the user's name and outputs the result to the console.

The final three lines cause the computer to wait for the user to press Enter before proceeding. These lines ensure that the user has time to read the output before the program continues:

```
// Wait for user to acknowledge the results.
Console.WriteLine("Press Enter to terminate...");
Console.Read();
```

This step can be important, depending on how you execute the program and depending on the environment. In particular, running your console app inside Visual Studio, or from Windows Explorer, makes the preceding lines necessary — otherwise, the console window closes so fast you can't read the output. If you open a console window and run the program from there, the window stays open regardless.

Introducing the Toolbox Trick

The key part of the program you create in the preceding section consists of the final two lines of code:

```
// Wait for user to acknowledge the results.
Console.WriteLine("Press Enter to terminate...");
Console.Read();
```

The easiest way to re-create those key lines in each future console application you write is described in the following sections.

Saving code in the Toolbox

The first step is to save those lines in a handy location for future use: the Toolbox window. With your Program1 console application open in Visual Studio, follow these steps:

1. In the Main() method of class Program, select the lines you want to save — in this case, the three lines mentioned previously.

2. Make sure the Toolbox window is open on the left. (If it isn't, open it by choosing View⇨Toolbox.)

3. Drag the selected lines into the General tab of the Toolbox window and drop them. (Or copy the lines and paste them into the Toolbox.)

   The Toolbox stores the lines there for you in perpetuity. Figure 1-6 shows the lines placed in the Toolbox.

FIGURE 1-6:
Setting up the
Toolbox with
some handy
saved text for
future use.

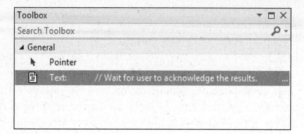

Reusing code from the Toolbox

Now that you have your template text stored in the Toolbox, you can reuse it in all console applications you write henceforth. Here's how to use it:

1. **In Visual Studio, create a new console application as described in the section "Creating the source program," earlier in this chapter.**

2. **Click in the editor at the spot where you'd like to insert some Toolbox text.**

3. **With the `Program.cs` file open for editing, make sure the Toolbox window is open.**

   If it isn't, see the procedure in the preceding "Saving code in the Toolbox" section.

4. **In the General tab of the Toolbox window (other tabs may be showing), find the saved text you want to use and double-click it.**

   The selected item is inserted at the insertion point in the editor window.

With that boilerplate text in place, you can write the rest of your application above those lines. That's it. You now have a finished console app. Try it for about 30 seconds. Then you can check out Chapter 2 of this minibook.

Chapter **2**

Living with Variability — Declaring Value-Type Variables

The most fundamental of all concepts in programming is that of the variable. A C# variable is like a small box in which you can store things, particularly numbers, for later use. (The term *variable* is borrowed from the world of mathematics.)

Unfortunately for programmers, C# places several limitations on variables — limitations that mathematicians don't have to consider. However, these limits are in place for a reason. They make it easier for C# to understand what you mean by a particular kind of variable and for you to find mistakes in your code. This chapter takes you through the steps for declaring, initializing, and using variables. It also introduces several of the most basic data types in C#.

Declaring a Variable

Mathematicians work with numbers in a precise manner, but in a way that C# could never understand. The mathematician is free to introduce the variables as needed to present an idea in a particular way. Mathematicians use algorithms, a set of procedural steps used to solve a problem, in a way that makes sense to other mathematicians to model real-world needs. Algorithms can appear quite complex, even to other humans, much less C#. For example, the mathematician may say this:

```
x = y² + 2y + y
if k = y + 1 then
x = k²
```

Programmers must define variables in a particular way that's more demanding than the mathematician's looser style. A programmer must tell C# the kind of value that a variable contains and then tell C# specifically what to place in that variable in a manner that C# understands. For example, a C# programmer may write the following bit of code:

```
int n;
n = 1;
```

The first line means, "Carve off a small amount of storage in the computer's memory and assign it the name n." This step is analogous to reserving one of those storage lockers at the train station and slapping the label n on the side. The second line says, "Store the value 1 in the variable n, thereby replacing whatever that storage location already contains." The train-locker equivalent is, "Open the train locker, rip out whatever happens to be in there, and shove a 1 in its place."

REMEMBER

The equals symbol (=) is called the *assignment operator.*

TECHNICAL STUFF

The mathematician says, "n equals 1." The C# programmer says in a more precise way, "Store the value 1 in the variable n." (Think about the train locker, and you see why that's easier for C# to understand.) C# operators, such as the assignment operator, tell the computer what you want to do. In other words, operators are verbs and not descriptors. The assignment operator takes the value on its right and stores it in the variable on the left. You discover more about operators in Chapter 4 of this minibook.

What's an int?

In C#, each variable has a fixed type. When you allocate one of those train lockers, you have to pick the size you need. If you pick an integer locker, for instance, you can't turn around and hope to stuff the entire state of Texas in it — maybe Rhode Island, but not Texas.

For the example in the preceding section of this chapter, you select a locker that's designed to handle an integer — C# calls it an int. Integers are the counting numbers 1, 2, 3, and so on, plus 0 and the negative numbers −1, −2, −3, and so on.

REMEMBER

Before you can use a variable, you must *declare* it, which means creating a variable with a specific name (label) using code and optionally assigning a value to that variable. After you declare a variable as int, it can hold integer values, as this example demonstrates:

```
// Declare a variable named n - an empty train locker.
int n;
// Declare an int variable m and initialize it with the value 2.
int m = 2;
// Assign the value stored in m to the variable n.
n = m;
```

The first line after the comment is a *declaration* that creates a little storage area, n, designed to hold an integer value. The initial value of n is not specified until it is *assigned* a value, so this locker is essentially empty. The second declaration not only declares an int variable m but also *initializes* it with a value of 2, all in one shot.

REMEMBER

The term *initialize* means to assign an initial value. To initialize a variable is to assign it a value for the first time. You don't know for sure what the value of a variable is until it has been initialized. Nobody knows. It's always an error to use a variable before you initialize it.

The final statement in the program assigns the value stored in m, which is 2, to the variable n. The variable n continues to contain the value 2 until it is assigned a new value. (The variable m doesn't lose its value when you assign its value to n. It's like cloning m.)

Rules for declaring variables

You can initialize a variable as part of the declaration, like this:

```
// Declare another int variable and give it the initial value of 1.
int p = 1;
```

This is equivalent to sticking a 1 into that `int` storage locker when you first rent it, rather than opening the locker and stuffing in the value later.

TIP

Initialize a variable when you declare it. In most (but not all) cases, C# initializes the variable for you — but don't rely on it to do that. For example, C# does place a 0 into an uninitialized `int` variable, but the compiler will still display an error if you try to use the variable before you initialize it. You may declare variables anywhere (well, almost anywhere) within a program.

WARNING

However, you may not use a variable until you declare it and set it to some value. Thus the last two assignments shown here are *not* legal:

```
// The following is illegal because m is not assigned
// a value before it is used.
int n
int m;
n = m;
// The following is illegal because p has not been
// declared before it is used.
p = 2;
int p;
```

Finally, you cannot declare the same variable twice in the same scope (a function, for example).

Variations on a theme: Different types of int

Most simple numeric variables are of type `int`. However, C# provides a number of twists to the `int` variable type for special occasions.

All integer variable types are limited to whole numbers. The `int` type suffers from other limitations as well. For example, an `int` variable can store values only in the range from roughly −2 billion to 2 billion.

A distance of 2 billion inches is greater than the circumference of the Earth. In case 2 billion isn't quite large enough for you, C# provides an integer type called `long` (short for `long int`) that can represent numbers almost as large as you can imagine. The only problem with a `long` is that it takes a larger train locker: A `long` consumes 8 bytes (64 bits) — twice as much as a garden-variety 4-byte (32-bit) `int`. C# provides several other integer variable types, as shown in Table 2-1.

TABLE 2-1   ## Size and Range of C# Integer Types

Type	Bytes	Range of Values	In Use
sbyte	1	–128 to 127	`sbyte sb = 12;`
byte	1	0 to 255	`byte b = 12;`
short	2	–32,768 to 32,767	`short sh = 12345;`
ushort	2	0 to 65,535	`ushort ush = 62345;`
int	4	–2 billion to 2 billion	`int n = 1234567890;`
uint	4	0 to 4 billion (exact values listed in the Cheat Sheet on this book's website)	`uint un = 3234567890U`
long	8	-10^{20} to 10^{20} — "a whole lot"	`long l = 123456789012L`
Ulong	8	0 to 2×10^{20}	`long ul = 123456789012UL`

As explained in the section entitled "Declaring Numeric Constants," later in this chapter, fixed values such as 1 also have a type. By default, a simple constant such as 1 is assumed to be an int. Constants other than an int must be marked with their variable type. For example, 123U is an unsigned integer, uint.

Most integer variables are called *signed*, which means they can represent negative values. Unsigned integers can represent only positive values, but you get twice the range in return. As you can see from Table 2-1, the names of most unsigned integer types start with a u, while the signed types generally don't have a prefix.

TIP

You don't need any unsigned integer versions in this book.

Representing Fractions

Integers are useful for most calculations. However, many calculations involve fractions, which simple integers can't accurately represent. The common equation for converting from Fahrenheit to Celsius temperatures demonstrates the problem, like this:

```
// Convert the temperature 41 degrees Fahrenheit.
int fahr = 41;
int celsius = (fahr - 32) * (5 / 9)
```

This equation works just fine for some values. For example, 41 degrees Fahrenheit is 5 degrees Celsius.

Okay, try a different value: 100 degrees Fahrenheit. Working through the equation, 100−32 is 68; 68 times $\frac{5}{9}$ is 37 when using integers. However, a closer answer is 37.78. Even that's wrong because it's really 37.777 . . . with the 7s repeating forever.

REMEMBER

An `int` can represent only integer numbers. The integer equivalent of 37.78 is 37. This lopping off of the fractional part of a number to get it to fit into an integer variable is called *integer truncation.*

TECHNICAL STUFF

Truncation is not the same thing as *rounding.* Truncation lops off the fractional part. Goodbye, Charlie. Rounding picks the closest integer value. Thus, truncating 1.9 results in 1. Rounding 1.9 results in 2.

For temperatures, 37 may be good enough. It's not like you wear short-sleeve shirts at 37.7 degrees but pull on a sweater at 37 degrees. But integer truncation is unacceptable for many, if not most, applications.

Actually, the problem is much worse than that. An `int` can't handle the ratio $\frac{5}{9}$ either; it always yields the value 0. Consequently, the equation as written in this example calculates `celsius` as 0 for all values of `fahr`.

Handling Floating-Point Variables

The limitations of an `int` variable are unacceptable for some applications. The range generally isn't a problem — the double-zillion range of a 64-bit-long integer should be enough for almost anyone. However, the fact that an `int` is limited to whole numbers is a bit harder to swallow.

In some cases, you need numbers that can have a nonzero fractional part. Mathematicians call these *real numbers.* (Somehow that always seemed like a ridiculous name for a number. Are integer numbers somehow unreal?)

REMEMBER

Note that a real number *can* have a nonzero fractional part — that is, 1.5 is a real number, but so is 1.0. For example, 1.0 + 0.1 is 1.1. Just keep that point in mind as you read the rest of this chapter.

Fortunately, C# understands real numbers. Real numbers come in two flavors: floating-point and decimal. Floating-point is the most common type. You can find a description of the decimal type in the section "Using the Decimal Type: Is It an Integer or a Float?" later in this chapter.

Declaring a floating-point variable

A floating-point variable carries the designation `float`, and you declare one as shown in this example:

```
float f = 1.0;
```

After you declare it as `float`, the variable `f` is a `float` for the rest of its natural instructions.

Table 2-2 describes the two kinds of floating-point types. All floating-point variables are signed. (There's no such thing as a floating-point variable that can't represent a negative value.)

TABLE 2-2 ## Size and Range of Floating-Point Variable Types

Type	Bytes	Range of Values	Accuracy to Number of Digits	In Use
float	8	$1.5 * 10^{-45}$ to $3.4 * 10^{38}$	6 to 7	`float f = 1.2F;`
double	16	$5.0 * 10^{-324}$ to $1.7 * 10^{308}$	15 to 16	`double d = 1.2;`

REMEMBER

You might think that `float` is the default floating-point variable type, but actually the `double` is the default in C#. If you don't specify the type for, say, 12.3, C# calls it a `double`.

The Accuracy column in Table 2-2 refers to the number of significant digits that such a variable type can represent. For example, $\frac{5}{9}$ is actually 0.555 . . . with an unending sequence of 5s. However, a `float` variable is said to have six significant digits of accuracy — which means that numbers after the sixth digit are ignored. Thus $\frac{5}{9}$ may appear this way when expressed as a `float`:

```
0.5555551457382
```

Here you know that all the digits after the sixth 5 are untrustworthy.

The same number — $\frac{5}{9}$ — may appear this way when expressed as a `double`:

```
0.55555555555555557823
```

The `double` packs a whopping 15 to 16 significant digits.

Use `double` variable types unless you have a specific reason to do otherwise. For example, here's the equation for converting from Fahrenheit to Celsius temperatures using floating-point variables:

```
double celsius = (fahr - 32.0) * (5.0 / 9.0)
```

Examining some limitations of floating-point variables

You may be tempted to use floating-point variables all the time because they solve the truncation problem so nicely. Sure, they use up a bit more memory. But memory is cheap these days, so why not? But floating-point variables also have limitations, which you discover in the following sections.

Counting

You can't use floating-point variables as counting numbers. Some C# structures need to count (as in 1, 2, 3, and so on). You know that 1.0, 2.0, and 3.0 are counting numbers just as well as 1, 2, and 3, but C# doesn't know that. For example, given the accuracy limitations of floating-points, how does C# know that you aren't *actually* saying 1.000001?

Whether you find that argument convincing, you can't use a floating-point variable when counting things.

Comparing numbers

You have to be careful when comparing floating-point numbers. For example, 12.5 may be represented as 12.500001. Most people don't care about that little extra bit on the end. However, the computer takes things extremely literally. To C#, 12.500000 and 12.500001 are not the same numbers.

So, if you add 1.1 to 1.1, you can't tell whether the result is 2.2 or 2.200001. And if you ask, "Is `doubleVariable` equal to 2.2?" you may not get the results you expect. Generally, you have to resort to some bogus comparison like this: "Is the absolute value of the difference between `doubleVariable` and 2.2 less than .000001?" In other words, "within an acceptable margin of error."

Modern processors play a trick to make this problem less troublesome than it otherwise may be: They perform floating-point arithmetic in an especially long `double` format — that is, rather than use 64 bits, they use a whopping 80 bits (or 128-bits in newer processors). When rounding off an 80-bit `float` into a 64-bit `float`, you (almost) always get the expected result, even if the 80-bit number was off a bit or two.

Calculation speed

Integers are always faster than floats to use because integers are less complex. Just as you can calculate the value of something using whole numbers a lot faster than using those pesky decimals, so can processors work faster with integers faster.

TECHNICAL STUFF

Intel processors perform integer math using an internal structure called a general-purpose register that can work only with integers. These same registers are used for counting. Using general-purpose registers is extremely fast. Floating-point numbers require use of a special area that can handle real numbers called the Arithmetic Logic Unit (ALU) and special floating-point registers that don't work for counting. Each calculation takes longer because of the additional handling that floating-point numbers require.

Unfortunately, modern processors are so complex that you can't know precisely how much time you save by using integers. Just know that using integers is generally faster, but that you won't actually see a difference unless you're performing a long list of calculations.

Not-so-limited range

In the past, a floating-point variable could represent a considerably larger range of numbers than an integer type. It still can, but the range of the `long` is large enough to render the point moot.

WARNING

Even though a simple `float` can represent a very large number, the number of significant digits is limited to about six. For example, `123,456,789F` is the same as `123,456,000F`. (For an explanation of the `F` notation at the end of these numbers, see "Declaring Numeric Constants," later in this chapter.)

Using the Decimal Type: Is It an Integer or a Float?

As explained in previous sections of this chapter, both the integer and floating-point types have their problems. Floating-point variables have rounding problems associated with limits to their accuracy, while `int` variables just lop off the fractional part of a variable. In some cases, you need a variable type that offers the best of two worlds:

>> Like a floating-point variable, it can store fractions.

>> Like an integer, numbers of this type offer exact values for use in computations — for example, 12.5 is really 12.5 and not 12.500001.

Fortunately, C# provides such a variable type, called decimal. A decimal variable can represent a number between 10^{-28} and 10^{28} — which represents a lot of zeros! And it does so without rounding problems.

Declaring a decimal

Decimal variables are declared and used like any variable type, like this:

```
decimal m1 = 100;    // Good
decimal m2 = 100M;   // Better
```

The first declaration shown here creates a variable m1 and initializes it to a value of 100. What isn't obvious is that 100 is actually of type int. Thus, C# must convert the int into a decimal type before performing the initialization. Fortunately, C# understands what you mean — and performs the conversion for you.

The declaration of m2 is the best. This clever declaration initializes m2 with the decimal constant 100M. The letter *M* at the end of the number specifies that the constant is of type decimal. No conversion is required. (See the section "Declaring Numeric Constants," later in this chapter.)

Comparing decimals, integers, and floating-point types

The decimal variable type seems to have all the advantages and none of the disadvantages of int or double types. Variables of this type have a very large range, they don't suffer from rounding problems, and 25.0 is 25.0 and not 25.00001.

The decimal variable type has two significant limitations, however. First, a decimal is not considered a counting number because it may contain a fractional value. Consequently, you can't use them in flow-control loops, as explained in Chapter 5 of this minibook.

The second problem with decimal variables is equally serious or even more so. Computations involving decimal values are significantly slower than those involving either simple integer or floating-point values. On a crude benchmark test of 300,000,000 adds and subtracts, the operations involving decimal variables were approximately 50 times slower than those involving simple int variables. The relative computational speed gets even worse for more complex operations. Besides that, most computational functions, such as calculating sines or exponents, are not available for the decimal number type.

Clearly, the decimal variable type is most appropriate for applications such as banking, in which accuracy is extremely important but the number of calculations is relatively small.

Examining the bool Type: Is It Logical?

Finally, a logical variable type, one that can help you get to the truth of the matter. The Boolean type bool can have two values: true or false.

WARNING

Former C and C++ programmers are accustomed to using the int value 0 (zero) to mean false and nonzero to mean true. That doesn't work in C#.

You declare a bool variable this way:

```
bool thisIsABool = true;
```

No conversion path exists between bool variables and any other types. In other words, you can't convert a bool directly into something else. (Even if you could, you shouldn't because it doesn't make any sense.) In particular, you can't convert a bool into an int (such as false becoming 0) or a string (such as false becoming the word "false").

Checking Out Character Types

A program that can do nothing more than spit out numbers may be fine for mathematicians, accountants, insurance agents with their mortality figures, and folks calculating cannon-shell trajectories. (Don't laugh. The original computers were built to generate tables of cannon-shell trajectories to help artillery gunners.) However, for most applications, programs must deal with letters as well as numbers.

C# treats letters in two distinctly different ways: individual characters of type char (usually pronounced *char*, as in singe or burn) and strings of characters — a type called, cleverly enough, string.

The char variable type

The char variable is a box capable of holding a single character. A character constant appears as a character surrounded by a pair of single quotation marks, as in this example:

```
char c = 'a';
```

You can store any single character from the Roman, Hebrew, Arabic, Cyrillic, and most other alphabets. You can also store Japanese katakana and hiragana characters, as well as many Japanese and Chinese kanjis.

In addition, char is considered a counting type. That means you can use a char type to control the looping structures described in Chapter 5 of this minibook. Character variables do not suffer from rounding problems.

WARNING

The character variable includes no font information. So you may store in a char variable what you think is a perfectly good kanji (and it may well be) — but when you view the character, it can look like garbage if you're not looking at it through the eyes of the proper font.

Special chars

Some characters within a given font are not printable, in the sense that you don't see anything when you look at them on the computer screen or printer. The most obvious example of this is the space, which is represented by the character ' ' (single quotation mark, space, single quotation mark). Other characters have no letter equivalent — for example, the tab character. C# uses the backslash to flag these characters, as shown in Table 2-3.

TABLE 2-3

Special Characters

Character Constant	Value
'\n'	New line
'\t'	Tab
'\0'	Null character
'\r'	Carriage return
'\\'	Backslash

The string type

Another extremely common variable type is the string. The following examples show how you declare and initialize string variables:

```
// Declare now, initialize later.
string someString1;
someString1 = "this is a string";
// Or initialize when declared - preferable.
string someString2 = "this is a string";
```

A string constant, often called a string *literal*, is a set of characters surrounded by double quotation marks. The characters in a string can include the special characters shown in Table 2-3. A string cannot be written across a line in the C# source file, but it can contain the newline character, as the following examples show (see boldface):

```
// The following is not legal.
string someString = "This is a line
and so is this";
// However, the following is legal.
string someString = "This is a line\nand so is this";
```

When written out with Console.WriteLine, the last line in this example places the two phrases on separate lines, like this:

```
This is a line
and so is this
```

A string is not a counting type. A string is also not a value-type — no "string" exists that's intrinsic (built in) to the processor. A computer processor understands only numbers, not letters. The letter *A* is actually the number 65 to the processor. Only one of the common operators works on string objects: The + operator concatenates two strings into one. For example:

```
string s = "this is a phrase"
        + " and so is this";
```

These lines of code set the string variable s equal to this character string:

```
"this is a phrase and so is this"
```

The string with no characters, written "" (two double quotation marks in a row), is a valid string, called an empty string (or sometimes a null string). A null string ("") is different from a null char ('\0') and from a string containing any amount of space, even one ("").

Best practice is to initialize strings using the String.Empty value, which means the same thing as "" and is less prone to misinterpretation:

```
string mySecretName = String.Empty;   // A property of the String type
```

By the way, all the other data types in this chapter are *value types*. The string type, however, is not a value type, as explained in the following section. Chapter 3 of this minibook goes into much more detail about the string type.

What's a Value Type?

The variable types described in this chapter are of fixed length — again with the exception of string. A fixed-length variable type always occupies the same amount of memory. So if you assign a = b, C# can transfer the value of b into a without taking extra measures designed to handle variable-length types. In addition, these kinds of variables are stored in a special location called the *stack* as actual values. You don't need to worry about the stack; you just need to know that it exists as a location in memory. This characteristic is why these types of variables are called *value types.*

The types int, double, and bool, and their close derivatives (like unsigned int) are intrinsic variable types built right into the processor. The intrinsic variable types plus decimal are also known as value types because variables store the actual data. The string type is neither — because the variable actually stores a sort of "pointer" to the string's data, called a *reference*. The data in the string is actually off in another location. Think of a reference type as you would an address for a house. Knowing the address tells you the location of the house, but you must actually go to the address to find the physical house.

The programmer-defined types explained in Chapter 8 of this minibook, known as reference types, are neither value types nor intrinsic. The string type is a reference type, although the C# compiler does accord it some special treatment because string types are so widely used.

Comparing string and char

Although strings deal with characters, the `string` type is amazingly different from the `char`. Of course, certain trivial differences exist. You enclose a character with single quotation marks, as in this example:

```
'a'
```

On the other hand, you put double quotation marks around a string:

```
"this is a string"
"a"    // So is this -- see the double quotes?
```

The rules concerning strings are not the same as those concerning characters. For one thing, you know right up front that a `char` is a single character, and that's it. For example, the following code makes no sense, either as addition or as concatenation:

```
char c1 = 'a';
char c2 = 'b';
char c3 = c1 + c2
```

TECHNICAL STUFF

Actually, this bit of code almost compiles — but with a completely different meaning from what was intended. These statements convert c1 into an `int` consisting of the numeric value of c1. C# also converts c2 into an `int` and then adds the two integers. The error occurs when trying to store the results back into c3 — numeric data may be lost storing an `int` into the smaller `char`. In any case, the operation makes no sense.

A string, on the other hand, can be any length. So concatenating two strings, as shown here, *does* make sense:

```
string s1 = "a";
string s2 = "b";
string s3 = s1 + s2;  // Result is "ab"
```

As part of its library, C# defines an entire suite of string operations. You find these operations described in Chapter 3 of this minibook.

NAMING CONVENTIONS

Programming is hard enough without programmers making it harder. To make your C# source code easier to wade through, adopt a naming convention and stick to it. As much as possible, your naming convention should follow that adopted by other C# programmers:

- **The names of things other than variables start with a capital letter, and variables start with a lowercase letter.** Make these names as descriptive as possible — which often means that a name consists of multiple words. These words should be capitalized but butted up against each other with no underscore between them — for example, ThisIsALongName. Names that start with a capital are *Pascal-cased,* from the way a 1970s-era language called Pascal named things.

- **The names of variables start with a lowercase letter.** A typical variable name looks like this: thisIsALongVariableName. This variable naming style is called *camel-casing* because it has humps in the middle.

Prior to the .NET era, it was common among Windows programmers to use a convention in which the first letter of the variable name indicated the type of the variable. Most of these letters were straightforward: f for float, d for double, s for string, and so on. The only one that was even the slightest bit different was n for int. One exception to this rule existed: For reasons that stretch way back into the Fortran programming language of the 1960s, the single letters i, j, and k were also used as common names for an int, and they still are in C#. This style of naming variables was called Hungarian notation, after Charles Simonyi, a famous Microsoftie who went to the International Space Station as a space tourist. (Martha Stewart packed his sack lunch.)

Hungarian notation has fallen out of favor, at least in .NET programming circles. With recent Visual Studio versions, you can simply rest the cursor on a variable in the debugger to have its data type revealed in a tooltip box. That makes the Hungarian prefix a bit less useful, although a few folks still hold out for Hungarian.

Calculating Leap Years: DateTime

What if you had to write a program that calculates whether this year is a leap year?

The algorithm looks like this:

```
It's a leap year if
   year is evenly divisible by 4
   and, if it happens to be evenly divisible by 100,
      it's also evenly divisible by 400
```

You don't have enough tools yet to tackle that in C#. But you could just ask the DateTime type (which is a value type, like `int`):

```
DateTime thisYear = new DateTime(2011, 1, 1);
bool isLeapYear = DateTime.IsLeapYear(thisYear.Year);
```

The result for 2016 is `true`, but for 2017, it's `false`. (For now, don't worry about that first line of code, which uses some things you haven't gotten to yet.)

With the DateTime data type, you can do something like 80 different operations, such as pull out just the month; get the day of the week; add days, hours, minutes, seconds, milliseconds, months, or years to a given date; get the number of days in a given month; and subtract two dates.

The following sample lines use a convenient property of DateTime called Now to capture the present date and time, and one of the numerous DateTime methods that let you convert one time into another:

```
DateTime thisMoment = DateTime.Now;
DateTime anHourFromNow = thisMoment.AddHours(1);
```

You can also extract specific parts of a DateTime:

```
int year = DateTime.Now.Year;                    // For example, 2007
DayOfWeek dayOfWeek = DateTime.Now.DayOfWeek;    // For example, Sunday
```

If you print that DayOfWeek object, it prints something like "Sunday." And you can do other handy manipulations of DateTimes:

```
DateTime date = DateTime.Today;                      // Get just the date part.
TimeSpan time = thisMoment.TimeOfDay;                // Get just the time part.
TimeSpan duration = new TimeSpan(3, 0, 0, 0);       // Specify length in days.
DateTime threeDaysFromNow = thisMoment.Add(duration);
```

The first two lines just extract portions of the information in a DateTime. The next two lines add a *duration* (length of time) to a DateTime. A duration differs from a moment in time; you specify durations with the TimeSpan class, and moments with DateTime. So the third line sets up a TimeSpan of three days, zero hours, zero minutes, and zero seconds. The fourth line adds the three-day duration to the DateTime representing right now, resulting in a new DateTime whose day component is three greater than the day component for thisMoment.

Subtracting a `DateTime` from another `DateTime` (or a `TimeSpan` from a `DateTime`) returns a `DateTime`:

```
TimeSpan duration1 = new TimeSpan(1, 0, 0);  // One hour later.
// Since Today gives 12:00:00 AM, the following gives 1:00:00 AM:
DateTime anHourAfterMidnight = DateTime.Today.Add(duration1);
Console.WriteLine("An hour after midnight will be {0}", anHourAfterMidnight);
DateTime midnight = anHourAfterMidnight.Subtract(duration1);
Console.WriteLine("An hour before 1 AM is {0}", midnight);
```

The first line of the preceding code creates a `TimeSpan` of one hour. The next line gets the date (actually, midnight this morning) and adds the one-hour span to it, resulting in a `DateTime` representing 1:00 a.m. today. The next-to-last line subtracts a one-hour duration from 1:00 a.m. to get 12:00 a.m. (midnight).

Declaring Numeric Constants

There are very few absolutes in life; however, C# does have an absolute: Every expression has a value and a type. In a declaration such as int n, you can easily see that the variable n is an `int`. Further, you can reasonably assume that the type of a calculation n + 1 is an `int`. However, what type is the constant 1?

The type of a constant depends on two things: its value and the presence of an optional descriptor letter at the end of the constant. Any integer type less than 2 billion is assumed to be an `int`. Numbers larger than 2 billion are assumed to be `long`. Any floating-point number is assumed to be a `double`.

Table 2-4 demonstrates constants that have been declared to be of a particular type. The case of these descriptors is not important; 1U and 1u are equivalent.

TABLE 2-4

Common Constants Declared along with Their Types

Constant	Type
1	int
1U	unsigned int
1L	long int (avoid lowercase l; it's too much like the digit 1)
1.0	double
1.0F	float

Constant	Type
`1M`	decimal
`true`	bool
`false`	bool
`'a'`	char
`'\n'`	char (the character newline)
`'\x123'`	char (the character whose numeric value is hex 123)[1]
`"a string"`	string
`""`	string (an empty string); same as `String.Empty`

[1]"hex" is short for hexadecimal (numbers in base 16 rather than in base 10).

Changing Types: The Cast

Humans don't treat different types of counting numbers differently. For example, a normal person (as distinguished from a C# programmer) doesn't think about the number 1 as being signed, unsigned, short, or long. Although C# considers these types to be different, even C# realizes that a relationship exists between them. For example, this bit of code converts an `int` into a `long`:

```
int intValue = 10;
long longValue;
longValue = intValue;  // This is OK.
```

An `int` variable can be converted into a `long` because any possible value of an `int` can be stored in a `long` — and because they are both counting numbers. C# makes the conversion for you automatically without comment. This is called an *implicit* type conversion.

A conversion in the opposite direction can cause problems, however. For example, this line is illegal:

```
long longValue = 10;
int intValue;
intValue = longValue;  // This is illegal.
```

TIP

Some values that you can store in a `long` don't fit in an `int` (4 billion, for example). If you try to shoehorn such a value into an `int`, C# generates an error because data may be lost during the conversion process. This type of bug is difficult to catch.

But what if you know that the conversion is okay? For example, even though longValue is a long, maybe you know that its value can't exceed 100 in this particular program. In that case, converting the long variable longValue into the int variable intValue would be okay.

You can tell C# that you know what you're doing by means of a cast:

```
long longValue = 10;
int intValue;
intValue = (int)longValue;  // This is now OK.
```

In a *cast*, you place the name of the type you want in parentheses and put it immediately in front of the value you want to convert. This cast forces C# to convert the long named longValue into an int and assumes that you know what you're doing. In retrospect, the assertion that you know what you're doing may seem overly confident, but it's often valid.

A counting number can be converted into a floating-point number automatically, but converting a floating-point into a counting number requires a cast:

```
double doubleValue = 10.0;
long longValue = (long)doubleValue;
```

All conversions to and from a decimal require a cast. In fact, all numeric types can be converted into all other numeric types through the application of a cast. Neither bool nor string can be converted directly into any other type.

TECHNICAL
STUFF

Built-in C# methods can convert a number, character, or Boolean into its string equivalent, so to speak. For example, you can convert the bool value true into the string "true"; however, you cannot consider this change a direct conversion. The bool true and the string "true" are completely different things.

Letting the C# Compiler Infer Data Types

So far in this book — well, so far in this chapter — when you declared a variable, you *always* specified its exact data type, like this:

```
int i = 5;
string s = "Hello C#";
double d = 1.0;
```

You're allowed to offload some of that work onto the C# compiler, using the var keyword:

```
var i = 5;
var s = "Hello C# 4.0";
var d = 1.0;
```

Now the compiler *infers* the data type for you — it looks at the stuff on the right side of the assignment to see what type the left side is.

TECHNICAL STUFF

For what it's worth, Chapter 3 of this minibook shows how to calculate the type of an expression like the ones on the right side of the assignments in the preceding example. Not that you need to do that — the compiler mostly does it for you. Suppose, for example, you have an initializing expression like this:

```
var x = 3.0 + 2 - 1.5;
```

The compiler can figure out that x is a double value. It looks at 3.0 and 1.5 and sees that they're of type double. Then it notices that 2 is an int, which the compiler can convert *implicitly* to a double for the calculation. All the additional terms in x's initialization expression end up as double types. So the *inferred type* of x is double.

But now, you can simply utter the magic word var and supply an initialization expression, and the compiler does the rest:

```
var aVariable = <initialization expression here>;
```

TECHNICAL STUFF

If you've worked with a scripting language such as JavaScript or VBScript, you may have gotten used to all-purpose-in-one data types. VBScript calls them Variant data types — and a Variant can be anything at all. But does var in C# signify a Variant type? Not at all. The object you declare with var definitely has a C# data type, such as int, string, or double. You just don't have to declare what it is.

What's really lurking in the variables declared in this example with var? Take a look at this:

```
var aString = "Hello C# 3.0";
Console.WriteLine(aString.GetType().ToString());
```

The mumbo jumbo in that WriteLine statement calls the String.GetType() method on aString to get its C# type. Then it calls the resulting object's

ToString() method to display the object's type. Here's what you see in the console window:

```
System.String
```

The output from this code proves that the compiler correctly inferred the type of aString.

TIP

Most of the time, the best practice is to not use var. Save it for when it's necessary. Being explicit about the type of a variable is clearer to anyone reading your code than using var.

You see examples later in which var is definitely called for, and you use it part of the time throughout this book, even sometimes where it's not strictly necessary. You need to see it used, and use it yourself, to internalize it.

TIP

You can see var used in other ways: with arrays and collections of data, in Chapter 6 of this minibook, and with anonymous types, in Book 2. Anonymous? Bet you can't wait.

What's more, a type in C# 4.0 and later is even more flexible than var: The dynamic type takes var a step further.

The var type causes the compiler to infer the type of the variable based on expected input. The dynamic keyword does this at runtime, using a set of tools called the Dynamic Language Runtime. You can find more about the dynamic type in Chapter 6 of Book 3.

» **Matching searching, trimming, splitting, and concatenating strings**

» **Parsing strings read into the program**

» **Formatting output strings manually or using the** `String.Format()` **method**

Chapter **3**

Pulling Strings

For many applications, you can treat a `string` like one of the built-in value-type variable types such as `int` or `char`. Certain operations that are otherwise reserved for these intrinsic types are available to strings:

```
Int i = 1;          // Declare and initialize an int.
string s = "abc";   // Declare and initialize a string.
```

In other respects, as shown in the following example, a `string` is treated like a user-defined class (Book 2 discusses classes):

```
string s1 = new String();
string s2 = "abcd";
int lengthOfString = s2.Length;
```

Which is it — a value type or a class? In fact, `String` is a class for which C# offers special treatment because strings are so widely used in programs. For example, the keyword `string` is synonymous with the class name `String`, as shown in this bit of code:

```
String s1 = "abcd"; // Assign a string literal to a String obj.
string s2 = s1;     // Assign a String obj to a string variable.
```

In this example, s1 is declared to be an object of class String (spelled with an uppercase S) whereas s2 is declared as a simple string (spelled with a lowercase s). However, the two assignments demonstrate that string and String are of the same (or compatible) types.

TECHNICAL STUFF

In fact, this same property is true of the other intrinsic variable types, to a more limited extent. Even the lowly int type has a corresponding class Int32, double has the class Double, and so on. The distinction here is that string and String truly are the same thing.

The rest of the chapter covers Strings and strings and all the tasks you can accomplish by using them.

The Union Is Indivisible, and So Are Strings

You need to know at least one thing that you didn't learn before the sixth grade: You can't change a string object after creating it. Even though you may see text that speaks of modifying a string, C# doesn't have an operation that modifies the actual string object. Plenty of operations appear to modify the string that you're working with, but they always return the modified string as a new object instead. The new string contains the modified text and has the same name as the existing string, but it really is a new string.

For example, the operation "His name is " + "Randy" changes neither of the two strings, but it generates a third string, "His name is Randy". One side effect of this behavior is that you don't have to worry about someone modifying a string that you create. Consider this example program:

```
using System;

// ModifyString -- The methods provided by class String do
//    not modify the object itself. (s.ToUpper() doesn't
//    modify 's'; rather it returns a new string that has
//    been converted.)
namespace ModifyString
{
  class Program
  {
    public static void Main(string[] args)
    {
      // Create a student object.
      Student s1 = new Student();
      s1.Name = "Jenny";
```

```
        // Now make a new object with the same name.
        Student s2 = new Student();
        s2.Name = s1.Name;

        // "Changing" the name in the s1 object does not
        // change the object itself because ToUpper() returns
        // a new string without modifying the original.
        s2.Name = s1.Name.ToUpper();
        Console.WriteLine("s1 - " + s1.Name + ", s2 - " + s2.Name);

        // Wait for user to acknowledge the results.
        Console.WriteLine("Press Enter to terminate...");
        Console.Read();
    }
}

// Student -- You just need a class with a string in it.
class Student
{
    public String Name;
}
}
```

Book 2 fully discusses classes, but for now, you can see that the Student class contains a data variable called Name, of type String. The Student objects s1 and s2 are set up so the student Name data in each points to the same string data. ToUpper() converts the string s1.Name to all uppercase characters. Normally, this would be a problem because both s1 and s2 point to the same object. However, ToUpper() does not change Name — it creates a new, independent uppercase string and stores it in the object s2. Now the two Students don't point to the same string data. Here's some sample output from this program:

```
s1 - Jenny, s2 - JENNY
Press Enter to terminate...
```

This property of strings is called *immutability* (meaning unchangeability).

**TECHNICAL
STUFF**

The immutability of strings is also important for string constants. A string such as "this is a string" is a form of a string constant, just as 1 is an int constant. A compiler may choose to combine all accesses to the single constant "this is a string". Reusing string constants can reduce the *footprint* of the resulting program (its size on disc or in memory) but would be impossible if anyone could modify the string.

Performing Common Operations on a String

C# programmers perform more operations on strings than Beverly Hills plastic surgeons do on Hollywood hopefuls. Virtually every program uses the addition operator that's used on strings, as shown in this example:

```
string name = "Randy";
Console.WriteLine("His name is " + name); // + means concatenate.
```

The String class provides this special operator. However, the String class also provides other, more direct methods for manipulating strings. You can see the complete list by looking up "String class" in the Visual Studio Help Index, and you'll meet many of the usual suspects in this chapter. Among the string-related tasks I cover here are the ones described in this list:

>> Comparing strings — for equality or for tasks like alphabetizing

>> Changing and converting strings in various ways: replacing part of a string, changing case, and converting between strings and other things

>> Accessing the individual characters in a string

>> Finding characters or substrings inside a string

>> Handling input from the command line

>> Managing formatted output

>> Working efficiently with strings using the StringBuilder

Comparing Strings

It's common to need to compare two strings. For example, did the user input the expected value? Or maybe you have a list of strings and need to alphabetize them. Best practice calls for avoiding the standard == and != comparison operators and to use the built-in comparison functions because strings can have nuances of difference between them, and these operators don't always work as expected. In addition, using the comparison functions makes the kind of comparison you want clearer and makes your code easier to maintain. The article at https://docs. microsoft.com/en-us/dotnet/csharp/programming-guide/strings/how-to- compare-strings provides some additional details on this issue, but the following sections tell you all you need to know about comparing two strings.

Equality for all strings: The Compare() method

Numerous operations treat a string as a single object — for example, the Compare() method. Compare(), with the following properties, compares two strings as though they were numbers:

» If the left string is *greater than* the right string, Compare(*left*, *right*) returns 1.

» If the left string is *less than* the right string, it returns –1.

» If the two strings are equal, it returns 0.

The algorithm works as follows when written in *notational* C# (that is, C# without all the details, also known as *pseudocode*):

```
compare(string s1, string s2)
{
  // Loop through each character of the strings until
  // a character in one string is greater than the
  // corresponding character in the other string.
  foreach character in the shorter string
    if (s1's character > s2's character when treated as a number)
      return 1
    if (s2's character < s1's character)
      return -1
  // Okay, every letter matches, but if the string s1 is longer,
  // then it's greater.
  if s1 has more characters left
    return 1
  // If s2 is longer, it's greater.
  if s2 has more characters left
    return -1
  // If every character matches and the two strings are the same
  // length, then they are "equal."
  return 0
}
```

Thus, "abcd" is greater than "abbd", and "abcde" is greater than "abcd". More often than not, you don't care whether one string is greater than the other, but only whether the two strings are equal. You *do* want to know which string is bigger when performing a sort.

The Compare() method returns 0 when two strings are identical (as shown by the code in boldface type in the following listing). The following test program uses the equality feature of Compare() to perform a certain operation when the program encounters a particular string or strings. BuildASentence prompts the user to enter lines of text. Each line is concatenated to the previous line to build a single sentence. This program ends when the user enters the word *EXIT*, *exit*, *QUIT*, or *quit*. (You'll see after the code what the code in bold does.)

```
using System;

// BuildASentence -- The following program constructs sentences
//    by concatenating user input until the user enters one of the
//    termination characters. This program shows when you need to look for
//    string equality.
namespace BuildASentence
{
  public class Program
  {
    public static void Main(string[] args)
    {
      Console.WriteLine("Each line you enter will be "
                   + "added to a sentence until you "
                   + "enter EXIT or QUIT");

      // Ask the user for input; continue concatenating
      // the phrases input until the user enters exit or
      // quit (start with an empty sentence).
      string sentence = "";

      for (; ; )
      {
        // Get the next line.
        Console.WriteLine("Enter a string ");
        string line = Console.ReadLine();

        // Exit the loop if line is a terminator.
        string[] terms = { "EXIT", "exit", "QUIT", "quit" };

        // Compare the string entered to each of the
        // legal exit commands.
        bool quitting = false;

        foreach (string term in terms)
        {
          // Break out of the for loop if you have a match.
          if (String.Compare(line, term) == 0)
          {
            quitting = true;
          }
```

```
    }
    if (quitting == true)
    {
      break;
    }

    // Otherwise, add it to the sentence.
    sentence = String.Concat(sentence, line);

    // Let the user know how she's doing.
    Console.WriteLine("\nyou've entered: " + sentence);
  }

  Console.WriteLine("\ntotal sentence:\n" + sentence);

  // Wait for user to acknowledge the results.
  Console.WriteLine("Press Enter to terminate...");
  Console.Read();
  }
 }
}
```

After prompting the user for what the program expects, the program creates an empty initial sentence string called sentence. From there, the program enters an infinite loop.

REMEMBER

The controls while(true) and for(;;) loop forever, or at least long enough for some internal break or return to break you out. The two loops are equivalent, and in practice, you'll see them both. (Looping is covered in Chapter 5 of this minibook.)

BuildASentence prompts the user to enter a line of text, which the program reads using the ReadLine() method. Having read the line, the program checks to see whether it is a terminator by using the code in boldface in the preceding example.

The termination section of the program defines an array of strings called terms and a bool variable quitting, initialized to false. Each member of the terms array is one of the strings you're looking for. Any of these strings causes the program to end.

WARNING

The program must include both "EXIT" and "exit" because Compare() considers the two strings to be different by default. (The way the program is written, these are the only two ways to spell *exit*. Strings such as "Exit" and "eXit" aren't recognized as terminators.) You can also use other string operations to check for various spellings of exit. You see how to perform this task in the next section.

The termination section loops through each of the strings in the array of target strings. If Compare() reports a match to any of the terminator phrases, quitting is set to true. If quitting remains false after the termination section and line is not one of the terminator strings, it is concatenated to the end of the sentence using the String.Concat() method. The program outputs the immediate result so that the user can see what's going on. Iterating through an array is a classic way to look for one of various possible values. (The next section shows you another way, and Book 2 gives you an even cooler way.) Here's a sample run of the BuildASentence program:

```
Each line you enter will be added to a
sentence until you enter EXIT or QUIT
Enter a string
Programming with

You've entered: Programming with
Enter a string
 C# is fun

You've entered: Programming with C# is fun
Enter a string
 (more or less)

You've entered: Programming with C# is fun (more or less)
Enter a string
EXIT


Total sentence:
Programming with C# is fun (more or less)
Press Enter to terminate...
```

Would you like your compares with or without case?

The Compare() method used in the previous example considers "EXIT" and "exit" different strings. However, the Compare() method has a second version that includes a third argument. This argument indicates whether the comparison should ignore the letter case. A true indicates "ignore."

The following version of the lengthy termination section in the BuildASentence example sets quitting to true whether the string passed is uppercase, lowercase, or a combination of the two:

```
// Indicate true if passed either exit or quit,
// irrespective of case.
```

```
if (String.Compare("exit", source, true) == 0) ||
    (String.Compare("quit", source, true) == 0)
{
    quitting = true;
}
}
```

This version is simpler than the previous looping version. This code doesn't need to worry about case, and it can use a single conditional expression because it now has only two options to consider instead of a longer list: any spelling variation of QUIT or EXIT.

What If I Want to Switch Case?

You may be interested in whether all the characters (or just one) in a string are uppercase or lowercase characters. And you may need to convert from one to the other.

Distinguishing between all-uppercase and all-lowercase strings

You can use the switch statement (see Chapter 5 of this minibook) to look for a particular string. Normally, you use the switch statement to compare a counting number to some set of possible values; however, switch does work on string objects as well. This version of the termination section in BuildASentence uses the switch construct:

```
switch(line)
{
    case "EXIT":
    case "exit":
    case "QUIT":
    case "quit":
        return true;
}
return false;
```

This approach works because you're comparing only a limited number of strings. The for loop offers a much more flexible approach for searching for string values. Using the case-less Compare() in the previous section gives the program greater flexibility in understanding the user.

Converting a string to upper- or lowercase

Suppose you have a string in lowercase and need to convert it to uppercase. You can use the `ToUpper()` method:

```
string lowcase = "armadillo";
string upcase = lowcase.ToUpper();  // ARMADILLO.
```

Similarly, you can convert uppercase to lowercase with `ToLower()`.

What if you want to convert just the first character in a string to uppercase? The following rather convoluted code will do it (but you can see a better way in the last section of this chapter):

```
string name = "chuck";
string properName =
   char.ToUpper(name[0]).ToString() + name.Substring(1, name.Length - 1);
```

The idea in this example is to extract the first char in `name` (that's `name[0]`), convert it to a one-character string with `ToString()`, and then tack on the remainder of `name` after removing the old lowercase first character with `Substring()`.

You can tell whether a string is uppercased or lowercased by using this scary-looking `if` statement:

```
if (string.Compare(line.ToUpper(CultureInfo.InvariantCulture),
                line, false) == 0) ...  // True if line is all upper.
```

Here the `Compare()` method is comparing an uppercase version of `line` to `line` itself. There should be no difference if `line` is already uppercase. The `Culture Info.InvariantCulture` property tells `Compare()` to perform the comparison without considering culture. You can read more about it at https://msdn.micro soft.com/library/system.globalization.cultureinfo.invariantculture. aspx. If you want to ensure that the string contains all lowercase characters, stick a not (`!`) operator in front of the `Compare()` call. Alternatively, you can use a loop, as described in the next section.

Looping through a String

You can access individual characters of a string in a `foreach` loop. The following code steps through the characters and writes each to the console — just another (roundabout) way to write out the string:

```
string favoriteFood = "cheeseburgers";
foreach(char c in favoriteFood)
{
  Console.Write(c);  // Could do things to the char here.
}
Console.WriteLine();
```

You can use that loop to solve the problem of deciding whether favoriteFood is all uppercase. (See the previous section for more about case.)

```
bool isUppercase = true;  // Assume that it's uppercase.
foreach(char c in favoriteFood)
{
  if(!char.IsUpper(c))
  {
    isUppercase = false;  // Disproves all uppercase, so get out.
    break;
  }
}
```

At the end of the loop, isUppercase will either be true or false. As shown in the final example in the previous section on switching case, you can also access individual characters in a string by using an array index notation.

REMEMBER

Arrays start with zero, so if you want the first character, you ask for index [0]. If you want the third, you ask for index [2].

```
char thirdChar = favoriteFood[2];   // First 'e' in "cheeseburgers"
```

Pulling Strings

Searching Strings

What if you need to find a particular word, or a particular character, inside a string? Maybe you need its index so that you can use Substring(), Replace(), Remove(), or some other method on it. In this section, you see how to find individual characters or substrings using favoriteFood from the previous section.

Can I find it?

The simplest task is finding an individual character with IndexOf():

```
int indexOfLetterS = favoriteFood.IndexOf('s');   // 4.
```

Class `String` also has other methods for finding things, either individual characters or substrings:

» `IndexOfAny()` takes an array of `char`s and searches the string for any of them, returning the index of the first one found.

```
char[] charsToLookFor = { 'a', 'b', 'c' };
int indexOfFirstFound = favoriteFood.IndexOfAny(charsToLookFor);
```

That call is often written more briefly this way:

```
int index = name.IndexOfAny(new char[] { 'a', 'b', 'c' });
```

» `LastIndexOf()` finds not the first occurrence of a character but the last.

» `LastIndexOfAny()` works like `IndexOfAny()`, but starting at the end of the string.

» `Contains()` returns `true` if a given substring can be found within the target string:

```
if(favoriteFood.Contains("ee")) ...            // True
```

» And `Substring()` returns the string (if it's there), or empty (if not):

```
string sub = favoriteFood.Substring(6, favoriteFood.Length - 6);
```

Is my string empty?

How can you tell if a target string is empty (`""`) or has the value `null`? (`null` means that no value has been assigned yet, not even to the empty string.) Use the `IsNullOrEmpty()` method, like this:

```
bool notThere = string.IsNullOrEmpty(favoriteFood);   // False
```

Notice how you call `IsNullOrEmpty()`: `string.IsNullOrEmpty(s)`. You can set a string to the empty string in these two ways:

```
string name = "";
string name = string.Empty;
```

Getting Input from the Command Line

A common task in console applications is getting the information that the user types when the application prompts for input, such as an interest rate or a name. The console methods provide all input in string format. Sometimes you need to parse the input to extract a number from it. And sometimes you need to process lots of input numbers.

Trimming excess white space

First, consider that in some cases, you don't want to mess with any white space on either end of the string. The term *white space* refers to the characters that don't normally display on the screen — for example, space, newline (or \n), and tab (\t). You may sometimes also encounter the carriage return character, \r.You can use the Trim() method to trim off the edges of the string, like this:

```
// Get rid of any extra spaces on either end of the string.
random = random.Trim();
```

Class String also provides TrimFront() and TrimEnd() methods for getting more specific, and you can pass an array of chars to include in the trimming process. For example, you might trim a leading currency sign, such as '$'. Cleaning up a string can make it easier to parse. The trim methods return a new string.

Parsing numeric input

A program can read from the keyboard one character at a time, but you have to worry about newlines and so on. An easier approach reads a string and then *parses* the characters out of the string.

Parsing characters out of a string is necessary at times, but some programmers abuse this technique. In some cases, they're too quick to jump into the middle of a string and start pulling out what they find there. This is particularly true of C++ programmers because that's the only way they could deal with strings — until the addition of a string class.

The ReadLine() method used for reading from the console returns a string object. A program that expects numeric input must convert this string. C# provides just the conversion tool you need in the Convert class. This class provides a conversion method from `string` to each built-in variable type. Thus, this code segment reads a number from the keyboard and stores it in an `int` variable:

```
string s = Console.ReadLine();   // Keyboard input is string data
int n = Convert.ToInt32(s);      // but you know it's meant to be a number.
```

The other conversion methods are a bit more obvious: `ToDouble()`, `ToFloat()`, and `ToBoolean()`. `ToInt32()` refers to a 32-bit, signed integer (32 bits is the size of a normal `int`), so this is the conversion method for `int`s. `ToInt64()` handles the size of a `long`.

When `Convert()` encounters an unexpected character type, it can generate unexpected results. Thus, you must know for sure what type of data you're processing and ensure that no extraneous characters are present.

Although you don't know much about methods yet (see Book 2), here's one anyway. The `IsAllDigits()` method returns `true` if the string passed to it consists of only digits. You can call this method prior to converting a string into an integer, assuming that a sequence of nothing but digits is a legal number.

Here's the method:

```
// IsAllDigits -- Return true if all characters
//    in the string are digits.
public static bool IsAllDigits(string raw)
{
  // First get rid of any benign characters at either end;
  // if there's nothing left, you don't have a number.
  string s = raw.Trim();  // Ignore white space on either side.
  if (s.Length == 0) return false;

  // Loop through the string.
  for(int index = 0; index < s.Length; index++)
  {
    // A nondigit indicates that the string probably isn't a number.
    if (Char.IsDigit(s[index]) == false) return false;
  }

  // No nondigits found; it's probably okay.
  return true;
}
```

To be truly complete, you need to include the decimal point for floating-point variables and include a leading minus sign for negative numbers.

The method IsAllDigits() first removes any harmless white space at either end of the string. If nothing is left, the string was blank and could not be an integer. The method then loops through each character in the string. If any of these characters turns out to be a nondigit, the method returns false, indicating that the string is probably not a number. If this method returns true, the probability is high that you can convert the string into an integer successfully. The following code sample inputs a number from the keyboard and prints it back out to the console.

```csharp
using System;

// IsAllDigits -- Demonstrate the IsAllDigits method.
namespace IsAllDigits
{
  class Program
  {
    public static void Main(string[] args)
    {
      // Input a string from the keyboard.
      Console.WriteLine("Enter an integer number");
      string s = Console.ReadLine();

      // First check to see if this could be a number.
      if (!IsAllDigits(s)) // Call the special method.
      {
        Console.WriteLine("Hey! That isn't a number");
      }
      else
      {
        // Convert the string into an integer.
        int n = Int32.Parse(s);

        // Now write out the number times 2.
        Console.WriteLine("2 * " + n + " = " + (2 * n));
      }

      // Wait for user to acknowledge the results.
      Console.WriteLine("Press Enter to terminate...");
      Console.Read();
    }
    // Place IsAllDigits here...
  }
}
```

The program reads a line of input from the console keyboard. If IsAllDigits() returns false, the program alerts the user. If not, the program converts the string into a number using an alternative to Convert.ToInt32(aString) — the

`Int32.Parse(aString)` call. Finally, the program outputs both the number and two times the number (the latter to prove that the program did, in fact, convert the string as advertised). Here's the output from a sample run of the program:

```
Enter an integer number
1A3
Hey! That isn't a number
Press Enter to terminate...
```

You could let `Convert()` try to convert garbage and handle any exception it may decide to throw. However, a better-than-even chance exists that it won't throw an exception but will just return incorrect results — for example, returning 1 when presented with 1A3. You should validate input data yourself.

You could instead use `Int32.TryParse(s, n)`, which returns `false` if the parse fails or `true` if it succeeds. If it does work, the converted number is found in the second parameter, an `int` that I named n. This method won't throw exceptions. See the next section for an example.

Handling a series of numbers

Often, a program receives a series of numbers in a single line from the keyboard. Using the `String.Split()` method, you can easily break the string into a number of substrings, one for each number, and parse them separately.

The `Split()` method chops a single string into an array of smaller strings using some delimiter. For example, if you tell `Split()` to divide a string using a comma (,) as the delimiter, `"1,2,3"` becomes three strings, `"1"`, `"2"`, and `"3"`. (The *delimiter* is whichever character you use to split collections.) The following program uses the `Split()` method to input a sequence of numbers to be summed. The code in bold shows the `Split()` method-specific code.

```
using System;

// ParseSequenceWithSplit; Input a series of numbers separated by commas,
// parse them into integers and output the sum.
namespace ParseSequenceWithSplit
{
  class Program
  {
    public static void Main(string[] args)
    {
      // Prompt the user to input a sequence of numbers.
      Console.WriteLine(
          "Input a series of numbers separated by commas:");
```

```
// Read a line of text.
string input = Console.ReadLine();
Console.WriteLine();

// Now convert the line into individual segments
// based upon either commas or spaces.
char[] dividers = {',', ' '};
string[] segments = input.Split(dividers);

// Convert each segment into a number.
int sum = 0;

foreach(string s in segments)
{
  // Skip any empty segments.
  if (s.Length > 0)
  {
    // Skip strings that aren't numbers.
    if (IsAllDigits(s))
    {
      // Convert the string into a 32-bit int.
      int num = 0;
      if (Int32.TryParse(s, out num))
      {
        Console.WriteLine("Next number = {0}", num);
        // Add this number into the sum.
        sum += num;
      }
      // If parse fails, move on to next number.
    }
  }
}

// Output the sum.
Console.WriteLine("Sum = {0}", sum);

// Wait for user to acknowledge the results.
Console.WriteLine("Press Enter to terminate...");
Console.Read();
}
// Place IsAllDigits here...
}
}
```

The ParseSequenceWithSplit program begins by reading a string from the keyboard. The program passes the dividers array of char to the Split() method to indicate that the comma and the space are the characters used to separate individual numbers. Either character will cause a split there.

The program iterates through each of the smaller subarrays created by Split() using the foreach loop statement. The program skips any zero-length subarrays. (This would result from two dividers in a row.) The program next uses the IsAllDigits() method to make sure that the string contains a number. (It won't if, for instance, you type ,.3 with an extra nondigit, nonseparator character.) Valid numbers are converted into integers and then added to an accumulator, sum. Invalid numbers are ignored. Here's the output of a typical run:

```
Input a series of numbers separated by commas:
1,2, a, 3 4

Next number = 1
Next number = 2
Next number = 3
Next number = 4
Sum = 10
Press Enter to terminate...
```

The program splits the list, accepting commas, spaces, or both as separators. It successfully skips over the a to generate the result of 10. In a real-world program, however, you probably don't want to skip over incorrect input without comment. You almost always want to draw the user's attention to garbage in the input stream.

Joining an array of strings into one string

Class String also has a Join() method. If you have an array of strings, you can use Join() to concatenate all the strings. You can even tell it to put a certain character string between each item and the next in the array:

```
string[] brothers = { "Chuck", "Bob", "Steve", "Mike" };
string theBrothers = string.Join(":", brothers);
```

The result in theBrothers is "Chuck:Bob:Steve:Mike", with the names separated by colons. You can put any separator string between the names: ", ", "\t", "   ". The first item is a comma and a space. The second is a tab character. The third is a string of several spaces.

Controlling Output Manually

Controlling the output from programs is an important aspect of string manipulation. Face it: The output from the program is what the user sees. No matter how elegant the internal logic of the program may be, the user probably won't be impressed if the output looks shabby.

The String class provides help in directly formatting string data for output. The following sections examine the Pad(), PadRight(), PadLeft(), Substring(), and Concat() methods.

Using the Trim() and Pad() methods

In the "Trimming excess white space" section, you see how to use Trim() and its more specialized variants, TrimFront() and TrimEnd(). This section discusses another common method for formatting output. You can use the Pad methods, which add characters to either end of a string to expand the string to some predetermined length. For example, you may add spaces to the left or right of a string to left- or right-justify it, or you can add "*" characters to the left of a currency number, and so on. The following small AlignOutput program uses both Trim() and Pad() to trim up and justify a series of names (the code specific to Trim() and Pad() appears in bold):

```
using System;
using System.Collections.Generic;

// AlignOutput -- Left justify and align a set of strings
//     to improve the appearance of program output.
namespace AlignOutput
{
  class Program
  {
    public static void Main(string[] args)
    {
      List<string> names = new List<string> {"Christa   ",
                                             "   Sarah",
                                             "Jonathan",
                                             "Sam",
                                             "   Schmekowitz "};

      // First output the names as they start out.
      Console.WriteLine("The following names are of "
                        + "different lengths");

      foreach(string s in names)
      {
        Console.WriteLine("This is the name '" + s + "' before");
      }
      Console.WriteLine();
```

```csharp
            // This time, fix the strings so they are
            // left justified and all the same length.
            // First, copy the source list into a list that you can manipulate.
            List<string> stringsToAlign = new List<string>();

            // At the same time, remove any unnecessary spaces from either end
            // of the names.
            for (int i = 0; i < names.Count; i++)
            {
                string trimmedName = names[i].Trim();
                stringsToAlign.Add(trimmedName);
            }

            // Now find the length of the longest string so that
            // all other strings line up with that string.
            int maxLength = 0;
            foreach (string s in stringsToAlign)
            {
                if (s.Length > maxLength)
                {
                    maxLength = s.Length;
                }
            }

            // Now justify all the strings to the length of the maximum string.
            for (int i = 0; i < stringsToAlign.Count; i++)
            {
                stringsToAlign[i] = stringsToAlign[i].PadRight(maxLength + 1);
            }

            // Finally output the resulting padded, justified strings.
            Console.WriteLine("The following are the same names "
                            + "normalized to the same length");

            foreach(string s in stringsToAlign)
            {
                Console.WriteLine("This is the name '" + s + "' afterwards");
            }

            // Wait for user to acknowledge.
            Console.WriteLine("\nPress Enter to terminate...");
            Console.Read();
        }
    }
}
```

AlignOutput defines a List<string> of names of uneven alignment and length. (You could just as easily write the program to read these names from the console or from a file.) The Main() method first displays the names as they are. Main() then aligns the names using the Trim() and PadRight() methods before redisplaying the resulting trimmed up strings:

```
The following names are of different lengths:
This is the name 'Christa  ' before
This is the name '  Sarah' before
This is the name 'Jonathan' before
This is the name 'Sam' before
This is the name ' Schmekowitz ' before

The following are the same names rationalized to the same length:
This is the name 'Christa   ' afterwards
This is the name 'Sarah     ' afterwards
This is the name 'Jonathan  ' afterwards
This is the name 'Sam       ' afterwards
This is the name 'Schmekowitz ' afterwards
```

The alignment process begins by making a copy of the input names list. The code loops through the list, calling Trim() on each element to remove unneeded white space on either end. The method loops again through the list to find the longest member. The code loops one final time, calling PadRight() to expand each string to match the length of the longest member in the list. Note how the padded names form a neat column in the output.

PadRight(10) expands a string to be at least ten characters long. For example, PadRight(10) adds four spaces to the right of a six-character string.

Finally, the code displays the list of trimmed and padded strings for output. Voilà.

Using the Concatenate() method

You often face the problem of breaking up a string or inserting some substring into the middle of another. Replacing one character with another is most easily handled with the Replace() method, like this:

```
string s = "Danger NoSmoking";
s = s.Replace(' ', '!')
```

This example converts the string into "Danger!NoSmoking". Replacing all appearances of one character (in this case, a space) with another (an exclamation mark) is especially useful when generating comma-separated strings for easier parsing. However, the more common and more difficult case involves breaking a single string into substrings, manipulating them separately, and then recombining them into a single, modified string.

The following RemoveWhiteSpace sample program uses the Replace() method to remove white space (spaces, tabs, and newlines — all instances of a set of special characters) from a string:

```csharp
using System;

// RemoveWhiteSpace -- Remove any of a set of chars from a given string.
//    Use this method to remove whitespace from a sample string.
namespace RemoveWhiteSpace
{
  public class Program
  {
    public static void Main(string[] args)
    {
      // Define the white space characters.
      char[] whiteSpace = {' ', '\n', '\t'};

      // Start with a string embedded with whitespace.
      string s = " this is a\nstring"; // Contains spaces & newline.
      Console.WriteLine("before:" + s);

      // Output the string with the whitespace missing.
      Console.Write("after:");

      // Start looking for the white space characters.
      for(;;)
      {
        // Find the offset of the character; exit the loop
        // if there are no more.
        int offset = s.IndexOfAny(whiteSpace);

        if (offset == -1)
        {
          break;
        }

        // Break the string into the part prior to the
        // character and the part after the character.
        string before = s.Substring(0, offset);
        string after  = s.Substring(offset + 1);

        // Now put the two substrings back together with the
        // character in the middle missing.
        s = String.Concat(before, after);

        // Loop back up to find next whitespace char in
        // this modified s.
      }
```

```
        Console.WriteLine(s);

        // Wait for user to acknowledge the results.
        Console.WriteLine("Press Enter to terminate...");
        Console.Read();
      }
    }
  }
```

The key to this program is the boldfaced loop. This loop continually refines a string consisting of the input string, s, removing every one of a set of characters contained in the array whiteSpace.

The loop uses IndexOfAny() to find the first occurrence of any of the chars in the whiteSpace array. It doesn't return until every instance of any of those chars has been removed. The IndexOfAny() method returns the index within the array of the first white space char that it can find. A return value of –1 indicates that no items in the array were found in the string.

The first pass through the loop removes the leading blank on the target string. IndexOfAny() finds the blank at index 0. The first Substring() call returns an empty string, and the second call returns the whole string after the blank. These are then concatenated with Concat(), producing a string with the leading blank squeezed out.

The second pass through the loop finds the space after "this" and squeezes that out the same way, concatenating the strings "this" and "is a\nstring". After this pass, s has become "thisis a\nstring".

The third pass finds the \n character and squeezes that out. On the fourth pass, IndexOfAny() runs out of white space characters to find and returns –1 (not found). That ends the loop.

The RemoveWhiteSpace program prints out a string containing several forms of white space. The program then strips out white space characters. The output from this program appears as follows:

```
before: this is a
string
after:thisisastring
Press Enter to terminate...
```

Let's Split() that concatenate program

The RemoveWhiteSpace program demonstrates the use of the Concat() and IndexOf() methods; however, it doesn't use the most efficient approach.

As usual, a little examination reveals a more efficient approach using our old friend Split(). The method that does the work is shown here:

```
// RemoveWhiteSpace -- The RemoveSpecialChars method removes every
//     occurrence of the specified characters from the string.
// Note: The rest of the program is not shown here.
public static string RemoveSpecialChars(string input, char[] targets)
{
  // Split the input string up using the target
  // characters as the delimiters.
  string[] subStrings = input.Split(targets);

  // output will contain the eventual output information.
  string output = "";

  // Loop through the substrings originating from the split.
  foreach(string subString in subStrings)
  {
    output = String.Concat(output, subString);
  }
  return output;
}
```

This version uses the Split() method to break the input string into a set of substrings, using the characters to be removed as delimiters. The delimiter is not included in the substrings created, which has the effect of removing the character(s). The logic here is much simpler and less error-prone.

The foreach loop in the second half of the program puts the pieces back together again using Concat(). The output from the program is unchanged. Pulling the code out into a method further simplifies it and makes it clearer.

Formatting Your Strings Precisely

The String class also provides the Format() method for formatting output, especially the output of numbers. In its simplest form, Format() allows the insertion of string, numeric, or Boolean input in the middle of a format string. For example, consider this call:

```
string myString = String.Format("{0} times {1} equals {2}", 2, 5, 2*5);
```

The first argument to Format() is known as the *format string* — the quoted string you see. The {n} items in the middle of the format string indicate that the nth argument following the format string is to be inserted at that point. {0} refers to the first argument (in this case, the value 2), {1} refers to the next (that is, 5), and so on. This code returns a string, myString. The resulting string is

```
"2 times 5 equals 10"
```

Unless otherwise directed, Format() uses a default output format for each argument type. Format() enables you to affect the output format by including *specifiers* (modifiers or controls) in the placeholders. See Table 3-1 for a listing of some of these specifiers. For example, {0:E6} says, "Output the number in exponential form, using six spaces for the fractional part."

TABLE 3-1   ## Format Specifiers Using String.Format()

Control	Example	Result	Notes
C — currency	{0:C} of 123.456	$123.45	The currency sign depends on the Region setting.
	{0:C} of –123.456	($123.45)	Specify Region in Windows control panel.
D — decimal	{0:D5} of 123	00123	Integers only.
E — exponential	{0:E} of 123.45	1.2345E+002	Also known as scientific notation.
F — fixed	{0:F2} of 123.4567	123.45	The number after the F indicates the number of digits after the decimal point.
N — number	{0:N} of 123456.789	123,456.79	Adds commas and rounds off to nearest 100th.
	{0:N1} of 123456.789	123,456.8	Controls the number of digits after the decimal point.
	{0:N0} of 123456.789	123,457	Controls the number of digits after the decimal point.
X — hexadecimal	{0:X} of 123	0x7B	7B hex = 123 decimal (integers only).
{0:0...}	{0:000.00} of 12.3	012.30	Forces a 0 if a digit is not already present.
{0:#...}	{0:###.##} of 12.3	12.3	Forces the space to be left blank; no other field can encroach on the three digits to the left and two digits after the decimal point (useful for maintaining decimal-point alignment).
	{0:##0.0#} of 0	0.0	Combining the # and zeros forces space to be allocated by the #s and forces at least one digit to appear, even if the number is 0.
{0:# or 0%}	{0:#00.#%} of .1234	12.3%	The % displays the number as a percentage (multiplies by 100 and adds the % sign).
	{0:#00.#%} of .0234	02.3%	The % displays the number as a percentage (multiplies by 100 and adds the % sign).

TIP

The `Console.WriteLine()` method uses the same placeholder system. The first placeholder, {0}, takes the first variable or value listed after the format string part of the statement, and so on. Given the exact same arguments as in the earlier `Format()` call, `Console.WriteLine()` would write the same string to the console. You also have access to the format specifiers. From now on, the examples use the formatted form of `WriteLine()` much of the time, rather than concatenate items to form the final output string with the + operator.

These format specifiers can seem a bit bewildering. Explore the topic "format specifiers" in C# Language Help Index for more information. To help you wade through these options, the following `OutputFormatControls` program enables you to enter a floating-point number followed by a specifier sequence. The program then displays the number, using the specified `Format()` control:

```
using System;

// OutputFormatControls -- Allow the user to reformat input numbers
//     using a variety of format specifiers input at run time.
namespace OutputFormatControls
{
  public class Program
  {
    public static void Main(string[] args)
    {
      // Keep looping -- inputting numbers until the user
      // enters a blank line rather than a number.
      for(;;)
      {
        // First input a number -- terminate when the user
        // inputs nothing but a blank line.
        Console.WriteLine("Enter a double number");
        string numberInput = Console.ReadLine();

        if (numberInput.Length == 0)
        {
          break;
        }

        double number = Double.Parse(numberInput);

        // Now input the specifier codes; split them
        // using spaces as dividers.
        Console.WriteLine("Enter the format specifiers"
                     + " separated by a blank "
                     + "(Example: C E F1 N0 0000000.00000)");
        char[] separator = {' '};
        string formatString = Console.ReadLine();
        string[] formats = formatString.Split(separator);
```

```
        // Loop through the list of format specifiers.
        foreach(string s in formats)
        {
          if (s.Length != 0)
          {
            // Create a complete format specifier
            // from the letters entered earlier.
            string formatCommand = "{0:" + s + "}";

            // Output the number entered using the
            // reconstructed format specifier.
            Console.Write(
                "The format specifier {0} results in ", formatCommand);
            try
            {
              Console.WriteLine(formatCommand, number);
            }
            catch(Exception)
            {
              Console.WriteLine("<illegal control>");
            }
            Console.WriteLine();
          }
        }
      }

      // Wait for user to acknowledge.
      Console.WriteLine("Press Enter to terminate...");
      Console.Read();
    }
  }
}
```

The `OutputFormatControls` program continues to read floating-point numbers into a variable `numberInput` until the user enters a blank line. (Because the input is a bit tricky, the application includes an example for the user to imitate as part of the message asking for input.) Note that the program doesn't include tests to determine whether the input is a legal floating-point number to keep the code simple.

The program then reads a series of specifier strings separated by spaces. Each specifier is then combined with a "{0}" string (the number before the colon, which corresponds to the placeholder in the format string) into the variable `formatCommand`. For example, if you entered **N4**, the program would store the specifier "{0:N4}". The following statement writes the number `number` using the newly constructed `formatCommand`:

```
Console.WriteLine(formatCommand, number);
```

In the case of the lowly N4, the command would be rendered this way:

```
Console.WriteLine("{0:N4}", number);
```

Typical output from the program appears this way:

```
Enter a double number
12345.6789
Enter the specifiers separated by a blank (Example: C E F1 N0 0000000.00000)
C E F1 N0 0000000.00000
The format specifier {0:C} results in $12,345.68

The format specifier {0:E} results in 1.234568E+004

The format specifier {0:F1} results in 12345.7

The format specifier {0:N0} results in 12,346

The format specifier {0:0000000.00000} results in 0012345.67890

Enter a double number
.12345
Enter the specifiers separated by a blank (Example: C E F1 N0 0000000.00000)
00.0%
The format specifier {0:00.0%} results in 12.3%
Enter a double number

Press Enter to terminate...
```

When applied to the number 12345.6789, the specifier N0 adds commas in the proper place (the N part) and lops off everything after the decimal point (the 0 portion) to render 12,346. (The last digit was rounded off, not truncated.)

Similarly, when applied to 0.12345, the control 00.0% outputs 12.3%. The percent sign multiplies the number by 100 and adds %. The 00.0 indicates that the output should include at least two digits to the left of the decimal point and only one digit after the decimal point. The number 0.01 is displayed as 01.0%, using the same 00.0% specifier.

TECHNICAL
STUFF

The mysterious try ... catch catches any errors that spew forth in the event you enter an illegal format command such as a D, which stands for decimal. (Chapter 9 of this minibook tells you about exceptions.)

StringBuilder: Manipulating Strings More Efficiently

Building longer strings out of a bunch of shorter strings can cost you an arm and its elbow. Because a string, after it's created, can't be changed; it's immutable, as described at the beginning of this chapter. This example doesn't tack "ly" onto s1:

```
string s1 = "rapid";
string s2 = s1 + "ly";              // s2 = rapidly.
```

It creates a new string composed of the combination. (s1 is unchanged.) Other operations that appear to modify a string, such as Substring() and Replace(), do the same.

The result is that each operation on a string produces yet another string. Suppose you need to concatenate 1,000 strings into one huge one. You're going to create a new string for each concatenation:

```
string[] listOfNames = ...  // 1000 pet names
string s = string.Empty;
for(int i = 0; i < 1000; i++)
{
  s += listOfNames[i];
}
```

To avoid such costs when you're doing lots of modifications to strings, use the companion class StringBuilder. Be sure to add this line at the top of your file:

```
using System.Text;  // Tells the compiler where to find StringBuilder.
```

REMEMBER

Unlike String manipulations, the manipulations you do on a StringBuilder directly change the underlying string. Here's an example:

```
StringBuilder builder = new StringBuilder("012");
builder.Append("34");
builder.Append("56");
string result = builder.ToString();  // result = 0123456
```

Create a StringBuilder instance initialized with an existing string, as just shown. Or create an empty StringBuilder with no initial value:

```
StringBuilder builder = new StringBuilder();  // Defaults to 16 characters
```

You can also create the `StringBuilder` with the capacity you expect it to need, which reduces the overhead of increasing the builder's capacity frequently:

```
StringBuilder builder = new StringBuilder(256); // 256 characters.
```

Use the `Append()` method to add text to the end of the current contents. Use `ToString()` to retrieve the string inside the `StringBuilder` when you finish your modifications. Here's the `StringBuilder` version of the loop just shown, with retrieval of the final concatenated string in boldface:

```
StringBuilder sb = new StringBuilder(20000);  // Allocate a bunch.
for(int i = 0; i < 1000; i++)
{
    sb.Append(listOfNames[i]);      // Same list of names as earlier
}
string result = sb.ToString();  // Retrieve the results.
```

`StringBuilder` has a number of other useful string manipulation methods, including `Insert()`, `Remove()`, and `Replace()`. It lacks many of `string`'s methods, though, such as `Substring()`, `CopyTo()`, and `IndexOf()`.

Suppose that you want to uppercase just the first character of a string, as in the earlier section "Converting a string to upper- or lowercase." With `StringBuilder`, it's much cleaner looking than the code I gave earlier.

```
StringBuilder sb = new StringBuilder("jones");
sb[0] = char.ToUpper(sb[0]);
string fixedString = sb.ToString();
```

This puts the lowercase string `"jones"` into a `StringBuilder`, accesses the first `char` in the `StringBuilder`'s underlying string directly with `sb[0]`, uses the `char.ToUpper()` method to uppercase the character, and reassigns the uppercased character to `sb[0]`. Finally, it extracts the improved string `"Jones"` from the `StringBuilder`.

The `BuildASentence` example presented in the section "Equality for all strings: The Compare() method," earlier in this chapter, could benefit from using a `StringBuilder`.

TIP

Book 2 introduces a C# feature called *extension methods*. The example there adds several handy methods to the `String` class. That minibook describes how to convert between `strings`, arrays of `char`, and arrays of `byte`. Those are operations you may need to do frequently.

Chapter **4**

Smooth Operators

Mathematicians create variables and manipulate them in various ways, adding them, multiplying them, and — here's a toughie — even integrating them. Chapter 2 of this minibook describes how to declare and define variables. However, it says little about how to use variables to get anything done after you declare them. This chapter looks at the operations you can perform on variables to do some work. Operations require *operators*, such as +, −, =, <, and &. This chapter also discusses arithmetic, logical, and other types of operators.

Performing Arithmetic

The set of arithmetic operators breaks down into several groups: the simple arithmetic operators, the assignment operators, and a set of special operators unique to programming. After you digest these, you also need to digest a separate set of logical operators. *Bon appétit!*

Simple operators

You most likely learned in elementary school how to use most of the simple operators. Table 4-1 lists them. *Note:* Computers use an asterisk (*), not the multiplication sign (×), for multiplication.

TABLE 4-1

Simple Operators

Operator	What It Means
– (unary)	Take the negative of
*	Multiply
/	Divide
+	Add
– (binary)	Subtract
%	Modulo

Most of these operators in the table are *binary* operators because they operate on two values: one on the left side of the operator and one on the right side. The lone exception is the unary negative. However, it's just as straightforward as the others, as shown in this example:

```
int n1 = 5;
int n2 = -n1;   // n2 now has the value -5.
```

The value of –n2 is the negative of the value of n1.

The modulo operator may not be quite as familiar to you as the others. Modulo is the remainder after division. Thus, 5 % 3 is 2 (5 / 3 = 1, remainder 2), and 25 % 3 is 1 (25 / 3 = 8, remainder 1). Read it "five modulo three" or simply "five mod three." Even numbers mod 2 are 0: 6 % 2 = 0 (6/2 = 3, remainder 0).

The arithmetic operators other than modulo are defined for all numeric types. The modulo operator isn't defined for floating-point numbers because you have no remainder after the division of floating-point values.

Operating orders

The value of some expressions may not be clear. Consider, for example, the following expression:

```
int n = 5 * 3 + 2;
```

Does the programmer mean "multiply 5 times 3 and then add 2," which is 17, or "multiply 5 times the sum of 3 and 2," which gives you 25?

REMEMBER

C# generally executes common operators from left to right and performs multiplication before addition. So, the preceding example assigns the value 17 to the variable n.

C# determines the value of n in the following example by first dividing 24 by 6 and then dividing the result of that operation by 2 (as opposed to dividing 24 by the ratio 6 over 2). The result is 2:

```
int n = 24 / 6 / 2
```

However, the various operators have a *hierarchy*, or order of precedence. C# scans an expression and performs the operations of higher precedence before those of lower precedence. For example, multiplication has higher precedence than addition. Many books take great pains to explain the order of precedence, but, frankly, that's a complete waste of time (and brain cells).

REMEMBER

Don't rely on yourself or someone else to know the precedence order. Use parentheses to make your meaning explicit to human readers of the code as well as to the compiler.

The value of the following expression is clear, regardless of the operators' order of precedence:

```
int n = (7 % 3) * (4 + (6 / 3));
```

Parentheses can override the order of precedence by stating exactly how the compiler is to interpret the expression. To find the first expression to evaluate, C# looks for the innermost parentheses, dividing 6 by 3 to yield 2:

```
int n = (7 % 3) * (4 + 2);    // 6 / 3 = 2
```

Then C# works its way outward, evaluating each set of parentheses in turn, from innermost to outermost:

```
int n = 1 * 6;    // (4 + 2) = 6
```

So the final result, and the value of n, is 6.

The assignment operator

C# has inherited an interesting concept from C and C++: Assignment is itself a binary operator. The assignment operator has the value of the argument to the right. The assignment has the same type as both arguments, which must match.

This view of the assignment operator has no effect on the other expressions described in this chapter:

```
n = 5 * 3;
```

In this example, 5 * 3 is 15 and an int. The assignment operator stores the int on the right into the int on the left and returns the value 15. However, this view of the assignment operator allows the following line:

```
m = n = 5 * 3;
```

Assignments are evaluated in series from right to left. The assignment on the right stores the value 15 into n and returns 15. The assignment on the left stores 15 into m and returns 15, which is then dropped, leaving the value of each variable as 15.

This strange definition for assignment makes the following rather bizarre expressions legal:

```
int n;
int m;
n = m = 2;
```

TIP

Avoid chaining assignments because it's less clear to human readers. Anything that can confuse people reading your code (including you) is worth avoiding because confusion breeds errors.

The increment operator

Of all the additions that you may perform in programming, adding 1 to a variable is the most common:

```
n = n + 1;  // Increment n by 1.
```

C# extends the simple operators with a set of operators constructed from other binary operators. For example, n += 1; is equivalent to n = n + 1;.

An assignment operator exists for just about every binary operator: +=, −=, *=, /=, %=, &=, |=, ^=. Look up *C# language, operators* in C# Language Help for full details on them.

Yet even n += 1 is not good enough. C# provides this even shorter version:

```
++n;        // Increment n by 1.
```

All these forms of incrementing a number are equivalent — they all increment n by 1.

The increment operator is strange enough, but believe it or not, C# has two increment operators: ++n and n++. The first one, ++n, is the *prefix increment* operator, and n++ is the *postfix increment* operator. The difference is subtle but important.

Remember that every expression has a type and a value. In the following code, both ++n and n++ are of type int:

```
int n;
n = 1;
int p = ++n;
n = 1;
int m = n++;
```

But what are the resulting values of m and p? (*Hint:* The choices are 1 and 2.) The value of p is 2, and the value of m is 1. That is, the value of the expression ++n is the value of n *after* being incremented, and the value of the expression n++ is the value of n *before* it's incremented. Either way, the resulting value of n itself is 2.

C# has equivalent decrement operators — n-- and --n. They work in exactly the same way as the increment operators.

Performing Logical Comparisons — Is That Logical?

C# provides a set of logical comparison operators, as shown in Table 4-2. These operators are *logical* comparisons because they return either a true or a false value of type bool.

Here's an example that involves a logical comparison:

```
int m = 5;
int n = 6;
bool b = m > n;
```

This example assigns the value false to the variable b because 5 is *not* greater than 6.

TABLE 4-2

Logical Comparison Operators

Operator	Operator Is True If
a == b	a has the same value as b.
a > b	a is greater than b.
a >= b	a is greater than or equal to b.
a < b	a is less than b.
a <= b	a is less than or equal to b.
a != b	a is not equal to b.

The logical comparisons are defined for all numeric types, including float, double, decimal, and char. All the following statements are legal:

```
bool b;
b = 3 > 2;        // true
b = 3.0 > 2.0;    // true
b = 'a' > 'b';    // false -- Alphabetically, later = greater.
b = 'A' < 'a';    // true  -- Upper A is less than lower a.
b = 'A' < 'b';    // true  -- All upper are less than all lower.
b = 10M > 12M;    // false
```

The comparison operators always produce results of type bool. The comparison operators other than == are not valid for variables of type string. (Not to worry: C# offers other ways to compare strings; see Chapter 3 of this minibook for details.)

Comparing floating-point numbers: Is your float bigger than mine?

Comparing two floating-point values can get dicey, and you need to be careful with these comparisons. Consider the following comparison:

```
float f1;
float f2;
f1 = 10;
f2 = f1 / 3;
bool b1 = (3 * f2) == f1;  // b1 is true if (3 * f2) equals f1.
f1 = 9;
f2 = f1 / 3;
bool b2 = (3 * f2) == f1;
```

Notice that both the fifth and eighth lines in the preceding example contain first an assignment operator (=) and then a logical comparison (==). These are different animals, so don't type = when you mean ==. C# does the logical comparison and then assigns the result to the variable on the left.

The only difference between the calculations of b1 and b2 is the original value of f1. So, what are the values of b1 and b2? The value of b2 is clearly true: 9 / 3 is 3; 3 * 3 is 9; and 9 equals 9. Voilà!

WARNING

The value of b1 isn't obvious: 10 / 3 is 3.333 . . . and 3.333 . . . * 3 is 9.999. . . . Is 9.999 . . . equal to 10? The manner in which math operations round values can affect comparisons, which means you need to exercise care when making assumptions about the outcome of math operations. Even though you might see two values as potentially equal, the computer won't. Consequently, using the == operator with floating-point values is generally frowned upon because of the potential to introduce errors into your code.

TECHNICAL STUFF

C# does provide some methods around the rounding error issue so that you can use the == operator when appropriate. For example, you can use the system absolute value method to compare f1 and f2:

```
Math.Abs(f1 - 3.0 * f2) < .00001; // Use whatever level of accuracy.
```

This calculation returns true for both cases. You can also use the constant Double. Epsilon instead of .00001 to produce the maximum level of accuracy. Epsilon is the smallest possible difference between two nonequal double variables.

For a self-guided tour of the System.Math class, where Abs and many other useful mathematical functions live, look for *math* in C# Language Help.

Compounding the confusion with compound logical operations

The bool variables have another set of operators defined just for them, as shown in Table 4-3.

REMEMBER

The ! operator (NOT) is the logical equivalent of the minus sign. For example, !a (read "not a") is true if a is false and false if a is true. Can that be true?

The next two operators in the table are straightforward. First, a & b is true only if both a and b are true. And a | b is true if either a or b is true (or both are). The exclusive or (xor) operator, or ^, is sort of an odd beast. An exclusive or is true if either a or b is true but not if both a and b are true. All three operators produce a logical bool value as their result.

Smooth Operators

TABLE 4-3 **The Compound Logical Operators**

Operator	Operator Is True If
!a	a is false (also known as the "not" operator).
a & b	a and b are true (also known as the "and" operator).
a | b	Either a or b or else both are true (also known as a *and/or* b).
a ^ b	a is true or b is true but not both (also known as *a xor b*, the *exclusive or* operator).
a && b	a is true and b is true with short-circuit evaluation.
a || b	a is true or b is true with short-circuit evaluation. (This section discusses short-circuit evaluation.)

TECHNICAL STUFF

The &, |, and ^ operators also have a *bitwise operator* version. When applied to int variables, these operators perform their magic on a bit-by-bit basis. Thus 6 & 3 is 2 (0110_2 & 0011_2 is 0010_2), 6 | 3 is 7 (0110_2 | 0011_2 is 0111_2), and 6 ^ 3 is 5 (0110_2 ^ 0011_2 is 0101_2). Binary arithmetic is cool but beyond the scope of this book. You can search for it at your favorite search engine.

The remaining two logical operators are similar to, but subtly different from, the first three. Consider the following example:

```
bool b = (boolExpression1) & (boolExpression2);
```

In this case, C# evaluates boolExpression1 and boolExpression2. It then looks to see whether they both are true before deciding the value of b. However, this may be a wasted effort. If one expression is false, there's no reason to perform the other. Regardless of the value of the second expression, the result will be false. Nevertheless, & goes on to evaluate both expressions.

The && operator avoids evaluating both expressions unnecessarily, as shown in the following example:

```
bool b = (boolExpression1) && (boolExpression2);
```

In this case, C# evaluates boolExpression1. If it's false, then b is set to false and the program continues on its merry way. On the other hand, if boolExpression1 is true, then C# evaluates boolExpression2 and stores the result in b. The && operator uses this *short-circuit evaluation* because it short-circuits around the second Boolean expression, if necessary.

TIP

Most programmers use the doubled forms most of the time. The || operator works the same way, as shown in the following expression:

```
bool b = (boolExpression1) || (boolExpression2);
```

If boolExpression1 is true, there's no point in evaluating boolExpression2 because the result is always true. You can read these operators as "short-circuit and" and "short-circuit or."

TECHNICAL STUFF

Some programmers do rely on the standard operators for specific tasks. For example, if the expressions perform a task other than provide just a value, it's important not to use the short-circuit operator or C# will never perform the second task when the first task is false. Don't worry about this particular case right now, but file it away as useful information for later. Sometimes, short-circuit operators produce unexpected results when you rely on the code to do more than just provide an evaluation of two values.

Matching Expression Types at TrackDownAMate.com

In calculations, an expression's type is just as important as its value. Consider the following expression:

```
int n;
n = (5 * 5) + 7;
```

My calculator says the resulting value of n is 32. However, that expression also has an overall type based on the types of its parts. Written in "type language," the preceding expression becomes

```
int [=] (int * int) + int;
```

To evaluate the type of an expression, follow the same pattern you use to evaluate the expression's value. Multiplication takes precedence over addition. An int times an int is an int. Addition comes next. An int plus an int is an int. In this way, you can reduce the preceding expression this way:

```
(int * int) + int
int + int
int
```

Calculating the type of an operation

Most operators come in various flavors. For example, the multiplication operator comes in the following forms (the arrow means "produces"):

```
int     * int     ⇨ int
uint    * uint    ⇨ uint
long    * long    ⇨ long
float   * float   ⇨ float
decimal * decimal ⇨ decimal
double  * double  ⇨ double
```

Thus, 2 * 3 uses the int * int version of the * operator to produce the int 6.

Implicit type conversion

The * symbol works well for multiplying two ints or two floats. But imagine what happens when the left and right arguments aren't of the same type. For example, consider what happens in this case:

```
int anInt = 10;
double aDouble = 5.0;
double result = anInt * aDouble;
```

First, C# doesn't have an int * double operation. C# could just generate an error message and leave it at that; however, it tries to make sense of the programmer's intention. C# has int * int and double * double versions of multiplication and could convert aDouble into its int equivalent, but that would involve losing any fractional part of the number (the digits to the right of the decimal point). Instead, in *implicit promotion*, C# converts the int anInt into a double and uses the double * double operator.

An implicit promotion is implicit because C# does it automatically, and it's a promotion because it involves the natural concept of uphill and downhill. The list of multiplication operators is in promotion order from int to double or from int to decimal — *from narrower type to wider type*. No implicit conversion exists between the floating-point types and decimal. Converting from the more capable type, such as double, to a less capable type, such as int, is known as a *demotion*.

WARNING

Implicit demotions aren't allowed; C# generates an error message.

Explicit type conversion — the cast

Imagine what happens if C# was wrong about implicit conversion and the programmer *wanted* to perform integer multiplication? You can change the type of any value-type variable by using the cast operator. A *cast* consists of a type enclosed in parentheses and placed immediately in front of the variable or expression in question. Thus the following expression uses the int * int operator:

```
int anInt = 10;
double aDouble = 5.0;
int result = anInt * (int)aDouble;
```

The cast of aDouble to an int is known as an *explicit demotion* or *downcast*. The conversion is explicit because of the programmer's explicit declaration of intent.

REMEMBER

You can make an explicit conversion between any two value types, whether it's up or down the promotion ladder.

TIP

Avoid implicit type conversion. Make any changes in value types explicit by using a cast. Doing so reduces the possibility of error and makes code much easier for humans to read.

Leave logical alone

C# offers no type conversion path to or from the bool type.

Assigning types

The same matching of types that you find in conversions applies to the assignment operator.

WARNING

Inadvertent type mismatches that generate compiler error messages usually occur in the assignment operator, not at the point of the mismatch. Consider the following multiplication example:

```
int n1 = 10;
int n2 = 5.0 * n1;
```

The second line in this example generates an error message because of a type mismatch, but the error occurs *at the assignment* — not at the multiplication. Here's the horrible tale: To perform the multiplication, C# implicitly converts n1 to a double. C# can then perform double multiplication, the result of which is the all-powerful double.

The type of the right and left operators of the assignment operator must match, but the type of the left operator cannot change. Because C# refuses to demote an expression implicitly, the compiler generates the error message Cannot implicitly convert type double to int. C# allows this expression with an explicit cast:

```
int n1 = 10;
int n2 = (int)(5.0 * n1);
```

(The parentheses are necessary because the cast operator has very high precedence.) This example works — *explicit* demotion is okay. The n1 is promoted to a double, the multiplication is performed, and the double result is demoted to an int. In this case, however, you would worry about the sanity of the programmer because 5 * n1 is so much easier for both the programmer and the C# compiler to read.

Changing how an operator works: Operator overloading

To further complicate matters, the behavior of any operator can be changed with a feature of C# called operator overloading. *Operator overloading* is essentially defining a new function that is run any time you use an operator in the same project where the overload is defined. Operation overloading is actually simpler than it sounds. If you code

```
var x = 2+2;
```

you'd expect x to equal 4 right? That's the way + works. Well, this is the twenty-first century, people, and answers are a matter of opinion! To make things interesting, you should give users more than they ask for on any transaction. For that reason, you may want to add a value of 1 to every addition operation.

To add a value of 1 to each addition operation, you need to create a custom class that your overloaded operator can use. This class will have some custom types and a method that you'll use for the overload operation. In short, if you add regular numbers, you'll get a regular answer; if you add the special AddOne numbers, you'll get one added:

```
public class AddOne
{
    public int x;

    public static AddOne operator +(AddOne a, AddOne b)
    {
        AddOne addone = new AddOne();
        addone.x = a.x + b.x + 1;
        return addone;
    }
}
```

After the operator is overloaded (with the operator tag in the listing), you can use it as usual:

```
public class Program{
        static void Main(string[] args)
        {
            AddOne foo = new AddOne();
            foo.x = 2;

            AddOne bar = new AddOne();
            bar.x = 3;

            //And 2 + 3 now is 6...
            Console.WriteLine((foo + bar).x.ToString());
            Console.Read();
        }
    }
```

The answer of course, will be 6, not 5. Operator overloading isn't useful for integers unless you're planning to rewrite the laws of mathematics. However, if you genuinely have two entities that you want to be able to add together, this technique may be useful. For instance, if you have a Product class, you can redefine the + operator for that class to add the prices.

Chapter **5**

Getting into the Program Flow

Consider this simple program:

```
using System;
namespace HelloWorld
{
  public class Program
  {
    // This is where the program starts.
    static void Main(string[] args)
    {
      // Prompt user to enter a name.
      Console.WriteLine("Enter your name, please:");

      // Now read the name entered.
      string name = Console.ReadLine();

      // Greet the user with the entered name.
      Console.WriteLine("Hello, " + name);
```

```
        // Wait for user to acknowledge the results.
        Console.WriteLine("Press Enter to terminate ... ");
        Console.Read();
    }
  }
}
```

Beyond introducing you to a few fundamentals of C# programming, this program is almost worthless. It simply spits back out whatever you entered. You can imagine more complicated program examples that accept input, perform some type of calculations, generate some type of output (otherwise, why do the calculations?), and then exit at the bottom. However, a program such as this one can be of only limited use.

One key element of any computer processor is its ability to make decisions, which means that the processor sends the flow of execution down one path of instructions if a condition is true or down another path if the condition is false (not true). Any programming language must offer this fundamental capability to control the flow of execution.

The three basic types of *flow control* are the if statement, the loop, and the jump. (Chapter 6 of this minibook describes the foreach looping control.)

Branching Out with if and switch

The basis of all C# decision-making capability is the if statement:

```
if (bool-expression)
{
    // Control goes here if the expression is true.
}
// Control passes to this statement whether the expression is true or not.
```

A pair of parentheses immediately following the keyword if contains a *conditional expression* of type bool. (See Chapter 2 of this minibook for a discussion of bool expressions.) Immediately following the expression is a block of code set off by a pair of braces. If the expression is true, the program executes the code within the braces; if the expression is not true, the program skips the code in the braces. (If the program executes the code in braces, it ends just after the closing brace and continues from there.)

The `if` statement is easier to understand by looking at a concrete example:

```
// Make sure that a is not negative:
// If a is less than 0 ...
if (a < 0)
{
    //  ... then assign 0 to it so that it's no longer negative.
    a = 0;
}
```

This segment of code ensures that the variable a is nonnegative — greater than or equal to 0. The `if` statement says, "If a is less than 0, assign 0 to a." (In other words, turn a into a positive value.)

TECHNICAL STUFF

The braces aren't required. C# treats `if(bool-expression) statement;` as though it had been written `if(bool-expression) {statement;}`. The general consensus is to always use braces for better clarity. In other words, don't ask — just do it.

Introducing the if statement

Consider a small program that calculates interest. The user enters the principal amount and the interest rate, and the program spits out the resulting value for each year. (This program isn't sophisticated.) The simplistic calculation appears as follows in C#:

```
// Calculate the value of the principal plus interest.
decimal interestPaid;
interestPaid = principal * (interest / 100);

// Now calculate the total.
decimal total = principal + interestPaid;
```

The first equation multiplies the principal `principal` times the interest `interest` to produce the interest to be paid — `interestPaid`. (You divide by 100 because interest is usually calculated by entering a percentage amount.) The interest to be paid is then added back into the principal, resulting in a new principal, which is stored in the variable `total`.

The program must anticipate almost anything when dealing with human input. For example, you don't want your program to accept a negative principal or interest amount (well, maybe a negative interest). The following `CalculateInterest` program includes checks to ensure that neither of these entries happens:

```csharp
using System;

// CalculateInterest -- Calculate the interest amount paid
//    on a given principal. If either the principal or the
//    interest rate is negative, generate an error message.
namespace CalculateInterest
{
  public class Program
  {
    public static void Main(string[] args)
    {
      // Prompt user to enter source principal.
      Console.Write("Enter principal: ");
      string principalInput = Console.ReadLine();
      decimal principal = Convert.ToDecimal(principalInput);

      // Make sure that the principal is not negative.
      if (principal < 0)
      {
        Console.WriteLine("Principal cannot be negative");
        principal = 0;
      }

      // Enter the interest rate.
      Console.Write("Enter interest: ");
      string interestInput = Console.ReadLine();
      decimal interest = Convert.ToDecimal(interestInput);

      // Make sure that the interest is not negative either.
      if (interest < 0)
      {
        Console.WriteLine("Interest cannot be negative");
        interest = 0;
      }

      // Calculate the value of the principal plus interest.
      decimal interestPaid = principal * (interest / 100);

      // Now calculate the total.
      decimal total = principal + interestPaid;

      // Output the result.
      Console.WriteLine();   // Skip a line.
      Console.WriteLine("Principal      = " + principal);
```

```
        Console.WriteLine("Interest      = " + interest + "%");
        Console.WriteLine();
        Console.WriteLine("Interest paid = " + interestPaid);
        Console.WriteLine("Total         = " + total);

        // Wait for user to acknowledge the results.
        Console.WriteLine("Press Enter to terminate ... ");
        Console.Read();
      }
    }
  }
}
```

The `CalculateInterest` program begins by prompting the user for a name using `WriteLine()` to write a `string` to the console. Tell the user exactly what you want and, if possible, specify the format. Users don't respond well to uninformative prompts, such as >.

The sample program uses the `ReadLine()` command to read in whatever the user types; the program returns the value entered, in the form of a `string`, when the user presses Enter. Because the program is looking for the principal in the form of a `decimal`, the input `string` must be converted using the `Convert.ToDecimal()` command. The result is stored in `principalInput`.

The `ReadLine()`, `WriteLine()`, and `ToDecimal()` commands are all examples of method calls. A *method call* delegates some work to another part of the program, called a method. Book 2 describes method calls in detail. For now, don't worry if you have problems understanding precisely how method calls work.

The next line in the example checks `principal`. If it's negative, the program outputs a polite message indicating the need for new input. The program does the same thing for the interest rate, and then it performs the simplistic interest calculation outlined earlier, in the "Introducing the if statement" section, and spits out the result, using a series of `WriteLine()` commands. Here's some example output from the program:

```
Enter principal: 1234
Enter interest: 21

Principal    = 1234
Interest     = 21%

Interest paid = 259.14
Total        = 1493.14
Press Enter to terminate ...
```

Executing the program with illegal input generates the following output:

```
Enter principal: 1234
Enter interest: –12.5
Interest cannot be negative

Principal    = 1234
Interest     = 0%

Interest paid = 0
Total         = 1234
Press Enter to terminate ...
```

TIP

Indent the lines within an `if` clause to enhance readability. This type of indentation is ignored by C# but is helpful to us humans. Most programming editors support autoindenting, whereby the editor automatically indents as soon as you enter the `if` command. To set autoindenting in Visual Studio, choose Tools⇨Options. Then expand the Text Editor node. From there, expand C#. Finally, click Tabs. On this page, enable Smart Indenting and set the number of spaces per indent to your preference. (The book uses two spaces per indent.) Set the tab size to the same value.

Examining the else statement

Sometimes, your code must check for mutually exclusive conditions. For example, the following code segment stores the maximum of two numbers, a and b, in the variable max:

```csharp
// Store the maximum of a and b into the variable max.
int max;

// If a is greater than b ...
if (a > b)
{
    // ... save a as the maximum.
    max = a;
}

// If a is less than or equal to b ...
if (a <= b)
{
    // ... save b as the maximum.
    max = b;
}
```

The second if statement causes needless processing because the two conditions are mutually exclusive. If a is greater than b, a can't possibly be less than or equal to b. C# defines an else clause for just this case. The else keyword defines a block of code that's executed if the if block is not. The code segment to calculate the maximum now appears this way:

```
// Store the maximum of a and b into the variable max.
int max;

// If a is greater than b ...
if (a > b)
{
    // ... save a as the maximum; otherwise ...
    max = a;
}
else
{
    // ... save b as the maximum.
    max = b;
}
```

If a is greater than b, the first block is executed; otherwise, the second block is executed. In the end, max contains the greater of a or b.

Avoiding even the else

Sequences of else clauses can become confusing. Some programmers like to avoid them when doing so doesn't cause even more confusion. You could write the maximum calculation like this:

```
// Store the maximum of a and b into the variable max.
int max;

// Start by assuming that a is greater than b.
max = a;

// If it is not ...
if (b > a)
{
    // ... then you can change your mind.
    max = b;
}
```

Programmers who like to be cool and cryptic often use the *ternary operator*, : ?, equivalent to an if/else on one line:

```
bool informal = true;
string name = informal : "Chuck" ? "Charles";  // Returns "Chuck"
```

This chunk evaluates the expression before the colon. If the expression is true, return the value after the colon but before the question mark. If the expression is false, return the value after the question mark. This process turns an if/else into an expression. Best practice advises using ternary only rarely because it truly *is* cryptic.

Nesting if statements

The CalculateInterest program warns the user of illegal input; however, continuing with the interest calculation, even if one of the values is illogical, doesn't seem quite right. It causes no real harm here because the interest calculation takes little or no time and the user can ignore the results, but some calculations aren't nearly as quick. In addition, why ask the user for an interest rate after entering an invalid value for the principal? The user knows that the results of the calculation will be invalid. (You'd be amazed at how much it infuriates users.) The program should ask the user for an interest rate only if the principal is reasonable and perform the interest calculation only if both values are valid. To accomplish this, you need two if statements, one within the other.

An if statement found within the body of another if statement is an *embedded*, or *nested*, statement. The following program, CalculateInterestWithEmbeddedTest, uses embedded if statements to avoid stupid questions if a problem is detected in the input:

```
using System;

// CalculateInterestWithEmbeddedTest -- Calculate the interest amount
//    paid on a given principal. If either the principal or the
//    interest rate is negative, then generate an error message
//    and don't proceed with the calculation.
namespace CalculateInterestWithEmbeddedTest
{
  public class Program
  {
    public static void Main(string[] args)
    {
      // Define a maximum interest rate.
      int maximumInterest = 50;
```

```
// Prompt user to enter source principal.
Console.Write("Enter principal: ");
string principalInput = Console.ReadLine();
decimal principal = Convert.ToDecimal(principalInput);

// If the principal is negative ...
if (principal < 0)
{
  // ... generate an error message ...
  Console.WriteLine("Principal cannot be negative");
}
else  // Go here only if principal was > 0: thus valid.
{
  //  ... otherwise, enter the interest rate.
  Console.Write("Enter interest: ");
  string interestInput = Console.ReadLine();
  decimal interest = Convert.ToDecimal(interestInput);

  // If the interest is negative or too large ...
  if (interest < 0 || interest > maximumInterest)
  {
    //  ... generate an error message as well.
    Console.WriteLine("Interest cannot be negative " +
                      "or greater than " + maximumInterest);
    interest = 0;
  }
  else  // Reach this point only if all is well.
  {
    // Both the principal and the interest appear to be legal;
    // calculate the value of the principal plus interest.
    decimal interestPaid;
    interestPaid = principal * (interest / 100);

    // Now calculate the total.
    decimal total = principal + interestPaid;

    // Output the result.
    Console.WriteLine();  // Skip a line.
    Console.WriteLine("Principal     = " + principal);
    Console.WriteLine("Interest      = " + interest + "%");
    Console.WriteLine();
    Console.WriteLine("Interest paid = " + interestPaid);
    Console.WriteLine("Total         = " + total);
  }
}
```

```
      // Wait for user to acknowledge the results.
      Console.WriteLine("Press Enter to terminate ... ");
      Console.Read();
   }
 }
}
```

The program first reads the principal from the user. If the principal is negative, the program outputs an error message and quits. If the principal is not negative, control passes to the else clause, where the program continues executing.

The interest rate test has been improved in this example. Here, the program requires an interest rate that's nonnegative (a mathematical law) and less than a maximum rate (a judiciary law). This if statement uses the following compound test:

```
if (interest < 0 || interest > maximumInterest)
```

This statement is true if interest is less than 0 or greater than maximumInterest. Notice the code declares maximumInterest at the top of the program rather than *hard-code* it as a constant number here. *Hard-coding* refers to using values directly in your code rather than creating a constant to hold them.

TIP

Define important constants at the top of your program. Giving a constant a descriptive name (rather than just a number) makes it easy to find and easier to change. If the constant appears ten times in your code, you still have to make only one change to change all references. Entering a correct principal but a negative interest rate generates this output:

```
Enter principal: 1234
Enter interest: -12.5
Interest cannot be negative or greater than 50.
Press Enter to terminate ...
```

Only when the user enters both a legal principal and a legal interest rate does the program generate the correct calculation:

```
Enter principal: 1234
Enter interest: 12.5

Principal    = 1234
Interest     = 12.5%

Interest paid = 154.250
Total        = 1388.250
Press Enter to terminate ...
```

Running the switchboard

You often want to test a variable for numerous different values. For example, maritalStatus may be 0 for unmarried, 1 for married, 2 for divorced, 3 for widowed, or 4 for none of your business. To differentiate among these values, you could use the following series of if statements:

```
if (maritalStatus == 0)
{
  // Must be unmarried ...
  // ... do something ...
}
else
{
  if (maritalStatus == 1)
  {
    // Must be married ...
    // ... do something else ...
```

You can see that these repetitive if statements grow tiresome quickly. Testing for multiple cases is such a common occurrence that C# provides a special construct to decide between a set of mutually exclusive conditions. This control, the switch, works as follows:

```
switch(maritalStatus)
{
  case 0:
          // ... do the unmarried stuff ...
          break;
  case 1:
          // ... do the married stuff ...
          break;
  case 2:
          // ... do the divorced stuff ...
          break;
  case 3:
          // ... do the widowed stuff ...
          break;
  case 4:
          // ... get out of my face ...
          break;
  default:
          // Goes here if it fails to pass a case;
          // this is probably an error condition.
          break;
}
```

The expression at the top of the `switch` statement is evaluated. In this case, the expression is simply the variable `maritalStatus`. The value of that expression is then compared against the value of each of the cases. Control passes to the `default` clause if no match is found. The argument to the `switch` statement can also be a `string`:

```
string s = "Davis";
switch(s)
{
  case "Davis":
          // ... control will actually pass here ...
          break;
  case "Smith":
          // ... do Smith stuff ...
          break;
  case "Jones":
          // ... do Jones stuff ...
          break;
  case "Hvidsten":
          // ... do Hvidsten stuff ...
          break;
  default:
          // Goes here if it doesn't pass any cases.
          break;
}
```

REMEMBER

Using the `switch` statement involves these restrictions:

» The argument to the `switch()` must be one of the counting types (including `char`) or a `string`. Floating-point values are excluded.

» The various case values must refer to values of the same type as the `switch` expression.

» The case values must be constant in the sense that their value must be known at compile time. (A statement such as `case x` isn't legal unless x is a type of constant.)

» Each clause must end in a `break` statement (or another exit command, such as `return`). The `break` statement passes control out of the `switch`.

You can omit a break statement if two cases lead to the same actions: A single case clause may have more than one case label, as in this example:

```
string s = "Davis";
switch(s)
{
```

```
    case "Davis":
    case "Hvidsten":
            // Do the same thing whether s is Davis or Hvidsten
            // since they're related.
            break;
    case "Smith":
            // ... do Smith stuff ...
            break;
    default:
            // Goes here if it doesn't pass any cases.
            break;
}
```

This approach enables the program to perform the same operation, whether the input is Davis or Hvidsten. The final section of this chapter supplies a small addendum to the switch story.

Here We Go Loop-the-Loop

The if statement enables a program to take different paths through the code being executed, depending on the results of a bool expression. This statement provides for drastically more interesting programs than programs without decision-making capability. Adding the ability to execute a set of instructions *repeatedly* adds another quantum jump in capability.

Consider the CalculateInterest program from the section "Introducing the if statement," earlier in this chapter. Performing this simple interest calculation by using a calculator (or by hand, using a piece of paper) would be much easier than writing and executing a program.

If you could calculate the amount of principal for each of several succeeding years, that would be even more useful. A simple macro in a Microsoft Excel spreadsheet is still easier to handle, but at least you're getting closer. What you need is a way for the computer to execute the same short sequence of instructions multiple times — known as a *loop*.

Looping for a while

The C# keyword `while` introduces the most basic form of execution loop:

```
while(bool-expression)
{
    // ... repeatedly executed as long as the expression is true.
}
```

When the `while` loop is first encountered, the `bool` expression is evaluated. If the expression is true, the code within the block is executed. When the block of code reaches the closed brace, control returns to the top, and the whole process starts over again. Control passes beyond the closed brace the first time the `bool` expression is evaluated and turns out to be false.

REMEMBER

If the condition is not true the first time the `while` loop is encountered, the set of commands within the braces is never executed.

WARNING

It's easy to become confused about how a `while` loop executes. You may feel that a loop executes until a condition is false, which implies that control passes outside the loop — no matter where the program happens to be executing — as soon as the condition becomes false. This definitely isn't the case. The program doesn't check whether the condition is still true until control specifically passes back to the top of the loop.

You can use the `while` loop to create the `CalculateInterestTable` program, a looping version of the `CalculateInterest` program. `CalculateInterestTable` calculates a table of principals showing accumulated annual payments:

```
using System;

// CalculateInterestTable -- Calculate the interest paid on a given
//      principal over a period of years.
namespace CalculateInterestTable
{
  public class Program
  {
    public static void Main(string[] args)
    {
        // Define a maximum interest rate.
        int maximumInterest = 50;

        // Prompt user to enter source principal.
        Console.Write("Enter principal: ");
        string principalInput = Console.ReadLine();
        decimal principal = Convert.ToDecimal(principalInput);
```

```csharp
// If the principal is negative ...
if (principal < 0)
{
  // ... generate an error message ...
  Console.WriteLine("Principal cannot be negative");
}
else  // Go here only if principal was > 0: thus valid.
{
  //  ... otherwise, enter the interest rate.
  Console.Write("Enter interest: ");
  string interestInput = Console.ReadLine();
  decimal interest = Convert.ToDecimal(interestInput);

  // If the interest is negative or too large ...
  if (interest < 0 || interest > maximumInterest)
  {
    //  ... generate an error message as well.
    Console.WriteLine("Interest cannot be negative " +
                      "or greater than " + maximumInterest);
    interest = 0;
  }
  else  // Reach this point only if all is well.
  {
    // Both the principal and the interest appear to be
    // legal; finally, input the number of years.
    Console.Write("Enter number of years: ");
    string durationInput = Console.ReadLine();
    int duration = Convert.ToInt32(durationInput);

    // Verify the input.
    Console.WriteLine();  // Skip a line.
    Console.WriteLine("Principal     = " + principal);
    Console.WriteLine("Interest      = " + interest + "%");
    Console.WriteLine("Duration      = " + duration + " years");
    Console.WriteLine();

    // Now loop through the specified number of years.
    int year = 1;
    while(year <= duration)
    {
      // Calculate the value of the principal plus interest.
      decimal interestPaid;
      interestPaid = principal * (interest / 100);

      // Now calculate the new principal by adding
      // the interest to the previous principal amount.
      principal = principal + interestPaid;
```

```
            // Round off the principal to the nearest cent.
            principal = decimal.Round(principal, 2);

            // Output the result.
            Console.WriteLine(year + "-" + principal);

            // Skip over to next year.
            year = year + 1;
          }
        }
      }

      // Wait for user to acknowledge the results.
      Console.WriteLine("\nPress Enter to terminate ... ");
      Console.Read();
    }
  }
}
```

The output from a trial run of `CalculateInterestTable` appears this way:

```
Enter principal: 1234
Enter interest: 12.5
Enter number of years: 10

Principal   = 1234
Interest    = 12.5%
Duration    = 10 years

1-1388.25
2-1561.78
3-1757.00
4-1976.62
5-2223.70
6-2501.66
7-2814.37
8-3166.17
9-3561.94
10-4007.18

Press Enter to terminate ...
```

Each value represents the total principal after the number of years elapsed, assuming simple interest compounded annually. For example, the value of $1,234 at 12.5 percent is $3,561.94 after nine years.

**TECHNICAL
STUFF**

Most of the values show two decimal places for the cents in the amount. Because trailing zeros aren't displayed in all versions of C#, some values may show only a single digit — or even no digit — after the decimal point. Thus, $12.70 may be displayed as 12.7. If so, you can fix the problem by using the special formatting characters described in Chapter 3 of this minibook. (C# 2.0 and later appear to show trailing zeros by default.)

The CalculateInterestTable program begins by reading the principal and interest values from the user and checking to make sure that they're valid. CalculateInterestTable then reads the number of years over which to iterate and stores this value in the variable duration.

Before entering the while loop, the program declares a variable year, which it initializes to 1. This will be the "current year" — that is, this number changes "each year" as the program loops. If the year number contained in year is less than the total duration contained in duration, the principal for "this year" is recalculated by calculating the interest based on the "previous year." The calculated principal is output along with the current-year offset.

**TECHNICAL
STUFF**

The statement decimal.Round() rounds the calculated value to the nearest fraction of a cent.

The key to the program lies in the last line within the block. The statement year = year + 1; increments year by 1. If year begins with the value 3, its value will be 4 after this expression. This incrementing moves the calculations along from one year to the next.

After the year has been incremented, control returns to the top of the loop, where the value year is compared to the requested duration. In the sample run, if the current year is less than 10, the calculation continues. After being incremented ten times, the value of year becomes 11, which is greater than 10, and program control passes to the first statement after the while loop — the program stops looping.

The counting variable year in CalculateInterestTable must be declared and initialized before the while loop in which it is used. In addition, the year variable must be incremented, usually as the last statement within the loop. As this example demonstrates, you have to look ahead to see which variables you need. This pattern is easier to use after you've written a few thousand while loops.

When writing `while` loops, don't forget to increment the counting variable, as shown in this example:

```
int nYear = 1;
while (nYear < 10)
{
    // ... whatever ...
}
```

This example doesn't increment `nYear`. Without the increment, `nYear` is always 1 and the program loops forever. The only way to exit this *infinite loop* is to terminate the program or reboot. (So nothing is truly infinite, with the possible exception of a particle passing through the event horizon of a black hole.)

Make sure that the terminating condition can be satisfied. Usually, this means your counting variable is being incremented properly. Otherwise, you're looking at an infinite loop, an angry user, bad press, and 50 years of drought. Infinite loops are a common mistake, so don't be embarrassed when you get caught in one.

Doing the do . . . while loop

A variation of the `while` loop is the `do ... while` loop. In this example, the condition isn't checked until the *end* of the loop:

```
int year = 1;
do
{
    // ... some calculation ...
    year = year + 1;
} while (year < duration);
```

In contrast to the `while` loop, the `do ... while` loop is executed at least once, regardless of the value of `duration`.

Breaking up is easy to do

You can use two special commands to bail out of a loop: `break` and `continue`. Executing the `break` command causes control to pass to the first expression immediately following the loop. The similar `continue` command passes control straight back up to the conditional expression at the top of the loop to start over and get it right this time.

Suppose that you want to take your money out of the bank as soon as the principal exceeds a certain number of times the original amount, irrespective of the duration in years. You could easily accommodate this amount by adding the following code (in bold) within the loop:

```
// Now loop through the specified number of years.
int year = 1;
while(year <= duration)
{
  // Calculate the value of the principal plus interest.
  decimal interestPaid;
  interestPaid = principal * (interest / 100);

  // Now calculate the new principal by adding
  // the interest to the previous principal amount.
  principal = principal + interestPaid;

  // Round off the principal to the nearest cent.
  principal = decimal.Round(principal, 2);

  // Output the result.
  Console.WriteLine(year + "-" + principal);

  // Skip over to next year.
  year = year + 1;

  // Determine whether we have reached our goal.
  if (principal > (maxPower * originalPrincipal))
  {
    break;
  }
}
```

The break clause isn't executed until the condition within the if comparison is true — in this case, until the calculated principal is maxPower times the original principal or more. Executing the break statement passes control outside the while(year <= duration) statement, and the program resumes execution immediately after the loop.

Looping until you get it right

The CalculateInterestTable program is smart enough to terminate in the event that the user enters an invalid balance or interest amount. However, jumping immediately out of the program just because the user mistypes something seems harsh.

A combination of `while` and `break` enables the program to be a little more flexible. The `CalculateInterestTableMoreForgiving` program demonstrates the principle this way:

```
using System;

// CalculateInterestTableMoreForgiving -- Calculate the interest paid on a
//     given principal over a period of years. This version gives the user
//     multiple chances to input the legal principal and interest.
namespace CalculateInterestTableMoreForgiving
{
  using System;
  public class Program
  {
    public static void Main(string[] args)
    {
      // Define a maximum interest rate.
      int maximumInterest = 50;

      // Prompt user to enter source principal; keep prompting
      // until the correct value is entered.
      decimal principal;
      while(true)
      {
        Console.Write("Enter principal: ");
        string principalInput = Console.ReadLine();
        principal = Convert.ToDecimal(principalInput);

        // Exit if the value entered is correct.
        if (principal >= 0)
        {
          break;
        }

        // Generate an error on incorrect input.
        Console.WriteLine("Principal cannot be negative");
        Console.WriteLine("Try again");
        Console.WriteLine();
      }

      // Now enter the interest rate.
      decimal interest;
      while(true)
      {
        Console.Write("Enter interest: ");
        string interestInput = Console.ReadLine();
        interest = Convert.ToDecimal(interestInput);
```

```
      // Don't accept interest that is negative or too large ...
      if (interest >= 0 && interest <= maximumInterest)
      {
        break;
      }

      //  ... generate an error message as well.
      Console.WriteLine("Interest cannot be negative " +
                        "or greater than " + maximumInterest);
      Console.WriteLine("Try again");
      Console.WriteLine();
    }

    // Both the principal and the interest appear to be
    // legal; finally, input the number of years.
    Console.Write("Enter number of years: ");
    string durationInput = Console.ReadLine();
    int duration = Convert.ToInt32(durationInput);

    // Verify the input.
    Console.WriteLine();  // Skip a line.
    Console.WriteLine("Principal     = " + principal);
    Console.WriteLine("Interest      = " + interest + "%");
    Console.WriteLine("Duration      = " + duration + " years");
    Console.WriteLine();

    // Now loop through the specified number of years.
    int year = 1;
    while(year <= duration)
    {
      // Calculate the value of the principal plus interest.
      decimal interestPaid;
      interestPaid = principal * (interest / 100);

      // Now calculate the new principal by adding
      // the interest to the previous principal.
      principal = principal + interestPaid;

      // Round off the principal to the nearest cent.
      principal = decimal.Round(principal, 2);

      // Output the result.
      Console.WriteLine(year + "-" + principal);

      // Skip over to next year.
      year = year + 1;
    }
```

```
        // Wait for user to acknowledge the results.
        Console.WriteLine("Press Enter to terminate ... ");
        Console.Read();
    }
  }
}
```

This program works largely the same way as do the examples in previous sections of this chapter, except in the area of user input. This time, a `while` loop replaces the `if` statement used in earlier examples to detect invalid input:

```
decimal principal;
while(true)
{
  Console.Write("Enter principal: ");
  string principalInput = Console.ReadLine();
  principal = Convert.ToDecimal(principalInput);

  // Exit when the value entered is correct.
  if (principal >= 0)
  {
    break;
  }

  // Generate an error on incorrect input.
  Console.WriteLine("Principal cannot be negative");
  Console.WriteLine("Try again");
  Console.WriteLine();
}
```

This section of code inputs a value from the user within a loop. If the value of the text is okay, the program exits the input loop and continues. However, if the input has an error, the user sees an error message and control passes back to the program flow to start over.

REMEMBER

The program continues to loop until the user enters the correct input. (In the worst case, the program could loop until an obtuse user dies of old age.)

Notice that the conditionals have been reversed because the question is no longer whether illegal input should generate an error message, but rather whether the correct input should exit the loop. In the interest section, for example, consider this test:

```
principal < 0 || principal > maximumInterest
```

This test changes to this:

```
interest >= 0 && interest <= maximumInterest
```

Clearly, `interest >= 0` is the opposite of `interest < 0`. What may not be as obvious is that the OR (`||`) operator is replaced with an AND (`&&`) operator. It says, "Exit the loop if the interest is greater than zero AND less than the maximum amount (in other words, if it is correct)." Note that the `principal` variable must be declared outside the loop because of scope rules, which is explained in the next section.

WARNING

It may sound obvious, but the expression `true` evaluates to `true`. Therefore, `while(true)` is your archetypical infinite loop. It's the embedded `break` command that exits the loop. Therefore, if you use the `while(true)` loop, make sure that your break condition can occur. The output from a sample execution of this program appears this way:

```
Enter principal: -1000
Principal cannot be negative
Try again

Enter principal: 1000
Enter interest: -10
Interest cannot be negative or greater than 50
Try again

Enter interest: 10
Enter number of years: 5

Principal    = 1000
Interest     = 10%
Duration     = 5 years

1-1100.0
2-1210.00
3-1331.00
4-1464.10
5-1610.51
Press Enter to terminate ...
```

The program refuses to accept a negative principal or interest amount and patiently explains the mistake on each loop.

WARNING

Explain exactly what the user did wrong before looping back for further input or else that person will become extremely confused. Showing an example may also help, especially for formatting problems. A little diplomacy can't hurt, either, as Grandma may have pointed out.

Focusing on scope rules

A variable declared within the body of a loop is *defined only within* that loop. Consider this code snippet:

```
int days = 1;
while(days < duration)
{
    int average = value / days;
    //  ... some series of commands ...
    days = days + 1;
}
```

TECHNICAL STUFF

The variable average isn't defined outside the while loop. Various reasons for this exist, but consider this one: The first time the loop executes, the program encounters the declaration int average and the variable is defined. On the second loop, the program again encounters the declaration for average, and were it not for scope rules, it would be an error because the variable is already defined. Suffice it to say that the variable average goes away, as far as C# is concerned, as soon as the program reaches the closed brace — and is redefined each time through the loop.

TIP

Experienced programmers say that the *scope* of the variable average is limited to the while loop.

Looping a Specified Number of Times with for

The while loop is the simplest and second most commonly used looping structure in C#. Compared to the for loop, however, the while loop is used about as often as metric tools in an American machine shop.

The for loop has this structure:

```
for(initExpression; condition; incrementExpression)
{
    // ... body of code ...
}
```

When the `for` loop is encountered, the program first executes the `initExpression` expression and then executes the `condition`. If the `condition` expression is true, the program executes the body of the loop, which is surrounded by the braces immediately following the `for` command. When the program reaches the closed brace, control passes to `incrementExpression` and then back to `condition`, where the next pass through the loop begins. In fact, the definition of a `for` loop can be converted into this `while` loop:

```
initExpression;
while(condition)
{
    //  ... body of code ...
    incrementExpression;
}
```

An example

You can better see how the `for` loop works in this example:

```
// Here is one C# expression or another.
a = 1;

// Now loop for awhile.
for(int year = 1; year < duration; year = year + 1)
{
    //  ... body of code ...
}

// The program continues here.
a = 2;
```

Assume that the program has just executed the `a = 1;` expression. Next, the program declares the variable `year` and initializes it to 1. Then the program compares `year` to `duration`. If `year` is less than `duration`, the body of code within the braces is executed. After encountering the closed brace, the program jumps back to the top and executes the `year = year + 1` clause before sliding back over to the `year < duration` comparison.

WARNING

The `year` variable is undefined outside the scope of the `for` loop. The loop's scope includes the loop's heading as well as its body.

Why do you need another loop?

Why do you need the `for` loop if C# has an equivalent `while` loop? The short answer is that you don't — the `for` loop doesn't bring anything to the table that the `while` loop can't already do.

However, the sections of the `for` loop exist for convenience — and to clearly establish the three parts that every loop should have: the setup, exit criteria, and increment. Not only is this arrangement easier to read, it's also easier to get right. (Remember that the most common mistakes in a `while` loop are forgetting to increment the counting variable and failing to provide the proper exit criteria.) The most important reason to understand the `for` loop is that it's the loop everyone uses — and it (along with its cousin, `foreach`) is the one you see 90 percent of the time when you're reading other people's code.

TECHNICAL STUFF

The `for` loop is designed so that the first expression initializes a counting variable and the last section increments it; however, the C# language doesn't enforce any such rule. You can do anything you want in these two sections; however, you would be ill advised to do anything *but* initialize and increment the counting variable.

The increment operator is particularly popular when writing `for` loops. (Chapter 4 of this minibook describes the increment operator along with other operators.) The previous `for` loop is usually written this way:

```
for(int year = 1; year < nDuration; year++)
{
    //  ... body of code ...
}
```

TIP

You almost always see the postincrement operator used in a `for` loop instead of the preincrement operator, although the effect in this case is the same. There's no reason other than habit and the fact that it looks cooler. (The next time you want to break the ice, just haul out your C# listing full of postincrement operators to show how cool you are. It almost never works, but it's worth a try.)

The `for` loop has one variation that you may find hard to understand. If the logical condition expression is missing, it's assumed to be `true`. Thus `for(;;)` is an infinite loop. You see `for(;;)` used as an infinite loop more often than `while(true)`.

Nesting Loops

An inner loop can appear within an outer loop, this way:

```
for( ...some condition ...)
{
  for( ...some other condition ...)
  {
    //  ... do whatever ...
  }
}
```

The inner loop is executed to completion after each pass through the outer loop. The loop variable (such as year) used in the inner for loop isn't defined outside the inner loop's scope.

REMEMBER

A loop contained within another loop is a *nested* loop. Nested loops cannot "cross." For example, the following code won't work:

```
do                 // Start a do..while loop.
{
  for( ...)        // Start some for loop.
  {
  } while( ...)  // End do..while loop.
}                  // End for loop.
```

REMEMBER

A break statement within a nested loop breaks out of the inner loop only. In the following example, the break statement exits loop B and goes back into loop A:

```
// for loop A
for( ...some condition ...)
{
  // for loop B
  for( ...some other condition ...)
  {
    //  ... do whatever ...
    if (something is true)
    {
      break;        // Breaks out of loop B and not loop A
    }
  }
}
```

C# doesn't have a break command that exits both loops simultaneously. You must use two separate break commands, one for each loop.

Having to use two break commands isn't as big a limitation as it sounds. In practice, the often-complex logic contained within such nested loops is better encapsulated in a method. Executing a return from within any of the loops exits the method, thereby bailing out of all loops, no matter how nested they are. Chapter 7 of this minibook describes methods and the return statement.

Don't goto Pieces

You can transfer control in an unstructured fashion by using the goto statement. It's followed by one of these items:

» A label

» A case in a switch statement

» The keyword default (the default clause of a switch statement)

The idea behind the latter two items is to "jump" from one case to another. This snippet demonstrates how the goto statement is used:

```
// If the condition is true ...
if (a > b)
{
  // ... control passes unconditionally from the goto to the label.
  goto exitLabel;
}
// ... whatever other code goes here ...
exitLabel:
  // Control continues here.
```

The goto statement is unpopular for the very reason that makes it such a powerful control: It is almost completely unstructured. Tracking the flow of control through anything larger than a trivial piece of code can be difficult if you use goto. (Can you say "spaghetti code"?)

Religious wars have sprung up over the use of the goto statement. In fact, the C# language itself has been criticized for its inclusion of the statement. Actually, goto is neither all that horrible nor necessary. Because you can almost always avoid using goto, I recommend staying away from it, other than *occasionally* using it to link two cases within a switch statement, like this:

```
switch(n)  // This example becomes gnarly in the logic department ...
{
  case 0:
    // Do something for the 0 case, then  ...
    goto 3;  // jump to another case; no break statement needed.
  case 1:
    // Do something for the 1 case.
    break;
  case 3:    // Case 0 jumps to here after doing its thing.
    // Add some case 3 stuff to what case 0 did, thus "chaining" the cases.
    break;
  default:
    // Default case.
    break;
}
```

Don't get addicted to goto, though. Really.

Chapter **6**

Lining Up Your Ducks with Collections

Simple one-value variables of the sort you may encounter in this book fall a bit short in dealing with lots of items of the same kind: ten ducks instead of just one, for example. C# fills the gap with two kinds of variables that store multiple items, generally called *collections.* The two species of collection are the *array* and the more general-purpose *collection class.*

REMEMBER

This book specifically uses the term *array* when discussing arrays. When working with the collection class, the book uses the term *collection class.* If the book refers to a *collection* or a *list,* the object in question can be either an array or a collection class.

An *array* is a data type that holds a list of objects of the same type. You can't create a single array that contains both int and double objects, for example. Every object must be of the same type.

C# gives you quite a collection of collection classes, and they come in various shapes, such as flexible lists (like strings of beads), queues (like the line at the bank), stacks (like a stack of pancakes), and more. Most collection classes are like arrays in that they can hold just apples or just oranges. But C# also gives you a few collection classes that can hold both apples and oranges at the same time — which is useful only rarely. (And you have much better ways to manage the feat than using these elderly collections.)

For now, if you can master arrays and the List collection, you'll do fine throughout most of this book. But circle back here later if you want to pump up your collection repertoire. This chapter does introduce two other collection types.

The C# Array

Variables that contain single values are plenty useful. Even class structures that can describe compound objects made up of parts (such as a vehicle with its engine and transmission) are critical. But you also need a construct for holding a bunch of objects, such as Bill Gates's extensive collection of vintage cars or a list of tunes in a music collection. The built-in class Array is a structure that can contain a series of elements of the same type (all int values and all double values, for example, or all Vehicle objects and Motor objects; you meet these latter sorts of objects in Chapter 7 of this minibook).

The argument for the array

Consider the problem of averaging a set of six floating-point numbers. Each of the six numbers requires its own double storage:

```
double d0 = 5;
double d1 = 2;
double d2 = 7;
double d3 = 3.5;
double d4 = 6.5;
double d5 = 8;
```

Computing the average of those variables might look like this (remember that averaging int variables can result in rounding errors, as described in Chapter 2 of this minibook):

```
double sum = d0 + d1 + d2 + d3 + d4 + d5;
double average = sum / 6;
```

Listing each element by name is tedious. Okay, maybe it's not so tedious when you have only 6 numbers to average, but imagine averaging 600 (or even 6 million) floating-point values.

The fixed-value array

Fortunately, you don't need to name each element separately. C# provides the array structure that can store a sequence of values. Using an array, you can put all your `doubles` into one variable, like this:

```
double[] doublesArray = {5, 2, 7, 3.5, 6.5, 8, 1, 9, 1, 3};
```

You can also declare an empty array without initializing it:

```
double[] doublesArray = new double[6];
```

This line allocates space for six `doubles` but doesn't initialize them.

REMEMBER

The `Array` class, on which all C# arrays are based, provides a special syntax that makes it more convenient to use. The paired brackets `[]` refer to the way you access individual elements in the array:

```
doublesArray[0] // Corresponds to d0 (that is, 5)
doublesArray[1] // Corresponds to d1 (that is, 2)
...
```

The 0th element of the array corresponds to d0, the 1th element to d1, the 2th element to d2, and so on. Programmers commonly refer to the 0th element as "`doublesArray` sub-0," to the first element as "`doublesArray` sub-1," and so on.

REMEMBER

The array's element numbers — 0, 1, 2, . . . — are known as the *index*.

REMEMBER

In C#, the array index starts at 0 and not at 1. Therefore, you typically don't refer to the element at index 1 as the first element but, rather, as the "oneth element" or the "element at index 1." *The first element is the zeroth element.* If you insist on using normal speech, just be aware that the first element is always at index 0 and the second element is at index 1.

The `doublesArray` variable wouldn't be much of an improvement, were it not for the possibility that the index of the array is a variable. Using a `for` loop is easier than writing out each element by hand, as this program demonstrates:

```
using System;

// FixedArrayAverage -- Average a fixed array of numbers using a loop.
namespace FixedArrayAverage
{
    public class Program
```

```
{
    public static void Main(string[] args)
    {
        double[] doublesArray = {5, 2, 7, 3.5, 6.5, 8, 1, 9, 1, 3};

        // Accumulate the values in the array into the variable sum.
        double sum = 0;
        for (int i = 0; i < 10; i++)
        {
            sum = sum + doublesArray[i];
        }

        // Now calculate the average.
        double average = sum / 10;
        Console.WriteLine(average);
        Console.WriteLine("Press Enter to terminate...");
        Console.Read();
    }
}
}
```

The program begins by initializing a variable sum to 0. Then it loops through the values stored in doublesArray, adding each one to sum. By the end of the loop, sum has accumulated the sum of all values in the array. The resulting sum is divided by the number of elements to create the average. The output from executing this program is the expected 4.6. (You can check it with your calculator.)

The variable-length array

The array used in the FixedArrayAverage program example suffers from these two serious problems:

>> The size of the array is fixed at ten elements.

>> Worse, the elements' values are specified directly in the program.

A program that could read in a variable number of values, perhaps determined by the user during execution, would be much more flexible. It would work not only for the ten values specified in FixedArrayAverage but also for any other set of values, regardless of their number. The format for declaring a variable-size array differs slightly from that of a fixed-size, fixed-value array:

```
double[] doublesArrayVariable = new double[N];   // Variable, versus ...
double[] doublesArrayFixed = new double[10];     // Fixed
```

CHECKING ARRAY BOUNDS

Fortunately, the FixedArrayAverage program (in the preceding section "The fixed-value array") loops through all ten elements. But what if you goof and don't iterate through the loop properly? You have these two cases to consider:

You iterate through only nine elements: C# doesn't consider it an error. If you want to read nine elements of a ten-element array, who is C# to say any differently? Of course, the average is incorrect, but the program doesn't know that.

You iterate through 11 (or more) elements: *Now* C# cares a lot. It doesn't let you index beyond the end of an array, for fear that you may overwrite an important value in memory. To test it, change the comparison in FixedArrayAverage's for loop to the following, replacing the value 10 with 11:

```
for(int i = 0; i < 11; i++)
```

When you execute the program, you see a dialog box with this error message:

```
IndexOutOfRangeException was unhandled
Index was outside the bounds of the array.
```

At first glance, this error message seems imposing. However, you can get the gist rather quickly: Clearly, the IndexOutOfRangeException tells you that the program tried to access an array beyond the end of its *range* — accessing element 11 in a 10-element array. (Chapter 9 of this minibook shows you how to find out more about that error.)

Here, N represents the number of elements to allocate. The updated program VariableArrayAverage enables the user to specify the number of values to enter. (N has to come from somewhere.) Because the program retains the values entered, not only does it calculate the average, it also displays the results in a pleasant format, as shown here:

```
using System;

// VariableArrayAverage -- Average an array whose size is
//     determined by the user at runtime, accumulating the values
//     in an array. Allows them to be referenced as often as
//     desired. In this case, the array creates an attractive output.
namespace VariableArrayAverage
{
  public class Program
  {
    public static void Main(string[] args)
```

```
{
    // First read in the number of doubles the user intends to enter.
    Console.Write("Enter the number of values to average: ");
    string numElementsInput = Console.ReadLine();
    int numElements = Convert.ToInt32(numElementsInput);
    Console.WriteLine();

    // Now declare an array of that size.
    double[] doublesArray = new double[numElements]; // Here's the 'N'.

    // Accumulate the values into an array.
    for (int i = 0; i < numElements; i++)
    {
      // Prompt the user for another double.
      Console.Write("enter double #" + (i + 1) + ": ");
      string val = Console.ReadLine();
      double value = Convert.ToDouble(val);
      // Add this to the array using bracket notation.
      doublesArray[i] = value;
    }

    // Accumulate 'numElements' values from
    // the array in the variable sum.
    double sum = 0;
    for (int i = 0; i < numElements; i++)
    {
      sum = sum + doublesArray[i];
    }

    // Now calculate the average.
    double average = sum / numElements;

    // Output the results in an attractive format.
    Console.WriteLine();
    Console.Write(average + " is the average of (" + doublesArray[0]);
    for (int i = 1; i < numElements; i++)
    {
      Console.Write(" + " + doublesArray[i]);
    }
    Console.WriteLine(") / " + numElements);

    // Wait for user to acknowledge the results.
    Console.WriteLine("Press Enter to terminate...");
    Console.Read();
  }
 }
}
```

Look at the following output of a sample run in which you enter five sequential values, 1 through 5, and the program calculates the average to be 3:

```
Enter the number of values to average:5

enter double #1: 1
enter double #2: 2
enter double #3: 3
enter double #4: 4
enter double #5: 5

3 is the average of (1 + 2 + 3 + 4 + 5) / 5
Press Enter to terminate...
```

The VariableArrayAverage program begins by prompting the user for the number of values to average. (That's the N mentioned earlier.) The result is stored in the int variable numElements. In the example, the number entered is 5.

The program continues by allocating an array doublesArray with the specified number of elements. In this case, the program allocates an array with five elements. The program loops the number of times specified by numElements, reading a new value from the user each time. After the last value, the program calculates the average.

TIP

Getting console output just right, as in this example, is a little tricky. Follow each statement in VariableArrayAverage carefully as the program outputs open parentheses, equals signs, plus signs, and each of the numbers in the sequence, and compare it with the output.

The VariableArrayAverage program probably doesn't completely satisfy your thirst for flexibility. You don't want to have to tell the program how many numbers you want to average. What you really want is to enter numbers to average as long as you want — and then tell the program to average what you entered. That's where the C# collections come in. They give you a powerful, flexible alternative to arrays. Getting input directly from the user isn't the only way to fill up your array or another collection, either.

The Length property

The for loop that's used to populate the array in the VariableArrayAverage program begins this way:

```
// Now declare an array of that size.
double[] doublesArray = new double[numElements];
```

```
// Accumulate the values into an array.
for (int i = 0; i < numElements; i++)
{
    ...
}
```

The doublesArray is declared to be numElements items long. Thus the clever programmer used a for loop to iterate through numElements items of the array. (*Iterate* means to loop through the array one element at a time, as with a for loop.)

It would be a shame and a crime to have to schlep around the variable numElements with doublesArray everywhere it goes just so that you know how long it is. Fortunately, that isn't necessary. An array has a property named Length that contains its length. doublesArray.Length has the same value as numElements.

The following for loop is preferable:

```
// Accumulate the values into an array.
for (int i = 0; i < doublesArray.Length; i++) ...
```

Initializing an array

The following lines show an array with its initializer and then one that allocates space but doesn't initialize the elements' values:

```
double[] initializedArray = {5, 2, 7, 3.5, 6.5, 8, 1, 9, 1, 3};
double[] blankArray = new double[10];
```

REMEMBER

Even though blankArray allocates space for the elements, you must still initialize its values. You could use a for loop to perform this task by assigning a value to each indexed element in turn or relying on the code shown for initializedArray.

Processing Arrays by Using foreach

Given an array of strings, the following loop averages their lengths:

```
public class Student  // Read about classes in Book 2.
{
    public string name;
    public double gpa;        // Grade point average
}
```

```
public class Program
{
  public static void Main(string[] args)
  {
    // ...create the array somehow ...

    // Now average the students you have.
    double sum = 0.0;
    for (int i = 0; i < students.Length; i++)
    {
      sum += students[i].gpa;
    }

    double avg = sum / students.Length;
    // ...do something with the average ...
  }
}
```

The for loop iterates through the members of the array. (Yes, you can have arrays of any sort of object, not just of simple types such as double and string. Book 2 formally introduces you to classes, so don't worry if the code doesn't quite make sense.) students.Length contains the number of elements in the array.

REMEMBER

C# provides another loop, named foreach, designed specifically for iterating through collections such as the array. It works this way:

```
// Now average the students that you have.
double sum = 0.0;
foreach (Student student in students)
{
  sum += student.gpa;  // This extracts the current student's GPA.
}

double avg = sum / students.Length;
```

The first time through the loop, foreach fetches the first Student object in the array and stores it in the variable student. On each subsequent pass, foreach retrieves the next element. Control passes out of the foreach loop when all elements in the array have been processed.

Notice that no index appears in the foreach statement. The lack of an index greatly reduces the chance of error and is simpler to write than the for statement, although sometimes that index is handy and you prefer a for loop.

TECHNICAL STUFF

The foreach loop is even more powerful than it would seem from the example. This statement works on other collection types in addition to arrays. In addition, foreach handles *multidimensional* arrays (arrays of arrays, in effect), a topic I don't describe in this book. To find out all about multidimensional arrays, look up *multidimensional arrays* in the C# Language Help Index.

Sorting Arrays of Data

A common programming challenge is the need to sort the elements within an array. Just because an array cannot grow or shrink doesn't mean that the elements within it cannot be moved, removed, or added. For example, the following code snippet swaps the location of two string elements within the array strings:

```
string temp = strings[i]; // Save the i'th string.
strings[i] = strings[k];  // Replace it with the kth.
strings[k] = temp;        // Replace kth with temp.
```

In this example, the object reference in the *i*th location in the strings array is saved so that it isn't lost when the second statement replaces it with another element. Finally, the temp variable is saved back into the *k*th location. Pictorially, this process looks like Figure 6-1.

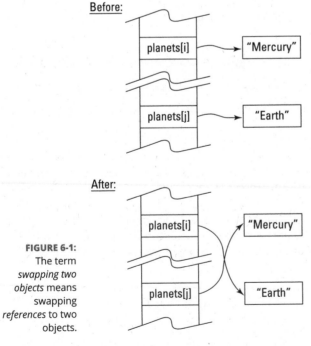

FIGURE 6-1: The term *swapping two objects* means swapping *references* to two objects.

The data collections discussed in the rest of this chapter are more versatile than the array for adding and removing elements. The following program demonstrates how to use the ability to manipulate elements within an array as part of a sort. This particular sorting algorithm is the *bubble sort*. Though it's not so great on large arrays with thousands of elements, it's simple and effective on small arrays:

```csharp
using System;

// BubbleSortArray -- Given a list of planets, sort their
//     names: first, in alphabetical order.
//     Second, by the length of their names, shortest to longest.
//     Third, from longest to shortest.
//     This demonstrates using and sorting arrays, working with
//     them by array index. Two sort algorithms are used:
//     1. The Sort algorithm used by class Array's Sort() method.
//     2. The classic Bubble Sort algorithm.
namespace BubbleSortArray
{
  class Program
  {
    static void Main(string[] args)
    {
      Console.WriteLine("The 5 planets closest to the sun, in order: ");
      string[] planets =
        new string[] { "Mercury", "Venus", "Earth", "Mars", "Jupiter" };

      foreach (string planet in planets)
      {
        // Use the special char \t to insert a tab in the printed line.
        Console.WriteLine("\t" + planet);
      }

      Console.WriteLine("\nNow listed alphabetically: ");

      // Array.Sort() is a method on the Array class.
      // Array.Sort() does its work in-place in the planets array,
      // which leaves you without a copy of the original array. The
      // solution is to copy the old array to a new one and sort it.
      string[] sortedNames = planets;
      Array.Sort(sortedNames);

      // This demonstrates that (a) sortedNames contains the same
      // strings as planets and (b) that they're now sorted.
      foreach (string planet in sortedNames)
      {
        Console.WriteLine("\t" + planet);
      }
```

```csharp
Console.WriteLine("\nList by name length - shortest first: ");

// This algorithm is called "Bubble Sort": It's the simplest
// but worst-performing sort. The Array.Sort() method is much
// more efficient, but you can't use it directly to sort the
// planets in order of name length because it sorts strings,
// not their lengths.
int outer;  // Index of the outer loop
int inner;  // Index of the inner loop

// Loop DOWN from last index to first: planets[4] to planets[0].
for (outer = planets.Length - 1; outer >= 0; outer--)
{

    // On each outer loop, loop through all elements BEYOND the
    // current outer element. This loop goes up, from planets[1]
    // to planets[4]. Using the for loop, you can traverse the
    // array in either direction.
    for (inner = 1; inner <= outer; inner++)
    {

        // Compare adjacent elements. If the earlier one is longer
        // than the later one, swap them. This shows how you can
        // swap one array element with another when they're out of
        // order.
        if (planets[inner - 1].Length > planets[inner].Length)
        {
            // Temporarily store one planet.
            string temp = planets[inner - 1];

            // Now overwrite that planet with the other one.
            planets[inner - 1] = planets[inner];

            // Finally, reclaim the planet stored in temp and put
            // it in place of the other.
            planets[inner] = temp;
        }
    }
}

foreach (string planet in planets)
{
    Console.WriteLine("\t" + planet);
}

Console.WriteLine("\nNow listed longest first: ");

// That is, just loop down through the sorted planets.
for(int i = planets.Length - 1; i >= 0; i--)
```

```
        {
            Console.WriteLine("\t" + planets[i]);
        }

        Console.WriteLine("\nPress Enter to terminate...");
        Console.Read();
    }
  }
}
```

The program begins with an array containing the names of the first five planets closest to the sun. (The example excludes the outer planets to keep the figures small.) The program then invokes the array's own Sort() method. The built-in Sort() method for arrays (and other collections) is, without a doubt, more efficient than the custom bubble sort. Don't roll your own unless you have good reason to.

After sorting with the built-in Sort() method on the Array class, the program sorts the lengths of the planets' names using a custom sort just to amaze you. The algorithm for the second sort works by continuously looping through the list of strings until the list is sorted. On each pass through the sortedNames array, the program compares each string to its neighbor. If the two are found to be out of order, the method swaps them and then flags the list as not sorted. Figures 6-2 through 6-5 show the planets list after each pass. In Figure 6-5, note that the next-to-last pass results in a sorted list and that the final pass terminates the sort because nothing changes.

| Mercury ◄——— And they're off and running! |
| Venus |
| Earth |
| Mars |
| Jupiter |

FIGURE 6-2:
Before starting
the bubble sort.

| Earth ◄——— Earth edges its way into the lead... |
| Mercury |
| Venus |
| Mars |
| Jupiter |

FIGURE 6-3:
After Pass 1 of
the bubble sort.

Earth	
Mars	← Mars jumps past Mercury and Venus for second place
Mercury	
Venus	
Jupiter	

Earth	← At the finish, it's Earth crossing the line in first place for the win...
Jupiter	← ...and Jupiter noses out Mars to place.
Mars	← Meanwhile, Mars struggles to show.
Mercury	
Venus	

Eventually, longer planet names "bubble" their way to the top of the list; hence the name *bubble sort*. Also note how the code gives single-item variables singular names, as in planet or student. The name of the variable should somehow include the name of the class, as in badStudent or goodStudent or sexyCoed Student. The code also gives arrays plural names, as in students or phoneNumbers.

Using var for Arrays

Traditionally, you used one of the following forms (which are as old as C#) to initialize an array:

```
int[] numbers = new int[3];              // Size but no initializer, or ...
int[] numbers = new int[] { 1, 2, 3 }; // Initializer but no size, or ...
int[] numbers = new int[3] { 1, 2, 3 };// Size and initializer, or ...
int[] numbers = { 1, 2, 3 };             // No 'new' keyword -- short form.
```

Chapter 2 of this minibook introduces the var keyword, which tells the C# compiler, "Determine the variable type from the initializer expression." Happily, var works with arrays, too:

```
// myArray is an int[] with 6 elements.
var myArray = new [] { 2, 3, 5, 7, 11, 13 };  // Initializer required!
```

The new syntax has only two changes:

>> var is used instead of the explicit type information for the numbers array on the left side of the assignment.

>> The int keyword is omitted before the brackets on the right side of the assignment. It's the part that the compiler can infer.

REMEMBER

In the var version, the initializer is required. The compiler uses it to infer the type of the array elements without the int keyword. Here are a few more examples:

```
var names = new [] { "John", "Paul", "George", "Ringo" };        // Strings
var averages = new [] { 3.0, 3.34, 4.0, 2.0, 1.8 };              // Doubles
var prez = new []{new President("FDR"), new President("JFK")};   // Presidents
```

REMEMBER

You can't use the short form for initializing an array when you use var. The following line doesn't compile:

```
var names = { "John", "Paul", "George", "Ringo" };  // Needs 'new []'
```

The var way is less concise, but when used in some other situations not involving arrays, it truly shines and in some cases is mandatory. (You can see examples in Book 1, Chapter 7.)

Loosening Up with C# Collections

Often an array is the simplest, most straightforward way to deal with a list of Students or a list of doubles. You also encounter many places in the .NET Framework class library that require the use of arrays. But arrays have a couple of fairly serious limitations that sometimes get in your way. At such times, you'll appreciate the extensive C# repertoire of more flexible collection classes. Although arrays have the advantage of simplicity and can have multiple dimensions, they suffer from two important limitations:

>> **A program must declare the size of an array when it's created.** Unlike Visual Basic, C# doesn't let you change the size of an array after it's defined. For example, you might not know up front how big the array needs to be.

>> **Inserting or removing an element in the middle of an array is wildly inefficient.** You have to move around all the elements to make room. In a big array, that can be a huge, time-consuming job.

Most collections, on the other hand, make it much easier to add, insert, or remove elements, and you can resize them as needed, right in midstream. In fact, most collections usually take care of resizing automatically.

TIP

If you need a multidimensional data structure, use an array. No collection allows multiple dimensions (although you can create some elaborate data structures, such as collections of arrays or collections of collections). Arrays and collections have some characteristics in common:

» Each can contain elements of only one type. You must specify that type in your code, at compile time, and after you declare the type, it can't change.

» As with arrays, you can access most collections with array-like syntax using square brackets to specify an index: myList[3] = "Joe".

» Both collections and arrays have methods and properties. Thus, to find the number of elements in the following smallPrimeNumbers array, you call its Length property:

```
var smallPrimeNumbers = new [] { 2, 3, 5, 7, 11, 13 };
int numElements = smallPrimeNumbers.Length;  // Result is 6.
```

With a collection, you call its Count property:

```
List<int> smallPrimes = new List<int> { 2, 3, 5, 7, 11, 13 };

// Collections have a Count property.
int numElements = smallPrimes.Count;
```

Check out class Array in C# Language Help to see what other methods and properties it has (7 public properties and 36 public methods).

Understanding Collection Syntax

In this section, you discover collection syntax and see the most important and most frequently used collection classes. Table 6-1 lists the main collection classes in C#. It's useful to think of collections as having various "shapes" — the list shape or dictionary shape, for example.

TABLE 6-1 **The Most Common Collection "Shapes"**

Class	Description
List<T>	This dynamic array contains objects of type T.
LinkedList<T>	This is a linked list of objects of type T.
Queue<T>	Start at the back end of the line and end up at the front.
Stack<T>	Always add or delete items at the "top" of the list, like a stack of cafeteria trays.
Dictionary<TKey, TValue>	This structure works like a dictionary. Look up a key (a word, for example) and retrieve its corresponding value (for example, definition).
HashSet<T>	This structure resembles a mathematical set, with no duplicate items. It works much like a list but provides mathematical set operations, such as union and intersection.

Figuring out <T>

In the mysterious-looking <T> notation you see in Table 6-1, <T> is a placeholder for a particular data type. To bring this symbolic object to life, *instantiate* it by inserting a real type, like this:

```
List<int> intList = new List<int>(); // Instantiating for int
```

REMEMBER

Instantiate is geekspeak for "Create an object (instance) of this type." For example, you might create different List<T> instantiations for types int, string, and Student. By the way, T isn't a sacred name. You can use anything you like — for instance, <dummy> or <aType>. It's common to use T, U, V, and so on.

Notice how Table 6-1 shows the Dictionary<TKey, TValue> collection. Here, two types are needed: one for the dictionary's keys and one for the values associated with the keys. The "Using Dictionaries" section, later in this chapter, describes how to use dictionaries.

Going generic

These modern collections are known as *generic* collections, in the sense that you can fill in a blank template, of sorts, with a type (or types) in order to create a custom collection. If the generic List<T> seems puzzling, check out Chapter 8 in this minibook. That chapter discusses the generic C# facilities in more detail.

Using Lists

Suppose you need to store a list of MP3 objects, each of which represents one item in your MP3 music collection. As an array, it might look like this:

```
MP3[] myMP3s = new MP3[50];          // Start with an empty array.
myMP3s[0] = new MP3("Norah Jones"); // Create and add an MP3 to the array.
// ... and so on.
```

With a list collection, it looks like this:

```
List<MP3> myMP3s = new List<MP3>();   // An empty list
myMP3s.Add(new MP3("Avril Lavigne")); // Add an MP3 to the list.
// ... and so on.
```

These examples look similar, and the list doesn't appear to provide any advantage over the array. But what happens when you add the 50th MP3 to the array and then want to add a 51st? You're out of room. Your only course is to declare a new, larger array and then copy all MP3s from the old array into the new one. Also, if you remove an MP3 from the array, your array is left with a gaping hole. What do you put into that empty slot to take the place of the MP3 you ditched? The value null, maybe?

The list collection sails happily on, in the face of those same obstacles. Want to add MP3 number 51? No problem. Want to junk your old Pat Boone MP3s? (Are there any?) No problem. The list takes care of healing itself after you delete old Pat.

WARNING

If your list (or array, for that matter) can contain null items, be sure to check for null when you're looping through with for or foreach. You don't want to call the Play() method on a null MP3 item. It results in an error. The following sections show how to deal with various situations using lists.

Instantiating an empty list

The following code shows how to instantiate a new, empty list for the string type. In other words, this list can hold only strings:

```
// List<T>: note angle brackets plus parentheses in
// List<T> declaration; T is a "type parameter",
// List<T> is a "parameterized type."
// Instantiate for string type.
List<string> nameList = new List<string>();
nameList.Add("one");
nameList.Add(3);                        // Compiler error here!
nameList.Add(new Student("du Bois"));   // Compiler error here!
```

You add items to a List<T> by using its Add( ) method. The preceding code snippet successfully adds one string to the list, but then it runs into trouble trying to add first an integer and then a Student. The list was instantiated for strings, so the compiler rejects both attempts.

Creating a list of type int

The following code fragment instantiates a new list for type int and then adds two int values to the list. Afterward, the foreach loop iterates the int list, printing out the ints:

```
// Instantiate for int.
List<int> intList = new List<int>();
intList.Add(3);                         // Fine.
intList.Add(4);
Console.WriteLine("Printing intList:");
foreach(int i in intList)  // foreach just works for all collections.
{
  Console.WriteLine("int i = " + i);
}
```

Creating a list to hold objects

The following bit of code instantiates a new list to hold Students and adds two students with its Add( ) method. (Don't worry about the "new Student" stuff. Book 2 discusses the topic of using objects.) But then notice the *array* of Students, which is added to the student list using its AddRange( ) method. AddRange( ) lets you add a whole array or (almost) any other collection to the list, all at once:

```
// Instantiate for Student.
List<Student> studentList = new List<Student>();
Student student1 = new Student("Vigil");
Student student2 = new Student("Finch");
studentList.Add(student1);
studentList.Add(student2);
Student[] students = { new Student("Mox"), new Student("Fox") };
studentList.AddRange(students); // Add whole array to List.
Console.WriteLine("Num students in studentList = " + studentList.Count);
```

List<T> also has a number of other methods for adding items, including methods to insert one or more items anywhere in the list and methods to remove items or clear the list.

Converting between lists and arrays

You can easily convert lists to arrays and vice versa. To put an array into a list, use the list's AddRange() method as just described. To convert a list to an array, call the list's ToArray() method:

```
Student[] students = studentList.ToArray();   // studentList is a List<Student>.
```

Counting list elements

To determine the number of elements in List<T> you use the Count property. This single nit can trip you up if you're used to the Length property on arrays and strings. For collections, it's Count.

Searching lists

There are several ways to search a list: IndexOf() returns the array-style index of an item within the list, if found, or –1 if not found. The code also demonstrates accessing an item with array-style indexing and via the Contains() method. Other searching methods include BinarySearch(), not shown:

```
// Search with IndexOf().
Console.WriteLine("Student2 at " + studentList.IndexOf(student2));
string name = studentList[3].Name;   // Access list by index.
if(studentList.Contains(student1))   // student1 is a Student object.
{
    Console.WriteLine(student1.Name + " contained in list");
}
```

Performing other list tasks

The code in this section demonstrates several more List<T> operations, including sorting, inserting, and removing items:

```
studentList.Sort(); // Assumes Student implements IComparable interface  (Ch
    14).
studentList.Insert(3, new Student("Ross"));
studentList.RemoveAt(3);  // Deletes the third element.
Console.WriteLine("removed " + name);          // Name defined above
```

That's only a sampling of the List<T> methods. You can look up the full list in C# Language Help. To look up generic collections you have to look in C# Language Help for the term *List<T>*. If you try searching for just *List*, you'll be lost in a list of lists of lists. If you want to see information about the whole set of collection classes (well, the generic ones), search the index for *generic collections*.

Using Dictionaries

You've no doubt used *Webster's* or another dictionary. It's organized as a bunch of words in alphabetical order. Associated with each word is a body of information including pronunciations, definitions, and other information. To use a dictionary, you look up a word and retrieve its information.

In C#, the dictionary "shape" differs from the list shape. Dictionaries are represented by the Dictionary<TKey, TValue> class. TKey represents the data type used for the dictionary's *keys* (similar to the words in a standard dictionary or the terms you look up). TValue represents the data type used to store the information or data associated with a key (similar to the word's definitions in *Webster's*). The following sections demonstrate how to work with dictionaries.

Creating a dictionary

The first piece of the code just creates a new Dictionary object that has string keys and string values. You aren't limited to strings, though. Either the key or the value, or both, can be any type. Note that the Add() method requires both a key and a value.

```
Dictionary<string, string> dict = new Dictionary<string, string>();
// Add(key, value).
dict.Add("C#", "cool");
dict.Add("C++", "like writing Sanskrit poetry in Morse code");
dict.Add("VB", "a simple but wordy language");
dict.Add("Java", "good, but not C#");
dict.Add("Fortran", "ancient");
dict.Add("Cobol", "even wordier and more verbose than VB");
```

Searching a dictionary

The ContainsKey() method tells you whether the dictionary contains a particular key. There's a corresponding ContainsValue() method, too:

```
// See if the dictionary contains a particular key.
Console.WriteLine("Contains C# " + dict.ContainsKey("C#"));     // True
Console.WriteLine("Contains Ruby " + dict.ContainsKey("Ruby")); // False
```

Dictionary pairs are in no particular order, and you can't sort a dictionary. It really is just like a bunch of buckets spread around the floor.

Iterating a dictionary

You can, of course, iterate the dictionary in a loop just as you can in any collection. But keep in mind that the dictionary is like a list of *pairs* of items. Think of each pair as an object that contains both the key and the value. So to iterate the whole dictionary with `foreach`, you need to retrieve one of the *pairs* each time through the loop. The pairs are objects of type `KeyValuePair<TKey, TValue>`. This `WriteLine()` call uses the pair's `Key` and `Value` properties to extract the items. Here's what it looks like:

```
// Iterate the dictionary's contents with foreach.
// Note that you're iterating pairs of keys and values.
Console.WriteLine("\nContents of the dictionary:");
foreach (KeyValuePair<string, string> pair in dict)
{
    // Because the key happens to be a string, we can call string methods on it.
    Console.WriteLine("Key: " + pair.Key.PadRight(8) + "Value: " + pair.Value);
}
```

The following code snippet shows how to iterate just the keys or just the values. The dictionary's `Keys` property returns another collection: a list-shaped collection of type `Dictionary<TKey, TValue>.KeyCollection`. Because the keys happen to be strings, you can iterate the keys as strings and call string methods on them. The `Values` property is similar. The final bit of code uses the dictionary's `Count` property to see how many key/value pairs it contains.

```
// List the keys, which are in no particular order.
Console.WriteLine("\nJust the keys:");

// Dictionary<TKey, TValue>.KeyCollection is a collection of just the
// keys,in this case strings. So here's how to retrieve the keys:
Dictionary<string, string>.KeyCollection keys = dict.Keys;
foreach(string key in keys)
{
    Console.WriteLine("Key: " + key);
}

// List the values, which are in same order as key collection above.
Console.WriteLine("\nJust the values:");
Dictionary<string, string>.ValueCollection values = dict.Values;
foreach (string value in values)
{
```

```
    Console.WriteLine("Value: " + value);
}

Console.Write("\nNumber of items in the dictionary: " + dict.Count);
```

Of course, that doesn't exhaust the possibilities for working with dictionaries. Look up *generic dictionary* in C# Language Help for all the details.

Array and Collection Initializers

This section summarizes initialization techniques for both arrays and collections — both old-style and new. You may want to bend the page corner.

Initializing arrays

REMEMBER

As a reminder, given the var syntax covered in the section "Using var for Arrays," earlier in this chapter, an array declaration can look like either of these examples:

```
int[] numbers = { 1, 2, 3 };            // Shorter form — can't use var.
var numbers = new [] { 1, 2, 3 };       // Full initializer mandatory with var.
```

Initializing collections

Meanwhile, the traditional way to initialize a collection, such as a List<T> — or a Queue<T> or Stack<T> — back in the C# 2.0 days (a number of years ago), was this:

```
List<int> numList = new List<int>();     // New empty list.
numbers.Add(1);                          // Add elements one at a time.
numbers.Add(2);
numbers.Add(3);                              // ...tedious!
```

Or, if you had the numbers in an array or another collection already, it went like this:

```
List<int> numList = new List<int>(numbers); // Initializing from an array or...
List<int> numList2 = new List<int>(numList);// from another collection or...
numList.AddRange(numbers);                   // using AddRange
```

Since C# 3.0, collection initializers resemble the new array initializers and are much easier to use than most of the earlier forms. The new initializers look like this:

```
List<int> numList = new List<int> { 1, 2, 3 };  // List
int[] intArray = { 1, 2, 3 };                    // Array
```

The key difference between the new array and collection initializers is that you still must spell out the type for collections — which means giving List<int> after the new keyword (see the boldface in the preceding example).

Of course, you can also use the var keyword with collections:

```
var list = new List<string> { "Head", "Heart", "Hands", "Health" };
```

You can also use the new dynamic keyword:

```
dynamic list = new List<string> { "Head", "Heart", "Hands", "Health" };
```

Initializing dictionaries with the new syntax looks like this:

```
Dictionary<int, string> dict =
    new Dictionary<int, string> { { 1, "Sam" }, { 2, "Joe" } };
```

Outwardly, this example looks the same as for List<T>, but inside the outer curly braces, you see a second level of curly-brace-enclosed items, one per entry in the dictionary. Because this dictionary dict has integer keys and string values, each inner pair of curly braces contains one of each, separated by a comma. The key/value pairs are separated by commas as well.

Initializing sets (see the next section) is much like initializing lists:

```
HashSet<int> biggerPrimes = new HashSet<int> { 19, 23, 29, 31, 37, 41 };
```

Using Sets

C# 3.0 added the collection type HashSet<T>. A *set* is an unordered collection with no duplicate items. The set concept comes from mathematics. Think of the set of genders (female and male), the set of days in a week, or the set of variations on the triangle (isosceles, equilateral, scalene, right, obtuse). Unlike math sets, C# sets can't be infinite, though they can be as large as available memory. The following sections tell you more about working with sets.

Performing special set tasks

You can do things to a set in common with other collections, such as add, delete, and find items. But you can also perform several specifically setlike operations, such as union and intersection that are good for combining and eliminating items (you can read more about set operations at `https://www.probabilitycourse.com/chapter1/1_2_2_set_operations.php`).

>> **Union:** Joins the members of two sets into one

>> **Intersection:** Finds the overlap between two sets and results in a set containing only the overlapping members

>> **Difference:** Determines which elements of one set do not appear in a second set

When would you use `HashSet<T>`? Anytime you're working with two or more collections and you want to find such items as the overlap (or create a collection that contains two other collections or exclude a group of items from a collection), sets can be useful. Many of the `HashSet<T>` methods can relate sets and other collection classes. You can do more with sets, of course, so look up the term *HashSet<T>* in C# Language Help.

Creating a set

To create a `HashSet<T>`, you can do this:

```
HashSet<int> smallPrimeNumbers = new HashSet<int>();
smallPrimeNumbers.Add(2);
smallPrimeNumbers.Add(3);
```

Or, more conveniently, you can use a collection initializer:

```
HashSet<int> smallPrimeNumbers = new HashSet<int> { 2, 3, 5, 7, 11, 13 };
```

Or create the set from an existing collection of any listlike kind, including arrays:

```
List<int> intList = new List<int> { 0, 1, 2, 3, 4, 5, 6, 7 };
HashSet<int> numbers = new HashSet<int>(intList);
```

Adding items to a set

If you attempt to add to a hash set an item that the set already contains, as in this example:

```
smallPrimeNumbers.Add(2);
```

the compiler doesn't treat the duplication as an error (and doesn't change the hash set, which can't have duplicates). Actually, Add() returns true if the addition occurred and false if it didn't. You don't have to use that fact, but it can be useful if you want to do something when an attempt is made to add a duplicate:

```
bool successful = smallPrimeNumbers.Add(2);
if(successful)
{
    // 2 was added, now do something useful.
}
// If successful is false, not added because it was already there
```

Performing a union

The following example shows off several HashSet<T> methods but, more important, demonstrates using a HashSet<T> *as a tool for working with other collections.* You can do strictly mathematical operations with HashSet<T>, but its capability to combine collections in various ways is quite handy.

To begin, the example starts with a List<string> and an array. Each contains color names. Though you could combine the two by simply calling the list's AddRange() method:

```
colors.AddRange(moreColors);
```

the resulting list contains some duplicates (yellow, orange). By using a HashSet<T> and the UnionWith() method, on the other hand, you can combine two collections and eliminate any duplicates in one shot, as the following example shows:

```
Console.WriteLine("Combining two collections with no duplicates:");

List<string> colors = new List<string> { "red", "orange", "yellow" };
string[] moreColors = { "orange", "yellow", "green", "blue", "violet" };

// Want to combine but without any duplicates.
// Following is just the first stage ...
HashSet<string> combined = new HashSet<string>(colors);
```

```
// ... now for the second stage.
// UnionWith() collects items in both lists that aren't duplicated,
// resulting in a combined collection whose members are all unique.
combined.UnionWith(moreColors);

foreach (string color in combined)
{
  Console.WriteLine(color);
}
```

The result given here contains "red", "orange", "yellow", "green", "blue", and "violet". The first stage uses the colors list to initialize a new HashSet<T>. The second stage then calls the set's UnionWith() method to add in the moreColors array — but only the colors that aren't already in the set. The set ends up containing just the colors in both original lists. Green, blue, and violet come from the second list; red, orange, and yellow come from the first. The moreColors array's orange and yellow would duplicate the ones already in the set, so they're screened out.

But suppose that you want to end up with a List<T> containing those colors, not a HashSet<T>. The next segment shows how to create a new List<T> initialized with the combined set:

```
Console.WriteLine("\nConverting the combined set to a list:");
// Initialize a new List from the combined set above.
List<string> spectrum = new List<string>(combined);
foreach(string color in spectrum)
{
  Console.WriteLine(color);
}
```

Performing an intersection

Imagine that you need to work with data from a presidential campaign with about ten early candidates in each major party. A good many of those candidates are also members of the U.S. Senate. How can you produce a list of just the candidates who are also in the Senate? The HashSet<T> IntersectWith() method gives you the overlapping items between the candidate list and the Senate list — items in both lists, but only those items:

```
Console.WriteLine("\nFinding the overlap in two lists:");
List<string> presidentialCandidates =
  new List<string> { "Clinton", "Edwards", "Giuliani", "McCain", "Obama",
    "Romney" };
List<string> senators = new List<string> { "Alexander", "Boxer", "Clinton",
    "McCain", "Obama", "Snowe" };
```

```
HashSet<string> senatorsRunning = new HashSet<string>(presidentialCandidates);
// IntersectWith() collects items that appear in both lists, eliminates others.
senatorsRunning.IntersectWith(senators);
foreach (string senator in senatorsRunning)
{
    Console.WriteLine(senator);
}
```

The result is "Clinton", "McCain", "Obama" because those are the only ones in both lists.

The following code segment uses the SymmetricExceptWith() method to create the opposite result from IntersectWith(). Whereas intersection gives you the overlapping items, SymmetricExceptWith() gives you the items in both lists *that don't overlap*. The uniqueToOne set ends up containing just 5, 3, 1, 12, and 10:

```
Console.WriteLine("\nFinding just the non-overlapping items in two lists:");
Stack<int> stackOne = new Stack<int>(new int[] { 1, 2, 3, 4, 5, 6, 7, 8 });
Stack<int> stackTwo = new Stack<int>(new int[] { 2, 4, 6, 7, 8, 10, 12 });
HashSet<int> nonoverlapping = new HashSet<int>(stackOne);
// SymmetricExceptWith() collects items that are in one collection but not
// the other: the items that don't overlap.
nonoverlapping.SymmetricExceptWith(stackTwo);
foreach(int n in nonoverlapping)
{
    Console.WriteLine(n.ToString());
}
Console.WriteLine("Press Enter to terminate...");
Console.Read();
}
```

The use of stacks here is a bit unorthodox because the code adds all members at one time rather than *pushes* each one individually, and removes a bunch at a time rather than *pops* each one individually. Those operations — pushing and popping — are the correct ways to interact with a stack.

TECHNICAL STUFF

Notice that all the HashSet<T> methods demonstrated in this chapter are void methods; they don't return a value. Thus the results are reflected directly in the hash set on which you call these methods: nonoverlapping in the preceding code example.

Performing a difference

The opposite trick is to remove any items that appear in both of two lists so that you end up with just the items in your target list that aren't duplicated in the other list. This calls for the HashSet<T> method ExceptWith():

```
Console.WriteLine("\nExcluding items from a list:");
Queue<int> queue =
  new Queue<int>(new int[] { 0, 1, 2, 3, 4, 5, 6, 7, 8, 9, 17 });
HashSet<int> unique = new HashSet<int> { 1, 3, 5, 7, 9, 11, 13, 15 };
// ExceptWith() removes items in unique that are also in queue: 1, 3, 5, 7.
unique.ExceptWith(queue);
foreach (int n in unique)
{
  Console.WriteLine(n.ToString());
}
```

After this code, unique excludes its own items that duplicate items in queue (1, 3, 5, 7, and 9) and also excludes items in queue that aren't in unique (0, 2, 4, 6, 8, and 17). You end up with 11, 13, and 15 in unique.

On Not Using Old-Fashioned Collections

Initially all collection classes were implemented as collections of type Object. You couldn't create a collection just for strings or just for ints. Such a collection lets you store any type of data, because all objects in C# are derived from class Object. Thus you can add both ints and strings to *the same collection* without seeing error messages (because of the inheritance and polymorphism of C#, discussed in Book 2).

But a serious drawback occurs in the Object-based arrangement: To extract the int that you know you put *into* a collection, you must cast out to an int the Object you get:

```
ArrayList ints = new ArrayList();  // An old-fashioned list of Objects
int myInt = (int)ints[0];          // Extract the first int in the list.
```

It's as though your ints were hidden inside Easter eggs. If you don't cast, you create errors because, for instance, Object doesn't support the + operation or other methods, properties, and operators that you expect on ints. You can work with these limitations, but this kind of code is error-prone, and it's just plain tedious to do all that casting. (Besides, as discussed in Book 1, Chapter 8, working with

Easter eggs adds some processing overhead because of the "boxing" phenomenon. Too much boxing slows your program.)

Also, if the collection happens to contain objects of more than one type — pomegranates and basketballs, say — the problem becomes tougher. Somehow, you have to detect that the object you fish out is a pomegranate or a basketball so that you can cast it correctly.

With those limitations on the older, nongeneric collections, the newer generic ones are a gale of fresh air. You never have to cast, and you always know what you're getting because you can put only one type into any given collection. But you still see the older collections occasionally, in code that other people write — and sometimes you may even have a legitimate reason to stick apples and oranges in the same collection.

REMEMBER

The nongeneric collections are found in the System.Collections and System.Collections.Specialized namespaces. The Specialized collections are interesting, sometimes useful, oddball collections, and mainly nongeneric. The modern, generic ones are found in System.Collections.Generic. (Book 2 explains namespaces and generics in the discussion of object-oriented programming).

Chapter **7**

Stepping through Collections

Chapter 6 in this minibook explores the *collection classes* provided by the .NET Framework class library for use with C# and other .NET languages. Collection classes are constructs in .NET that can be instantiated to hold groups of items (see Chapter 6).

The first part of this chapter extends the notion of *collections* a bit. For instance, consider the following collections: a file as a collection of lines or records of data, and a directory as a collection of files. Thus, this chapter builds on both the collection material in Chapter 6 of this minibook and the file material in Book 3.

However, the focus in this chapter is on several ways to step through, or *iterate*, all sorts of collections, from file directories to arrays and lists of all sorts.

Iterating through a Directory of Files

Sometimes you want to skim a directory of files, looking for something. The following LoopThroughFiles program looks at all files in a given directory, reading each file and dumping its contents in hexadecimal format to the console. That may sound like a silly thing to do, but this program also demonstrates how to write out a file in a format other than just `string` types. (You can find a description of hexadecimal format in the "Getting hexed" sidebar.)

Using the LoopThroughFiles program

From the command line, the user specifies the directory to use as an argument to the program. The following command "hex-dumps" each file in the `temp` directory (including binary files as well as text files):

```
loopthroughfiles c:\temp
```

If you don't enter a directory name, the program uses the current directory by default. (A *hex dump* displays the output as numbers in the hexadecimal — base 16 — system. See the nearby sidebar "Getting hexed.")

WARNING

If you run this program in a directory with lots of files, the hex dump can take a while. Also, long files take a while to loop through. Either pick a directory with few files or stop a lengthy program run by pressing Ctrl+C. This command interrupts a program running in any console window.

The following example shows what happens when the user specifies the invalid directory x:

```
Directory "x" invalid
Could not find a part of the path "C:\C#Programs\LoopThroughFiles\bin\Debug\x".

No files left
Press Enter to terminate...
```

GETTING HEXED

Like binary numbers (0 and 1), hexadecimal, or "hex," numbers are fundamental to computer programming. In base 16, the digits are 0 through 9 and then A, B, C, D, E, F — where A=10, B=11 . . . F=15. To illustrate (using the zero-x prefix to indicate hex):

```
0xD = 13 decimal
0x10 = 16 decimal: 1*16 + 0*1
0x2A = 42 decimal: 2*16 + A*1 (where A*1 = 10*1)
```

The alphabetic digits can be uppercase or lowercase: *C* is the same as *c*. It's weird, but quite useful, especially when you're debugging or working close to the metal with memory contents.

Getting started

As with all examples in this book, you begin with a basic program structure, as shown in the following code. Note that you must include a separate using statement for the System.IO namespace. To this basic structure, you add the individual functions described in the sections that follow.

```
using System;
using System.IO;

// LoopThroughFiles -- Loop through all files contained in a directory;
//    this time perform a hex dump, though it could have been anything.
namespace LoopThroughFiles
{
  public class Program
  {
  }
}
```

Obtaining the initial input

Every console application begins with a Main() function, as previous chapters indicate. Don't worry for now if you don't quite understand how the Main() function is supposed to work as part of the console application. For now, just know that the first function that C# calls is the Main() function of your console application, as shown in the following code.

```
public static void Main(string[] args)
{
  // If no directory name provided...
  string directoryName;
  if (args.Length == 0)
  {
    // ...get the name of the current directory...
    directoryName = Directory.GetCurrentDirectory();
  }
  else
  {
    // ...otherwise, assume that the first argument
    // is the name of the directory to use.
    directoryName = args[0];
  }
  Console.WriteLine(directoryName);
```

```
      // Get a list of all files in that directory.
      FileInfo[] files = GetFileList(directoryName);

      // Now iterate through the files in that list,
      // performing a hex dump of each file.
      foreach(FileInfo file in files)
      {
        // Write the name of the file.
        Console.WriteLine("\n\nhex dump of file {0}:", file.FullName);

        // Now "dump" the file to the console.
        DumpHex(file);

        // Wait before outputting next file.
        Console.WriteLine("\nenter return to continue to next file");
        Console.ReadLine();
      }

      // That's it!
      Console.WriteLine("\no files left");

      // Wait for user to acknowledge the results.
      Console.WriteLine("Press Enter to terminate...");
      Console.Read();
    }
```

The first line in `LoopThroughFiles` looks for a program argument. If the argument list is empty (`args.Length` is zero), the program calls `Directory.GetCurrentDirectory()`. If you run inside Visual Studio rather than from the command line, that value defaults to the `bin\Debug` subdirectory of your `LoopThroughFiles` project directory.

The `Directory` class gives the user a set of methods for manipulating directories. The `FileInfo` class provides methods for moving, copying, and deleting files, among other tasks.

The program then creates a list of all files in the specified directory by calling the local `GetFileList()`. This method returns an array of `FileInfo` objects. Each `FileInfo` object contains information about a file — for example, the filename (with the full path to the file, `FullName`, or without the path, `Name`), the creation date, and the last modified date. `Main()` iterates through the list of files using your old friend, the `foreach` statement. It displays the name of each file and then passes off the file to the `DumpHex()` method for display to the console. At the end of the loop, it pauses to allow the programmer a chance to gaze on the output from `DumpHex()`.

Creating a list of files

Before you can process a list of files, you need to create one. The GetFileList() method begins by creating an empty FileInfo list. This list is the one it returns in the event of an error. Here's the required code.

```
// GetFileList -- Get a list of all files in a specified directory.
public static FileInfo[] GetFileList(string directoryName)
{
  // Start with an empty list.
  FileInfo[] files = new FileInfo[0];
  try
  {
    // Get directory information.
    DirectoryInfo di = new DirectoryInfo(directoryName);

    // That information object has a list of the contents.
    files = di.GetFiles();
  }
  catch(Exception e)
  {
    Console.WriteLine("Directory \"{0}\" invalid", directoryName);
    Console.WriteLine(e.Message);
  }
  return files;
}
```

GetFileList() then creates a DirectoryInfo object. Just as its name implies, a DirectoryInfo object contains the same type of information about a directory that a FileInfo object does about a file: name, rank, and serial-number-type stuff. However, the DirectoryInfo object has access to one thing that a FileInfo doesn't: a list of the files in the directory, in the form of a FileInfo array.

As usual, GetFileList() wraps the directory- and file-related code in a big try block. (For an explanation of try and catch, see Chapter 9 in this minibook.) The catch at the end traps any errors that are generated. Just to embarrass you further, the catch block flaunts the name of the directory (which probably doesn't exist, because you entered it incorrectly).

WARNING

The final step is to return files, which contains the list of files the code collection. Be careful about returning a reference to an object. For instance, don't return a reference to one of the underlying queues wrapped up in the PriorityQueue class, described in Chapter 8 of this minibook — unless you want to invite folks to mess with those queues through the reference instead of through your class methods, that is. That's a sure ticket to a corrupt, unpredictable queue. But GetFileList() doesn't expose the innards of one of your classes here, so it's okay.

Formating the output lines

You can do anything you want with the list of files you collect. This example displays the content of each file in hexadecimal format, which can be useful in certain circumstances, such as when you need to know how files are actually put together. Before you can create a line of hexadecimal output, however, you need to create individual output lines. The DumpHex() method, shown here, is a little tricky only because of the difficulties in formatting the output just right.

```csharp
// DumpHex -- Given a file, dump the file contents to the console.
public static void DumpHex(FileInfo file)
{
  // Open the file.
  FileStream fs;
  BinaryReader reader;
  try
  {
    fs = file.OpenRead();
    // Wrap the file stream in a BinaryReader.
    reader = new BinaryReader(fs);
  }
  catch(Exception e)
  {
    Console.WriteLine("\ncan't read from \"{0}\"", file.FullName);
    Console.WriteLine(e.Message);
    return;
  }

  // Iterate through the contents of the file one line at a time.
  for(int line = 1; true; line++)
  {
    // Read another 10 bytes across (all that will fit on a single
    // line) -- return when no data remains.
    byte[] buffer = new byte[10];
    // Use the BinaryReader to read bytes.
    // Note: Using FileStream is just as easy in this case.
    int numBytes = reader.Read(buffer, 0, buffer.Length);
    if (numBytes == 0)
    {
      return;
    }

    // Write the data in a single line preceded by line number.
    Console.Write("{0:D3} - ", line);
    DumpBuffer(buffer, numBytes);
```

```
        // Stop every 20 lines so that the data doesn't scroll
        // off the top of the Console screen.
        if ((line % 20) == 0)
        {
            Console.WriteLine("Enter return to continue another 20 lines");
            Console.ReadLine();
        }
    }
}
```

DumpHex() starts by opening file. A FileInfo object contains information about the file — it doesn't open the file. DumpHex() gets the full name of the file, including the path, and then opens a FileStream in read-only mode using that name. The catch block throws an exception if FileStream can't read the file for some reason.

DumpHex() then reads through the file, 10 bytes at a time. It displays every 10 bytes in hexadecimal format as a single line. Every 20 lines, it pauses until the user presses Enter. The code uses the modulo operator, %, to accomplish that task.

TIP

Vertically, a console window has room for 25 lines by default. (The user can change the window's size, of course, allowing more or fewer lines.) That means you have to pause every 20 lines or so. Otherwise, the data just streams off the top of the screen before the user can read it.

The modulo operator (%) returns the remainder after division. Thus (line % 20) == 0 is true when line equals 20, 40, 60, 80 — you get the idea. This trick is valuable, useful in all sorts of looping situations where you want to perform an operation only so often.

Displaying the hexadecimal output

After you have a single line of output to display, you can output it in hexadecimal form. DumpBuffer() writes each member of a byte array using the X2 format control. Although X2 sounds like the name of a secret military experiment, it *simply* means "display a number as two hexadecimal digits."

```
    // DumpBuffer -- Write a buffer of characters as a single line in hex
    format.
    public static void DumpBuffer(byte[] buffer, int numBytes)
    {
        for(int index = 0; index < numBytes; index++)
        {
```

```
        byte b = buffer[index];
        Console.Write("{0:X2}, ", b);
    }
    Console.WriteLine();
}
```

The range of a byte is 0 to 255, or 0xFF — two hex digits per byte. Here are the first 20 lines of an example file:

```
Hex dump of file C:\Temp\output.txt:
001 - 53, 74, 72, 65, 61, 6D, 20, 28, 70, 72,
002 - 6F, 74, 65, 63, 74, 65, 64, 29, 0D, 0A,
003 - 20, 20, 46, 69, 6C, 65, 53, 74, 72, 65,
004 - 61, 6D, 28, 73, 74, 72, 69, 6E, 67, 2C,
005 - 20, 46, 69, 6C, 65, 4D, 6F, 64, 65, 2C,
006 - 20, 46, 69, 6C, 65, 41, 63, 63, 65, 73,
007 - 73, 29, 0D, 0A, 20, 20, 4D, 65, 6D, 6F,
008 - 72, 79, 53, 74, 72, 65, 61, 6D, 28, 29,
009 - 3B, 0D, 0A, 20, 20, 4E, 65, 74, 77, 6F,
010 - 72, 6B, 53, 74, 72, 65, 61, 6D, 0D, 0A,
011 - 20, 20, 42, 75, 66, 66, 65, 72, 53, 74,
012 - 72, 65, 61, 6D, 20, 2D, 20, 62, 75, 66,
013 - 66, 65, 72, 73, 20, 61, 6E, 20, 65, 78,
014 - 69, 73, 74, 69, 6E, 67, 20, 73, 74, 72,
015 - 65, 61, 6D, 20, 6F, 62, 6A, 65, 63, 74,
016 - 0D, 0A, 0D, 0A, 42, 69, 6E, 61, 72, 79,
017 - 52, 65, 61, 64, 65, 72, 20, 2D, 20, 72,
018 - 65, 61, 64, 20, 69, 6E, 20, 76, 61, 72,
019 - 69, 6F, 75, 73, 20, 74, 79, 70, 65, 73,
020 - 20, 28, 43, 68, 61, 72, 2C, 20, 49, 6E,
Enter return to continue another 20 lines
```

You could reconstruct the file as a string from the hex display. The 0x61 value is the numeric equivalent of the character *a*. The letters of the alphabet are arranged in order, so 0x65 should be the character *e*; 0x20 is a space. The first line in this example (after the line number) is s)\n\r Nemo, where \n is a new line and \r is a carriage return. Intriguing, eh? You can search Google or another search engine for *ASCII table* to obtain additional insights.

The output codes are also valid for the lower part of the much vaster Unicode character set, which C# uses by default. (You can look on a search engine on the web for the term *Unicode characters*.)

Iterating foreach Collections: Iterators

In the rest of this chapter, you see three different approaches to the general problem of iterating a collection. This section continues discussing the most traditional approach (at least for C# programmers), the iterator class, or enumerator, which implements the IEnumerator interface.

The terms *iterator* and *enumerator* are synonymous. The term *iterator* is more common despite the name of the interface, but *enumerator* has been popular at Microsoft. Verb forms of these two nouns are also available: You iterate or enumerate through a container or collection. Note that the indexers and the new iterator blocks discussed later in this chapter are other approaches to the same problem.

Accessing a collection: The general problem

Different collection types may have different accessing schemes. Not all types of collections can be accessed efficiently with an index like an array's — the linked list, for example. A linked list just contains a reference to the next item in the list and is made to be consecutively — not randomly — accessed. Differences between collection types make it impossible to write a method such as the following without special provisions:

```
// Pass in any kind of collection:
void MyClearMethod(Collection aColl, int index)
{
  aColl[index] = 0; // Indexing doesn't work for all types of collections.
  // ...continues...
}
```

Each collection type can (and does) define its own access methods. For example, a linked list may offer a GetNext() method to fetch the next element in the chain of objects or a stack collection may offer a Push() and Pop() to add and remove objects.

A more general approach is to provide for each collection class a separate *iterator class,* which is wise in the ways of navigating that particular collection. Each collection X defines its own class IteratorX. Unlike X, IteratorX offers a common IEnumerator interface, the gold standard of iterating. This technique uses a second object, the *iterator,* as a kind of pointer, or cursor, into the collection. The iterator (enumerator) approach offers these advantages:

>> Each collection class can define its own iteration class. Because the iteration class implements the standard IEnumerator interface, it's usually straightforward to code.

>> The application code doesn't need to know how the collection code works. As long as the programmer understands how to use the iterator, the iteration class can handle the details. That's good encapsulation.

>> The application code can create multiple independent iterator objects for the same collection. Because the iterator contains its own state information ("knows where it is," in the iteration), each iterator can navigate through the collection independently. You can have several iterations going at one time, each one at a different location in the collection.

To make the foreach loop possible, the IEnumerator interface must support all different types of collections, from arrays to linked lists. Consequently, its methods must be as general as possible. For example, you can't use the iterator to access locations within the collection class randomly because most collections don't provide random access. (You'd need to invent a different enumeration interface with that capability, but it wouldn't work with foreach.) IEnumerator provides these three methods:

>> Reset(): Sets the enumerator to point to the beginning of the collection.
Note: The generic version of IEnumerator, IEnumerator<T>, doesn't provide a Reset() method. With .NET's generic LinkedList, for example, just begin with a call to MoveNext(). That generic LinkedList is found in System. Collections.Generic.

>> MoveNext(): Moves the enumerator from the current object in the collection to the next one.

>> Current: A property, rather than a method, that retrieves the data object stored at the current position of the enumerator.

The following method demonstrates this principle. The programmer of the MyCollection class (not shown) creates a corresponding iterator class — say, IteratorMyCollection (using the IteratorX naming convention described earlier in this chapter). The application programmer stores ContainedDataObjects in MyCollection. The following code segment uses the three standard IEnumerator methods to read these objects:

```
// The MyCollection class holds ContainedDataObject type objects as data.
void MyMethod(MyCollection myColl)
{
    // The programmer who created the MyCollection class also
    // creates an iterator class IteratorMyCollection;
    // the application program creates an iterator object
    // in order to navigate through the myColl object.
    IEnumerator iterator = new IteratorMyCollection(myColl);
```

```
    // Move the enumerator to the "next location" within the collection.
    while(iterator.MoveNext())
    {
        // Fetch a reference to the data object at the current location
        // in the collection.
        ContainedDataObject contained;  // Data
        contained = (ContainedDataObject)iterator.Current;

        // ...use the contained data object...
    }
}
```

The method MyMethod() accepts as its argument the collection of Contained DataObjects. It begins by creating an iterator of class IteratorMyCollection. The method starts a loop by calling MoveNext(). On this first call, MoveNext() moves the iterator to the first element in the collection. On each subsequent call, MoveNext() moves the pointer "over one position." MoveNext() returns false when the collection is exhausted and the iterator cannot be moved any farther.

The Current property returns a reference to the data object at the current location of the iterator. The program converts the object returned into a ContainedData Object before assigning it to contained. Calls to Current are invalid if the MoveNext() method didn't return true on the previous call or if MoveNext() hasn't yet been called.

Letting C# access data foreach container

The IEnumerator methods are standard enough that C# uses them automatically to implement the foreach statement. The foreach statement can access any class that implements IEnumerable or IEnumerable<T>. This section discusses foreach in terms of IEnumerable<T> as shown in this general method that is capable of processing any such class, from arrays to linked lists to stacks and queues:

```
void MyMethod(IEnumerable<T> containerOfThings)
{
    foreach(string s in containerOfThings)
    {
        Console.WriteLine("The next thing is {0}", s);
    }
}
```

A class implements IEnumerable<T> by defining the method GetEnumerator(), which returns an instance of IEnumerator<T>. Under the hood, foreach invokes the GetEnumerator() method to retrieve an iterator. It uses this iterator to make its way through the collection. Each element it retrieves has been cast appropriately before continuing into the block of code contained within the braces.

Note that `IEnumerable<T>` and `IEnumerator<T>` are different, but related, interfaces. C# provides nongeneric versions of both as well, but you should prefer the generic versions for their increased type safety. `IEnumerable<T>` looks like this:

```
interface IEnumerable<T>
{
  IEnumerator<T> GetEnumerator();
}
```

while `IEnumerator<T>` looks like this:

```
interface IEnumerator<T>
{
  bool MoveNext();
  T Current { get; }
}
```

The nongeneric `IEnumerator` interface adds a `Reset()` method that moves the iterator back to the beginning of the collection, and its `Current` property returns type `Object`. Note that `IEnumerator<T>` inherits from `IEnumerator` — and recall that interface inheritance (covered in Book 2, Chapter 8) is different from normal object inheritance.

C# arrays (embodied in the `Array` class they're based on) and all the .NET collection classes already implement both interfaces. So it's only when you're writing your own custom collection class that you need to take care of implementing these interfaces. For built-in collections, you can just use them. See the `System.Collections.Generic` namespace topic in Help. Thus you can write the `foreach` loop this way:

```
foreach(int nValue in myCollection)
{
  // ...
}
```

Accessing Collections the Array Way: Indexers

Accessing the elements of an array is simple: The command `container[n]` (read "container sub-n") accesses the *n*th element of the `container` array. The value in brackets is a *subscript.* If only indexing into other types of collections were so simple.

C# enables you to write your own implementation of the index operation. You can provide an index feature for collections that wouldn't otherwise enjoy such a feature. In addition, you can index on subscript types other than the simple integers to which C# arrays are limited. For example, by writing your own index feature, you can interact with `string` types. As another example, you could create an index feature for a programming construct like `container["Joe"]`. (The "Indexers" section of Book 2, Chapter 12 shows how to add an indexer to a `struct`.)

Indexer format

The indexer looks much like an ordinary `get`/`set` property, except for the appearance of the keyword `this` and the index operator `[]` instead of the property name, as shown in this bit of code:

```
class MyArray
{
  public string this[int index]    // Notice the "this" keyword.
  {
    get
    {
      return array[index];
    }
    set
    {
      array[index] = value;
    }
  }
}
```

Under the hood, the expression `s = myArray[i];` invokes the `get` accessor method, passing it the value of `i` as the index. In addition, the expression `myArray[i] = "some string";` invokes the `set` accessor method, passing it the same index `i` and `"some string"` as `value`.

An indexer program example

The index type isn't limited to `int`. You may choose to index a collection of houses by their owners' names, by house address, or by any number of other indices. In addition, the indexer property can be overloaded with multiple index types, so you can index on a variety of elements in the same collection. The following sections discuss the `Indexer` program, which generates the virtual array class `KeyedArray`. This virtual array looks and acts like an array except that it uses a `string` value as the index.

Performing the required class setup

This example relies on a special class, which means you must create a class framework for it. Here is the framework used to hold the class methods you find discussed in sections that follow.

```
using System;

// Indexer -- This program demonstrates the use of the index operator
//    to provide access to an array using a string as an index.
//    This version is nongeneric, but see the IndexerGeneric example.
namespace Indexer
{
  public class KeyedArray
  {
    // The following string provides the "key" into the array --
    // the key is the string used to identify an element.
    private string[] _keys;

    // The object is the actual data associated with that key.
    private object[] _arrayElements;

    // KeyedArray -- Create a fixed-size KeyedArray.
    public KeyedArray(int size)
    {
      _keys = new string[size];
      _arrayElements = new object[size];
    }
  }
}
```

The class KeyedArray holds two ordinary arrays. The _arrayElements array of objects contains the actual KeyedArray data. The string types that inhabit the _keys array act as identifiers for the object array. The *i*th element of _keys corresponds to the *i*th entry of _arrayElements. The application program can then index KeyedArray via string identifiers that have meaning to the application. A noninteger index is referred to as a *key*.

The line that reads public KeyedArray(int size) is the start of a special kind of function called a *constructor*. Think of a constructor as an instruction to build an instance of the class. You don't need to worry about it for now, but the constructor actually assigns values to _keys and _arrayElements.

Working with indexers

At this point, you need to define an indexer to make your code work, as shown in the following code. Note that the indexer, public object this[string key], requires the use of two functions, Find() and FindEmpty().

```
// Find -- Find the index of the element corresponding to the
//    string targetKey (return a negative if it can't be found).
private int Find(string targetKey)
{
  for(int i = 0; i < _keys.Length; i++)
  {
    if (String.Compare(_keys[i], targetKey) == 0)
    {
      return i;
    }
  }
  return -1;
}

// FindEmpty -- Find room in the array for a new entry.
private int FindEmpty()
{
  for (int i = 0; i < _keys.Length; i++)
  {
    if (_keys[i] == null)
    {
      return i;
    }
  }

  throw new Exception("Array is full");
}

// Look up contents by string key -- this is the indexer.
public object this[string key]
{
  set
  {
    // See if the string is already there.
    int index = Find(key);
    if (index < 0)
    {
      // It isn't -- find a new spot.
      index = FindEmpty();
      _keys[index] = key;
    }

    // Save the object in the corresponding spot.
    _arrayElements[index] = value;
  }
```

```
get
{
  int index = Find(key);
  if (index < 0)
  {
    return null;
  }
  return _arrayElements[index];
}
}
```

The set[string] indexer starts by checking to see whether the specified index already exists by calling the method Find(). If Find() returns an index, set[] stores the new data object into the corresponding index in _arrayElements. If Find() can't find the key, set[] calls FindEmpty() to return an empty slot in which to store the object provided.

The get[] side of the index follows similar logic. It first searches for the specified key using the Find() method. If Find() returns a nonnegative index, get[] returns the corresponding member of _arrayElements where the data is stored. If Find() returns –1, get[] returns null, indicating that it can't find the provided key anywhere in the list.

The Find() method loops through the members of _keys to look for the element with the same value as the string targetKey passed in. Find() returns the index of the found element (or –1 if none was found). FindEmpty() returns the index of the first element that has no key element.

Testing your new class

The Main() method, which is part of the Indexer program and not part of the class, demonstrates the KeyedArray class in a trivial way:

```
public class Program
{
  public static void Main(string[] args)
  {
    // Create an array with enough room.
    KeyedArray ma = new KeyedArray(100);

    // Save the ages of the Simpson kids.
    ma["Bart"] = 8;
    ma["Lisa"] = 10;
    ma["Maggie"] = 2;
```

```
    // Look up the age of Lisa.
    Console.WriteLine("Let's find Lisa's age");
    int age = (int)ma["Lisa"];
    Console.WriteLine("Lisa is {0}", age);

    // Wait for user to acknowledge the results.
    Console.WriteLine("Press Enter to terminate...");
    Console.Read();
  }
}
```

The program creates a KeyedArray object ma of length 100 (that is, with 100 free elements). It continues by storing the ages of the children in *The Simpsons* TV show, indexed by each child's name. Finally, the program retrieves Lisa's age using the expression ma["Lisa"] and displays the result. The expression ma["Lisa"] is read as "ma sub-Lisa."

Notice that the program has to cast the value returned from ma[] because KeyedArray is written to hold any type of object. The cast wouldn't be necessary if the indexer were written to handle only int values — or if the KeyedArray were generic. (For more information about generics, see Chapter 8 in this minibook.) The output of the program is simple yet elegant:

```
Let's find Lisa's age
Lisa is 10
Press Enter to terminate...
```

Looping Around the Iterator Block

In previous versions of C#, the linked list discussed in the section "Accessing Collections the Array Way: Indexes," earlier in this chapter, was the primary practice for moving through collections, just as it was done in C++ and C before this. Although that solution does work, it turns out that C# versions 2.0 and above have simplified this process so that

>> You don't have to call GetEnumerator() (and cast the results).

>> You don't have to call MoveNext().

>> You don't have to call Current and cast its return value.

>> You can simply use foreach to iterate the collection. (C# does the rest for you under the hood — it even writes the enumerator class.)

> Well, to be fair, foreach works for the LinkedList class in.NET, too. That comes from providing a GetEnumerator() method. But you still have to write the LinkedListIterator class yourself. The new wrinkle is that you can skip that part in your roll-your-own collection classes, if you choose.

Rather than implement all those interface methods in collection classes that you write, you can provide an iterator block — and you don't have to write your own iterator class to support the collection. You can use iterator blocks for a host of other chores, too, as shown in the next example.

Creating the required iterator block framework

The best approach to iteration now uses iterator blocks. When you write a collection class — and the need still exists for custom collection classes such as KeyedList and PriorityQueue — you implement an iterator block in its code rather than implement the IEnumerator interface. Then users of that class can simply iterate the collection with foreach. Here is the basic framework used for this example, which contains the functions that follow in the upcoming sections.

```csharp
using System;

// IteratorBlocks -- Demonstrates using the C# 2.0 iterator
//    block approach to writing collection iterators
namespace IteratorBlocks
{
  class IteratorBlocks
  {
    //Main -- Demonstrate five different applications of
    //   iterator blocks.
    static void Main(string[] args)
    {
      // Instantiate a MonthDays "collection" class.
      MonthDays md = new MonthDays();

      // Iterate it.
      Console.WriteLine("Stream of months:\n");
      foreach (string month in md)
      {
        Console.WriteLine(month);
      }

      // Instantiate a StringChunks "collection" class.
      StringChunks sc = new StringChunks();
```

```
// Iterate it: prints pieces of text.
// This iteration puts each chunk on its own line.
Console.WriteLine("\nstream of string chunks:\n");
foreach (string chunk in sc)
{
  Console.WriteLine(chunk);
}


// And this iteration puts it all on one line.
Console.WriteLine("\nstream of string chunks on one line:\n");
foreach (string chunk in sc)
{
  Console.Write(chunk);
}
Console.WriteLine();


// Instantiate a YieldBreakEx "collection" class.
YieldBreakEx yb = new YieldBreakEx();


// Iterate it, but stop after 13.
Console.WriteLine("\nstream of primes:\n");
foreach (int prime in yb)
{
  Console.WriteLine(prime);
}



// Instantiate an EvenNumbers "collection" class.
EvenNumbers en = new EvenNumbers();


// Iterate it: prints even numbers from 10 down to 4.
Console.WriteLine("\nstream of descending evens :\n");
foreach (int even in en.DescendingEvens(11, 3))
{
  Console.WriteLine(even);
}


// Instantiate a PropertyIterator "collection" class.
PropertyIterator prop = new PropertyIterator();


// Iterate it: produces one double at a time.
Console.WriteLine("\nstream of double values:\n");
foreach (double db in prop.DoubleProp)
{
  Console.WriteLine(db);
}
```

```
      // Wait for the user to acknowledge.
      Console.WriteLine("Press enter to terminate...");
      Console.Read();


    }
  }
}
```

The Main() method shown provides basic testing functions for the iterator block code. Each of the sections the follow tell you how the code in the Main() method interacts with the iterator block. For now, just know that the Main() method is just one function, and the following sections break it apart so that you can understand it better.

Iterating days of the month: A first example

The following class provides an iterator (shown in bold) that steps through the months of the year:

```
//MonthDays -- Define an iterator that returns the months
//   and their lengths in days -- sort of a "collection" class.
class MonthDays
{
  // Here's the "collection."
  string[] months =
          { "January 31", "February 28", "March 31",
            "April 30", "May 31", "June 30", "July 31",
            "August 31", "September 30", "October 31",
            "November 30", "December 31" };

  //GetEnumerator -- Here's the iterator. See how it's invoked
  //   in Main() with foreach.
  public System.Collections.IEnumerator GetEnumerator()
  {
    foreach (string month in months)
    {
      // Return one month per iteration.
      yield return month;
    }
  }
}
```

Here's part of a `Main()` method that iterates this collection using a `foreach` loop:

```
// Instantiate a MonthDays "collection" class.
MonthDays md = new MonthDays();

// Iterate it.
foreach (string month in md)
{
  Console.WriteLine(month);
}
```

This collection class is based on an array, as `KeyedArray` is. The class contains an array whose items are `string` types. When a client iterates this collection, the collection's iterator block delivers `string` types one by one. Each `string` contains the name of a month (in sequence), with the number of days in the month tacked on to the `string`.

The class defines its own iterator block, in this case as a method named `GetEnumerator()`, which returns an object of type `System.Collections.IEnumerator`. Now, it's true that you had to write such a method before, but you also had to write your own enumerator class to support your custom collection class. Here, you just write a fairly simple method to return an enumerator based on the new `yield return` keywords. C# does the rest for you: It creates the underlying enumerator class and takes care of calling `MoveNext()` to iterate the array. You get away with much less work and much simpler code.

REMEMBER

Your class containing the `GetEnumerator()` method no longer needs to implement the `IEnumerator` interface. In fact, you don't want it to. In the following sections, you discover several varieties of iterator blocks:

>> Ordinary iterators

>> Named iterators

>> Class properties implemented as iterators

Note that class `MonthDays' GetEnumerator()` method contains a `foreach` loop to yield the `string` types in its inner array. Iterator blocks often use a loop of some kind to do this, as you can see in several later examples. In effect, you have in your own calling code an inner `foreach` loop serving up item after item that can be iterated in another `foreach` loop outside `GetEnumerator()`.

What a collection is, really

Take a moment to compare the little collection in this example with an elaborate LinkedList collection. Whereas LinkedList has a complex structure of nodes connected by pointers, this little months collection is based on a simple array — with canned content, at that. The example expands the *collection* notion a bit and then develops it even more before this chapter concludes.

Your collection class may not contain canned content — most collections are designed to hold things you put into them via Add() methods and the like. The KeyedArray class in the earlier section "Accessing Collections the Array Way: Indexers," for example, uses the [] indexer to add items. Your collection could also provide an Add() method as well as add an iterator block so that it can work with foreach.

The point of a collection, in the most general sense, is to store multiple objects and to allow you to iterate those objects, retrieving them one at a time sequentially — and sometimes randomly, or apparently randomly, as well, as in the Indexer example. (Of course, an array can do that, even without the extra apparatus of a class such as MonthDays, but iterators go well beyond the MonthDays example.)

More generally, regardless of what an iterable collection does under the hood, it produces a "stream" of values, which you get at with foreach. To drive home the point, here's another simple collection class from IteratorBlocks, one that stretches the idea of a collection about as far as possible (you may think):

```
//StringChunks -- Define an iterator that returns chunks of text,
//   one per iteration -- another oddball "collection" class.
class StringChunks
{
  //GetEnumerator -- This is an iterator; see how it's invoked
  //   (twice) in Main.
  public System.Collections.IEnumerator GetEnumerator()
  {
    // Return a different chunk of text on each iteration.
    yield return "Using iterator ";
    yield return "blocks ";
    yield return "isn't all ";
    yield return "that hard";
    yield return ".";
  }
}
```

Oddly, the StringChunks collection *stores* nothing in the usual sense. It doesn't even contain an array. So where's the collection? It's in that sequence of yield return calls, which use a special syntax to return one item at a time until all have been returned. The collection "contains" five objects, each a simple string much like the ones stored in an array in the previous MonthDays example. And, from outside the class, in Main(), you can iterate those objects with a simple foreach loop because the yield return statements deliver one string at a time, in sequence. Here's part of a simple Main() method that iterates a StringChunks collection:

```
// Instantiate a StringChunks "collection" class.
StringChunks sc = new StringChunks();

// Iterate it: prints pieces of text.
foreach (string chunk in sc)
{
  Console.WriteLine(chunk);
}
```

Iterator syntax gives up so easily

As of C# 2.0, the language introduced two new bits of iterator syntax. The yield return statement resembles the old combination of MoveNext() and Current for retrieving the next item in a collection. The yield break statement resembles the C# break statement, which lets you break out of a loop or switch statement.

Yield return: Okay, I give up

The yield return syntax works this way:

1. The first time it's called, it returns the first value in the collection.

2. The next time it's called, it returns the second value.

3. And so on. . . .

Using yield is much like calling an old-fashioned iterator's MoveNext() method explicitly, as in a LinkedList. Each MoveNext() call produces a new item from the collection. But here you don't need to call MoveNext(). (You can bet, though, that it's being done for you somewhere behind that yield return syntax.)

You might wonder what's meant by "the next time it's called". Here again, the foreach loop is used to iterate the StringChunks collection:

```
foreach (string chunk in sc)
{
  Console.WriteLine(chunk);
}
```

Each time the loop obtains a new chunk from the iterator (on each pass through the loop), the iterator stores the position it has reached in the collection (as all iterators do). On the next pass through the foreach loop, the iterator returns the next value in the collection, and so on.

Yield break: I want out of here!

You needto understand one bit of syntax related to yield. You can stop the progress of the iterator at some point by specifying the yield break statement in the iterator. Say that a threshold is reached after testing a condition in the collection class's iterator block, and you want to stop the iteration at that point. Here's a brief example of an iterator block that uses yield break in just that way:

```
//YieldBreakEx -- Another example of the yield break keyword
class YieldBreakEx
{
  int[] primes = { 2, 3, 5, 7, 11, 13, 17, 19, 23 };

  //GetEnumerator -- Returns a sequence of prime numbers
  //   Demonstrates yield return and yield break
  public System.Collections.IEnumerator GetEnumerator()
  {
    foreach (int prime in primes)
    {
      if (prime > 13) yield break;
      yield return prime;
    }
  }
}
```

In this case, the iterator block contains an if statement that checks each prime number as the iterator reaches it in the collection (using another foreach inside the iterator, by the way). If the prime number is greater than 13, the block invokes yield break to stop producing primes. Otherwise, it continues — with each yield return giving up another prime number until the collection is exhausted.

TIP

Besides using iterator blocks in formal collection classes, using them to implement enumerators, you could simply write any of the iterator blocks in this chapter as, say, static methods parallel to Main() in the Program class. In cases such as many of the examples in this chapter, the collection is inside the method. Such special-purpose collections can have many uses, and they're typically quick and easy to write.

TIP

You can also write an *extension method* on a class (or another type) that behaves as an iterator block. That can be quite useful when you have a class that can be thought of in some sense as a collection. Book 2 covers extension methods.

Iterator blocks of all shapes and sizes

In earlier examples in this chapter, iterator blocks have looked like this:

```
public System.Collections.IEnumerator GetEnumerator()
{
  yield return something;
}
```

But iterator blocks can also take a couple of other forms:

» Named iterators

» Class properties

An iterator named Fred

Rather than always write an iterator block presented as a method named GetEnumerator(), you can write a *named iterator* — a method that returns the System.Collections.IEnumerable interface instead of IEnumerator and that you don't have to name GetEnumerator() — you can name it something like MyMethod() instead. For example, you can use this simple method to iterate the even numbers from a top value that you specify down to a stop value — yes, in *descending* order. Iterators can do just about anything:

```
//EvenNumbers -- Define a named iterator that returns even numbers
//   from the "top" value you pass in DOWN to the "stop" value.
//   Another oddball "collection" class
class EvenNumbers
{
  //DescendingEvens -- This is a "named iterator."
  //   Also demonstrates the yield break keyword
  //   See how it's invoked in Main() with foreach.
  public System.Collections.IEnumerable DescendingEvens(int top,
                                                        int stop)
  {
    // Start top at nearest lower even number.
    if (top % 2 != 0) // If remainder after top / 2 isn't 0.
      top -= 1;

    // Iterate from top down to nearest even above stop.
    for (int i = top; i >= stop; i -= 2)
    {
      if (i < stop)
        yield break;
```

```
            // Return the next even number on each iteration.
         yield return i;
      }
   }
}
```

The `DescendingEvens()` method takes two parameters (a handy addition), which set the upper limit of even numbers that you want to start from and the lower limit where you want to stop. The first even number that's generated will equal the top parameter or, if `top` is odd, the nearest even number below it. The last even number generated will equal the value of the `stop` parameter (or if `stop` is odd, the nearest even number above it). The method doesn't return an `int` itself, however; it returns the `IEnumerable` interface. But it still contains a `yield return` statement to return one even number and then waits until the next time it's invoked from a `foreach` loop. That's where the `int` is yielded up.

REMEMBER

This example shows another collection with no underlying collection — such as `StringChunks`, mentioned earlier in this chapter. Note that this one is *computed* — the method "yield returns" a computed value rather than a stored or hard-coded value. That's another way to implement a collectionless collection. (You can also retrieve items from a data source or web service.) And, finally, the example shows that you can iterate a collection pretty much any way you like: down instead of up or by steps of two instead of one, for example.

TIP

An iterator needn't be finite, either. Consider the following iterator, which delivers a new number as long as you care to request them:

```
public System.Collections.IEnumerable PositiveIntegers()
{
   for (int i = 0; ; i++)
   {
      yield return i;
   }
}
```

WARNING

This example is, in effect, an infinite loop. You might want to pass a value used to stop the iteration. Here's how you would call `DescendingEvens()` from a `foreach` loop in `Main()`. (Calling `PositiveIntegers()` in the preceding example would work similarly.) This example demonstrates what happens if you pass odd numbers as the limit values, too — another use of the `%` operator:

```
// Instantiate an EvenNumbers "collection" class.
EvenNumbers en = new EvenNumbers();

// Iterate it: prints even numbers from 10 down to 4.
Console.WriteLine("\nstream of descending evens :\n");
foreach (int even in en.DescendingEvens(11, 3))
{
  Console.WriteLine(even);
}
```

This call produces a list of even-numbered integers from 10 down through 4. Notice also how the foreach is specified. You have to instantiate an EvenNumbers object (the collection class). Then, in the foreach statement, you invoke the named iterator method through that object:

```
EvenNumbers en = new EvenNumbers();
foreach(int even in en.DescendingEvens(nTop, nStop)) ...
```

TIP

If DescendingEvens() were static, you wouldn't even need the class instance. You would call it through the class itself, as usual:

```
foreach(int even in EvenNumbers.DescendingEvens(nTop, nStop)) ...
```

It's a regular wetland out there!

If you can produce a "stream" of even numbers with a foreach statement, think of all the other useful things you may produce with special-purpose collections like these: streams of powers of two or of terms in a mathematical series such as prime numbers or squares — or even something exotic such as Fibonacci numbers. Or, how about a stream of random numbers (that's what the Random class already does) or of randomly generated objects?

Iterated property doesn't mean "a house that keeps getting sold"

You can also implement an iterator block as a *property* of a class — specifically in the get() accessor for the property. In this simple class with a DoubleProp property, the property's get() accessor acts as an iterator block to return a stream of double values:

```
//PropertyIterator -- Demonstrate implementing a class
//    property's get accessor as an iterator block.
class PropertyIterator
{
  double[] doubles = { 1.0, 2.0, 3.5, 4.67 };
```

```csharp
// DoubleProp -- A "get" property with an iterator block
public System.Collections.IEnumerable DoubleProp
{
  get
  {
    foreach (double db in doubles)
    {
      yield return db;
    }
  }
}
```

You write the `DoubleProp` header in much the same way as you write the `DescendingEvens()` method's header in the named iterators example. The header returns an `IEnumerable` interface, but as a property it has no parentheses after the property name and it has a `get()` accessor — though no `set()`. The `get()` accessor is implemented as a `foreach` loop that iterates the collection and uses the standard `yield return` to yield up, in turn, each item in the collection of `doubles`. Here's the way the property is accessed in `Main()`:

```csharp
// Instantiate a PropertyIterator "collection" class.
PropertyIterator prop = new PropertyIterator();

// Iterate it: produces one double at a time.
Console.WriteLine("\nstream of double values:\n");
foreach (double db in prop.DoubleProp)
{
  Console.WriteLine(db);
}
```

TIP

You can also have a generic iterator. Look up *iterators, using* in C# Language Help. The "Using Iterators" topic for C# includes an example of a named iterator that also happens to be generic.

Chapter **8**

Buying Generic

The problem with collections is that you need to know exactly what you're sending to them. Can you imagine a recipe that accepts only the exact listed ingredients and no others? No substitutions — nothing even named differently? That's how most collections treat you, but not generics.

As with prescriptions at your local pharmacy, you can save big by opting for the generic version. *Generics*, introduced in C# 2.0, are fill-in-the-blanks classes, methods, interfaces, and delegates. For example, the List<T> class defines a generic array-like list that's quite comparable to the older, nongeneric ArrayList — but better! When you pull List<T> off the shelf to instantiate your own list of, say, ints, you replace T with int:

```
List<int> myList = new List<int>();  // A list limited to ints
```

The versatile part is that you can instantiate List<T> for *any single* data type (string, Student, BankAccount, CorduroyPants — whatever), and it's still type-safe like an array, without nongeneric costs. It's the superarray. (This chapter explains type-safety and the costs of using nongeneric collections before you discover how to create a generic class because knowing what these terms mean is essential.)

Generics come in two flavors in C#: the built-in generics, such as List<T>, and a variety of roll-your-own items. After a quick tour of generic concepts, this chapter covers roll-your-own generic classes, generic methods, and generic interfaces and delegates.

Writing a New Prescription: Generics

What's so hot about generics? They excel for two reasons: safety and performance.

Generics are type-safe

REMEMBER

When you declare an array, you must specify the exact type of data it can hold. If you specify int, the array can't hold anything other than ints or other numeric types that C# can convert implicitly to int. You see compiler errors at build-time if you try to put the wrong kind of data into an array. Thus the compiler enforces *type-safety*, enabling you to fix a problem before it ever gets out the door.

A compiler error beats the heck out of a runtime error. Compiler errors are useful because they help you spot problems now.

REMEMBER

The old-fashioned nongeneric collections aren't type-safe. In C#, everything IS_A Object because Object is the base type for all other types, both value-types and reference-types. But when you store *value-types* (numbers, chars, bools, and structs) in a collection, they must be *boxed* going in and *unboxed* coming back out. It's as though you're putting items in an egg carton and having to stuff them inside the eggs so that they fit and then breaking the eggshells to get the items back out. (Reference-types such as string, Student, and BankAccount don't undergo boxing.)

The first consequence of nongenerics lacking type-safety is that you need a cast, as shown in the following code, to get the original object out of the ArrayList because it's hidden inside an Object:

```
ArrayList aList = new ArrayList();
// Add five or six items, then ...
string myString = (string)aList[4];   // Cast to string.
```

WARNING

Fine, but the second consequence is this: You can put eggs in the carton, sure. But you can also add marbles, rocks, diamonds, fudge — you name it. An ArrayList can hold many *different types* of objects *at the same time*. So it's legal to write this:

```
ArrayList aList = new ArrayList();
aList.Add("a string");      // string -- OK
aList.Add(3);               // int -- OK
aList.Add(aStudent);        // Student -- OK
```

However, if you put a mixture of incompatible types into an ArrayList (or another nongeneric collection), how do you know what type is in, say, aList[3]? If it's a `Student` and you try to cast it to `string`, you get a runtime error. It's just like Harry Potter reaching into a box of Bertie Botts's Every Flavor Beans: He doesn't know whether he'll grab raspberry beans or earwax.

To be safe, you have to resort to using the `is` operator (discussed in Book 2) or the alternative, the `as` operator:

```
// See if the object is the right type, then cast it ...
if(aList[i] is Student)                  // Is the object there a Student?
{
  Student aStudent = (Student)aList[i];  // Yes, so it's safe to cast.
}
// Or do the conversion and see if it went well...
Student aStudent = aList[i] as Student;  // Extract a Student, if present;
if(aStudent != null)                     // if not, "as" returns null.
{
  // OK to use aStudent; "as" operator worked.
}
```

You can avoid all this extra work by using generics. Generic collections work like arrays: You specify the one and only type they can hold when you declare them.

Generics are efficient

Polymorphism allows the type `Object` to hold any other type, as with the egg carton analogy in the previous section. But you can incur a penalty by putting in value-type objects — numeric, `char`, and `bool` types and `struct`s — and taking them out. That's because value-type objects that you add have to be boxed. (See Book 2 for more on polymorphism.)

Boxing isn't worrisome unless your collection is big (although the amount of boxing going on can startle you and be more costly than you imagined). If you're stuffing a thousand, or a million, `int`s into a nongeneric collection, it takes about 20 times as long, plus extra space on the memory heap, where reference-type objects are stored. Boxing can also lead to subtle errors that will have you tearing your hair out. Generic collections eliminate boxing and unboxing.

Classy Generics: Writing Your Own

Besides the built-in generic collection classes, C# lets you write your own generic classes, regardless of whether they're collections. The point is that you can create generic versions of classes that *you* design.

Picture a class definition full of ⟨T⟩ notations. When you instantiate such a class, you specify a type to replace its generic placeholders, just as you do with the generic collections. Note how similar these declarations are:

```
LinkedList<int> aList = new LinkedList<int>(); // Built-in LinkedList class
MyClass<int> aClass = new MyClass<int>();       // Custom class
```

Both are instantiations of classes — one built-in and one programmer-defined. Not every class makes sense as a generic; in the section "Writing generic code the easy way," later in this chapter, you see an example of one that does.

REMEMBER

Classes that logically could do the same things for different types of data make the best generic classes. Collections of one sort or another are the prime example. If you find yourself mumbling, "I'll probably have to write a version of this for Student objects, too," it's probably a good candidate for generics.

To show you how to write your own generic class, the following example develops a special kind of queue collection class, a priority queue.

Shipping packages at OOPs

Here's the scene for an example: a busy shipping warehouse similar to UPS or FedEx. Packages stream in the front door at OOPs, Inc., and are shipped out the back as soon as they can be processed. Some packages need to be delivered by way of superfast, next-day teleportation; others can travel a tiny bit slower, by second-day cargo pigeon; and most can take the snail route: ground delivery in your cousin Fred's '82 Volvo.

But the packages don't arrive at the warehouse in any particular order, so as they come in, you need to expedite some of them as next-day or second-day. Because some packages are more equal than others, they are prioritized, and the folks in the warehouse give the high-priority packages special treatment.

Except for the priority aspect, this situation is tailor-made for a queue data structure. A queue is perfect for anything that involves turn-taking. You've stood (or driven) in thousands of queues in your life, waiting for your turn to buy Twinkies or pay too much for prescription medicines. You know the drill.

The shipping warehouse scenario is similar: New packages arrive and go to the back of the line — normally. But because some have higher priorities, they're privileged characters, like those Premium Class folks at the airport ticket counter. They get to jump ahead, either to the front of the line or not far from the front.

Queuing at OOPs: PriorityQueue

The shipping queue at OOPs deals with high-, medium-, and low-priority packages coming in. Here are the queuing rules:

>> **High-priority packages** (next-day) go to the front of the queue — but behind any other high-priority packages that are already there.

>> **Medium-priority packages** (second-day) go as far forward as possible — but behind all the high-priority packages, even the ones that a laggard will drop off later, and also behind other medium-priority packages that are already in the queue.

>> **Low-priority ground-pounders** must join at the back of the queue. They get to watch all the high priorities sail by to cut in front of them — sometimes, *way* in front of them.

C# comes with built-in queues, even generic ones. But it doesn't come with a priority queue, so you have to build your own. How? A common approach is to embed several actual queues within a wrapper class, sort of like this:

```
class Wrapper        // Or PriorityQueue
{
    Queue queueHigh   = new Queue ();
    Queue queueMedium = new Queue ();
    Queue queueLow    = new Queue ();
    // Methods to manipulate the underlying queues...
```

Wrappers are classes (or methods) that encapsulate complexity. A wrapper may have an interface quite different from the interfaces of what's inside it — that's an *adapter*.

The wrapper encapsulates three actual queues here (they could be generic), and the wrapper must manage what goes into which underlying queue and how. The standard interface to the Queue class, as implemented in C#, includes these two key methods:

>> Enqueue() (pronounced "N-Q") inserts items into a queue *at the back.*

>> Dequeue() (pronounced "D-Q") removes items from the queue *at the front.*

TECHNICAL STUFF

For the shipping-priority queue, the wrapper provides the same interface as a normal queue, thus pretending to be a normal queue itself. It implements an Enqueue() method that determines an incoming package's priority and decides which underlying queue it gets to join. The wrapper's Dequeue() method finds the highest-priority Package in any of the underlying queues. The formal name of this wrapper class is PriorityQueue. Here is the complete source for the example so that you can see how things work together, but you see the individual pieces explained in the sections that follow.

```
using System;
using System.Collections.Generic;

// PriorityQueue -- Demonstrates using lower-level queue collection
//     objects (generic ones at that) to implement a higher-level generic
//     Queue that stores objects in priority order
namespace PriorityQueue
{
  class Program
  {
    // Main -- Fill the priority queue with packages, then
    // remove a random number of them.
    static void Main(string[] args)
    {
      Console.WriteLine("Create a priority queue:");
      PriorityQueue<Package> pq = new PriorityQueue<Package>();
      Console.WriteLine(
        "Add a random number (0 - 20) of random packages to queue:");
      Package pack;
      PackageFactory fact = new PackageFactory();

      // You want a random number less than 20.
      Random rand = new Random();
      int numToCreate = rand.Next(20); // Random int from 0 - 20
      Console.WriteLine("\tCreating {0} packages: ", numToCreate);

      for (int i = 0; i < numToCreate; i++)
      {
        Console.Write("\t\tGenerating and adding random package {0}", i);
        pack = fact.CreatePackage();
        Console.WriteLine(" with priority {0}", pack.Priority);
        pq.Enqueue(pack);
      }

      Console.WriteLine("See what we got:");
      int total = pq.Count;
      Console.WriteLine("Packages received: {0}", total);

      Console.WriteLine("Remove a random number of packages (0-20): ");
      int numToRemove = rand.Next(20);
      Console.WriteLine("\tRemoving up to {0} packages", numToRemove);

      for (int i = 0; i < numToRemove; i++)
      {
```

```
        pack = pq.Dequeue();
        if (pack != null)
        {
          Console.WriteLine("\t\tShipped package with priority {0}",
              pack.Priority);
        }
      }

      // See how many were "shipped."
      Console.WriteLine("Shipped {0} packages", total - pq.Count);

      // Wait for user to acknowledge the results.
      Console.WriteLine("Press Enter to terminate...");
      Console.Read();
    }
  }


// Priority enumeration -- Defines a set of priorities
//     instead of priorities like 1, 2, 3, ... these have names.
//     For information on enumerations,
//     see the article "Enumerating the Charms of the Enum"
//     on csharp102.info.
enum Priority
{
  Low, Medium, High
}


// IPrioritizable interface -- Defines ability to prioritize.
//     Define a custom interface: Classes that can be added to
//     PriorityQueue must implement this interface.
interface IPrioritizable
{
  Priority Priority { get; } // Example of a property in an interface
}


//PriorityQueue -- A generic priority queue class
// Types to add to the queue *must* implement IPrioritizable interface.
class PriorityQueue<T> where T : IPrioritizable
{
  //Queues -- the three underlying queues: all generic!
  private Queue<T> _queueHigh = new Queue<T>();
  private Queue<T> _queueMedium = new Queue<T>();
  private Queue<T> _queueLow = new Queue<T>();

  //Enqueue -- Prioritize T and add an item of type T to correct queue.
  //    The item must know its own priority.
  public void Enqueue(T item)
  {
```

```csharp
    switch (item.Priority) // Require IPrioritizable for this property.
    {
      case Priority.High:
        _queueHigh.Enqueue(item);
        break;
      case Priority.Medium:
        _queueMedium.Enqueue(item);
        break;
      case Priority.Low:
        _queueLow.Enqueue(item);
        break;
      default:
        throw new ArgumentOutOfRangeException(
          item.Priority.ToString(),
          "bad priority in PriorityQueue.Enqueue");
    }
}

//Dequeue -- Get T from highest-priority queue available.
public T Dequeue()
{
  // Find highest-priority queue with items.
  Queue<T> queueTop = TopQueue();
  // If a non-empty queue is found.
  if (queueTop != null & queueTop.Count > 0)
  {
    return queueTop.Dequeue(); // Return its front item.
  }
  // If all queues empty, return null (you could throw exception).
  return default(T); // What's this? See discussion.
}

//TopQueue -- What's the highest-priority underlying queue with items?
private Queue<T> TopQueue()
{
  if (_queueHigh.Count > 0)    // Anything in high-priority queue?
    return _queueHigh;
  if (_queueMedium.Count > 0) // Anything in medium-priority queue?
    return _queueMedium;
  if (_queueLow.Count > 0)    // Anything in low-priority queue?
    return _queueLow;
  return _queueLow;            // All empty, so return an empty queue.
}

//IsEmpty -- Check whether there's anything to deqeue.
public bool IsEmpty()
{
  // True if all queues are empty
```

```csharp
        return (_queueHigh.Count == 0) & (_queueMedium.Count == 0) &
            (_queueLow.Count == 0);
    }


    //Count -- How many items are in all queues combined?
    public int Count  // Implement this one as a read-only property.
    {
        get { return _queueHigh.Count + _queueMedium.Count +
            _queueLow.Count; }
    }
}


//Package -- An example of a prioritizable class that can be stored in
//   the priority queue; any class that implements
//   IPrioritizable would look something like Package.
class Package : IPrioritizable
{
    private Priority _priority;

    //Constructor
    public Package(Priority priority)
    {
        this._priority = priority;
    }


    //Priority -- Return package priority -- read-only.
    public Priority Priority
    {
        get { return _priority; }
    }


    // Plus ToAddress, FromAddress, Insurance, etc.
}


//PackageFactory -- You need a class that knows how to create a new
//   package of any desired type on demand; such a class
//   is a factory class.
class PackageFactory
{
    //A random-number generator
    Random _randGen = new Random();

    //CreatePackage -- The factory method selects a random priority,
    //   then creates a package with that priority.
    //   Could implement this as iterator block.
    public Package CreatePackage()
    {
        // Return a randomly selected package priority.
```

```
      // Need a 0, 1, or 2 (values less than 3).
      int rand = _randGen.Next(3);

      // Use that to generate a new package.
      // Casting int to enum is clunky, but it saves
      // having to use ifs or a switch statement.
      return new Package((Priority)rand);
   }
 }
}
```

TIP

When you run PriorityQueue, run it several times. Because it's built around random numbers, you get varying results on each run. Sometimes it may "receive" zero packages, for instance. (Slow days happen.)

Unwrapping the package

This example relies on a simplified example package. Class Package focuses on the priority part, although a real Package object would include other members. Here's the code for Class Package:

```
//Package -- An example of a prioritizable class that can be stored in
//   the priority queue; any class that implements
//   IPrioritizable would look something like Package.
class Package : IPrioritizable
{
  private Priority _priority;

  //Constructor
  public Package(Priority priority)
  {
    this._priority = priority;
  }

  //Priority -- Return package priority -- read-only.
  public Priority Priority
  {
    get { return _priority; }
  }

  // Plus ToAddress, FromAddress, Insurance, etc.
}
```

All that `Package` needs for the example are:

>> A private data member to store its priority

>> A constructor to create a package with a specific priority

>> A method (implemented as a read-only property here) to return the priority

Two aspects of class `Package` require some explanation: the `Priority` type and the `IPrioritizable` interface that `Package` implements.

Specifying the possible priorities

Priorities are measured with an enumerated type, or enum, named `Priority`. The `Priority` enum looks like this:

```
//Priority -- Instead of priorities like 1, 2, 3, they have names.
enum Priority
{
   Low, Medium, High
}
```

Implementing the IPrioritizable interface

Any object going into the `PriorityQueue` must "know" its own priority. (A general object-oriented principle states that objects should be responsible for themselves.)

TIP

You can informally "promise" that class `Package` has a member to retrieve its priority, but you should make it a requirement that the compiler can enforce. You require any object placed in the `PriorityQueue` to have such a member. One way to enforce this requirement is to insist that all shippable objects implement the `IPrioritizable` interface, which follows:

```
//IPrioritizable -- Define a custom interface: Classes that can be added to
//                  PriorityQueue must implement this interface.
interface IPrioritizable  // Any class can implement this interface.
{
   Priority Priority { get; }
}
```

The notation { get; } is how to write a property in an interface declaration (as described in Book 2, Chapter 8. Class Package implements the interface by providing a fleshed-out implementation for the Priority property:

```
public Priority Priority
{
  get { return _priority; }
}
```

You encounter the other side of this enforceable requirement in the declaration of class PriorityQueue, in the later section "Saving PriorityQueue for last."

Touring Main()

Before you spelunk the PriorityQueue class, it's useful to get an overview of how it works in practice at OOPs, Inc. Here's the Main() method for the PriorityQueue example:

```
static void Main(string[] args)
{
  Console.WriteLine("Create a priority queue:");
  PriorityQueue<Package> pq = new PriorityQueue<Package>();
  Console.WriteLine(
    "Add a random number (0 - 20) of random packages to queue:");
  Package pack;
  PackageFactory fact = new PackageFactory();

  // You want a random number less than 20.
  Random rand = new Random();
  int numToCreate = rand.Next(20); // Random int from 0-20.
  Console.WriteLine("\tCreating {0} packages: ", numToCreate);

  for (int i = 0; i < numToCreate; i++)
  {
    Console.Write("\t\tGenerating and adding random package {0}", i);
    pack = fact.CreatePackage();
    Console.WriteLine(" with priority {0}", pack.Priority);
    pq.Enqueue(pack);
  }

  Console.WriteLine("See what we got:");
  int total = pq.Count;
  Console.WriteLine("Packages received: {0}", total);
```

```
Console.WriteLine("Remove a random number of packages (0-20): ");
int numToRemove = rand.Next(20);
Console.WriteLine("\tRemoving up to {0} packages", numToRemove);

for (int i = 0; i < numToRemove; i++)
{
  pack = pq.Dequeue();
  if (pack != null)
  {
    Console.WriteLine("\t\tShipped package with priority {0}",
        pack.Priority);
  }
}

// See how many were "shipped."
Console.WriteLine("Shipped {0} packages", total - pq.Count);

// Wait for user to acknowledge the results.
Console.WriteLine("Press Enter to terminate...");
Console.Read();
}
```

Here's what happens in `Main()`:

1. **Instantiate a** `PriorityQueue` **object for type** `Package`.

2. **Create a** `PackageFactory` **object whose job is to create new packages with randomly selected priorities, on demand.**

   A *factory* is a class or method that creates objects for you. You tour `PackageFactory` in the section "Using a (nongeneric) Simple Factory class," later in this chapter.

3. **Use the .NET library class** `Random` **to generate a random number and then call** `PackageFactory` **to create that number of new** `Package` **objects with random priorities.**

4. **Add each package to the** `PriorityQueue` **by using** `pq.Enqueue(pack)`.

5. **Write the number of packages created and then randomly remove some of them from the** `PriorityQueue` **by using** `pq.Dequeue()`.

6. **End after displaying the number of packages removed.**

Writing generic code the easy way

Now you have to figure out how to write a generic class, with all those <T>s. Looks confusing, doesn't it? Well, it's not so hard, as this section demonstrates.

TIP

The simple way to write a generic class is to write a nongeneric version first and then substitute the `<T>`s. For example, you can write the `PriorityQueue` class for `Package` objects, test it, and then "genericize" it. Here's a small piece of a nongeneric `PriorityQueue`, to illustrate:

```
public class PriorityQueue
{
  //Queues -- The three underlying queues: all generic!
  private Queue<Package> _queueHigh   = new Queue<Package>();
  private Queue<Package> _queueMedium = new Queue<Package>();
  private Queue<Package> _queueLow    = new Queue<Package>();
  //Enqueue -- Prioritize a Package and add it to correct queue.
  public void Enqueue(Package item)
  {
    switch(item.Priority)  // Package has this property.
    {
      case Priority.High:
        queueHigh.Enqueue(item);
        break;
      case Priority.Low:
        queueLow.Enqueue(item);
        break;
      case Priority.Medium:
        queueMedium.Enqueue(item);
        break;
    }
  }
  // And so on ...
```

Testing the logic of the class is easier when you write the class nongenerically first. When all the logic is straight, you can use find-and-replace to replace the name `Package` with `T`.

Saving PriorityQueue for last

Why would a priority queue be last? It may seem a little backward, but you've seen the code that relies on the priority queue to perform tasks. Now it's time to examine the `PriorityQueue` class. This section shows the code and then walks you through it so that you see how to deal with a couple of small issues. Take it a piece at a time.

The underlying queues

`PriorityQueue` is a wrapper class that hides three ordinary `Queue<T>` objects, one for each priority level. Here's the first part of `PriorityQueue`, showing the three underlying queues (now generic):

```
//PriorityQueue -- A generic priority queue class
// Types added to the queue *must* implement IPrioritizable interface.
class PriorityQueue<T> where T : IPrioritizable
{
  // Queues -- the three underlying queues: all generic!
  private Queue<T> _queueHigh = new Queue<T>();
  private Queue<T> _queueMedium = new Queue<T>();
  private Queue<T> _queueLow = new Queue<T>();
  // The rest will follow shortly ...
```

The lines in bold declare three private data members of type Queue<T> and initialize them by creating the Queue<T> objects. The later "Tending to unfinished business" section in this chapter talks about that odd-looking class declaration line above the "subqueue" declarations.

The Enqueue() method

Enqueue() adds an item of type T to the PriorityQueue. This method's job is to look at the item's priority and put it into the correct underlying queue. In the first line, it gets the item's Priority property and switches based on that value. To add the item to the high-priority queue, for example, Enqueue() turns around and enqueues the item in the underlying queueHigh. Here's PriorityQueue's Enqueue() method:

```
//Enqueue -- Prioritize T and add it to correct queue; an item of type T.
//   The item must know its own priority.
public void Enqueue(T item)
{
  switch (item.Priority) // Require IPrioritizable for this property.
  {
    case Priority.High:
      _queueHigh.Enqueue(item);
      break;
    case Priority.Medium:
      _queueMedium.Enqueue(item);
      break;
    case Priority.Low:
      _queueLow.Enqueue(item);
      break;
    default:
      throw new ArgumentOutOfRangeException(
        item.Priority.ToString(),
        "bad priority in PriorityQueue.Enqueue");
  }
}
```

The Dequeue() method

Dequeue()'s job is a bit trickier than Enqueue()'s: It must locate the highest-priority underlying queue that has contents and then retrieve the front item from that subqueue. Dequeue() delegates the first part of the task, finding the highest-priority queue that isn't empty, to a private TopQueue() method (described in the next section). Then Dequeue() calls the underlying queue's Dequeue() method to retrieve the frontmost object, which it returns. Here's how Dequeue() works:

```
//Dequeue -- Get T from highest-priority queue available.
public T Dequeue()
{
  // Find highest-priority queue with items.
  Queue<T> queueTop = TopQueue();

  // If a non-empty queue is found
  if (queueTop != null & queueTop.Count > 0)
  {
    return queueTop.Dequeue(); // Return its front item.
  }

  // If all queues empty, return null (you could throw exception).
  return default(T); // What's this? See discussion.
}
```

A difficulty arises only if none of the underlying queues have any packages — in other words, the whole PriorityQueue is empty. What do you return in that case? Dequeue() returns null. The client — the code that calls Priority-Queue.Dequeue() — should check the Dequeue() return value in case it's null. Where's the null it returns? It's that odd duck, default(T), at the end. The later "Determining the null value for type T: default(T)" section deals with default(T).

The TopQueue() utility method

Dequeue() relies on the private method TopQueue() to find the highest-priority, nonempty underlying queue. TopQueue() just starts with queueHigh and asks for its Count property. If it's greater than zero, the queue contains items, so TopQueue() returns a reference to the whole underlying queue that it found. (The TopQueue() return type is Queue<T>.) On the other hand, if queueHigh is empty, TopQueue() tries queueMedium and then queueLow. What happens if all subqueues are empty? TopQueue() could return null, but it's more useful for it to simply return one of the empty queues. When Dequeue() then calls the returned queue's Dequeue() method, it returns null. TopQueue() works like this:

```
//TopQueue -- What's the highest-priority underlying queue with items?
private Queue<T> TopQueue()
{
  if (_queueHigh.Count > 0)    // Anything in high-priority queue?
    return _queueHigh;
  if (_queueMedium.Count > 0) // Anything in medium-priority queue?
    return _queueMedium;
  if (_queueLow.Count > 0)    // Anything in low-priority queue?
    return _queueLow;
  return _queueLow;           // All empty, so return an empty queue.
}
```

The remaining PriorityQueue members

PriorityQueue is useful when it knows whether it's empty and, if not, how many items it contains. (An object should be responsible for itself.) Look at PriorityQueue's IsEmpty() method and Count property in the earlier listing. You might also find it useful to include methods that return the number of items in each of the underlying queues. *Be careful:* Doing so may reveal too much about how the priority queue is implemented. Keep your implementation private.

Using a (nongeneric) Simple Factory class

The "Saving PriorityQueue for last" section, earlier in this chapter, uses a Simple Factory object to generate an endless stream of Package objects with randomized priority levels. At long last, that simple class can be revealed:

```
// PackageFactory -- You need a class that knows how to create a new
//      package of any desired type on demand; such a
//      class is a factory class.
class PackageFactory
{
  Random _randGen = new Random();  // C#'s random-number generator

  //CreatePackage -- This factory method selects a random priority,
  //   then creates a package with that priority.
  public Package CreatePackage()
  {
    // Return a randomly selected package priority:
    // need a 0, 1, or 2 (values less than 3).
    int rand = _randGen.Next(3);

    // Use that to generate a new package.
    // Casting int to enum is clunky, but it saves
```

```
        // having to use ifs or a switch statement.
        return new Package((Priority)rand);
    }
}
```

Class `PackageFactory` has one data member and one method. (You can just as easily implement a simple factory as a method rather than as a class — for example, a method in class `Program`.) When you instantiate a `PackageFactory` object, it creates an object of class `Random` and stores it in the data member `rand`. `Random` is a .NET library class that generates random numbers.

Using PackageFactory

To generate a randomly prioritized `Package` object, you call your factory object's `CreatePackage()` method this way:

```
PackageFactory fact = new PackageFactory();
IPrioritizable pack = fact.CreatePackage(); // Note the interface here.
```

`CreatePackage()` tells its random-number generator to generate a number from 0 to 2 (inclusive) and uses the number to set the priority of a new `Package`, which the method returns (to a `Package` or, better, to an `IPrioritizable` variable).

REMEMBER

Note that `CreatePackage` returns a reference to `IPrioritizable`, which is more general than returning a reference to `Package`. This example shows *indirection*: `Main()` refers to a `Package` indirectly, through an interface that `Package` implements. Indirection insulates `Main()` from the details of what `CreatePackage` returns. You then have greater freedom to alter the underlying implementation of the factory without affecting `Main()`.

More about factories

Factories are helpful for generating lots of test data. (A factory needn't use random numbers — that's just what was needed for the `PriorityQueue` example.) Factories improve programs by isolating object creation. Every time you mention a specific class by name in your code, you create a *dependency* on that class. The more such dependencies you have, the more *tightly coupled* (bound together) your classes become.

Programmers have long known that they should avoid tight coupling. (One of the more *decoupled* approaches is to use the factory indirectly via an interface, such as `IPrioritizable`, rather than a concrete class, such as `Package`.) Programmers still create objects directly all the time, using the `new` operator, and that's fine. But factories can make code less coupled — and therefore more flexible.

Tending to unfinished business

PriorityQueue needs to a couple of small issues. Here are the issues:

>> By itself, PriorityQueue wouldn't prevent you from trying to instantiate it for, say, int or string or Student — elements that don't have priorities. You need to *constrain* the class so that it can be instantiated only for types that implement IPrioritizable. Attempting to instantiate for a non-IPrioritizable class should result in a compiler error.

>> The Dequeue() method for PriorityQueue returns the value null instead of an actual object. But generic types such as <T> don't have a natural default null value the way elements such as int types, string types, and down-and-out object references do. That part of it needs to be genericized, too.

Adding constraints

PriorityQueue must be able to ask an object what its priority is. To make it work, all classes that are storable in PriorityQueue must implement the IPrioritizable interface, as Package does. Package lists IPrioritizable in its class declaration heading, like this:

```
class Package : IPrioritizable
```

Then it implements IPrioritizable's Priority property.

REMEMBER

A matching limitation is needed for PriorityQueue. You want the compiler to squawk if you try to instantiate for a type that doesn't implement IPrioritizable. In the nongeneric form of PriorityQueue (written specifically for type Package, say), the compiler squeals automatically when one of your priority queue methods tries to call a method that Package doesn't have. But, for generic classes, you can go to the next level with an explicit *constraint*. Because you could instantiate the generic class with literally any type, you need a way to tell the compiler which types are acceptable — because they're guaranteed to have the right methods.

REMEMBER

You add the constraint by specifying IPrioritizable in the heading for PriorityQueue, like this:

```
class PriorityQueue<T> where T: IPrioritizable
```

Did you notice the where clause earlier? This boldfaced where clause specifies that T must implement IPrioritizable. *That's the enforcer.* It means, "Make sure that T implements the IPrioritizable interface — or else!"

You specify constraints by listing *one or more* of the following elements (separated by commas) in a `where` clause:

>> The name of a required base class that T must derive from (or be).

>> The name of an interface that T must implement, as shown in the previous example.

>> You can see more — Table 8-1 has the complete list.

For information about these constraints, look up *Generics [C#], constraints* in C# Language Help.

TABLE 8-1 ## Generic Constraint Options

Constraint	Meaning	Example
MyBaseClass	T must be, or extend, MyBaseClass.	where T: MyBaseClass
IMyInterface	T must implement IMyInterface.	where T: IMyInterface
struct	T must be any value type.	where T: struct
class	T must be any reference type.	where T: class
new()	T must have a parameterless constructor.	where T: new()

Note the `struct` and `class` options in particular. Specifying `struct` means that T can be any value type: a numeric type, a `char`, a `bool`, or any object declared with the `struct` keyword. Specifying `class` means that T can be any reference type: any *class* type.

These constraint options give you quite a bit of flexibility for making your new generic class behave just as you want. And a well-behaved class is a pearl beyond price. You aren't limited to just one constraint, either. Here's an example of a hypothetical generic class declared with multiple constraints on T:

```
class MyClass<T> : where T: class, IPrioritizable, new()
{ ... }
```

In this line, T must be a class, not a value type; it must implement `IPrioritizable`; and it must contain a constructor without parameters. Strict!

You might have two generic parameters and both need to be constrained. (Yes, you can have more than one generic parameter — think of `Dictionary<TKey, TValue>`.) Here's how to use two `where` clauses:

```
class MyClass<T, U> : where T: IPrioritizable, where U: new()
```

You see two `where` clauses, separated by a comma. The first constrains `T` to any object that implements the `IPrioritizable` interface. The second constrains `U` to any object that has a default (parameterless) constructor.

Determining the null value for type T: default(T)

In case you read the last paragraph in the previous section and are confused, well, each type has (as mentioned earlier) a default value that signifies "nothing" for that type. For `int`s, `double`s, and other types of numbers, it's 0 (or 0.0). For `bool`, it's `false`. And, for all reference types, such as `Package`, it's `null`. As with all reference types, the default for `string` is `null`.

But because a generic class such as `PriorityQueue` can be instantiated for almost any data type, C# can't predict the proper `null` value to use in the generic class's code. For example, if you use the `Dequeue()` method of `PriorityQueue`, you may face this situation: You call `Dequeue()` to get a package, but none is available. What do you return to signify "nothing"? Because `Package` is a class type, it should return `null`. That signals the caller of `Dequeue()` that there was nothing to return (and the caller must check for a `null` return value).

REMEMBER

The compiler can't make sense of the `null` keyword in a generic class because the class may be instantiated for all sorts of data types. That's why `Dequeue()` uses this line instead:

```
return default(T);   // Return the right null for whatever T is.
```

This line tells the compiler to look at `T` and return the right kind of `null` value for that type. In the case of `Package`, which as a class is a reference type, the right `null` to return is, well, `null`. But, for some other `T`, it may be different and the compiler can figure out what to use.

Revising Generics

The generics model implemented in C# 2.0 was incomplete. Generics are fine for making the programmer's life easier, but they did little in that version to make the analyst's life easier. It used to be very hard to model an actual business model using Generics, and that changed in C# 4.0. Although parameters in C# 2.0 all allowed for variance in several directions, generics did not.

Variance has to do with types of parameters and return values. *Covariance* means that an instance of a subclass can be used when an instance of a parent class is expected, while *contravariance* means that an instance of a superclass can be used when an instance of a subclass is expected. When neither is possible, it is called *invariance*.

All fourth-generation languages support some kind of variance. In C# 3.0 and earlier versions, parameters are covariant, and return types are contravariant. So, this works because string and integer parameters are covariant to object parameters:

```
public static void MessageToYou(object theMessage)
{
    if (theMessage != null)
        Console.Writeline(theMessage)
}
//then:
MessageToYou("It's a message, yay!");
MessageToYou(4+6.6);
```

And this works because object return types are contravariant to string and integer return types (for example):

```
object theMessage =  MethodThatGetsTheMessage();
```

Generics are invariant in C# 2.0 and 3.0. This means that if Basket<apple> is of type Basket<fruit>, those Baskets are not interchangeable as strings and objects are in the preceding example.

Variance

If you look at a method like the following one:

```
public static void WriteMessages()
{
    List<string> someMessages = new List<string>();
    someMessages.Add("The first message");
    someMessages.Add("The second message");
    MessagesToYou(someMessages);
}
```

and then you try to call that method as you did earlier in this chapter with a string type

```
//This doesn't work in C#3!!
public static void MessagesToYou(IEnumerable<object> theMessages)
{
```

```
        foreach (var item in theMessages)
            Console.WriteLine(item);
}
```

it will fail. Generics are invariant in C# 3.0. But, in Visual Studio 2010 and later this complies because IEnumerable<T> is covariant — you can use a more derived type as a substitute for a higher-order type. The next section shows a real example.

Contravariance

A scheduling application could have Events, which have a date, and then a set of subclasses, one of which is Course. A Course is an Event. Courses know their own number of students. One of these methods is MakeCalendar:

```
public void MakeCalendar(IEnumerable<Event> theEvents)
{
    foreach (Event item in theEvents)
    {
        Console.WriteLine(item.WhenItIs.ToString());
    }
}
```

Pretend that it makes a calendar. For now, all it does is print the date to the console. MakeCalendar is systemwide, so it expects some enumerable list of events.

The application also has a sort algorithm at the main system called EventSorter that passes a sorted collection into the Sort method. It expects a call from a list of Events. Here is the EventSorter class:

```
class EventSorter : IComparer<Event>
{
    public int Compare(Event x, Event y)
    {
        return x.WhenItIs.CompareTo(y.WhenItIs);
    }
}
```

The event manager makes a list of courses, sorts them, and then makes a calendar. ScheduleCourses creates the list of courses and then calls courses.Sort() with EventSorter as an argument, as shown here:

```
public void ScheduleCourses()
{
    List<Course> courses = new List<Course>()
    {
```

```
            new Course(){NumberOfStudents=20,
                    WhenItIs = new DateTime(2018,2,1)},
        new Course(){NumberOfStudents=14,
                    WhenItIs = new DateTime(2018,3,1)},
        new Course(){NumberOfStudents=24,
                    WhenItIs = new DateTime(2018,4,1)},
    };

    //Pass an ICompare<Event> class to the List<Course> collection.
    //It should be an ICompare<Course>, but it can use ICompare<Event>
    // because of contravariance
    courses.Sort(new EventSorter());


    //Pass a List of courses, where a List of Events was expected.
    //We can do this because generic parameters are covariant
    MakeCalendar(courses);
}
```

But wait, this is a list of courses that calls Sort(), not a list of events. Doesn't matter — IComparer<Event> is a contravariant generic for T (its return type) as compared to IComparer<Course>, so it's still possible to use the algorithm.

Now the application passes a list into the MakeSchedule method, but that method expects an enumerable collection of Events. Because parameters are covariant for generics now, it's possible to pass in a List of courses, as Course is covariant to Event.

There is another example of contravariance, using parameters rather than return values. If you have a method that returns a generic list of courses, you can call that method expecting a list of Events, because Event is a superclass of Course.

You know how you can have a method that returns a String and assign the return value to a variable that you have declared an object? Now you can do that with a generic collection, too.

In general, the C# compiler makes assumptions about the generic type conversion. As long as you're working up the chain for parameters or down the chain for return types, C# will just magically figure the type out.

Covariance

The application now passes the list into the MakeSchedule method, but that method expects an enumerable collection of Events. Because parameters are covariant for generics now, it's possible to pass in a List of courses, as Course is covariant to Event. This is covariance for parameters.

Chapter **9**

Some Exceptional Exceptions

t's difficult to accept, but occasionally a method doesn't do what it's supposed to do, which results in an error. (If you need to learn about methods, read the third chapter of Book 2). Users are notoriously unreliable as well. No sooner do you ask for an `int` than a user inputs a `double`, which also results in an error. Sometimes the method goes merrily along, blissfully ignorant that it is spewing out garbage. However, good programmers write their methods to anticipate problems and report them as they occur.

REMEMBER

This chapter discusses runtime errors, not compile-time errors, which C# spits out when you try to build your program. *Runtime errors* occur when the program is running, not at compile time.

The C# *exception mechanism* is a means for reporting these errors in a way that the calling method can best understand and use to handle the problem. This mechanism has a lot of advantages over the ways that programmers handled errors in the, uh, good old days. This chapter walks you through the fundamentals of exception handling. You have a lot to digest here, so lean back in your old, beat-up recliner.

Using an Exceptional Error-Reporting Mechanism

C# introduces a completely different mechanism for capturing and handling errors: the *exception*. This mechanism is based on the keywords try, catch, throw, and finally. In outline form, it works like this: A method will try to execute a piece of code. If the code detects a problem, it will throw an error indication, which your code can catch, and no matter what happens, it finally executes a special block of code at the end, as shown in this snippet:

```
public class MyClass
{
  public void SomeMethod()
  {
    // Set up to catch an error.
    try
    {
      // Call a method or do something that could throw an exception.
      SomeOtherMethod();
      // ... make whatever other calls you want ...
    }
    catch(Exception e)
    {
      // Control passes here in the event of an error anywhere
      // within the try block.
      // The Exception object e describes the error in detail.
    }
    finally
    {
      // Clean up here: close files, release resources, etc.
      // This block runs even if an exception was caught.
    }
  }
  public void SomeOtherMethod()
  {
    // ... error occurs somewhere within this method ...
    // ... and the exception bubbles up the call chain.
    throw new Exception("Description of error");
    // ... method continues if throw didn't happen ...
  }
}
```

REMEMBER

The combination of try, catch, and (possibly) finally is an *exception handler*. The SomeMethod() method surrounds a section of code in a block labeled with the keyword try. Any method called within the call tree within the block is part of the try block. If you have a try block, you must have either a catch block or a finally block, or both.

WARNING

A variable declared inside a try, catch, or finally block isn't accessible from outside the block. If you need access, declare the variable outside, before the block:

```
int aVariable;  // Declare aVariable outside the block.

try
{
  aVariable = 1;
  // Declare aString inside the block.
  string aString = aVariable.ToString(); // Use aVariable in block.
}

// aVariable is visible here; aString is not.
```

About try blocks

Think of using the try block as putting the C# runtime on alert. If an error occurs while executing any code within this block, the C# runtime throws an exception. Exceptions bubble up through the code until the exception encounters a catch block or the application ends. A try block incorporates a lot of code, including all methods called by its contents.

About catch blocks

A try block is usually followed immediately by the keyword catch, which is followed by the catch keyword's block. Control passes to the catch block in the event of an error anywhere within the try block. The argument to the catch block is an object of class Exception or, more likely, a subclass of Exception as shown here:

```
catch(Exception e)  // No object specified here (no "Exception e")
{
  // Display the error
  Console.WriteLine(e.ToString());
}
```

If your catch doesn't need to access any information from the exception object it catches, you can specify only the exception type:

```
catch(SomeException)  // No object specified here (no "Exception e")
{
    // Do something that doesn't require access to exception object.
}
```

However, a catch block doesn't have to have arguments: A bare catch catches any exception, equivalent to catch(Exception):

```
catch
{
}
```

About finally blocks

A finally block, if you supply one, runs regardless of whether the try block throws an exception. The finally block is called after a successful try or after a catch. You can use finally even if you don't have a catch. For example, you use the finally block to clean up before moving on so that files aren't left open. A common use of finally is to clean up after the code in the try block, regardless of whether an exception occurs. So you often see code that looks like this:

```
try
{
    ...
}
finally
{
    // Clean up code, such as close a file opened in the try block.
}
```

In fact, you should use finally blocks liberally — only one per try.

TECHNICAL STUFF

A method can have multiple try/catch handlers. You can even nest a try/catch inside a try, a try/catch inside a catch, or a try/catch inside a finally — or all the above. (And you can substitute try/finally for all the above.)

What happens when an exception is thrown

When an exception occurs, a variation of this sequence of events takes place:

1. **An exception is thrown.**

Somewhere deep in the bowels of SomeOtherMethod( ), an error occurs. Always at the ready, the method reports a runtime error with the throw of an Exception object back to the first block that knows enough to catch and handle it.

Note that because an exception is a *runtime error,* not a compile error, it occurs as the program executes. So an error can occur after you release your masterpiece to the public. Oops!

2. **C# "unwinds the call stack," looking for a catch block.**

The exception works its way back to the calling method, and then to the method that called that method, and so on, even all the way to the top of the program in Main( ) if no catch block is found to handle the exception. Figure 9-1 shows the path that's followed as C# searches for an exception handler.

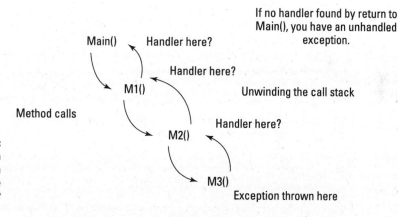

FIGURE 9-1: Where, oh where can a handler be found?

3. **If an appropriate catch block is found, it executes.**

An *appropriate* catch block is one that's looking for the right exception class (or any of its base classes). This catch block might do any of a number of things. As the stack unwinds, if a given method doesn't have enough context —

that is, doesn't know enough — to correct the exceptional condition, it simply doesn't provide a catch block for that exception. The right catch may be high up the stack.

REMEMBER

The exception mechanism beats the old-fashioned error-return mechanism all hollow, for these reasons:

- When the calling method gets an old-style return value and can't do anything useful, it must explicitly return the error itself to *its* caller, and so on. If the method that can handle the problem is far up the call chain, returning a return that returned a return that . . . becomes awkward, leading to some ugly design kludge. (*Kludge* is an engineer's term for something that works but is lame and ugly. Think "spit and baling wire.")

- With exceptions, in contrast, the exception automatically climbs the call chain until it runs into an exception handler. You don't have to keep forwarding the message, which eliminates a lot of kludgy code.

4. **If a finally block accompanies the try block, it executes, whether an exception was caught or not.**

The finally is called before the stack unwinds to the next-higher method in the call chain. *All* finally blocks anywhere up the call chain also execute.

5. **If no catch block is found anywhere, the program crashes.**

If C# gets to Main() and doesn't find a catch block there, the user sees an "unhandled exception" message, and the program exits. This is a *crash*. However, you can deal with exceptions not caught elsewhere by using an exception handler in Main(). See the section "Grabbing Your Last Chance to Catch an Exception," later in this chapter.

This exception mechanism is undoubtedly more complex and difficult to handle than using error codes. You have to balance the increased difficulty against these considerations, as shown in Figure 9-1:

- » Exceptions provide a more "expressive" model — one that lets you express a wide variety of error-handling strategies.

- » An exception object carries far more information with it, thus aiding in debugging — far more than error codes ever could.

- » Exceptions lead to more readable code — and less code.

- » Exceptions are an integral part of C# rather than an ad hoc, tacked-on afterthought such as error-code schemes, no two of which are much alike. A consistent model promotes understanding.

Throwing Exceptions Yourself

If classes in the .NET class library can throw exceptions, so can you. To throw an exception when you detect an error worthy of an exception, use the throw keyword:

```
throw new ArgumentException("Don't argue with me!");
```

You have as much right to throw things as anybody. Because the .NET class library has no awareness of your custom BadHairDayException, who will throw it but you?

TIP

If one of the .NET predefined exceptions fits your situation, throw it. But if none fits, you can invent your own custom exception class.

TECHNICAL STUFF

.NET has some exception types that you should never catch: StackOverflow Exception, OutOfMemoryException, ExecutionEngineException, and a few more advanced items related to working with non-.NET code. These exceptions represent a kind of ultimate failure. For example, if you're out of stack space, StackOverflowException, you simply don't have any memory to continue executing the program. Given that exception handling occurs on the stack, you don't even have enough memory to continue with the exception handling. Like-wise, the OutOfMemoryException defines a condition in which your application is out of heap space (used for reference variables). And if the exception engine, ExecutionEngineException, isn't working at all, there isn't any point in con-tinuing because you have no way to handle this error.

Knowing What Exceptions Are For

REMEMBER

Software that can't complete what it set out to do should throw exceptions. If a method is supposed to process all of an array, for example, or read all of a file, and for some reason can't complete the job, it should throw an appropriate exception.

A method can fail at its task for various reasons: bad input values or unexpected conditions (such as a missing or smaller than expected file), for example. The task is incomplete or can't even be undertaken. If any of these conditions occurs in your methods, you should throw an exception.

REMEMBER

The overall point here is that whoever called the method needs to know that its task wasn't completed. Throwing an exception is almost always better than using any error-return code. However, if you can handle the exception within the method, you need to do that rather than use an exception in place of good code.

The article at https://docs.microsoft.com/dotnet/standard/exceptions/best-practices-for-exceptions provides additional ideas on how to use exceptions correctly.

Can I Get an Exceptional Example?

The following FactorialException program demonstrates the key elements of the exception mechanism:

```
using System;

// FactorialException -- Create a factorial program that reports illegal
//    Factorial() arguments using an Exception.
namespace FactorialException
{
  // MyMathFunctions -- A collection of mathematical functions
  //    we created (it's not much to look at yet)
  public class MyMathFunctions
  {
    // Factorial -- Return the factorial of the provided value.
    public static int Factorial(int value)
    {
      // Don't allow negative numbers.
      if (value < 0)
      {
        // Report negative argument.
        string s = String.Format(
            "Illegal negative argument to Factorial {0}", value);

        throw new ArgumentException(s);
      }

      // Begin with an "accumulator" of 1.
      int factorial = 1;

      // Loop from value down to 1, each time multiplying
      // the previous accumulator value by the result.
      do
      {
        factorial *= value;
      } while(--value > 1);
```

```
        // Return the accumulated value.
        return factorial;
    }
}

public class Program
{
    public static void Main(string[] args)
    {
        // Here's the exception handler.
        try
        {
            // Call factorial in a loop from 6 down to -6.
            for (int i = 6; i > -6; i--)
            {
                // Calculate the factorial of the number.
                int factorial = MyMathFunctions.Factorial(i);

                // Display the result of each pass.
                Console.WriteLine("i = {0}, factorial = {1}",
                                    i, factorial);
            }
        }
        catch(ArgumentException e)
        {
            // This is a "last-chance" exception handler.
            // Probably all you can do here is alert the user before quitting.
            Console.WriteLine("Fatal error:");

            // When you're ready to release the program, change this
            // output to something in plain English, preferably with guide-
            // lines for what to do about the problem.
            Console.WriteLine(e.ToString());
        }

        // Wait for user to acknowledge.
        Console.WriteLine("Press Enter to terminate...");
        Console.Read();
    }
}
```

This "exceptional" version of Main() wraps almost its entire contents in a try block. The catch block at the end of Main() catches the ArgumentException object and uses its ToString() method to display most of the error information contained within the exception object in a single string. The example uses the ArgumentException because it most accurately describes the problem: an unacceptable argument to Factorial().

Knowing what makes the example exceptional

The version of the Factorial() method in the preceding section includes a check for a negative argument. If its argument is negative, Factorial() can't continue, so it formats an error message that describes the problem, including the value it found to be offensive. Factorial() then bundles this information into a newly created ArgumentException object, which it throws back to the calling method.

TIP

You can use the debugger to watch the exception occur in real time. (Book 4 tells you more about the debugger.) The output from this program appears as follows (the error messages are trimmed to make them more readable):

```
i = 6, factorial = 720
i = 5, factorial = 120
i = 4, factorial = 24
i = 3, factorial = 6
i = 2, factorial = 2
i = 1, factorial = 1
i = 0, factorial = 0
Fatal error:
System.ArgumentException: Illegal negative argument to Factorial -1
    at Factorial(Int32 value) in c:\c#programs\Factorial\Program.cs:line 21
    at FactorialException.Program.Main(String[] args) in c:\c#programs\Factorial\
        Program.cs:line 49
Press Enter to terminate...
```

The first few lines display the actual factorial of the numbers 6 through 0. Attempting to calculate the factorial of –1 generates the message starting with Fatal error — that doesn't sound good.

The first line in the error message was formatted back in Factorial() itself. This line describes the nature of the problem, including the offending value of –1.

Tracing the stack

The remainder of the output is a *stack trace*. The first line of the stack trace describes where the exception was thrown. In this case, the exception was thrown in Factorial(Int32 value) — more specifically, Line 21 within the source file Program.cs. Factorial() was invoked in the method Main(string[] args) on Line 49 within the same file. The stack trace stops with Main() because that's the module in which the exception was caught.

You have to admit that this process is impressive — the message describes the problem and identifies the offending argument. The stack trace tells you where the exception was thrown and how the program got there. Using that information, you should be drawn to the culprit like a tornado to a trailer park.

TIP

If you run the previous example and examine the stack trace it prints to the console, you see `Main()` at the *bottom* of the listing and deeper methods above it. The trace builds upward from `Main()`, so, technically, unwinding the call stack goes *down* the trace toward `Main()`. You should think of it the other way around, though: Callers are higher in the call chain (refer to Figure 9-1).

TIP

Returning geeky information such as the stack trace works just fine during development, but you would probably want real users to see more intelligible information. Still, you may want to write the stack trace to a log file somewhere.

TIP

While the program is running in the debugger, the stack trace is available in one of the Visual Studio debugger windows.

Assigning Multiple catch Blocks

Earlier in the chapter you learn that you can define your own custom exception types. Suppose that you want to define a `CustomException` class. The class might look something like this:

```
public class CustomException : System.Exception
{
    // Default constructor
    public CustomException() : base()
    {
    }

    // Argument constructor
    public CustomException(String message) : base(message)
    {
    }

    // Argument constructor with inner exception
    public CustomException(String message, Exception innerException) :
        base(message, innerException)
    {
    }
```

```
   // Argument constructor with serialization support
   protected CustomException(
      SerializationInfo info, StreamingContext context) :
      base(info, context)
   {
   }
}
```

You can use this basic setup for any custom exception that you want to create. There is no special code (unless you want to add it) because the base() entries mean that the code relies on the code found in System.Exception. What you're seeing here is the work of inheritance, something you see quite a lot in Book 2. In other words, for now, you don't have to worry too much about how this custom exception works. Now consider the catch clause used here:

```
public void SomeMethod()
{
  try
  {
    SomeOtherMethod();
  }
  catch(CustomException ce)
  {
  }
}
```

What if SomeOtherMethod() had thrown a simple Exception or another non-CustomException type of exception? It would be like trying to catch a football with a baseball glove — the catch doesn't match the throw.

REMEMBER

Fortunately, C# enables the program to define numerous catch clauses, each designed for a different type of exception. Assuming that this is the right place to handle the other exceptions, you can tack on one after another. You must line up the multiple catch clauses for different exception types nose to tail after the try block. C# checks each catch block sequentially, comparing the object thrown with the catch clause's argument type, as shown in this chunk of code:

```
public void SomeMethod()
{
  try
  {
    SomeOtherMethod();
  }
  catch(CustomException ce)  // Most specific exception type
  {
    // All CustomException objects are caught here.
  } // You could insert other exception types between these two.
```

```
catch(Exception e)            // Most general exception type
{
    // All otherwise uncaught exceptions are caught here.
    // Not that you should always do so -- but when it makes sense ...
}
}
```

Were `SomeOtherMethod()` to throw an `Exception` object, it would pass over the `catch(CustomException)` because an `Exception` isn't a type of `Custom Exception`. It would be caught by the next `catch` clause: the `catch(Exception)`.

WARNING

Always line up the `catch` clauses from most specific to most general. Never place the more general `catch` clause first, as in this fairly awful bit of code:

```
public void SomeMethod()
{
    try
    {
        SomeOtherMethod();
    }
    catch(Exception e)   // Most general first -- not good!
    {
        // All exceptions are caught here.
        // The dingo ate everything.
    }
    catch(CustomException ce)
    {
        // No exception ever gets this far, because it's
        // caught and consumed by the more general catch clause.
    }
}
```

The more general `catch` clause starves the `catch` clause that follows by intercepting any `throw`. The compiler alerts you to this error.

REMEMBER

Any class that inherits `CustomException` IS_A `CustomException`:

```
class MySpecialException : CustomException
{
    // ... whatever ...
}
```

Given the chance, a `CustomException` catch grabs a `MySpecialException` object like a frog nabs flies.

Planning Your Exception-Handling Strategy

It makes sense to have a plan for how your program will deal with errors. Choosing to use exceptions instead of error codes is just one choice to make.

Some questions to guide your planning

Several questions should be on your mind as you develop your program:

- **What could go wrong?** Ask this question about each bit of code you write.

- **If it does go wrong, can I fix it?** If so, you may be able to recover from the problem, and the program may be able to continue. If not, you probably need to pack your bags and get out of town.

- **Does the problem put user data at risk?** If so, you must do everything in your power to keep from losing or damaging that data. Knowingly releasing code that can mangle user data is akin to software malpractice.

- **Where should I put my exception handler for this problem?** Trying to handle an exception in the method where it occurs may not be the best approach. Often, another method higher up in the chain of method calls has better information and may be able to do something more intelligent and useful with the exception. Put your try/catch there so that the try block surrounds the call that leads to the place where the exception can occur.

- **Which exceptions should I handle?** Catch any exception that you can recover from somehow. Try hard to find a way to recover. Then, during development and testing, the unhandled exceptions will reach the top of your program. Before you release the program to real users, fix the underlying causes of any exceptions that go unhandled — if you can. But sometimes an exception *should* require terminating the program prematurely because things are hopelessly fouled up.

- **What about exceptions that slip through the cracks and elude my handlers?** The section "Grabbing Your Last Chance to Catch an Exception," later in this chapter, describes providing a "last-chance" exception handler to catch strays.

- **How robust (unbreakable) does my code need to be?** You never know where your code is going to end up. You might have designed it as a simple utility, but if it does something useful, it could end up in an air-traffic-control system. With this need in mind, you need to make your code as bulletproof as possible every time you write code.

Guidelines for code that handles errors well

You should keep the questions in the previous section in mind as you work. These guidelines may help, too:

>> **Protect the user's data at all costs.** This is the Top Dog guideline. See the next bullet item.

>> **Don't crash.** Recover if you can, but be prepared to go down as gracefully as possible. Don't let your program just squeak out a cryptic, geeky message and go belly up. *Gracefully* means that you provide clear messages containing as much helpful information as possible before shutting down. Users truly hate crashes. But you probably knew that.

>> **Don't let your program continue running if you can't recover from a problem.** The program could be unstable or the user's data left in an inconsistent state. When all is most certainly lost, you can display a message and call `System.Environment.FailFast()` to terminate the program immediately rather than throw an exception. It isn't a crash — it's deliberate.

>> **Treat class libraries differently from applications.** In *class libraries*, let exceptions reach the caller, which is best equipped to decide how to deal with the problem. Don't keep the caller in the dark about problems. But in *applications*, handle any exceptions you can. Your goal is to keep the code running if possible and protect the user's data without putting a lot of inconsequential messages in the user's face.

>> **Throw exceptions when, for any reason, a method can't complete its task.** The caller needs to know about the problem. (The caller may be a method higher up the call stack in your code or a method in code by another developer using your code.) If you check input values for validity before using them and they aren't valid — such as an unexpected `null` value — fix them and continue if you can. Otherwise, throw an exception.

Try to write code that doesn't need to throw exceptions — and correct bugs when you find them — rather than rely on exceptions to patch up the code. But use exceptions as your main method of reporting and handling errors.

>> **In most cases, don't catch exceptions in a particular method unless you can handle them in a useful way, preferably by recovering from the error.** Catching an exception that you can't handle is like catching a wasp in your bare hand. Now what? Most methods don't contain exception handlers.

>> **Test your code thoroughly,** especially for any category of bad input you can think of. Can your method handle negative input? Zero? A very large value? An empty string? A `null` value? What could the user do to cause an exception? What fallible resources, such as files, databases, or URLs, does your code use? See the two previous bullet paragraphs.

>> **Catch the most specific exception you can.** Don't write many catch blocks for high-level exception classes such as Exception or ApplicationException. You risk starving handlers higher up the chain.

>> **Always put a last-chance exception handler block in** Main( ) — or wherever the "top" of your program is (except in reusable class libraries). You can catch type Exception in this block. Catch and handle the ones you can and let the last-chance exception handler pick up any stragglers. (The "Grabbing Your Last Chance to Catch an Exception" section explains last-chance handlers.)

>> **Don't use exceptions as part of the normal flow of execution.** For example, don't throw an exception as a way to get out of a loop or exit a method.

>> **Consider writing your own custom exception classes** if they bring something to the table — such as more information to help in debugging or more meaningful error messages for users.

The rest of this chapter gives you the tools needed to follow these guidelines. For more information, look up *exception handling, design guidelines* in the C# Language Help system, but be prepared for some technical reading.

REMEMBER

If a public method throws any exceptions that the caller may need to catch, those exceptions are part of your class's public interface. You need to document them, preferably with the XML documentation comments discussed in Chapter 1 of Book 4.

How to analyze a method for possible exceptions

In the following method, which is the first step in setting up exception handlers, consider which exceptions it can throw:

```csharp
public string FixNamespaceLine(string line)
{
  const string COMPANY_PREFIX = "CMSCo";
  int spaceIndex = line.IndexOf(' ');
  int nameStart = GetNameStartAfterNamespaceKeyword(line, spaceIndex);
  string newline = string.Empty;
  newline = PlugInNamespaceCompanyQualifier(line, COMPANY_PREFIX, nameStart);
  return newline.Trim();
}
```

Given a C# file, this method is part of some code intended to find the `namespace` keyword in the file and insert a string representing a company name (one of ours) as a prefix on the namespace name. (See Book 2, Chapter 10 for information about namespaces.) The following example illustrates where the `namespace` keyword is likely to be found in a C# file:

```
using System;
namespace SomeName
{
    // Code within the namespace ...
}
```

Running the `FixNamespaceLine()` method on this type of file converts the first line into the second:

```
namespace SomeName
namespace CmsCo.SomeName
```

The overall program reads .CS files. Then it steps through the lines one by one, feeding each one to the `FixNamespaceLine()` method. Given a line of code, the method calls `String.IndexOf()` to find the index of the namespace name (normally, 10). Then it calls `GetNameStartAfterNamespaceKeyword()` to locate the beginning of the namespace name. Finally, it calls another method, `PlugInNamespaceCompanyQualifier()`, to plug the company name into the correct spot in the line, which it then returns. Much of the work is done by the subordinate methods.

First, even without knowing what this code is for or what the two called methods do, consider the input. The `line` argument could have at least one problem for the call to `String.IndexOf()`. If `line` is `null`, the `IndexOf()` call results in an `ArgumentNullException`. You can't call a method on a `null` object. Also, at first blush, will calling `IndexOf()` on an empty string work? It turns out that it will, so no exception occurs there, but what happens if you pass an empty `line` to one of those methods with the long names? The recommended fix is a guard clause before the first line of code in `FixNamespaceLine()` — and at least checking for `null`:

```
if(String.IsNullOrEmpty(name))  // A handy string method
{
    return name; // You can get away with a reasonable return value here
              // instead of throwing an exception.
}
```

Second, after you're safely past the `IndexOf()` call, one of the two method calls can throw an exception, even with `line` carefully checked out first. If `spaceIndex` turns out to be −1 (not found) — as can happen because the line that's passed in doesn't usually contain a namespace keyword — passing it to the first method can be a problem. You can guard for that outcome, of course, like this:

```
if(spaceIndex > -1) ...
```

If spaceIndex is negative, the line doesn't contain the namespace keyword. *That's not an error.* You just skip that line by returning the original line and then move on to the next line. In any event, don't call the subordinate methods.

Method calls in your method require exploring each one to see which exceptions it can throw and then digging into any methods that those methods call, and so on, until you reach the bottom of this particular call chain.

With this possibility in mind, and given that FixNamespaceLine() needs additional bulletproofing guard clauses first, where might you put an exception handler?

You may be tempted to put most of FixNamespaceLine() in a try block. But you have to consider whether this the best place for it. This method is low-level, so it should just throw exceptions as needed — or just pass on any exceptions that occur in the methods it calls. The best practice is to look up the call chain to see which method might be a good location for a handler.

As you move up the call chain, ask yourself the questions in the earlier section "Some questions to guide your planning." What would be the consequences if FixNamespaceLine() threw an exception? That depends on how its result is used higher up the chain. Also, how dire would the results need to be? If you can't "fix" the namespace line for the current file, does the user lose anything major? Maybe you can get away with an occasional unfixed file, in which case you might choose to "swallow" the exception at some level in the call chain and just notify the user of the unprocessed file. Or maybe not. You get the idea. The moral is that correctly setting up exception handlers requires some analysis and thought.

REMEMBER

However, keep in mind that *any* method call can throw exceptions — for example, the application *could* run out of memory, or the assembly it's in might not be found and loaded. You can't do much about that.

How to find out which methods throw which exceptions

TIP

To find out whether calling a particular method in the .NET class libraries, such as String.IndexOf() — or even one of your own methods — can throw an exception, consider these guidelines:

- » **Visual Studio provides immediate help with tooltips.** When you hover the mouse pointer over a method name in the Visual Studio editor, a yellow tooltip window lists not only the method's parameters and return type but also the exceptions it can throw.

- » **If you have used XML comments to comment your own methods,** Visual Studio shows the information in those comments in its IntelliSense tool tips just as it does for .NET methods. If you documented the exceptions your method can throw (see the previous section), you see them in a tooltip. Plug in the ‹exception› line inside your ‹summary› comment to make it show in the tooltip.

- » **The C# Language Help files provide even more.** When you look up a .NET method in C# Language Help, you find a list of exceptions that the method can throw, along with additional descriptions not provided via the yellow Visual Studio tooltip. To open the C# Language Help page for a given method, click the method name in your code and press F1. You can also supply similar help for your own classes and methods.

You should look at each of the exceptions you see listed, decide how likely it is to occur, and (if warranted for your program) guard against it using the techniques covered in the rest of this chapter.

Grabbing Your Last Chance to Catch an Exception

The FactorialException example in the earlier section "Can I Get an Exceptional Example?" wraps all of Main(), except for the final console calls, in an outer, "last-chance" exception handler.

REMEMBER

If you're writing an application, always sandwich the contents of Main() in a try block because Main() is the starting point for the program and thus the ending point as well. (If you're writing a class library intended for reuse, don't worry about unhandled exceptions — whoever is using your library needs to know about all exceptions, so let them bubble up through your methods.)

Any exception not caught somewhere else percolates up to Main(). This is your last opportunity to grab the error before it ends up back in Windows, where the error message is much harder to interpret and may frustrate — or scare the bejabbers out of — the program's user.

All the serious code in FactorialException's Main() is inside a try block. The associated catch block catches any exception whatsoever and outputs a message to the console, and the application exits.

This catch block serves to prevent hard crashes by intercepting all exceptions not handled elsewhere. And it's your chance to explain why the application is quitting.

To see why you need this last-chance handler, deliberately throw an exception in a little program without handling it. You see what the user would see without your efforts to make the landing a bit softer.

REMEMBER

During development, you *want* to see exceptions that occur as you test the code, in their natural habitat — so you want all the geekspeak. In the version you release, convert the programmerish details to normal English, display the message to the user, including, if possible, what the user might do to run successfully next time, and exit stage right. Make this plain-English version of the exception handler one of the last chores you complete before you release your program into the wild. Your last-chance handler should certainly log the exception information somehow, for later forensic analysis.

Throwing Expressions

C# versions prior to 7.0 have certain limits when it comes to throwing an exception as part of an expression. In these previous versions, you essentially had two choices. The first choice was to complete the expression and then check for a result, as shown here:

```
var myStrings = "One,Two,Three".Split(',');
var numbers = (myStrings.Length > 0) ? myStrings : null
if(numbers == null){throw new Exception("There are no numbers!");}
```

The second option was to make throwing the exception part of the expression, as shown here:

```
var numbers = (myStrings.Length > 0) ?
   myStrings :
   new Func<string[]>(() => {
      throw new Exception("There are no numbers!"); })();
```

C# 7.0 and above includes a new null coalescing operator, ?? (two question marks). Consequently, you can compress the two previous examples so that they look like this:

```
var numbers = myStrings ?? throw new Exception("There are no numbers!");
```

In this case, if myStrings is null, the code automatically throws an exception. You can also use this technique within a conditional operator (like the second example):

```
var numbers = (myStrings.Length > 0)? myStrings :
  throw new Exception("There are no numbers!");
```

The capability to throw expressions also exists with expression-bodied members. You might have seen these members in one of the two following forms (if not, you find them covered completely in Book 2, so don't worry too much about the specifics for now):

```
public string getMyString()
{
  return " One,Two,Three ";
}
```

or

```
public string getMyString() => "One,Two,Three";
```

However, say that you don't know what content to provide. In this case, you had these two options before version 7.0:

```
public string getMyString() => return null;
```

or

```
public string getMyString() {throw NotImplementedException();}
```

Both of these versions have problems. The first example leaves the caller without a positive idea of whether the method failed — a null return might be the expected value. The second version is cumbersome because you need to create a standard function just to throw the exception. Because of the new additions to C# 7.0 and above, it's now possible to throw an expression. The previous lines become

```
public string getMyString() => throw new NotImplementedException();
```

Chapter **10**

Creating Lists of Items with Enumerations

To *enumerate* means to specify individual items as in a list. For example, you might create an enumeration of colors and then list individual colors, such as red, blue, green, and so on. Using enumerations in programming makes sense because you can list individual items as part of a common collection. For example, `Colors.Blue` would indicate the color blue, and `Colors.Red` would indicate the color red. Because enumerations are so handy, you see them used all the time in the actual world, which is why you also see them in applications. Code should model the real world to provide useful functionality in an easy-to-understand form.

The `enum` keyword lets you create enumerations in C#. This chapter begins by discussing basic `enum` usage but then moves on to some interesting additions you can make. For example, you can use *initializers* to determine the initial value of each enumeration element.

Flags give you a compact way to track small configuration options — normally on or off, but you can make them more complicated than that. You see them used a lot in older applications because they make memory usage significantly more efficient. C# applications use flags to group like options and make them easier to find and work with. You can use a single flag variable to determine precisely how some objects work.

Enumerations also see use as part of C# switches. Book 1, Chapter 5 introduces you to the switch statement, but this chapter takes you a little further by demonstrating how using enumerations can make your switch statements even easier to read and understand.

Seeing Enumerations in the Real World

A problem with many programming constructs is relating them to the real world, and such can be the case with enumerations. An enumeration is any permanent collection of items. As previously mentioned, colors are one of the more common enumerations, and you use them often in the real world. However, if you were to look up color enumerations online, you'd find a stack of programming-specific references and not a single real-world reference. Instead of a color enumeration, look for a color wheel; that's how people in the real world enumerate colors and create collections of color types. People often organize the color sets by their position on the color wheel, such as complimentary or analogous colors. (See https://www.sessions.edu/color-calculator/ for a color calculator and description of the color wheel.)

Collections take many forms, and you may not even realize that you've created one. For example, the site at http://www.softschools.com/science/biology/ classification_of_living_things/ tells you about the classification of living organisms. Because these classifications follow a pattern and tend not to change much, you could express them as an enumeration within an application. For example, the list of five kingdoms is unlikely to change ever. Even the list of phylums within each kingdom is unlikely to change, so you could express them as enumerations as well.

Practical, everyday uses for enumerations include lists of items or information that everyone needs. For example, you can't mail something without knowing which state the package is supposed to go to. An enumeration of states within an application saves everyone time and ensures that the address appears without errors. You use enumerations to represent actual objects correctly. People make mistakes, and enumerations reduce errors; also, because they save time, people really want to use them.

REMEMBER

Enumerations work only under certain circumstances. In fact, situations arise in which you should most definitely not use an enumeration. The following list offers some rules of thumb to use when deciding whether to create an enumeration:

>> **Collection stability:** The collection must present a stable, unchanging list of members. A list of states is stable and unlikely to change frequently. A list of

the top ten songs on the Billboard chart isn't stable and can change almost daily.

>> **Member stability:** Each member within the collection must also remain stable and present a recognizable, consistent value. A list of area codes, even though quite large, is also consistent and recognizable, so you could create such an enumeration, should you decide to do so. A list of people's first names is a bad idea because people change the spelling of names constantly and add new names at the drop of a hat.

>> **Consistent value:** Enumerations exchange numeric values that a program can understand for word values that a human can understand. If the numeric value associated with a particular word changes, the enumeration won't work because you can't rely on a dependable association between the numeric value and the word used to represent it.

Working with Enumerations

The basic idea behind enumerations is relatively simple. All you really need to do is create a list of names and assign the collection a name. However, you can make additions to a basic enumeration that enhances flexibility and your ability to use enumerations in a wide range of scenarios. The following sections describe how to create various kinds of enumerations.

Using the enum keyword

You use the `enum` keyword to create an enumeration. For example, the following code creates an enumeration named `Colors`.

```
enum Colors {Red, Orange, Yellow, Green, Blue, Purple};
```

REMEMBER

C# offers multiple ways to access the enumeration. If you need just a single value, you can use the color name. The output you get depends on how you access the value, as shown here:

```
// Display the color name.
Console.WriteLine(Colors.Blue);

// Display the color value.
Console.WriteLine((int)Colors.Blue);
```

If you were to execute this code, you'd see Blue as the output for the first line and 4 for the output of the second line. When creating an enumeration, the values begin at 0 and proceed sequentially from there. Because Blue is the fifth element of Colors, its value is 4.

You might need to access the entire list of enumerated values at some point. To perform this task, you use a foreach statement, like this:

```
// Display all the elements starting with names.
foreach (String Item in Enum.GetNames(typeof(Colors)))
    Console.WriteLine(Item);

// Display the values too.
foreach (Colors Item in Enum.GetValues(typeof(Colors)))
    Console.WriteLine("{0} = {1}", Item, (int)Item);
```

However, you might actually need only a range of values. In this case, you could also use a for statement, like this:

```
// Display a range of names.
for (Colors Item = Colors.Orange; Item <= Colors.Blue; Item++)
    Console.WriteLine("{0} = {1}", Item, (int)Item);
```

In this case, you see only a range of the values that Colors provides. The output is

```
Orange = 1
Yellow = 2
Green = 3
Blue = 4
```

Creating enumerations with initializers

Using the default values that the enum keyword provides works fine in most cases because you don't really care about the value — you care about the human-readable form of the value. However, sometimes you really do need to assign specific values to each of the enumeration elements. In this case, you need an initializer. An *initializer* simply specifies the specific value assigned to each element member, like this:

```
enum Colors2
{
    Red = 5,
    Orange = 10,
    Yellow = Orange + 5,
```

```
    Green = 5 * 4,
    Blue = 0x19,
    Purple = Orange | Green
}
```

To assign a value to each element, just add an equals sign, followed by a value. You must provide a numeric value. For example, you can't assign a value of "Hello" to one of the elements.

REMEMBER

You might be thinking to yourself that those last four initializers look strange. The fact is that an initializer can equate to anything that ends up being a number. In the first case, you add 5 to the value of Orange to initialize Yellow. Green is the result of a math equation. Meanwhile, Blue uses hexadecimal format instead of decimal. Finally, Purple is the result of performing a logical or of Orange and Green. You use the same techniques as before to enumerate an enum that uses initializers:

```
foreach (Colors2 Item in Enum.GetValues(typeof(Colors2)))
    Console.WriteLine("{0} = {1}", Item, (int)Item);
```

Here are the results:

```
Red = 5
Orange = 10
Yellow = 15
Green = 20
Blue = 25
Purple = 30
```

Specifying an enumeration data type

The default enumeration data type is int. However, you might not want to use an int; you might need some other value, such as a long or a short. You can, in fact, use the byte, sbyte, short, ushort, int, uint, long, and ulong types to create an enumeration. The type you choose depends on how you plan to use the enum and how many values you plan to store in it.

To define an enum data type, you add a colon and type name after the enumeration name. Here's an example:

```
enum Colors3: byte {Red, Orange, Yellow, Green, Blue, Purple};
```

The `Colors3` enumeration is supposedly of type `byte`. Of course, you don't know for certain that it is until you test it. The following code shows how to perform the testing:

```
foreach (Colors3 Item in Enum.GetValues(typeof(Colors3)))
    Console.WriteLine("{0} is {1} = {2}",
        Item, Item.GetTypeCode(), (int)Item);
```

REMEMBER

Note that you must use the `Item.GetTypeCode()` method, not the `Item.GetType()` method, to obtain the underlying enumeration type. If you use `Item.GetType()` instead, C# tells you that `Item` is of type `Colors3`. Here's the output from this example:

```
Red is Byte = 0
Orange is Byte = 1
Yellow is Byte = 2
Green is Byte = 3
Blue is Byte = 4
Purple is Byte = 5
```

Creating Enumerated Flags

Flags provide an interesting way to work with data. You can use them in various ways to perform tasks such as defining options that aren't exclusive. For example, you can buy a car that has air conditioning, GPS, Bluetooth, and a number of other features. Each of these features is an addition, but they all fall within the category of optional accessories.

REMEMBER

When working with flags, you must think in terms of bits. For example, most people would think of a `byte` as being able to hold values up to 255, or they might think of a byte as being eight bits long. However, what you need to think about when working with flags is that the `byte` can hold eight individual bit values. So, a value of 1 might indicate that the person wants air conditioning. A value of 2 might indicate a desire for GPS. Likewise, a value of 4 might indicate a need for Bluetooth — with all using bit positions, as shown here:

```
0000 0001 Air Conditioning
0000 0010 GPS
0000 0100 Bluetooth
```

By reserving bit positions and associating them each with a particular option, you can start to perform bit manipulation using and (&), or (|), and exclusive or (^).

For example, a value of 3, which equates to 0000 0011, would tell someone that a buyer needs both air conditioning and GPS.

REMEMBER

The most common way to work with bit values is using hexadecimal, which can represent 16 different values directly, which equates to four bit positions. Consequently, 0x11 would appear as 0001 0001 in bit form. Hexadecimal values range from 0 through F, where A = 10, B = 11, C = 12, D = 13, E = 14, and F = 15 in decimal form. Here's an example of an enumerated flag:

```
[Flags]
enum Colors4
{
    Red = 0x01,
    Orange = 0x02,
    Yellow = 0x04,
    Green = 0x08,
    Blue = 0x10,
    Purple = 0x20
}
```

Note the [Flags] attribute that appears immediately before the enum keyword. An attribute tells the C# compiler how to react to a common structure in a special way. In this case, you tell the C# compiler that this isn't a standard enumeration; this enumeration defines flag values.

TIP

You should also see that the individual elements rely on hexadecimal initializers (see the "Creating enumerations with initializers" section, earlier in this chapter, for details). C# doesn't require that you use hexadecimal initializers, but doing so makes your code significantly easier to read. The following code shows how an enumerated flag might work:

```
// Create a variable containing three color options.
Colors4 myColors = Colors4.Red | Colors4.Green | Colors4.Purple;

// Display the result.
Console.WriteLine(myColors);
Console.WriteLine("0x{0:X2}", (int)myColors);
```

The code begins by creating myColors, which contains three options, Colors4.Red, Colors4.Green, and Colors4.Purple. To create an additive option list, you always or the values together using the | operator. Normally, myColors would contain a value of 41. However, the next two lines of code show the effects of the [Flags] attribute:

```
Red, Green, Purple
0x29
```

The output shows the individual options when you display myColors. Because myColors represents flag values, the example also outputs the myColors value of 41 as a hexadecimal value of 0x29. The addition of the X2 format string to the format argument outputs the value in hexadecimal, rather than decimal form with two significant digits. The format argument and the format string are separated with a colon (:). You can read more about format types (which include format strings) at https://docs.microsoft.com/dotnet/standard/base-types/formatting-types.

Defining Enumerated Switches

When working with a switch statement, the reason for a decision can be quite unclear if you use a numeric value. For example, the following code doesn't really tell you much about the decision-making process:

```
// Create an ambiguous switch statement.
int mySelection = 2;
switch (mySelection)
{
    case 0:
        Console.WriteLine("You chose red.");
        break;
    case 1:
        Console.WriteLine("You chose orange.");
        break;
    case 2:
        Console.WriteLine("You chose yellow.");
        break;
    case 3:
        Console.WriteLine("You chose green.");
        break;
    case 4:
        Console.WriteLine("You chose blue.");
        break;
    case 5:
        Console.WriteLine("You chose purple.");
        break;
}
```

This code leaves you wondering why mySelection has a value of 2 assigned to it and what those output statements are all about. The code works, but the reasoning behind it is muddled. To make this code more readable, you can use an enumerated switch, like this:

```
// Create a readable switch statement.
Colors myColorSelection = Colors.Yellow;
switch (myColorSelection)
{
    case Colors.Red:
        Console.WriteLine("You chose red.");
        break;
    case Colors.Orange:
        Console.WriteLine("You chose orange.");
        break;
    case Colors.Yellow:
        Console.WriteLine("You chose yellow.");
        break;
    case Colors.Green:
        Console.WriteLine("You chose green.");
        break;
    case Colors.Blue:
        Console.WriteLine("You chose blue.");
        break;
    case Colors.Purple:
        Console.WriteLine("You chose purple.");
        break;
}
```

The output is the same in both cases: "You chose yellow." However, in the second case, the code is infinitely more readable. Simply by looking at the code, you know that myColorSelection has a color value assigned to it. In addition, the use of a Colors member for each case statement makes the choice clear. You understand why the code takes a particular path.

2

Object-Oriented
C# Programming

Contents at a Glance

Chapter **1**

Object-Oriented Programming — What's It All About?

O bject orientation is an essential part of modern programming because it helps you model the real world by using code, which is a better way to resolve difficult coding problems than by using procedural programming techniques. This chapter answers two essential questions: "What are the concepts behind object-oriented programming, and how do they differ from the procedural concepts covered in Book 1?" You begin by considering the abstraction that object orientation offers to help create a real-world model in code. The chapter then considers the whole issue of classification and how you use object orientation to create applications faster and easier than by using procedural techniques.

Object-Oriented Concept #1: Abstraction

You get into your car intending to drive somewhere. You start the car, put the car in gear, and then press the accelerator to move forward. The brake lets you temporarily stop the car so that you don't hit pedestrians or break any other laws.

When you arrive at your destination, you take the car out of gear and turn it off. During this whole scenario, there are things you don't do:

>> Open the engine compartment to manually adjust the flow of gas and air in an effort to control engine speed.

>> Modify the way the car works so that pressing the accelerator stops the car and pressing the brake causes it to move forward.

>> Create an entirely new system of lights to signal your intentions to other drivers.

REMEMBER

These observations aren't profound: You can deal with only so much stress in your life. To reduce the number of issues you deal with, you work at a certain level of detail. In object-oriented (OO) computerese, the level of detail at which you're working is the *level of abstraction*. To introduce another OO term, you *abstract away* the details of the car's innards.

Happily, computer scientists — and thousands of geeks — have invented object orientation and numerous other concepts that reduce the level of complexity at which programmers have to work. Using powerful abstractions makes the job simpler and far less error-prone than it used to be. In a sense, that's what the past half-century or so of computing progress has been about: managing ever more complex concepts and structures with ever fewer errors.

When you drive your car, you view it as a box. (While driving to the market or the theater, you can't afford to worry about the innards of the car and still avoid hitting those pesky pedestrians, much less elude the nuisance of a ticket.) As long as you use the car only by way of its interface (the various controls), nothing you can do should cause the car to enter an inconsistent state and crash or, worse, turn your car into a blackened, flaming mass.

Preparing procedural trips

Suppose you want to create a procedure for using a car for a quick trip. You might include these items in the procedure:

1. Start the car.
2. Get out into the lane of traffic.
3. Drive to the desired location.
4. Avoid obstacles along the way.

5. Follow the required traffic laws.

6. Park the car on arrival.

7. Stop the car.

That description is straightforward and complete. But it isn't the way a procedural programmer would code a program to make a trip somewhere. Procedural programmers live in a world devoid of objects such as cars, traffic laws, and pedestrians. They tend to worry about flowcharts with their myriad procedural paths. In a procedural solution to the driving problem, the programmer would need to describe the actual interactions between components, such as how pressing the accelerator increases the flow of gas. It wouldn't take long for the whole process to become a nightmare of small interactions that don't have much to do with driving anywhere.

In that world of procedural programming, you can't easily think in terms of levels of abstraction. You have no objects and no abstractions behind which to hide inherent complexity.

Preparing object-oriented trips

In an object-oriented approach to taking a trip, you first identify the types of objects in the problem: car, accelerator, brake, turn indicators, pedestrians, and so on. Then you begin the task of modeling those objects in software, without regard for the details of how they might be used in the final program. For example, you can model the accelerator as an object in isolation from the other objects and then combine it with the brake, turn indicator, and other components to make them interact. (And you might decide that some of these objects don't need to be objects in the software: pedestrians, for instance.)

While you do that, you're said to be working (and thinking) at the level of the basic objects. You need to think about making a useful car, but you don't have to think about the logical process of pushing the accelerator pedal — yet. After all, the car designers didn't think about the specific problem of your making a left turn. Rather, they set about solving the problem of designing and building a useful car.

After you successfully code and test the objects you need, you can ratchet up to the next level of abstraction and start thinking at the trip-making level rather than at the car-making level. At this point, you can begin creating your dream car to make a trip to your favorite location.

Object-Oriented Concept #2: Classification

Critical to the concept of abstraction is that of classification. When discussing a car, you can easily see it simply as a wheeled vehicle. However, that wheeled vehicle has certain characteristics. For example, a car with four tires will work; a car with only two tires (with two missing) won't. On the other hand, a motorcycle is also a type of wheeled vehicle, but it works just fine using only two wheels. *Classification* helps define types of objects to model in software.

REMEMBER

In object-oriented computerese, the car is an *instance* of the class car. The class car is a *subclass* of the class wheeledVehicle, which is a subclass of the class vehicle. Likewise, a motorcycle is an instance of the class motorcycle, which is also a subclass of wheeledVehicle, which is a subclass of vehicle. However, a boat would be an instance of the class boat, which is a subclass of floatingVehicle, which is a subclass of vehicle. So, cars, motorcycles, and boats are all vehicles, but they're specific kinds of vehicles.

Humans classify. Everything about the world is ordered into taxonomies. Humans do this to reduce the number of items they have to remember. For example, the first time you saw an SUV, the advertisement probably referred to the SUV as "revolutionary, the likes of which have never been seen." But you and I know that it just isn't so. You may like the looks of certain SUVs (others need to go back to take another crack at it), but hey, an SUV is a car. As such, it shares all (or at least most of) the properties of other cars. It has a steering wheel, seats, a motor, and brakes, for example. You can likely even drive one without reading the user's manual first.

You don't have to clutter the limited amount of storage space in your head with all the features that an SUV has in common with other cars. All you have to remember is "An SUV is a car that . . ." and tack on those few characteristics that are unique to an SUV (such as the price tag).

Why Classify?

Why should you classify? It sounds like a lot of trouble. Besides, people have been using the procedural approach for a long time — why change now?

Designing and building a car specifically for making local trips (rather than also allowing for extended trips) may seem easier than building a separate, more generic wheeled vehicle object. Suppose that you want to build a car that has just one control for moving, rather than separate accelerator and brake controls, which are pretty much required when you drive long distances. You might not even place these controls on the floor; they could appear as a lever next to the driver's hand (similar to those used by garden tractors and mowers). Unfortunately, the resulting vehicle, while simpler, would also be less capable. The procedural approach has these problems:

>> **It's too complex.** You don't want the details of car-building mixed into the details of taking a trip. If you can't define the objects and pull them from the morass of details to deal with separately, you must deal with all the complexities of the problem at the same time.

>> **It isn't flexible.** Someday, you may need to replace the car with another type of wheeled vehicle, or perhaps one that flies instead. You should be able to do so as long as the two vehicles have the same interface (or the flying vehicle is a true *superset,* having additional controls, of the wheeled vehicle). Without being clearly delineated and developed separately, one object type can't be cleanly removed and replaced with another.

>> **It isn't reusable.** Cars are used to make lots of different trip types. You don't want to create a new car every time you encounter a new destination. Having solved a problem once, you want to be able to reuse the solution in other places within the program. If you're lucky, you may be able to reuse it in future programs as well.

Object-Oriented Concept #3: Usable Interfaces

An object must be able to project an external interface that is sufficient but as simple as possible. This concept is sort of the reverse of Concept #4 (described in the next section). If the device interface is insufficient, users may start ripping the top off the device in hopes of achieving better results. Knowing that a device has capabilities that the interface doesn't address is frustrating. On the flip side, if the device interface is too complex, no one will buy the device — or at least no one will use all its features.

People complain continually that their DVD players are too complex, though it's less of a problem with today's onscreen controls. These devices have too many buttons with too many different functions. Often, the same button has different functions, depending on the state of the machine. In addition, no two DVD players seem to have the same interface. For whatever reason, the DVD player projects an interface that's too difficult and nonstandard for most people to use beyond the bare basics.

Compare the VCR with an automobile. You'd have difficulty arguing that a car is less complicated than a VCR. However, people don't seem to have much trouble driving cars.

All automobiles offer more or less the same controls in more or less the same place. For example, you might buy a car that has the headlight control on the left side of the steering wheel, where the turn signal handle normally lives. You push down on the light lever to turn off the lights, and you raise the lever to turn them on. This difference may seem trivial, but most people will never learn to turn left in that car at night without turning off the lights.

A well-designed auto doesn't use the same control to perform more than one operation, depending on the state of the car. Of course, for every good example, there is one exception to this rule: Some buttons on most cruise controls are overloaded with multiple functions.

Object-Oriented Concept #4: Access Control

Some devices do allow for multiple combinations of control access, such as a microwave oven. A microwave oven must be built so that no combination of keystrokes that you can enter on the front keypad can cause the oven to hurt you. Certainly, some combinations don't do anything. However, no sequence of keystrokes should

>> **Break the device:** You may be able to put the device into a strange state in which it doesn't do anything until you reset it (say, by throwing an internal breaker). However, you shouldn't be able to break the device by using the front panel — unless, of course, you throw it to the ground in frustration. The manufacturer of this type of device would probably have to send out some type of fix for it.

>> **Cause the device to catch fire and burn down the house:** As bad as it may be for the device to break itself, catching fire is much worse. You live in a litigious society. The manufacturer's corporate officers would likely end up in jail, especially if the user has anything to say about it.

However, to enforce these two rules, you have to take some responsibility. You can't make modifications to the inside of the device.

Almost all kitchen devices of any complexity, including microwave ovens, have a small seal to keep consumers from reaching inside them. If the seal is broken, indicating that the cover of the device has been removed, the manufacturer no longer bears responsibility. If you modify the internal workings of an oven, you're responsible if it subsequently catches fire and burns down the house.

Similarly, a class must be able to control access to its data members. No sequence of calls to class members should cause your program to crash. The class cannot possibly ensure control of this access if external elements have access to the internal state of the class. The class must be able to keep critical data members inaccessible to the outside world.

How C# Supports Object-Oriented Concepts

Okay, how does C# implement object-oriented programming? In a sense, this is the wrong question. C# is an object-oriented language; however, it doesn't implement object-oriented programming — the programmer does. You can certainly write a non-object-oriented program in C# or any other language (by, for instance, writing all of Microsoft Word in Main()). Something like "you can lead a horse to water" comes to mind. But you can easily write an object-oriented program in C#. These C# features are necessary for writing object-oriented programs:

>> **Controlled access:** C# controls the way in which class members can be accessed. C# keywords enable you to declare some members wide open to the public, whereas internal members are protected from view and some secrets are kept private. Notice the little hints. Access control secrets are revealed in Chapter 5 of this minibook.

>> **Specialization:** C# supports specialization through a mechanism known as *class inheritance.* One class inherits the members of another class. For example, you can create a Car class as a particular type of Vehicle. Chapter 6 in this minibook specializes in specialization.

>> **Polymorphism:** This feature enables an object to perform an operation the way it wants to. The Rocket type of Vehicle may implement the Start operation much differently from the way the Car type of Vehicle does. But all Vehicles have a Start operation, and you can rely on that. Chapter 7 in this minibook finds its own way of describing polymorphism.

>> **Indirection.** Objects frequently use the services of other objects — by calling their public methods. But classes can "know too much" about the classes they use. The two classes are then said to be "too tightly coupled," which makes the using class too dependent on the used class. The design is too brittle — liable to break if you make changes. But change is inevitable in software, so you should find more *indirect* ways to connect the two classes. That's where the C# interface construct comes in. (You can get the scoop on interfaces in Chapter 8 of this minibook.)

Chapter **2**

Showing Some Class

Y ou can freely declare and use all the intrinsic data types — such as int, double, and bool — to store the information necessary to make your program the best it can be. For some programs, these simple variables are enough. However, most programs need a way to bundle related data into a neat package.

As shown in Book 1, C# provides arrays and other collections for gathering into one structure groups of *like-typed* variables, such as string or int. A hypothetical college, for example, might track its students by using an array. But a student is much more than just a name — how should this type of program represent a student?

Some programs need to bundle pieces of data that logically belong together but aren't of the same type. A college enrollment application handles students, each of whom has a name, rank (grade-point average), and serial number. Logically, the student's name may be a string; the grade-point average, a double; and the serial number, a long. That type of program needs a way to bundle these three different types of variables into a single structure named Student. Fortunately, C# provides a structure known as the *class* for accommodating groupings of unlike-typed variables.

Defining a Class and an Object

A *class* is a bundling of unlike data and functions that logically belong together into one tidy package. C# gives you the freedom to foul up your classes any way you want, but good classes are designed to represent *concepts.*

Computer science models the world via structures that represent concepts or things in the world, such as bank accounts, tic-tac-toe games, customers, game boards, documents, and products. Analysts say that "a class maps concepts from the problem into the program." For example, your problem might be to build a traffic simulator that models traffic patterns for the purpose of building streets, intersections, and highways.

Any description of a problem concerning traffic would include the term *vehicle* in its solution. Vehicles have a top speed that must be figured into the equation. They also have a weight, and some of them are clunkers. In addition, vehicles stop and vehicles go. Thus, as a concept, *vehicle* is part of the problem domain.

A good C# traffic-simulator program would necessarily include the class Vehicle, which describes the relevant properties of a vehicle. The C# Vehicle class would have properties such as topSpeed, weight, and isClunker.

Because the class is central to C# programming, the rest of Book 2 discusses the ins and outs of classes in much more detail. This chapter gets you started.

Defining a class

An example of the class Vehicle may appear this way:

```
public class Vehicle
{
    public string model;          // Name of the model
    public string manufacturer;   // Name of the manufacturer
    public int numOfDoors;        // The number of doors on the vehicle
    public int numOfWheels;       // You get the idea.
}
```

A class definition begins with the words public class, followed by the name of the class — in this case, Vehicle. Like all names in C#, the name of the class is case sensitive. C# doesn't enforce any rules concerning class names, but an unofficial rule holds that the name of a class starts with a capital letter.

The class name is followed by a pair of open and closed braces. Within the braces, you have zero or more *members*. The members of a class are variables that make up the parts of the class. In this example, class Vehicle starts with the member model of type string, which contains the name of the model of the vehicle. If the vehicle were a car, its model name could be Trooper II. The second member of this Vehicle class example is manufacturer of type string. The other two properties are the number of doors and the number of wheels on the vehicle, both of which are type int.

As with any variable, make the names of the members as descriptive as possible. A good variable name usually says it all. However, adding comments, as shown in this example, can make the purpose and usage of the members clearer.

The public modifier in front of the class name makes the class universally accessible throughout the program. Similarly, the public modifier in front of the member names makes them accessible to everything else in the program. Other modifiers are possible. (Chapter 5 in this minibook covers the topic of accessibility in more detail and shows how you can hide some members.)

The class definition should describe the properties of the object that are salient to the problem at hand. That's a little hard to do right now because you don't know what the problem is, but it becomes clearer as you work through the problem.

What's the object?

Defining a Vehicle design isn't the same task as building a car. Someone has to cut some sheet metal and turn some bolts before anyone can drive an actual car. A class object is declared in a similar (but not identical) fashion to declaring an intrinsic object such as an int.

The term *object* is used universally to mean a "thing." Okay, that isn't helpful. An int variable is an int object. A car is a Vehicle object. The following code segment creates a car of class Vehicle:

```
Vehicle myCar;
myCar = new Vehicle();
```

The first line declares a variable myCar of type Vehicle, just as you can declare a somethingOrOther of class int. (Yes, a class is a type, and all C# objects are defined as classes.) The new Vehicle() command creates a specific object of type Vehicle and stores the location in memory of that object into the variable myCar. The new has nothing to do with the age of myCar. (My car could qualify for an antique license plate if it weren't so ugly.) The new operator creates a new block of memory in which your program can store the properties of myCar.

REMEMBER

In C# terms, you say that myCar is an object of type Vehicle. You also say that myCar is an instance of Vehicle. In this context, *instance* means "an example of" or "one of." You can also use the word *instance* as a verb, as in *instantiating* myCar. That's what *new* does. Compare the declaration of myCar with that of an int variable named num:

```
int num;
num = 1;
```

The first line declares the variable num, and the second line assigns an already created constant, 1, of type int into the location of the variable num.

TECHNICAL
STUFF

The intrinsic num and the object myCar are stored differently in memory. The first uses the *stack* and the second uses the *heap*. The variable num actually contains the value 1 rather than a memory location. The new Vehicle() expression allocates the memory necessary on the heap. The variable myCar contains a memory reference rather than the actual values used to describe a Vehicle.

Accessing the Members of an Object

Each object of class Vehicle has its own set of members. The following expression stores the number 1 into the numberOfDoors member of the object referenced by myCar:

```
myCar.numberOfDoors = 1;
```

TECHNICAL
STUFF

Every C# operation must be evaluated by type as well as by value. The object myCar is an object of type Vehicle. The variable Vehicle.numberOfDoors is of type int. (Look again at the definition of the Vehicle class.) The constant 5 is also of type int, so the type of the variable on the right side of the assignment operator matches the type of the variable on the left. Similarly, the following code stores a reference to the strings describing the model and manufacturer name of myCar:

```
myCar.manufacturer = "BMW";      // Don't get your hopes up.
myCar.model = "Isetta";          // The Urkel-mobile
```

The Isetta was a small car built during the 1950s with a single door that opened the entire front of the car. You can search for *Urkel* by using your favorite search engine.

An Object-Based Program Example

The simple VehicleDataOnly program performs these tasks:

>> Define the class Vehicle.

>> Create an object myCar.

>> Assign properties to myCar.

>> Retrieve those values from the object for display.

Here's the code for the VehicleDataOnly program:

```
using System;

// VehicleDataOnly -- Create a Vehicle object, populate its
//      members from the keyboard, and then write it back out.
namespace VehicleDataOnly
{
  public class Vehicle
  {
    public string model;        // Name of the model
    public string manufacturer; // Ditto
    public int numOfDoors;      // The number of doors on the vehicle
    public int numOfWheels;     // You get the idea.
  }

  public class Program
  {
    // This is where the program starts.
    static void Main(string[] args)
    {
      // Prompt user to enter a name.
      Console.WriteLine("Enter the properties of your vehicle");

      // Create an instance of Vehicle.
      Vehicle myCar = new Vehicle();

      // Populate a data member via a temporary variable.
      Console.Write("Model name = ");
      string s = Console.ReadLine();
      myCar.model = s;

      // Or you can populate the data member directly.
      Console.Write("Manufacturer name = ");
      myCar.manufacturer = Console.ReadLine();
```

```
        // Enter the remainder of the data.
        // A temp is useful for reading ints.
        Console.Write("Number of doors = ");
        s = Console.ReadLine();
        myCar.numOfDoors = Convert.ToInt32(s);
        Console.Write("Number of wheels = ");
        s = Console.ReadLine();
        myCar.numOfWheels = Convert.ToInt32(s);

        // Now display the results.
        Console.WriteLine("\nYour vehicle is a ");
        Console.WriteLine(myCar.manufacturer + " " + myCar.model);
        Console.WriteLine("with " + myCar.numOfDoors + " doors, "
                    + "riding on " + myCar.numOfWheels
                    + " wheels.");

        // Wait for user to acknowledge the results.
        Console.WriteLine("Press Enter to terminate...");
        Console.Read();
    }
  }
}
```

REMEMBER

The program listing begins with a definition of the Vehicle class. The definition of a class can appear either before or after class Program — it doesn't matter. However, you should adopt a style and stick with it. Book 4, which talks about Visual Studio, shows the more conventional technique of creating a separate .cs file to contain each class, but just put the extra class in your Program.cs file for now.

The program creates an object myCar of class Vehicle and then populates each field by reading the appropriate data from the keyboard. (The input data isn't — but should be — checked for legality.) The program then writes myCar's properties in a slightly different format. Here's some example output from executing this program:

```
Enter the properties of your vehicle
Model name = Metropolitan
Manufacturer name = Nash
Number of doors = 2
Number of wheels = 4

Your vehicle is a
Nash Metropolitan
with 2 doors, riding on 4 wheels
Press Enter to terminate...
```

TIP

The calls to Read() as opposed to ReadLine() leave the cursor directly after the output string, which makes the user's input appear on the same line as the prompt. In addition, inserting the newline character '\n' in a write generates a blank line without the need to execute WriteLine() separately.

Discriminating between Objects

Detroit car manufacturers can track every car they make without getting the cars confused. Similarly, a program can create numerous objects of the same class, as shown in this example:

```
Vehicle car1 = new Vehicle();
car1.manufacturer = "Studebaker";
car1.model = "Avanti";

// The following has no effect on car1.
Vehicle car2 = new Vehicle();
car2.manufacturer = "Hudson";
car2.model = "Hornet";
```

Creating an object car2 and assigning it the manufacturer name Hudson has no effect on the car1 object (with the manufacturer name Studebaker). That's because car1 and car2 appear in totally separate memory locations. In part, the ability to discriminate between objects is the real power of the class construct. The object associated with the Hudson Hornet can be created, manipulated, and dispensed with as a single entity, separate from other objects, including the Avanti. (Both are classic automobiles, especially the latter.)

Can You Give Me References?

The dot operator and the assignment operator are the only two operators defined on reference types:

```
// Create a null reference.
Vehicle yourCar;

// Assign the reference a value.
yourCar = new Vehicle();
```

```
// Use dot to access a member.
yourCar.manufacturer = "Rambler";

// Create a new reference and point it to the same object.
Vehicle yourSpousalCar = yourCar;
```

The first line creates an object yourCar without assigning it a value. A reference that hasn't been initialized is said to point to the *null object*. Any attempt to use an uninitialized (null) reference generates an immediate error that terminates the program.

The C# compiler can catch most attempts to use an uninitialized reference and generate a warning at build-time. If you somehow slip one past the compiler, accessing an uninitialized reference terminates the program immediately.

The second statement creates a new Vehicle object and assigns it to yourCar. The last statement in this code snippet assigns the reference yourSpousalCar to the reference yourCar. This action causes yourSpousalCar to refer to the same object as yourCar. This relationship is shown in Figure 2-1.

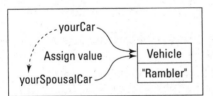

FIGURE 2-1:
Two references to the same object.

The following two calls have the same effect:

```
// Build your car.
Vehicle yourCar = new Vehicle();
yourCar.model = "Kaiser";

// It also belongs to your spouse.
Vehicle yourSpousalCar = yourCar;

// Changing one changes the other.
yourSpousalCar.model = "Henry J";
Console.WriteLine("Your car is a " + yourCar.model);
```

Executing this program would output Henry J and not Kaiser. Notice that yourSpousalCar doesn't point to yourCar; rather, both yourCar and your SpousalCar refer to the same vehicle (the same memory location). In addition, the reference yourSpousalCar would still be valid, even if the variable yourCar were somehow "lost" (if it went out of scope, for example), as shown in this chunk of code:

```
// Build your car.
Vehicle yourCar = new Vehicle();
yourCar.model = "Kaiser";

// It also belongs to your spouse.
Vehicle yourSpousalCar = yourCar;

// When your spouse takes your car away ...
yourCar = null;              // yourCar now references the "null object."

// ...yourSpousalCar still references the same vehicle
Console.WriteLine("your car was a " + yourSpousalCar.model);
```

Executing this program generates the output Your car was a Kaiser, even though the reference yourCar is no longer valid. The object is no longer *reachable* from the reference yourCar because yourCar no longer contains a reference to the required memory location. The object doesn't become completely unreachable until both yourCar and yourSpousalCar are "lost" or nulled out.

At some point, the C# *garbage collector* steps in and returns the space formerly used by that particular Vehicle object to the pool of space available for allocating more Vehicles (or Students, for that matter). (A sidebar at the end of Chapter 6 of this minibook says more about garbage collection.)

TIP

Making one *object variable* (a variable of a reference type, such as Vehicle or Student, rather than one of a simple type such as int or double) point to a different object — as shown here — makes storing and manipulating reference objects in arrays and collections quite efficient. Each element of the array stores a reference to an object, and when you swap elements within the array, you're just moving references, not the objects themselves. References have a fixed size in memory, unlike the objects they refer to.

Classes That Contain Classes Are the Happiest Classes in the World

The members of a class can themselves be references to other classes. For example, vehicles have motors, which have power and efficiency factors, including displacement. You could throw these factors directly into the class this way:

```
public class Vehicle
{
  public string model;          // Name of the model
  public string manufacturer;   // Ditto
  public int numOfDoors;        // The number of doors on the vehicle
  public int numOfWheels;       // You get the idea.

  // New stuff:
  public int power;             // Power of the motor [horsepower]
  public double displacement;   // Engine displacement [liter]
}
```

However, power and engine displacement aren't properties of the car. For example, your friend's Jeep might be supplied with two different motor options that have drastically different levels of horsepower. The 2.4-liter Jeep is a snail, and the same car outfitted with the 4.0-liter engine is quite peppy. The motor is a concept of its own and deserves its own class:

```
public class Motor
{
  public int power;             // Power [horsepower]
  public double displacement;   // Engine displacement [liter]
}
```

You can combine this class into the Vehicle (see boldfaced text):

```
public class Vehicle
{
  public string model;          // Name of the model
  public string manufacturer;   // Ditto
  public int numOfDoors;        // The number of doors on the vehicle
  public int numOfWheels;       // You get the idea.
  public Motor motor;
}
```

Creating myCar now appears this way:

```
// First create a Motor.
Motor largerMotor = new Motor();
largerMotor.power = 230;
largerMotor.displacement = 4.0;

// Now create the car.
Vehicle friendsCar = new Vehicle();
friendsCar.model = "Cherokee Sport";
friendsCar.manufacturer = "Jeep";
friendsCar.numOfDoors = 2;
friendsCar.numOfWheels = 4;

// Attach the motor to the car.
friendsCar.motor = largerMotor;
```

From Vehicle, you can access the motor displacement in two stages. You can take one step at a time, as this bit of code shows:

```
Motor m = friendsCar.motor;
Console.WriteLine("The motor displacement is " + m.displacement);
```

Or, you can access it directly, as shown here:

```
Console.Writeline("The motor displacement is " + friendsCar.motor.displacement);
```

Either way, you can access the displacement only through the Motor.

Generating Static in Class Members

Most data members of a class are specific to their containing object, not to any other objects. Consider the Car class:

```
public class Car
{
  public string licensePlate;      // The license plate ID
}
```

Because the license plate ID is an *object property*, it describes each object of class Car uniquely. For example, your spouse's car will have a different license plate from your car, as shown here:

```
Car spouseCar = new Car();
spouseCar.licensePlate = "XYZ123";

Car yourCar = new Car();
yourCar.licensePlate = "ABC789";
```

However, some properties exist that all cars share. For example, the number of cars built is a property of the class Car but not of any single object. These *class properties* are flagged in C# with the keyword static:

```
public class Car
{
    public static int numberOfCars; // The number of cars built
    public string licensePlate;       // The license plate ID
}
```

REMEMBER

Static members aren't accessed through the object. Instead, you access them by way of the class itself, as this code snippet demonstrates:

```
// Create a new object of class Car.
Car newCar = new Car();
newCar.licensePlate = "ABC123";

// Now increment the count of cars to reflect the new one.
Car.numberOfCars++;
```

The object member newCar.licensePlate is accessed through the object newCar, and the class (static) member Car.numberOfCars is accessed through the class Car. All Cars share the same numberOfCars member, so each car contains exactly the same value as all other cars.

REMEMBER

Class members are static members. Nonstatic members are specific to each "instance" (each individual object) and are *instance members*. The italicized phrases you see here are the generic way to refer to these types of members.

Defining const and readonly Data Members

One special type of static member is the const data member, which represents a constant. You must establish the value of a const variable in the declaration, and you cannot change it anywhere within the program, as shown here:

```
class Program
{
  // Number of days in the year (including leap day)
  public const int daysInYear = 366;  // Must have initializer.

  public static void Main(string[] args)
  {
    // This is an array, covered later in this chapter.
    int[] maxTemperatures = new int[daysInYear];
    for(int index = 0; index < daysInYear; index++)
    {
      //  ...accumulate the maximum temperature for each
      // day of the year ...
    }
  }
}
```

You can use the constant daysInYear in place of the value 366 anywhere within your program. The const variable is useful because it can replace a mysterious number such as 366 with the descriptive name daysInYear to enhance the readability of your program. C# provides another way to declare constants — you can preface a variable declaration with the readonly modifier, like so:

```
public readonly int daysInYear = 366;  // This could also be static.
```

As with const, after you assign the initial value, it can't be changed. Although the reasons are too technical for this book, the readonly approach to declaring constants is usually preferable to const.

You can use const with class data members like those you might have seen in this chapter and inside class methods. But readonly isn't allowed in a method. Chapter 3 of this minibook dives into methods.

An alternative convention also exists for naming constants. Rather than name them like variables (as in daysInYear), many programmers prefer to use uppercase letters separated by underscores, as in DAYS_IN_YEAR. This convention separates constants clearly from ordinary read-write variables.

Chapter **3**

We Have Our Methods

Programmers need to be able to break large programs into smaller chunks that are easy to handle. For example, the programs contained in previous chapters of this minibook reach the limit of the amount of programming information a person can digest at one time.

REMEMBER

C# lets you divide your class code into chunks known as *methods.* A method is equivalent to a function, procedure, or subroutine in other languages. The difference is that a method is always part of a class. Properly designed and implemented methods can greatly simplify the job of writing complex programs.

Defining and Using a Method

Consider the following example:

```
class Example
{
  public int anInt;                // Nonstatic
  public static int staticInt      // Static
  public void InstanceMethod()     // Nonstatic
  {
    Console.WriteLine("this is an instance method");
  }
```

```
  public static void ClassMethod()    // Static
  {
    Console.WriteLine("this is a class method");
  }
}
```

The element `anInt` is a *data member,* just like those shown in Book 1. However, the element `InstanceMethod()` is new. `InstanceMethod()` is known as an *instance method,* which is a set of C# statements that you can execute by referencing the method's name. This concept is best explained by example. (`Main()` and `WriteLine()` are used in nearly every example in this book, and they're methods.)

Note: The distinction between static and nonstatic members is important. This chapter covers part of the story, but you get more detail in Chapter 4 of this minibook, which focuses on nonstatic, or instance, methods.

REMEMBER

To invoke a nonstatic — instance — method, you need an instance of the class. To invoke a static — class — method, you call via the class name, not an instance. The following code snippet assigns a value to the object data member `anInt` and the class, or static, member `staticInt`:

```
Example example = new Example(); // Create an instance of class Example.
example.anInt = 1;                // Initialize instance member.
Example.staticInt = 2;            // Initialize class member.
```

The following snippet defines and accesses `InstanceMethod()` and `Class Method()` in almost the same way:

```
Example example = new Example(); // Create an instance.
example.InstanceMethod();         // Invoke the instance method.
Example.ClassMethod();            // Invoke the class method.

// The following lines won't compile.
example.ClassMethod();            // No class method access via instance.
Example.InstanceMethod();         // No instance method access via a class.
```

REMEMBER

Every instance of a class has its own, private copy of any instance members. But all instances of the same class share the same class members — both data members and methods — and their values.

The expression `example.InstanceMethod()` passes control to the code contained within the method. C# follows an almost identical process for `Example.ClassMethod()`. Executing the lines just shown (after commenting out the last two lines, which don't compile) generates this output:

```
this is an instance method
this is a class method
```

REMEMBER

After a method completes execution, it returns control to the point where it was called. That is, control moves to the next statement after the call.

The bit of C# code given in the two sample methods does nothing more than write a silly `string` to the console, but methods generally perform useful (and sometimes complex) operations such as calculate sines, concatenate two `strings`, sort an array of students. A method can be as large and complex as you want, but try to strive for shorter methods, using the approach described next.

TIP

This book includes the parentheses when describing methods in text — as in `InstanceMethod()` — to make them a little easier to recognize. Otherwise, you might become confused in trying to understand the text.

A Method Example for Your Files

This section divides the monolithic `CalculateInterestTable` programs from Book 1, Chapter 5 into several reasonable methods; the demonstration shows how the proper definition of methods can help make a program easier to write and understand. The process of dividing working code this way is known as *refactoring*, and versions of Visual Studio 2012 and above provide a handy Refactor menu that automates the most common refactorings. When working with Visual Studio 2017, you choose Edit⇨Refactor to access the refactoring options.

USING COMMENTS

By reading the comments *with the C# code removed*, you should be able to get a good idea of a program's intention. If you can't, you aren't commenting properly. Conversely, if you can't strip out most comments and still understand the intention from the method and variable names, you aren't naming your methods clearly enough or aren't making them small enough (or both). Smaller methods are preferable, and using good method names beats using comments. (That's why real-world code has far fewer comments than the code examples in this book. The book's code uses heavy commenting to explain more.)

REMEMBER

You find the exact details of method definitions and method calls in later sections of this chapter. This example simply gives an overview. In outline form, the CalculateInterestTable program appears this way:

```
public static void Main(string[] args)
{
    // Prompt user to enter source principal.
    // If the principal is negative, generate an error message.
    // Prompt user to enter the interest rate.
    // If the interest is negative, generate an error message.
    // Finally, prompt user to input the number of years.
    //
    // Display the input back to the user.
    //
    // Now loop through the specified number of years.
    while(year <= duration)
    {
        // Calculate the value of the principal plus interest.
        // Output the result.
    }
}
```

This bit of code illustrates a good technique for planning a method. If you stand back and study the program from a distance, you can see that it's divided into these three sections:

>> An initial input section in which the user inputs the principal, interest, and duration information

>> A section mirroring the input data so that the user can verify the entry of the correct data

>> A section that creates and outputs the table

Use this list to start looking for ways to refactor the program. In fact, if you further examine the input section of that program, you can see that the same basic code is used to input these amounts:

>> Principal

>> Interest

>> Duration

Your observation gives you another good place to look. Alternatively, you can write empty methods for some of those comments and then fill them in one by one. That's *programming by intention*. You can use these techniques to plan a method to create the following version of the `CalculateInterestTableWithMethods` program:

```csharp
using System;

// CalculateInterestTableWithMethods -- Generate an interest table
//    much like the other interest table programs, but this time using a
//    reasonable division of labor among several methods.
namespace CalculateInterestTableWithMethods
{
  public class Program
  {
    public static void Main(string[] args)
    {
      // Section 1 -- Input the data you need to create the table.
      decimal principal = 0M;
      decimal interest = 0M;
      decimal duration = 0M;
      InputInterestData(ref principal, ref interest, ref duration);

      // Section 2 -- Verify the data by mirroring it back to the user.
      Console.WriteLine();  // Skip a line.
      Console.WriteLine("Principal    = " + principal);
      Console.WriteLine("Interest     = " + interest + "%");
      Console.WriteLine("Duration     = " + duration + " years");
      Console.WriteLine();

      // Section 3 -- Finally, output the interest table.
      OutputInterestTable(principal, interest, duration);
      // Wait for user to acknowledge the results.
      Console.WriteLine("Press Enter to terminate...");
      Console.Read();
    }

    // InputInterestData -- Retrieve from the keyboard the
    //    principal, interest, and duration information needed
    //    to create the future value table. (Implements Section 1.)
    public static void InputInterestData(ref decimal principal,
                                         ref decimal interest,
                                         ref decimal duration)
    {
      // 1a -- Retrieve the principal.
      principal = InputPositiveDecimal("principal");

      // 1b -- Now enter the interest rate.
      interest = InputPositiveDecimal("interest");
```

```csharp
    // 1c -- Finally, the duration
    duration = InputPositiveDecimal("duration");
}

// InputPositiveDecimal -- Return a positive decimal number
//      from the keyboard.
public static decimal InputPositiveDecimal(string prompt)
{
    // Keep trying until the user gets it right.
    while(true)
    {
        // Prompt the user for input.
        Console.Write("Enter " + prompt + ":");

        // Retrieve a decimal value from the keyboard.
        string input = Console.ReadLine();
        decimal value = Convert.ToDecimal(input);

        // Exit the loop if the value that's entered is correct.
        if (value >= 0)
        {
            // Return the valid decimal value entered by the user.
            return value;
        }

        // Otherwise, generate an error on incorrect input.
        Console.WriteLine(prompt + " cannot be negative");
        Console.WriteLine("Try again");
        Console.WriteLine();
    }
}

// OutputInterestTable -- Given the principal and interest,
//      generate a future value table for the number of periods
//      indicated in duration. (Implements Section 3.)
public static void OutputInterestTable(decimal principal,
                                       decimal interest,
                                       decimal duration)
{
    for (int year = 1; year <= duration; year++)
    {
        // Calculate the value of the principal plus interest.
        decimal interestPaid;
        interestPaid = principal * (interest / 100);

        // Now calculate the new principal by adding
        // the interest to the previous principal.
        principal = principal + interestPaid;
```

```
        // Round off the principal to the nearest cent.
        principal = decimal.Round(principal, 2);

        // Output the result.
        Console.WriteLine(year + "-" + principal);
      }
    }
  }
}
```

The example divides `Main()` into three clearly distinguishable parts, each marked with boldfaced comments. It further divides the first section into subsections labeled 1a, 1b, and 1c.

REMEMBER

Normally, you don't include the boldfaced comments. If you did, the listings would grow rather complicated because of all the numbers and letters. In practice, those types of comments aren't necessary if the methods are well thought out and their names clearly express the intent of each one.

Part 1 calls the method `InputInterestData()` to input the three variables the program needs in order to create the table: `principal`, `interest`, and `duration`. Part 2 displays these three values for verification just as earlier versions of the program do. Part 3 outputs the table via the method `OutputInterestTable()`.

From the bottom and working upward, the `OutputInterestTable()` method contains an output loop with the interest rate calculations. This loop is the same one used in the inline, nonmethod `CalculateInterestTable` program. The advantage of this version, however, is that when writing this section of code, you don't need to concern yourself with any details of inputting or verifying data. When writing this method, think of it this way: "Given the three numbers — `principal`, `interest`, and `duration` — output an interest table," and that's it. After you're done, you can return to the line that called the `OutputInterestTable()` method and continue from there. `OutputInterestTable()` offers a target for trying the Visual Studio 2012 Refactor menu. Take these steps to give it a whirl:

1. **Using the** `CalculateInterestTableMoreForgiving` **example from Book 1, Chapter 5 as a starting point, select the code from the declaration of the** `year` **variable through the end of the** `while` **loop:**

```
int year = 0;              // You grab the loop variable
while(year <= duration)    // and the entire while loop.
{
  //...
}
```

2. Choose Edit⇨Refactor⇨Extract Method.

3. When you see the Rename: New Method dialog box, type OutputInterestTable in the highlighted part of the editing area.

Notice that every location where the new method is referenced automatically changes as you type. The proposed signature for the new method begins with the `private static` keywords and includes `principal`, `interest`, and `duration` in parentheses. (Book 1 introduces `private`, an alternative to `public`. For now, you can make the method `public` after the refactoring, if you like.)

```
private static decimal OutputInterestTable(decimal principal,
    decimal interest, int duration)
```

4. Click Apply to complete the Extract Method refactoring.

The code you selected in Step 1 is located below `Main( )` and named `OutputInterestTable( )`. In the spot that it formerly occupied, you see this method call:

```
principal = OuputInterestTable(principal, interest, duration);
```

Suppose that the previous refactoring did something you don't like, such place `principal` in the wrong position in the parameter list. (Because this situation is possible, you must always check a refactoring to be certain that it's what you want. If, after refactoring, you suffer "buyer's remorse," click Undo or press Ctrl+Z.)

You can use the Edit⇨Refactor⇨Reorder Parameters refactoring to fix this problem. In the Change Signature dialog box, click the `principal` line to select it. Then click the ↑ button as needed to move `principal` to the top of the list. Click OK. The result of all this refactoring consists of these two pieces:

» A new `private static` method below `Main( )`, named `OutputInterestTable( )`

» The following line of code within `Main( )` where the extracted code was:

```
principal = OutputInterestTable(principal, interest, duration);
```

TIP

Because C# supports named parameters, you can call the parameters in which-ever order you want, by specifying the name of the expected parameter before the value when calling a method. You discover more about this topic later in Book 2, but for now, just know that in C# 4.0 and above, reordering parameters is less of an issue.

For `InputInterestData()`, you can focus solely on inputting the three deci-mal values. However, in this case, you realize that inputting each one involves identical operations on three different input variables. The `InputPositive Decimal()` method bundles these operations into a set of general code that you can apply to principal, interest, and duration alike. Notice that the three `while` loops that take input in the original program are collapsed into one `while` loop inside `InputPositiveDecimal()`. This process reduces code duplication.

This `InputPositiveDecimal()` method displays the prompt it was given and awaits input from the user. The method returns the value to the caller if it isn't negative. If the value is negative, the method outputs an error message and loops back to try again. From the user's standpoint, the modified program acts exactly the same as the inline version, which is just the point:

```
Enter principal:100
Enter interest:-10
interest cannot be negative
Try again

Enter interest:10
Enter duration:10

Principal    = 100
Interest     = 10%
Duration     = 10 years


1-110.0
2-121.00
3-133.10
4-146.41
5-161.05
6-177.16
7-194.88
8-214.37
9-235.81
10-259.39
Press Enter to terminate...
```

WHY YOU SHOULD BOTHER WITH METHODS

When FORTRAN introduced the function concept — methods, in C# — during the 1950s, its sole purpose was to avoid duplication of code by combining similar sections into a common element. Suppose that you were to write a program to calculate ratios in multiple places. Your program could call the `CalculateRatio()` method when needed, for more or less the sole purpose of avoiding duplicate code. The savings may not seem important for a method as small as `CalculateRatio()`, but methods can grow much larger. Besides, a common method such as `WriteLine()` may be invoked in hundreds of different places.

Quickly, a second advantage became obvious: Coding a single method correctly is easier than coding many — and is doubly easier if the method is small. The `CalculateRatio()` method includes a check to ensure that the denominator isn't zero. If you repeat the calculation code throughout your program, you can easily remember this test in some cases — and easily forget it in others.

Not as obvious is a third advantage: A carefully crafted method reduces the complexity of the program. A well-defined method should stand for a concept. You should be able to describe the purpose of the method without using the words *and* or *or*. The method should do only one thing.

A method such as `CalculateSin()` is an ideal example. The programmer who's tasked with this assignment can implement this complex operation with no concern about how it may be used. The applications programmer can use `CalculateSin()` with no concern about how this operation is performed internally, which greatly reduces the number of issues the programmer must monitor. After the number of "variables" is reduced, a large job is accomplished by implementing two smaller, easier jobs.

Large programs, such as word processors, are built up from many layers of methods at ever-increasing levels of abstraction. For example, a `RedisplayDocument()` method would undoubtedly call a `Reparagraph()` method to redisplay the paragraphs within the document. `Reparagraph()` would need to invoke a `CalculateWordWrap()` method to decide where to wrap the lines that make up the paragraph. `CalculateWordWrap()` would have to call a `LookUpWordBreak()` method to decide where to break a word at the end of the line, to make the sentences wrap more naturally. Each of these methods was described in a single, simple sentence. (Notice that these methods are well named.)

Without the capability to *abstract* complex concepts, someone writing programs of even moderate complexity would find that the task becomes almost impossible — and all the more so when creating an operating system such as Windows, a utility such as WinZip, a word processor such as WordPerfect, or a game such as *Halo*.

Having Arguments with Methods

A method such as the following example is about as useful as Bill Sempf's hairbrush because no data passes into or out of the method:

```
public static void Output()
{
    Console.WriteLine("this is a method");
}
```

Compare this example to real-world methods that *do* something. For example, the mathematical sine operation requires some type of input — after all, you have to calculate the sine of something. Similarly, to concatenate two strings, you need two strings. So the Concatenate() method requires at least two strings as input. You need to find a way to move data into and out of a method.

Passing an argument to a method

The values you input to a method are *method* arguments, or *parameters*. Most methods require some type of arguments if they're going to do something. You pass arguments to a method by listing them in the parentheses that follow the method name. Consider this small addition to the earlier Example class:

```
public class Example
{
    public static void Output(string someString)
    {
        Console.WriteLine("Output() was passed the argument: " + someString);
    }
}
```

You could invoke this method from within the same class, like this:

```
Output("Hello");
```

You'd then see this not-too-exciting output:

```
Output() was passed the argument: Hello
```

The program passes to the method `Output()` a reference to the `string` "Hello". The method receives the reference and assigns it the name `someString`. The `Output()` method can use `someString` within the method just as it would use any other `string` variable. Try changing the example in one minor way:

```
string myString = "Hello";
Output(myString);
```

This code snippet assigns the variable `myString` to reference the `string` "Hello". The call `Output(myString)` passes the object referenced by `myString`, which is your old friend "Hello". Figure 3-1 depicts this process. From there, the effect is the same as before.

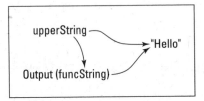

TECHNICAL STUFF

The placeholders you specify for arguments when you write a method — for example, `someString` in `Output()` — are *parameters*. The values you pass to a method via a parameter are *arguments*. This book uses the terms more or less interchangeably.

A similar idea is passing arguments to a program. For example, you may have noticed that `Main()` usually takes an array argument.

Passing multiple arguments to methods

You can define a method with multiple arguments of varying types. Consider the following sample method `AverageAndDisplay()`:

```
using System;

// AverageAndDisplay -- Demonstrate argument passing.
namespace Example
{
  public class Program
  {
    public static void Main(string[] args)
    {
      // Access the member method.
      AverageAndDisplay("grade 1", 3.5, "grade 2", 4.0);
```

```
        // Wait for user to acknowledge.
        Console.WriteLine("Press Enter to terminate...");
        Console.Read();
    }


    // AverageAndDisplay -- Average two numbers with their
    //     labels and display the results.
    public static void AverageAndDisplay(string s1, double d1,
                                         string s2, double d2)
    {
        double average = (d1 + d2) / 2;
        Console.WriteLine("The average of "   + s1
                    + " whose value is " + d1
                    + " and "                + s2
                    + " whose value is " + d2
                    + " is " + average);
    }
  }
}
```

Executing this simple program generates this output:

```
The average of grade 1 whose value is 3.5 and grade 2 whose value is 4 is 3.75
Press Enter to terminate...
```

The method `AverageAndDisplay()` is declared with several parameters in the order in which arguments are to be passed to them.

As usual, execution of the sample program begins with the first statement after `Main()`. The first noncomment line in `Main()` invokes the method `AverageAndDisplay()`, passing the two `string`s "grade 1" and "grade 2" and the two `double` values 3.5 and 4.0.

The method `AverageAndDisplay()` calculates the average of the two `double` values, d1 and d2, passed to it along with their names contained in s1 and s2, and the calculated average is stored in `average`.

TIP

Changing the value of an argument inside the method can lead to confusion and errors, so be wise and assign the value to a temporary variable and modify it instead.

Matching argument definitions with usage

Each argument in a method call must match the method definition in both type *and order* if you call them without naming them. The following (illegal) example generates a build-time error:

```
using System;

// AverageWithCompilerError -- This version does not compile!
namespace Example
{
  public class Program
  {
    public static void Main(string[] args)
    {
      // Access the member method.
      AverageAndDisplay("grade 1", "grade 2", 3.5, 4.0);

      // Wait for user to acknowledge.
      Console.WriteLine("Press Enter to terminate...");
      Console.Read();
    }

    // AverageAndDisplay -- Average two numbers with their
    //     labels and display the results.
    public static void AverageAndDisplay(string s1, double d1,
                                         string s2, double d2)
    {
      // var okay here, but it's really double.
      var average = (d1 + d2) / 2;
      Console.WriteLine("The average of " + s1
                      + " whose value is " + d1
                      + " and "            + s2
                      + " whose value is " + d2
                      + " is " + average);
    }
  }
}
```

C# can't match the type of each argument in the call to AverageAndDisplay() with the corresponding argument in the method definition. The string "grade 1" matches the first string in the method definition; however, the method definition calls for a double as its second argument rather than the string that's passed.

You can easily see that the code transposes the second and third arguments. To fix the problem, swap the second and third arguments.

Overloading a method doesn't mean giving it too much to do

TIP

You can give two methods within a given class the same name — known as *overloading* the method name — as long as their arguments differ. This example demonstrates overloading:

```
using System;

// AverageAndDisplayOverloaded -- This version demonstrates that
//      the AverageAndDisplay method can be overloaded.
namespace AverageAndDisplayOverloaded
{
  public class Program
  {
    public static void Main(string[] args)
    {
      // Access the first version of the method.
      AverageAndDisplay("my GPA", 3.5, "your GPA", 4.0);
      Console.WriteLine();

      // Access the second version of the method.
      AverageAndDisplay(3.5, 4.0);

      // Wait for user to acknowledge.
      Console.WriteLine("Press Enter to terminate...");
      Console.Read();
    }

    // AverageAndDisplay -- Average two numbers with their
    //      labels and display the results.
    public static void AverageAndDisplay(string s1, double d1,
                                         string s2, double d2)
    {
      double average = (d1 + d2) / 2;
      Console.WriteLine("The average of "  + s1
                  + " whose value is " + d1);
      Console.WriteLine("and "            + s2
                  + " whose value is " + d2
                  + " is " + average);
    }

    public static void AverageAndDisplay(double d1, double d2)
    {
      double average = (d1 + d2) / 2;
      Console.WriteLine("The average of " + d1
```

```
                      + " and "           + d2
                      + " is " + average);
      }
    }
  }
```

This program defines two versions of `AverageAndDisplay()`. The program invokes one and then the other by passing the proper arguments. C# can tell which method the program wants by comparing the call with the definition. The program compiles properly and generates this output when executed:

```
The average of my GPA whose value is 3.5
and your GPA whose value is 4 is 3.75

The average of 3.5 and 4 is 3.75
Press Enter to terminate...
```

C# generally doesn't allow two methods in the same class to have the same name unless the number or type of the methods' arguments differs (or if both differ). Thus C# differentiates between these two methods:

>> `AverageAndDisplay(string, double, string, double)`

>> `AverageAndDisplay(double, double)`

When you say it that way, it's clear that the two methods are different.

Implementing default arguments

In some cases, a method needs a *default argument*, a predefined value, to make it easier to use. If most of the developers using the method require a particular value, a default value makes sense. Providing a value for the argument then becomes one of flexibility so that developers who need other values still have the option of supplying one. Often, you want to supply two (or more) versions of a method. Developers take two common routes:

TECHNICAL
STUFF

>> **Complicated:** Provides complete flexibility but requires numerous arguments from the calling routine, several of which the user may not even understand.

The word *user* doesn't always refer to the user of a program. References to the user of a method often mean, in practice, the programmer who is making use of the method. Another term is *client* (which is often you).

>> **Acceptable (if somewhat bland):** Assumes default values for certain arguments.

You can easily implement default arguments using method overloading. Consider this pair of DisplayRoundedDecimal() methods:

```
// MethodsWithDefaultArguments -- Provide variations of the same methods,
//    some with default arguments, by overloading the method name.
using System;
namespace MethodsWithDefaultArguments
{
  public class Program
  {
    public static void Main(string[] args)
    {
      // Access the member method.
      Console.WriteLine(DisplayRoundedDecimal(12.345678M, 3));

      // Wait for user to acknowledge.
      Console.WriteLine("Press Enter to terminate...");
      Console.Read();
    }

    // DisplayRoundedDecimal -- Convert a decimal value into a string
    //    with the specified number of signficant digits.
    public static string DisplayRoundedDecimal(decimal value,
                                    int numberOfSignificantDigits)
    {
      // First round off the number to the specified number
      // of significant digits.
      decimal roundedValue =
                decimal.Round(value,
                            numberOfSignificantDigits);

      // Convert that to a string.
      string s = Convert.ToString(roundedValue);
      return s;
    }

    public static string DisplayRoundedDecimal(decimal value)
    {
      // Invoke DisplayRoundedDecimal(decimal, int) specifying
      // the default number of digits.
      string s = DisplayRoundedDecimal(value, 2);
      return s;
    }
  }
}
```

The DisplayRoundedDecimal(decimal, int) method converts the decimal value that's provided into a string with the specified number of digits after the decimal point. Because decimals are often used to display monetary values, the most common choice is to place two digits after the decimal point. Therefore, the DisplayRoundedDecimal(decimal) method provides the same conversion service — but defaults the number of significant digits to two, thereby removing any worry about the meaning of the second argument.

REMEMBER The generic (decimal) version of the method calls the more specific (decimal, int) version to perform its magic. This stacked method calling is more common than not because it reduces duplication. The generic methods simply provide arguments that the programmer doesn't have the inclination to find in the documentation, and shouldn't have to unless needed.

WARNING Having to unnecessarily consult the reference documentation for the meanings of normally defaulted arguments distracts the programmer from the main job at hand — thereby making it more difficult, wasting time, and increasing the likelihood of mistakes.

Providing default arguments does more than just save lazy programmers from exerting a tiny bit of effort (programming requires lots of concentration). The author of the method understands the relationship between the arguments — and therefore bears the onus of providing friendlier, overloaded versions of methods.

Visual Basic, C, and C++ programmers should be accustomed to supplying a default value for a parameter directly in the method signature. Until C# 4.0 was released, you couldn't do that in C#. Now you can.

For instance, although overloading the method in the preceding example is a perfectly acceptable way to implement a default parameter, you can also give default parameters by using the equals sign (=), just as in Visual Basic:

```
using System;

// MethodsWithDefaultArguments2-- Provide optional parameters to a method
// to avoid overloading. It's another way to do the same thing.
namespace MethodsWithDefaultArguments2
{
  public class Program
  {
    public static void Main(string[] args)
    {
      // Access the member method.
      Console.WriteLine(DisplayRoundedDecimal(12.345678M, 3));
```

```
        // Wait for user to acknowledge.
        Console.WriteLine("Press Enter to terminate...");
        Console.Read();
    }


    // DisplayRoundedDecimal -- Convert a decimal value into a string
    //    that has the specified number of signficant digits. That argument
    //    is optional and has a default value. If you call the method
    //    without the second argument, it uses the default value.
    public static string DisplayRoundedDecimal(decimal value,
                                 int numberOfSignificantDigits = 2)
    {
      // First round off the number to the specified number
      // of significant digits.
      decimal roundedValue =
                decimal.Round(value,
                                  numberOfSignificantDigits);

      // Convert that to a string.
      string s = Convert.ToString(roundedValue);
      return s;
    }
  }
}
```

TECHNICAL STUFF

Why would Microsoft make these changes? The answer is COM. The Component Object Model (COM) was the architectural paradigm of choice for Microsoft products before .NET was released, and it's still quite prevalent. Office, for one, is entirely developed using COM. COM applications are developed in C++ or Visual Basic 6 and earlier, and methods from those classes allow for optional parameters. Thus, communicating with COM without using optional parameters can become difficult. To address this imbalance, optional parameters (along with a number of other features) were added to C# 4.0. Book 2, Chapter 11 covers named and optional parameters.

Returning Values after Christmas

Many real-world operations create values to return to the caller. For example, Sin() accepts an argument and returns the trigonometric sine. A method can return a value to the caller in two ways — most commonly via the return statement; however, a second method uses the *call-by-reference* feature.

Returning a value via return postage

The following code snippet demonstrates a small method that returns the average of its input arguments:

```csharp
public class Example
{
  public static double Average(double d1, double d2)
  {
    double average = (d1 + d2) / 2;
    return average;
  }

  public static void Main(string[] args)
  {
    double v1 = 1.0;
    double v2 = 3.0;
    double averageValue = Average(v1, v2);

    Console.WriteLine("The average of " + v1
                + " and " + v2 + " is "
                + averageValue);

    // This also works.
    Console.WriteLine("The average of " + v1
                + " and " + v2 + " is "
                + Average(v1, v2));
  }
}
```

Notice the example declares the method as `public static double Average()` first — the `double` in front of its name indicates that the `Average()` method returns a double-precision value to the caller. The `Average()` method applies the names d1 and d2 to the double values passed to it. This method creates a variable `average` to which it assigns the average of d1 and d2 and returns to the caller the value contained in `average`.

WARNING

People sometimes use this careless but common shorthand: "The method returns `average`." Saying that `average` or any other variable is passed or returned anywhere is imprecise. In this case, the *value* contained within `average` is returned to the caller.

The call to `Average()` from the `Test()` method appears the same as any other method call; however, the `double` value returned by `Average()` via the `return` keyword is stored in the variable `averageValue`.

REMEMBER

A method that returns a value, such as Average(), cannot return to the caller by merely encountering the closed brace of the method. If it did, C# wouldn't know which value to return. You need a return statement.

Defining a method with no value

The declaration public static double Average(double, double) declares a method Average() that returns the average of its arguments as a double. Some methods don't need to return a value to the caller. An earlier method, AverageAndDisplay(), displays the average of its input arguments but doesn't return that average to the caller. Rather than leave the return type blank, you declare a method such as AverageAndDisplay() this way:

```
public void AverageAndDisplay(double, double)
```

The keyword void, where the return type is normally used, means *nontype*. That is, the declaration void indicates that the AverageAndDisplay() method returns no value to the caller. (Regardless, every method declaration specifies a return type, even if it's void.)

REMEMBER

A *void method* returns no value. This definition doesn't mean that the method is empty or that it's used for medical or astronautical purposes; it simply refers to the initial keyword. By comparison, a method that returns a value is a *nonvoid method.*

A nonvoid method must pass control back to the caller by executing a return followed by the value to return to the caller. A void method has no value to return. A void method returns when it encounters a return with no value attached. Or, by default (if no return exists), a void method exits automatically when control reaches the closing brace of the method. Consider this DisplayRatio() method:

```
public class Example
{
  public static void DisplayRatio(double numerator,
                                  double denominator)
  {
    // If the denominator is zero ...
    if (denominator == 0.0)
    {
      //  ...output an error message and ...
      Console.WriteLine("The denominator of a ratio cannot be 0");

      //  ...return to the caller.
      return;  // An early return due to the error
    }
```

```
      // This code is executed only if denominator is nonzero.
      double ratio = numerator / denominator;
      Console.WriteLine("The ratio of " + numerator
                  + " over " + denominator
                  + " is " + ratio);
   } // If the denominator isn't zero, the method exits here.
}
```

THE WriteLine() METHOD

You may have noticed that the WriteLine() construct used in program examples
earlier in this book is nothing more than a method call that's invoked by a Console
class:

```
Console.WriteLine("this is a method call");
```

WriteLine() is one of many predefined methods provided by the .NET Framework
library. The Console predefined class refers to the application console (also known as
the command prompt or command window).

The argument to the WriteLine() method used until now is a single string. The +
operator enables the programmer to combine strings, or to combine a string and
an intrinsic variable, before the sum is passed to WriteLine():

```
string s = "Sarah"
Console.WriteLine("My name is " + s + " and my age is " + 3);
```

All that WriteLine() sees in this case is "My name is Sarah and my age is 3."

A second form of WriteLine() provides a more flexible set of arguments:

```
Console.WriteLine("My name is {0} and my age is {1}.", "Sarah", 3);
```

The first argument is a format string. The string "Sarah" is inserted where the symbol {0}
appears — 0 refers to the first argument after the format string. The integer 3 is inserted
at the position marked by {1}. This form is more efficient than in the previous example
because concatenating strings isn't as easy as it might sound. It's a time-consuming
business.

The `DisplayRatio()` method checks whether the `denominator` value is zero:

>> **If the value is zero:** The program displays an error message and returns to the caller without attempting to calculate a ratio. Doing so would divide the numerator value by zero and cause a CPU processor fault.

>> **If the value is nonzero:** The program displays the ratio. The closed brace immediately following `WriteLine()` is the closed brace of the method `DisplayRatio()` and therefore acts as the return point for the program.

If that were the only difference, it wouldn't be much to write home about. However, the second form of `WriteLine()` also provides a number of controls on the output format. Book 1, Chapter 3 describes these format controls.

Returning Multiple Values Using Tuples

In versions of C# prior to C# 7.0, every return value was a single object. It could be a really complex object, but it was still a single object. In C# 7.0, you can actually return multiple values using tuples. A tuple is a kind of dynamic array nominally containing two items that you can interpret as a key and value pair (but it isn't strictly required). In C#, you can also create tuples containing more than two items. Many languages, such as Python, use tuples to simplify coding and to make interacting with values considerably easier.

C# 4.x actually introduced the concept of a Tuple as part of dynamic programming techniques. However, C# 7.0 advances the use of tuples to allow returning multiple values rather than just one object. This book doesn't provide extensive coverage of tuples, but they work so well in returning complex data that you definitely need to know something about this use of tuples.

Using a single-entry tuple

A tuple relies on the `Tuple` data type, which can accept either one or two inputs, with two being the most common (otherwise, you can simply return a single object). The best way to work with tuples is to provide the data types of the variables you plan to provide as part of the declaration. Here's an example of a method that returns a tuple:

```
static Tuple<string, int> getTuple()
{
    // Return a single value using the tuple.
    return new Tuple<string, int>("Hello", 123);
}
```

The code begins by specifying that getTuple() returns a Tuple consisting of two items, a string and an int. You use the new keyword to create an instance of Tuple, specify the data types in angle brackets, <string, int>, and then provide the data values. The getTuple() method effectively returns two values that you can manipulate individually, as shown here:

```
// This is where your program starts.
static void Main(string[] args)
{
    // Obtain a single entry tuple.
    Console.WriteLine(
        getTuple().Item1 + " " + getTuple().Item2);

    // Wait for user to acknowledge the results.
    Console.WriteLine("Press Enter to terminate...");
    Console.Read();
}
```

To access a single-entry tuple like this one, you call getTuple(), add a period, and then specify which item to use, Item1 or Item2. This example just demonstrates how tuples work, so it's simple. The output looks like this:

```
Hello 123
Press Enter to terminate...
```

TIP

Using a tuple lets you return two values without resorting to complex data types or other odd structures. It makes your code simpler when the output requirements fit within the confines of a tuple. For example, when performing certain math operations, you need to return a result and a remainder or the real part and the imaginary part of a complex number.

Relying on the Create() method

An alternative way to create a tuple is to rely on the Create() method. The result is the same as when working with the method found in the previous section. Here's an example of using the Create() method:

```
// Use the Create() method.
var myTuple = Tuple.Create<string, int>("Hello", 123);
Console.WriteLine(myTuple.Item1 + "\t" + myTuple.Item2);
```

This approach isn't quite as safe as using the method shown in the previous section because myTuple could end up with anything inside. You could further eliminate the <string, int> portion of the constructor to force the compiler to ascertain what myTuple should receive as input.

Using a multi-entry tuple

The true value of a tuple is in creating datasets using extremely easy coding methods. This is where you might choose to view Item1 as a key and Item2 as a value. Many dataset types today rely on the key and value paradigm and viewing a tuple in this way does make it incredibly useful. The following example shows the creation and return of a tuple dataset.

```
static Tuple<string, int>[] getTuple()
{
    // Create a new tuple.
    Tuple<string, int>[] aTuple =
    {
        new Tuple<string, int>("One", 1),
        new Tuple<string, int>("Two", 2),
        new Tuple<string, int>("Three", 3)
    };

    // Return a list of values using the tuple.
    return aTuple;
}
```

As in the previous section, you specify the return types of the Tuple data type. However, this example adds a pair of square brackets ([]) similar to those used for an array. The square brackets tell C# that this version of getTuple() returns multiple tuples, not just one.

To create a tuple dataset, you begin with the variable declaration as shown for aTuple. Each new entry into the tuple requires a new Tuple declaration with the requisite inputs as shown. The entire thing is placed within curly brackets and you end it with a semicolon. To return the tuple, you simply use the return statement as normal.

Accessing the tuple requires use of an enumerator, and you can do anything you would normally do with an enumerator, such as interact with the individual values using foreach. The following code shows how you might perform this task just for experimentation purposes:

```
static void Main(string[] args)
{
    // Obtain a multiple entry tuple.
    Tuple<string, int>[] myTuple = getTuple();

    // Output the values.
    foreach (var Item in myTuple)
```

```
    {
        Console.WriteLine(Item.Item1 + "\t" + Item.Item2);
    }

    // Wait for user to acknowledge the results.
    Console.WriteLine("Press Enter to terminate...");
    Console.Read();
}
```

The foreach statement places individual items from myTuple into Item. You then access the data elements individually by using Item1 and Item2 as before. Here's the output from this example:

```
One     1
Two     2
Three   3
Press Enter to terminate...
```

Creating tuples with more than two items

Tuples can have one to eight items. If you want more than eight items, the eighth item must contain another tuple. Nesting tuples enables you to return an almost infinite number of items, but at some point you really do need to look at the complexity of your code and see whether you can keep the number of return items down. Otherwise, you find that your application executes slowly and uses a lot of resources. Here is an example of a version of the code found in the previous section that uses three items:

```
static Tuple<string, int, bool>[] getTuple()
{
    // Create a new tuple.
    Tuple<string, int, bool>[] aTuple =
    {
        new Tuple<string, int, bool>("One", 1, true),
        new Tuple<string, int, bool>("Two", 2, false),
        new Tuple<string, int, bool>("Three", 3, true)
    };

    // Return a list of values using the tuple.
    return aTuple;
}
```

The technique follows the same pattern as before. The only difference is that you provide more values for each tuple. It also doesn't matter whether you create a single tuple or a tuple array used as a dataset. Either choice allows you to use up to eight items per tuple.

Chapter **4**

Let Me Say This about this

This chapter moves from the static methods emphasized in Chapter 3 in this minibook to the nonstatic methods of a class. Static methods belong to the whole class, and nonstatic methods belong to each instance created from the class. Important differences exist between static and nonstatic class members.

Passing an Object to a Method

You pass object references as arguments to methods in the same way as you pass value-type variables, with one difference: You always pass objects by reference. The following small program demonstrates how you pass objects — to methods, that is:

```
using System;

// PassObject -- Demonstrate how to pass an object to a method.
namespace PassObject
{
```

```
public class Student
{
  public string name;
}

public class Program
{
  public static void Main(string[] args)
  {
    Student student = new Student();

    // Set the name by accessing it directly.
    Console.WriteLine("The first time:");
    student.name = "Madeleine";
    OutputName(student);

    // Change the name using a method.
    Console.WriteLine("After being modified:");
    SetName(student, "Willa");
    OutputName(student);

    // Wait for user to acknowledge.
    Console.WriteLine("Press Enter to terminate...");
    Console.Read();
  }

  // OutputName -- Output the student's name.
  public static void OutputName(Student student)
  {
    // Output current student's name.
    Console.WriteLine("Student's name is {0}", student.name);
  }

  // SetName -- Modify the student object's name.
  public static void SetName(Student student, string name)
  {
    student.name = name;
  }
}
```

The program creates a student object consisting of nothing but a name. The program first sets the name of the student directly and passes the *student object* to the output method OutputName(). OutputName() displays the name of any Student object it receives.

The program then updates the name of the student by calling SetName(). Because all reference-type objects are passed by reference in C#, the changes made to student are retained in the calling method. When Main() outputs the student object again, the name has changed, as shown in this bit of code:

```
The first time:
Student's name is Madeleine
After being modified:
Student's name is Willa
Press Enter to terminate...
```

The SetName() method can change the name within the Student object and make it stick.

TECHNICAL STUFF

You don't use the ref keyword when passing a *reference-type* object. Yet the effect is that the object's contents can be modified through the *reference*. However, if SetName() tries to assign a whole new Student object to its Student parameter, it doesn't affect the original Student object outside the method, as this chunk of code shows:

```
Student student = new Student();
SetName(student, "Pam");
Console.WriteLine(student.name);  // Still "Pam"
...
// A revised SetName():
public static void SetName(Student student, string name)
{
  student = new Student(); // Doesn't replace student outside SetName().
  student.Name = name;
}
```

Defining Methods

A class is supposed to collect the elements that describe a real-world object or concept. For example, a Vehicle class may contain data elements for maximum velocity, weight, and carrying capacity. However, a Vehicle has active properties — *behaviors* — as well: the capability to start and stop and the like. These active properties are described by the methods related to that vehicular data. These methods are just as much a part of the Vehicle class as the data elements.

Defining a static method

You could rewrite the program from the previous section in a slightly better way:

```csharp
using System;

// StudentClassWithMethods -- Demonstrate putting methods that
//    operate on a class's data inside the class. A class is
//    responsible for its own data and any operations on it.
namespace StudentClassWithMethods
{
  // Now the OutputName and SetName methods are members of
  // class Student, not class Program.
  public class Student
  {
    public string name;

    // OutputName -- Output the student's name.
    public static void OutputName(Student student)
    {
      // Output current student's name.
      Console.WriteLine("Student's name is {0}", student.name);
    }

    // SetName -- Modify the student object's name.
    public static void SetName(Student student, string name)
    {
      student.name = name;
    }
  }

  public class Program
  {
    public static void Main(string[] args)
    {
      Student student = new Student();

      // Set the name by accessing it directly.
      Console.WriteLine("The first time:");
      student.name = "Madeleine";
      Student.OutputName(student); // Method now belongs to Student.

      // Change the name using a method.
      Console.WriteLine("After being modified:");
      Student.SetName(student, "Willa");
      Student.OutputName(student);
```

```
        // Wait for user to acknowledge.
        Console.WriteLine("Press Enter to terminate...");
        Console.Read();
      }
    }
  }
```

Other than its name, this program has only one significant change from the PassObject program in the previous section: the OutputName() and SetName() methods appear in the Student class. Because of that change, Main() must reference the Student class in the calls to SetName() and OutputName(). The methods are now members of the class Student and not Program, the class in which Main() resides.

This step is small but significant. Placing OutputName() within the class leads to a higher level of reuse: Outside methods that need to display the object can find OutputName() right there as part of the class. It doesn't have to be written separately by each program using the Student class.

This solution is also better on a philosophical level. Class Program shouldn't need to worry about how to initialize the name of a Student object nor about how to output important material. The Student class should contain that information. Objects are responsible for themselves. In fact, Main() shouldn't initialize the name to Madeleine in the first place. It should call SetName() instead.

From within Student, one member method can invoke another without explicitly applying the class name. SetName() could invoke OutputName() without needing to reference the class name. If you leave off the class name, C# assumes that the method being accessed is in or on the same class.

Defining an instance method

Although OutputName() and SetName() are static methods, they could as easily be nonstatic, or *instance*, methods.

REMEMBER

All static members of a class are *class members,* and all nonstatic members are *instance members.* This includes methods.

The nonstatic *data members* of an object — an instance of a class — are accessed with the object and not with the class. Thus, you may say

```
Student student = new Student(); // Create an instance of Student.
student.name = "Madeleine";      // Access the member via the instance.
```

C# enables you to invoke nonstatic member methods in the same way:

```
student.SetName("Madeleine");
```

The following example demonstrates this technique:

```
using System;

// InvokeMethod -- Invoke a member method through the object.
namespace InvokeMethod
{
  class Student
  {
    // The name information to describe a student
    public string firstName;
    public string lastName;

    // SetName -- Save name information. (Nonstatic.)
    public void SetName(string fName, string lName)
    {
      firstName = fName;
      lastName  = lName;
    }

    // ToNameString -- Convert the student object into a
    //    string for display. (Nonstatic.)
    public string ToNameString()
    {
      string s = firstName + " " + lastName;
      return s;
    }
  }

  public class Program
  {
    public static void Main()
    {
      Student student = new Student();
      student.SetName("Stephen", "Davis"); // Call instance method.
      Console.WriteLine("Student's name is "
                        + student.ToNameString());

      // Wait for user to acknowledge.
      Console.WriteLine("Press Enter to terminate...");
      Console.Read();
    }
  }
}
```

The output from this program is this simple line:

```
Student's name is Stephen Davis
```

Other than having a much shorter name, this program is quite similar to the earlier StudentClassWithMethods program. This version uses *nonstatic* methods to manipulate both a first and last name.

The program begins by creating a new Student object, student. The program then invokes the SetName() method, which stores the two strings, "Stephen" and "Davis", into the data members firstName and lastName. Finally, the program calls the member method ToNameString(), which returns the name of the student by concatenating the two strings.

Look again at the SetName() method, which updates the first and last name fields in the Student object. To see which object SetName() modifies, consider this example:

```
Student christa = new Student();   // Here's one student.
Student sarah = new Student();     // And here's a completely different one.
christa.SetName("Christa", "Smith");
sarah.SetName("Sarah", "Jones");
```

The first call to SetName() updates the first and last name of the christa object. The second call updates the sarah object.

TIP

Thus, C# programmers say that a method operates on the *current* object. In the first call, the current object is christa; in the second, it's sarah.

Expanding a method's full name

A subtle but important problem exists with the description of method names in the example in the previous section. To see the problem, consider this sample code snippet:

```
public class Person
{
  public void Address()
  {
    Console.WriteLine("Hi");
  }
}
```

```
public class Letter
{
  string address;

  // Store the address.
  public void Address(string newAddress)
  {
    address = newAddress;
  }
}
```

Any subsequent discussion of the Address() method is now ambiguous. The Address() method within Person has nothing to do with the Address() method in Letter. If an application needs to access the Address() method, which Address() does it access? The problem lies not with the methods themselves, but rather with the description. In fact, no Address() method exists as an independent entity — only a Person.Address() and a Letter.Address() method. Attaching the class name to the beginning of the method name clearly indicates which method is intended.

This description is quite similar to people's names. At home, you might not ever experience any ambiguity because you're the only person who has your name. However, at work, you might respond to a yell when someone means to attract the attention of another person with the same name as yours. Of course, this is the reason that people resort to using last names. Thus, you can consider Address() to be the first name of a method, with its class as the family name.

Accessing the Current Object

Consider the following Student.SetName() method:

```
class Student
{
  // The name information to describe a student
  public string firstName;
  public string lastName;

  // SetName — Save name information.
  public void SetName(string firstName, string lastName)
  {
    firstName = firstName;
    lastName  = lastName;
  }
}
```

```
public class Program
{
  public static void Main()
  {
    Student student1 = new Student();
    student1.SetName("Joseph", "Smith");

    Student student2 = new Student();
    student2.SetName("John", "Davis");
  }
}
```

The method `Main()` uses the `SetName()` method to update first `student1` and then `student2`. But you don't see a reference to either `Student` object *within SetName() itself*. In fact, no reference to a `Student` object exists. A method is said to operate on "the current object." How does a method know which one is the current object? Will the real current object please stand up? The answer is simple. The current object is passed as an implicit argument in the call to a method. For example:

```
student1.SetName("Joseph", "Smith");
```

This call is equivalent to the following:

```
Student.SetName(student1, "Joseph", "Smith"); // Equivalent call,
                                 // (but this won't build properly).
```

The example isn't saying that you can invoke `SetName()` in two different ways; just that the two calls are semantically equivalent. The object identifying the current object — the hidden first argument — is passed to the method, just as other arguments are. Leave that task to the compiler.

Passing an object implicitly is easy to swallow, but what about a reference from one method to another? The following code snippet illustrates calling one method from another:

```
public class Student
{
  public string firstName;
  public string lastName;

  public void SetName(string firstName, string lastName)
  {
    SetFirstName(firstName);
    SetLastName(lastName);
  }
```

```
  public void SetFirstName(string name)
  {
    firstName = name;
  }

  public void SetLastName(string name)
  {
    lastName = name;
  }
}
```

No object appears in the call to SetFirstName(). The current object continues to be passed along silently from one method call to the next. An access to any member from within an object method is assumed to be with respect to the current object. The upshot is that a method knows which object it belongs to. *Current object* (or *current instance*) means something like *me*.

What is the this keyword?

Unlike most arguments, the current object doesn't appear in the method argument list, so it isn't assigned a name by the programmer. Instead, C# assigns this object the less-than-imaginative name this, which is useful in the few situations in which you need to refer directly to the current object. Thus you could write the previous example this way:

```
public class Student
{
  public string firstName;
  public string lastName;

  public void SetName(string firstName, string lastName)
  {
    // Explicitly reference the "current object" referenced by this.
    this.SetFirstName(firstName);
    this.SetLastName(lastName);
  }

  public void SetFirstName(string name)
  {
    this.firstName = name;
  }

  public void SetLastName(string name)
  {
    this.lastName = name;
  }
}
```

Notice the explicit addition of the keyword this. Adding it to the member references doesn't add anything because this is assumed. However, when Main() makes the following call, this references student1 throughout SetName() and any other method it may call:

```
student1.SetName("John", "Smith");
```

You can't use the C# keyword this for any other purpose.

When is this explicit?

You don't normally need to refer to this explicitly because it is understood where necessary by the compiler. However, two common cases require this. You may need it when initializing data members, as in this example:

```
class Person
{
  public string name;   // This is this.name below.
  public int id;        // And this is this.id below.

  public void Init(string name, int id)  // These are method arguments.
  {
    this.name = name;  // Argument names same as data member names
    this.id = id;
  }
}
```

The arguments to the Init() method are named name and id, which match the names of the corresponding data members. The method is then easy to read because you know immediately which argument is stored where. The only problem is that the name name in the argument list obscures the name of the data member. The compiler complains about it.

The addition of this clarifies which name is intended. Within Init(), the name name refers to the method argument, but this.name refers to the data member. You also need this when storing the current object for use later or by some other method. Consider this program example:

```
using System;

// ReferencingThisExplicitly -- Demonstrates how to explicitly use
//     the reference to 'this'.
namespace ReferencingThisExplicitly
{
```

```csharp
public class Program
{
  public static void Main(string[] strings)
  {
    // Create a student.
    Student student = new Student();
    student.Init("Stephen Davis", 1234);

    // Now enroll the student in a course.
    Console.WriteLine
          ("Enrolling Stephen Davis in Biology 101");
    student.Enroll("Biology 101");

    // Display student course.
    Console.WriteLine("Resulting student record:");
    student.DisplayCourse();

    // Wait for user to acknowledge the results.
    Console.WriteLine("Press Enter to terminate...");
    Console.Read();
  }
}

// Student -- The class for university students.
public class Student
{
  // All students have a name and an id.
  public string _name;
  public int _id;

  // The course in which the student is enrolled
  CourseInstance _courseInstance;

  // Init -- Initialize the student object.
  public void Init(string name, int id)
  {
    this._name = name;
    this._id = id;
    _courseInstance = null;
  }

  // Enroll -- Enroll the current student in a course.
  public void Enroll(string courseID)
  {
    _courseInstance = new CourseInstance();
    _courseInstance.Init(this, courseID); // The explicit reference.
  }
```

```
      // Display the name of the student and the course.
      public void DisplayCourse()
      {
        Console.WriteLine(_name);
        _courseInstance.Display();
      }
    }

    // CourseInstance -- A combination of a student with
    //    a university course.
    public class CourseInstance
    {
      public Student _student;
      public string _courseID;

      // Init -- Tie the student to the course.
      public void Init(Student student, string courseID)
      {
        this._student = student;
        this._courseID = courseID;
      }

      // Display -- Output the name of the course.
      public void Display()
      {
        Console.WriteLine(_courseID);
      }
    }
  }
```

This program is fairly mundane. The Student object has room for a name, an ID, and a single instance of a university course (this is not an industrious student). Main() creates the student instance and then invokes Init() to initialize the instance. At this point, the _courseInstance reference is set to null because the student isn't yet enrolled in a class.

The Enroll() method enrolls the student by initializing _courseInstance with a new object. However, the CourseInstance.Init() method takes an instance of Student as its first argument along with the course ID as the second argument. Which Student should you pass? Clearly, you need to pass the current Student — the Student referred to by this. (Thus you can say that Enroll() enrolls this student in the CourseInstance.)

TIP

Some programmers like to differentiate data members from other variables more clearly by prefixing an underscore to the name of each data member, like this: _name. The book adopts this convention most of the time, but it's only a convention, and you may do as you like. If you use the convention, you don't need to preface the item with this, as in this._id. It's completely unambiguous with just the underscore prefix.

What happens when you don't have this?

Mixing class (static) methods and instance (nonstatic) methods is like mixing sheepmen and ranchers. Fortunately, C# gives you some ways around the problems between the two. To see the problem, consider this program snippet:

```
using System;

// MixingStaticAndInstanceMethods -- Mixing class (static) methods
//      and instance (nonstatic) methods can cause problems.
namespace MixingStaticAndInstanceMethods
{
  public class Student
  {
    public string _firstName;
    public string _lastName;

    // InitStudent -- Initialize the student object.
    public void InitStudent(string firstName, string lastName)
    {
      _firstName = firstName;
      _lastName = lastName;
    }

    // OutputBanner (static) -- Output the introduction.
    public static void OutputBanner()
    {
      Console.WriteLine("Aren't we clever:");
      // Console.WriteLine(? what student do we use ?);  ← The problem!
    }

    // OutputBannerAndName (nonstatic) -- Output intro.
    public void OutputBannerAndName()
    {
      // The class Student is implied but no this
      // object is passed to the static method.
      OutputBanner();

      // The current Student object is passed explicitly.
      OutputName(this);
    }
```

```csharp
    // OutputName -- Output the student's name.
    public static void OutputName(Student student)
    {
      // Here, the Student object is referenced explicitly.
      Console.WriteLine("Student's name is {0}",
                  student.ToNameString());
    }

    // ToNameString -- Fetch the student's name.
    public string ToNameString()
    {
      // Here, the current object is implicit --
      // this could have been written:
      // return this._firstName + " " + this._lastName;
      return _firstName + " " + _lastName;
    }
  }

  public class Program
  {
    public static void Main(string[] args)
    {
      Student student = new Student();
      student.InitStudent("Madeleine", "Cather");

      // Output the banner and name statically.
      Student.OutputBanner();
      Student.OutputName(student);
      Console.WriteLine();

      // Output the banner and name again using instance.
      student.OutputBannerAndName();

      // Wait for user to acknowledge.
      Console.WriteLine("Press Enter to terminate...");
      Console.Read();
    }
  }
}
```

Start at the bottom of the program with Main() so that you can better see the problems. The program begins by creating a Student object and initializing its name. The program now wants to do nothing more than output the name preceded by a short message and banner.

Main() first outputs the banner and message using the class or static method approach. The program invokes the OutputBanner() method for the banner line and the OutputName() method to output the message and the student name. The method OutputBanner() outputs a simple message to the console. Main() passes the student object as an argument to OutputName() so that it can display the student's name.

Next, Main() uses the instance method approach to outputting the banner and message by calling student.OutputBannerAndName(). OutputBannerAndName() first invokes the static method OutputBanner(). The class Student is assumed. No object is passed because the static OutputBanner doesn't need one. Next, OutputBannerAndName() calls the OutputName() method. OutputName() is also a static method, but it takes a Student object as its argument. OutputBanner AndName() passes this for that argument.

A more interesting case is the call to ToNameString() from within OutputName(). OutputName() is declared static and therefore has no this. It has an explicit Student object, which it uses to make the call.

The OutputBanner() method would probably like to call ToNameString() as well; however, it has no Student object to use. It has no this reference because it's a static method and wasn't passed an object explicitly. Note the boldfaced line in the sample code: The static method cannot call the instance method.

REMEMBER

A static method cannot call a nonstatic method without explicitly providing an object. No object, no call. In general, static methods cannot access any nonstatic items in the class. But nonstatic (instance) methods can access static as well as instance items: static data members and static methods.

Using Local Functions

Even with all the methods of making code smaller and easier to work with that you have seen so far, sometimes a method might prove complex and hard to read anyway. A local function enables you to declare a function within the scope of a method to help promote further encapsulation. You use this approach when you need to perform a task a number of times within a method, but no other method within the application performs this particular task. Here's a simple example of a local function:

```
static void Main(string[] args)
{
    //Create a local function
    int Sum(int x, int y)
    {
        return x + y;
    }

    // Use the local function to output some sums.
    Console.WriteLine(Sum(1, 2));
    Console.WriteLine(Sum(5, 6));

    // Wait for user to acknowledge.
    Console.WriteLine("Press Enter to terminate...");
    Console.Read();
}
```

The Sum() method is relatively simple, but it demonstrates how a local function could work. The function encapsulates some code that only Main() uses. Because Main() performs the required task more than once, using Sum() makes sense to make the code more readable, easier to understand, and easier to maintain.

TIP

Local functions have all the functionality of any method except that you can't declare them as static. A local function has access to all the variables found within the enclosing method, so if you need a variable found in Main(), you can access it from Sum().

Chapter **5**

Holding a Class Responsible

A class must be held responsible for its actions. Just as a microwave oven shouldn't burst into flames if you press the wrong key, so a class shouldn't allow itself to roll over and die when presented with incorrect data.

To be held responsible for its actions, a class must ensure that its initial state is correct and then control its subsequent state so that it remains valid. C# provides both these capabilities.

Restricting Access to Class Members

Simple classes define all their members as `public`. Consider a `BankAccount` program that maintains a `balance` data member to retain the balance in each account. Making that data member `public` puts everyone on the honor system.

Most banks aren't nearly so forthcoming as to leave a pile of money and a register for you to mark down every time you add money to or take money away from the pile. After all, you may forget to mark your withdrawals in the register. Controlling access avoids little mistakes, such as forgetting to mark a withdrawal here or there, and manages to avoid some truly big mistakes with withdrawals.

You might think that you can protect the data by ensuring that no one can access the balance member directly. That approach may work in theory, but in practice it never does. People start with good intentions, but those intentions get crushed under the weight of schedule pressures to get the product out the door.

A public example of public BankAccount

The following BankAccount class example declares all its methods public but declares its data members, including _accountNumber and _balance, as private. The example leaves the variables in an incorrect state to make a point. The following code chunk doesn't compile correctly yet:

```
using System;

// BankAccount -- Create a bank account using a double variable
//    to store the account balance (keep the balance in a private
//    variable to hide its implementation from the outside world).
// Note: Until you correct it, this program fails to compile
// because Main() refers to a private member of class BankAccount.
namespace BankAccount
{
  public class Program
  {
    public static void Main(string[] args)
    {
      Console.WriteLine("This program doesn't compile.");

      // Open a bank account.
      Console.WriteLine("Create a bank account object");
      BankAccount ba = new BankAccount();
      ba.InitBankAccount();

      // Accessing the balance via the Deposit() method is okay --
      // Deposit() has access to all the data members.
      ba.Deposit(10);

      // Accessing the data member directly is a compile-time error.
      Console.WriteLine("Just in case you get this far the following is "
                    + "supposed to generate a compile error");
      ba._balance += 10;
```

```
      // Wait for user to acknowledge the results.
      Console.WriteLine("Press Enter to terminate...");
      Console.Read();
    }
}


// BankAccount -- Define a class that represents a simple account.
public class BankAccount
{
  private static int _nextAccountNumber = 1000;
  private int _accountNumber;

  // Maintain the balance as a double variable.
  private double _balance;

  // Init -- Initialize a bank account with the next
  //    account id and a balance of 0.
  public void InitBankAccount()
  {
    _accountNumber = ++_nextAccountNumber;
    _balance = 0.0;
  }

  // GetBalance -- Return the current balance.
  public double GetBalance()
  {
    return _balance;
  }

  // AccountNumber
  public int GetAccountNumber()
  {
    return _accountNumber;
  }

  public void SetAccountNumber(int accountNumber)
  {
    this._accountNumber = accountNumber;
  }

  // Deposit -- Any positive deposit is allowed.
  public void Deposit(double amount)
  {
    if (amount > 0.0)
    {
      _balance += amount;
    }
}
```

```
// Withdraw -- You can withdraw any amount up to the
//    balance; return the amount withdrawn.
public double Withdraw(double withdrawal)
{
  if (_balance <= withdrawal)
  {
    withdrawal = _balance;
  }
  _balance -= withdrawal;
  return withdrawal;
}

// GetString -- Return the account data as a string.
public string GetString()
{
  string s = String.Format("#{0} = {1:C}",
                           GetAccountNumber(), GetBalance());

  return s;
}
}
}
```

The BankAccount class provides an InitBankAccount() method to initialize the members of the class, a Deposit() method to handle deposits, and a Withdraw() method to perform withdrawals. The Deposit() and Withdraw() methods even provide some rudimentary rules, such as "You can't deposit a negative number" and "You can't withdraw more than you have in your account" (both good rules for a bank, as I'm sure you'll agree). However, everyone's on the honor system as long as _balance is accessible to external methods. (In this context, *external* means external to the class but within the same program.) The honor system can be a problem on big programs written by teams of programmers. It can even be a problem for you (and me), given general human fallibility.

REMEMBER

Well-written code with rules that the compiler can enforce saves everyone from the occasional bullet to the big toe. Before you get too excited, however, notice that the program doesn't build. Attempts to do so generate this error message:

```
'BankAccount.BankAccount._balance' is inaccessible due to its protection level.
```

The error message seems a bit hard to understand because that's how error messages are, for the most part (writing a truly understandable error message is incredibly tough). The crux of the problem is that _balance is private, which means no one can see it. The statement `ba._balance += 10;` is illegal because `_balance` isn't accessible to `Main()`, a method outside the `BankAccount` class. Replacing this line with `ba.Deposit(10)` solves the problem. The `BankAccount.Deposit()` method is public and therefore accessible to `Main()` and other parts of your program.

REMEMBER

The default access type is `private`. Not declaring a class member's access type explicitly is the same as declaring it `private`. However, you should include the `private` keyword to remove any doubt. Good programmers make their intentions explicit, which is another way to reduce errors.

Jumping ahead — other levels of security

WARNING

Understanding this section depends on your having some knowledge of inheritance (see Chapter 6 in this minibook) and namespaces (see Chapter 10 in this minibook). You can skip this section for now if you want, but just know that it's here when you need it. C# provides these levels of security:

>> A `public` member is accessible to any class in the program.

>> A `private` member is accessible only from the current class.

>> A `protected` member is accessible from the current class and any of its subclasses.

>> An `internal` member is accessible from any class within the same program module or assembly.

TECHNICAL STUFF

   A C# *module,* or *assembly,* is a separately compiled piece of code, either an executable program in an .EXE file or a supporting library module in a .DLL file. A single namespace can extend across multiple assemblies. (Chapter 10 in this minibook explains C# assemblies and namespaces and discusses access levels other than `public` and `private`.)

>> An `internal protected` member is accessible from the current class and any subclass, and from classes within the same module.

Keeping a member hidden by declaring it `private` offers the maximum amount of security. However, in many cases, you don't need that level of security. After all, the members of a subclass already depend on the members of the base class, so `protected` offers a comfortable level of security.

Why You Should Worry about Access Control

Declaring the internal members of a class `public` is a bad idea for at least these reasons:

> » **With all data members `public`, you can't easily determine when and how data members are being modified.** Why bother building safety checks into the `Deposit()` and `Withdraw()` methods? In fact, why even bother with these methods? Any method of any class can modify these elements at any time. If other methods can access these data members, they almost certainly will.
>
> Your `BankAccount` program may execute for an hour or so before you notice that one of the accounts has a negative balance. The `Withdraw()` method would have ensured that this situation didn't happen, so obviously another method accessed the balance without going through `Withdraw()`. Figuring out which method is responsible and under which conditions is a difficult problem.

> » **Exposing all data members of the class makes the interface too complicated.** As a programmer using the `BankAccount` class, you don't want to know about the internal workings of the class. You just need to know that you can deposit and withdraw funds. It's like a candy machine that has 50 buttons versus one with just a few buttons — the ones you need.

> » **Exposing internal elements leads to a distribution of the class rules.** For example, my `BankAccount` class doesn't allow the balance to be negative under any circumstances. That required business rule should be isolated within the `Withdraw()` method. Otherwise, you have to add this check everywhere the balance is updated.
>
> Sometimes a bank decides to change the rules so that valued customers are allowed to carry slightly negative balances for a short period, to avoid unintended overdrafts. Then you have to search through the program to update every section of code that accesses the balance, to ensure that the safety checks are changed.

TIP

Make your classes and methods no more accessible than necessary. This advice isn't meant to cause paranoia about snoopy hackers so much as it is to suggest a prudent step that helps reduce errors as you code. Use `private`, if possible, and then escalate to `protected`, `internal`, `internal protected`, or `public` as necessary.

Accessor methods

If you look more carefully at the BankAccount class, you see a few other methods. One, GetString(), returns a string version of the account fit for presentation to any Console.WriteLine() for display. However, displaying the contents of a BankAccount object may be difficult if its contents are inaccessible. The class should have the right to decide how it is displayed.

In addition, you see two *getter* methods, GetBalance() and GetAccountNumber(), and one *setter* method, SetAccountNumber(). You may wonder why it's important to declare a data member such as _balance private, but to provide a public GetBalance() method to return its value:

» GetBalance() **doesn't provide a way to modify _balance — it merely returns its value.** The balance is read-only. To use the analogy of an actual bank, you can look at your balance any time you want; you just can't withdraw money from your account without using the bank's withdrawal mechanism.

» GetBalance() **hides the internal format of the class from external methods.** GetBalance() may perform an extensive calculation by reading receipts, adding account charges, and accounting for any other amounts your bank may want to subtract from your balance. External methods don't know and don't care. Of course, you care which fees are being charged — you just can't do anything about them, short of changing banks.

Finally, GetBalance() provides a mechanism for making internal changes to the class without the need to change the users of BankAccount. If the Federal Deposit Insurance Corporation (FDIC) mandates that your bank store deposits differently, the mandate shouldn't change the way you access your account.

Access control to the rescue — an example

The following DoubleBankAccount program demonstrates a potential flaw in the BankAccount program. The following listing shows Main() — the only portion of the program that differs from the earlier BankAccount program:

```
using System;

// DoubleBankAccount -- Create a bank account using a double variable
//     to store the account balance (keep the balance in a private
//     variable to hide its implementation from the outside world).
namespace DoubleBankAccount
```

```
{
  public class Program
  {
    public static void Main(string[] args)
    {
      // Open a bank account.
      Console.WriteLine("Create a bank account object");
      BankAccount ba = new BankAccount();
      ba.InitBankAccount();

      // Make a deposit.
      double deposit = 123.454;
      Console.WriteLine("Depositing {0:C}", deposit);
      ba.Deposit(deposit);

      // Account balance
      Console.WriteLine("Account = {0}", ba.GetString());

      // Here's the problem.
      double fractionalAddition = 0.002;
      Console.WriteLine("Adding {0:C}", fractionalAddition);
      ba.Deposit(fractionalAddition);

      // Resulting balance
      Console.WriteLine("Resulting account = {0}", ba.GetString());

      // Wait for user to acknowledge the results.
      Console.WriteLine("Press Enter to terminate...");
      Console.Read();
    }
  }
}
```

The Main() method creates a bank account and then deposits $123.454, an amount that contains a fractional number of cents. Main() then deposits a small fraction of a cent to the balance and displays the resulting balance. The output from this program appears this way:

```
Create a bank account object
Depositing $123.45
Account = #1001 = $123.45
Adding $0.00
Resulting account = #1001 = $123.46
Press Enter to terminate...
```

Users start to complain: "I just can't reconcile my checkbook with my bank statement." Apparently, the program has a bug.

The problem, of course, is that $123.454 shows up as $123.45. To avoid the problem, the bank decides to round deposits and withdrawals to the nearest cent. Deposit $123.454 and the bank takes that extra 0.4 cent. On the other side, the bank gives up enough 0.4 amounts that everything balances out in the long run. Well, in theory, it does.

The easiest way to solve the rounding problem is by converting the bank accounts to decimal and using the Decimal.Round() method, as shown in this DecimalBankAccount program:

```
using System;

// DecimalBankAccount -- Create a bank account using a decimal
//      variable to store the account balance.
namespace DecimalBankAccount
{
  public class Program
  {
    public static void Main(string[] args)
    {
      // Open a bank account.
      Console.WriteLine("Create a bank account object");
      BankAccount ba = new BankAccount();
      ba.InitBankAccount();

      // Make a deposit.
      double deposit = 123.454;
      Console.WriteLine("Depositing {0:C}", deposit);
      ba.Deposit(deposit);

      // Account balance
      Console.WriteLine("Account = {0}", ba.GetString());

      // Now add in a very small amount.
      double fractionalAddition = 0.002;
      Console.WriteLine("Adding {0:C}", fractionalAddition);
      ba.Deposit(fractionalAddition);

      // Resulting balance.
      Console.WriteLine("Resulting account = {0}", ba.GetString());

      // Wait for user to acknowledge the results.
      Console.WriteLine("Press Enter to terminate...");
      Console.Read();
    }
  }
}
```

```csharp
// BankAccount -- Define a class that represents a simple account.
public class BankAccount
{
  private static int _nextAccountNumber = 1000;
  private int _accountNumber;

  // Maintain the balance as a single decimal variable.
  private decimal _balance;

  // Init -- Initialize a bank account with the next
  //    account id and a balance of 0.
  public void InitBankAccount()
  {
    _accountNumber = ++_nextAccountNumber;
    _balance = 0;
  }

  // GetBalance -- Return the current balance.
  public double GetBalance()
  {
    return (double)_balance;
  }

  // AccountNumber
  public int GetAccountNumber()
  {
    return _accountNumber;
  }

  public void SetAccountNumber(int accountNumber)
  {
    this._accountNumber = accountNumber;
  }

  // Deposit -- Any positive deposit is allowed.
  public void Deposit(double amount)
  {
    if (amount > 0.0)
    {
      // Round off the double to the nearest cent before depositing.
      decimal temp = (decimal)amount;
      temp = Decimal.Round(temp, 2);
      _balance += temp;
    }
  }
}
```

```
// Withdraw -- You can withdraw any amount up to the
//    balance; return the amount withdrawn.
public double Withdraw(double withdrawal)
{
  // Convert to decimal and work with the decimal version.
  decimal decWithdrawal = (decimal)withdrawal;
  if (_balance <= decWithdrawal)
  {
    decWithdrawal = _balance;
  }
  _balance -= decWithdrawal;
  return (double)decWithdrawal;  // Return a double.
}

// GetString -- Return the account data as a string.
public string GetString()
{
  string s = String.Format("#{0} = {1:C}",
                       GetAccountNumber(), GetBalance());

  return s;
}
}
}
```

This version of the example changes all internal representations to decimal values, a type better adapted to handling bank account balances than double in any case. The Deposit( ) method now uses the Decimal.Round( ) method to round the deposit amount to the nearest cent before making the deposit. The output from the program is now as expected:

```
Create a bank account object
Depositing $123.45
Account = #1001 = $123.45
Adding $0.00
Resulting account = #1001 = $123.45
Press Enter to terminate...
```

So what?

You could argue that the BankAccount program should have used decimal input arguments to begin with. But the point is that many development projects make the same sort of mistakes. Other applications were written using double as the form of storage. A problem arose. The BankAccount class was able to fix the problem internally and make no changes to the application software. (Notice that the class's public interface didn't change: Balance( ) and Withdraw( ) still return doubles, and Deposit( ) and Withdraw( ) still take a double parameter.)

In this case, the only calling method potentially affected was Main(), but the effects could have extended to dozens of methods that accessed bank accounts, and those methods could have been spread over hundreds of assemblies. None of those methods would have to change, because the fix was within the confines of the BankAccount class, whose *public interface* (its public methods) didn't outwardly change. This solution wouldn't have been possible if the internal members of the class had been exposed to external methods.

Internal changes to a class still require some retesting of other code, even though you didn't have to modify that code.

Defining Class Properties

The GetX() and SetX() methods demonstrated in the BankAccount programs in the previous section are *access methods*, or simply *accessors*. Although they signify good programming habits in theory, access methods can become clumsy in practice. For example, the following code line is necessary to increment _accountNumber by 1:

```
SetAccountNumber(GetAccountNumber() + 1);
```

C# defines a construct known as a *property*, which makes using access methods much easier than making them methods. The following code snippet defines a read-write property, AccountNumber (it's both a getter and a setter):

```
public int AccountNumber          // No parentheses here.
{
  // The "read" part. Curly braces and semicolon.
  get{ return _accountNumber; }

  // The "write" part. 'value' is a keyword.
  set{ _accountNumber = value; }
}
```

The get section is called whenever the property is read, and the set section is invoked on the write. The following Balance property is read-only because only the get section is defined (using a less compact notation):

```
public double Balance
{
  get
  {
    return (double)_balance;
  }
}
```

In use, these properties appear as follows:

```
BankAccount ba = new BankAccount();

// Set the account number property.
ba.AccountNumber = 1001;

// Get both properties.
Console.WriteLine("#{0} = {1:C}", ba.AccountNumber, ba.Balance);
```

The properties AccountNumber and Balance look much like public data members, in both appearance and use. However, properties enable the class to protect internal members (Balance is a read-only property) and hide their implementation (the underlying _balance data member is private). Notice that Balance performs a conversion — it could have performed any number of calculations. Properties don't necessarily use just one line of code; as with any other part of C#, a property can do things like verify input or manipulate incoming data.

By convention, the name of a property begins with a capital letter. Note that properties don't have parentheses: It's Balance, not Balance().

TIP

Properties aren't necessarily inefficient. The C# compiler can optimize a simple accessor to the point that it generates no more machine code than accessing the data member directly does. This concept is important, not only to an application program but also to C# itself. The C# library uses properties throughout, and you should, too. Use properties to access class data members, even from methods in the same class.

TECHNICAL STUFF

Static properties

A static (class) data member may be exposed through a static property, as shown in this simplistic example (note its compact layout):

```
public class BankAccount
{
    private static int _nextAccountNumber = 1000;
    public static int NextAccountNumber { get { return _nextAccountNumber; } }
    // ...
}
```

The NextAccountNumber property is accessed through the class as follows because it isn't an instance property (it's declared static):

```
// Read the account number property.
int value = BankAccount.NextAccountNumber;
```

(In this example, value is outside the context of a property, so it isn't a reserved word.)

Properties with side effects

A get operation can perform extra work other than simply retrieving the associated property, as shown here:

```
public static int AccountNumber
{
  // Retrieve the property and set it up for the
  // next retrieval by incrementing it.
  get{ return ++_nextAccountNumber; }
}
```

This property increments the static account number member before returning the result. This action probably isn't a good idea, however, because the user of the property receives no clue that anything is happening other than the actual reading of the property. The incrementation is a side effect.

REMEMBER

Like the accessor methods that they mimic, properties shouldn't change the state of the class other than, say, setting a data member's value. Both properties and methods generally should avoid side effects because they can lead to subtle bugs. Change a class as directly and explicitly as possible.

Letting the compiler write properties for you

Most properties described in the previous section are utterly routine, and writing them is tedious (though simple):

```
private string _name;  // An underlying data member for the property
public string Name { get { return _name; } set { _name = value; } }
```

Because you write this same boilerplate code repeatedly, since C# 3.0, the compiler now does it for you. All you have to write for the previous property (including the private data member) is this line:

```
public string Name { get; set; }
```

This line is sort of equivalent to

```
private string <somename>;  // What's <somename>? Don't know or care.
public string Name { get { return <somename>; } set { <somename> = value; } }
```

The compiler creates a mysterious data member, which shall be nameless, along with the accessor boilerplate code. This style encourages using the property even inside other members of its containing class because the property name is all you know. For that reason, you must have both `get` and `set` when you write the shortcut property. You can initialize such properties using the property syntax:

```
public int AnInt { get; set; } // Compiler provides a private variable.
...
AnInt = 2; // Initialize compiler-written instance variable via property.
```

Accessors with access levels

Accessor properties don't necessarily have to be declared `public`. You can declare them at any appropriate level, even `private`, if the accessor is used only inside its class. (The upcoming example marks the `Name` property `internal`.)

You can even adjust the access levels of the `get` and `set` portions of an accessor individually. Suppose that you don't want to expose the `set` accessor outside your class — it's for internal use only. You can write the property like this:

```
internal string Name { get; private set; }
```

Getting Your Objects Off to a Good Start — Constructors

REMEMBER

Controlling class access is only half the problem: An object needs a good start in life if it is to grow. A class can supply an initialization method that the application calls to get things started, but the application could forget to call the method. The class starts out with garbage, and the situation gets no better after that. If you want to hold the class accountable, you have to ensure that it has a chance to start out correctly. C# solves that problem by calling the initialization method for you — for example:

```
MyObject mo = new MyObject();
```

REMEMBER

In other words, this statement not only grabs an object from a special memory area but also initializes that object's members. Keep the terms class and object separate in your mind. `Cat` is a class. An instance of `Cat` named `Striper` is an object of class `Cat`.

The C#-Provided Constructor

C# keeps track of whether a variable has been initialized and doesn't allow you to use an uninitialized variable. For example, the following code chunk generates a compile-time error:

```
public static void Main(string[] args)
{
  int n;
  double d;
  double calculatedValue = n + d;
}
```

C# tracks the fact that the local variables n and d haven't been assigned a value and doesn't allow them to be used in the expression. Compiling this tiny program generates these compiler errors:

```
Use of unassigned local variable 'n'
Use of unassigned local variable 'd'
```

By comparison, C# provides a default constructor that initializes the data members of an object to

>> 0 for numbers

>> false for Booleans

>> null for object references

Consider the following simple program example:

```
using System;

namespace Test
{
  public class Program
  {
    public static void Main(string[] args)
    {
      // First create an object.
      MyObject localObject = new MyObject();
      Console.WriteLine("localObject.n is {0}", localObject.n);
```

```
      if (localObject.nextObject == null)
      {
        Console.WriteLine("localObject.nextObject is null");
      }

      // Wait for user to acknowledge the results.
      Console.WriteLine("Press Enter to terminate...");
      Console.Read();
    }
  }

  public class MyObject
  {
    internal int n;
    internal MyObject nextObject;
  }
}
```

This program defines a class MyObject, which contains both a simple data member n of type int and a reference to an object, nextObject (both declared internal). The Main() method creates a MyObject and then displays the initial contents of n and nextObject. The output from executing the program appears this way:

```
localObject.n is 0
localObject.nextObject is null
Press Enter to terminate...
```

When the object is created, C# executes a small piece of code that the compiler provides to initialize the object and its members. Left to their own devices, the data members localObject.n and nextObject would contain random, garbage values.

REMEMBER

The code that initializes values when they're created is the default constructor. It constructs the class, in the sense of initializing its members. Thus C# ensures that an object starts life in a known state: all zeros, nulls, or false values, depending on type. This concept affects only data members of the class, not local variables in a method.

Replacing the Default Constructor

Although the compiler automatically initializes all instance variables to the appropriate values, for many classes (probably most classes), the default value isn't a valid state. Consider the following BankAccount class from earlier in this chapter:

```
public class BankAccount
{
  private int _accountNumber;
  private double _balance;
  // ...other members
}
```

Although an initial balance of 0 is probably okay, an account number of 0 definitely isn't the hallmark of a valid bank account.

At this point in the chapter, the BankAccount class includes the InitBankAccount() method to initialize the object. However, this approach puts too much responsibility on the application software using the class. If the application fails to invoke the InitBankAccount() method, the bank account methods may not work, through no fault of their own.

REMEMBER

A class shouldn't rely on external methods such as InitBankAccount() to start the object in a valid state. To work around this problem, you can have your class provide its own explicit *class constructor* that C# calls automatically when the object is created. The constructor could have been named Init(), Start(), or Create(), but C# requires the constructor to carry the name of the class. Thus a constructor for the BankAccount class appears this way:

```
public void Main(string[] args)
{
  BankAccount ba = new BankAccount();  // This invokes the constructor.
}

public class BankAccount
{
  // Bank accounts start at 1000 and increase sequentially.
  private static int _nextAccountNumber = 1000;

  // Maintain the account number and balance for each object.
  private int _accountNumber;
  private double _balance;

  // BankAccount constructor -- Here it is -- ta-da!
  // Parentheses, possible arguments, no return type
  public BankAccount()
```

```
    {
        _accountNumber = ++_nextAccountNumber;
        _balance = 0.0;
    }


    // ... other members ...
}
```

The contents of the BankAccount constructor are the same as those of the original Init...() method. However, the way you declare and use the constructor differs:

>> The constructor always carries the same name as the class.

>> The constructor can take parameters (or not).

>> The constructor never has a return type, not even void.

>> Main() doesn't need to invoke any extra method to initialize the object when it's created; no Init() is necessary.

REMEMBER

If you provide your own constructor, C# no longer supplies a default constructor. Your constructor replaces the default and becomes the only way to create an instance of your class.

Constructing something

Try out a constructor thingie. Consider the following program, Demonstrate CustomConstructor:

```
using System;

// DemonstrateCustomConstructor -- Demonstrate how you can replace the
// C# default constructor with your own, custom constructor. Creates
// a class with a constructor and then steps through a few scenarios.
namespace DemonstrateCustomConstructor
{
    // MyObject -- Create a class with a noisy custom constructor
    //    and an internal data object.
    public class MyObject
    {
        // This data member is a property of the class (it's static).
        private static MyOtherObject _staticObj = new MyOtherObject();

        // This data member is a property of each instance.
        private MyOtherObject _dynamicObj;
```

```
    // Constructor (a real chatterbox)
    public MyObject()
    {
      Console.WriteLine("MyObject constructor starting");
      Console.WriteLine("(Static data member constructed before " +
                        "this constructor)");
      Console.WriteLine("Now create nonstatic data member dynamically:");
      _dynamicObj = new MyOtherObject();
      Console.WriteLine("MyObject constructor ending");
    }
}

// MyOtherObject -- This class also has a noisy constructor but
//    no internal members.
public class MyOtherObject
{
  public MyOtherObject()
  {
    Console.WriteLine("MyOtherObject constructing");
  }
}

public class Program
{
  public static void Main(string[] args)
  {
    Console.WriteLine("Main() starting");
    Console.WriteLine("Creating a local MyObject in Main():");
    MyObject localObject = new MyObject();

    // Wait for user to acknowledge the results.
    Console.WriteLine("Press Enter to terminate...");
    Console.Read();
  }
}
```

Executing this program generates the following output:

```
Main() starting
Creating a local MyObject in Main():
MyOtherObject constructing
MyObject constructor starting
(Static data member constructed before this constructor)
Now create nonstatic data member dynamically:
MyOtherObject constructing
MyObject constructor ending
Press Enter to terminate...
```

The following steps reconstruct what just happened:

1. **The program starts, and** Main( ) **outputs the initial message and announces that it's about to create a local** MyObject.

2. Main( ) **creates a** localObject **of type** MyObject.

3. MyObject **contains a static member** _staticObj **of class** MyOtherObject.

REMEMBER

All static data members are initialized before the first MyObject( ) constructor runs. In this case, C# populates _staticObj with a newly created MyOtherObject before passing control to the MyObject constructor. This step accounts for the third line of output.

4. **The constructor for** MyObject **is given control. It outputs the initial message,** MyObject constructor starting, **and then notes that the static member was already constructed before the** MyObject( ) **constructor began:**

```
(Static data member constructed before this constructor)
```

5. **After announcing its intention with** Now create nonstatic data member dynamically, **the** MyObject **constructor creates an object of class** MyOtherObject **using the** new **operator, generating the second** MyOtherObject constructing **message as the** MyOtherObject **constructor is called.**

6. **Control returns to the** MyObject **constructor, which returns to** Main( ).

Initializing an object directly with an initializer

Besides letting you initialize data members in a constructor, C# enables you to initialize data members directly by using initializers. Thus, you could write the BankAccount class as follows:

```csharp
public class BankAccount
{
    // Bank accounts start at 1000 and increase sequentially.
    private static int _nextAccountNumber = 1000;

    // Maintain the account number and balance for each object.
    private int _accountNumber = ++_nextAccountNumber;
    private double _balance = 0.0;

    // ... other members ...
}
```

Here's the initializer business. Both _accountNumber and _balance are assigned a value as part of their declaration, which has the same effect as a constructor but without having to do the work in it.

Be clear about exactly what's happening. You may think that this statement sets _balance to 0.0 right now. However, _balance exists only as a part of an object. Thus, the assignment isn't executed until a BankAccount object is created. In fact, this assignment is executed every time an object is created.

Note that the static data member _nextAccountNumber is initialized the first time the BankAccount class is accessed, that's the first time you access any method or property of the object owning the static data member, including the constructor.

REMEMBER

After the static member is initialized, it isn't reinitialized every time you construct a BankAccount instance. That's different from the nonstatic members. Initializers are executed in the order of their appearance in the class declaration. If C# encounters both initializers and a constructor, the initializers are executed before the body of the constructor.

Seeing that construction stuff with initializers

In the DemonstrateCustomConstructor program, move the call new MyOtherObject() from the MyObject constructor to the declaration itself, as follows (see the bold text), modify the second WriteLine() statement as shown, and then rerun the program:

```csharp
public class MyObject
{
  // This member is a property of the class (it's static).
  private static MyOtherObject _staticObj = new MyOtherObject();

  // This member is a property of each instance.
  private MyOtherObject _dynamicObj = new MyOtherObject();  // <- Here.

  public MyObject()
  {
    Console.WriteLine("MyObject constructor starting");
    Console.WriteLine(
      "Both data members initialized before this constructor)");
    // _dynamicObj construction was here, now moved up.
    Console.WriteLine("MyObject constructor ending");
  }
}
```

Compare the following output from this modified program with the output from its predecessor, DemonstrateCustomConstructor:

```
Main() starting
Creating a local MyObject in Main():
MyOtherObject constructing
MyOtherObject constructing
MyObject constructor starting
(Both data members initialized before this constructor)
MyObject constructor ending
Press Enter to terminate...
```

Initializing an object without a constructor

Suppose that you have a little class to represent a Student:

```
public class Student
{
  public string Name { get; set; }
  public string Address { get; set; }
  public double GradePointAverage { get; set; }
}
```

A Student object has three public properties, Name, Address, and GradePointAverage, which specify the student's basic information. Normally, when you create a new Student object, you have to initialize its Name, Address, and GradePointAverage properties like this:

```
Student randal = new Student();
randal.Name = "Randal Sphar";
randal.Address = "123 Elm Street, Truth or Consequences, NM 00000";
randal.GradePointAverage = 3.51;
```

If Student had a constructor, you could do something like this:

```
Student randal = new Student
    ("Randal Sphar", "123 Elm Street, Truth or Consequences, NM, 00000", 3.51);
```

Sadly, however, Student lacks a constructor, other than the default one that C# supplies automatically — which takes no parameters.

In C# 3.0 and later, you can simplify that initialization with something that looks suspiciously like a constructor — well, sort of:

```
Student randal = new Student
  { Name = "Randal Sphar",
    Address = "123 Elm Street, Truth or Consequences, NM 00000",
    GradePointAverage = 3.51
  };
```

The last two examples are different in this respect: The first one, using a constructor, shows parentheses containing two strings and one `double` value separated by commas, and the second one, using the new object-initializer syntax, has instead curly braces containing three assignments separated by commas. The syntax works something like this:

```
new LatitudeLongitude
  { assignment to Latitude, assignment to Longitude };
```

The object-initializer syntax lets you assign to any accessible *set* properties of the `LatitudeLongitude` object in a code block (the curly braces). The block is designed to initialize the object. Note that you can set only accessible properties this way, not private ones, and you can't call any of the object's methods or do any other work in the initializer.

The object-initializer syntax is much more concise: one statement versus three. Also, it simplifies the creation of initialized objects that don't let you do so through a constructor. The new object-initializer syntax doesn't gain you much of anything besides convenience, but convenience when you're coding is high on any programmer's list. So is brevity. Besides, the feature becomes essential when you read about anonymous classes.

TIP

Use the new object-initializer syntax to your heart's content. The book uses it frequently, so you have plenty of examples. Look up the term *object initializer* in C# Language Help to determine the kinds of properties it works with.

Using Expression-Bodied Members

Expression-bodied members first appeared in C# 6.0 as a means to make methods and properties easier to define. In C# 7.0, expression-bodied members also work with constructors, destructors, property accessors, and event accessors.

Creating expression-bodied methods

The following example shows how you might have created a method before C# 6.0:

```
public int RectArea(Rectangle rect)
{
    return rect.Height * rect.Width;
}
```

When working with an expression-bodied member, you can reduce the number of lines of code to just one line, like this:

```
public int RectArea(Rectangle rect) => rect.Height * rect.Width;
```

Even though both versions perform precisely the same task, the second version is much shorter and easier to write. The trade-off is that the second version is also terse and can be harder to understand.

Defining expression-bodied properties

Expression-bodied properties work similarly to methods: You declare the property using a single line of code, like this:

```
public int RectArea => _rect.Height * _rect.Width;
```

The example assumes that you have a private member named _rect defined and that you want to get the value that matches the rectangle's area.

Defining expression-bodied constructors and destructors

In C# 7.0, you can use this same technique when working with a constructor. In earlier versions of C#, you might create a constructor like this one:

```
public EmpData()
{
    _name = "Harvey";
}
```

In this case, the EmpData class constructor sets a private variable, _name, equal to "Harvey". The C# 7.0 version uses just one line but accomplishes the same task:

```
public EmpData() => _name = "Harvey";
```

Destructors work much the same as constructors. Instead of using multiple lines, you use just one line to define them.

Defining expression-bodied property accessors

Property accessors can also benefit from the use of expression-bodied members. Here is a typical C# 6.0 property accessor with both get and set methods:

```
private int _myVar;
public MyVar
{
  get
  {
    return _myVar;
  }
  set
  {
    SetProperty(ref _myVar, value);
  }
}
```

When working in C# 7.0, you can shorten the code using an expression-bodied member, like this:

```
private int _myVar;
public MyVar
{
  get => _myVar;
  set => SetProperty(ref _myVar, value);
}
```

Defining expression-bodied event accessors

As with property accessors, you can create an event accessor form using the expression-bodied member. Here's what you might have used for C# 6.0:

```
private EventHandler _myEvent;
public event EventHandler MyEvent
{
    add
    {
        _myEvent += value;
    }
    remove
    {
        _myEvent -= value;
    }
}
```

The expression-bodied member form of the same event accessor in C# 7.0 looks like this:

```
private EventHandler _myEvent;
public event EventHandler MyEvent
{
    add => _myEvent += value;
    remove => _myEvent -= value;
}
```

Chapter **6**

Inheritance: Is That All I Get?

Object-oriented programming is based on four principles: the capability to control access (encapsulation), inherit from other classes, respond appropriately (polymorphism), and refer from one object to another indirectly (interfaces).

Inheritance is a common concept. You are a human. You inherit certain properties from the class Human, such as your ability to converse and your dependence on air, food, and beverages. The class Human inherits its dependencies on air, water, and nourishment from the class Mammal, which inherits from the class Animal.

The capability to pass down properties is a powerful one. You can use it to describe items in an economical way. For example, if your son asks, "What's a duck?" you can say, "It's a bird that quacks." Despite what you may think, that answer conveys a considerable amount of information. Your son knows what a bird is, and now he knows all those same characteristics about a duck plus the duck's additional property of "quackness."

Object-oriented languages express this inheritance relationship by allowing one class to inherit properties from another. This feature enables object-oriented languages to generate a model that's closer to the real world than the model generated by languages that don't support inheritance.

Class Inheritance

In the following InheritanceExample program, the class SubClass inherits from the class BaseClass:

```csharp
using System;

// InheritanceExample -- Provide the simplest possible
//    demonstration of inheritance.
namespace InheritanceExample
{
  public class BaseClass
  {
    public int _dataMember;
    public void SomeMethod()
    {
      Console.WriteLine("SomeMethod()");
    }
  }

  public class SubClass : BaseClass
  {
    public void SomeOtherMethod()
    {
      Console.WriteLine("SomeOtherMethod()");
    }
  }

  public class Program
  {
    public static void Main(string[] args)
    {
```

```
      // Create a base class object.
      Console.WriteLine("Exercising a base class object:");
      BaseClass bc = new BaseClass();
      bc._dataMember = 1;
      bc.SomeMethod();

      // Now create a subclass object.
      Console.WriteLine("Exercising a subclass object:");
      SubClass sc = new SubClass();
      sc._dataMember = 2;

      // Execute some subclass-specific code.
      sc.SomeMethod();
      sc.SomeOtherMethod();

      // Wait for user to acknowledge the results.
      Console.WriteLine("Press Enter to terminate...");
      Console.Read();
    }
  }
}
```

The class BaseClass is defined with a data member and the simple method SomeMethod(). Main() creates and exercises the BaseClass object bc. The class SubClass inherits from BaseClass by placing the name of the class, BaseClass, after a colon in the class definition:

```
public class SubClass : BaseClass
```

REMEMBER

SubClass gets all members of BaseClass as its own, plus any members it may add to the pile. Main() demonstrates that SubClass now has a data member, _dataMember, and a member method, SomeMethod(), to join the brand-new member of the family, little method SomeOtherMethod(). The program produces the following expected output:

```
Exercising a base class object:
SomeMethod()
Exercising a subclass object:
SomeMethod()
SomeOtherMethod()
Press Enter to terminate...
```

INHERITANCE IS AMAZING

To make sense of their surroundings, humans build extensive taxonomies. For example, Fido is a special case of dog, which is a special case of canine, which is a special case of mammal — and so it goes. This ability to classify items shapes the human understanding of the world.

In an object-oriented language such as C#, you say that the class Student inherits from the class Person. You also say that Person is a base class of Student and that Student is a subclass of Person. Finally, you say that a Student IS_A Person. (Using all caps and an underscore is a common way of expressing this unique relationship.)

Notice that the IS_A property isn't reflexive: Although Student IS_A Person, the reverse isn't true. A Person IS_NOT_A Student. A statement such as this one always refers to the general case. A particular Person might be, in fact, a Student — but lots of people who are members of the class Person aren't members of the class Student. In addition, the class Student has properties that it doesn't share with the class Person. For example, Student has a grade-point average, but the ordinary Person quite happily does not.

The inheritance property is transitive. For example, if I define a new class GraduateStudent as a subclass of Student, GraduateStudent is also a Person. It must be that way: If a GraduateStudent IS_A Student and a Student IS_A Person, a GraduateStudent IS_A Person.

Why You Need Inheritance

Inheritance serves several important functions. You may think, for example, that inheritance reduces the amount of typing. In a way, it does — you don't need to repeat the properties of a Person when you're describing a Student class. A more important, related issue is the major buzzword *reuse*. Computer scientists have known for some time that starting from scratch with each new project and rebuilding the same software components makes little sense.

Compare the situation in software development to that of other industries. Think about the number of car manufacturers that start by building their own wrenches and screwdrivers before they construct a car. Of those who do that, estimate how many would start over completely and build all new tools for the next model. Practitioners in other industries have found that starting with existing screws, bolts, nuts, and even larger off-the-shelf components such as motors and compressors makes more sense than starting from scratch.

Inheritance enables you to tweak existing software components. You can adapt existing classes to new applications without making internal modifications. The existing class is inherited into — or, as programmers often say, *extended* by — a new subclass that contains the necessary additions and modifications. If someone else wrote the base class, you may not be able to modify it, so inheritance can save the day.

This capability carries with it a third benefit of inheritance. Suppose that you inherit from — extend — an existing class. Later, you find that the base class has a bug you must correct. If you modified the class to reuse it, you must manually check for, correct, and retest the bug in each application separately. If you inherited the class without changes, you can generally stick the updated class into the other application with little hassle.

But the biggest benefit of inheritance is that it describes the way life is. Items inherit properties from each other. There's no getting around it.

Inheriting from a BankAccount Class (a More Complex Example)

A bank maintains several types of accounts. One type, the savings account, has all the properties of a simple bank account plus the ability to accumulate interest. The following SimpleSavingsAccount program models this relationship in C#.

```csharp
using System;

// SimpleSavingsAccount -- Implement SavingsAccount as a form of
//    bank account; use no virtual methods.
namespace SimpleSavingsAccount
{
  // BankAccount -- Simulate a bank account, each of which
  //    carries an account ID (which is assigned
  //    on creation) and a balance.
  public class BankAccount    // The base class
  {
    // Bank accounts start at 1000 and increase sequentially.
    public static int _nextAccountNumber = 1000;

    // Maintain the account number and balance for each object.
    public int _accountNumber;
    public decimal _balance;
```

```csharp
// Init -- Initialize a bank account with the next account ID and the
//    specified initial balance (default to zero).
public void InitBankAccount()
{
  InitBankAccount(0);
}

public void InitBankAccount(decimal initialBalance)
{
  _accountNumber = ++_nextAccountNumber;
  _balance = initialBalance;
}

// Balance property.
public decimal Balance
{
  get { return _balance;}
}

// Deposit -- any positive deposit is allowed.
public void Deposit(decimal amount)
{
  if (amount > 0)
  {
    _balance += amount;
  }
}

// Withdraw -- You can withdraw any amount up to the
//    balance; return the amount withdrawn.
public decimal Withdraw(decimal withdrawal)
{
  if (Balance <= withdrawal) // Use Balance property.
  {
    withdrawal = Balance;
  }
  _balance -= withdrawal;
  return withdrawal;
}

// ToString - Stringify the account.
public string ToBankAccountString()
{
  return String.Format("{0} - {1:C}",
    _accountNumber, Balance);
}
}
```

```csharp
// SavingsAccount -- A bank account that draws interest
public class SavingsAccount : BankAccount    // The subclass
{
  public decimal _interestRate;

  // InitSavingsAccount -- Input the rate expressed as a
  //    rate between 0 and 100.
  public void InitSavingsAccount(decimal interestRate)
  {
    InitSavingsAccount(0, interestRate);
  }

  public void InitSavingsAccount(decimal initialBalance,
                                  decimal interestRate)
  {
    InitBankAccount(initialBalance);  // Note call to base class.
    this._interestRate = interestRate / 100;
  }

  // AccumulateInterest -- Invoke once per period.
  public void AccumulateInterest()
  {
    _balance = Balance + (decimal)(Balance * _interestRate);
  }

  // ToString -- Stringify the account.
  public string ToSavingsAccountString()
  {
    return String.Format("{0} ({1}%)",
      ToBankAccountString(), _interestRate * 100);
  }
}

public class Program
{
  public static void Main(string[] args)
  {
    // Create a bank account and display it.
    BankAccount ba = new BankAccount();
    ba.InitBankAccount(100M); // M suffix indicates decimal.
    ba.Deposit(100M);
    Console.WriteLine("Account {0}", ba.ToBankAccountString());

    // Now a savings account
    SavingsAccount sa = new SavingsAccount();
    sa.InitSavingsAccount(100M, 12.5M);
    sa.AccumulateInterest();
    Console.WriteLine("Account {0}", sa.ToSavingsAccountString());
```

```
          // Wait for user to acknowledge the results.
          Console.WriteLine("Press Enter to terminate...");
          Console.Read();
        }
      }
    }
```

The BankAccount class is not unlike some that appear in other chapters of this book. It begins with an overloaded initialization method InitBankAccount(): one for accounts that start out with an initial balance and another for which an initial balance of zero will have to suffice. Notice that this version of BankAccount doesn't take advantage of the latest and greatest constructor advances. The final version of BankAccount in this chapter overcomes the constructor issue, but the simpler version is used for illustration purposes now.

The Balance property allows other people to read the balance without letting them modify it. The Deposit() method accepts any positive deposit. Withdraw() lets you take out as much as you want, as long as you have enough money in your account. ToBankAccountString() creates a string that describes the account.

The SavingsAccount class inherits all that good stuff from BankAccount. It also adds an interest rate and the capability to accumulate interest at regular intervals.

Main() does about as little as it can. It creates a BankAccount, displays the account, creates a SavingsAccount, accumulates one period of interest, and displays the result, with the interest rate in parentheses:

```
Account 1001 - $200.00
Account 1002 - $112.50 (12.500%)
Press Enter to terminate...
```

TIP

Notice that the InitSavingsAccount() method invokes InitBankAccount(). It initializes the bank account–specific data members. The InitSavingsAccount() method could have initialized these members directly; however, a better practice is to allow BankAccount to initialize its own members. A class should be responsible for itself.

IS_A versus HAS_A — I'm So Confused_A

The relationship between SavingsAccount and BankAccount is the fundamental IS_A relationship in inheritance. In the following sections, I show you why, and then I show you what the alternative, the HAS_A relationship, would look like in comparison.

The IS_A relationship

The IS_A relationship between SavingsAccount and BankAccount is demonstrated by the modification to the class Program in the SimpleSavingsAccount program from the preceding section:

```
public class Program
{
  // Add this:
  // DirectDeposit -- Deposit my paycheck automatically.
  public static void DirectDeposit(BankAccount ba, decimal pay)
  {
    ba.Deposit(pay);
  }

  public static void Main(string[] args)
  {
    // Create a bank account and display it.
    BankAccount ba = new BankAccount();
    ba.InitBankAccount(100M);
    DirectDeposit(ba, 100M);
    Console.WriteLine("Account {0}", ba.ToBankAccountString());

    // Now a savings account
    SavingsAccount sa = new SavingsAccount();
    sa.InitSavingsAccount(12.5M);
    DirectDeposit(sa, 100M);
    sa.AccumulateInterest();
    Console.WriteLine("Account {0}", sa.ToSavingsAccountString());

    // Wait for user to acknowledge the results.
    Console.WriteLine("Press Enter to terminate...");
    Console.Read();
  }
}
```

In effect, nothing has changed. The only real difference is that all deposits are now being made through the local method DirectDeposit(), which isn't part of class BankAccount. The arguments to this method are the bank account and the amount to deposit.

REMEMBER

Notice that Main() could pass either a bank account or a savings account to DirectDeposit() because a SavingsAccount IS_A BankAccount and is accorded all the same rights and privileges. Because SavingsAccount IS_A BankAccount, you can assign a SavingsAccount to a BankAccount-type variable or method argument.

Gaining access to BankAccount by using containment

The class SavingsAccount could have gained access to the members of BankAccount in a different way, as shown in the following code, where the key lines are shown in boldface:

```csharp
// SavingsAccount -- A bank account that draws interest
public class SavingsAccount_   // Notice the underscore: this isn't
                               // the SavingsAccount class.
{
  // Notice this, the contained BankAccount.
  public BankAccount _bankAccount;
  public decimal _interestRate;

  // InitSavingsAccount -- Input the rate expressed as a
  //    rate between 0 and 100.
  public void InitSavingsAccount(BankAccount bankAccount,
                                 decimal interestRate)
  {
    this._bankAccount = bankAccount;
    this._interestRate = interestRate / 100;
  }

  // AccumulateInterest -- Invoke once per period.
  public void AccumulateInterest()
  {
    _bankAccount._balance = _bankAccount.Balance
                  + (_bankAccount.Balance * interestRate);
  }

  // Deposit -- Any positive deposit is allowed.
  public void Deposit(decimal amount)
  {
    // Delegate to the contained BankAccount object.
    _bankAccount.Deposit(amount);
  }

  // Withdraw -- You can withdraw any amount up to the
  //    balance; return the amount withdrawn.
  public double Withdraw(decimal withdrawal)
  {
    return _bankAccount.Withdraw(withdrawal);
  }
}
```

In this case, the class SavingsAccount_ *contains* a data member _bankAccount (as opposed to inheriting from BankAccount). The _bankAccount object contains the balance and account number information needed by the savings account. The SavingsAccount_ class retains the data unique to a savings account and *delegates* to the contained BankAccount object as needed. That is, when the SavingsAccount needs, say, the balance, it asks the contained BankAccount for it.

In this case, you say that the SavingsAccount_ HAS_A BankAccount. Hard-core object-oriented jocks say that SavingsAccount *composes* a BankAccount. That is, SavingsAccount is partly composed of a BankAccount.

The HAS_A relationship

The HAS_A relationship is fundamentally different from the IS_A relationship. This difference doesn't seem so bad in the following application-code segment example:

```
// Create a new savings account.
BankAccount ba = new BankAccount()

// HAS_A version of SavingsAccount
SavingsAccount_ sa = new SavingsAccount_();
sa.InitSavingsAccount(ba, 5);

// And deposit 100 dollars into it.
sa.Deposit(100M);

// Now accumulate interest.
sa.AccumulateInterest();
```

The problem is that this modified SavingsAccount_ cannot be used as a BankAccount because it doesn't inherit from BankAccount. Instead, it *contains* a BankAccount — not the same concept. For example, this code example fails:

```
// DirectDeposit -- Deposit my paycheck automatically.
void DirectDeposit(BankAccount ba, int pay)
{
  ba.Deposit(pay);
}

void SomeMethod()
{
  // The following example fails.
  SavingsAccount_ sa = new SavingsAccount_();
  DirectDeposit(sa, 100);
  // ... continue ...
}
```

REMEMBER

DirectDeposit() can't accept a SavingsAccount_ in lieu of a BankAccount. No obvious relationship between the two exists, as far as C# is concerned, because inheritance isn't involved. Don't think, though, that this situation makes containment a bad idea. You just have to approach the concept a bit differently in order to use it.

When to IS_A and When to HAS_A

The distinction between the IS_A and HAS_A relationships is more than just a matter of software convenience. This relationship has a corollary in the real world.

For example, a Ford Explorer IS_A car. An Explorer HAS_A motor. If your friend says, "Come on over in your car" and you show up in an Explorer, he has no grounds for complaint. He may have a complaint if you show up carrying your Explorer's engine in your arms, however. (Or at least *you* will.) The class Explorer should extend the class Car, not only to give Explorer access to the methods of a Car but also to express the fundamental relationship between the two.

Unfortunately, the beginning programmer may have Car inherit from Motor, as an easy way to give the Car class access to the members of Motor, which the Car needs in order to operate. For example, Car can inherit the method Motor.Go(). However, this example highlights a problem with this approach: Even though humans become sloppy in their speech, making a car go isn't the same thing as making a motor go. The car's go operation certainly relies on that of the motor's, but they aren't the same thing — you also have to put the transmission in gear, release the brake, and complete other tasks. Perhaps even more than that, inheriting from Motor misstates the facts. A car simply isn't a type of motor.

REMEMBER

Elegance in software is a goal worth achieving in its own right. It enhances understandability, reliability, and maintainability.

TIP

Hard-core object-oriented jocks recommend preferring HAS_A over IS_A for simpler program designs. But use inheritance when it makes sense, as it probably does in the BankAccount hierarchy.

Other Features That Support Inheritance

C# implements a set of features designed to support inheritance. The following sections discuss these features.

Substitutable classes

A program can use a subclass object where a base class object is called for. In fact, you may have already seen this concept in one of the examples. SomeMethod() can pass a SavingsAccount object to the DirectDeposit() method, which expects a BankAccount object. You can make this conversion more explicit:

```
BankAccount ba;

// The original, not SavingsAccount_
SavingsAccount sa = new SavingsAccount();

// OK:
ba = sa;                   // Implicitly convert subclass to base class.
ba = (BankAccount)sa;      // But the explicit cast is preferred.

// Not OK:
sa = ba;                   // Implicitly convert base class to subclass.
sa = (SavingsAccount)ba;   // An explicit cast is allowed, however.
```

The first line stores a SavingsAccount object into a BankAccount variable. C# converts the object for you. The second line uses a cast to explicitly convert the object.

The final two lines attempt to convert the BankAccount object back into SavingsAccount. You can complete this operation explicitly, but C# doesn't do it for you. It's like trying to convert a larger numeric type, such as double, to a smaller one, such as float. C# doesn't do it implicitly because the process involves a loss of data.

REMEMBER

The IS_A property isn't reflexive. That is, even though an Explorer is a car, a car isn't necessarily an Explorer. Similarly, a BankAccount isn't necessarily a SavingsAccount, so the implicit conversion isn't allowed. The final line is allowed because the programmer has indicated a willingness to "chance it."

Invalid casts at runtime

Generally, casting an object from BankAccount to SavingsAccount is a dangerous operation. Consider this example:

```
public static void ProcessAmount(BankAccount bankAccount)
{
    // Deposit a large sum to the account.
    bankAccount.Deposit(10000.00M);
```

```
    // If the object is a SavingsAccount, collect interest now.
    SavingsAccount savingsAccount = (SavingsAccount)bankAccount;
    savingsAccount.AccumulateInterest();
}

public static void TestCast()
{
    SavingsAccount sa = new SavingsAccount();
    ProcessAmount(sa);

    BankAccount ba = new BankAccount();
    ProcessAmount(ba);
}
```

ProcessAmount() performs a few operations, including invoking the
AccumulateInterest() method. The cast of ba to a SavingsAccount is necessary because the bankAccount parameter is declared to be a BankAccount. The
program compiles properly because all type conversions are made by explicit cast.

All goes well with the first call to ProcessAmount() from within TestCast(). The
SavingsAccount object sa is passed to the ProcessAmount() method. The cast
from BankAccount to SavingsAccount causes no problem because the ba object
was originally a SavingsAccount anyway.

The second call to ProcessAmount() isn't as lucky, however. The cast to Savings
Account cannot be allowed. The ba object doesn't have an AccumulateInterest()
method.

WARNING

An incorrect conversion generates an error during the execution of the program (a
runtime error in the form of an exception). Runtime errors are much more difficult
to find and fix than compile-time errors. Worse, they can happen to a user other
than you, which users tend not to appreciate.

Avoiding invalid conversions with the is operator

The ProcessAmount() method would work if it could ensure that the object passed
to it is a SavingsAccount object before performing the conversion. C# provides
two keywords for this purpose: is and as.

The is operator accepts an object on the left and a type on the right. The is operator returns true if the runtime type of the object on the left is compatible with the
type on the right. Use it to verify that a cast is legal before you attempt the cast.

You can modify the example in the previous section to avoid the runtime error by using the `is` operator:

```
public static void ProcessAmount(BankAccount bankAccount)
{
  // Deposit a large sum to the account.
  bankAccount.Deposit(10000.00M);

  // If the object is a SavingsAccount ...
  if (bankAccount is SavingsAccount)
  {
    // ...then collect interest now (cast is guaranteed to work).
    SavingsAccount savingsAccount = (SavingsAccount)bankAccount;
    savingsAccount.AccumulateInterest();
  }

  // Otherwise, don't do the cast -- but why is BankAccount not what
  // you expected? This could be an error situation.
}
public static void TestCast()
{
  SavingsAccount sa = new SavingsAccount();
  ProcessAmount(sa);

  BankAccount ba = new BankAccount();
  ProcessAmount(ba);
}
```

The added `if` statement checks the `bankAccount` object to ensure that it's of the class `SavingsAccount`. The `is` operator returns `true` when `ProcessAmount()` is called the first time. When passed a `BankAccount` object in the second call, however, the `is` operator returns `false`, avoiding the illegal cast. This version of the program doesn't generate a runtime error.

TIP

A best practice is to protect all casts with the `is` operator to avoid the possibility of a runtime error. However, you should avoid casts altogether, if possible.

Avoiding invalid conversions with the as operator

The `as` operator works a bit differently from `is`. Rather than return a `bool` if the cast should work (but doesn't), it converts the type on the left to the type on the right. It safely returns `null` if the conversion fails — rather than cause a runtime error. You should always use the result of casting with the as operator only if it isn't null. So, using as looks like this:

```
SavingsAccount savingsAccount = bankAccount as SavingsAccount;
if(savingsAccount != null)
{
    // Go ahead and use savingsAccount.
}
// Otherwise, don't use it: generate an error message yourself.
```

REMEMBER

Generally, you should prefer as because it's more efficient. The conversion is already done with the as operator, whereas you must complete two steps when you use is: First test with is and then complete the cast with the cast operator.

WARNING

Unfortunately, as doesn't work with value-type variables, so you can't use it with types such as int, long, or double or with char. When you're trying to convert a value-type object, prefer the is operator.

The object Class

Consider these related classes:

```
public class MyBaseClass {}
public class MySubClass : MyBaseClass {}
```

The relationship between the two classes enables the programmer to make the following runtime test:

```
public class Test
{
    public static void GenericMethod(MyBaseClass mc)
    {
        // If the object truly is a subclass ...
        MySubClass msc = mc as MyBaseClass;
        if(msc != null)
        {
            // ...then handle as a subclass.
            // ... continue ...
        }
    }
}
```

In this case, the method GenericMethod() differentiates between subclasses of MyBaseClass using the as keyword.

REMEMBER

To help you differentiate between seemingly unrelated classes using the same as operator, C# extends all classes from the common base class object. That is, any class that doesn't specifically inherit from another class inherits from the class object. Thus the following two statements declare classes with the same base class — object — and are equivalent:

```
class MyClass1 : object {}
class MyClass1 {}
```

Sharing the common base class of object provides for this generic method:

```
public class Test
{
  public static void GenericMethod(object o)
  {
    MyClass1 mc1 = o as MyClass1;
    if(mc1 != null)
    {
      // Use the converted object mc1.
      // ...
    }
  }
}
```

GenericMethod() can be invoked with any type of object. The as keyword can convert o to MyClass1 from object.

Inheritance and the Constructor

The InheritanceExample program described in the "Class Inheritance" section, earlier in this chapter, relies on those awful Init...() methods to initialize the BankAccount and SavingsAccount objects to a valid state. Outfitting these classes with constructors is definitely the right way to go, but it introduces some complexity. The following sections show how to overcome the issues involved with using Init...() methods.

Invoking the default base class constructor

The default base class constructor is invoked any time a subclass is constructed. The constructor for the subclass automatically invokes the constructor for the base class, as this simple program demonstrates:

```csharp
using System;

// Inheriting A Constructor - Demonstrate that the base class
// constructor is invoked automatically.
namespace InheritingAConstructor
{
  public class Program
  {
    public static void Main(string[] args)
    {
      Console.WriteLine("Creating a BaseClass object");
      BaseClass bc = new BaseClass();

      Console.WriteLine("Now creating a SubClass object");
      SubClass sc = new SubClass();

      // Wait for user to acknowledge.
      Console.WriteLine("Press Enter to terminate...");
      Console.Read();
    }
  }

  public class BaseClass
  {
    public BaseClass()
    {
      Console.WriteLine("\tConstructing BaseClass");
    }
  }

  public class SubClass : BaseClass
  {
    public SubClass()
    {
      Console.WriteLine("\tConstructing SubClass");
    }
  }
}
```

The constructors for BaseClass and SubClass do nothing more than output a message to the command line. Creating the BaseClass object invokes the default BaseClass constructor. Creating a SubClass object invokes the BaseClass constructor before invoking its own constructor. Here's the output from this program:

```
Creating a BaseClass object
        Constructing BaseClass
Now creating a SubClass object
        Constructing BaseClass
        Constructing SubClass
Press Enter to terminate...
```

REMEMBER

A *hierarchy* of inherited classes is much like the floor layout of a building. Each class is built on the classes it extends, as upper floors build on lower ones, and for a clear reason: Each class is responsible for itself. A subclass shouldn't be held responsible for initializing the members of the base class. The BaseClass must be given the opportunity to construct its members before the SubClass members are given a chance to access them. You want the horse well out in front of the cart.

Passing arguments to the base class constructor

The subclass invokes the default constructor of the base class unless specified otherwise — even from a subclass constructor other than the default. The following slightly updated example demonstrates this feature:

```
using System;

namespace Example
{
  public class Program
  {
    public static void Main(string[] args)
    {
      Console.WriteLine("Invoking SubClass() default");
      SubClass sc1 = new SubClass();

      Console.WriteLine("\nInvoking SubClass(int)");
      SubClass sc2 = new SubClass(0);

      // Wait for user to acknowledge.
      Console.WriteLine("Press Enter to terminate...");
      Console.Read();
    }
  }
```

```
public class BaseClass
{
  public BaseClass()
  {
    Console.WriteLine("Constructing BaseClass (default)");
  }

  public BaseClass(int i)
  {
    Console.WriteLine("Constructing BaseClass (int)");
  }
}

public class SubClass : BaseClass
{
  public SubClass()
  {
    Console.WriteLine("Constructing SubClass (default)");
  }

  public SubClass(int i)
  {
    Console.WriteLine("Constructing SubClass (int)");
  }
}
```

Executing this program generates the following result:

```
Invoking SubClass()
Constructing BaseClass (default)
Constructing SubClass (default)

Invoking SubClass(int)
Constructing BaseClass (default)
Constructing SubClass (int)
Press Enter to terminate...
```

The program first creates a default object. As expected, C# invokes the default SubClass constructor, which first passes control to the default BaseClass constructor. The program then creates an object, passing an integer argument. Again as expected, C# invokes the SubClass(int). This constructor invokes the default BaseClass constructor, just as in the earlier example, because it has no data to pass.

Getting specific with base

A subclass constructor can invoke a specific base class constructor using the keyword base. This feature is similar to the way that one constructor invokes another within the same class by using the this keyword. For example, consider this small program, InvokeBaseConstructor:

```
using System;

// InvokeBaseConstructor -- Demonstrate how a subclass can
//     invoke the base class constructor of its choice using
//     the base keyword.
namespace InvokeBaseConstructor
{
  public class BaseClass
  {
    public BaseClass()
    {
      Console.WriteLine("Constructing BaseClass (default)");
    }

    public BaseClass(int i)
    {
      Console.WriteLine("Constructing BaseClass({0})", i);
    }
  }

  public class SubClass : BaseClass
  {
    public SubClass()
    {
      Console.WriteLine("Constructing SubClass (default)");
    }

    public SubClass(int i1, int i2) : base(i1)
    {
      Console.WriteLine("Constructing SubClass({0}, {1})", i1, i2);
    }
  }

  public class Program
  {
    public static void Main(string[] args)
    {
      Console.WriteLine("Invoking SubClass()");
      SubClass sc1 = new SubClass();
```

```
      Console.WriteLine("\ninvoking SubClass(1, 2)");
      SubClass sc2 = new SubClass(1, 2);

      // Wait for user to acknowledge.
      Console.WriteLine("Press Enter to terminate...");
      Console.Read();
    }
  }
}
```

The output from this program is

```
Invoking SubClass()
Constructing BaseClass (default)
Constructing SubClass (default)

Invoking SubClass(1, 2)
Constructing BaseClass(1)
Constructing SubClass(1, 2)
Press Enter to terminate...
```

This version begins the same as the previous examples do by creating a default SubClass object using the default constructor of both BaseClass and SubClass.

The second object is created with the expression new SubClass(1, 2). C# invokes the SubClass(int, int) constructor, which uses the base keyword to pass one of the values to the BaseClass(int) constructor. SubClass passes the first argument to the base class for processing and then uses the second value itself.

The Updated BankAccount Class

The program ConstructorSavingsAccount is an updated version of the SimpleBankAccount program. In this version, however, the SavingsAccount constructor can pass information back to the BankAccount constructors. Only Main() and the constructors themselves are shown here:

```
using System;

// ConstructorSavingsAccount -- Implement a SavingsAccount as
//     a form of BankAccount; use no virtual methods, but
//     implement the constructors properly.
namespace ConstructorSavingsAccount
{
```

```
// BankAccount -- Simulate a bank account, each of which carries an
//      account ID (which is assigned upon creation) and a balance.
public class BankAccount
{
  // Bank accounts start at 1000 and increase sequentially.
  public static int _nextAccountNumber = 1000;

  // Maintain the account number and balance for each object.
  public int _accountNumber;
  public decimal _balance;

  // Constructors
  public BankAccount() : this(0)
  {
  }

  public BankAccount(decimal initialBalance)
  {
    _accountNumber = ++_nextAccountNumber;
    _balance = initialBalance;
  }

  public decimal Balance
  {
    get { return _balance; }
    // Protected setter lets subclass use Balance property to set.
    protected set { _balance = value; }
  }

  // Deposit -- Any positive deposit is allowed.
  public void Deposit(decimal amount)
  {
    if (amount > 0)
    {
      Balance += amount;
    }
  }

  // Withdraw -- You can withdraw any amount up to the
  //      balance; return the amount withdrawn.
  public decimal Withdraw(decimal withdrawal)
  {
    if (Balance <= withdrawal)
    {
      withdrawal = Balance;
    }
```

```csharp
      Balance -= withdrawal;
      return withdrawal;
    }

    // ToString -- Stringify the account.
    public string ToBankAccountString()
    {
      return String.Format("{0} - {1:C}",
        _accountNumber, Balance);
    }
  }


// SavingsAccount -- A bank account that draws interest
public class SavingsAccount : BankAccount
{
  public decimal _interestRate;
  // InitSavingsAccount -- Input the rate expressed as a
  //   rate between 0 and 100.
  public SavingsAccount(decimal interestRate) : this(interestRate, 0)
  { }
  public SavingsAccount(decimal interestRate, decimal initial) :
                        base(initial)
  {
    this._interestRate = interestRate / 100;
  }

  // AccumulateInterest -- Invoke once per period.
  public void AccumulateInterest()
  {
    // Use protected setter and public getter via Balance property.
    Balance = Balance + (decimal)(Balance * _interestRate);
  }

  // ToString -- Stringify the account.
  public string ToSavingsAccountString()
  {
    return String.Format("{0} ({1}%)",
      ToBankAccountString(), _interestRate * 100);
  }
}

public class Program
{
  // DirectDeposit -- Deposit my paycheck automatically.
  public static void DirectDeposit(BankAccount ba, decimal pay)
  {
    ba.Deposit(pay);
  }
```

```
    public static void Main(string[] args)
    {
        // Create a bank account and display it.
        BankAccount ba = new BankAccount(100M);
        DirectDeposit(ba, 100M);
        Console.WriteLine("Account {0}", ba.ToBankAccountString());

        // Now a savings account
        SavingsAccount sa = new SavingsAccount(12.5M);
        DirectDeposit(sa, 100M);
        sa.AccumulateInterest();
        Console.WriteLine("Account {0}", sa.ToSavingsAccountString());

        // Wait for user to acknowledge the results.
        Console.WriteLine("Press Enter to terminate...");
        Console.Read();
    }
  }
}
```

BankAccount defines two constructors: one that accepts an initial account balance and the default constructor, which does not. To avoid duplicating code within the constructor, the default constructor invokes the BankAccount(initial balance) constructor using the this keyword.

The SavingsAccount class also provides two constructors. The SavingsAccount (interest rate) constructor invokes the SavingsAccount(interest rate, initial balance) constructor, passing an initial balance of 0. This most general constructor passes the initial balance to the BankAccount(initial balance) constructor using the base keyword, as shown in Figure 6-1.

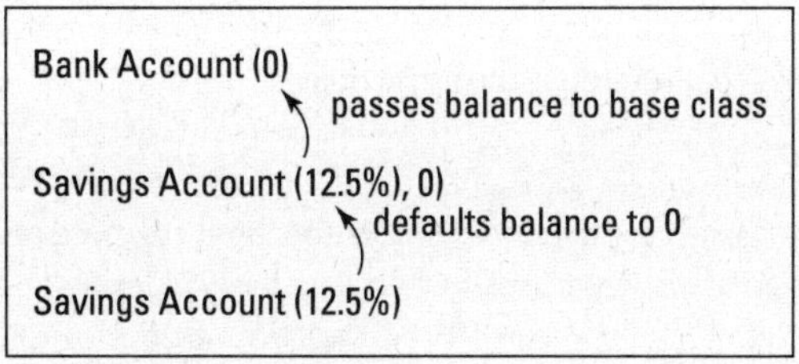

FIGURE 6-1:
The path for
constructing an
object using
the default
constructor.

Bank Account (0)
    ↖ passes balance to base class

Savings Account (12.5%), 0)
    ↖ defaults balance to 0

Savings Account (12.5%)

The example modifies Main() to get rid of the Init...() methods and replace them with constructors instead. The output from this program is the same.

TIP

Notice the `Balance` property in `BankAccount`, which has a `public` getter but a `protected` setter. Using `protected` here prevents use from outside of `BankAccount` but permits using the `protected` setter in subclasses, which occurs in `SavingsAccount.AccumulateInterest`, with `Balance` on the left side of the assignment operator. (Properties and the `protected` keyword appear in Chapter 5 in Book 2.)

GARBAGE COLLECTION AND THE C# DESTRUCTOR

C# provides a method that's inverse to the constructor: the *destructor*. It carries the name of the class with a tilde (~) in front. For example, the `~BaseClass()` method is the destructor for `BaseClass`.

C# invokes the destructor when it is no longer using the object. The default destructor is the only destructor that can be created because the destructor cannot be invoked directly. In addition, the destructor is always virtual.

When an inheritance ladder of classes is involved, destructors are invoked in reverse order of constructors. That is, the destructor for the subclass is invoked before the destructor for the base class.

The destructor method in C# is much less useful than it is in other object-oriented languages, such as C++, because C# has *nondeterministic destruction*. Understanding what that term means — and why it's important — requires some explanation.

The memory for an object is borrowed from the heap when the program executes the `new` command, as in `new SubClass()`. This block of memory remains reserved as long as any valid references to that memory are used by any running programs. You may have several variables that reference the same object.

The memory is said to be *unreachable* when the last reference goes out of scope. In other words, no one can access that block of memory after no more references to it exist. C# doesn't do anything in particular when a memory block first becomes unreachable. A low-priority system task executes in the background, looking for unreachable memory blocks. To avoid negatively affecting program performance, this garbage collector executes when little is happening in your program. As the garbage collector finds unreachable memory blocks, it returns them to the heap.

Normally, the garbage collector operates silently in the background. The garbage collector takes over control of the program for only a short period when heap memory begins to run out.

The C# destructor — for example, ~BaseClass( ) — is nondeterministic because it isn't invoked until the object is garbage-collected, and that task can occur long after the object is no longer being used. In fact, if the program terminates before the object is found and returned to the heap, the destructor is never invoked. *Nondeterministic* means you can't predict when the object will be garbage-collected. It could be quite a while before the object is garbage-collected and its destructor called.

C# programmers seldom use the destructor. C# has other ways to return borrowed system resources when they're no longer needed, using a Dispose( ) method, a topic that's beyond the scope of this book. (You can search for the term *Dispose method* in C# Language Help.)

Chapter **7**

Poly-what-ism?

I n inheritance, one class adopts the members of another. Thus it's possible to create a class SavingsAccount that inherits data members, such as account id, and methods, such as Deposit(), from a base class BankAccount. That's useful, but this definition of inheritance isn't sufficient to mimic what's going on out there in the business world. (See Chapter 6 of this minibook if you don't know or remember much about class inheritance.)

A microwave oven is a type of oven, not because it looks like an oven, but rather because it performs the same functions as an oven. A microwave oven may perform additional functions, but it performs, at the least, the base oven functions, such as heating food. It's not important to know what the oven must do internally to make that happen, any more than it's important to know what type of oven it is, who made it, or whether it was on sale when purchased.

From a human vantage point, the relationship between a microwave oven and a conventional oven doesn't seem like such a big deal, but consider the problem from the oven's point of view. The steps that a conventional oven performs internally are completely different from those that a microwave oven may take.

REMEMBER

The power of inheritance lies in the fact that a subclass doesn't *have* to inherit every single method from the base class just the way it's written. A subclass can inherit the essence of the base class method while implementing the details differently.

Overloading an Inherited Method

As described in Chapter 3 of this minibook (look up *overloading* in C# Language Help), two or more methods can have the same name as long as the number or type of arguments differs (or as long as both differ).

It's a simple case of method overloading

REMEMBER

Giving two methods the same name is *overloading*. The arguments of a method become a part of its extended name, as this example demonstrates:

```csharp
public class MyClass
{
  public static void AMethod()
  {
    // Do something.
  }

  public static void AMethod(int)
  {
    // Do something else.
  }

  public static void AMethod(double d)
  {
    // Do something even different.
  }

  public static void Main(string[] args)
  {
    AMethod();
    AMethod(1);
    AMethod(2.0);
  }
}
```

C# can differentiate the methods by their arguments. Each of the calls within Main() accesses a different method.

REMEMBER

The return type isn't part of the extended name. You can't have two methods that differ only in their return types.

Different class, different method

Not surprisingly, the class to which a method belongs is also a part of its extended name. Consider this code segment:

```
public class MyClass
{
  public static void AMethod1();
  public void AMethod2();
}

public class UrClass
{
  public static void AMethod1();
  public void AMethod2();
}

public class Program
{
  public static void Main(string[] args)
  {
    UrClass.AMethod1();  // Call static method.

    // Invoke the MyClass.AMethod2() instance method:
    MyClass mcObject = new MyClass();
    mcObject.AMethod2();
  }
}
```

The name of the class is a part of the extended name of the method. The method `MyClass.AMethod1()` has nothing to do with `UrClass.AMethod1()`.

Peek-a-boo — hiding a base class method

So a method in one class can overload another method in its own class by having different arguments. As it turns out, a method can also overload a method in its own base class. Overloading a base class method is known as *hiding* the method.

Suppose that your bank adopts a policy that makes savings account withdrawals different from other types of withdrawals. Suppose, just for the sake of argument, that withdrawing from a savings account costs $1.50.

Taking the procedural approach, you could implement this policy by setting a flag (variable) in the class to indicate whether the object is a `SavingsAccount` or just a simple BankAccount. Then the withdrawal method would have to check the flag to decide whether it needs to charge $1.50, as shown here:

```csharp
public class BankAccount
{
  private decimal _balance;
  private bool _isSavingsAccount;  // The flag

  // Indicate the initial balance and whether the account
  // you're creating is a savings account.
  public BankAccount(decimal initialBalance, bool isSavingsAccount)
  {
    _balance = initialBalance;
    _isSavingsAccount = isSavingsAccount;
  }

  public decimal Withdraw(decimal amountToWithdraw)
  {
    // If the account is a savings account ...
    if (_isSavingsAccount)
    {
      // ...then skim off $1.50.
      _balance -= 1.50M;
    }

    // Continue with the usual withdraw code:
    if (amountToWithdraw > _balance)
    {
      amountToWithdraw = _balance;
    }

    _balance -= amountToWithdraw;
    return amountToWithdraw;
  }
}

class MyClass
{
  public void SomeMethod()
  {
    // I want to create a savings account:
    BankAccount ba = new BankAccount(0, true);
  }
}
```

Your method must tell the BankAccount whether it's a SavingsAccount in the constructor by passing a flag. The constructor saves that flag and uses it in the Withdraw() method to decide whether to charge the extra $1.50.

The more object-oriented approach hides the method `Withdraw()` in the base class `BankAccount` with a new method of the same name in the `SavingsAccount` class:

```
using System;

// HidingWithdrawal -- Hide the withdraw method in the base
//    class with a method in the subclass of the same name.
namespace HidingWithdrawal
{
  // BankAccount -- A very basic bank account
  public class BankAccount
  {
    protected decimal _balance;
    public BankAccount(decimal initialBalance)
    {
      _balance = initialBalance;
    }

    public decimal Balance
    {
      get { return _balance; }
    }

    public decimal Withdraw(decimal amount)
    {
      // Good practice means avoiding modifying an input parameter.
      // Modify a copy.
      decimal amountToWithdraw = amount;

      if (amountToWithdraw > Balance)
      {
        amountToWithdraw = Balance;
      }

      _balance -= amountToWithdraw;
      return amountToWithdraw;
    }
  }

  // SavingsAccount -- A bank account that draws interest
  public class SavingsAccount : BankAccount
  {
    public decimal _interestRate;

    // SavingsAccount -- Input the rate expressed as a
    //    rate between 0 and 100.
    public SavingsAccount(decimal initialBalance, decimal interestRate)
      : base(initialBalance)
```

```
    {
      _interestRate = interestRate / 100;
    }

    // AccumulateInterest -- Invoke once per period.
    public void AccumulateInterest()
    {
      _balance = Balance + (Balance * _interestRate);
    }

    // Withdraw -- You can withdraw any amount up to the
    //    balance; return the amount withdrawn.
    public decimal Withdraw(decimal withdrawal)
    {
      // Take the $1.50 off the top.
      base.Withdraw(1.5M);

      // Now you can withdraw from what's left.
      return base.Withdraw(withdrawal);
    }
  }
}
public class Program
{
  public static void Main(string[] args)
  {
    BankAccount ba;
    SavingsAccount sa;

    // Create a bank account, withdraw $100, and
    // display the results.
    ba = new BankAccount(200M);
    ba.Withdraw(100M);

    // Try the same trick with a savings account.
    sa = new SavingsAccount(200M, 12);
    sa.Withdraw(100M);
    // Display the resulting balance.
    Console.WriteLine("When invoked directly:");
    Console.WriteLine("BankAccount balance is {0:C}", ba.Balance);
    Console.WriteLine("SavingsAccount balance is {0:C}", sa.Balance);

    // Wait for user to acknowledge the results.
    Console.WriteLine("Press Enter to terminate...");
    Console.Read();
  }
}
}
```

`Main()` in this case creates a `BankAccount` object with an initial balance of $200 and then withdraws $100. `Main()` repeats the trick with a `SavingsAccount` object. When `Main()` withdraws money from the base class, `BankAccount.Withdraw()` performs the withdraw function with great aplomb. When `Main()` then withdraws $100 from the savings account, the method `SavingsAccount.Withdraw()` tacks on the extra $1.50.

TIP

Notice that the `SavingsAccount.Withdraw()` method uses `BankAccount.Withdraw()` rather than manipulate the balance directly. If possible, let the base class maintain its own data members.

Making the hiding approach better than adding a simple test

On the surface, adding a flag to the `BankAccount.Withdraw()` method may seem simpler than all this method-hiding stuff. After all, it's just four little lines of code, two of which are nothing more than braces.

The problems are manifold. One problem is that the `BankAccount` class has no business worrying about the details of `SavingsAccount`. More formally, it's known as "breaking the encapsulation of `SavingsAccount`." Base classes don't normally know about their subclasses, which leads to the real problem: Suppose that your bank subsequently decides to add a `CheckingAccount` or a `CDAccount` or a `TBillAccount`. All those likely additions have different withdrawal policies, each requiring its own flag. After adding three or four different types of accounts, the old `Withdraw()` method starts looking complicated. Each of those types of classes should worry about its own withdrawal policies and leave `BankAccount.Withdraw()` alone. Classes are responsible for themselves.

Accidentally hiding a base class method

Oddly enough, you can hide a base class method accidentally. For example, you may have a `Vehicle.TakeOff()` method that starts the vehicle rolling. Later, someone else extends your `Vehicle` class with an `Airplane` class. Its `TakeOff()` method is entirely different. In airplane lingo, "take off" means more than just "start moving." Clearly, this is a case of mistaken identity — the two methods have no similarity other than their identical name. Fortunately, C# detects this problem.

C# generates an ominous-looking warning when it compiles the earlier `HidingWithdrawal` program example. The text of the warning message is long, but here's the important part:

```
'...SavingsAccount.Withdraw(decimal)' hides inherited member
  '...BankAccount.Withdraw(decimal)'.
  Use the new keyword if hiding was intended.
```

C# is trying to tell you that you've written a method in a subclass that has the same name as a method in the base class. Is that what you meant to do?

TIP

This message is just a warning — you don't even notice it unless you switch over to the Error List window to take a look. But you must sort out and fix all warnings. In almost every case, a warning is telling you about something that can bite you if you don't fix it.

The descriptor new, shown in the following sample code, tells C# that the hiding of methods is intentional and not the result of an oversight (and it makes the warning disappear):

```
// No withdraw() pains now.
new public decimal Withdraw(decimal withdrawal)
{
   // ... no change internally ...
}
```

TIP

This use of the keyword new has nothing to do with the same word new that's used to create an object. (C# even overloads itself!)

Calling back to base

Check out the SavingsAccount.Withdraw() method in the HidingWithdrawal example, shown earlier in this chapter. The call to BankAccount.Withdraw() from within this new method includes the new keyword base. The following version of the method without the base keyword doesn't work:

```
new public decimal Withdraw(decimal withdrawal)
{
  decimal amountWithdrawn = Withdraw(withdrawal);
  amountWithdrawn += Withdraw(1.5);
  return amountWithdrawn;
}
```

The preceding call has the same problem as this one:

```
void fn()
{
  fn(); // Call yourself.
}
```

The call to fn() from within fn() ends up calling itself (*recursing*) repeatedly. Similarly, a call to Withdraw() from within the method calls itself in a loop, chasing its tail until the program eventually crashes.

Somehow, you need to indicate to C# that the call from within SavingsAccount.Withdraw() is meant to invoke the base class BankAccount.Withdraw() method. One approach is to cast the this reference into an object of class BankAccount before making the call:

```
// Withdraw -- This version accesses the hidden method in the base
//     class by explicitly recasting the this object.
new public decimal Withdraw(decimal withdrawal)
{
  // Cast the this reference into an object of class BankAccount.
  BankAccount ba = (BankAccount)this;

  // Invoking Withdraw() using this BankAccount object
  // calls the method BankAccount.Withdraw().
  decimal amountWithdrawn = ba.Withdraw(withdrawal);
  amountWithdrawn += ba.Withdraw(1.5);
  return amountWithdrawn;
}
```

This solution works: The call ba.Withdraw() now invokes the BankAccount method, just as intended. The problem with this approach is the explicit reference to BankAccount. A future change to the program may rearrange the inheritance hierarchy so that SavingsAccount no longer inherits directly from BankAccount. This type of rearrangement breaks this method in a way that future programmers may not easily find.

You need a way to tell C# to call the `Withdraw()` method from the class immediately above in the hierarchy without naming it explicitly. That would be the class that `SavingsAccount` extends. C# provides the keyword `base` for this purpose.

This keyword `base` is the same one that a constructor uses to pass arguments to its base class constructor. The C# keyword `base`, shown in the following chunk of code, is similar to `this`, but is automatically recast to the base class no matter what that class may be:

```
// Withdraw -- You can withdraw any amount up to the
//    balance; return the amount withdrawn.
new public decimal Withdraw(decimal withdrawal)
{
  // Take the $1.50 off the top.
  base.Withdraw(1.5M);

  // Now you can withdraw from what's left.
  return base.Withdraw(withdrawal);
}
```

The call `base.Withdraw()` now invokes the `BankAccount.Withdraw()` method, thereby avoiding the recursive "invoking itself" problem. In addition, this solution doesn't break if the inheritance hierarchy is changed.

Polymorphism

You can overload a method in a base class with a method in the subclass. As simple as this process sounds, it introduces considerable capability, and with capability comes danger.

Here's a thought experiment: Should you make the decision to call `BankAccount.Withdraw()` or `SavingsAccount.Withdraw()` at compile-time or at runtime? To illustrate the difference, the following example changes the previous `Hiding Withdrawal` program in a seemingly innocuous way. (The `HidingWithdrawal Polymorphically` version streamlines the listing by leaving out the stuff that doesn't change.) The new version is shown here:

```
// HidingWithdrawalPolymorphically -- Hide the Withdraw() method in the
//    base class with a method in the subclass of the same name.
public class Program
{
  public static void MakeAWithdrawal(BankAccount ba, decimal amount)
```

```
  {
    ba.Withdraw(amount);
  }

  public static void Main(string[] args)
  {
    BankAccount ba;
    SavingsAccount sa;

    // Create a bank account, withdraw $100, and
    // display the results.
    ba = new BankAccount(200M);
    MakeAWithdrawal(ba, 100M);

    // Try the same trick with a savings account.
    sa = new SavingsAccount(200M, 12);
    MakeAWithdrawal(sa, 100M);

    // Display the resulting balance.
    Console.WriteLine("When invoked through intermediary:");
    Console.WriteLine("BankAccount balance is {0:C}", ba.Balance);
    Console.WriteLine("SavingsAccount balance is {0:C}", sa.Balance);

    // Wait for user to acknowledge the results.
    Console.WriteLine("Press Enter to terminate...");
    Console.Read();
  }
}
```

The following output from this program may or may not be confusing, depending on what you expected:

```
When invoked through intermediary
BankAccount balance is $100.00
SavingsAccount balance is $100.00
Press Enter to terminate...
```

This time, rather than perform a withdrawal in Main(), the program passes the bank account object to the method MakeAWithdrawal().

The first question is fairly straightforward: Why does the MakeAWithdrawal() method even accept a SavingsAccount object when it clearly states that it's looking for a BankAccount? The answer is obvious: "Because a SavingsAccount IS_A BankAccount." (See Chapter 6 of this minibook.)

The second question is subtle. When passed a BankAccount object, MakeAWithdrawal() invokes BankAccount.Withdraw() — that's clear enough. But when passed a `SavingsAccount` object, `MakeAWithdrawal()` calls the same method. Shouldn't it invoke the `Withdraw()` method in the subclass?

The prosecution intends to show that the call `ba.Withdraw()` should invoke the method `BankAccount.Withdraw()`. Clearly, the `ba` object is a `BankAccount`. To do anything else would merely confuse the state. The defense has witnesses back in `Main()` to prove that although the `ba` object is declared `BankAccount`, it is in fact a `SavingsAccount`. The jury is deadlocked. Both arguments are equally valid.

In this case, C# comes down on the side of the prosecution: The safer of the two possibilities is to go with the declared type because it avoids any miscommunication. The object is declared to be a `BankAccount` and that's that. However, that may not be what you want.

Using the declared type every time (Is that so wrong?)

In some cases, you don't want to choose the declared type. What you want is to make the call based on the *real type* — the runtime type — as opposed to the declared type. For example, you want to use the `SavingsAccount` stored in a `BankAccount` variable. This capability to *decide at runtime* is known as *polymorphism*, or *late binding*. Using the declared type every time is called *early binding* because it sounds like the opposite of *late binding.*

The term *polymorphism* comes from the Greek language: *Poly* means more than one, *morph* means transform, and *ism* relates to an ideology or philosophy. Consequently, polymorphism is the idea or concept of transforming a single object, `BankAccount`, into many different objects, `BankAccount` or `SavingsAccount` (in this case). Polymorphism and late binding aren't exactly the same concept — but the difference is subtle:

>> *Polymorphism* refers to the general ability to decide which method to invoke at runtime.

>> *Late binding* refers to the specific way a language implements polymorphism.

Polymorphism is the key to the power of object-oriented (OO) programming. It's so important that languages that don't support it can't advertise themselves as OO languages.

Languages that support classes but not polymorphism are *object-based languages.* Visual Basic 6.0 (not VB.NET) is an example of such a language.

Without polymorphism, inheritance has little meaning. As another example, suppose that you had written a great program that uses a class named Student. After months of design, coding, and testing, you release this application to rave reviews from colleagues and critics alike.

Time passes, and your boss asks you to add to this program the capability of handling graduate students, who are similar but not identical to undergraduate students. (The graduate students probably claim that they aren't similar in any way.) Suppose that the formula for calculating the tuition amount for a graduate student is completely different from the formula for an undergrad. Now, your boss doesn't know or care that, deep within the program, are numerous calls to the member method CalcTuition(). The following example shows one of those many calls to CalcTuition():

```
void SomeMethod(Student s)  // Could be grad or undergrad
{
  // ... whatever it might do ...
  s.CalcTuition();
  // ... continues on ...
}
```

If C# didn't support late binding, you would need to edit someMethod() to check whether the student object passed to it is a GraduateStudent or a Student. The program would call Student.CalcTuition() when s is a Student and GraduateStudent.CalcTuition() when it's a GraduateStudent. Editing someMethod() doesn't seem so bad, except for two problems:

>> You're assuming use by only one method. Suppose that CalcTuition() is called from many places.

>> CalcTuition() might not be the only difference between the two classes. The chances aren't good that you'll find all items that need to be changed.

Using polymorphism, you can let C# decide which method to call.

Using is to access a hidden method polymorphically

C# provides one approach to manually solving the problem of making your program polymorphic, using the keyword is. (Chapter 6 of this minibook introduces is, and its cousin as.) The expression ba is SavingsAccount returns true or false depending on the runtime class of the object. The declared type may be

BankAccount, but which type is it really? The following code chunk uses is to access the SavingsAccount version of Withdraw() specifically:

```csharp
public class Program
{
  public static void MakeAWithdrawal(BankAccount ba, decimal amount)
  {
    if(ba is SavingsAccount)
    {
      SavingsAccount sa = (SavingsAccount)ba;
      sa.Withdraw(amount);
    }
    else
    {
      ba.Withdraw(amount);
    }
  }
}
```

Now, when Main() passes the method a SavingsAccount object, MakeA Withdrawal() checks the runtime type of the ba object and invokes Savings Account.Withdraw().

As an alternative, the programmer could have performed the cast and the call for a SavingsAccount in the following single line:

```csharp
((SavingsAccount)ba).Withdraw(amount);   // Notice locations of parentheses.
```

You often see this technique used in programs written by experienced developers who hate typing any more than necessary. Although you can use this approach, it's more difficult to read than when you use multiple lines, as shown in the example code. Anything written confusingly or cryptically tends to be more error-prone, too.

The is approach works, but it's a bad idea. It requires MakeAWithdrawal() to be aware of all the different types of bank accounts and which of them is represented by different classes. That puts too much responsibility on poor old MakeA Withdrawal(). Right now, your application handles only two types of bank accounts, but suppose that your boss asks you to implement a new account type, CheckingAccount, and it has different Withdraw() requirements. Your program doesn't work properly if you don't search out and find every method that checks the runtime type of its argument.

Declaring a method virtual and overriding it

As the author of `MakeAWithdrawal()`, you don't want to know about all the different types of accounts. You want to leave to the programmers who use `MakeAWithdrawal()` the responsibility to know about their account types and just leave you alone. You want C# to make decisions about which methods to invoke based on the runtime type of the object.

You tell C# to make the runtime decision of the version of `Withdraw()` by marking the base class method with the keyword `virtual` and marking each subclass version of the method with the keyword `override`.

The following example relies on polymorphism. It has output statements in the `Withdraw()` methods to prove that the proper methods are indeed being invoked. Here's the `PolymorphicInheritance` program:

```
using System;

// PolymorphicInheritance -- Hide a method in the
//    base class polymorphically. Show how to use
//    the virtual and override keywords.
namespace PolymorphicInheritance
{
  // BankAccount -- A basic bank account
  public class BankAccount
  {
    protected decimal _balance;

    public BankAccount(decimal initialBalance)
    {
      _balance = initialBalance;
    }

    public decimal Balance
    {
      get { return _balance; }
    }

    public virtual decimal Withdraw(decimal amount)
    {
      Console.WriteLine("In BankAccount.Withdraw() for ${0}...", amount);
      decimal amountToWithdraw = amount;
      if (amountToWithdraw > Balance)
```

```
      {
        amountToWithdraw = Balance;
      }
      _balance -= amountToWithdraw;
      return amountToWithdraw;
  }
}
// SavingsAccount -- A bank account that draws interest
public class SavingsAccount : BankAccount
{
  public decimal _interestRate;

  // SavingsAccount -- Input the rate expressed as a
  //    rate between 0 and 100.
  public SavingsAccount(decimal initialBalance, decimal interestRate)
                         : base(initialBalance)
  {
    _interestRate = interestRate / 100;
  }

  // AccumulateInterest -- Invoke once per period.
  public void AccumulateInterest()
  {
    _balance = Balance + (Balance * _interestRate);
  }

  // Withdraw -- You can withdraw any amount up to the
  //    balance; return the amount withdrawn.
  override public decimal Withdraw(decimal withdrawal)
  {
    Console.WriteLine("In SavingsAccount.Withdraw()...");
    Console.WriteLine("Invoking base-class Withdraw twice...");

    // Take the $1.50 off the top.
    base.Withdraw(1.5M);

    // Now you can withdraw from what's left.
    return base.Withdraw(withdrawal);
  }
}

public class Program
{
  public static void MakeAWithdrawal(BankAccount ba, decimal amount)
  {
    ba.Withdraw(amount);
  }
```

```
    public static void Main(string[] args)
    {
      BankAccount ba;
      SavingsAccount sa;

      // Display the resulting balance.
      Console.WriteLine("Withdrawal: MakeAWithdrawal(ba, ...)");
      ba = new BankAccount(200M);
      MakeAWithdrawal(ba, 100M);
      Console.WriteLine("BankAccount balance is {0:C}", ba.Balance);
      Console.WriteLine("Withdrawal: MakeAWithdrawal(sa, ...)");

      sa = new SavingsAccount(200M, 12);
      MakeAWithdrawal(sa, 100M);
      Console.WriteLine("SavingsAccount balance is {0:C}", sa.Balance);

      // Wait for user to acknowledge the results.
      Console.WriteLine("Press Enter to terminate...");
      Console.Read();
    }
  }
}
```

The output from executing this program is shown here:

```
Withdrawal: MakeAWithdrawal(ba, ...)
In BankAccount.Withdraw() for $100...
BankAccount balance is $100.00
Withdrawal: MakeAWithdrawal(sa, ...)
In SavingsAccount.Withdraw()...
Invoking base-class Withdraw twice...
In BankAccount.Withdraw() for $1.5...
In BankAccount.Withdraw() for $100...
SavingsAccount balance is $98.50
Press Enter to terminate...
```

REMEMBER

The Withdraw() method is flagged as virtual in the base class BankAccount, and the Withdraw() method in the subclass is flagged with the keyword override. The MakeAWithdrawal() method is unchanged, yet the output of the program is different because the call ba.Withdraw() is resolved based on the ba runtime type.

TIP

Choose sparingly which methods to make virtual. Each one has a cost, so use the virtual keyword only when necessary. It's a trade-off between a class that's highly flexible and can be overridden (lots of virtual methods) and a class that isn't flexible enough (hardly any virtuals).

Getting the most benefit from polymorphism

Much of the power of polymorphism springs from polymorphic objects sharing a common interface. For example, given a hierarchy of Shape objects — Circles, Squares, and Triangles, for example — you can count on all shapes having a Draw() method. Each object's Draw() method is implemented quite differently, of course. But the point is that, given a collection of these objects, you can freely use a foreach loop to call Draw() or any other method in the polymorphic interface on the objects.

The Class Business Card: ToString()

All classes inherit from a common base class that carries the clever name Object. However, it's worth mentioning here that Object includes a method, ToString(), that converts the contents of the object into a string. The idea is that each class should override the ToString() method to display itself in a meaningful way. The examples up to this point use the GetString() method to avoid discussing inheritance issues (see Chapter 6 of this minibook). After you understand inheritance, the virtual keyword, and overriding, you can describe ToString(). By overriding ToString() for each class, you give each class the ability to display itself in its own way. For example, a useful, appropriate Student.ToString() method may display the student's name and ID.

Most methods — even those built into the C# library — use the ToString() method to display objects. Thus, overriding ToString() has the useful side effect of displaying the object in its own, unique format, no matter who does the displaying.

C# During Its Abstract Period

A duck is a type of bird. So are the cardinal and the hummingbird. In fact, every bird out there is a subtype of bird. The flip side of that argument is that no bird exists that *isn't* a subtype of Bird. That statement doesn't *sound* profound, but in a way, it is. The software equivalent of that statement is that all bird objects are instances of the Bird subclasses — there's never an instance of class Bird. What's a bird? It's always a robin or a grackle or another specific species.

Different types of birds share many properties (otherwise, they wouldn't be birds), yet no two types share every property. If they did, they wouldn't be different types. For example, not all birds Fly() the same way. Ducks have one style, cardinals another. The hummingbird's style is completely different. But if not all birds fly the same way and there's no such thing as an instance of a generic Bird, what the heck is Bird.Fly()? The Bird.Fly() method would need to be different for each subclass of Bird. The following sections discuss this issue in detail.

Class factoring

People generate taxonomies of objects by factoring out commonalities. To see how factoring works, consider the two classes HighSchool and University, shown in Figure 7-1. This figure uses the Unified Modeling Language (UML), a graphical language that describes a class along with the relationship of that class to others. UML has become universally popular with programmers and is worth learning (to a reasonable extent) in its own right.

FIGURE 7-1:
A UML
description of
the HighSchool
and University
classes.

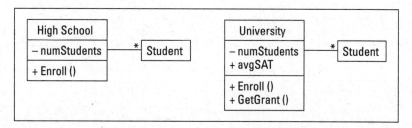

High schools and universities have several similar properties — many more than you may think (refer to Figure 7-1). Both schools offer a publicly available Enroll() method for adding Student objects to the school. In addition, both classes offer a private member, numStudents, which indicates the number of students attending the school. Another common feature is the relationship between students: One school can have any number of students — a student can attend only a single school at one time. Even high schools and most universities offer more than described, but only one of each type of member is needed for illustration.

In addition to the features of a high school, the university contains a method GetGrant() and a data member avgSAT. High schools have no SAT entrance requirements and receive no federal grants.

UML LITE

The Unified Modeling Language (UML) is an expressive language that's capable of clearly defining the relationships of objects within a program. One advantage of UML is that you can ignore the more specific language features without losing its meaning entirely. The essential features of UML are

- Classes are represented by a box divided vertically into three sections. The name of the class appears in the uppermost section.

- The data members of the class appear in the middle section, and the methods of the class in the bottom. You can omit either the middle or bottom section if the class has no data members or methods or if you want just a high-level classes-only view.

- Members with a plus sign (+) in front are public; those with a minus sign (–) are private. To provide protected and internal visibility, most people use the pound sign (#) and the tilde (~), respectively.

  A private member is accessible only from other members of the same class. A public member is accessible to all classes. See Chapter 5 in this minibook.

- The label {abstract} next to a name indicates an abstract class or method.

  UML uses a different symbol for an abstract method, but doing so isn't essential. You can also just show abstract items in italics.

- An arrow between two classes represents a relationship between the two classes. A number above the line expresses cardinality — the number of items you can have at each end of the arrow. The asterisk symbol (*) means *any number*. If no number is present, the cardinality is assumed to be 1. Thus you can see that a single university has any number of students — a one-to-many relationship (refer to Figure 7-1).

- A line with a large, open arrowhead, or a triangular arrowhead, expresses the IS_A relationship (inheritance). The arrow points *up* the class hierarchy to the base class. Other types of relationships include the HAS_A relationship (a line with a filled diamond at the owning end).

To explore UML in depth, check out *UML 2 For Dummies,* by Michael Jesse Chonoles and James A. Schardt (Wiley).

Figure 7-1 is acceptable, as far as it goes, but lots of information is duplicated, and duplication in code (and UML diagrams) stinks. You can reduce the duplication by allowing the more complex class University to inherit from the simpler HighSchool class, as shown in Figure 7-2.

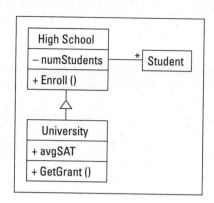

FIGURE 7-2:
Inheriting
HighSchool
simplifies the
University class
but introduces
problems.

The HighSchool class is left unchanged, but the University class is easier to describe. You say that "a University is a HighSchool that also has an avgSAT and a GetGrant() method." But this solution has a fundamental problem: A university isn't a high school with special properties.

You say, "So what? Inheriting works, and it saves effort." True, but the problems are more than stylistic trivialities. This type of misrepresentation is confusing to the programmer, both now and in the future. Someday, a programmer who is unfamiliar with your programming tricks will have to read and understand what your code does. Misleading representations are difficult to reconcile and understand.

In addition, this type of misrepresentation can lead to problems down the road. Suppose that the high school decides to name a "favorite" student at the prom. The clever programmer adds the NameFavorite() method to the HighSchool class, which the application invokes to name the favorite Student object.

But now you have a problem: Most universities don't name a favorite student. However, as long as University inherits from HighSchool, it inherits the NameFavorite() method. One extra method may not seem like a big deal. "Just ignore it," you say. However, one method is just one more brick in the wall of confusion. Extra methods and properties accumulate over time, until the University class is carrying lots of extra baggage. Pity the poor software developer who has to understand which methods are "real" and which aren't.

REMEMBER

Inheritances of convenience lead to another problem. The way it's written, Figure 7-2 implies that a University and a HighSchool have the same enrollment procedure. As unlikely as that statement sounds, assume that it's true. The program is developed, packaged up, and shipped off to the unwitting public. Months pass before the school district decides to modify its enrollment procedure. It isn't obvious to anyone that modifying the high school enrollment procedure also modifies the sign-up procedure at the local college.

To fix the source of the problem you must consider that a university isn't a particular type of high school. A relationship exists between the two, but neither IS_A or HAS_A are the right ones. Instead, both high schools and universities are special types of schools. That's what they have the most in common.

Figure 7-3 describes a better relationship. The newly defined class School contains the common properties of both types of schools, including the relationship they both have with Student objects. School even contains the common Enroll() method, although it's abstract because HighSchool and University usually don't implement Enroll() the same way.

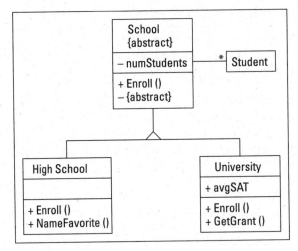

FIGURE 7-3:
Base both
HighSchool and
University on
a common
School class.

The classes HighSchool and University now inherit from a common base class. Each contains its unique members: NameFavorite() in the case of HighSchool, and GetGrant() for the University. In addition, both classes override the Enroll() method with a version that describes how that type of school enrolls students. In effect, the example extracts a superclass, or base class, from two similar classes, which now become subclasses. The introduction of the School class has at least two big advantages:

>> **It corresponds with reality.** A University is a School, but it isn't a HighSchool. Matching reality is nice but not conclusive.

>> **It isolates one class from changes or additions to the other.** Adding the CommencementSpeech() method to the University class doesn't affect HighSchool.

This process of culling common properties from similar classes is known as *factoring*. This feature of object-oriented languages is important for the reasons described earlier in this minibook, plus one more: reducing redundancy.

WARNING

Factoring is legitimate only if the inheritance relationship corresponds to reality. Factoring together a class `Mouse` and `Joystick` because they're both hardware pointing devices is legitimate. Factoring together a class `Mouse` and `Display` because they both make low-level operating-system calls is not.

Factoring can and usually does result in multiple levels of abstraction. For example, a program written for a more developed school hierarchy may have a class structure more like the one shown in Figure 7-4.

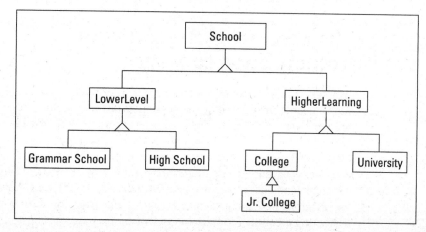

FIGURE 7-4:
Class factoring usually results in added layers of inheritance hierarchy.

You can see that Figure 7-4 inserts a pair of new classes between `University` and `School`: `HigherLearning` and `LowerLevel`. It subdivides the new class `Higher Learning` into `College` and `University`. This type of multitiered class hierarchy is common and desirable when factoring out relationships. They correspond to reality, and they can teach you subtle features of your solution.

Note, however, that no Unified Factoring Theory exists for any given set of classes. The relationship shown in Figure 7-4 seems natural, but suppose that an application cared more about differentiating types of schools administered by local politicians from those that aren't. This relationship, shown in Figure 7-5, is a more natural fit for that type of problem. No correct factoring exists: The proper way to break down the classes is partially a function of the problem being solved.

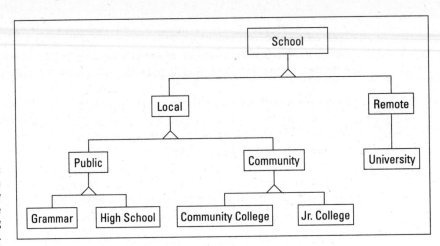

FIGURE 7-5:
Breaking down
classes is partially
a function of the
problem being
solved.

The abstract class: Left with nothing but a concept

As intellectually satisfying as factoring is, it reveals a problem of its own. Revisit BankAccount, introduced at the beginning of this chapter. Think about how you may go about defining the different member methods defined in BankAccount.

Most BankAccount member methods are no problem to refactor because both account types implement them in the same way. You should implement those common methods in BankAccount. Withdraw() is different, however. The rules for withdrawing from a savings account differ from those for withdrawing from a checking account. You have to implement SavingsAccount.Withdraw() differently from CheckingAccount.Withdraw(). But how are you supposed to implement BankAccount.Withdraw()? Ask the bank manager for help. This is the conversation that could take place:

> "What are the rules for making a withdrawal from an account?" you ask, expectantly.
>
> "Which type of account? Savings or checking?" comes the reply.
>
> "From an account," you say. "Just an account."
>
> [Blank look.] (You might say a "blank bank look." Then again, maybe not.)

The problem is that the question doesn't make sense. No such thing as "just an account" exists. All accounts (in this example) are either checking accounts or savings accounts. The concept of an account is *abstract*: It factors out properties common to the two concrete classes. It's incomplete because it lacks the critical property Withdraw(). (After you delve into the details, you may find other properties that a simple account lacks.)

How do you use an abstract class?

Abstract classes are used to describe abstract concepts. An *abstract class* is a class with one or more abstract methods. An abstract method is a method marked `abstract` and has no implementation because it has no method body. You create the method body when you subclass from the abstract class. Consider the following stripped-down demonstration program:

```
using System;

// AbstractInheritance -- The BankAccount class is abstract because
//     there is no single implementation for Withdraw.
namespace AbstractInheritance
{
  // AbstractBaseClass -- Create an abstract base class with nothing
  //     but an Output() method. You can also say "public abstract."
  abstract public class AbstractBaseClass
  {
    // Output -- Abstract method that outputs a string
    abstract public void Output(string outputString);
  }

  // SubClass1 -- One concrete implementation of AbstractBaseClass
  public class SubClass1 : AbstractBaseClass
  {
    override public void Output(string source) // Or "public override"
    {
      string s = source.ToUpper();
      Console.WriteLine("Call to SubClass1.Output() from within {0}", s);
    }
  }

  // SubClass2 -- Another concrete implementation of AbstractBaseClass
  public class SubClass2 : AbstractBaseClass
  {
    public override void Output(string source)  // Or "override public"
    {
      string s = source.ToLower();
      Console.WriteLine("Call to SubClass2.Output() from within {0}", s);
    }
  }

  class Program
  {
    public static void Test(AbstractBaseClass ba)
    {
      ba.Output("Test");
    }
```

```
  public static void Main(string[] strings)
  {
    // You can't create an AbstractBaseClass object because it's
    // abstract. C# generates a compile-time error if you
    // uncomment the following line.
    // AbstractBaseClass ba = new AbstractBaseClass();

    // Now repeat the experiment with Subclass1.
    Console.WriteLine("\ncreating a SubClass1 object");
    SubClass1 sc1 = new SubClass1();
    Test(sc1);

    // And, finally, a Subclass2 object
    Console.WriteLine("\ncreating a SubClass2 object");
    SubClass2 sc2 = new SubClass2();
    Test(sc2);

    // Wait for user to acknowledge.
    Console.WriteLine("Press Enter to terminate... ");
    Console.Read();
  }
}
}
```

The program first defines the class AbstractBaseClass with a single abstract Output() method. Because it's declared abstract, Output() has no implementation — that is, no method body. Two classes inherit from AbstractBaseClass: SubClass1 and SubClass2. Both are concrete classes because they override the Output() method with real methods and contain no abstract methods themselves.

TIP

A class can be declared abstract regardless of whether it has abstract members; however, a class can be concrete only when all abstract methods in any base class above it have been overridden with full methods.

The two subclass Output() methods differ in a trivial way: Both accept input strings, which they send back to users. However, one converts the string to all caps before output and the other converts it to all-lowercase characters. The following output from this program demonstrates the polymorphic nature of AbstractBaseClass:

```
Creating a SubClass1 object
Call to SubClass1.Output() from within TEST

Creating a SubClass2 object
Call to SubClass2.Output() from within test
Press Enter to terminate...
```

TIP

An abstract method is automatically virtual, so you don't add the `virtual` keyword to an abstract method.

Creating an abstract object — not!

Notice something about the `AbstractInheritance` program: It isn't legal to create an `AbstractBaseClass` object, but the argument to `Test()` is declared to be an object of the class `AbstractBaseClass` or one of its subclasses. It's the subclasses clause that's critical here. The `SubClass1` and `SubClass2` objects can be passed because each one is a concrete subclass of `AbstractBaseClass`. The IS_A relationship applies. This powerful technique lets you write highly general methods.

Sealing a Class

You may decide that you don't want future generations of programmers to be able to extend a particular class. You can lock the class by using the keyword `sealed`. A sealed class cannot be used as the base class for any other class. Consider this code snippet:

```
using System;

public class BankAccount
{
  // Withdrawal -- You can withdraw any amount up to the
  //    balance; return the amount withdrawn
  virtual public void Withdraw(decimal withdrawal)
  {
    Console.WriteLine("invokes BankAccount.Withdraw()");
  }
}

public sealed class SavingsAccount : BankAccount
{
  override public void Withdraw(decimal withdrawal)
  {
    Console.WriteLine("invokes SavingsAccount.Withdraw()");
  }
}

public class SpecialSaleAccount : SavingsAccount  // Oops!
{
  override public void Withdraw(decimal withdrawal)
```

Poly-what-ism?

```
    {
        Console.WriteLine("invokes SpecialSaleAccount.Withdraw()");
    }
}
```

This snippet generates the following compiler error:

```
'SpecialSaleAccount' : cannot inherit from sealed class 'SavingsAccount'
```

You use the `sealed` keyword to protect your class from the prying methods of a subclass. For example, allowing a programmer to extend a class that implements system security enables someone to create a security back door.

Sealing a class prevents another program, possibly somewhere on the Internet, from using a modified version of your class. The remote program can use the class as is, or not, but it can't inherit bits and pieces of your class while overriding the rest.

Chapter **8**

Interfacing with the Interface

A class can contain a reference to another class, which describes the simple HAS_A relationship. One class can extend another class by using inheritance — that's the IS_A relationship. The C# interface implements another, equally important association: the CAN_BE_USED_AS relationship. This chapter introduces C# interfaces and shows some of the numerous ways they increase the power and flexibility of object-oriented programming.

Introducing CAN_BE_USED_AS

If you want to jot a note, you can scribble it with a pen, type it into your smartphone, or pound it out on your laptop's keyboard. You can fairly say that all three objects — pen, smartphone, and computer — implement the TakeANote operation. Suppose that you use the magic of inheritance to implement this concept in C#:

```
abstract class ThingsThatRecord          // The base class
{
  abstract public void TakeANote(string note);
}
```

```
public class Pen : ThingsThatRecord       // A subclass
{
  override public void TakeANote(string note)
  {
    // ... scribble a note with a pen ...
  }
}

public class PDA : ThingsThatRecord       // Another subclass
{
  override public void TakeANote(string note)
  {
    // ... stroke a note on the PDA ...
  }
}

public class LapTop : ThingsThatRecord   // A third subclass
{
  override public void TakeANote(string note)
  {
    // ... tap, tap, tap ...
  }
}
```

TIP

If the term *abstract* has you stumped, see Chapter 7 of this minibook and, later in this chapter, read the discussion in the section "Abstract or concrete: When to use an abstract class and when to use an interface." If the whole concept of inheritance is a mystery, check out Chapter 6 of this minibook. The following simple method shows the inheritance approach working just fine:

```
void RecordTask(ThingsThatRecord recorder) // Parameter type is base class.
{
  // All classes that extend ThingsThatRecord have a TakeANote method.
  recorder.TakeANote("Shopping list");
  // ... and so on.
}
```

The parameter type is ThingsThatRecord, so you can pass any subclasses to this method, making the method quite general. That might seem like a good solution, but it has two big drawbacks:

» **A fundamental problem:** Do Pen, PDA, and LapTop truly have an IS_A relationship? Are those three items all the same type in real life? The issue is that ThingsThatRecord makes a poor base class here.

>> **A purely technical problem:** You might reasonably derive both LapTop and PDA as subclasses of Computer. But nobody would say that a Pen IS_A Computer. You have to characterize a pen as a type of MechanicalWritingDevice or DeviceThatStainsYourShirt. But a C# class can't inherit from two different base classes at the same time — a C# class can be only one type of item.

So the Pen, PDA, and LapTop classes have in common only the characteristic that they CAN_BE_USED_AS recording devices. Inheritance doesn't apply.

Knowing What an Interface Is

An *interface* in C# resembles a class with no data members and nothing but abstract methods, almost like an abstract class — almost:

```
interface IRecordable
{
    void TakeANote(string note);
}
```

The interface begins with the interface keyword. It contains nothing but abstract methods. It has no data members and no implemented methods.

TECHNICAL STUFF

Interfaces can contain a few other features, including properties (covered in Chapter 5 of this minibook), events (covered in Chapter 9 of this minibook), and indexers (covered in Chapter 7 of Book 1). Among the elements that a C# interface cannot exhibit are

>> Access specifiers, such as public or private (see Chapter 5 of this minibook)

>> Keywords such as virtual, override, or abstract (see Chapter 7 of this minibook)

>> Data members (see Chapter 2 of this minibook)

>> Implemented methods — nonabstract methods with bodies

All members of a C# interface are public (you can't even mention access specifiers in defining interface methods), and a C# interface isn't involved in normal inheritance; hence, it has none of those keywords. (An interface itself can be public, protected, internal, or private.)

Unlike an abstract class, a C# interface isn't a class. It can't be subclassed, and none of the methods it contains can have bodies.

How to implement an interface

To put a C# interface to use, you implement it with one or more classes or structures. The class and structure headings look like this:

```
// Looks like inheritance, but isn't
class Pen : IRecordable
struct PenDescription : IRecordable
```

REMEMBER

A C# interface specifies that classes or structures which implement the interface must provide specific implementations. For example, any class that implements the IRecordable interface must provide an implementation for the TakeANote method. The method that implements TakeANote doesn't use the override keyword. Using an interface isn't like overriding a virtual method in classes. Class Pen might look like this:

```
class Pen : IRecordable
{
    public void TakeANote(string note)    // Interface method implementations
    {                                     // MUST be declared public.
        // ... scribble a note with a pen ...
    }
}
```

This example fulfills two requirements: Note that the class implements IRecordable and provides a method implementation for TakeANote().

The syntax indicating that a class inherits a base class, such as ThingsThat Record, is essentially no different from the syntax indicating that the class implements a C# interface such as IRecordable:

```
public class PDA : ThingsThatRecord ...
public class PDA : IRecordable ...
```

TIP

Visual Studio can help you implement an interface. Hover the cursor over the interface name in the class heading. A little underline appears underneath the first character of the interface name — it's a Smart Tag. Move the cursor until a menu opens and then choose Implement Interface *Book*. Presto! A skeleton framework appears; you fill in the details.

How to name your interface

The .NET naming convention for interfaces precedes the name with the letter I. Interface names are typically adjectives, such as IRecordable.

Why C# includes interfaces

REMEMBER

The bottom line with interfaces is that an interface describes a capability, such as Swim Safety Training or Class A Driver's License. A class implements the IRecordable interface when it contains a full version of the TakeANote method.

More than that, an interface is a *contract.* If you agree to implement every method defined in the interface, you get to claim its capability. Not only that, but a client using your class in an application knows calling those methods is possible. Implementing an interface is a promise, enforced by the compiler. (Enforcing promises through the compiler reduces errors.)

Mixing inheritance and interface implementation

Unlike some languages, such as C++, C# doesn't allow *multiple inheritance* — a class inheriting from two or more base classes. Think of class HouseBoat inheriting from House and Boat. Just don't think of it in C#.

But although a class can inherit from only one base class, it can in addition implement as many interfaces as needed. After defining IRecordable as an interface, a couple of the recording devices looked like this:

```
public class Pen : IRecordable          // Base class is Object.
{
  public void TakeANote(string note)
  {
    // Record the note with a pen.
  }
}

public class PDA : ElectronicDevice, IRecordable
{
  public void TakeANote(string note)
  {
    // Record the note with your thumbs or a stylus.
  }
}
```

Class PDA inherits from a base class and implements an interface.

And he-e-e-re's the payoff

To begin to see the usefulness of an interface such as IRecordable, consider this example:

```
public class Program
{
  static public void RecordShoppingList(IRecordable recorder)
  {
    // Jot it down, using whatever device was passed in.
    recorder.TakeANote(...);
  }

  public static void Main(string[] args)
  {
    PDA pda = new PDA();
    RecordShoppingList(pda);  // Oops, battery's low ...

    Pen pen = new Pen();
    RecordShoppingList(pen);
  }
}
```

The IRecordable parameter is an instance of any class that implements the IRecordable interface. RecordShoppingList() makes no assumptions about the exact type of recording object. Whether the device is a PDA or a type of Electronic Device isn't important, as long as the device can record a note.

That concept is immensely powerful because it lets the RecordShoppingList() method be highly general — and thus possibly reusable in other programs. The method is even more general than using a base class such as ElectronicDevice for the argument type, because the interface lets you pass almost arbitrary objects that don't necessarily have anything in common other than implementing the interface. They don't even have to come from the same class hierarchy, which truly simplifies the designing of hierarchies, for example.

TECHNICAL STUFF

Overworked word alert: Programmers use the term interface in more than one way. You can see the C# keyword interface and how it's used. People also talk about a class's *public interface,* or the public methods and properties that it exposes to the outside world. This book keeps the distinction clear by saying *C# interface* most of the time when that's what is meant, and saying *public interface* when referring to a class's set of public methods.

Using an Interface

In addition to your being able to use a C# interface for a parameter type, an interface is useful as

>> A method return type

>> The base type of a highly general array or collection

>> A more general kind of object reference for variable types

The previous section explains the advantage of using a C# interface as a method. The following sections tell you about other interface uses.

As a method return type

You farm out the task of creating key objects you need to a factory method. Suppose that you have a variable like this one:

```
IRecordable recorder = null;  // Yes, you can have interface-type variables.
```

Somewhere, maybe in a constructor, you call a factory method to deliver a particular kind of IRecordable object:

```
recorder = MyClass.CreateRecorder("Pen");  // A factory method is often static.
```

where CreateRecorder() is a method, often on the same class, that returns not a reference to a Pen but, rather, an IRecordable reference:

```
static IRecordable CreateRecorder(string recorderType)
{
   if(recorderType == "Pen") return new Pen();
   ...
}
```

You can find more about the factory idea in the section "Hiding Behind an Interface," later in this chapter. But note that the return type for CreateRecorder() is an interface type.

As the base type of an array or collection

Suppose that you have two classes, Animal and Robot, and that both are abstract. You want to set up an array to hold both thisCat (an Animal) and thatRobot (a Robot). The only way is to fall back on type Object, the ultimate base class in

C# and the only base class that's common to both Animal and Robot as well as to their subclasses:

```
object[] things = new object[] { thisCat, thatRobot };
```

That's poor design for lots of reasons. But suppose that you're focused on the objects' movements. You can have each class implement an IMovable interface:

```
interface IMovable
{
    void Move(int direction, int speed, int distance);
}
```

and then set up an array of IMovables to manipulate your otherwise incompatible objects:

```
IMovable[] movables = { thisCat, thatRobot };
```

The interface gives you a commonality that you can exploit in collections.

As a more general type of object reference

The following variable declaration refers to a specific, physical, concrete object (see the later section "Abstract or concrete: When to use an abstract class and when to use an interface"):

```
Cat thisCat = new Cat();
```

One alternative is to use a C# interface for the reference:

```
IMovable thisMovableCat = (IMovable)new Cat();  // Note the required cast.
```

Now you can put any object into the variable that implements IMovable. This practice has wide, powerful uses in object-oriented programming, as you can see in the next section.

Using the C# Predefined Interface Types

Because interfaces are extremely useful, you find a considerable number of interfaces in the .NET class library. Among the dozen or more interfaces in the System namespace alone are IComparable, IComparable<T>, IDisposable, and IFormattable. The System.Collections.Generics namespace includes

IEnumerable<T>, IList<T>, ICollection<T>, and IDictionary<TKey, TValue>. And there are many more. Those with the <T> notation are generic interfaces. Book 1, Chapter 6 explains the <T> notation in the discussion of collection classes.

TIP

The C# Language Help files show all the ISomething<T> types with little tick marks added (IList`1), but look for "IList<T>" in C# Language Help.

Two interfaces that are commonly used are IComparable and IEnumerable — largely superseded now by their generic versions IComparable<T> (read as "IComparable of T") and IEnumerable<T>.

The "Implementing the incomparable IComparable<T> interface" section, later in this chapter, shows you the IComparable<T> interface. This interface lets you compare all sorts of objects, such as Students, to each other, and enables the Sort() method that all arrays and most collections supply. IEnumerable<T> makes the powerful foreach loop work. Most collections implement IEnumerable<T>, so you can iterate the collections with foreach. You can find an additional major use for IEnumerable<T>, as the basis for C# 3.0 and above query expressions, described in Book 1.

Looking at a Program That CAN_BE_USED_ AS an Example

Interfaces help you perform tasks in ways that classes can't because you can implement as many interfaces as you want, but you can inherit only a single class. The SortInterface program that appears in the following sections demonstrates the use of multiple interfaces and how you can use multiple interfaces effectively. To fully understand the impact of working with multiple interfaces, it's important to break the SortInterface program into sections to demonstrate various principles.

Creating your own interface at home in your spare time

The following IDisplayable interface is satisfied by any class that contains a Display() method (and declares that it implements IDisplayable, of course). Display() returns a string representation of the object that can be displayed using WriteLine().

```
// IDisplayable -- Any object that implements the Display() method
interface IDisplayable
```

Interfacing with the Interface

```
{
  // Return a description of yourself.
  string Display();
}
```

The following Student class implements IDisplayable:

```
class Student : IDisplayable
{
  public Student(string name, double grade)
  { Name = name; Grade = grade; }
  public string Name { get; private set; }
  public double Grade { get; private set; }

  public string Display()
  {
    string padName = Name.PadRight(9);
    return String.Format("{0}: {1:N0}", padName, Grade);
  }
}
```

Display() uses String's PadRight() and Format() methods, covered in Book 1, Chapter 3, to return a neatly formatted string.

The following DisplayArray() method takes an array of any objects that implement the IDisplayable interface. Each of those objects is guaranteed (by the interface) to have its own Display() method (the entire program appears in the later section "Putting it all together"):

```
// DisplayArray -- Display an array of objects that implement
//    the IDisplayable interface.
public static void DisplayArray(IDisplayable[] displayables)
{
  foreach(IDisplayable disp in displayables)
  {
    Console.WriteLine("{0}, disp.Display());
  }
}
```

The following example shows the output from DisplayArray():

```
Homer    : 0
Marge    : 85
Bart     : 50
Lisa     : 100
Maggie   : 30
```

Implementing the incomparable IComparable<T> interface

C# defines the interface IComparable<T> this way:

```
interface IComparable<T>
{
  // Compare the current T object to the object 'item'; return a
  // 1 if larger, -1 if smaller, and 0 if the same.
  int CompareTo(T item);
}
```

A class implements the IComparable<T> interface by implementing a CompareTo() method. Notice that CompareTo() takes an argument of type T, a type you supply when you instantiate the interface for a particular data type, as in this example:

```
class SoAndSo : IComparable<SoAndSo>  // Make me comparable.
```

When you implement IComparable<T> for your class, its CompareTo() method should return 0 if the two items (of your class type) being compared are "equal" in a way that you define. If not, it should return 1 or –1, depending on which object is "greater."

It seems a little Darwinian, but you could say that one Student object is "greater than" another Student object if the subject student's grade-point average is higher. Implementing the CompareTo() method implies that the objects have a sorting order. If one student is greater than another, you must be able to sort the students from least to greatest. In fact, most collection classes (including arrays but not dictionaries) supply a Sort() method something like this:

```
void Sort(IComparable<T>[] objects);
```

This method sorts a collection of objects that implement the IComparable<T> interface. It doesn't even matter which class the objects belong to. For example, they could even be Student objects. Collection classes such as arrays or List<T> could even sort this version of Student:

```
// Student -- Description of a student with name and grade
class Student : IComparable<Student>, IDisplayable   // Instantiation
{
  // Constructor -- initialize a new student object.
  public Student(double grade)
  { Grade = grade; }
```

```
public double Grade { get; private set; }

// Implement the IComparable<T> interface:
// CompareTo -- Compare another object (in this case, Student objects)
//    and decide which one comes after the other in the sorted array.
public int CompareTo(Student rightStudent)
{
    // Compare the current Student (call her 'left') against the other
    // student (call her 'right').
    Student leftStudent = this;

    // Generate a -1, 0 or 1 based on the Sort criteria (the student's
    // grade). You could use class Double's CompareTo() method instead).
    if (rightStudent.Grade < leftStudent.Grade)
    {
        return -1;
    }

    if (rightStudent.Grade > leftStudent.Grade)
    {
        return 1;
    }

    return 0;
}
```

Sorting an array of Students is reduced to this single call:

```
// Where Student implements IComparable<T>
void MyMethod(Student[] students)
{
    Array.Sort(students); // Sort array of IComparable<Student>s
}
```

You provide the comparator (CompareTo()), and Array does all the work.

Putting it all together

This is the moment you've been waiting for: the complete SortInterface program that uses the features described earlier in this chapter:

```
using System;

// SortInterface - Demonstrates how the interface concept can be used
//    to provide an enhanced degree of flexibility in factoring
```

```
//    and implementing classes.
namespace SortInterface
{
  // IDisplayable - An object that can convert itself into a displayable
  //    string format. (This duplicates what you can do by overriding
  //    ToString(), but it helps me make a point.)
  interface IDisplayable
  {
    // Display - return a string representation of yourself.
    string Display();
  }

  class Program
  {
    public static void Main(string[] args)
    {
      // Sort students by grade...
      Console.WriteLine("Sorting the list of students");

      // Get an unsorted array of students.
      Student[] students = Student.CreateStudentList();

      // Use the IComparable interface to sort the array.
      Array.Sort(students);

      // Now the IDisplayable interface to display the results.
      DisplayArray(students);

      // Now sort an array of birds by name using the same routines even
      // though the classes Bird and Student have no common base class.
      Console.WriteLine("\nsorting the list of birds");
      Bird[] birds = Bird.CreateBirdList();

      // Notice that it's not  necessary to cast the objects explicitly
      // to an array of IDisplayables (and wasn't for Students either) ...
      Array.Sort(birds);
      DisplayArray(birds);

      // Wait for user to acknowledge the results.
      Console.WriteLine("Press Enter to terminate...");
      Console.Read();
    }

    // DisplayArray - Display an array of objects that
    //    implement the IDisplayable interface.
```

```csharp
  public static void DisplayArray(IDisplayable[] displayables)
  {
    foreach(IDisplayable displayable in displayables)
    {
      Console.WriteLine("{0}", displayable.Display());
    }
  }
}

// ----------- Students - Sort students by grade -------
// Student - Description of a student with name and grade.
class Student : IComparable<Student>, IDisplayable
{
  // Constructor - initialize a new student object.
  public Student(string name, double grade)
  {
    this.Name = name;
    this.Grade = grade;
  }

  // CreateStudentList - To save space here, just create
  // a fixed list of students.
  static string[] names = {"Homer", "Marge", "Bart", "Lisa", "Maggie"};

  static double[] grades = {0, 85, 50, 100, 30};
  public static Student[] CreateStudentList()
  {
    Student[] students = new Student[names.Length];
    for (int i = 0; i < names.Length; i++)
    {
      students[i] = new Student(names[i], grades[i]);
    }
    return students;
  }

  // Access read-only properties.
  public string Name { get; private set; }
  public double Grade { get; private set; }

  // Implement the IComparable interface:
  // CompareTo - Compare another object (in this case, Student objects)
  //    and decide which one comes after the other in the sorted array.
  public int CompareTo(Student rightStudent)
  {
    // Compare the current Student (let's call her 'left') against
    // the other student (we'll call her 'right').
    Student leftStudent = this;
```

```
    // Generate a -1, 0 or 1 based upon the Sort criteria (the student's
    // grade). Double's CompareTo() method would work too.
    if (rightStudent.Grade < leftStudent.Grade)
    {
      return -1;
    }
    if (rightStudent.Grade > leftStudent.Grade)
    {
      return 1;
    }
    return 0;
  }


  // Implement the IDisplayable interface:
  // Display - Return a representation of the student.
  public string Display()
  {
    string padName = Name.PadRight(9);
    return String.Format("{0}: {1:N0}", padName, Grade);
  }
}


// -----------Birds - Sort birds by their names--------
// Bird - Just an array of bird names.
class Bird : IComparable<Bird>, IDisplayable
{
  // Constructor - initialize a new Bird object.
  public Bird(string name) { Name = name; }

  // CreateBirdList - Return a list of birds to the caller;
  //    Use a canned list here to save space.
  static string[] birdNames =
      { "Oriole", "Hawk", "Robin", "Cardinal", "Bluejay", "Finch", "Sparrow"};
  public static Bird[] CreateBirdList()
  {
    Bird[] birds = new Bird[birdNames.Length];
    for(int i = 0; i < birds.Length; i++)
    {
      birds[i] = new Bird(birdNames[i]);
    }
    return birds;
  }

  // Access read-only property.
  public string Name { get; private set; }

  // Implement the IComparable interface:
  // CompareTo - Compare the birds by name; use the
```

```
    //     built-in String class compare method.
    public int CompareTo(Bird rightBird)
    {
      // We'll compare the "current" bird to the
      // "right-hand object" bird.
      Bird leftBird = this;

      return String.Compare(leftBird.Name, rightBird.Name);
    }

    // Implement the IDisplayable interface:
    // Display - returns the name of the bird.
    public string Display() { return Name; }
  }
}
```

The `Student` class (it's in the middle of the program listing) implements the `IComparable<T>` and `IDisplayable` interfaces, as described earlier. The `CompareTo()` method compares the students by grade, which results in the students being sorted by grade. `Student`'s `Display()` method returns the name and grade of the student.

The other methods of `Student` include the read-only `Name` and `Grade` properties, a simple constructor, and a `CreateStudentList()` method. This method just returns a fixed list of students for the code to work on.

The `Bird` class at the bottom of the listing also implements the interfaces `IComparable<T>` and `IDisplayable`. The class implements `CompareTo()` by comparing the names of the birds using `String.Compare()`. So one bird is greater than another if its name is greater. `Bird.CompareTo()` alphabetizes the list. `Bird`'s `Display()` method just returns the name of the bird.

Getting back to the Main() event

If you've followed along so far, you're set up for the good part, back in `Main()`. The `CreateStudentList()` method is used to return an unsorted list, which is stored in the array `students`. You might think it necessary to cast the array of students into an array of `comparableObjects` so that you can pass the students to `Array`'s `Sort()` method:

```
IComparable<Student>[] comparables = (IComparable<Student>[])students;
```

But not so: `Sort()` sees that the array passed in consists of objects that implement `IComparable<something>` and simply calls `CompareTo()` on each `Student` object to sort them. The sorted array of `Student` objects is then passed to the locally defined `DisplayArray()` method. `DisplayArray()` uses `foreach` to iterate through an array of objects that implement a `Display()` method (guaranteed by the objects' having implemented `IDisplayable`). In the loop, it calls `Display()` on each object and displays the result to the console using `WriteLine()`.

The program in `Main()` continues by sorting and displaying birds! Of course, birds have nothing to do with students. Yet the same `Sort()` and `DisplayArray()` methods work on `Bird` as on `Student`.

The output from the program appears:

```
Sorting the list of students
Lisa    : 100
Marge   : 85
Bart    : 50
Maggie  : 30
Homer   : 0

Sorting the list of birds
Bluejay
Cardinal
Finch
Hawk
Oriole
Robin
Sparrow
Press Enter to terminate...
```

Unifying Class Hierarchies

Figure 8-1 shows the `Robot` and `Animal` hierarchies. Some, but not all, of the classes in each hierarchy not only inherit from the base classes, `Robot` or `Animal`, but also implement the `IPet` interface (not all animals are pets).

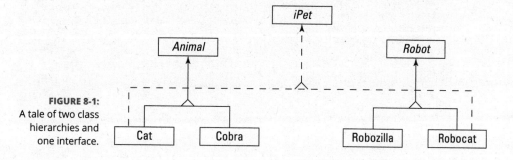

FIGURE 8-1:
A tale of two class hierarchies and one interface.

The following code shows how to implement the hierarchy. Note the properties in IPet. That's how you specify properties in interfaces. If you need both getter and setter, just add set; after get;.

```csharp
// Two abstract base classes and one interface
abstract class Animal
{
  abstract public void Eat(string food);
  abstract public void Sleep(int hours);
  abstract public int NumberOfLegs { get; }
  public void Breathe() { ... } // Nonabstract, implementation not shown.
}

abstract class Robot
{
  public virtual void Speak(string whatToSay) { ... } // Impl not shown
  abstract public void LiftObject(object o);
  abstract public int NumberOfLegs { get; }
}

interface IPet
{
  void AskForStrokes();
  void DoTricks();
  int NumberOfLegs { get; }  // Properties in interfaces look like this.
  string Name { get; set; }  // get/set must be public in implementations.
}

// Cat -- This concrete class inherits (and partially implements)
//     class Animal and also implements interface IPet.
class Cat : Animal, IPet
{
  public Cat(string name) { Name = name; }

  // 1. Overrides and implements Animal members (not shown).
  // 2. Provides additional implementation for IPet.
  // Inherits NumberOfLegs property from base class, thus meeting
  // IPet's requirement for a NumberOfLegs property.
  #region IPet Members
  public void AskForStrokes() ...
  public void DoTricks() ...
  public string Name { get; set; }
  #endregion IPet Members

  public override string ToString() { return Name; }
}
```

```
class Cobra : Animal
{
  // 1. Inherits or overrides all Animal methods only (not shown).
}

class Robozilla : Robot     // Not IPet
{
  // 1. Override Speak.
  public override void Speak(string whatToSay)
  { Console.WriteLine("DESTROY ALL HUMANS!"); }

  // 2. Implement LiftObject and NumberOfLegs, not all shown.
  public override void LiftObject(object o) ...
  public override int NumberOfLegs { get { return 2; } }
}

class RoboCat : Robot, IPet
{
  public RoboCat(string name) { Name = name; }

  // 1. Override some Robot members, not all shown:
  #region IPet Members
  public void AskForStrokes() ...
  public void DoTricks() ...
  public string Name { get; set; }
  #endregion IPet Members
}
```

The code shows two concrete classes that inherit from Animal and two that inherit from Robot. However, you can see that neither class Cobra nor class Robozilla implements IPet — probably for good reasons. Most people don't plan to watch TV with a pet cobra beside them on the couch, and a robozilla sounds nasty, too. Some of the classes in both hierarchies exhibit what you might call "petness" and some don't.

The point of this section is that any class can implement an interface, as long as it provides the right methods and properties. Robocat and Robodog can carry out the AskForStrokes() and DoTricks() actions and have the NumberOfLegs property, as can Cat and Dog in the Animal hierarchy — all while other classes in the same hierarchies don't implement IPet.

Hiding Behind an Interface

Often this book discusses code that (a) you write but (b) someone else (a client) uses in a program (you may be the client yourself, of course). Sometimes you have a complex or tricky class whose entire public interface you would truly rather not expose to clients. For various reasons, however, it includes some dangerous operations that nonetheless have to be public. Ideally, you would expose a safe subset of your class's public methods and properties and hide the dangerous ones. C# interfaces can do that, too.

Here's a different Robozilla class, with several methods and properties that amateurs can use safely and enjoyably. But Robozilla also has some advanced features that can be, well, scary:

```
public class Robozilla  // Doesn't implement IPet!
{
    public void ClimbStairs();                    // Safe
    public void PetTheRobodog();                  // Safe? Might break it.
    public void Charge();                         // Maybe not safe
    public void SearchAndDestroy();               // Dangerous
    public void LaunchGlobalThermonuclearWar();   // Catastrophic
}
```

You want to expose only the two safer methods while hiding the last three dangerous ones. Here's how you can do that by using a C# interface:

1. Design a C# interface that exposes only the safe methods:

```
public interface IRobozillaSafe
{
    void ClimbStairs();
    void PetTheRobodog();
}
```

2. Modify the Robozilla class to implement the interface. Because it already has implementations for the required methods, all you need is the : IRobozillaSafe notation on the class heading:

```
public class Robozilla : IRobozillaSafe  ...
```

Now you can just keep Robozilla itself a secret from everybody and give most users the IRobozillaSafe interface. Give your clients a way to instantiate a new Robozilla, but return to them a reference to the interface (in this example, by using a static factory method added to class Robozilla):

```
// Creates a Robozilla but returns only an interface reference to it.
public static IRobozillaSafe CreateRobozilla(<parameter list>)
{
    return (IRobozillaSafe)new Robozilla(<parameter list>);
}
```

Clients then use Robozilla like this:

```
IRobozillaSafe myZilla = Robozilla.CreateRobozilla(...);
myZilla.ClimbStairs();
myZilla.PetTheRobodog();
```

It's that simple. Using the interface, they can call the Robozilla methods that it specifies — but not any other Robozilla methods. However, expert programmers can defeat this ploy with a simple cast:

```
Robozilla myKillaZilla = (Robozilla)myZilla;
```

Doing so is usually a bad idea, though. The interface has a purpose: to keep bugs at bay. In real life, programmers sometimes use this hand-out-an-interface technique with the complex DataSet class used in ADO.NET to interact with databases. A DataSet can return a set of database tables loaded with records — such as a table of Customers and a table of Orders. (Modern relational databases, such as Oracle and SQL Server, contain tables linked by various relationships. Each table contains lots of records, where each record might be, for example, the name, rank, and serial number of a Customer.)

Unfortunately, if you hand a client a DataSet reference (even through a read-only property's get clause), the client can muddle the situation by reaching into the DataSet and modifying elements that you don't want modified. One way to prevent such mischief is to return a DataView object, which is read-only. Alternatively, you can create a C# interface to expose a safe subset of the operations available on the DataSet. Then you can subclass DataSet and have the subclass (call it MyDataSet) implement the interface. Finally, give clients a way to obtain an interface reference to a live MyDataSet object and let them have at it in relative safety — through the interface.

TIP

You usually shouldn't return a reference to a collection, either, because it lets anyone alter the collection outside the class that created it. Remember that the reference you hand out can still point to the original collection inside your class. That's why List<T>, for instance, provides an AsReadOnly() method. This method returns a collection that can't be altered:

```
private List<string> _readWriteNames = ...  // A modifiable data member
...
ReadonlyCollection<string> readonlyNames = _readWriteNames.AsReadOnly();
return readonlyNames; // Safer to return this than _readWriteNames.
```

Although it doesn't qualify as using an interface, the purpose is the same.

Inheriting an Interface

A C# interface can inherit the methods of another interface. However, interface inheritance may not always be true inheritance, no matter how it may appear. The following interface code lists a base interface, much like a base class, in its heading:

```
interface IRobozillaSafe : IPet   // Base interface
{
  // Methods not shown here ...
}
```

By having IRobozillaSafe "inherit" IPet, you can let this subset of Robozilla implement its own petness without trying to impose petness inappropriately on all of Robozilla:

```
class PetRobo : Robozilla, IRobozillaSafe // (also an IPet by inheritance)
{
  // Implement Robozilla operations.
  // Implement IRobozillaSafe operations, then ...
  // Implement IPet operations too (required by the inherited IPet interface).
}
...
// Hand out only a safe reference, not one to PetRobo itself.
IPet myPetRobo = (IPet)new PetRobo();
// ... now call IPet methods on the object.
```

The IRobozillaSafe interface inherits from IPet. Classes that implement IRobozillaSafe must therefore also implement IPet to make their implementation of IRobozillaSafe complete. This type of inheritance isn't the same concept as class inheritance. For instance, class PetRobo in the previous example can have a constructor, but no equivalent of a base-class constructor exists for IRobozillaSafe or IPet. Interfaces don't have constructors. More important, polymorphism doesn't work the same way with interfaces. Though you can call a method of a subclass through a reference to the base class (class polymorphism), the parallel operation involving interfaces (interface polymorphism) doesn't work: You can't call a method of the derived interface (IRobozillaSafe) through a base interface reference (IPet).

Although interface inheritance isn't polymorphic in the same way that class inheritance is, you can pass an object of a derived interface type (IRobozillasafe) through a parameter of its base interface type (IPet). Therefore, you can also put IRobozillasafe objects into a collection of IPet objects.

Using Interfaces to Manage Change in Object-Oriented Programs

Interfaces are the key to object-oriented programs that bend flexibly with the winds of change. Your code will laugh in the face of new requirements.

REMEMBER

You've no doubt heard it said, "Change is a constant." When you hand a new program to a bunch of users, they soon start requesting changes. Add this feature, please. Fix that problem, please. The RoboWarrior has feature *X*, so why doesn't Robozilla? Many programs have a long shelf life. Thousands of programs, especially old Fortran and Cobol programs, have been in service for 20 or 30 years, or longer. They undergo lots of maintenance in that extended time span, which makes planning and designing for change one of your highest priorities.

Here's an example: In the Robot class hierarchy, suppose that all robots can move in one way or another. Robocats saunter. Robozillas charge — at least when operated by a power (hungry) user. And Robosnakes slither. One way to implement these different modes of travel involves inheritance: Give the base class, Robot, an abstract Move() method. Then each subclass overrides the Move() method to implement it differently:

```
abstract public class Robot
{
  abstract public void Move(int direction, int speed);
  // ...
}

public class Robosnake : Robot
{
  public override void Move(int direction, int speed)
  {
    // A real Move() implementation here: slithering.
    ... some real code that computes angles and changes
    snake's location relative to a coordinate system, say ...
  }
}
```

But suppose that you often receive requests to add new types of movement to existing Robot subclasses. "Please make Robosnake undulate rather than slither," maybe. Now you have to open up the Robosnake class and modify its Move() method directly.

REMEMBER

After the Move() method is working correctly for slithering, most programmers would prefer not to meddle with it. Implementing slithering is difficult, and changing the implementation can introduce brand-new bugs. If it ain't broke, don't fix it.

Making flexible dependencies through interfaces

There must be a way to implement Move() that doesn't require you to open a can of worms every time a client wants wriggling instead. You can use interfaces, of course! Look at the following code that uses HAS_A, a now-familiar relationship between two classes in which one class contains the other:

```
public class Robot
{
   // This object is used to implement motion.
   protected Motor _motor = new Motor(); // Refers to Motor by name
   // ...
}

internal class Motor { ... }
```

The point about this example is that the contained object is of type Motor, where Motor is a concrete object. (That is, it represents a real item, not an abstraction.) HAS_A sets up a dependency between classes Robot and Motor: Robot depends on the concrete class Motor. A class with concrete dependencies is tightly coupled to them: When you need to replace Motor with something else, code that depends directly on Motor like this has to change, too. Instead, insulate your code by relying only on the public interface of dependencies, which you can do with interfaces.

Abstract or concrete: When to use an abstract class and when to use an interface

In Chapter 7 of this minibook, the discourse about birds says, "Every bird out there is a subtype of Bird." In other words, a duck is an instance of a subclass Duck. You never see an instance of Bird itself — Bird is an abstraction. Instead, you always see concrete, physical ducks, sparrows, or hummingbirds. Abstractions are concepts. As living creatures, ducks are real, concrete objects. Also, concrete objects are instances of concrete classes. (A *concrete class* is a class that you can instantiate. It lacks the abstract keyword, and it implements all methods.)

REMEMBER

You can represent abstractions in two ways in C#: with abstract classes or with C# interfaces. The two have differences that can affect your choice of which one to use:

>> **Use an abstract class** when you can profitably share an implementation with subclasses — the abstract base class can contribute real code that its sub-classes can use by inheritance. For instance, maybe class Robot can handle part of the robot's tasks, just not movement.

An abstract class doesn't have to be completely abstract. Though it has to have at least one abstract, unimplemented method or property, some can provide implementations (bodies). Using an abstract class to provide an implementation for its subclasses to inherit prevents duplication of code. That's always a good thing.

>> **Use an interface** when you can't share any implementation or your imple-menting class already has a base class.

C# interfaces are purely, totally abstract. A C# interface supplies no imple-mentation of any of its methods. Yet it can also add flexibility that isn't otherwise possible. The abstract class option may not be available because you want to add a capability to a class that already has a base class (that you can't modify). For example, class Robot may already have a base class in a library that you didn't write and therefore can't alter. Interfaces are especially helpful for representing completely abstract capabilities, such as movability or displayability, that you want to add to multiple classes that may otherwise have nothing in common — for example, being in the same class hierarchy.

Doing HAS_A with interfaces

You discovered earlier in this chapter that you can use interfaces as a more general reference type. The containing class can refer to the contained class not with a reference to a concrete class but, rather, with a reference to an abstraction. Either an abstract class or a C# interface will work:

```
AbstractDependentClass dependency1 = ...;
ISomeInterface dependency2 = ...;
```

Suppose that you have an IPropulsion interface:

```
interface IPropulsion
{
    void Movement(int direction, int speed);
}
```

Class Robot can contain a data member of type IPropulsion instead of the concrete type Motor:

```
public class Robot
{
  private IPropulsion _propel;     //<--Notice the interface type here.

  // Somehow, you supply a concrete propulsion object at runtime ...
  // Other stuff and then:
  public void Move(int speed, int direction)
  {
    // Use whatever concrete propulsion device is installed in _propel.
    _propel.Movement(speed, direction); // Delegate to its methods.
  }
}
```

Robot's Move() method delegates the real work to the object referred to through the interface. Be sure to provide a way to install a concrete Motor or Engine or another implementer of IPropulsion in the data member. Programmers often install that concrete object — "inject the dependency" — by passing it to a constructor:

```
Robot r = new Robosnake(someConcreteMotor);  // Type IPropulsion
```

or by assigning it via a setter property:

```
r.PropulsionDevice = someConcreteMotor;      // Invokes the set clause
```

Another approach to dependency injection is to use a factory method (discussed in the "As a method return type" section, earlier in this chapter, and illustrated in the section "Hiding Behind an Interface"):

```
IPropulsion _propel = CreatePropulsion();    // A factory method
```

Chapter **9**

Delegating Those Important Events

This chapter looks into a corner of C# that has been around since the birth of the language. The ability to create a *callback*, a method used to handle events, is essential for C# applications of all sorts. In fact, the callback appears in applications of every kind today. Even web-based applications must have some sort of callback mechanism to allow them to work properly.

The alternative is to hold up the application while you wait for something to happen, which means that the application won't respond to anything but the anticipated input. That's how the console applications used in examples to this point work. The `Console.Read()` call essentially stops the application until the user does something. A console application can work in this manner, but when a user could click any button on a form, you must have something better — a callback mechanism. In C#, you implement a callback by using a *delegate*, which is a description of what a callback method requires to handle an event. The delegate acts as a method reference type. In addition to callback methods, this chapter also helps you understand how to create and use delegates.

E.T., Phone Home — The Callback Problem

If you've seen the Steven Spielberg movie *E.T., the Extraterrestrial* (1982), you watched the cute but ugly little alien stranded on Earth try to build an apparatus from old toy parts with which he could "phone home." He needed his ship to pick him up.

It's a big jump from *E.T.* to C#, but code sometimes needs to phone home, too. For example, you may have wondered how the Windows progress bar works. It's the horizontal "bar" that gradually fills up with coloring to show progress during a lengthy operation, such as copying files. The progress bar is based on a lengthy operation's periodic pause to "phone home." In programmerese, it's a *callback*. Usually, the lengthy operation estimates how long its task should take and then checks frequently to see how far it has progressed. Periodically, the progress bar sends a signal by calling a *callback method* back on the mother ship — the class that kicked off the long operation. The mother ship can then update its progress bar. The trick is that you have to supply this callback method for the long operation to use.

That callback method may be in the same class as the lengthy operation — such as phoning your sister on the other side of the house. Or, more often, it's in another class that knows about the progress bar — such as phoning Aunt Maxie in Minnesota. Somehow, at its start, the lengthy operation has been handed a mechanism for phoning home — sort of like giving your kid a cellphone so that she can call you at 10 p.m.

REMEMBER

This chapter talks about how your code can set up this callback mechanism and then invoke it to phone home when needed. Callbacks are used a lot in Windows programming, typically for a piece of code, down in your program's guts, to notify a higher-level module that the task has finished, to ask for needed data, or to let that module take a useful action, such as write a log entry or update a progress bar. However, the place where you use callbacks the most is with the user interface. When the user does something with the user interface, such as click a button, it generates an event. The callback method handles the event.

Defining a Delegate

C# provides *delegates* for making callbacks — and a number of other tasks. Delegates are the C# way (the .NET way, really, because any .NET language can use them) for you to pass around methods as though they were data. You're saying, "Here, execute this method when you need it" (and then handing over the method to execute). This chapter helps you get a handle on that concept, see its usefulness, and start using it yourself.

You may be an experienced coder who will recognize immediately that delegates are similar to C/C++ function pointers — only much, much better. But this section assumes that you aren't and you don't.

Think of a delegate as a vehicle for passing a callback method to a "workhorse" method that needs to call you back or needs help with that action, as in doing the same action to each element of a collection. Because the collection doesn't know about your custom action, you need a way to provide the action for the collection to carry out. Figure 9-1 shows how the parts of this scheme fit together.

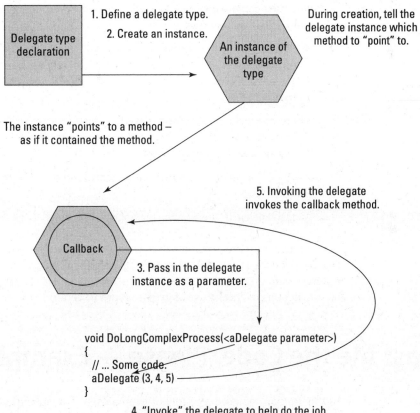

FIGURE 9-1:
Sending your
delegate to the
bungee-jump on
your behalf.

A delegate is a data type, similar to a class. As with a class, you create an instance of the delegate type in order to use the delegate. Figure 9-1 shows the sequence of events in the delegate's life cycle as you complete these steps:

1. **Define the delegate type (in much the same way as you would define a class).**

   Sometimes, C# has already defined a delegate you can use. Much of the time, though, you need to define your own, custom delegates.

   Under the surface, a delegate *is* a class, derived from the class `System.MulticastDelegate`, which knows how to store one or more "pointers" to methods and invoke them for you. Relax: The compiler writes the class part of it for you.

2. **Create an instance of the delegate type — such as instantiating a class.**

   During creation, you hand the new delegate instance the name of a method that you want it to use as a callback or an action method.

3. **Pass the delegate instance to a workhorse method, which has a parameter of the delegate type.**

   That's the doorway through which you insert the delegate instance into the workhorse method. It's like smuggling a candy bar into a movie theater — except that in this example, the movie theater expects, even invites, the contraband candy.

4. **When the workhorse method is ready — for example, when it's time to update the progress bar — the workhorse invokes the delegate, passing it any expected arguments.**

5. **Invoking the delegate in turn invokes (calls) the callback method that the delegate "points" to.**

   Using the delegate, the workhorse phones home.

This fundamental mechanism solves the callback problem — and has other uses, too. Delegate types can also be generic, allowing you to use the same delegate for different data types, much as you can instantiate a `List<T>` collection for `string` or `int`. Book 1 covers the use of generic types in detail.

Pass Me the Code, Please — Examples

In this section, you see a couple of examples — and solve the callback problem discussed at the beginning of this chapter.

Delegating the task

In this section, you walk through two examples of using a callback — a delegate instance phoning home, like *E.T.*, to the object that created it. But first take a look at some common variations on what you can use a callback delegate for:

>> **To notify the delegate's home base of an event:** A lengthy operation has finished or made some progress or perhaps run into an error. "Mother, this is E.T. Can you come get me at Elliot's house?"

>> **To call back to home base to ask for the necessary data to complete a task:** "I'm at the store. Should I get white bread or wheat?"

REMEMBER

>> **More generally, to customize a method:** The method you're customizing provides a framework, and its caller supplies a delegate to do the work. "Take this grocery list to the store and follow it exactly." The delegate method carries out a task that the customized method needs done (but can't handle by itself). The customized method is responsible for invoking the delegate at the appropriate moment.

First, a simple example

The `SimpleDelegateExample` program demonstrates a simple delegate. The delegate-related parts of this example are highlighted in boldface.

```
using System;

// SimpleDelegateExample -- Demonstrate a simple delegate callback.
namespace SimpleDelegateExample
{
  class Program
  {
    // Inside class or inside namespace
    delegate int MyDelType(string name);

    static void Main(string[] args)
    {
      // Create a delegate instance pointing to the CallBackMethod below.
      // Note that the callback method is static, so you prefix the name
      // with the class name, Program.
      MyDelType del = new MyDelType(Program.CallBackMethod);

      // Call a method that will invoke the delegate.
      UseTheDel(del, "hello");
```

```
        // Wait for user to acknowledge results.
        Console.WriteLine("Press Enter to terminate...");
        Console.Read();
    }


    // UseTheDel -- A "workhorse" method that takes a MyDelType delegate
    //      argument and invokes the delegate. arg is a string to pass
    //      to the delegate invocation.
    private static void UseTheDel(MyDelType del, string arg)
    {
        if (del == null) return; // Don't invoke a null delegate!

        // Here's where you invoke the delegate.
        // What's written here? A number representing the length of arg.
        Console.WriteLine("UseTheDel writes {0}", del(arg));
    }


    // CallBackMethod -- A method that conforms to the MyDelType
    //      delegate signature (takes a string, returns an int).
    //      The delegate will call this method.
    public static int CallBackMethod(string stringPassed)
    {
        // Leave tracks to show you were here.
        // What's written here? stringPassed.
        Console.WriteLine("CallBackMethod writes: {0}", stringPassed);

        // Return an int.
        return stringPassed.Length;  // Delegate requires an int return.
    }
}
```

First you see the delegate definition. MyDelType defines a *signature* — you can pass any method with the delegate; such a method must take a string argument and return an int. Second, the CallBackMethod(), defined at the bottom of the listing, matches that signature. Third, Main() creates an instance of the delegate, called del, and then passes the delegate instance to a "workhorse" method, UseTheDel(), along with some string data, "hello", that the delegate requires. In that setup, here's the sequence of events:

1. UseTheDel() takes two arguments, a MyDelType delegate, and a string that it calls arg. So, when Main() calls UseTheDel(), it passes the delegate instance to be used inside the method. When you create the delegate instance, del, in Main(), you pass the name of the CallBackMethod() as the method to call. Because CallBackMethod() is static, you have to prefix the name with the class name, Program.

2. Inside `UseTheDel()`, the method ensures that the delegate isn't `null` and then starts a `WriteLine()` call. Within that call, before it finishes, the method invokes the delegate by calling `del(arg)`. `arg` is just something you can pass to the delegate, which causes the `CallBackMethod()` to be called.

3. Inside `CallBackMethod()`, the method writes its own message, including the string that was passed when `UseTheDel()` invoked the delegate. Then `CallBackMethod()` returns the length of the string it was passed, and that length is written out as the last part of the `WriteLine()` in `UseTheDel()`.

The output looks like this:

```
CallBackMethod writes: hello
UseTheDel writes 5
Press Enter to terminate...
```

`UseTheDel()` phones home and `CallBackMethod()` answers the call.

A More Real-World Example

For a more realistic example than `SimpleDelegateExample`, the following example shows you how to write a little app that puts up a progress bar and updates it every time a lengthy method invokes a delegate. You can access the example code for this chapter in the `\CSAIO4D\BK02\CH09` folder in the downloadable source, as explained in the Introduction.

Getting an overview of the bigger example

The `SimpleProgress` example demonstrates the Windows Forms `ProgressBar` control. (By the way, this example of Windows *graphical* programming is nearly the only one in this book — even if it's simple-minded — so the example steps through it carefully. It's a good idea to complete the steps as provided.)

The example displays a small dialog-box-style window with two buttons and a progress bar. When you load the solution example into Visual Studio and then build it, run it, and click the upper button, marked Click to Start, the progress bar runs for a few seconds. You see it gradually fill up, one-tenth of its length at a time. When it's completely full, you can click the Close button to end the program or click Click to Start again.

Putting the app together

To create the sample app on your own and experience a bit of Windows graphical programming, follow these steps, working first in *design mode,* in which you're just laying out the appearance of your app. First, create the project and position the necessary controls on your "window":

1. **Choose File⇨New Project and select Windows Classic Desktop on the left, under C#.**

You see a list of potential applications, like those shown in Figure 9-2.

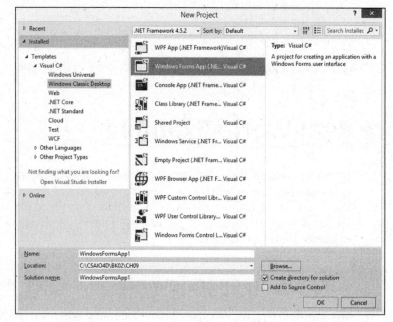

FIGURE 9-2:
The Windows Classic Desktop folder contains older project types.

2. **Select Windows Forms App in the middle pane.**

3. **Type** SimpleProgress **in the Name field and click OK.**

The first thing you see is the *form:* a window that you lay out yourself using several *controls.*

4. **Choose View ⇨ Toolbox and open Common Controls group.**

You see the list of controls shown in Figure 9-3.

FIGURE 9-3:
The Common
Controls Group
contains the
controls you use
most often.

5. **Drag a** ProgressBar **control to the form and drop it; then drag two** Button**s onto the form.**

6. **Position the buttons and the** ProgressBar **so that they look somewhat like the one shown in Figure 9-4.**

   Note the handy guide lines that help with positioning.

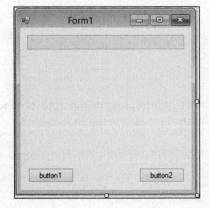

FIGURE 9-4:
Create the
form you use
to demonstrate
the use of a
progress bar.

Next, set properties for these controls: Choose View⇨Properties, select a control on the form, and set the control's properties:

1. **For the progress bar — named** progressBar1 **in the code — make sure that the** Minimum **property is 0, the** Maximum **property is 100, the** Step **property is 10, and the** Value **property is 0.**

2. **For button1, change the** Text **property to** "Click to Start" **and drag the sizing handles on the button image until it looks right and shows all its text.**

3. **For button2, change the** Text **property to** "Close" **and adjust the button's size to your liking.**

TIP

In this simple example, you're putting all code in the *form* class. (The form is your window; its class — here, named Form1 — is responsible for all things graphical.) Generally, you should put all "business" code — the code that does your calculations, data access, and other important work — in other classes. Reserve the form class for code that's intimately involved with displaying elements on the form and responding to its controls. I break that rule here — but the delegate works no matter where its callback method is.

Now, still in design mode, add a *handler method* for each button:

1. **On the form, double-click the new Close button.**

   This action generates a method in the "code behind the form" (or, simply, "the code-behind") — the code that makes the form work. It looks like this (you add the boldfaced code):

   ```
   private void button2_Click(object sender, EventArgs e)
   {
     Close();
   }
   ```

TIP

To toggle between the form's code and its image, just change tabs in the main panel.

2. **Double-click the new Click to Start button to generate its handler method, which looks like the following in the code-behind:**

   ```
   private void button1_Click(object sender, EventArgs e)
   {
     UpdateProgressCallback callback =
       new UpdateProgressCallback(this.DoUpdate);
   ```

```
    // Do something that needs periodic progress reports. This
    // passes a delegate instance that knows how to update the bar.
    DoSomethingLengthy(callback);

    // Clear the bar so that it can be used again.
    progressBar1.Value = 0;
    }
```

You see red underlines beneath UpdateProgressCallback and DoSomethingLengthy, which indicate errors. Ignore these errors for now — later steps will fix them.

3. **Add the following callback method to the form class:**

```
private void DoUpdate()
{
    // Tells progress bar to update itself
    progressBar1.PerformStep();
}
```

The next section walks you through the remaining code, all of it on the form class. Later in the chapter, you see other variations on the delegate that's passed.

Looking at the code

The remaining bits of code tucked into the Form1 class consist of the parts of the delegate life cycle, covered earlier in this chapter. You see the class and then the various delegate components. The boldfaced lines are new code that you add beyond the items you added in the previous section:

```
using System;
using System.Windows.Forms;

namespace SimpleProgress
{
  public partial class Form1 : Form
  {
    // Declare the delegate. This one is void.
    delegate void UpdateProgressCallback();

    public Form1()
    {
      InitializeComponent();
    }
```

```csharp
    // DoSomethingLengthy -- My workhorse method takes a delegate.
    private void DoSomethingLengthy(UpdateProgressCallback updateProgress)
    {
      int duration = 2000;
      int updateInterval = duration / 10;

      for (int i = 0; i < duration; i++)
      {
        Console.WriteLine("Something or other");

        // Update every tenth of the duration.
        if ((i % updateInterval) == 0 && updateProgress != null)
        {
          updateProgress();  // Invoke the delegate.
        }

if(updateProgress !=null)updateProgress();
    }
  }


  // DoUpdate -- The callback method
  private void DoUpdate()
  {
    progressBar1.PerformStep();
  }

  private void button1_Click(object sender, EventArgs e)
  {
    // Instantiate the delegate, telling it what method to call.
    UpdateProgressCallback callback =
      new UpdateProgressCallback(this.DoUpdate);

    // Do something that needs periodic progress reports.
    // This passes a delegate instance that knows how to update the bar.
    DoSomethingLengthy(callback);

    // Clear the bar so that it can be used again.
    progressBar1.Value = 0;
  }

  private void button2_Click(object sender, EventArgs e)
  {
    this.Close();
  }
 }
}
```

REMEMBER

The class declaration is interesting as an aside:

```
public partial class Form1 : Form
```

The `partial` keyword indicates that this line is only part of the full class. The rest can be found in the `Form1.Designer.cs` file listed in Solution Explorer. (Take a look at it.) Later, in the "Stuff Happens — C# Events" section, you revisit that file to discover a couple of things about *events*. Partial classes, which were introduced in C# 2.0, let you split a class between two or more files. The compiler generates the `Form1.Designer.cs` file, so don't modify its code directly. You can modify it indirectly, however, by changing elements on the form. `Form1.cs` is *your* part.

Tracking the delegate life cycle

Look at the example through the parts of the delegate life cycle:

1. You define the `UpdateProgressCallback` **delegate near the top of the class:**

```
delegate void UpdateProgressCallback();
```

Methods that this delegate can "point" to will be `void`, with no parameters. After the `delegate` keyword, the rest defines the *signature* of any method that the delegate can point to: its return type and the number, order, and types of its parameters. Delegates don't have to be `void` — you can write delegates that return any type and take any arguments.

Defining a delegate defines a *type,* just as `class Student {...}` does. You can declare your delegate `public`, `internal`, `protected`, or even `private`, as needed.

TIP

It's considered good form to append the name `Callback` to the name of a delegate type that defines a callback method, though C# couldn't care less.

2. **You instantiate the delegate and then pass the instance to the** `DoSomethingLengthy()` **method in the** `button1_Click()` **method:**

```
UpdateProgressCallback callback =
  new UpdateProgressCallback(this.DoUpdate);

// Do something that needs periodic progress reports. This
// passes a delegate instance that knows how to update the bar.
DoSomethingLengthy(callback);
```

Delegating Those
Important Events

This delegate "points" to a method on this class (and this is optional). To point to a method on another class, you need an instance of that class (if the method is an instance method), and you pass the method like this:

```
SomeClass sc = new SomeClass();
UpdateProgressCallback callback =
  new UpdateProgressCallback(sc.DoUpdate);
```

But if the method is a static method (located anywhere), pass it like this:

```
UpdateProgressCallback callback =
  new UpdateProgressCallback(SomeClass.DoUpdate);
```

What you're passing in the instantiation is just the method's *name*, no parameters. What you pass to DoSomethingLengthy() is the delegate instance, callback (which points to the method).

3. **Your** DoSomethingLengthy() **method does some "lengthy processing" and periodically pauses to call back to the form so that it can update its progress bar.**

Invoking the delegate inside DoSomethingLengthy() looks like calling a method, complete with parameters, if any:

```
updateProgress();  // Invoke the delegate instance passed in.
```

DoSomethingLengthy() looks like this:

```
private void DoSomethingLengthy(UpdateProgressCallback updateProgress)
{
  int duration = 2000;
  int updateInterval = duration / 10;

  for (int i = 0; i < duration; i++)
  {
    Console.WriteLine("Something or other");

    // Update the form periodically.
    if ((i % updateInterval) == 0 && updateProgress != null)
    {
      updateProgress();  // Invoke the delegate.
    }

    if(updateProgress != null) updateProgress();
  }
}
```

The lengthy process doesn't do much. It sets the duration variable to 2,000 loop iterations — a few seconds at runtime, which is more than enough for this demo. Next, the method computes an update interval of 200 iterations by dividing the overall duration into tenths. Then the for loop ticks off those 2,000 iterations. For each one, it checks whether it's time to update the user interface, or UI. Most times through the loop, no update occurs. But whenever the if condition is true, the method invokes the UpdateProgressCallback instance that was passed to its updateProgress parameter. The modulo expression, i % updateInterval, produces a 0 remainder, thus satisfying the if condition, once every 200 iterations.

REMEMBER

Always check a newly instantiated delegate for null before invoking it.

4. **When** DoSomethingLengthy() **invokes the delegate, the delegate in turn invokes the method you pointed it at — in this case, the** DoUpdate() **method on the** Form1 **class.**

5. **When called via the delegate,** DoUpdate() **carries out the update by calling a method on the** ProgressBar **class named** PerformStep()**:**

```
private void DoUpdate()
{
    progressBar1.PerformStep();
}
```

PerformStep(), in turn, fills another 10 percent increment of the bar with color, the amount dictated by its Step property, set to 10 at the outset.

6. **Finally, control returns to** DoSomethingLengthy(), **which continues looping. When the loop runs its course,** DoSomethingLengthy() **exits, returning control to the** button1_Click() **method. That method then clears the** ProgressBar **by setting its** Value **property to 0. And the app settles down to wait for another click on one of its buttons (or its Close box).**

And there you have it. Using the delegate to implement a callback, the program keeps its progress bar up to date. See the list of uses for delegates in the earlier section "Delegating the task." Write a *custom* delegate when you need to define a type for delegate-type parameters so that you can implement a callback. Use *predefined* delegates for events and the collection classes' Find() and ForEach() methods.

Shh! Keep It Quiet — Anonymous Methods

After you have the gist of using delegates, take a quick look at Microsoft's *first* cut at simplifying delegates in C# 2.0 a couple of years ago. To cut out some of the delegate rigamarole, you can use an anonymous method. Anonymous methods are just written in more traditional notation. Although the syntax and a few details are different, the effect is essentially the same whether you use a raw delegate, an anonymous method, or a lambda expression.

An anonymous method creates the delegate instance and the method it "points" to at the same time — right in place, on the fly, *tout de suite*. Here are the guts of the DoSomethingLengthy() method again, this time rewritten to use an anonymous method (boldfaced):

```csharp
private void DoSomethingLengthy()  // No arguments needed this time.
{
  ...
  for (int i = 0; i < duration; i++)
  {
    if ((i % updateInterval) == 0)
    {
      // Create delegate instance.
      UpdateProgressCallback anon = delegate()
      {
        progressBar1.PerformStep();          // Method 'pointed' to
      };

      if(anon != null) anon();               // Invoke the delegate.
    }
  }
}
```

The code looks like standard delegate instantiations, except that after the = sign, you see the delegate keyword, any parameters to the anonymous method in parentheses (or empty parentheses if none), and the method body. The code that used to be in a separate DoUpdate() method — the method that the delegate "points" to — has moved inside the anonymous method — no more pointing. And this method is utterly nameless. You still need the UpdateProgressCallback delegate type definition, and you're still invoking a delegate instance, named anon in this example.

Needless to say, this description doesn't cover everything there is to know about anonymous methods, but it's a start. Look up the term *anonymous method* in C# Language Help to see more anonymous method examples in the Delegate Examples program on the website. The best advice is to keep your anonymous methods short.

Stuff Happens — C# Events

One more application of delegates deserves discussion in this section: the C# *event,* which is implemented with delegates. An event is a variation on a callback but provides a simpler mechanism for alerting the application whenever an important event occurs. An event is especially useful when more than one method is waiting for a callback. Events are widely used in C#, especially for connecting the objects in the user interface to the code that makes them work. The buttons in the `SimpleProgress` example, presented earlier in this chapter, illustrate this use.

The Observer design pattern

It's extremely common in programming for various objects in the running program to have an interest in events that occur on other objects. For example, when the user clicks a button, the form that contains the button wants to know about it. Events provide the standard mechanism in C# and .NET for notifying any interested parties of important actions.

TIP

The event pattern is so common that it has a name: the Observer design pattern. It's one of many common *design patterns* that people have published for anyone to use in their own code. To begin learning about other design patterns, you can consult *Design Patterns: Elements of Reusable Object-Oriented Software,* by Erich Gamma, Richard Helm, Ralph Johnson, and John Vlissides (Addison-Wesley Professional).

The Observer pattern consists of an Observable object — the object with interesting events (sometimes called the Subject) — and any number of Observer objects: those interested in a particular event. The observers register themselves with the Observable in some way and, when events of interest occur, the Observable notifies all registered observers. You can implement this pattern in numerous ways without events (such as callbacks and interfaces), but the C# way is to use events.

TIP

An alternative name for *observers* that you may encounter is *listeners.* Listeners listen for events. And that's not the last of the alternatives.

What's an event? Publish/Subscribe

One analogy for events is your local newspaper. You and many other people contact the paper to subscribe, and then the paper delivers current newspapers to you. The newspaper company is the Publisher, and its customers are Subscribers, so this variation of Observer is often called *Publish/Subscribe* pattern. That's the analogy used in the chapter, but remember that the Observer pattern *is* the Publish/Subscribe pattern, with different terminology. Observers are subscribers, and the Observable object that they observe is a publisher.

In C#, when you have a class on which interesting events arise, you advertise the availability of notifications to any classes that may have an interest in knowing about such events by providing an *event object* (usually public).

REMEMBER

The term *event* has two meanings in C#. You can think of the word *event* as meaning both "an interesting occurrence" and a specific kind of C# object. The former is the real-world concept, and the latter is the way it's set up in C#, using the event keyword.

How a publisher advertises its events

REMEMBER

To advertise for subscribers, a class declares a delegate and a corresponding event, something like this:

```
public class PublisherOfInterestingEvents
{
    // A delegate type on which to base the event. Should be
    // declared 'internal' if all subscribers are in the same assembly.
    public delegate void NewEditionEventHandler(object sender,
                                                NewEditionEventArgs e);
    // The event:
    public event NewEditionEventHandler NewEdition;
    // ... other code.
}
```

The delegate and event definitions announce to the world: "Subscribers welcome!" You can think of the NewEdition event as similar to a variable of the New EditionEventHandler delegate type. (So far, no events have been sent. This is just the infrastructure for them.)

TIP

It's considered good practice to append EventHandler to the name of a delegate type that is the basis for events. A common example, which you can see in the SimpleProgress code example, discussed earlier in this chapter, is a Button advertising its various events, including a Click event. In C#, class Button exposes this event as

```
event _dispCommandBarControlEvents_ClickEventHandler Click;
```

where the second, long item is a delegate defined somewhere in .NET.

REMEMBER

Because events are used so commonly, .NET defines two event-related delegate types for you, named EventHandler and EventHandler<TEventArgs>. You can change NewEditionEventHandler in the previous code to EventHandler or to the generic EventHandler<TEventArgs>, and you don't need your own delegate type.

The rest of this chapter pretends to use the built-in `EventHandler<TEventArgs>` delegate type mentioned earlier, not `EventHandler` or a custom type, `NewEdition EventHandler`. You should prefer this form, too:

```
event EventHandler<NewEditonEventArgs> NewEdition;
```

How subscribers subscribe to an event

To receive a particular event, subscribers sign up something like this:

```
publisher.EventName +=
  new EventHandler<some EventArgs type here>(some method name here);
```

where `publisher` is an instance of the publisher class, `EventName` is the event name, and `EventHandler<TEventArgs>` is the delegate underneath the event. More specifically, the code in the previous example might be

```
myPublisher.NewEdition += new EventHandler<NewEditionEventArgs>(MyPubHandler);
```

Because an event object is a delegate under its little hood, the += syntax is adding a method to the list of methods that the delegate will call when you invoke it.

TIP

Any number of objects can subscribe this way (and the delegate will hold a list of all subscribed "handler" methods) — even the object on which the event was defined can subscribe, if you like. (And yes, this example shows that a delegate can "point" to more than one method.) In the `SimpleProgress` program, look in the `Form1.Designer.cs` file for how the form class registers itself as a subscriber to the buttons' `Click` events.

How to publish an event

When the publisher decides that something worthy of publishing to all subscribers has occurred, it *raises* (sends) the event. This situation is analogous to a real newspaper putting out the Sunday edition. To publish the event, the publisher would have code like this in one of its methods (but see the later section "A recommended way to raise your events"):

```
NewEditionEventArgs e =
  new NewEditionEventArgs(<args to constructor here>);

// Raise the event -- 'this' is the publisher object.
NewEdition(this, e);
```

Or for the Button example, though this is hidden in class Button:

```
EventArgs e = new EventArgs();   // See next section for more on this topic.
Click(this, e);                  // Raise the event.
```

In each of these examples, you set up the necessary arguments — which differ from event to event; some events need to pass along a lot of info. Then you raise the event by "calling" its name (like invoking a delegate!):

```
// Raising an event (distributing the newspaper)
eventName(<argumentlist>);
NewEdition(this, e);
```

Events can be based on different delegates with different signatures, that have different parameters, as in the earlier NewEditionEventHandler example, but providing the sender and e parameters is conventional for events. The built-in EventHandler and EventHandler<TEventArgs> delegate types define them for you.

Passing along a reference to the event's sender (the object that raises the event) is useful if the event-handling method needs to get more information from it. Thus a particular Button object, button1, can pass a reference to the Form class the button is a part of. The button's Click event handler resides in a Form class, so the sender is the form: You would pass this.

You can raise an event in any method on the publishing class. But when? Raise it whenever appropriate. The "A recommended way to raise your events" section says more about raising events.

How to pass extra information to an event handler

The e parameter to an event handler method is a custom subclass of the System. EventArgs class. You can write your own NewEditionEventArgs class to carry whatever information you need to convey:

```
public class NewEditionEventArgs : EventArgs
{
  public NewEditionEventArgs(DateTime date, string majorHeadline)
    { PubDate = date; Head = majorHeadline; }
  public DateTime PubDate { get; private set; }
  public string Head { get; private set; }
}
```

You should implement this class's members as properties, as shown in the previous code example. The constructor uses the private setter clauses on the properties. Often, your event doesn't require any extra arguments, and you can just fall back on the EventArgs base class, as shown in the next section. If you don't need a special EventArgs-derived object for your event, just pass:

```
NewEdition(this, EventArgs.Empty);  // Raise the event.
```

A recommended way to raise your events

The earlier section "How to publish an event" shows the bare bones of raising an event. However, you should always define a special event raiser method, like this:

```
protected virtual void OnNewEdition(NewEditionEventArgs e)
{
  EventHandler<NewEditionEventArgs> temp = NewEdition;
  if(temp != null)
  {
    temp(this, e);
  }
}
```

Providing this method ensures that you always remember to complete two steps:

1. **Store the event in a temporary variable.**

   This step makes your event more usable in situations in which multiple "threads" try to use it at the same time. Threads divide your program into a foreground task and one or more background tasks, which run simultaneously (concurrently).

2. **Check the event for null before you try to raise it.**

   If it's null, trying to raise it causes an error. Besides, null also means that no other objects have shown an interest in your event (none is subscribed), so why bother raising it? *Always* check the event for null, regardless of whether you write this On*SomeEvent* method.

Making the method protected and virtual allows subclasses to override it. That's optional. After you have that method, which always takes the same form (making it easy to write quickly), you call the method when you need to raise the event:

```
void SomeMethod()
{
  // Do stuff here and then:
  NewEditionEventArgs e =
    new NewEditionEventArgs(DateTime.Today, "Peace Breaks Out!");
  OnNewEdition(e);
}
```

How observers "handle" an event

The subscribing object specifies the name of a *handler method* when it subscribes — it's the argument to the constructor (boldfaced):

```
button1.Click += new EventHandler<EventArgs>(button1_Click);
```

This line sort of says, "Send my paper to this address, please." Here's a handler for the NewEdition event:

```
myPublisher.NewEdition += new EventHandler<NewEditionEventArgs>(NewEdHandler);
...
void NewEdHandler(object sender, NewEditionEventArgs e)
{
  // Do something in response to the event.
}
```

For example, a BankAccount class can raise a custom TransactionAlert event when anything occurs in a BankAccount object, such as a deposit, withdrawal, or transfer or even an error. A Logger observer object can subscribe and log these events to a file or a database as an audit trail.

REMEMBER

When you create a button handler in Visual Studio (by double-clicking the button on your form), Visual Studio generates the subscription code in the Form1. Designer.cs file. You shouldn't edit the subscription, but you can delete it and replace it with the same code written in your half of the partial form class. Thereafter, the form designer knows nothing about it.

In your subscriber's handler method, you do whatever is supposed to happen when your class learns of this kind of event. To help you write that code, you can cast the sender parameter to the type you know it to be:

```
Button theButton = (Button)sender;
```

TIP

WHEN TO DELEGATE, WHEN TO EVENT, WHEN TO GO ON THE LAMBDA

Events: Use events when you may have multiple subscribers or when communicating with client software that uses your classes.

Delegates: Use delegates or anonymous methods when you need a callback or need to customize an operation.

Lambdas: A *lambda expression* is, in essence, just a short way to specify the method you're passing to a delegate. You can use lambdas instead of anonymous methods.

and then call methods and properties of that object as needed. Because you have a reference to the sending object, you can ask the subscriber questions and carry out operations on it if you need to — like the person who delivers your newspaper knocking on your door to collect the monthly subscription fees. And, you can extract information from the e parameter by getting at its properties in the same way:

```
Console.WriteLine(e.HatSize);
```

You don't always need to use the parameters, but they can be handy.

Chapter **10**

Can I Use Your Namespace in the Library?

C# gives you a variety of ways to break code into meaningful, workable units. These methods include programmatic breaks, such as methods and classes, and structural breaks, such as libraries, assemblies, and namespaces.

You can use a method to divide a long string of code into separate, maintainable units. Use the class structure to group both data and methods in meaningful ways to further reduce the complexity of the program. Programs are complex already, and humans become confused easily, so we need all the help we can get.

C# provides another level of grouping: You can group similar classes into a separate library. Beyond writing your own libraries, you can use anybody's libraries in your programs. These programs contain multiple modules known as *assemblies*. This chapter describes libraries and assemblies.

Meanwhile, the access-control story in Chapter 5 of this minibook leaves a few untidy loose ends — the protected, internal, and protected internal keywords — and is slightly complicated further by the use of *namespaces*, another way to group similar classes and allow the use of duplicate names in two parts of a program. This chapter covers namespaces as well.

Dividing a Single Program into Multiple Source Files

The programs in this book are for demonstration purposes only. Each program is no more than a few dozen lines long and contains no more than a few classes. An industrial-strength program, complete with all the necessary bells and whistles, can include hundreds of thousands of lines of code, spread over a hundred or more classes.

Consider an airline ticketing system: You have the interface to the reservations agent whom you call on the phone, another interface to the person behind the gate counter, the Internet (in addition to the part that controls aircraft seat inventory plus the part that calculates fares, including taxes); the list goes on and on. A program such as this one grows huge before it's all over. Putting all those classes into one big Program.cs source file quickly becomes impractical. It's awkward for these reasons:

>> **You have to keep the classes straight.** A single source file can become extremely difficult to understand. Getting a grip on modules such as these, for example, is much easier:

- Aircraft.cs

- Fare.cs

- GateAgent.cs

- GateAgentInterface.cs

- ResAgent.cs

- ResAgentInterface.cs

They also make the task of finding things easier.

>> **The work of creating large programs is usually spread among numerous programmers.** Two programmers can't edit the same file at the same time; each programmer requires exclusive file access or else chaos ensues. You may have 20 or 30 programmers working on a large project at one time. One file containing a single class would limit 24 programmers to one hour of editing a day, around the clock. If you divide the program into multiple classes and then place each class into its own file, orchestrating the same 24 programmers becomes much easier.

>> **Compiling a large file may take a considerable length of time.** You can draw out a coffee break for only so long before the boss starts getting suspicious. You certainly wouldn't want to rebuild all the instructions that make up a big system just because a programmer changed a single line. Visual Studio 2017 can rebuild a single project (an individual module of the whole program, which may contain numerous projects). That's quicker and easier than building an entire big program at one time.

For these reasons, the smart C# programmer divides a program into multiple .cs source files, which are compiled and built together into a single executable .exe file.

REMEMBER

A *project file* contains the instructions about which files should be used together and how they're combined. You can combine project files to generate combinations of programs that depend on the same user-defined classes. For example, you may want to couple a write program with its corresponding read program. That way, if one changes, the other is rebuilt automatically. One project would describe the write program while another describes the read program. A set of project files is known as a *solution*. (The FileRead and FileWrite programs covered in Book 3 could rely on a single combined solution, but they don't.)

TIP

Visual C# programmers use the Visual Studio Solution Explorer to combine multiple C# source files into projects within the Visual Studio 2017 environment. Book 4 describes Solution Explorer.

Dividing a Single Program into Multiple Assemblies

In Visual Studio, and in C#, Visual Basic .NET, and the other .NET languages, one project equals one compiled *module* — otherwise known as an *assembly* in .NET. The words module and assembly have somewhat different technical meanings, but only to advanced programmers. In this book, you can just equate the two terms.

Executable or library?

C# can produce two basic assembly types:

>> **Executable (.EXE):** A program in its own right that contains a Main() method. You can double-click a .EXE file in Windows Explorer, for example, and cause it to run. This book is full of executables in the form of console

applications. Executable assemblies often use supporting code from libraries in other assemblies.

>> **Class library (.DLL):** A compiled library of functionality that can be used by other programs. All programs in this book also use libraries. For example, the System namespace (the home of classes such as String, Console, Exception, Math, and Object) exists in a set of library assemblies. Every program needs System classes. Libraries are housed in DLL assemblies.

REMEMBER

Libraries aren't executable — you can't make them run directly. Instead, you must call their code from an executable or another library. The Common Language Runtime (CLR), which runs C# programs, loads library assemblies into memory as needed.

The important concept to know is that you can easily write your own class libraries. The "Putting Your Classes into Class Libraries" section of this chapter shows you how to perform this task.

Assemblies

Assemblies, which are the compiled versions of individual projects, contain the project's code in a special format, along with a bunch of *metadata*, or detailed information about the classes in the assembly.

This section introduces assemblies because they round out your understanding of the C# build process — and they come into play in the discussion of namespaces and access keywords such as protected and internal. (You find these namespaces and these keywords covered later in this chapter.) Assemblies also play a big part in understanding class libraries. It's all covered in the later section "Putting Your Classes into Class Libraries."

TECHNICAL
STUFF

The C# compiler converts the project's C# code to Common Intermediate Language (usually called IL) that's stored in the appropriate type of assembly file. IL resembles assembly language (one step beyond the 1s and 0s used in machine language) that hardcore programmers have used for decades to get down "close to the metal" because their higher-level languages couldn't do what they needed or the compilers couldn't produce the most efficient code possible.

One major consequence of compiling from .NET to IL, regardless of language, is that a program can use assemblies written in different languages. For example, a C# program can call methods in an assembly originally written in Visual Basic or C++ or the C# program can subclass a VB class.

Executables

You can run executable assemblies in a variety of ways:

>> Run them in Visual Studio: Choose Debug⇨Start Debugging (F5) or Debug⇨Start without Debugging (Ctrl+F5).

>> Double-click the assembly file (.EXE) in Windows Explorer.

>> Right-click the file in Windows Explorer and choose Run or Open from the pop-up menu.

>> Type the assembly's name (and path) into a console window.

>> If the program takes arguments, such as filenames, from the command line, drag the files to the executable file in Windows Explorer.

REMEMBER

A solution in Visual Studio can contain multiple projects — some .DLL and some .EXE. If a solution contains more than one .EXE project, you must tell Visual Studio which project is the *start-up project*; the one runs from the Debug menu. To specify a start-up project, right-click that project in Solution Explorer and choose Set As Startup Project. The start-up project's name appears in boldface in Solution Explorer.

Think of a solution containing two .EXE assemblies as two separate programs that happen to use the same library assemblies. For example, you might have in a solution a console executable and a Windows Forms executable plus some libraries. If you make the console app the start-up project and compile the code, you produce a console app. If you make the Windows Forms app the start-up — well, you get the idea.

Class libraries

A *class library* contains one or more classes, usually ones that work together in some way. Often, the classes in a library are in their own namespaces. (The "Putting Classes into Namespaces" section, later in this chapter, explains namespaces.) You may build a library of math routines, a library of string-handling routines, and a library of input/output routines, for example.

Sometimes, you even build a whole solution that is nothing but a class library, rather than a program that can be executed on its own. (Typically, while developing this type of library, you also build an accompanying .EXE project to test your library during development. But when you release the library for programmers to use, you release just the .DLL (not the .EXE) — and documentation for it, which you can generate by writing XML comments in the code. XML comments are described in Book 4, which is all about Visual Studio.) The next section shows you how to write your own class libraries.

Putting Your Classes into Class Libraries

REMEMBER

The simplest definition of a *class library project* is one whose classes contain no Main() method. Can that definition be correct? It can and is. The existence of Main() distinguishes a class library from an executable. C# libraries are much easier to write and use than similar libraries were in C or C++.

The following sections explain the basic concepts involved in creating your own class libraries. Don't worry: C# does the heavy lifting. Your end of it is quite simple.

Creating the projects for a class library

You can create the files for a new class library project and its test application in either of two ways:

>> **Create the class library project first and then add the test application project to its solution.** You might take this approach if you were writing a stand-alone class library assembly. The next section describes how to create the class library project.

>> **Create a test application first and then add one or more library projects to its solution.** Thus you might first create the test application as a console application or a graphical Windows Forms (or Windows Presentation Foundation) application. Then you would add class library projects to that solution.

This approach is the one to take if you want to add a supporting library to an ongoing application. In that case, the test application could be either the ongoing program or a special test application project added to the solution just to test the library. For testing, you set the test application project as the start-up project as described in the earlier section "Executables."

Creating a stand-alone class library

If your whole purpose is to develop a stand-alone class library that can be used in various other programs, you can create a solution that contains a class library project from scratch. Here's how simple it is:

1. Choose File⇨New⇨Project.

You see a New Project dialog box, shown in Figure 10-1.

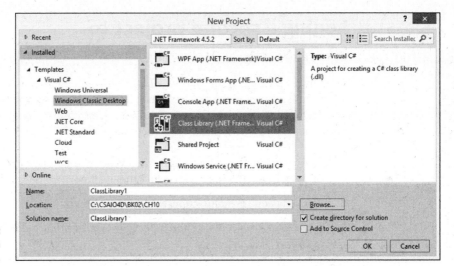

FIGURE 10-1:
A new library in Solution Explorer.

2. **Select the Class Library template in the Visual C#\Windows Classic Desktop folder.**

Figure 10-1 shows what Solution Explorer looks like at this point.

3. **Type a name for your class library in the Name field and then click OK.**

The example uses TestClass as the project name. Visual Studio creates the new project for you. You see the Class1.cs file open so that you can begin adding mode for your class library. After you have a class library project, you can add a test application project (or a unit test project or both) using the approach described in the next section.

TIP

Look in Solution Explorer and you see that the name of the file for your class is Class1.cs, which isn't very descriptive. Use these steps to correct the situation:

1. **Right-click the Class1.cs entry and choose Rename from the context menu.**

The entry changes so that you can type a new name.

2. **Type a new name for your file and press Enter.**

You see a dialog box stating that you're renaming a file and asking whether you'd like to rename the class to match.

3. **Click Yes.**

Visual Studio automatically renames all Class1 references to match the new filename you provide.

Can I Use Your Namespace in the Library?

Adding a second project to an existing solution

If you have an existing solution — whether it's an ongoing application or a class library project such as the one described in the previous section — you can easily add a second project to your solution: either a class library project or an executable project, such as a test application. Follow these steps:

1. **After your existing solution is open in Visual Studio, right-click the solution node (the top node) in Solution Explorer.**

2. **From the pop-up menu, choose Add⇨New Project.**

3. **In the New Project dialog box, select the type of project you want to add.**

   Select a class library, a console application, a Windows Forms application, or another available type on the right side of the dialog box.

4. **Use the Location box to navigate to the folder where you want the project.**

   The location you navigate to depends on how you want to organize your solution. You can put the new project's folder in either of two places:

   - **All-in-one-folder:** Navigate into the main project folder, making the added project a subfolder. (See Figure 10-2.)

Main project folder

Added project folder

   - **Side-by-side:** Navigate to the folder that contains the main project folder so that the two projects are at the same level. (See Figure 10-3.)

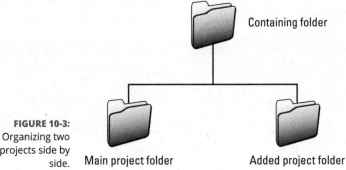

Containing folder

Main project folder

Added project folder

FIGURE 10-3:
Organizing two
projects side by
side.

5. **Name your project and click OK.**

The example uses TestApplication and a Console App template. If the new project is a library project, choose its name carefully — it will become the name of the library's .DLL file and the name of the namespace containing the project's classes.

TIP

If you need to give the library project the same name as another project or even the main project, you can distinguish it by appending the suffix Lib, as in MyConversionLib.

If the project you're adding is intended to stand on its own and be usable in other programs, use the side-by-side approach.

The TestClass example in this section (like most examples in this book) takes the all-in-one-folder approach. The point is that although the folders don't have to be in the same place, putting them there can be convenient. After you create Test Application, right-click its entry in Solution Explorer and choose Set as StartUp Project from the context menu.

The task of selecting the location is independent of adding the new project directly to the TestClass solution. The two project folders can be in the same solution while still being located in different places.

Creating classes for the library

After you have a class library project, create the classes that make up the library. The following TestClass example shows a simple class library:

```
using System;

namespace TestClass
{
    public class DoMath
```

```
    {
        public int DoAdd(int Num1, int Num2)
        {
            return Num1 + Num2;
        }

        public int DoSub(int Num1, int Num2)
        {
            return Num1 - Num2;
        }

        public int DoMul(int Num1, int Num2)
        {
            return Num1 * Num2;
        }

        public int DoDiv(int Num1, int Num2)
        {
            return Num1 / Num2;
        }
    }
}
```

Libraries can contain any C# type: class, structure, delegate, interface, and enumeration. You find structures discussed in Chapter 12 of this minibook, delegates appear in Chapter 9 of this minibook, interfaces are in Chapter 8 of this minibook, and Book 1, Chapter 10 discusses enumerations.

REMEMBER

In class library code, you normally shouldn't catch exceptions. Let them bubble up from the library to the client code that's calling into the library. Clients need to know about these exceptions and handle them in their own ways. Book 1 covers exceptions.

Using a test application to test a library

By itself, the class library doesn't do anything, so you need a *test application*, a small executable program that tests the library code during development by calling its methods. In other words, write a program that uses classes and methods from the library. You see this behavior in the TestApplication program example.

REMEMBER

To use your class library from within the test application, you must add a reference to it. To perform this task, right-click References in the TestApplication section of Solution Explorer and choose Add Reference. You see a Reference Manager dialog box like the one shown in Figure 10-4. Choose Projects\Solution in the left pane, select TestClass in the center pane, and click to add the reference.

FIGURE 10-4:
Add a reference
for your class
library.

The following chunk of code continues the previous code listing. This one adds a
new project with one class that contains a Main() method, and you can write code
to exercise your library inside Main():

```
using System;

// Add a reference to your class library.
using TestClass;

namespace TestApplication
{
    class Program
    {
        static void Main(string[] args)
        {
            // Create a DoMath object.
            DoMath math = new DoMath();

            // Test the DoMath library functions.
            Console.WriteLine("6 + 2 = {0}", math.DoAdd(6, 2));
            Console.WriteLine("6 - 2 = {0}", math.DoSub(6, 2));
            Console.WriteLine("6 * 2 = {0}", math.DoMul(6, 2));
            Console.WriteLine("6 / 2 = {0}", math.DoDiv(6, 2));

            // Wait for user to acknowledge the results.
            Console.WriteLine("Press Enter to terminate...");
            Console.Read();
        }
    }
}
```

Here's the output from the test application:

```
6 + 2 = 8
6 - 2 = 4
6 * 2 = 12
6 / 2 = 3
Press Enter to terminate...
```

TIP

Libraries often provide only `static` methods. In that case, you don't need to instantiate the library object. Just call the methods through the class.

Going Beyond Public and Private: More Access Keywords

Dividing a program into multiple assemblies, as discussed in the previous sections, has a bearing on which code in `AssemblyB` you can access from `AssemblyA`. The access control examples in Chapter 5 of this minibook do a good job of illustrating the `public` and `private` keywords. But that chapter doesn't say a lot about the other access keywords: `protected`, `internal`, and the combination `protected internal`. The following sections rectify this situation, assuming that you understand inheritance and method overriding as well as `public` and `private`. To ensure that this section makes sense, you might need to read (or reread) Chapter 5.

Internal: For CIA eyes only

Suppose that a program has these two projects:

>> `InternalLimitsAccess`: An executable whose class `Congress` contains the `Main()` method that kicks off program execution. (No law requires the `Main()` class to be named `Program`.)

>> `CIAAssembly`: The class library project.

In real life, the U.S. Congress has the annoying habit of expecting the Central Intelligence Agency (CIA) to reveal its secrets — just to members of Congress and senators, of course. ("We won't leak your secrets — honest.") Meanwhile, those overly secretive spooks at the CIA have secrets they would prefer to hang on to.

(Maybe they know the secret formula for Coca-Cola or Colonel Sanders's secret herbs and spices or a more sinister entity.) Exactly what Secret X is doesn't matter here, but the CIA wants to keep Secret X, well, secret.

There's a problem, though. Everybody at the CIA needs to know Secret X. In the InternalLimitsAccess example, the CIA is divided into several classes — class GroupA and class GroupB, for example. Think of them as sections of the CIA that (sometimes) communicate and share with each other. Suppose that GroupA is the holder of Secret X, so the group marked it private. The code looks something like this:

```
// In assembly InternalLimitsAccess:
class Congress
{
  static void Main(...)
  {
    // Code to oversee CIA
  }
}


// In assembly CIAAssembly:
public class GroupA
{
  private string _secretFormulaForCocaCola; // Secret X
  internal GroupA() { _secretFormulaForCocaCola = "lots of sugar";}
}


public class GroupB
{
  public void DoSomethingWithSecretX()
  {
    // Do something with Secret X, if only you could access it.
  }
}
```

Now GroupB can't see Secret X, but suppose that it has a legitimate need to know it. GroupA can, of course, bump Secret X to public status, but if it does, the secret isn't much of a secret anymore. If GroupB can see the secret, so can those snoops over in Congress. Even worse, CNN knows it too, not to mention Fox, ABC, and other networks. And you know how well those folks keep secrets. Oh, right — Russia can see Secret X, too.

REMEMBER

Luckily, C# also has the `internal` keyword. Using `internal` is just one step down from `public` and well above `private`. If you mark the `GroupA` class and its "public" methods — the ones that are visible outside the class — with the `internal` keyword instead, everybody at the CIA can see and access Secret X — as long as you either mark the secret itself (a data member) as `internal` or provide an `internal` property to get it with, as shown in this version:

```
// In assembly CIAAssembly:
internal class GroupA
{
  private string _secretFormulaForCocaCola; // Secret X
  internal string SecretX { get { return _secretFormulaForCocaCola; } }
  internal GroupA() { _secretFormulaForCocaCola = "lots of sugar";}
}

public class GroupB
{
  public void DoSomethingWithSecretX()
  {
    // Do something with Secret X, now that we can see it:
    Console.WriteLine("I know Secret X, which is {0} characters long, "
        + "but I'm not telling.", GroupA.SecretX.Length);
  }
}
```

Now class `GroupB` has the access it needs — and it isn't giving up the secret (even under threat of waterboarding). All it tells `Congress`, over in `Main()`, is that it knows Secret X, and Secret X has 11 characters. Here's that chunk of code:

```
class Congress
{
  static void Main(string[] args)
  {
    // Code to oversee CIA
    // The following line doesn't compile because GroupA isn't accessible
    // outside CIAAssembly. Congress can't get at GroupA over at CIA.

    // CIAAssembly.GroupA groupA = new CIAAssembly.GroupA();

    // Class Congress can access GroupB because it's declared public.
    // GroupB is willing to admit to knowing the secret, but it's
    // not telling -- except for a small hint.
    GroupB groupB = new GroupB();
    groupB.DoSomethingWithSecretX();
```

```
      // Wait for user to acknowledge results.
      Console.WriteLine("Press Enter to terminate...");
      Console.Read();
   }
}
```

From `Main()`, `GroupA` is now invisible, so an attempt to construct an instance of it doesn't compile. But because `GroupB` is public, `Main()` can access it and call its public method `DoSomethingWithSecretX()`.

Wait! CIA does have to talk to Congress about certain topics, but on a need-to-know basis, limited to selected members of Congress and senators, of course. They can do so already, via `GroupB`, as long as they present the proper credentials, although you need to add them to the code:

```
public string DoSomethingWithSecretXUsingCredentials(string credentials)
{
    if (credentials == "congressman with approved access")
    {
      return GroupA.SecretX;
    }
    return string.Empty;
}
```

REMEMBER

The `internal` keyword makes classes and their members accessible only inside their own assembly. But within the assembly, the internal items are effectively "public" to all local classes.

REMEMBER

You can mark a method inside an `internal` class as `public`, though it isn't truly public. A class member can't be more accessible than its class, so the so-called "public" member is just `internal`.

CIA can still keep its deepest, darkest secrets ultra-hush-hush by declaring them private inside their owning class. That strategy makes them accessible only in that class.

Protected: Sharing with subclasses

The main purpose of `private` is to hide information. In particular, `private` hides a class's internal implementation details. (Classes who know classes too intimately aren't the luckiest classes in the world. In fact, they're the unluckiest.) Classes with a lot of implementation details are said to be "too tightly coupled" with the classes they know too much about. If class A is aware of the internal workings of class B, A can come to rely too much on those details. If they ever change, you end up having to modify both classes.

The less the other classes — and assemblies — know about how class B performs its magic, the better. Chapter 5 of this minibook uses the example of a BankAccount class. The bank doesn't want forgetful folks or forgetful classes to be able to change a balance directly. That balance is properly part of the BankAccount class's implementation. It's private. BankAccount provides access to the balance — but only through a carefully controlled public interface. In the BankAccount class, the public interface consists of three public methods:

>> Balance: Provides a read-only way to find out the current balance. You can't use Balance to modify the underlying balance.

>> Deposit(): Lets someone outside the class add to the balance in a controlled way.

>> Withdraw(): Lets someone (presumably the account owner) subtract from the balance, but within carefully controlled limits. Withdraw() enforces the business rule that you can't withdraw more than you have.

Access control considerations other than private and public arise in programming. The previous section explains how the internal keyword opens a class — but only to other classes in its own assembly.

However, suppose that the BankAccount class has a subclass, SavingsAccount. Methods in SavingsAccount need access to that balance defined in the base class. Of course, other classes, even in the same assembly, probably don't. Luckily, SavingsAccount can use the same public interface, the same access, as outsiders: using Balance, Deposit(), and Withdraw().

Sometimes, though, the base class doesn't supply such access methods for its subclasses (and others) to use. What if the _balance data member in BankAccount is private and the class doesn't provide the Balance property?

REMEMBER

Enter the protected keyword: If the _balance instance variable in the base class is declared protected rather than private, outsiders can't see it — it's effectively private to them. But subclasses can see it just fine.

TIP

An even better solution is to mark _balance private in BankAccount as before and then provide a Balance property marked protected. Subclasses such as SavingsAccount can access _balance by using the Balance property. But the balance is invisible to outsiders, which protects the BankAccount implementation even from its subclasses.

If the balance does indeed need to be accessible (read-only) to outsiders, you should, of course, provide the public Balance property to get the balance (read-only). However, you may still need to set the balance from inside SavingsAccount itself. To do that, you can give the set accessor of Balance protected access — accessible from SavingsAccount and other subclasses but inaccessible to outsiders. The discussion of properties in Chapter 5 of this minibook shows how to do it, and here's what the code looks like:

```
// In BankAccount:
public decimal Balance
{
  get { return _balance; }            // Public
  protected set { _balance = value; }  // Not public
}
```

TECHNICAL STUFF

You can even subclass BankAccount in a different assembly, and the subclass has access to anything declared protected in BankAccount. The capability to extend (subclass) a class from outside the base class's assembly has implications for security, which is why many classes should be marked sealed. Sealing a class prevents outsiders from gaining access by subclassing it. That's why you're advised to make classes extendable (nonsealed) only if they need to be subclassable. One way to give other code in the same assembly access to a base class's members — including a subclass in the same assembly — is to mark those members internal rather than protected. That way, you gain the desired level of access from a local subclass while preventing access from an external subclass. Of course, access is then allowed from other classes in the assembly. This solution may not be ideal, but it should be more secure — if that's a consideration.

Protected internal: Being a more generous protector

Making items in the BankAccount base class protected internal, rather than just protected, simply adds a new dimension to the accessibility of those items in your program. Using protected alone allows a subclass (in any assembly in the program) to access protected items in the base class. Adding internal extends the items' accessibility to any class, as long as they're in the same assembly as BankAccount or at least a subclass in some other assembly.

REMEMBER

Make items as inaccessible as possible. Start with private. If some parts of your code need more access than that, increase it selectively. Maybe just protected will work (that's all a subclass needs). Maybe other classes in the same assembly truly do need access. If so, increase it to internal. If subclasses and other classes in the same assembly need access, use protected internal. Use public only for classes (and their members) that should be accessible to every class in the program, regardless of assembly.

TIP

The same advice that applies to whole classes also applies to class members: Keep them as inaccessible as possible. Little *helper classes,* or classes that support the implementation of more public classes, can be limited to no more than `internal`. If a class or other type needs to be `private`, `protected`, or `protected internal`, nest it, if you can, inside the class that needs access to it.

Putting Classes into Namespaces

Namespaces exist to put related classes in one bag and to reduce collisions between names used in different places. For example, you may compile all math-related classes into a `MathRoutines` namespace. A single file can be (but isn't commonly) divided into multiple namespaces:

```
// In file A.cs:
namespace One
{
}

namespace Two
{
}
```

More commonly, you group multiple files. For example, the file `Point.cs` may contain the class `Point`, and the file `ThreeDSpace.cs` contains class `ThreeDSpace` to describe the properties of a Euclidean space (like a cube). You can combine `Point.cs` and `ThreeDSpace.cs` and other C# source files into the `MathRoutines` namespace (and, possibly, a `MathRoutines` library assembly). Each file would wrap its code in the same namespace. (It's the classes in those files, rather than the files themselves, that make up the namespace. Which files the classes are in is irrelevant for namespaces. Nor does it matter which assembly they're in: A namespace can span multiple assemblies.)

```
// In file Point.cs:
namespace MathRoutines
{
  class Point { }
}

// In file ThreeDSpace.cs:
namespace MathRoutines
{
  class ThreeDSpace { }
}
```

REMEMBER

If you don't wrap your classes in a namespace, C# puts them in the *global namespace*, the base (unnamed) namespace for all other namespaces. A better practice, though, is to use a specific namespace. The namespace serves these purposes:

» **A namespace puts oranges with oranges, not with apples.** As an application programmer, you can reasonably assume that the classes that comprise the MathRoutines namespace are all math related. By the same token, when looking for just the perfect math method, you first would look in the classes that make up the MathRoutines namespace.

» **Namespaces avoid the possibility of name conflicts.** For example, a file input/output library may contain a class Convert that converts the representation in one file type to that of another. At the same time, a translation library may contain a class of the same name. Assigning the namespaces FileIO and TranslationLibrary to the two sets of classes avoids the problem: The class FileIO.Convert clearly differs from the class TranslationLibrary. Convert.

Declaring a namespace

You declare a namespace using the keyword namespace followed by a name and an open and closed curly-braces block. The classes (and other types) within that block are part of the namespace:

```
namespace MyStuff
{
    class MyClass {}
    class UrClass {}
}
```

In this example, both MyClass and UrClass are part of the MyStuff namespace.

REMEMBER

Namespaces are implicitly public, and you can't use access specifiers on namespaces, not even public.

Besides classes, namespaces can contain other types, including these:

» delegate

» enum

» interface

» struct

A namespace can also contain *nested namespaces,* which are namespaces within other namespaces, to any depth of nesting. You may have `Namespace2` nested inside `Namespace1`, as in this example:

```
namespace Namespace1
{
  // Classes in Namespace1 here ...
  // Then the nested namespace:
  namespace Namespace2
  {
    // Classes in Namespace2
    public class Class2
    {
      public void AMethod() { }
    }
  }
}
```

To call a method in `Class2`, inside `Namespace2`, from somewhere outside `Namespace1`, you specify this line:

```
Namespace1.Namespace2.Class2.AMethod();
```

Imagine these namespaces strung together with dots as a sort of logical path to the desired item. "Dotted names," such as `System.IO`, look like nested namespaces, but they name only one namespace. So `System.Data` is a complete namespace name, not the name of a `Data` namespace nested inside `System`. This convention makes it easier to have several related namespaces, such as `System.IO`, `System.Data`, and `System.Text`, and make the family resemblance obvious. In practice, nested namespaces and namespaces with dotted names are indistinguishable.

TECHNICAL STUFF

Prefixing all namespaces in a program with your company name is conventional — making the company name the front part of multiple segments separated by dots: `MyCompany.MathRoutines`. (That statement is true if you have a company name; you can also use just your own name.) Adding a company name prevents name clashes if your code uses two third-party code libraries that happen to use the same basic namespace name, such as `MathRoutines`.

TIP

The Visual Studio New Project dialog box runs an Application Wizard that puts all code it generates in namespaces. The wizard names these namespaces after the project directory it creates. Look at any of the programs in this book, each of which was created by the Application Wizard. For example, the `AlignOutput` program is created in the `AlignOutput` folder. The name of the source file is `Program.cs`, which matches the name of the default class. The name of the namespace containing `Program.cs` is the same as that of the folder: `AlignOutput`.

TIP

You can change the name of any namespace by typing a new name. However, this method of performing the change can cause problems if you're not careful. A better way is to right-click the namespace name and choose Rename from the context menu. This approach forces Visual Studio to do the work for you and ensures that you get more consistent results.

Relating namespaces to the access keyword story

REMEMBER

In addition to helping package your code into a more usable form, namespaces extend the notion of access control presented in Chapter 5 of this minibook (which introduces the `public`, `private`, `protected`, `internal`, and `protected internal` keywords). Namespaces extend access control by further limiting which members of a class you can access from where.

However, namespaces affect visibility more than accessibility. By default, classes and methods in `NamespaceA` are invisible to classes in `NamespaceB`, regardless of their access-control specifiers. But you can make one namespace's classes and methods visible to another namespace in a couple of ways. The bottom line is that you can access only what is visible to you and is public enough. This issue involves access control, extended earlier in this chapter and covered in the discussion of access specifiers in Chapter 5 of this minibook.

Determining whether the class and method you need are visible and accessible to you

To determine whether `Class1` in `NamespaceA` can call `NamespaceB.Class2.AMethod()`, consider these two questions:

>> **Is `Class2` over in `NamespaceB` visible to the calling class, `Class1`?**

This issue involves namespace visibility, discussed at the end of this list.

>> **If the answer to the first question is True, are `Class2` and its `AMethod()` also "public enough" for `Class1` to access?**

If `Class2` is in a different assembly from `Class1`, it must be `public` for `Class1` to access its members. `Class2`, in the same assembly needs to be declared at least `internal`. Classes can only be `public`, `protected`, `internal`, or `private`.

Likewise, the `Class2` method must have at least a certain level of access in each of those situations. Methods add the `protected internal` option to the list of access specifiers that classes have. Chapter 5 in this minibook and the earlier section "Going Beyond Public and Private: More Access Keywords" supply the gory details.

You need to answer Yes to both questions before `Class1` can call the `Class2` method.

Making classes and methods in another namespace visible

C# provides two ways to make items in NamespaceB visible in NamespaceA:

>> **Fully qualify names from** NamespaceB **wherever you use them in** NamespaceA. This method results in code such as the following line, which starts with the namespace name and then adds the class and lists the method:

```
System.Console.WriteLine("my string");
```

>> **Eliminate the need for fully qualified names in** NamespaceA **by giving your files a** using **directive for** NamespaceB:

```
using System;    // These are namespace names.
using NamespaceB;
```

Programs throughout this book make items in NamespaceB visible in NamespaceA with the using directive. The next two sections discuss full qualification and using directives.

Using fully qualified names

The namespace of a class is a part of the extended class name, which leads to the first way to make classes in one namespace visible in another. This example doesn't have any using directives to simplify referring to classes in other namespaces:

```
namespace MathRoutines  // Broken into two segments -- see below.
{
  class Sort
  {
    public void SomeMethod(){}
  }
}

namespace Paint
{
  public class PaintColor
```

```
  {
    public PaintColor(int nRed, int nGreen, int nBlue) {}
    public void Paint() {}
    public static void StaticPaint() {}
  }
}

namespace MathRoutines  // Another piece of this namespace
{
  public class Test
  {
    static public void Main(string[] args)
    {
      // Create an object of type Sort from the same namespace
      // we're in and invoke a method.
      Sort obj = new Sort();
      obj.SomeMethod();

      // Create an object in another namespace -- notice that the
      // namespace name must be included explicitly in every
      // class reference.
      Paint.PaintColor black = new Paint.PaintColor(0, 0, 0);
      black.Paint();
      Paint.PaintColor.StaticPaint();
    }
  }
}
```

Normally, Sort and Test would be in different C# source files that you build together into one program. In this case, the two classes Sort and Test are contained within the same namespace, MathRoutines, even though they appear in different declarations within the file (or in different files). That namespace is broken into two parts.

The method Test.Main() can reference the Sort class without specifying the namespace because the two classes are in the same namespace. However, Main() must specify the Paint namespace when referring to PaintColor, as in the call to Paint.PaintColor.StaticPaint(). This process is known as *fully qualifying* the name.

Notice that you don't need to take any special steps when referring to black. Paint(), because the class of the black object is specified, namespace and all, in the black declaration.

Chapter **11**

Improving Productivity with Named and Optional Parameters

Parameters, as you probably remember, are the inputs to methods. They're the values that you put in so that you get a return value. Sometimes, the return values are parameters, too, which confuses things.

In older versions of C# and most C-derived languages, parameters can't be optional. Instead of making parameters optional, you are required to make a separate overload for every version of the method you expect your users to need. This pattern works well, but there are some problems that are explored in this chapter. Many VB programmers point to flexible parameterization as a strong reason to use VB over C#.

C# 4.0 and above have optional parameters. *Optional parameters* are parameters that have a default value right in the method signature — just like the VB.NET implementation. This is one more step toward language parity, and again in the name of COM programming. It's the same control-versus-productivity issue that Book 3, Chapter 6 shows you about the dynamic type. Optional parameters give you just enough rope to hang yourself. A programmer can easily make mistakes.

Exploring Optional Parameters

Optional parameters depend on having a default value set in order to be optional. For instance, if you're searching for a phone number by name and city, you can default the city name to your city, making the parameter optional.

```
public static string searchForPhoneNumber(string name, string city = "Columbus")
   {...}
```

In C# 3.0 (and older), you must implement this with two overloaded implementations of the search method. One of them includes the name and the city as parameters. The second has only the name as a parameter. It sets the city in the body of the method and calls the first method. The code looks like this:

```
public static string searchForPhoneNumber(string name, string city) {...}
public static string searchForPhoneNumber(string name) {
   string city = "Columbus";
   return searchForPhoneNumber(name, city);
}
```

The canonical example of this is the addit method. It's silly, but it illustrates the realities of multiple overloads. So, previously you had this:

```
public static int addit(int z, int y)
{
    return z + y;
}

public static int addit(int z, int y, int x)
{
    return z+y+x;
}

public static int addit(int z, int y, int x, int w)
{
    return z + y + x + w;
}

public static int addit(int z, int y, int x, int w, int v)
{
    return z + y + x + w + v;
}
```

With optional parameters, you now have this:

```
public static int addit(int z, int y, int x = 0, int w = 0, int v = 0)
{
    return z + y + x + w + v;
}
```

If you need to add two numbers, you can do it easily.

```
int answer = addit(10, 4),
```

If you need to add four numbers, you have no problems, either.

```
int answer = addit(10, 4, 5, 12);
```

So why are optional parameters dangerous? Because sometimes default values can have unintended consequences. For instance, you don't want to make a divideit method and set the default parameters to 0. Someone could call it and get an undebuggable division by zero error. Setting the optional values in additall to 1 inside the method body would be bad.

```
public static int addit(int z, int y, int x = 0, int w = 0, int v = 1)
{
    //You CLEARLY don't want this
    return z + y + x + w + v;
}
```

And sometimes problems can be subtle, so use optional parameters carefully. For instance, say you have a base class and then derive a class that implements the base, like this:

```
public abstract class Base
{
    public virtual void SomeFunction(int x = 0)
    {...}
}

public sealed class Derived : Base
{
    public override void SomeFunction(int x = 1)
    {...}
}
```

What happens if you declare a new instance?

```
Base ex1 = new Base();
ex1. SomeFunction ();                    // SomeFunction (0)

Base ex2 = new Derived();
ex2. SomeFunction ();                    // SomeFunction (0)

Derived ex3 = new Derived();
ex3. SomeFunction ();                    // SomeFunction (1)
```

What happened here? Depending on how you implement the classes, the default value for the optional parameter is set differently. The first example, ex1, is an implementation of Base, and the default optional parameter is 0. In the second example, ex2 is cast to a type of Derived (which is legal because Derived is a subclass of Base), and the default value is also 0. However, in the third example, Derived is instantiated directly, and the default value is 1. This isn't expected behavior. No matter how you slice it, it's a gotcha and something to watch out for.

Reference types

A reference type, as Book 1 discusses, types a variable that stores a reference to actual data, instead of the data itself. Reference types are usually referred to as objects. New reference types are implemented with

>> Class

>> Interface

>> Delegate

These need to be built before you use them; class itself isn't a reference type, but the Calendar class is. There are three built-in reference types in the .NET Framework:

>> String (who knows why this isn't a static type)

>> Object

>> Dynamic

You can pass a reference type into a method just as you can pass a static type. It is still considered a parameter. You still use it inside the method as you do with any other variable.

But can reference types be passed, as static types can? Let's try. For instance, if you have a `Schedule` method for your `Calendar` class, you could pass in the `CourseId`, or you could pass in the whole `Course`. It all depends on how you structure the application.

```
public class Course
{
    public int CourseId;
    public string Name;
    public void Course(int id, string name)
    {
        CourseId = id;
        Name = name;
    }
}

public class Calendar
{
    public static void Schedule(int courseId)
    {
    }
    public static void Schedule(Course course)
    {
        //Something interesting happens here
    }
}
```

In this example, you have an overloaded method for `Schedule` — one that accepts a `CourseId` and one that accepts a `Course` reference type. The second is a reference type, because `Course` is a class, rather than a static type, like the `Integer` of the `CourseId`.

What if you want the second `Schedule` method to support an optional `Course` parameter? Say, if you want it to create a `New Course` by default, you omit the parameter. This would be similar to setting a static integer to "0" or whatever, wouldn't it?

```
public static void Schedule(Course course = New Course())
{
    //Implementation here
}
```

This isn't allowed, however. Visual Studio allows optional parameters only on static types, and the compiler tells you so. If you want to do this, you have to accept the `CourseId` in the `Schedule` method and construct a new `Course` in the body of the event.

Output parameters

Output parameters are parameters in the method signature that actually change the value of the variable that is passed into them by the user. The parameter references the location of the original variable, rather than creating a working copy. Output parameters are declared in a method signature with the out keyword. You can have as many as you like (well, within reason), although if you use more than a few, you probably should use something else (a generic list, maybe?). An output parameter might look like this in a method declaration:

```
public static void Schedule(int courseId, out string name,
                            out DateTime scheduledTime)
{
    name = "something";
    scheduledTime = DateTime.Now;
}
```

Following the rules, you should be able to make one of these parameters optional by presetting a value. Unlike reference parameters, it makes sense that output parameters don't support default values. The output parameter is exactly that — output, and setting the value should happen inside the method body. Because output parameters aren't expecting a value coming in any way, it doesn't benefit the programmer to have default values.

Looking at Named Parameters

Hand in hand with the concept of optional parameters are named parameters. If you have more than one default parameter, you need a way to tell the compiler which parameter you're supplying! For example, look at the additall method earlier in this chapter, after optional parameters are implemented:

```
public static int addit(int z, int y, int x = 0, int w = 0, int v = 0)
{
    return z + y + x + w + v;
}
```

Clearly, the order of the parameters doesn't matter in this implementation, but if this were in a class library, you might not know that the order of the parameters is a non-issue! How would you tell the compiler to skip x and w if you want to supply v? In the old days, you would do this:

```
int answer = additall(3,7, , ,4);
```

Fortunately, you don't have to do that anymore. Now, with named parameters, you can say

```
int answer = additall(z:3, y:7, v:4);
```

The non-optional parameters don't have to be named; the position is assumed because they're required anyway. Nonetheless, naming them is good practice. If you skip naming them, you have this instead:

```
int answer = additall(3, 7, v:4);
```

You have to admit that this is a little harder to read. One would have to go back to the method signature to figure out what is happening.

Dealing with Overload Resolution

Problems begin when you have optional arguments and overloaded methods in the same method signature. Because C# allows for differently named parameters in overloads, things can get sort of hairy. Take, for example,

```
class Course
{
        public void New(object course)
        {
        }

        public void New(int courseId)
        {
        }
}
```

Try calling the New method with something like this:

```
Course course = new Course();
course.New(10);
```

Here, the runtime picks the second overload because 10 better matches an int than an object. The same is true when dealing with overloaded method signatures with optional parameters. The tiebreaker goes to the overload with the fewest casts required to make it work.

Using Alternative Methods to Return Values

C# 7.0 changes the way return values work. You can now work with out and reference variables in new ways. The following sections discuss these new techniques.

Working with out variables

The "Output parameters" section of the chapter discusses the common methods of working with the out variable. However, consider the following example, which has just one out variable.

```
static void MyCalc(out int x)
{
    x = 2 + 2;
}
```

In this case, you could call the MyCalc() method the old way by using the following code:

```
static void DisplayMyCalc()
{
    int p;
    MyCalc(out p);
    Console.WriteLine($"{nameof(p)} = {p}");
}
```

The output of the DisplayMyCalc() function is: p = 4. Note that MyCalc() assigns a value of 4 to p. C# provides a shorter way to accomplish the same task:

```
static void DisplayMyCalc()
{
    MyCalc(out int p);
    Console.WriteLine($"{nameof(p)} = {p}");
}
```

The output is the same as before. However, you don't need to declare p before using it. The declaration occurs as part of the call to MyCalc().

TIP

Of course, if your method returns just one output parameter, it's normally best to use a return value instead. This example uses just one so that you get a better idea of how the new technique works.

REMEMBER

A more interesting addition to C# 7.0 is that you can now use the `var` keyword with `out` parameters. For example, this call is perfectly acceptable in C# 7.0.

```
static void DisplayMyCalc()
{
    MyCalc(out var p);
    Console.WriteLine($"{nameof(p)} = {p}");
}
```

Returning values by reference

You can return values by reference in older versions of C#. However, you have to create your code carefully to do it, as shown here:

```
static ref int ReturnByReference()
{
    int[] arrayData = { 1, 2 };
    ref int x = ref arrayData[0];
    return ref x;
}
```

In C# 7.0, you can reduce the code used to perform this task to this:

```
static ref int ReturnByReference()
{
    int[] arrayData = { 1, 2 };
    return ref arrayData;
}
```

REMEMBER

However, notice that you're returning an entire array now, instead of a single `int` value. The array is a reference type; the `int` is a value type. You can't return value types by using this technique. To make returning a value type possible, you must pass it in as a parameter, like this:

```
static ref int ReturnByReference(ref int myInt)
{
    myInt = 1;
    return ref myInt;
}
```

Chapter **12**

Interacting with Structures

Structures are an important addition to C# because they provide a means for defining complex data entities, akin to records from a database. Because of the way you use structures to develop applications, a distinct overlap exists between structures and classes. This overlap causes problems for many developers because it can become difficult to determine when to use a structure versus a class. Consequently, the first order of business in this chapter is to discuss the differences between the two and offer some best practices.

Creating structures requires use of the `struct` keyword. A structure can contain many of the same elements found in classes: constructors, constants, fields, methods, properties, indexers, operators, events, and even nested types. This chapter helps you understand the nuances of creating structures with these elements so that you can fully access all the flexibility that structures have to offer.

REMEMBER

Even though structures do have a great deal to offer, the most common way to use them is to represent a kind of data record. The final section of this chapter provides a discussion of the structure as a record-holding object. You discover how to use structures in this manner for single records and for multiple records as part of a collection.

Comparing Structures to Classes

For many developers, the differences between structures and classes are confusing, to say the least. In fact, many developers use classes alone and forget about structures. However, not using structures is a mistake because they fulfill a definite purpose in your programming strategy. Using structures can make the difference between an application that performs well and one that does the job, but does so more slowly than it could.

REMEMBER

You find many schools of thought on the use of structures. This book doesn't even attempt to cover them all. It does give you a good overview of how structures can help you create better applications. After you have this information, you can begin using structures and discover for yourself precisely how you want to interact with them.

Considering struct limits

Structures are a value type, which means that C# allocates memory for them differently than classes. Most of the `struct` limits come from this difference. Here are some things to consider when you think about using a `struct` in place of a class. A structure

>> Can have constructors, but not destructors. This means that you can perform all the usual tasks required to create a specific data type, but you don't have control over cleaning up through a destructor.

>> Cannot inherit from other structures or classes (meaning they're stand alone).

>> Can implement one or more interfaces, but with the limits imposed by the elements they support (see "Including common struct elements," later in this chapter, for details).

>> Cannot be defined as `abstract`, `virtual`, or `protected`.

Understanding the value type difference

When working with structures, you must remember that they're a value type, not a reference type like classes. This means that structures have certain inherent advantages over classes. For example, they're much less resource intensive. In addition, because structures aren't garbage-collected, they tend to require less time to allocate and deallocate.

TIP

The differences in resource use and in both allocation and deallocation time is compounded when working with arrays. An array of reference types incurs a huge penalty because the array contains just pointers to the individual objects. To access the object, the application must then look for it on the heap.

Value types are also deterministic. You know that C# deallocates them the moment they go out of scope. Waiting for C# to garbage-collect reference types means that you can't quite be sure how memory is used in your application.

Determining when to use struct versus class

Opinions abound as to when to use a `struct` versus a `class`. For the most part, it all ends up being a matter of what you're trying to achieve and what you're willing to pay in terms of both resource usage and application speed to achieve it. In most cases, you use `class` far more often than you use `struct` simply because `class` is more flexible and tends to incur fewer penalties in some situations.

As with all value types, structures must be boxed and unboxed when cast to a reference type or when required by an interface they implement. Too much boxing and unboxing will actually make your application run slower. This means that you should avoid using structures when you need to perform tasks with reference types. In this case, using a class is the best idea.

REMEMBER

Using a value type also changes the way in which C# interacts with the variable. A reference type is passed by reference during a call so that any changes made to the reference type appear in all instances that point to that reference. A value type is copied when you pass it because it's passed by value. This means that changes you make to the value type in another method don't appear in the original variable. This is possibly the most confusing aspect of using structures for developers because passing an object created by a class is inherently different from passing a variable created by a structure. This difference makes classes generally more efficient to pass than structures.

It's true that structures do have a definite advantage when working with arrays. However, you must exercise care when working with structures in collection types because the structure may require boxing and unboxing. If a collection works with objects, you need to consider using a class instead.

Avoid using structures when working with objects. Yes, you can place object types within a structure, but then the structure will contain a reference to the object, rather than the object itself. References reduce the impact of any resource and time savings that a structure can provide. Keep structures limited to other value types such as int and double when possible. Of course, many structures still use reference types such as String.

Creating Structures

Creating a structure is similar to creating a class in many respects. Of course, you use the struct keyword instead of the class keyword, and a structure has the limitations described in the "Considering struct limits" section, earlier in this chapter. However, even with these differences, if you know how to create a class, you can also create a structure. The following sections describe how to work with structures in greater detail.

Defining a basic struct

A basic struct doesn't contain much more than the fields you want to use to store data. For example, consider a struct used to store messages from people requesting the price of certain products given a particular quantity. It might look like this:

```
public struct Message
{
    public int MsgID;
    public int ProductID;
    public int Qty;
    public double Price;
}
```

To use this basic structure, you might follow a process like this:

```
// Create the struct.
Message myMsg = new Message();

// Create a message.
myMsg.MsgID = 1;
myMsg.ProductID = 22;
myMsg.Qty = 5;

// Compute the price.
myMsg.Price = 5.99 * myMsg.Qty;

// Display the struct on screen.
Console.WriteLine(
    "In response to Msg {0}, you can get {1} of {2} for {3}.",
    myMsg.MsgID, myMsg.Qty, myMsg.ProductID, myMsg.Price);
```

Note that the process used to create and use a structure is much the same as creating and using a class. In fact, you could possibly look at the two processes as being the same for the most part (keeping in mind that structures do have differences). The output from this example looks like this:

```
In response to Msg 1, you can get 5 of 22 for 29.95.
```

Obviously, this is a simplified example, and you'd never create code like this for a real application, but it does get the process you use across. When working with structures, think about the processes you use with classes, but with a few differences that can make structures far more efficient to use.

Including common struct elements

Structures can include many of the same elements as classes do. The "Defining a basic struct" section of the chapter introduces you to the use of fields. As previously noted, fields cannot be abstract, virtual, or protected. However, their default scope is private, and you can set them to public, as shown in the code. Obviously, classes contain far more than fields and so do structures. The following sections take you through the common struct elements so that you can use structures efficiently in your code.

Constructors

As with a class, you can create a struct with a constructor. Here's an example of the Message struct with a constructor included:

```
public struct Message
{
    public int MsgID;
    public int ProductID;
    public int Qty;
    public double Price;

    public Message(
        int msgId, int productId = 22, int qty = 5)
    {
        // Provided by the user.
        MsgID = msgId;
        ProductID = productId;
        Qty = qty;
```

```
        // Defined by the application.
        if (ProductID == 22)
        {
            Price = 5.99 * qty;
        }
        else
        {
            Price = 6.99 * qty;
        }
    }
}
```

Note that the constructor accepts default values, so you can use a single constructor in more than one way. When you use the new version of Message, IntelliSense
shows both the default constructor (which, in contrast to a class, doesn't go away)
and the new constructor that you created, as shown here:

```
// Create the struct using a constructor.
Message myMsg2 = new Message(2);

// Display the struct on screen.
Console.WriteLine(
    "In response to Msg {0}, you can get {1} of {2} for {3}.",
    myMsg2.MsgID, myMsg2.Qty, myMsg2.ProductID, myMsg2.Price);
```

Thanks to the use of default parameters, you can create a new message by simply
providing the message number. The default parameters assign the other values.
Of course, you can choose to override any of the values to create a unique object.

Constants

As with all other areas of C#, you can define constants in structures to serve as
human readable forms of values that don't change. For example, you might choose
to create a generic product constant like this:

```
public const int genericProduct = 22;
```

The Message constructor might then change to look like this:

```
public Message(
    int msgId, int productId = genericProduct, int qty = 5)
```

The new form is easier to read. However, it doesn't produce different results.

Methods

Structures can often benefit from the addition of methods that help you perform specific tasks with them. For example, you might want to provide a method for calculating the Message Price field, rather than perform the task manually every time. Using a method would ensure that a change in calculation method appears only once in your code, rather than each time the application requires the calculation. The CalculatePrice() method looks like this:

```
public static double CalculatePrice(double SinglePrice, int Qty)
{
    return SinglePrice * Qty;
}
```

Obviously, most calculations aren't this simple, but you get the idea. Moving the code to a method means that you can change the other parts of the code to make its meaning clearer. For example, the Message() constructor if statement now looks like this:

```
// Defined by the application.
if (ProductID == 22)
{
    Price = CalculatePrice(5.99, qty);
}
else
{
    Price = CalculatePrice(6.99, qty);
}
```

REMEMBER

Note that you must declare the method static or you receive an error message. A structure, like a class, can have both struct and instance methods. The instance methods become available only after you create an instance of the structure.

Properties

You can also use properties with structures. In fact, using properties is the recommended approach in many cases because using properties lets you ensure that input values are correct. Fortunately, if you are using C# 7.0 and originally created public fields, you can turn them into properties quite easily using these steps:

1. **Place the cursor (insertion point) anywhere on the line of code you want to turn into a property.**

   In this case, place it anywhere on the line of code that reads: public int MsgID;. A lightbulb icon appears in the left margin of the editing area.

2. **Hover your mouse cursor over the top of the lightbulb to show the down arrow next to the icon and click the down arrow.**

You see the options shown in Figure 12-1. The highlighted option, Encapsulate Field: 'MsgID' (And Use Property), lets you turn MsgID into a property and use it appropriately in your code.

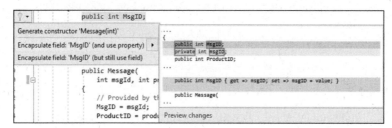

FIGURE 12-1:
Turn the MsgID field into the MsgID property.

3. **Click the option shown highlighted in Figure 12-1.**

Visual Studio turns the field into a property by making the changes shown in bold in the following code:

```
private int msgID;
public int ProductID;
public int Qty;
public double Price;
public const int genericProduct = 22;

public int MsgID { get => msgID; set => msgID = value; }
```

TIP

At this point, you can work with the property as needed to safeguard your data. However, one other issue is still there. If you try to compile the code now, you see a CS0188 error code in the constructor telling you that you're trying to use the property before the fields are assigned. To correct this problem, change the assignment MsgID = msgId; in the constructor to msgID = msgId;. The difference is that you assign a value to the private field now, rather than use the public property.

Indexers

An indexer allows you to treat a structure like an array. In fact, you must use many of the same techniques with it, but you must also create a lot of the features from scratch because your structure indexer has flexibility that an array doesn't provide. Here's the code for a structure, ColorList, that has the basic features required for an indexer:

```
public struct ColorList
{
    private string[] names;

    public string this[int i]
    { get => names[i]; set => names[i] = value; }

    public void Add(string ColorName)
    {
        if (names == null)
        {
            names = new string[1];
            names[0] = ColorName;
        }
        else
        {
            names = names.Concat<string>(
                new string[] { ColorName }).ToArray();
        }
    }

    public int Length
    { get => names.Length; }
}
```

REMEMBER

Starting from the top of the listing, an indexer implies that you have an array somewhere in the structure, which is names in this case. To access names using an indexer, you must also create a this property of the type shown in the example. The this property enables you to access specific names array elements. Note that this example is using a really simple this property; a production version would add all sorts of checks, including verifying that names isn't null and that the requested value actually exists.

When working with an indexer associated with a class, you assign a starting value to the array. However, you can't do that in this case because this is a structure, so names remains uninitialized. Another problem is that you also can't override the default constructor, so you can't initialize names there, either. The Add() method provides the solution. To add a new member to names, a caller must provide a string that adds the value to names as shown.

Note that when names is null, Add() first initializes the array and then adds the color to the first element (given that there are no other elements). However, when names already has values, the code concatenates a new single element string array to names. You must call ToArray() to convert the enumerable type used with Concat() to an array for storage in names.

To use ColorList in a real application, you must also provide a means of obtaining the array length. The read-only Length property accomplishes this task by exposing the names.Length property value. Here is an example of ColorList in action:

```
// Create a color list.
ColorList myList = new ColorList();

// Fill it with values.
myList.Add("Yellow");
myList.Add("Blue");

// Display each of the elements in turn.
for (int i = 0; i < myList.Length; i++)
    Console.WriteLine("Color = " + myList[i]);
```

The code works much as you might expect for a custom array. You create a new ColorList, rely on Add() to add values to it, and then use Length within a for loop to display the values. Here's the output from this code:

```
Color = Yellow
Color = Blue
```

Operators

Structures can also contain operators. For example, you might choose to create a method for adding two ColorList structures together. You do that by creating a + operator. Note that you're creating, not overriding, the + operator, as shown here:

```
public static ColorList operator + (ColorList First, ColorList Second)
{
    ColorList Output = new ColorList();

    for (int i = 0; i < First.Length; i++)
        Output.Add(First[i]);

    for (int i = 0; i < Second.Length; i++)
        Output.Add(Second[i]);

    return Output;
}
```

You can't create an instance operator. It must appear as part of the struct as shown. The process follows the same technique you use to create a ColorList in the first place. The difference is that you iterate through both ColorList variables to perform the task using a for loop. Here's some code that uses the + operator to add two ColorList variables.

```
// Create and fill a second color list.
ColorList myList2 = new ColorList();
myList2.Add("Red");
myList2.Add("Purple");

// Add the first list to the second.
ColorList myList3 = myList + myList2;

// Display each of the elements in turn.
for (int i = 0; i < myList3.Length; i++)
    Console.WriteLine("myList3 Color = " + myList3[i]);
```

As you can see, myList3 is the result of adding two other ColorList variables, not of creating a new one. The output is as you'd expect:

```
myList3 Color = Yellow
myList3 Color = Blue
myList3 Color = Red
myList3 Color = Purple
```

Using Structures as Records

The main reason to work with structures in most code is to create records that contain custom data. You use these custom data records to hold complex information and pass it around as needed within your application. It's easier and faster to pass a single record than it is to pass a collection of data values, especially when your application performs the task regularly. The following sections show how to use structures as a kind of data record.

Managing a single record

Passing structures to methods is cleaner and easier than passing a collection of individual data values. Of course, the values in the structure must be related in order for this strategy to work well. However, consider the following method:

```
static void DisplayMessage(Message msg)
{
    Console.WriteLine(
        "In response to Msg {0}, you can get {1} of {2} for {3}.",
        msg.MsgID, msg.Qty, msg.ProductID, msg.Price);
}
```

TIP

In this case, the `DisplayMessage()` method receives a single input of type `Message` instead of the four variables that the method would normally require. Using the Message structure produces these positive results in the code:

>> The receiving method can assume that all the required data values are present.

>> The receiving method can assume that all the variables are initialized.

>> The caller is less likely to create erroneous code.

>> Other developers can read the code with greater ease.

>> Code changes are easier to make.

Adding structures to arrays

Applications rarely use a single data record for every purpose. In most cases, applications also include database-like collections of records. For example, an application is unlikely to receive just one `Message`. Instead, the application will likely receive a group of `Message` records, each of which it must process.

TECHNICAL STUFF

You can add structures to any collection. However, most collections work with objects, so adding a structure to them would incur a performance penalty because C# must box and unbox each structure individually. As the size of the collection increases, the penalty becomes quite noticeable. Consequently, it's always a better idea to restrict collections of data records that rely on structures to arrays in your application when speed is the most important concern.

Working with an array of structures is much like working with an array of anything else. You could use code like this to create an array of `Message` structures:

```
// Display all the messages on screen.
Message[] Msgs = { myMsg, myMsg2 };
DisplayMessages(Msgs);
```

In this case, `Msgs` contains two records, `myMsg` and `myMsg2`. The code then processes the messages by passing the array to `DisplayMessages()`, which is shown here:

```
static void DisplayMessages(Message[] msgs)
{
    foreach (Message item in msgs)
```

```
    {
        Console.WriteLine(
            "In response to Msg {0}, you can get {1} of {2} for {3}.",
            item.MsgID, item.Qty, item.ProductID, item.Price);
    }
}
```

The DisplayMessages() method uses a foreach loop to separate the individual Message records. It then processes them using the same approach as DisplayMessage() in the previous section of the chapter.

Overriding methods

REMEMBER

Structures provide a great deal of flexibility that many developers assign exclusively to classes. For example, you can override methods, often in ways that make the structure output infinitely better. A good example is the ToString() method, which outputs a somewhat unhelpful (or something similar):

```
Structures.Program+Messages
```

The output isn't useful because it doesn't tell you anything. To garner anything useful, you must override the ToString() method by using code like this:

```
public override string ToString()
{
    // Create a useful output string.
    return "Message ID:\t" + MsgID +
        "\r\nProduct ID:\t" + ProductID +
        "\r\nQuantity:\t" + Qty +
        "\r\nTotal Price:\t" + Price;
}
```

Now when you call ToString(), you obtain useful information. In this case, you see the following output when calling myMsg.ToString():

```
Message ID:    1
Product ID:    22
Quantity:      5
Total Price:   29.95
```

3

Designing for C#

Contents at a Glance

Chapter **1**

Writing Secure Code

S ecurity is a big topic. Ignoring for a moment all the buzzwords surrounding security, you likely realize that you need to protect your application from being used by people who shouldn't use it. You also need to prevent your application from being used for things it shouldn't be used for.

At the beginning of the electronic age, security was usually performed by *obfuscation*. If you had an application that you didn't want people peeking at, you just hid it, and no one would know where to find it. Thus, it would be secure. (Remember *War Games*, the movie in which the military assumed that no one would find the phone number needed to connect to its mainframes — but Matthew Broderick's character did?)

Using obfuscation obviously doesn't cut it anymore; now you need to consider security as an integral requirement of every system that you write. Your application might not contain sensitive data, but can it be used to get to other information on the machine? Can it be used to gain access to a network that it shouldn't? The answers to these questions matter.

The two main parts to security are authentication and authorization. *Authentication* is the process of making sure a user is authentic — that the user identity is genuine. The most common method of authentication is to require the use of a username and password, though other ways exist, such as thumbprint scans. *Authorization* is the act of ensuring that a user has the authority to perform specific tasks. File permissions are a good example of this — users can't delete system-only files, for instance.

It's never possible to identify a specific user with complete assurance. Hackers can steal usernames and passwords with ease. In fact, biometric devices, such as thumbprint scanners, are exceptionally easy to beat as well. The article at `http://www.instructables.com/id/How-To-Fool-a-Fingerprint-Security-System-As-Easy-/` details just how easy it is to overcome thumbprint security. The best you can ever hope to achieve is to authenticate a user identity, never the user. You don't actually ever know that you're dealing with a particular person; it could be a hacker in disguise.

The silent partner of security makes it harder to fool your system into believing a user identity is authentic or authorized. Because of this requirement, there is more to security than inserting username and password text boxes in your program. In this chapter, you discover the tools that are available in the .NET Framework to help you make sure that your applications are secure.

Designing Secure Software

Security takes a fair amount of work to accurately design. If you break the process into pieces, you find that it's a lot easier to accomplish. The Patterns and Practices team (a group of software architects at Microsoft who devise programming best practices) have created a systematic approach to designing secure programs, described in the following sections, that you should find straightforward.

Determining what to protect

Different applications have different artifacts that need protection, but all applications share something that needs protection. If you have a database in your application, that is the most important item to protect. If your application is a server-based application, the server should rate fairly high when you're determining what to protect.

REMEMBER

Even if your program is just a little single-user application, the software should do no wrong. An outsider shouldn't be able to use the application to break into the user's computer.

Documenting the components of the program

If you think this section's title sounds similar to part of the design process, you're right. A lot of threat modeling is just understanding how the application works and describing it well.

First, describe what the application does. This description becomes a functional overview. If you follow the commonly accepted Software Development Life Cycle (SDLC), the use cases, requirements, or user stories documents (depending on your personal methodology) should give you a good starting point.

Next, describe how the application accomplishes all those tasks at the highest level. A Software Architecture Overview (SAO) diagram is a useful way to do it. This diagram shows which machines and services do what in your software. Sometimes the SAO is a simple diagram. If you have a stand-alone Windows Forms (also known as WinForms) program, such as a game, that's all there is! A stand-alone program has no network connection and no communication between software parts. Therefore, the software architecture diagram contains only one instance.

Decomposing components into functions

After you create a document that describes what the software is doing and how, you need to break out the individual functional pieces of the software. If you've set up your software in a component fashion, the classes and methods show the functional decomposition. It's simpler than it sounds.

The end result of breaking the software into individual pieces is having a decent matrix of which components need to be protected, which parts of the software interact with each component, which parts of the network and hardware system interact with each component, and which functions of the software do what with each component.

Identifying potential threats in functions

After you create the list of components that you need to protect, you tackle the tough part: Put two and two together. Identifying threats is the process that gets the security consultants the big bucks, and it's almost entirely a factor of experience.

For instance, if your application connects to a database, you have to imagine that the connection could be intercepted by a third party. If you use a file to store sensitive information, the file could, theoretically, be compromised.

To create a threat model, you need to categorize the potential threats to your software. An easy way to remember the different categories of threats is as the acronym STRIDE:

>> **Spoofing identity:** Users pretend to be someone they are not.

>> **Tampering with data or files:** Users edit something that shouldn't be edited.

- **Repudiation of action:** Users have the opportunity to say they didn't do something that they actually did do.

- **Information disclosure:** Users see something that shouldn't be seen.

- **Denial of service:** Users prevent legitimate users from accessing the system.

- **Elevation of privilege:** Users get access to something that they shouldn't have access to.

All these threats must be documented in an outline under the functions that expose the threat. This strategy not only gives you a good, discrete list of threats but also focuses your security hardening on those parts of the application that pose the greatest security risk.

Rating the risk

The final step in the process is to rate the risks. Microsoft uses the DREAD model to assess risk to its applications. The acronym DREAD represents five key attributes used to measure each vulnerability:

- **Damage potential:** The dollar cost to the company for a breach

- **Reproducibility:** Special conditions to the breach that might make it harder or easier to find

- **Exploitability:** A measure of how far into a corporate system a hacker can get

- **Affected users:** The number of users who are affected and who they are

- **Discoverability:** The ease with which you can find the potential breach

You can research the DREAD model at http://msdn.microsoft.com/security or position your threat model to consider those attributes. The key is to determine which threats are most likely to cause problems and then mitigate them.

Building Secure Windows Applications

The .NET framework lives in a tightly controlled sandbox when running on a client computer. Because of the realities of this sandbox, the configuration of security policy for your application becomes important.

The first place you need to look for security in writing Windows applications is in the world of authentication and authorization. *Authentication* confirms the user identity (but not the user), and *authorization* determines the tasks that the user can perform (both inside and outside the application). For example, gaining access to an application feature that the user shouldn't use is a security breach inside the application. Deleting a required file using operating system features is a security breach outside the application.

When you're threat modeling, you can easily consider all the possible authentication and authorization threats using the STRIDE acronym. (See the earlier section "Identifying potential threats in functions" for more about STRIDE.)

Authentication using Windows login

To be straightforward, the best way for an application to authorize a user is to make use of the Windows login. Various arguments arise about this strategy and others, but the key is simplicity: Simple things are more secure.

For much of the software developed with Visual Studio, the application will be used in an office by users who have different roles in the company; for example, some users might be in the Sales or Accounting department. In many environments, the most privileged users are managers or administrators — yet another set of roles. In most offices, all employees have their own user accounts, and users are assigned to the Windows groups that are appropriate for the roles they play in the company.

REMEMBER

Using Windows security works only if the Windows environment is set up correctly. You can't effectively build a secure application in a workspace that has a bunch of Windows XP machines with everyone logging on as the administrator, because you can't tell who is in what role.

Building a Windows application to take advantage of Windows security is straightforward. The goal is to check to see who is logged on (authentication) and then check that user's role (authorization). The following steps show you how to create an application that protects the menu system for each user by showing and hiding buttons. Even though this sample application relies on the Windows Forms App template, the techniques also work with other application types, such as a Windows Presentation Foundation (WPF) app. To successfully run this code, you must have an environment that has Accounting, Sales, and Management user groups.

1. **Choose File⇨New⇨Project.**

   You see the New Project dialog box.

2. **Select the Visual C#\Windows Classic Desktop folder in the left pane.**

3. **Highlight the Windows Forms App template in the center pane.**

4. Type SecureButton **in the Name field and click OK.**

Visual Studio creates a new Windows Forms application for you and displays the designer, where you can add controls.

5. **Add three buttons to your form from the Toolbox — one for Sales Menu, one for Accounting Menu, and one for Manager Menu.**

Figure 1-1 shows one method for configuring the form. You change the button caption using the Text property found in the Properties window for each of the buttons.

FIGURE 1-1:
The Windows
Security
application
sample.

6. **Set the** (Name) **property for each of the buttons to match their role name:** SalesButton, AccountingButton, **and** ManagerButton.

Giving the buttons a recognizable name makes them easier to work with.

7. **Set every button's visible properties to** False **so that they aren't shown on the form by default.**

8. **Double-click the form to reach the** Form1_Load **event handler.**

9. **Above the** Namespace **statement, import the** System.Security.Principal **namespace this way:**

```
using System.Security.Principal;
```

10. **In the** Form1_Load **event handler, instantiate a new** Identity **object that represents the current user with the** GetCurrent **method of the** WindowsIdentity **object by adding this bit of code:**

```
WindowsIdentity myIdentity = WindowsIdentity.GetCurrent();
```

11. Get a reference to this identity with the `WindowsPrincipal` **class:**

```
WindowsPrincipal myPrincipal = new WindowsPrincipal(myIdentity);
```

12. Hover the mouse next to the `using` statements.

You see a light-bulb icon when using C# 7.0. This icon tells you that there are ways to make your code more efficient.

13. Choose Remove Unnecessary Usings.

Visual Studio removes the unnecessary `using` statements. This action makes your code load faster and use resources more efficiently.

14. Finally, also in the `Form1_Load` **subroutine, code a little** `If/Then` **statement to determine which button to show.**

The code is shown in Listing 1-1.

LISTING 1-1: **The Windows Security Application Code**

```csharp
using System;
using System.Windows.Forms;
using System.Security.Principal;

namespace SecureButton
{
    public partial class Form1 : Form
    {
        public Form1()
        {
            InitializeComponent();
        }

        private void Form1_Load(object sender, EventArgs e)
        {
            // Get the user's identity.
            WindowsIdentity myIdentity = WindowsIdentity.GetCurrent();

            // Obtain information about the user's rights.
            WindowsPrincipal myPrincipal =
                new WindowsPrincipal(myIdentity);

            // Determine which buttons to show based on
            // the user's rights.
```

(continued)

LISTING 1-1: *(continued)*

```
            if (myPrincipal.IsInRole("Accounting"))
            {
                AccountingButton.Visible = true;
            }
            else if (myPrincipal.IsInRole("Sales"))
            {
                SalesButton.Visible = true;
            }
            else if (myPrincipal.IsInRole("Management"))
            {
                ManagerButton.Visible = true;
            }
        }
    }
}
```

In some cases, you don't need this kind of role diversification. Sometimes you just need to know whether the user is in a standard role, which System.Security provides for. Using the WindowsBuiltInRole enumerator, you describe actions that should take place when, for example, the administrator is logged on:

```
if (myPrincipal.IsInRole(WindowsBuiltInRole.Administrator))
    {
        //Do something
    }
```

Encrypting information

Encryption is, at its core, an insanely sophisticated process. Five namespaces are devoted to different algorithms. Because encryption is so complex, this book doesn't get into details. Nonetheless, it's important that you understand one cryptographic element for a key element of security — encrypting files. When you work with a file in a Windows Forms application, you risk someone loading it up in a text editor and looking at it, unless you have encrypted the program.

The common encryption scheme Advanced Encryption Standard (AES) is implemented in .NET in Visual Studio 2008 (C# 3.0) and above. Older versions of Visual Studio rely on the Data Encryption Standard (DES), which isn't the strongest encryption in these days of 64-bit desktop machines. Use AES whenever possible to gain the highest level of encryption for your application. You can find the methods to encrypt for DES in the DESCryptoServiceProvider in the System.Security.Cryptography namespace.

Deployment security

If you deploy your application using `ClickOnce`, you need to define the access to the PC that the application will request. `ClickOnce` is a web server–based deployment strategy that allows users to run Windows Forms applications from a web browser by using the Windows Security tab in the My Project configuration file, shown in Figure 1-2. (For example, in the example project, you access this dialog box by choosing Project⇨SecureButton Properties.)

Here, you can define the features that your application uses so that the user installing it receives a warning at installation rather than a security error when running the application.

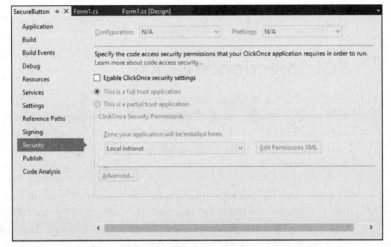

FIGURE 1-2:
The Windows
Security tab of
the My Project
configuration file.

Building Secure Web Forms Applications

Web Forms applications are disconnected, loosely coupled programs that expose a server to potential attacks through the exposed ports used by the applications. A *loosely coupled* application has a transact-and-wait relationship with the server. The request is issued, and then the requestor waits for the response.

Because of this coupling, building for security becomes more important than ever with a Web Forms application. A side effect is that your application can become less functional.

When building web-based applications, you spend less time worrying about authentication (especially if your application is made publicly available) and more time worrying about hackers. Because you're making a server — usually something you keep private — available to the public, your programs are subject to a whole new set of security rules.

The key to protecting a public server is honesty. You have to be honest with yourself about the weaknesses of the system. Don't think, "Well, a hacker could figure out the password by doing XYZ, but no one would ever do that." Trust me, someone will figure it out. The two main types of attacks to be concerned about for a Web Forms application are

>> SQL Injection attacks

>> Script exploits

SQL Injection attacks

A *SQL Injection attack* happens when a hacker enters a line of SQL code into an input field used to query a database in a form on a web page (such as the username and password text boxes in a login form). Malicious SQL code causes the database to act in an unexpected way or to allow the hacker to gain access to, alter, or damage the database.

The best way to understand how a hacker uses a SQL Injection is to see an example. For instance, a web page has code that accepts a Product ID from the user in a text box and returns product details based on the Product ID the user entered. The code on the server might look like this:

```
//Get productId from user
string ProductId = TextBox1.Text;

//Get information from the database
string SelectString = "SELECT * FROM Items WHERE ProductId = '" +
    ProductId + "';";
SqlCommand cmd = new SqlCommand(SelectString, conn);
conn.Open();
SqlDataReader myReader = cmd.ExecuteReader();

//Process results
myReader.Close();
conn.Close();
```

Normally, a user enters the appropriate information into the text box. But a hacker attempting a SQL Injection attack would enter the following string into textBox1:

```
"FOOBAR';DELETE FROM Items;--"
```

The SQL code that would be run by your code would look like this:

```
SELECT * FROM Items WHERE ProductID = 'FOOBAR';DELETE FROM Items;--'
```

The SQL Server executes some code you didn't expect; in this case, the code deleted everything in the Items table.

REMEMBER

The easiest way to prevent SQL Injection is to never use string concatenation to generate SQL. Use a stored procedure and SQL parameters. You can read more about that in Chapter 2 of this minibook.

Script exploits

A *script exploit* is a security flaw that takes advantage of the JavaScript engine in a user's web browser. Script exploits take advantage of one of the more common features of public Web Forms applications: enabling interaction among users. For instance, a Web Forms application may enable a user to post a comment that other users of the site can view, or it may allow a user to fill out an online profile.

If a malicious user were to put some script code in a profile or comment, that hacker could take over the browser of the next user who comes to the site. Several outcomes are possible, none of them good.

For instance, the cookies collection is available to JavaScript when a user comes to your site. A malicious user would put some script code in the profile that could copy the cookie for your site to a remote server. This could give the malicious user access to the current user's session because the session identifier is stored as a cookie. The malicious user would then be able to spoof the current user's identity.

Fortunately, ASP.NET prevents users from typing most script code into a form field and posting it to the server. Try it with a basic Web Forms project by following these steps (you see the error shown in Figure 1-4):

1. **Choose File⇨New⇨Project.**

   You see the New Project dialog box.

2. **Select the Visual C#\Web folder in the left pane.**

3. **Highlight the ASP.NET Web Application template in the center pane.**

4. **Type** SecureForm **in the Name field and click OK.**

   Visual Studio displays a New ASP.NET Web Application dialog box like the one shown in Figure 1-3.

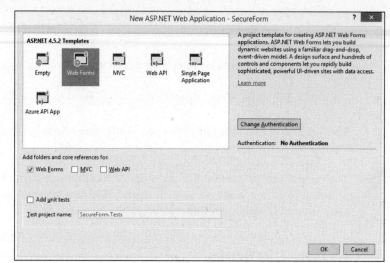

5. **Select Web Forms and then click OK.**

   Visual Studio creates a new Web Forms application for you.

6. **Double-click Default.aspx in the Solution Explorer.**

   You see a form designer. The form designer has all sorts of controls on it, but don't worry about them for now.

7. **Select the Design tab and add a text box and a button to the default page.**

8. **Run the project.**

9. **Type** <script>msgbox()</script> **into the text box.**

10. **Click the button.**

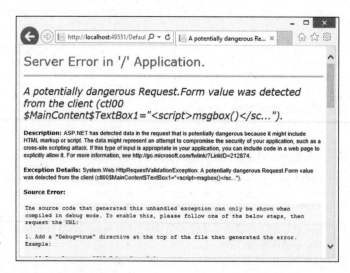

Best practices for securing Web Forms applications

Aside from making sure that your Web Forms application will prevent SQL Injection attacks and script exploits, you should keep in mind some good practices for securing your web applications. The following list runs down some of the most important practices for securing your web applications:

» Keep your Internet Information Server (IIS) box up to date.

» Back up everything.

» Avoid using a Querystring variable (the values after the page name in a URL).

» Don't leave HTML comments in place. Any user can view the HTML code and see your comments by choosing View⇨Source in a browser.

» Don't depend on client-side validation for security — it can be faked.

» Use strong passwords.

» Don't assume what the user sent you came from your form and is safe. It is easy to fake a form post.

» Make sure that error messages don't give the user any information about your application. Email yourself the error messages instead of displaying them to the user.

» Use Secure Sockets Layer.

» Don't store anything useful in a cookie.

» Close all unused ports on your web server.

» Turn off SMTP on IIS unless you need it.

» Run a virus checker if you allow uploads.

» Don't run your application as Administrator.

» Use temporary cookies, if possible, by setting the expiration date to a past date. The cookie will stay alive only for the length of the session.

» Put a size limit on file uploads. You can do it in the Web.Config file:

```
<configuration>
    <system.web>
        <httpRuntime maxRequestLength="4096"/>
    </system.web>
</configuration>
```

» Remember that the ViewState of Web Forms is easily viewable.

Using System.Security

Although many of the security tools are built into the classes that use them, some classes defy description or classification. For that reason, System.Security is the holding pot for stuff that doesn't fit anywhere else.

The more common namespaces for System.Security are described in Table 1-1. I show how to use the Security.Principal namespace in the earlier section "Authentication using Windows login."

TABLE 1-1 **Common Namespaces in System.Security**

Namespace	Description	Common Classes
Security	Base classes for security	CodeAccessPermission, SecureString
AccessControl	Sophisticated control for authorization	AccessRule, AuditRule
Authorization	Enumerations that describe the security of an application	CipherAlgorithmType
Cryptography	Contains several namespaces that help with encryption	CryptoConfig, DESCryptoServiceProvider
Permissions	Controls access to resources	PrincipalPermission, SecurityPermission
Policy	Defends repudiation with classes for evidence	Evidence, Site, Url
Principal	Defines the object that represents the current user context	WindowsIdentity, WindowsPrincipal

Chapter **2**

Accessing Data

Not to predispose you to the contents of this chapter, but you'll probably find that data access is the most important part of your use of the .NET Framework. You'll likely use the various features of the System.Data namespace more than any other namespace.

Unquestionably, one of the most common uses of Visual Studio is the creation of business applications. Business applications are about data. This is the black and white of development with Visual Studio. Understanding a little of everything is important, but complete understanding of the System.Data namespace is essential when you're building business applications.

Until the .NET Framework became popular in the 2003 time frame, most business applications built using Microsoft products used FoxPro or Visual Basic. C# has unquestionably replaced those languages as the business programmer's language of choice over the past several years. You can look at the data tools in C# in three ways:

» **Database connectivity:** Getting information out of and into a database is a primary part of the System.Data namespace.

» **Holding data in containers within your programs:** The DataSet, DataView, and DataTable containers are useful mechanisms for accomplishing the holding of data. If you're a Visual Basic 6 or ASP programmer, you may remember Recordsets, which have been replaced by the new constructs.

REMEMBER

The Language Integrated Query (LINQ) enables you to get the data out of the data containers using Structured Language Queries (SQL) rather than complicated object-oriented language (OOL).

» **Integration with data controls:** The System.Web and System.Windows namespaces function to integrate with the data controls. Data control integration uses database connectivity and data containers extensively. This makes data controls a great target for your reading in this chapter.

Getting to Know System.Data

Data in .NET is different from data in any other Microsoft platform. Microsoft has and continues to change the way data is manipulated in the .NET Framework. ADO.NET, whose implementation is contained in the new data library System.Data, provides yet another new way to think about data from a development perspective:

» **Disconnected:** After you get data from a data source, your program is no longer connected to that data source. You have a copy of the data. This cures one problem and causes another:

- You no longer have a row-locking problem. Because you have a copy of the data, you don't have to constrain the database from making changes.

- You have the *last in wins* problem. If two instances of a program get the same data, and they both update it, the last one back to the database overwrites the changes made by the first program.

» **XML driven:** The data copy that's collected from the data source is XML under the hood. It might be moved around in a custom format when Microsoft deems it necessary for performance, but it is just XML either way, making movement between platforms or applications or databases much easier.

» **Database-generic containers:** The containers don't depend on the type of database at all — they can be used to store data from anywhere.

» **Database-specific adapters:** Connections to the database are specific to the database platform, so if you want to connect to a specific database, you need the components that work with that database.

The process for getting data has changed a little, too. You used to have a connection and a command, which returned a Recordset. Now you have an adapter, which uses a connection and a command to fill a DataSet container. What has changed is the way the user interface helps you get the job done.

`System.Data` has the classes to help you connect to a lot of different databases and other types of data. These classes are broken up into the namespaces in Table 2-1.

TABLE 2-1   ## The System.Data Namespaces

Namespace	Purpose	Most Used Classes
System.Data	Classes common to all of ADO.NET	The containers DataSet, DataView, DataTable, DataRow
System.Data.Common	Utility classes used by database-specific classes	DbCommand, DbConnection
System.Data.ODBC	Classes for connections to ODBC databases such as dBASE	OdbcCommand, OdbcAdapter
System.Data.OleDb	Classes for connections to OleDb databases such as Access	OleDbCommand, OleDbAdapter
System.Data.OracleClient	Classes for connections to Oracle	OracleCommand, OracleAdapter
System.Data.SqlClient	Classes for connections to Microsoft SQL Server	SqlCommand, SqlDataAdapter
System.Data.SqlTypes	For referencing the native types common to SQL Server	SqlDateTime

Though there is a lot to the `System.Data` namespace and related tools, this chapter focuses on the way Visual Studio implements these tools. In previous versions of the development software of all makes and models, the visual tools just made things harder because of the black box problem.

TECHNICAL STUFF

The *black box problem* is that of having a development environment do some things for you over which you have no control. Sometimes it's nice to have things done for you, but when the development environment doesn't build them exactly how you need them, code is generated that isn't useful.

Fortunately, that isn't the case anymore. Visual Studio now generates completely open and sensible C# code when you use the visual data tools. You should be pleased with the results.

Accessing Data

How the Data Classes Fit into the Framework

The data classes are all about information storage. Book 1 talks about collections, which are for storage of information while an application is running. Hashtables are another example of storing information. *Collections* hold lists of objects, and *hashtables* hold name and value pairs. The data containers hold data in larger amounts and help you manipulate that data. Here are the data containers:

>> DataSet: Kind of the granddaddy of them all, the DataSet container is an in-memory representation of an entire database.

>> DataTable: A single table of data stored in memory, the DataTable container is the closest thing you can find to a Recordset, if you're a VB 6 programmer and are looking. DataSet containers are made up of DataTable containers.

>> DataRow: Unsurprisingly, a row in a DataTable container.

>> DataView: A copy of a DataTable that you can use to sort and filter data for viewing purposes.

>> DataReader: A read-only, forward-only stream of data used for one-time processes, such as filling up list boxes. Usually called a *fire hose*.

Getting to Your Data

Everything in the System.Data namespace revolves around getting data from a database such as Microsoft SQL Server and filling these data containers. You can get to this data manually. Generally speaking, the process goes something like this:

1. You create an adapter.

2. You tell the adapter how to get information from the database (the connection).

3. The adapter connects to the database.

4. You tell the adapter which information to get from the database (the command).

5. The adapter fills the DataSet container with data.

6. The connection between the adapter and the database is closed.

7. You now have a disconnected copy of the data in your program.

Not to put too fine a point on it, but you shouldn't have to go through that process at all. Visual Studio does a lot of the data management for you if you let it. Best practice is to use as much automation as possible.

Using the System.Data Namespace

The System.Data namespace is another namespace that gets mixed up between the code world and the visual tools world. Though it is more of a relationship between the form controls and the Data namespace, it often seems that the data lives right inside the controls, especially when you're dealing with Windows Forms.

In the following sections, you deal primarily with the visual tools, which are as much a part of the C# experience as the code. First, you discover how to connect to data sources, and then you see how to write a quick application using one of those connections. Finally, you uncover a little of the code side.

To make all of this work, you need to have some kind of schema set up in your database. It can be a local project of your own creation or a sample schema. The next section tells you how.

Setting up a sample database schema

To get started, direct your browser to http://msftdbprodsamples.codeplex. com/releases/view/55330. If this URL doesn't work, search the web for *SQL Server 2012 samples* and find the nearest CodePlex link.

USING OLDER DATABASE VERSIONS

You might wonder why this book doesn't use the latest versions of the SQL Server databases. The World Wide Importers database at https://docs.microsoft.com/ en-us/sql/sample/microsoft-sql-server-samples is for SQL Server 2016 and the AdventureWorks 2014 database appears at https://msftdbprodsamples. codeplex.com/releases/view/125550. In both cases, you need an actual copy of SQL Server (of the right version) installed to use the sample databases. Using the older AdventureWorks 2012 database makes things simpler because you can access it without problem directly from C#. Making things simple in the learning environment is always a good idea, so that's the direction this book takes.

This page offers a whole bunch of sample listings — sample applications and sample schemas, as well as reporting databases and Online Transaction Processing (OLTP) bits and a bunch of other stuff. The sample applications are full-blown applications that show complete end-to-end implementation of data-driven software built using .NET. Some are in C#; others are in Visual Basic. The sample schemas are databases only and are designed for database administrators to practice getting experience in handling the system.

Any of the sample schemas will work. If you want exactly the same one used in the examples here, choose the AdventureWorks2012 Data File. Other options may be a better fit for the work you're doing. To install, download the MDF file and put it somewhere that makes sense to you. You'll eventually reference it in your project, so a local location like C:\Databases might be good. If you're familiar with SQL Server, you can add a database to your local install and point to it there. In case you aren't a DBA, you can also point a data provider directly to a file. That's the approach used for the rest of this chapter.

Connecting to a data source

There is more to connecting to a database than establishing a simple connection to SQL Server these days. C# developers have to connect to mainframes, text files, unusual databases, web services, and other programs. All these disparate systems get integrated into windows and web screens, with create, read, update, and delete (CRUD) functionality to boot.

REMEMBER

Getting to these data sources is mostly dependent on the Adapter classes of the individualized database namespaces. Oracle has its own, as does SQL Server. Databases that are ODBC (Open Database Connectivity) compliant (such as Microsoft Access) have their own Adapter classes; the newer OLEDB (Object Linking and Embedding Database) protocol has one, too.

Fortunately, a wizard handles most of this. The Data Source Configuration Wizard is accessible from the Data Sources panel, where you spend much of your time when working with data. To get started with the Data Source Configuration Wizard, follow these steps:

1. Choose File⇨New⇨Project.

You see the New Project dialog box.

2. Select the Visual C#\Windows Classic Desktop folder in the left pane.

3. Highlight the Windows Forms App template in the center pane.

4. Type AccessData **in the Name field and click OK.**

Visual Studio creates a new Windows Forms (also known as WinForms) application for you and displays the designer where you can add controls. At this point, you can create a data source to use for the example application.

5. Choose View⇨Other Windows⇨Data Sources or press Shift+Alt+D.

The Data Sources panel tells you that you have no data sources.

6. Click the Add New Data Source link in the Data Sources panel.

You see the Data Source Configuration Wizard, shown in Figure 2-1. The wizard has a variety of data source types to choose from. The most interesting of these is the Object source, which gives you access to an object in an assembly to bind your controls to.

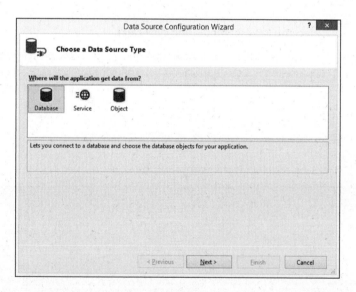

FIGURE 2-1:
Choose a source
type for the
application data.

7. Select the Database data source type and click Next.

You see the database model selections shown in Figure 2-2. The number of selections you have depends on the version of Visual Studio you use. As a minimum, you have access to the Dataset model.

Accessing Data

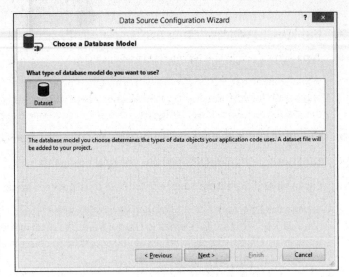

FIGURE 2-2:
Choose a
database model
to use to model
the data.

8. Select the Dataset model and click Next.

You see the option to choose a data connection, as shown in Figure 2-3. Because this is a new application, you shouldn't see any connections.

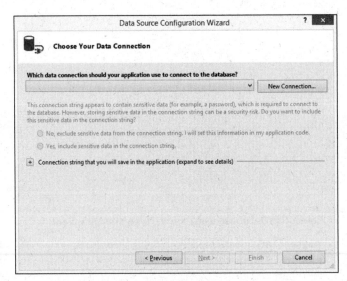

FIGURE 2-3:
Choosing your
data connection.

9. **Click the New Connection button.**

Visual Studio asks you to create a new connection by using the Choose Data Source dialog box, shown in Figure 2-4. This example relies on a direct connection to a Microsoft SQL Server Database File, which is the easiest kind of connection to create. Note that you can create direct connections to Microsoft Access database files as well, and can create connections to an assortment of other databases using a database adapter.

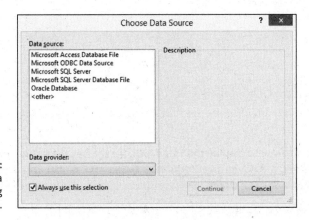

FIGURE 2-4:
The Choose Data
Source dialog
box.

TIP

The Data Provider field may provide more than one data provider. The wizard normally chooses the most efficient data provider for you. However, other data providers may have functionality you require for a specific application type. Always verify that you select the best data provider for your particular application needs.

The steps that follow are specific to using a Microsoft SQL Server database file. Other types of data sources may require that you perform other steps to create a connection.

10. **Select Microsoft SQL Server Database File and click Continue.**

You see the Add Connection dialog box, shown in Figure 2-5.

Accessing Data

FIGURE 2-5:
Specify the location of the database file used for this example.

11. **Click Browse to display the Select SQL Server Database File dialog box, highlight the AdventureWorks2012_Data.mdf file that you downloaded earlier, and click Open.**

The wizard adds the location to the Database File Name field.

12. **Click OK.**

You may be asked by Visual Studio to upgrade the database file, which is totally fine. Simply click Yes to complete the process. After a few moments, you see the connection added to the Data Source Configuration Wizard dialog box, shown previously in Figure 2-5.

13. **Click Next.**

The wizard may ask whether you want to copy the data file to your current project. If you're working through this book in an isolated project, that's fine. If you're on a development effort with others, check to make sure that it's appropriate to your life cycle methodology. For this example, click No because you're the only one using this data source and there isn't a good reason to create another copy. The wizard displays the connection string filename, as shown in Figure 2-6, and asks whether you want to save it to the application.

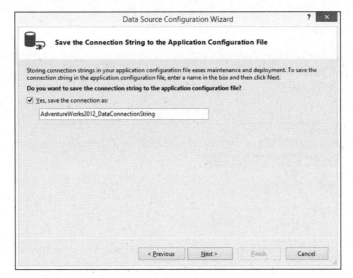

FIGURE 2-6:
Save the
connection string
file to use the
database in your
application.

14. Click Next.

You see the Choose Your Database Objects and Settings dialog box. You can choose the tables, views, or stored procedures that you want to use.

15. Under Tables, select Product and ProductCategory.

The Choose Your Database Objects and Settings dialog box should look similar to the one shown in Figure 2-7.

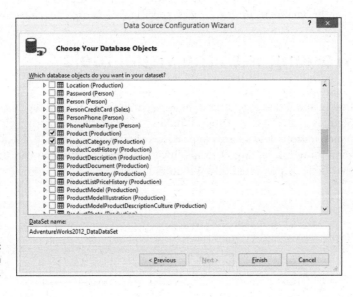

FIGURE 2-7:
Selecting data
objects.

16. **Click Finish.**

You're done! If you look at the Data Sources pane, you can see that a DataSet was added to your project with the two tables you requested, as shown in Figure 2-8.

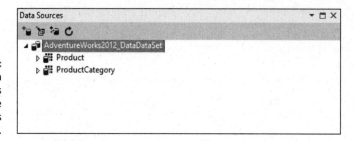

FIGURE 2-8:
New data
connections
appear in the
Data Sources
panel to the left.

By following the preceding steps, you create two significant entities in Visual Studio:

» You create a connection to the database, shown in the Server Explorer. You find that it sticks around — it's specific to this installation of Visual Studio.

» You also create a dataset, which is specific to this project and won't be there if you start another project.

Both of them are important, and they provide different functionality. In this chapter, you focus on the project-specific data source displayed in the dataset.

Working with the visual tools

The Rapid Application Development (RAD) data tools for C# in Visual Studio are usable and do what you need, and they write decent code for you. Select the Data Sources panel (View⇨Other Windows⇨Data Sources) and click a table in the panel, a drop-down arrow appears, as shown in Figure 2-9. Click it, and you see something interesting: A drop-down list appears, and you can then choose how that table is integrated into Windows Forms.

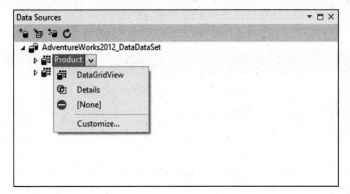

Change the Product table to Details View. It's used to create a detail type form — one that easily enables users to view and change data. Then drag the table to the form, and Details View is created for you, as shown in Figure 2-10. (The screen-shot doesn't show the entire form because it's too long.)

Accessing Data

A whole lot of things happened when you dropped the table on your form:

>> The fields and the field names were added.

>> The fields are in the most appropriate format.

>> The field name is a label.

>> Visual Studio automatically adds a space where the case changes.

TIP

Note that each field gets a SmartTag that enables you to specify a query for the values in the text box. You can also preset the control that's used by changing the values in the Data Sources pane (refer to Figure 2-9). Five completely code-based objects are added in the Component Tray at the bottom of the page: the DataSet (adventureWorks2012_DataDataSet); the BindingSource (productBindingSource); the TableAdapter (productTableAdapter); the TableAdapterManager (tableAdapterManager); and the BindingNavigator (productBindingNavigator) objects.

The VCR Bar (technically called the BindingNavigator) is added to the top of the page. When you run the application, you can use the VCR Bar to cycle among the records in the table. Click the Start button to see the VCR Bar work. You can walk through the items in the database with no problems, as shown in Figure 2-11.

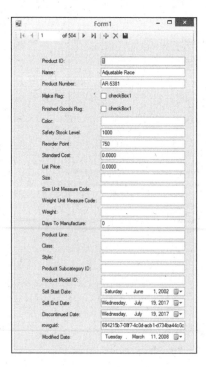

FIGURE 2-11:
Running the example.

Writing data code

In most enterprise development environments, however, you won't be using the visual tools to build data access software. Generally, an infrastructure is already in place because enterprise software often has specific requirements, and the easiest way to manage those specifications is with unique and customized code. In short, some organizations don't want things done the way Microsoft does them.

Output of the visual tools

Visual tools often aren't used in enterprise environments because the code the tools put out is rather sophisticated. Double click `Form1.Designer.cs` in Solution Explorer to see the code behind for the form controls. Figure 2-12 shows what you see when you first get in there. The box marking the region near the top of the code window is marked as `Windows Form Designer generated code`, and you can't help but notice that the line number before that section is in the twenties and the number after that is in the seven hundreds. That's a lot of generated code.

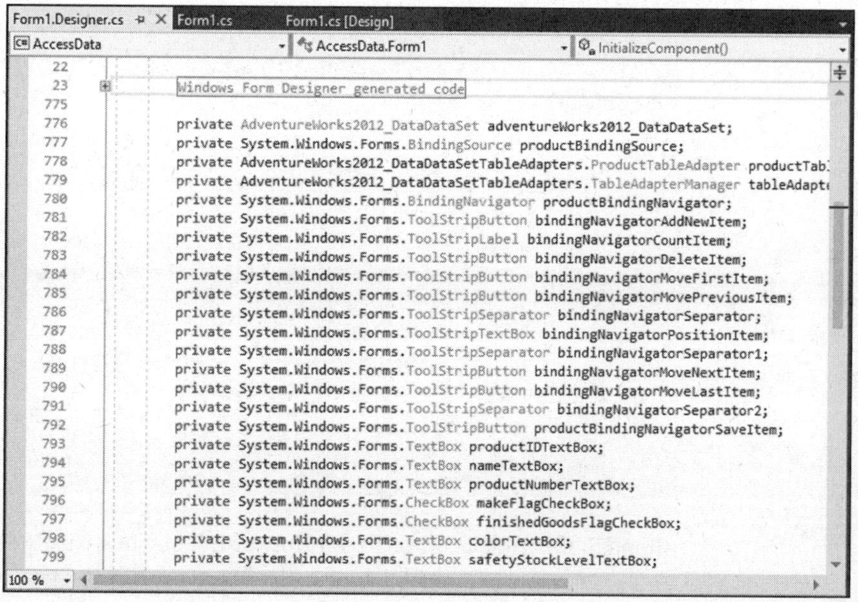

FIGURE 2-12: Generated code. Huh?

Nothing is wrong with this code, but it is purposely generic to support anything that anyone might want to do with it. Enterprise customers often want to make sure that everything is done the same way. For this reason, they often define a specific data code format and expect their software developers to use that, rather than the visual tools.

Basic data code

The code of the sample project is simple:

```
using System;
using System.Windows.Forms;

namespace AccessData
{
    public partial class Form1 : Form
    {
        public Form1()
        {
            InitializeComponent();
        }

        private void productBindingNavigatorSaveItem_Click(object sender,
            EventArgs e)
        {
            this.Validate();
            this.productBindingSource.EndEdit();
            this.tableAdapterManager.UpdateAll(
                this.adventureWorks2012_DataDataSet);

        }

        private void Form1_Load(object sender, EventArgs e)
        {
            // TODO: This line of code loads data into the
            // 'adventureWorks2012_DataDataSet.Product' table.
            // You can move, or remove it, as needed.
            this.productTableAdapter.Fill(
                this.adventureWorks2012_DataDataSet.Product);

        }
    }
}
```

Although this code is fairly straightforward, it obviously isn't everything that you need. The rest of the code is in the file that generates the visual form itself, supporting the visual components.

The time may come when you want to connect to a database without using visual tools. The "How the Data Classes Fit into the Framework" section, earlier in this chapter, discusses the required steps and here is the code to go with it:

```
1. SqlConnection mainConnection = new SqlConnection();
2. mainConnection.ConnectionString = "server=(local);database=Assets_
     Maintenance;Trusted_Connection=True"
3. SqlDataAdapter partsAdapter = new SqlDataAdapter("SELECT * FROM Parts",
     mainConnection)
4. DataSet partsDataSet = new DataSet();
5. mainConnection.Open();
6. partsAdapter.Fill(partsDataSet);
7. mainConnection.Close();
```

TIP

This approach becomes useful especially when you want to build a web service or a class library — though you should note that you can still use the visual tools in those project types. The following paragraphs discuss this code a line at a time.

Line 1 sets up a new data connection, and line 2 populates it with the connection string. You can get this from your Database Administrator (DBA) or from the Properties panel for the data connection.

Line 3 has a SQL Query in it. Chapter 1 of this minibook talks about how this coding technique is a bad deal, and you should use Stored Procedures. A Stored Procedure is a database artifact that allows you to use a parameterized query from ADO. NET, rather than dynamically generated SQL Strings. Don't use inline SQL for production systems.

Line 4 builds a new dataset. This is where the schema of the returned data is held and what you use to navigate the data.

Lines 5, 6, and 7 perform the magic: Open the connection, contact the database, fill the dataset using the adapter, and then close the database. It's all straightforward in this simple example. More complex examples make for more complex code.

After running this code, you would have the Products table in a DataSet container, just as you did in the visual tools in the earlier section, "How the Data Classes Fit into the Framework." To access the information, you set the value of a text box to the value of a cell in the DataSet container, like this:

```
TextBox1.Text = myDataSet.Tables[0].Rows[0]["name"]
```

To change to the next record, you need to write code that changes the Rows[0] to Rows[1] in the next example. As you can see, it would be a fair amount of code. That's why few people use the basic data code to get the databases. Either you use the visual tools or you use an Object Relationship Model of some sort, such as Entity Framework.

Accessing Data

Using the Entity Framework

Object models (which you see discussed in much of this book) and databases just don't go together. They're two different ways of thinking of the same information. The problem mostly lies in inheritance, discussed in Book 2. If you have a class called ScheduledEvent, which has certain properties, and a bunch of classes that inherit from it, like Courses, Conferences, and Parties, there just isn't a good way to show this in a relational type of database.

If you make a big table for ScheduledEvents with all possible types of properties and just make a Type property so that you can tell the Courses from the Parties, you have a lot of empty table cells. If you make a table for just the properties that are in ScheduledEvents and then separate tables for Courses and Parties, you make the database remarkably complex. To address this problem, Microsoft created the Entity Framework.

Object Role Modelers try to take the whole shootin' match and turn it on its head. The goal is to design the database first and then make an object model to work with it automatically. Then, keep it up to date.

The Entity Framework does an acceptable job at that process. It generates a context for you that you can use to communicate with your data in a way that looks more like an object model than it does a database.

Generating the entity model

To get started, you need the model itself. Just follow these steps to generate the entity model:

1. **Create a new project.**

   I used a Windows Forms project again, called EntityFramework.

2. **Right-click the EntityFramework entry in Solution Explorer and click Add⇨New Item in the context menu. Select the Data folder in the left pane.**

   You see the Add New Item dialog box, shown in Figure 2-13.

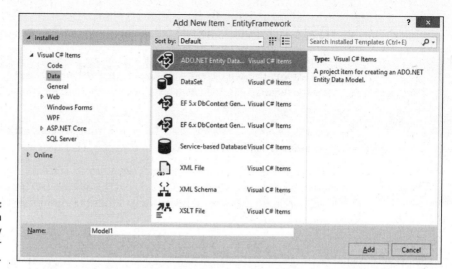

FIGURE 2-13:
Create a
new Entity
Framework for
your application.

3. **Select ADO.NET Entity Data Model and name it** PartsDatabase. **Click Add.**

You see the Entity Data Model Wizard dialog box, shown in Figure 2-14.

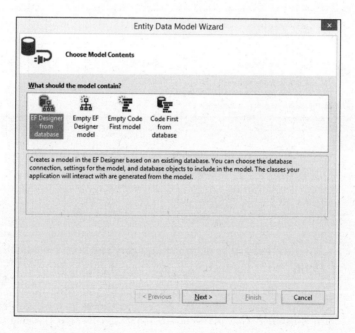

FIGURE 2-14:
Choose a method
for creating the
Entity Framework
model.

4. **Choose Code First from Database in the Choose Model Contents window and then click Next.**

   The wizard asks you to choose a database connection. In this case, you should see the required information in place because you already created it for the AccessData application.

5. **Select the** `AdventureWorks2012_Data.mdf` **from the Connection drop-down list; then click Next.**

   If it isn't there, see the earlier section "Connecting to a data source." If you get a message asking whether you'd like to copy the database into the project, select No. The wizard asks you to choose the database objects you want to use, as shown in Figure 2-15.

6. **Select the Product and ProductCategory and keep the default name. Click Finish.**

   Visual Studio generates the required code for you. When working with certain versions of Visual Studio, you see designer canvas for the Class Designer. However, this book doesn't go into detail with the Class Designer because it's a complex topic that could require an entire book by itself.

Writing code for the entity model

After you have an interesting addition to your coding environment and the database is meshed nicely into the C# object model, you can code with the objects provided in this new entity model. To start, follow these steps:

1. **Go back to the** `Form1` **designer and double-click** `Form1` **to go to Code View.**

2. **In the** `Form1_Load( )` **event handler, type** PartsDatabase part = new PartsDatabase();.

3. **In the next line, type** part. **and check out the IntelliSense.**

    It contains all columns in the Parts table as properties to the class.

What you now have is a context to work against. No complex Linq queries — they're all done under the covers. No inline SQL. No stored procedures. You can do it all with a scoped object.

Chapter **3**

Fishing the File Stream

C atching fish in a stream can prove to be quite a thrill to those who engage in fishing. Anglers often boast of the difficulty of getting that one special fish out of the stream and into a basket. Fishing the "file stream" with C# isn't quite so thrilling, but it's one of those indispensable programming skills.

File access refers to the storage and retrieval of data on the disk. This chapter covers basic text-file input/output. Reading and writing data from databases are covered in Chapter 2 of this minibook, and reading and writing information to the Internet are covered in Chapter 4.

Going Where the Fish Are: The File Stream

The console application programs in this book mostly take their input from, and send their output to, the console. Programs outside this chapter have better — or at least different — things to bore you with than file manipulation. It's important not to confuse their message with the extra baggage of involved input/output (I/O). However, console applications that don't perform file I/O aren't very common.

The I/O classes are defined in the System.IO namespace. The basic file I/O class is FileStream. In days past, the programmer would open a file. The open command would prepare the file and return a *handle.* Usually, this handle was nothing more than a number, like the one they give you when you place an order at a Burger Shop. Every time you wanted to read from or write to the file, you presented this ID.

Streams

C# uses a more intuitive approach, associating each file with an object of class FileStream. The constructor for FileStream opens the file and manages the underlying handle. The methods of FileStream perform the file I/O.

TIP

FileStream isn't the only class that can perform file I/O. However, it represents your good ol' basic file that covers 90 percent of your file I/O needs. This primary class is the one described in this chapter.

The *stream* concept is fundamental to C# I/O. Think of a parade, which "streams" by you, first the clowns, and then the floats, and then a band or two, some horses, a troupe of Customer objects, a BankAccount, and so on. Viewing a file as a stream of bytes (or characters or strings) is much like a parade. You "stream" the data in and out of your program.

The .NET classes used in C# include an abstract Stream base class and several subclasses, for working with files on the disk, over a network, or already sitting as chunks of data in memory. Some stream classes specialize in encrypting and decrypting data; some are provided to help speed up I/O operations that might be slow using one of the other streams; and you're free to extend class Stream with your own subclass if you come up with a great idea for a new stream (although extending Stream is arduous). The "Exploring More Streams than Lewis and Clark" section, later in this chapter, gives you a tour of the stream classes.

Readers and writers

FileStream, the stream class you'll probably use the most, is a basic class. Open a file, close a file, read a block of bytes, and write a block — that's about all you have. But reading and writing files down at the byte level is a lot of work. Fortunately, the .NET class library introduces the notion of *readers* and *writers.* Objects of these types greatly simplify file (and other) I/O.

When you create a new *reader* (of one of several available types), you associate a stream object with it. It's immaterial to the reader whether the stream connects to a file, a block of memory, a network location, or the Mississippi. The reader requests input from the stream, which gets it from — well, wherever. Using *writers* is quite similar, except that you're sending output to the stream rather than asking for input. The stream sends it to a specified destination. Often that's a file, but not always. The System.IO namespace contains classes that wrap around FileStream (or other streams) to give you easier access:

REMEMBER

>> TextReader/TextWriter: A pair of abstract classes for reading characters (text). These classes are the base for two flavors of subclasses: String Reader/StringWriter and StreamReader/StreamWriter.

Because TextReader and TextWriter are abstract, you'll use one of their subclass pairs, usually StreamReader/StreamWriter, to do actual work. Book 2 explains abstract classes.

>> StreamReader/StreamWriter: A more sophisticated text reader and writer for the more discriminating palate — not to mention that they aren't abstract, so you can even read and write with them. For example, Stream Writer has a WriteLine() method much like that in the Console class. StreamReader has a corresponding ReadLine() method and a handy ReadToEnd() method that grabs the whole text file in one gulp, returning the characters read as a string — which you could then use with a StringReader (discussed later), a foreach loop, the String.Split() method, and so on. Check out the various constructors for these classes in C# Language Help. You see StreamReader and StreamWriter in action in the next two sections.

One nice thing about reader/writer classes such as StreamReader and Stream Writer is that you can use them with any kind of stream. This makes reading from and writing to a MemoryStream no harder than reading from and writing to the kind of FileStream discussed in earlier sections of this chapter. (The "Exploring More Streams than Lewis and Clark" section later in this chapter covers Memory Stream.) See the later section "More Readers and Writers" for additional reader/writer pairs.

The following sections provide the FileWrite and FileRead programs, which demonstrate ways to use these classes for text I/O the C# way.

ASYNCHRONOUS I/O: IS IT WORTH WAITING FOR?

Normally, a program waits for a file I/O request to complete before continuing. Call a read( ) method, and you generally don't get control back until the file data is safely in the boat. This is known as *synchronous I/O*. Think of *synchronous* as meaning "while you wait."

The C# System. IO classes also support *asynchronous* I/O. Using asynchronous I/O, the read( ) call returns immediately to allow the program to continue doing something else while the I/O request is completed in the background. The program can check a "done" flag at its leisure to decide when the I/O has completed.

This is sort of like cooking hamburgers. Using synchronous I/O, you put the meat in the pan on the stovetop and stand there watching it until the meat has completely cooked before you go off and start cutting the onions that go on the burgers.

Using asynchronous I/O, you can start cutting up the onions while the hamburger patties are cooking. Every once in a while, you peek over to see whether the meat is done. When it is, you stop cutting, take the meat off the stove, and slap it on the buns.

Asynchronous I/O, and other async functionality, is a core part of C# 7.0. Any operation that should take more than 50 milliseconds to complete should be asynchronous in the Windows Store. Of course, web applications or your local WPF apps don't have to follow that standard.

StreamWriting for Old Walter

In the movie *On Golden Pond*, Henry Fonda spent his retirement years trying to catch a monster trout that he named Old Walter. You aren't out to drag in the big fish, but you should at least cast a line into the stream. This section covers writing to files. Programs generate two kinds of output:

>> **Binary:** Some programs write blocks of data as bytes in pure binary format. This type of output is useful for storing objects in an efficient way — for example, a file of Student objects that you need to *persist* (keep on disk in a permanent file). See the later section "More Readers and Writers" for the BinaryReader and BinaryWriter classes.

A sophisticated example of binary I/O is the persistence of groups of objects that refer to each other (using the HAS_A relationship). Writing an object to disk involves writing identifying information (so its type can be reconstructed when you read the object back in), and then each of its data members, some of which may be references to connected objects, each with its own identifying information and data members. Persisting objects this way is called *serialization.*

>> **Text:** Most programs read and write human-readable text: you know, letters, numbers, and punctuation, like Notepad. The human-friendly `StreamWriter` and `StreamReader` classes are the most flexible ways to work with the stream classes. For some details, see the earlier section "Readers and writers."

Human-readable data was formerly known as American Standard Code for Information Interchange (ASCII) text or, slightly later, American National Standards Institute (ANSI) text. These two monikers refer to the standards organization that defined them. However, ANSI encoding doesn't provide the alphabets east of Austria and west of Hawaii; it can handle only Roman letters, like those used in English. It has no characters for Russian, Hebrew, Arabic, Hindi, or any other language using a non-Roman alphabet, including Asian languages such as Chinese, Japanese, and Korean. The modern, more flexible Unicode character format is "backward-compatible" — including the familiar ANSI characters at the beginning of its character set, but still provides a large number of other alphabets, including everything you need for all the languages just listed. Unicode comes in several variations, called *encodings;* however, Unicode Transformation Format (8-Bit) (UTF8) is the default encoding for C#. You can read more about Unicode encodings at `http://unicodebook.readthedocs.io/unicode_encodings.html`. Other popular encodings are: UTF7, UTF16, and UTF32, where the number after UTF specifies the number of bits used in the encoding.

Using the stream: An example

The following `FileWrite` program reads lines of data from the console and writes them to a file of the user's choosing. This is pseudocode — it isn't meant to compile. It appears only as an example.

```
using System;
using System.IO;

// FileWrite -- Write input from the Console into a text file.
namespace FileWrite
{
  public class Program
  {
    public static void Main( string[] args )
```

```
{
    StreamWriter sw = null;
    string fileName = "";

    // Get a filename from the user -- the while loop lets you
    // keep trying with different filenames until you succeed.
    while ( true ) {
      try {
        // Enter output filename (simply hit Enter to quit).
        Console.Write( "Enter filename "
                       + "(Enter blank filename to quit):" );
        fileName = Console.ReadLine();

        if ( fileName.Length == 0 ) {
          // No filename -- this jumps beyond the while
          // loop to safety. You're done.
          break;
        }

        // Call a method (below) to set up the StreamWriter.
        sw = GetWriterForFile( fileName );

        // Read one string at a time, outputting each to the
        // FileStream open for writing.
        WriteFileFromConsole( sw );

        // Done writing, so close the file you just created.
        sw.Close(); // A very important step. Closes the file too.
        sw = null;  // Give it to the garbage collector.
      }
      catch ( IOException ioErr ) {
        // Ooops -- Error occurred during the processing of the
        // file -- tell the user the full name of the file:
        // Tack the name of the default directory to the filename.

        // Directory class
        string dir = Directory.GetCurrentDirectory();

        // System.IO.Path class
        string path = Path.Combine( dir, fileName );
        Console.WriteLine( "Error on file {0}", path );

        // Now output the error message in the exception.
        Console.WriteLine( ioErr.Message );
      }
    }
```

```
    // Wait for user to acknowledge the results.
    Console.WriteLine( "Press Enter to terminate..." );
    Console.Read();
}


// GetWriterForFile -- Create a StreamWriter set up to write
//    to the specified file.
private static StreamWriter GetWriterForFile( string fileName )
{
  StreamWriter sw;

  // Open file for writing in one of these modes:
  //    FileMode.CreateNew to create a file if it
  //        doesn't already exist or throw an
  //        exception if file exists.
  //    FileMode.Append to append to an existing file
  //        or create a new file if it doesn't exist.
  //    FileMode.Create to create a new file or
  //        truncate an existing file.

  //    FileAccess possibilities are:
  //        FileAccess.Read,
  //        FileAccess.Write,
  //        FileAccess.ReadWrite.
  FileStream fs = File.Open( fileName,
                            FileMode.CreateNew,
                            FileAccess.Write );

  // Generate a file stream with UTF8 characters.
  // Second parameter defaults to UTF8, so can be omitted.
  sw = new StreamWriter( fs, System.Text.Encoding.UTF8 );
  return sw;
}

// WriteFileFromConsole -- Read lines of text from the console
//    and spit them back out to the file.
private static void WriteFileFromConsole( StreamWriter sw )
{
  Console.WriteLine( "Enter text; enter blank line to stop" );

  while ( true ) {
    // Read next line from Console; quit if line is blank.
    string input = Console.ReadLine();

    if ( input.Length == 0 ) {
      break;
    }
```

```
        // Write the line just read to output file.
        sw.WriteLine( input );

        // Loop back up to get another line and write it.
      }
    }
  }
}
```

FileWrite uses the System.IO namespace as well as System. System.IO contains the file I/O classes.

Revving up a new outboard StreamWriter

The FileWrite program starts in Main() with a while loop containing a try block. This is common for a file-manipulation program. Encase all file I/O activity in a try block. File I/O can be prone to errors, such as missing files or directories, bad paths, and so on. See Book 1 for more on exception handling. The while loop serves two functions:

» It allows the program to go back and retry in the event of an I/O failure. For example, if the program can't find a file that the user wants to read, the program can ask for the filename again before blowing off the user.

» Executing a break command from within the program breezes you right past the try block and dumps you off at the end of the loop. This is a convenient mechanism for exiting a method or program. Keep in mind that break only gets you out of the loop it's called in. (Chapter 5 in Book I covers loops and break.)

The FileWrite program reads the name of the file to create from the console. The program terminates by breaking out of the while loop if the user enters an empty filename. The key to the program occurs in the call to a GetWriterForFile() method; you can find the method below Main(). The key lines in GetWriter ForFile() are

```
FileStream fs = File.Open(fileName, FileMode.CreateNew, FileAccess.Write);
// ...
sw = new StreamWriter(fs, System.Text.Encoding.UTF8);
```

In the first line, the program creates a FileStream object that represents the output file on the disk. The FileStream constructor used here takes three arguments:

>> **The filename:** This is clearly the name of the file to open. A simple name like `filename.txt` is assumed to be in the current directory (for `FileWrite`, working inside Visual Studio, that's the `\bin\Debug` subdirectory of the project directory; it's the directory containing the `.EXE` file after you build the program). A filename that starts with a backslash, like `\some directory\ filename.txt`, is assumed to be the full path on the local machine. Filenames that start with two slashes — for example, `\\your machine\some directory\ filename.txt` — are resident on other machines on your network. The filename encoding gets rapidly more complicated from here and is beyond the scope of this minibook.

>> **The file mode:** This argument specifies what you want to do to the file. The basic write modes are create (`CreateNew`), append (`Append`), and overwrite (`Create`). `CreateNew` creates a new file but throws an `IOException` if the file already exists. `Create` mode creates the file if it doesn't exist but overwrites ("truncates") the file if it exists. Just as it sounds, `Append` adds to the end of an existing file or creates the file if it doesn't exist.

>> **The access type:** A file can be opened for reading, writing, or both.

TIP

`FileStream` has numerous constructors, each of which defaults one or both of the mode and access arguments. However, you should specify these arguments explicitly because they have a strong effect on the program's clarity. That's good advice in general. Defaults can be convenient for the programmer but confusing for anyone reading the code.

In the penultimate code line of the `GetWriterForFile()` method, the program "wraps" the newly opened `FileStream` object in a `StreamWriter` object, `sw`. The `StreamWriter` class wraps around the `FileStream` object to provide a set of text-friendly methods. This `StreamWriter` is what the method returns.

The first argument to the `StreamWriter` constructor is the `FileStream` object. There's the wrapping. The second argument specifies the encoding to use. The default encoding is UTF8.

TECHNICAL STUFF

You don't need to specify the encoding when reading a file. `StreamWriter` writes out the encoding type in the first three bytes of the file. The `StreamReader` reads these three bytes when the file is opened to determine the encoding. Hiding this kind of detail is an advantage that good software libraries provide.

WRAP MY FISH IN NEWSPAPER

This kind of wrapping one class around another is a useful software pattern — the `StreamWriter` *wraps* (contains a reference to) another class, `FileStream`, and extends the `FileStream`'s interface with some nice amenities. The `StreamWriter` methods *delegate* to (call) the methods of the inner `FileStream` object. This is the HAS_A relationship discussed in Book 2, so anytime you use HAS_A, you're wrapping. Thus, in effect, you tell the `StreamWriter`, the wrapper, what to do, and it translates your simple instructions into the more complex ones needed by the wrapped `FileStream`. `StreamWriter` hands these translated instructions to the `FileStream` for action. Wrapping is a powerful, frequently used technique in programming. A `Wrapper` class looks like this:

```
class Wrapper
{
  private Wrapped _wrapped;
  public Wrapper(Wrapped w)
  {
    _w = w; // Now Wrapper has a reference to Wrapped.
  }
}
```

This example uses class `Wrapper`'s constructor to install the wrapped object, letting the caller provide the wrapped object. You might install it through a `SetWrapped()` method or by some other means, such as creating the wrapped object inside a constructor. You can also wrap one *method* around another, like so:

```
void WrapperMethod()
{
  _wrapped.DoSomething();
}
```

In this example, `WrapperMethod()`'s class HAS_A reference to whatever the _wrapped object is. In other words, the class wraps that object. `WrapperMethod()` delegates all or part of the evening chores to the `DoSomething()` method on the _wrapped object.

Think of wrapping as a way to translate one model into another. The wrapped item may be complicated, so that you want to provide a simpler version, or the wrapped item may have an inconvenient interface that you want to make over into a more convenient one. Generally speaking, wrapping illustrates the Adapter design pattern (which you can find using your favorite search engine). You can see it in the relationship between `StreamWriter` and `FileStream`. In many cases, you can wrap one stream around another stream in order to convert one kind of stream into another.

Finally, you're writing!

After setting up its `StreamWriter`, the `FileWrite` program begins reading lines of text input from the console (this code is in the `WriteFileFromConsole()` method, called from `Main()`). The program quits reading when the user enters a blank line; until then, it gobbles up whatever it's given and spits it into the `StreamWriter` `sw` using that class's `WriteLine()` method. Finally, the stream is closed with the `sw.Close()` expression. This is important to do, because it also closes the file.

TIP

Notice that the program nulls the `sw` reference after closing `StreamWriter`. A file object is useless after the file has been closed. It's good programming practice to null a reference after it becomes invalid so that you won't try to use it again. (If you do, your code will throw an exception, letting you know about it!) Closing the file and nulling the reference lets the garbage collector claim it (see Book 2 to meet the friendly collector on your route) and leaves the file available for other programs to open.

The `catch` block is like a soccer goalie: It's there to catch any file error that may have occurred in the program. The `catch` outputs an error message, including the name of the errant file. But it doesn't output just a simple filename — it outputs the entire filename, including the path, for your reading pleasure. It does this by using the `Path.Combine()` method to tack the current directory name, obtained through the `Directory` class, onto the front of the filename you entered. (`Path` is a class designed to manipulate path information. `Directory` provides properties and methods for working with directories.) Book 1 gives you the goods on exceptions, including the exceptions to exceptions, the exceptions to those.

TECHNICAL STUFF

WORKING WITH PATH CHARACTERS

The `Combine()` method is smart enough to realize that for a file like `c:\test.txt`, the path isn't in the current directory. `Path.Combine()` is also the safest way to ensure that the two path segments being combined will combine correctly, including a path separator character between them.

In Windows, the normal path separator character is \, but you can make the / character used on Linux systems work fine in most cases. You can obtain the correct separator for whatever operating system your code is running on, whether it's Windows or some brand of Linux, by using `Path.DirectorySeparatorChar`. The .NET Framework library is full of features like that, clearly aimed at writing C# programs that run on multiple operating systems.

The *path* is the full name of the file folder. For example, in the filename `c:\user\temp directory\text.txt`, the path is `c:\user\temp directory`.

Upon encountering the end of the `while` loop, either by successfully completing the `try` block or by being vectored through the `catch`, the program returns to the top of the `while` loop to allow the user to write to another file. A few sample runs of the program appear as follows. The test input is boldfaced:

```
Enter filename (Enter blank filename to quit):TestFile1.txt
Enter text; enter blank line to stop
This is some stuff
So is this
As is this

Enter filename (Enter blank filename to quit):TestFile1.txt
Error on file C:\C#Programs\FileWrite\bin\Debug\TestFile1.txt
The file 'C:\C#Programs\FileWrite\bin\Debug\TestFile1.txt' already exists.

Enter filename (Enter blank filename to quit):TestFile2.txt
Enter text; enter blank line to stop
I messed up back there. I should have called it
TestFile2.

Enter filename (Enter blank filename to quit):
Press Enter to terminate...
```

Everything goes smoothly when entering random text into `TestFile1.txt`. When you try to open `TestFile1.txt` again, however, the program spits out a message, the gist of which is `The file already exists`, with the filename attached. The path to the file is tortured because the "current directory" is the directory in which Visual Studio put the executable file. To correct the mistake, you enter an acceptable filename — such as `TestFile2.txt` — without complaint.

Using some better fishing gear: The using statement

Now that you've seen `FileStream` and `StreamWriter` in action, it's important to point out the usual way to do stream writing in C# — inside a `using` statement:

```
using(<someresource>)
{
    // Use the resource.
}
```

The using statement is a construct that automates the process of cleaning up after using a stream. On encountering the closing curly brace of the using block, C# manages "flushing" the stream and closing it for you. (To *flush* a stream is to push any last bytes left over in the stream's buffer out to the associated file before it gets closed. Think of pushing a handle to drain the last water out of your . . . trout stream.) Using using eliminates the common error of forgetting to flush and close a file after writing to it. Don't leave open files lying around. Without using, you'd need to write

```
Stream fileStream = null;
TextWriter writer = null;
try
{
  // Create and use the stream, then ...
}
finally
{
  stream.Flush();
  stream.Close();
  stream = null;
}
```

Note how the code declares the stream and writer above the try block (so they're visible throughout the method). It also declares the fileStream and writer variables using abstract base classes rather than the concrete types FileStream and StreamWriter. That's a good practice. The code sets them to null so that the compiler won't complain about uninitialized variables. The preferred way to write the key I/O code in the FileWrite example looks more like this:

```
// Prepare the file stream.
FileStream fs = File.Open(fileName,
                          FileMode.CreateNew,
                          FileAccess.Write);

// Pass the fs variable to the StreamWriter constructor in the using statement.
using (StreamWriter sw = new StreamWriter(fs))

{
  // sw exists only within the using block, which is a local scope.

  // Read one string at a time from the console, outputting each to the
  // FileStream open for writing.
  Console.WriteLine("Enter text; enter blank line to stop");

  while (true)
  {
```

```
    // Read next line from Console; quit if line is blank.
    string input = Console.ReadLine();

    if (input.Length == 0)
    {
      break;
    }

    // Write the line just read to output file via the stream.
    sw.WriteLine(input);

    // Loop back up to get another line and write it.
  }
} // sw goes away here, and fs is now closed. So ...

fs = null;  // Make sure you can't try to access fs again.
```

The items in parentheses after the using keyword are its "resource acquisition" section, where you allocate one or more resources such as streams, readers/ writers, fonts, and so on. (If you allocate more than one resource, they have to be of the same type.) Following that section is the enclosing block, bounded by the outer curly braces.

The using statement's block is not a loop. The block only defines a local scope, like the try block or a method's block. (Variables defined within the block, including its head, don't exist outside the block. Thus the StreamWriter sw isn't visible outside the using block.) Book 1 discusses scope.

At the top of the preceding example, in the resource-acquisition section, you set up a resource — in this case, create a new StreamWriter wrapped around the already-existing FileStream. Inside the block is where you carry out all your I/O code for the file.

At the end of the using block, C# automatically flushes the StreamWriter, closes it, and closes the FileStream, also flushing any bytes it still contains to the file on disk. Ending the using block also *disposes* (signifies that the object is no longer needed to the garbage collector) the StreamWriter object — see the warning and the technical discussion coming up.

It's a good practice to wrap most work with streams in using statements. Wrapping the StreamWriter or StreamReader in a using statement, for example, has the same effect as putting the use of the writer or reader in a try/finally exception-handling block. (See Book 1 for exceptions.) In fact, the compiler translates the using block into the same code it uses for a try/finally, which guarantees that the resources get cleaned up:

```
try
{
  // Allocate the resource and use it here.
}
finally
{
  // Close and dispose of the resource here.
}
```

WARNING

After the using block, the StreamWriter no longer exists, and the FileStream object can no longer be accessed. The fs variable still exists, assuming that you created the stream outside the using statement, rather than on the fly like this:

```
using(StreamWriter sw = new StreamWriter(new FileStream(...)) ...
```

Flushing and closing the writer has flushed and closed the stream as well. If you try to carry out operations on the stream, you get an exception telling you that you can't access a closed object. Notice that in the FileWrite code earlier in this section the code sets the FileStream object, fs, to null after the using block to ensure the code won't try to use fs again. After that, the FileStream object is handed off to the garbage collector.

Of course, the file you wrote to disk exists. Create and open a new file stream to the file if you need to work with it again.

TECHNICAL STUFF

Specifically, using is aimed at managing the cleanup of objects that implement the IDisposable interface (see Book 2 for information on interfaces). The using statement ensures that the object's Dispose() method gets called. Classes that implement IDisposable guarantee that they have a Dispose() method. IDisposable is mainly about disposing non-.NET resources, mainly stuff in the outside world of the Windows operating system, such as file handles and graphics resources. FileStream, for example, wraps a Windows file handle that must be released. (Many classes and structs implement IDisposable; your classes can, too, if necessary.)

This book doesn't delve into IDisposable, but you should plan to become more familiar with it as your C# powers grow. Implementing it correctly has to do with the kind of indeterminate garbage disposal mentioned briefly in Book 2 and can be complex. So using is for use with classes and structs that implement IDisposable, something that you can check in C# Language Help. It won't help you with just *any* old kind of object. *Note:* The intrinsic C# types — int, double, char, and such — do *not* implement IDisposable. Class TextWriter, the base class for StreamWriter, does implement the interface. In C# Language Help, that looks like this:

```
public abstract class TextWriter : MarshalByRefObject, IDisposable
```

When in doubt, check C# Language Help to see whether the classes or `struct`s you plan to use implement `IDisposable`.

Pulling Them Out of the Stream: Using StreamReader

Writing to a file is cool, but it's sort of worthless if you can't read the file later. The following `FileRead` program puts the *input* back into the phrase *file I/O*. This program reads a text file like the ones created by `FileWrite` or by Notepad — it's sort of `FileWrite` in reverse (note this code doesn't rely on `using`):

```
using System;
using System.IO;

// FileRead -- Read a text file and write it out to the Console.
namespace FileRead
{
  public class Program
  {
    public static void Main(string[] args)
    {
      // You need a file reader object.
      StreamReader sr = null;
      string fileName = "";

      try
      {
        // Get a filename from the user.
        sr = GetReaderForFile(fileName);

        // Read the contents of the file.
        ReadFileToConsole(sr);
      }
      catch (IOException ioErr)
      {
        //TODO: Replace with a more user friendly message before release.
        Console.WriteLine("{0}\n\n", ioErr.Message);
      }
      finally  // Clean up.
      {
        if (sr != null) // Guard against trying to Close()a null object.
```

```
        {
            sr.Close();   // Takes care of flush as well
            sr = null;
        }
    }

    // Wait for user to acknowledge the results.
    Console.WriteLine("Press Enter to terminate...");
    Console.Read();
}

// GetReaderForFile -- Open the file and return a StreamReader for it.
private static StreamReader GetReaderForFile(string fileName)
{
    StreamReader sr;

    // Enter input filename.
    Console.Write("Enter the name of a text file to read:");
    fileName = Console.ReadLine();

    // User didn't enter anything; throw an exception
    // to indicate that this is not acceptable.
    if (fileName.Length == 0)
    {
        throw new IOException("You need to enter a filename.");
    }

    // Got a name -- open a file stream for reading; don't create the
    // file if it doesn't already exist.
    FileStream fs = File.Open(fileName, FileMode.Open, FileAccess.Read);

    // Wrap a StreamReader around the stream -- this will use
    // the first three bytes of the file to indicate the
    // encoding used (but not the language).
    sr = new StreamReader(fs, true);
    return sr;
}

// ReadFileToConsole -- Read lines from the file represented
//     by sr and write them out to the console.
private static void ReadFileToConsole(StreamReader sr)
{
    Console.WriteLine("\nContents of file:");

    // Read one line at a time.
    while(true)
```

```
    {
        // Read a line.
        string input = sr.ReadLine();

        // Quit when you don't get anything back.
        if (input == null)
        {
            break;
        }

        // Write whatever you read to the console.
        Console.WriteLine(input);
    }
  }
 }
}
```

WARNING

Recall that the current directory that FileRead uses is the \bin\Debug subdi-rectory under your FileRead project (not the \bin\Debug directory under the FileWrite program's directory, which is where you used FileWrite to create some test files in the preceding section). Before you run FileRead to try it, place any plain-text file (.TXT extension) in FileRead's \bin\Debug directory and note its name so that you can open it. A copy of the TestFile1.txt file created in the FileWrite example would be good.

In FileRead, the user reads one and only one file. The user must enter a valid file-name for the program to output. No second chances. After the program has read the file, it quits. The user will have to run the program again to peek into a second file. That's a design choice you might make differently.

The program starts out with all its serious code wrapped in an exception han-dler. In the try block, this handler tries to call two methods, first to get a Stream Reader for the file and then to read the file and dump its lines to the console. In the event of an exception, the catch block writes the exception message. Finally, whether the exception occurred or not, the finally block makes sure the stream and its file are closed and the variable sr is nulled so the garbage collector can reclaim it (see Book 2). I/O exceptions could occur in either method called from the try block. These percolate up to Main() looking for a handler. (No need for exception handlers in the methods.)

TIP

Note the //TODO: comment in the catch block. This is a reminder to make the message more user friendly before releasing the program. Comments marked this way appear in the Visual Studio Task List window. In that window, select Com-ments from the drop-down list at the upper left. Double-click an item there to open the editor to that comment in the code.

TECHNICAL STUFF

Because the variable sr is used inside an exception block, you have to set it to null initially — otherwise, the compiler complains about using an uninitialized variable in the exception block. Likewise, check whether sr is already (or still) null before trying to call its Close() method. Better still, convert the program to use using.

Within the GetReaderForFile() method, the program gives the user one chance to enter a filename. If the name of the file entered at the console is nothing but a blank, the program throws its own error message: You need to enter a file name. If the filename isn't empty, it's used to open a FileStream object in read mode. The File.Open() call here is the same as the one used in FileWrite:

>> The first argument is the name of the file.

>> The second argument is the file mode. The mode FileMode.Open says, "Open the file if it exists, and throw an exception if it doesn't." The other option is OpenNew, which creates a zero-length file if the file doesn't exist.

>> The final argument defines which FileStream to use. The other alternatives are Write and ReadWrite.

The resulting FileStream object fs is then wrapped in a StreamReader object sr to provide convenient methods for accessing the text file. The StreamReader is finally passed back to Main() for use.

When the file-open process is done, the FileRead program calls the ReadFileTo Console() method, which loops through the file reading lines of text using the ReadLine() call. The program echoes each line to the console with the ubiquitous Console.WriteLine() call before heading back up to the top of the loop to read another line of text. The ReadLine() call returns a null when the program reaches the end of the file. When this happens, the method breaks out of the read loop and then returns. Main() then closes the object and terminates. (You might say that the reading part of this reader program is wrapped within a while loop inside a method that's in a try block wrapped in an enigma.)

The catch block in Main() exists to keep the exception from propagating up the food chain and aborting the program. If the program throws an exception, the catch block writes a message and then simply swallows (ignores) the error. You're in Main(), so there's nowhere to rethrow the exception to, and nothing to do but close the stream and close up shop. The catch is there to let the user know why the program failed and to prevent an unhandled exception. You could have the program loop back up and ask for a different filename, but this program is so small that it's simpler to let the user run it again.

Providing an exception handler with a `catch` block that swallows the exception keeps a program from aborting over an unimportant error. However, use this technique and swallow the exception only if an error would be truly, no fake, nondamaging. See the more extensive discussion in Book 2. Here are a few sample runs:

```
Enter the name of a text file to read:yourfile.txt
Could not find file 'C:\C#Programs\FileRead\bin\Debug\yourfile.txt'.

Press Enter to terminate...

Enter the name of a text file to read:
You need to enter a filename.

Press Enter to terminate...

Enter the name of a text file to read:myfile.txt

Contents of file:
Dave?
What are you doing, Dave?
Press Enter to terminate...
```

For an example of reading arbitrary *bytes* from a file — which could be either binary or text — see the `LoopThroughFiles` example in Book 1, Chapter 7. The program actually loops through all files in a target directory, reading each file and dumping its contents to the console, so it gets tedious if there are lots of files. Feel free to terminate it by pressing Ctrl+C or by clicking the console window's close box. See the discussion of `BinaryReader` in the next section.

More Readers and Writers

Earlier in this chapter, you see the `StreamReader` and `StreamWriter` classes that you'll probably use for the bulk of your I/O needs. However, .NET also makes several other reader/writer pairs available:

>> `BinaryReader`/`BinaryWriter`: A pair of stream classes that contain methods for reading and writing each value type: `ReadChar()`, `WriteChar()`, `ReadByte()`, `WriteByte()`, and so on. (These classes are a little more primitive: They don't offer `ReadLine()`/`WriteLine()` methods.) The classes are useful for reading or writing an object in binary (nonhuman-readable) format, as opposed to text. You can use an array of bytes to work with the binary data as raw bytes. For example, you may need to read or write the bytes that make up a bitmap graphics file.

Experiment: Open a file with a .EXE extension using Notepad. You may see some readable text in the window, but most of it looks like some sort of garbage. That's binary data.

Chapter 7 in Book 1 includes an example, mentioned earlier, that reads binary data. The example uses a BinaryReader with a FileStream object to read chunks of bytes from a file and then writes out the data on the console in hexadecimal (base 16) notation, which is explained in that chapter. Although it wraps a FileStream in the more convenient BinaryReader, that example could just as easily have used the FileStream itself. The reads are identical. Although the BinaryReader brings nothing to the table in that example, it's used there to provide an example of this reader. The example does illustrate reading raw bytes into a *buffer* (an array big enough to hold the bytes read).

» StringReader/StringWriter: And now for something a little more exotic: simple reader and writer classes that are limited to reading and writing strings. They let you treat a string like a file, an alternative to accessing a string's characters in the usual ways, such as with a foreach loop

```
foreach(char c in someString) { Console.Write(c); }
```

or with array-style bracket notation ([ ])

```
char c = someString[3];
```

or with String methods like Split(), Concatenate(), and IndexOf(). With StringReader/StringWriter, you read from and write to a string much as you would to a file. This technique is useful for long strings with hundreds or thousands of characters (such as an entire text file read into a string) that you want to process in bunches, and it provides a handy way to work with a StringBuilder.

When you create a StringReader, you initialize it with a string to read. When you create a StringWriter, you can pass a StringBuilder object to it or create it empty. Internally, the StringWriter stores a StringBuilder — either the one you passed to its constructor or a new, empty one. You can get at the internal StringBuilder's contents by calling StringWriter's ToString() method.

Each time you read from the string (or write to it), the "file pointer" advances to the next available character past the read or write. Thus, as with file I/O, you have the notion of a "current position." When you read, say, 10 characters from a 1,000-character string, the position is set to the eleventh character after the read.

The methods in these classes parallel those described earlier for the Stream Reader and StreamWriter classes. If you can use those, you can use these.

Exploring More Streams than Lewis and Clark

File streams are not the only kinds of `Stream` classes available. The flood of `Stream` classes includes (but probably is not limited to) those in the following list. Note that unless otherwise specified, these stream classes all live in the `System.IO` namespace.

>> `FileStream`: For reading and writing files on a disk.

>> `MemoryStream`: Manages reading and writing data to a block of memory. You see this technique sometimes in unit tests, to avoid actually interacting with the (slow, possibly troublesome) file system. In this way, you can fake a file when testing code that reads and writes.

TECHNICAL STUFF

>> `BufferedStream`: *Buffering* is a technique for speeding up input/output operations by reading or writing bigger chunks of data at a time. Lots of small reads or writes mean lots of slow disk access — but if you read a much bigger chunk than you need now, you can then continue to read your small chunks out of the buffer — which is far faster than reading the disk. When a `Buffered Stream`'s underlying buffer runs out of data, it reads in another big chunk — maybe even the whole file. Buffered writing is similar.

Class `FileStream` automatically buffers its operations, so `BufferedStream` is for special cases, such as working with a `NetworkStream` to read and write bytes over a network. In this case, you wrap the `BufferedStream` around the `NetworkStream`, effectively "chaining" streams. When you write to the `BufferedStream`, it writes to the underlying `NetworkStream`, and so on.

When you're wrapping one stream around another, you're *composing streams*. (You can look it up in C# Language Help for more information.) The earlier sidebar, "Wrap my fish in newspaper," discusses wrapping.

>> `NetworkStream`: Manages reading and writing data over a network. See `BufferedStream` for a simplified discussion of using it. `NetworkStream` is in the `System.Net.Sockets` namespace because it uses a technology called *sockets* to make connections across a network.

>> `UnmanagedMemoryStream`: Lets you read and write data in unmanaged blocks of memory. *Unmanaged* means, basically, "not .NET" and not managed by the .NET runtime and its garbage collector. This is advanced stuff, dealing with interaction between .NET code and code written under the Windows operating system.

>> `CryptoStream`: Located in the `System.Security.Cryptography` namespace, this stream class lets you pass data to and from an encryption or decryption transformation.

Chapter **4**

Accessing the Internet

he reason that Microsoft had to create the .NET Framework in the first place was the lack of Internet interoperability within its existing infrastructure. The Component Object Model (COM) just couldn't handle the Internet. The Internet works differently than most platforms, such as PCs. The Internet is based on *protocols* — carefully defined and agreed upon ways to get things like mail and file transfers working. Microsoft's environment before 2002 distinctly didn't handle those as well.

As you can see throughout this book, the .NET Framework is designed from the ground up to take the Internet and networking in general into consideration. Not surprisingly, that is nowhere more clear than it is in the System.Net namespace. The Internet takes first chair here, with web tools taking up nine of the classes in the namespace.

In version 4.7 of the .NET Framework (the one that ships with Visual Studio 2017), even more Internet functionality is baked in. Although in version 1.x the focus was on tools used to build other tools (low-level functions), now it contains features that are useful to you, such as web, mail, and File Transfer Protocol (FTP). Secure Sockets Layer — the Internet's transport security — is much easier to use in this version, as are FTP and mail, which previously required other, harder-to-use classes.

`System.Net` is a big, meaty namespace, and finding your way around it can be difficult. This chapter discusses tasks that you perform often and shows the basics. It then gives you the tools to research complex features of the classes.

Networking is a big part of the .NET Framework, and all the functionality is in this namespace — a whole book can be (and has been) written on the subject. For the purposes of this introduction to networking with C#, this chapter shows you these features:

>> Getting a file from the network

>> Sending email

>> Logging transfers

>> Checking the status of the network around your running application

Keep in mind that sockets and IPv6 and other advanced Internet protocols are important, but most developers don't currently use them every day. This chapter talks about the parts of the namespace that you will use every day. As always, there is more to discover about `System.Net`.

Getting to Know System.Net

The `System.Net` namespace is full of classes that are confusing if viewed in the documentation, but make a lot of sense when used in an application. The namespace removes all the complexity of dealing with the various protocols used on the Internet.

There are more than 2,000 RFCs for Internet protocols (an *RFC* is a Request For Comments, a document that is sent to a standards body for review by peers before it becomes a standard). If you have to learn all the RFCs separately, you'll never complete your project. The `System.Net` namespace is about making network coding less painful.

`System.Net` isn't just for web projects. Like everything else in the base class library, you can use `System.Net` with all kinds of projects. You can:

>> Get information from web pages on the Internet and use them on your programs.

>> Move files via the Internet using FTPs.

>> Send email easily.

>> Use more advanced network structures.

>> Secure communications over the Internet using the SSL protocol.

If you need to check on the connectivity of a computer from a Windows application, you can use System.Net. If you need to build a class that will download a file from a website, System.Net is the namespace you need. Just because most classes relate to the Internet doesn't mean that only web applications can use it. That's the magic of System.Net. Any application can be a connected application. While some parts of the namespace function to make the development of web applications easier, the namespace in general is designed to make any application work with networks that adhere to web standards (including an intranet accessible within your organization).

How Net Classes Fit into the Framework

The System.Net namespace contains a large number of classes (see https://msdn.microsoft.com/en-us/library/system.net(v=vs.110).aspx) and smaller namespaces (https://msdn.microsoft.com/en-us/library/gg145039(v=vs.110).aspx). The number of classes and namespaces increases with each version of the .NET Framework, so it pays to look after each update to see what new goodies are present. The number may seem overwhelming. However, if you look closely, you can see patterns.

The classes are well named, and you will note that a few protocols get a number of classes each. After you translate, you can narrow down what you need based on the way the protocol is named:

>> Authentication and Authorization: These classes provide security.

>> Cookie: This class manages cookies from web browsers and usually is used in ASP.NET pages.

>> DNS (Domain Name Services): These classes help to resolve domain names into IP addresses.

>> Download: This class is used to get files from servers.

>> EndPoint: This class helps to define a network node.

>> FileWeb: This brilliant set of classes describes network file servers as local classes.

>> FtpWeb: This class is a simple File Transfer Protocol implementation.

» Http (HyperText Transfer Protocol): This class is the web protocol.

» IP (Internet Protocol): This class helps to define network endpoints that are specifically Internet related.

» IrDA: This class is an infrared endpoint. Infrared ports are networks, too!

» NetworkCredential: This class is another security implementation.

» Service: This class helps manage network connections.

» Socket: This class deals with the most primitive of network connections.

» Upload: This set of classes helps you upload information to the Internet.

» Web: These classes help with the World Wide Web — largely implementations of the http classes that are more task oriented.

This list is extensive because the classes build on each other. The EndPoint classes are used by the socket classes to define certain network specifics, and the IP classes make them specific to the Internet. The Web classes are specific to the World Wide Web. You will rarely use the highest-level classes, but it's often tough to see what is needed when. Most of the functions that you use every day, though, are encapsulated within seven mostly new namespaces under the System.Net namespace:

» Cache: This function has a lot of enumerators that manage the browser and network caching functions built into the namespace.

» Configuration: This function grants access to the properties that you need to set to make many of the other System.Net classes work.

» Mail: This function takes over for System.Web.Mail to facilitate the sending of Internet email.

» Mime: This function bundles file attachments with the Mail namespace using Multipurpose Internet Mail Extensions (MIME).

» NetworkInformation: This function gets details about the network around your application.

» Security: This function implements the network security managed by many classes of System.Net.

» Sockets: This function utilizes the most basic network connections available to Windows.

Using the System.Net Namespace

The System.Net namespace is *code oriented*, which means that few implementations are specifically for user interfaces. Almost everything that you do with these classes is behind the scenes. You have few drag-and-drop user controls — the System.Net namespace is used in the Code view. To demonstrate this fact, the examples in the remainder of the chapter build a Windows Forms application that has the following requirements:

>> Check the network status.

>> Get a specific file from the Internet.

>> Email it to a specific email address (or addresses).

>> Log the whole transaction.

This is not an insignificant set of requirements. In fact, in the 1.0 and 1.1 versions of C#, this would be difficult. One of the main goals of the System.Net namespace in this version is to make common tasks much easier. You can start by loading the sample code or by starting a new project and following the steps in the following sections.

Checking the network status

First, you need to inform the user about network connectivity by following these steps:

1. **Choose File➪New➪Project.**

   You see the New Project dialog box.

2. **Select the Visual C#\Windows Classic Desktop folder in the left pane.**

3. **Highlight the Windows Forms App template in the center pane.**

4. **Type** NetworkTools **in the Name field and click OK.**

   Visual Studio creates a new Windows Form application for you and displays the designer where you can add controls. At this point, you can start adding controls to the example application.

5. **Add a** StatusStrip **control to the lower left of the form by dragging it from the Menus & Toolbars group of the Toolbox.**

   The StatusStrip automatically takes up the entire bottom area of the form.

6. **Select the SmartTag that appears on the left side of the** StatusStrip **and add a** StatusLabel.

   Figure 4-1 shows how the SmartTag entries appear when you click the down arrow in the box.

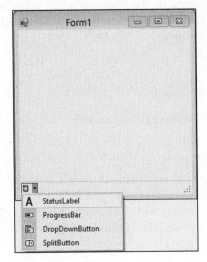

FIGURE 4-1:
Many controls
come with
SmartTags that
let you configure
them easily.

7. **Double-click the form.**

   Visual Studio creates the Form1_Load() method and displays the code editor for you.

8. **Reference the** System.Net **namespace by adding the line** using System. NET.NetworkInformation; **to the top of the code.**

9. **Add the code in bold from the following listing to test whether the network is available and display it on the status bar:**

```
using System;
using System.Windows.Forms;
using System.Net.NetworkInformation;

namespace NetworkTools
{
    public partial class Form1 : Form
    {
        public Form1()
        {
            InitializeComponent();
        }
```

```
private void Form1_Load(object sender, EventArgs e)
{
    if (NetworkInterface.GetIsNetworkAvailable())
    {
        toolStripStatusLabel1.Text = "Connected";
    }
    else
    {
        toolStripStatusLabel1.Text = "Disconnected";
    }
}
```

That's all there is to it. The NetworkInformation class contains a bunch of information about the status of the network, current IP addresses, the gateway being used by the current machine, and more.

TIP

Keep in mind that the NetworkInformation class will work only on a local machine. If you use this class in an ASP.NET Web Forms application, you will get information about the server.

Downloading a file from the Internet

You can get a file from the Internet in one of several ways, and one of the most common is by using File Transfer Protocol (FTP). The lightweight FTP protocol is favored because it's secure and supported on many systems. To build an application that uses FTP, start with the example from the previous section and follow these steps:

1. Drag a Button **control onto the form from the Toolbox.**

2. **Double-click the button.**

Visual Studio creates the button1_Click() method and displays the code editor for you.

3. **Add the following imports to the top of the coding area:**

```
using System.Net;
using System.IO;
```

4. Create a new method called DownloadFile **that accepts a** remoteFile **and a** localFile **as type** string.

5. Type the following code into the DownloadFile() **method:**

```csharp
private void DownLoadFile(string remoteFile, string localFile)
{
    // Create the stream and request objects.
    FileStream localFileStream =
        new FileStream(localFile, FileMode.OpenOrCreate);
    FtpWebRequest ftpRequest =
        (FtpWebRequest)WebRequest.Create(remoteFile);

    // Configure the request.
    ftpRequest.Method = WebRequestMethods.Ftp.DownloadFile;
    ftpRequest.Credentials =
        new NetworkCredential("Anonymous", "");

    // Configure the response to the request.
    WebResponse ftpResponse = ftpRequest.GetResponse();
    Stream ftpResponseStream = ftpResponse.GetResponseStream();
    byte[] buffer = new byte[1024];

    // Process the response by downloading data.
    int bytesRead = ftpResponseStream.Read(buffer, 0, 1024);
    while (bytesRead > 0)
    {
        localFileStream.Write(buffer, 0, bytesRead);
        bytesRead = ftpResponseStream.Read(buffer, 0, 1024);
    }

    // Close the streams.
    localFileStream.Close();
    ftpResponseStream.Close();
}
```

The code follows a process of establishing a connection, configuring the connection, configuring a response to that connection, and then performing a task. In this case, the task is to download a file from the FTP site. When providing a network credential for an FTP site, you often need to provide your email address as the password (the second parameter, which is blank in the example). You must always close the streams when you finish performing a task.

6. Call the DownloadFile() **method from the** button1_Click() **event handler by using the following code:**

```csharp
private void button1_Click(object sender, EventArgs e)
{
```

```
DownLoadFile(@"ftp://ftp.yourftpsite.com/afile.txt",
    @"c:\temp\afile.txt");
}
```

To use this example, you must replace the first string with the location of a file on your FTP site and the second string with the location on your hard drive where you want the file to go. In this FTP example, the WebRequest and WebResponse classes in the System.Net namespace are fully utilized to create the more complete FtpWebRequest. Properties such as the Method of download and Credentials make it an easy call.

In fact, the toughest part of this process is dealing with a FileStream object, which is still the best way to move files and is not specific to the System.Net namespace. Streams are discussed in Chapter 3 of this minibook, which covers the System.IO namespace, but they have significance to the network classes too. Streams represent a flow of data of some kind, and a flow of information from the Internet qualifies.

That's what you are doing when you get a web page or a file from the Internet — gathering a flow of data. If you think about it, it makes sense that this is a flow, because the status bar in an application shows a percentage of completion. Just like pouring water into a glass, the flow of data is a stream, so the concept is named Stream.

This concept holds true for getting a file from the World Wide Web, as well. HTTP, the web protocol, is just another protocol that defines how a document is moved from a server on the Internet to your local machine. In fact, the code looks strikingly similar to the FTP example, as you can see in the following bit of code. The same stream is recovered; only the formatting is different.

```
private void DownLoadWebFile(string remoteFile, string localFile)
{
    FileStream localFileStream =
        new FileStream(localFile, FileMode.OpenOrCreate);
    WebRequest webRequest = WebRequest.Create(remoteFile);
    webRequest.Method = WebRequestMethods.Http.Get;

    WebResponse webResponse = webRequest.GetResponse();
    Stream webResponseStream = webResponse.GetResponseStream();

    byte[] buffer = new byte[1024];
    int bytesRead = webResponseStream.Read(buffer, 0, 1024);
```

```
        while (bytesRead > 0)
        {
            localFileStream.Write(buffer, 0, bytesRead);
            bytesRead = webResponseStream.Read(buffer, 0, 1024);
        }

        localFileStream.Close();
        webResponseStream.Close();
    }
```

You need to pass in a web address, so your subroutine call looks like this:

```
DownloadWebFile(@"http://your.ftp.server.com/sampleFile.bmp",
    @"c:\sampleFile.bmp");
```

There are a few differences in this code. webRequest is now a WebRequest rather than an FtpWebRequest. Also, the Method property of webRequest has been changed to WebRequestMethods.Http.Get. Finally, the Credentials property has been removed because the credentials are no longer required.

Emailing a status report

Email is a common requirement of networked systems. If you are working in an enterprise environment, you are going to write a larger scale application to handle all email requirements, rather than make each individual application email-aware. However, if you are writing a stand-alone product, it might require email support.

Email is a server-based operation, so if you don't have an email server that you can use to send from, this might be hard. Many ISPs no longer allow *relaying*, which is sending an outgoing message without first having an account and logging in. Therefore, you might have trouble running this part of the sample.

If you are in a corporate environment, however, you can usually talk to your email administrator and get permission to use the email server. Because outgoing requests are usually only harnessed inside the firewall, relaying is often available. To build your email function, follow these steps:

1. **Add a TextBox control to the default form in Design view and then change to Code view.**

2. **Add the following imports to the top of the coding area:**

    ```
    using System.Net.Mail;
    ```

3. **Create a new method called** SendEmail **that accepts** fromAddress, toAddress, subject, **and** body, **all of type** string.

It should accept the from email address, the to email address, the subject of the email, and the body of the email.

4. **Type the following code into the** SendEmail() **method:**

```
private void SendEmail(string fromAddress, string toAddress,
    string subject, string body)
{
    // Define the message.
    MailMessage message =
        new MailMessage(fromAddress, toAddress, subject, body);

    // Create the connection and send the message.
    SmtpClient mailClient = new SmtpClient("localhost");
    mailClient.Send(message);

    // Release the message and client.
    message = null;
    mailClient = null;
}
```

The example follows a process that starts by creating a message. It then creates a client that provides the connection to the host and sends the message to the host. The last step is to release the message and client so that the garbage collector can reclaim them.

Notice that code uses localhost as the email server name. If you have email server software installed locally, even IIS 6.0 with SMTP, this will work. Most of the time, you'll have to put another email server name in the SmtpClient constructor. The email server name can often be found in your Outlook preferences.

After you have written your method, you need to call it after the file is downloaded in the Button1_Click event handler. Change the code of that subroutine to the following to call that method:

```
private void button1_Click(object sender, EventArgs e)
{
    // Obtain the file.
    DownLoadFile(@"ftp://ftp.yourftpsite.com/afile.txt",
        @"c:\temp\afile.txt");
```

```
// Send a success message.
SendEmail(textBox1.Text, textBox1.Text,
    "FTP Successful", "FTP Successfully downloaded");
}
```

The example uses the value of the text box twice: once for the to address, and once for the from address. This isn't always necessary, because you may have a situation in which you want the email to come only from a webmaster address or to go only to your address.

You should have enough code in place to run the application now. However, the example won't run as downloaded; you must provide location information for an FTP and an SMTP server. Press F5 to launch the application in debug mode and give it a try.

When you click the button, the application should download the file to the local drive and then email you to inform you that the download is complete. A host of things can go wrong with network applications, though, and you should be aware of them. Here are a few:

>> For most network activity, the machine running the software must be connected to a network. This isn't a problem for you as the developer, but you need to be conscious of the end users, who may need connectivity to have access to the features they want to use. Use of the network status code can help inform users about the availability of those features.

>> Firewalls and other network appliances sometimes block network traffic from legitimate applications. Some examples of this include:

- FTP is often blocked from corporate networks.

- Network analysis features of .NET are often blocked on corporate servers. If the server is available to the public, these openings can cause holes for hackers to crawl through.

- Speaking of hackers, make sure that if you use incoming network features in your application, you have adequately secured your application. More on this can be found in the excellent book *Writing Secure Code,* Second Edition, by Michael Howard and David C. LeBlanc (published by Microsoft Press).

- Email is especially fragile. Often, Internet service providers will block email from an address that is not registered on a mail server. This means that if you are using your localhost server your ISP might block the email.

>> Network traffic is notoriously hard to debug. For instance, if the sample application works, but you never receive an email from the SmtpServer you coded, what went wrong? You may never know. XML web services have a similar problem — it's spectacularly tough to see the actual code in the *SOAP*

Logging network activity

This brings you to the next topic, which is network logging. Because network activity problems are so hard to debug and reproduce, Microsoft has built in several tools for the management of tracing network activity.

What's more, as with the ASP.NET tracing available, the System.Net namespace tracing is completely managed using the configuration files. To be able to use the functions, therefore, you don't need to change and recompile your code. In fact, with a little management, you can even show debug information to the user by managing the config files your application uses.

Each kind of application has a different kind of configuration file. For Windows Forms applications, which you are using here, the file is called app.config and is stored in the development project directory. When you compile, the name of the file is changed to the name of the application, and it's copied into the bin directory for running.

If you open your app.config file now by double-clicking its entry in Solution Explorer, you see that it has practically nothing in it (as shown in Listing 4-1). This is fairly new for .NET, which used to have very involved configuration. You will add some content to the configuration to get tracing turned on.

LISTING 4-1: **The Default app.config File**

```
<?xml version="1.0" encoding="utf-8" ?>
<configuration>
    <startup>
        <supportedRuntime version="v4.0"
                          sku=".NETFramework,Version=v4.5.2"/>
    </startup>
</configuration>
```

First, you need to add a new source for the System.Net namespace. Next, you add a switch to the Switches section for the source you added. Finally, you add a SharedListener to that section and set the file to flush the tracing information automatically. The finished app.config file, with the adds in bold, is shown in Listing 4-2.

LISTING 4-2: **The Finished app.config File**

```xml
<?xml version="1.0" encoding="utf-8" ?>
<configuration>
    <startup>
        <supportedRuntime version="v4.0"
                          sku=".NETFramework,Version=v4.5.2"/>
    </startup>
    <system.diagnostics>
      <sources>
        <source name="System.Net">
          <listeners>
            <add name="System.Net"/>
          </listeners>
        </source>
      </sources>
      <switches>
        <add name="System.Net" value="Verbose" />
      </switches>
      <sharedListeners>
        <add name="System.Net"
             type="System.Diagnostics.TextWriterTraceListener"
             initializeData="my.log"/>
      </sharedListeners>
      <trace autoflush="true" />
    </system.diagnostics>
</configuration>
```

Run the application again and watch the Output window. Advanced logging information is shown there because of your changes to the configuration file. Additionally, a log file was written. In the development environment, this is in the bin/debug directory of your project. You might have to click the Show All Files button at the top of the Solution Explorer to see it.

In that folder, you should see the file named my.log, where the SharedListener you added to the app.config file directed the logging information. Listing 4-3 shows how the content of this file could appear. The specific URLs, reference numbers, and other object values will differ in your output, but you should see something similar to the output shown in the listing.

LISTING 4-3: **The Log Information**

```
System.Net Information: 0 : WebRequest::Create(ftp://ftp.csharpfordummies.net/
    sample.bmp)
System.Net Information: 0 : Exiting WebRequest::Create() ->
    FtpWebRequest#37460558
System.Net Information: 0 : FtpWebRequest#37460558::GetResponse()
```

```
System.Net Information: 0 : Exiting FtpWebRequest#37460558::GetResponse()
System.Net Information: 0 : Associating Message#59487907 with
   HeaderCollection#23085090
System.Net Information: 0 : HeaderCollection#23085090::Set(mime-version=1.0)
System.Net Information: 0 : Associating MailMessage#6964596 with Message#59487907
System.Net Information: 0 : SmtpClient::.ctor(host=24.123.157.3)
System.Net Information: 0 : Associating SmtpClient#17113003 with
   SmtpTransport#30544512
System.Net Information: 0 : Exiting SmtpClient::.ctor()        ->
   SmtpClient#17113003
System.Net Information: 0 : SmtpClient#17113003::Send(MailMessage#6964596)
System.Net Information: 0 : SmtpClient#17113003::Send(DeliveryMethod=Network)
System.Net Information: 0 : Associating SmtpClient#17113003 with
   MailMessage#6964596
System.Net Information: 0 : Associating SmtpTransport#30544512 with
   SmtpConnection#44365459
System.Net Information: 0 : Associating SmtpConnection#44365459 with
   ServicePoint#7044526
System.Net Information: 0 : Associating SmtpConnection#44365459 with
   SmtpPooledStream#20390146
System.Net Information: 0 : HeaderCollection#30689639::Set(content-transfer-
   encoding=base64)
System.Net Information: 0 : HeaderCollection#30689639::Set(content-transfer-
   encoding=quoted-printable)
System.Net Information: 0 : HeaderCollection#23085090::Remove(x-receiver)
System.Net Information: 0 : HeaderCollection#23085090::Set(from=bill@sempf.net)
System.Net Information: 0 : HeaderCollection#23085090::Set(to=bill@sempf.net)
System.Net Information: 0 : HeaderCollection#23085090::Set(date=1 Apr 2010
   16:32:32 -0500)
System.Net Information: 0 : HeaderCollection#23085090::Set(subject=FTP
   Successful)
System.Net Information: 0 : HeaderCollection#23085090::Get(mime-version)
System.Net Information: 0 : HeaderCollection#23085090::Get(from)
System.Net Information: 0 : HeaderCollection#23085090::Get(to)
System.Net Information: 0 : HeaderCollection#23085090::Get(date)
System.Net Information: 0 : HeaderCollection#23085090::Get(subject)
System.Net Information: 0 : HeaderCollection#30689639::Get(content-type)
System.Net Information: 0 : HeaderCollection#30689639::Get(content-transfer-
   encoding)
System.Net Information: 0 : Exiting SmtpClient#17113003::Send()
```

Reading this file, you can see that the reference numbers that match the requests on the server all appear, dramatically improving the ease of debugging. Also, because everything is in order of action, finding out exactly where the error occurred in the process is much easier.

Chapter **5**

Creating Images

N
o one is going to write the next edition of *Bioshock* using C#. It just isn't the kind of language you use to write graphics-intensive applications like shoot-'em-up games.

Still, C# packs a fair amount of power into the System.Drawing classes. Though these classes are somewhat primitive in some areas, and using them might cause you to have to write a few more lines of code than you should, there isn't much that these classes can't do with sufficient work.

The drawing capability provided by the .NET Framework is divided into four logical areas by the namespace design provided by Microsoft. All the general drawing capability is in the System.Drawing namespace. Then there are some specialized namespaces:

» System.Drawing.2D has advanced vector drawing functionality.

» System.Drawing.Imaging is mostly about using bitmap graphic formats, like .bmp and .jpg files.

» System.Drawing.Text deals with advanced typography.

This chapter focuses on the base namespace and covers only the basics of drawing in C#. (Discussing every aspect of drawing could easily fill an entire book.)

Getting to Know System.Drawing

Even at the highest level, graphics programming consists of drawing polygons, filling them with color, and labeling them with text — all on a canvas of some sort. Unsurprisingly, this leaves you with four objects that form the core of the graphics code you write: graphics, pens, brushes, and text.

Graphics

Generally speaking, the Graphics class creates an object that is your palette. It's the canvas. All the methods and properties of the Graphics object are designed to make the area you draw upon more appropriate for your needs.

Also, most of the graphics- and image-related methods of other classes in the framework provide the Graphics object as output. For instance, you can call the System.Web.Forms.Control.CreateGraphics method from a Windows Forms application and get a Graphics object back that enables you to draw in a form control in your project. You can also handle the Paint event of a form, and check out the Graphics property of the event.

Graphics objects use pens and brushes (discussed later in this chapter, in the "Pens" and "Brushes" sections) to draw and fill. Graphics objects have methods such as these:

» DrawRectangle

» FillRectangle

» DrawCircle

» FillCircle

» DrawBezier

» DrawLine

These methods accept pens and brushes as parameters. You might think, "How can a circle help me?" but you must remember that even complex graphic objects such as the Covenant in *Halo 3* are made up of circles and rectangles — thousands of them. The trick to useful art is using math to put together lots of circles and squares until you have a complete image. The sample application described later in this chapter is a simple example of just that.

Pens

You use pens to draw lines and curves. Complex graphics are made up of polygons, and those polygons are made of lines, and those lines are generated by pens. Pens have properties such as

- » Color
- » DashStyle
- » EndCap
- » Width

You get the idea: You use pens to draw things. These properties are used by the pens to determine how things are drawn.

Brushes

Brushes paint the insides of polygons. Though you use the pens to draw the shapes, you use brushes to fill in the shapes with gradients, patterns, or colors. Brushes are usually passed in as parameters to a DrawWhatever method of the pen objects. When the pen draws the shape it was asked to draw, it uses the brush to fill in the shape — just as you did in kindergarten with crayons and coloring books. (The brush object always stays inside the lines, though.)

Don't look for the Brush class, however. It's a holding area for the real brushes, which have kind of strange names. Brushes are made to be customized, but you can do a lot with the brushes that come with the framework as is. Some of the brushes include

- » SolidBrush
- » TextureBrush
- » HatchBrush
- » PathGradientBrush

Although the pens are used to pass into the Draw methods of the Graphics object, brushes are used to pass into the Fill methods that form polygons.

Text

Text is painted with a combination of fonts and brushes. Just like pens, the Font class uses brushes to fill in the lines of a text operation.

System.Drawing.Text has collections of all the fonts installed in the system running your program, or installed as part of your application. System.Drawing.Font has all the properties of the typography, such as

>> Bold

>> Size

>> Style

>> Underline

The Graphics object, again, provides the writing of the text on the palette.

PRINTING A FORM

In VB6, and earlier, one of the most common ways to get information to paper was to print a form. This functionality was lacking in .NET but came back in a Power Pack and now is built into Visual Studio 2008 and above. It's available to all languages, but VB programmers miss it the most.

If you need to build a report, you should use Microsoft Report Viewer, which isn't covered in this book. If you just want to get some text and images to the user's printer, though, the PrintForm component should do the trick.

To use the PrintForm component, drag it from the Toolbox onto your form in Design View. It will appear in the component tray. In the event handler for your print function (the MenuItem.Click function, for instance), set up the Form property of the component, the Print Action, and then call the Print command. It looks like this:

```
using PrintForm printForm = new PrintForm
    .Form =TheFormIWantPrinted
    .PrintAction = PrintToPrinter
    .Print()
end using
```

The form will be sent to the windows Print function, just as though you had used the Print dialog box to print a file.

How the Drawing Classes Fit into the Framework

The `System.Drawing` namespace breaks drawing into two steps:

1. Create a `System.Drawing.Graphics` **object.**

2. Use the tools in the `System.Drawing` **namespace to draw on it.**

It seems straightforward, and it is. The first step is to get a `Graphics` object. `Graphics` objects come from two main places — existing images and Windows Forms.

To get a `Graphics` object from an existing image, look at the `Bitmap` object. The `Bitmap` object is a great tool that enables you to create an object using an existing image file. This gives you a new palette that is based on a bitmap image (a JPEG file, for example) that is already on your hard drive. It's a convenient tool, especially for web images.

```
Bitmap currentBitmap = new Bitmap(@"c:\images\myImage.jpg");
Graphics palette = Graphics.FromImage(currentBitmap);
```

Now the object `myPalette` is a `Graphics` object whose height and width are based on the image in `myBitmap`. What's more, the base of the `myPalette` image looks exactly like the image referenced in the `myBitmap` object.

You can use the pens, brushes, and fonts in the `Graphics` class to draw directly on that image, as though it were a blank canvas. It's possible to use a font to put text on images before showing them on web pages and to use other `Graphics` elements to modify the format of images on the fly, too.

Another way to get a `Graphics` object is to get it from Windows Forms. The method you want is `System.Windows.Forms.Control.CreateGraphics`. This method gives you a new palette that is based on the drawing surface of the control being referenced. If it's a form, it inherits the height and width of the form and has the form background color. You can use pens and brushes to draw right on the form.

When you have a `Graphics` object, the options are endless. Sophisticated drawing isn't out of the question, though you would have to do a ton of work to create graphics like you see in *Halo* using Visual Studio. (There isn't a Master Chief class that you can just generate automatically.)

Nonetheless, even the most complex 3D graphics are just colored polygons, and you can make those with the `System.Drawing` class. The following sections build a cribbage board with a `Graphics` object, pens, brushes, and fonts.

Using the System.Drawing Namespace

Good applications come from strange places. Many people enjoy games, and one favorite in the United States (and many other places) is the card game cribbage. Say that you're on vacation and have the urge to play. You have the cards, but not a cribbage board.

You do have your laptop, Visual Studio, and the `System.Drawing` namespace. After just a few hours of work, you could build an application that serves as a working cribbage board! The example in the following sections isn't quite complete (which would require a whole lot of code), but it does include enough code to get you started, and it's operational enough to let you play a game.

Getting started

Cribbage is a card game where hands are counted up into points, and the first player to score 121 points wins. It's up to the players to count the points, and the score is kept on a board.

Cribbage boards are made up of two lines of holes for pegs, usually totaling 120, but sometimes 60 holes are used and you play through twice. Figure 5-1 shows a typical cribbage board. Cribbage boards come in a bunch of styles — check out `www.cribbage.org` if you're curious; it has a great gallery of almost 100 boards, from basic to whimsical.

In this example, you create the board image for an application that keeps score of a cribbage game — but it wouldn't be beyond C# to write the cards into the game, too! So the board for this application has 40 holes on each of three pairs of lines, which is the standard board setup for two players playing to 120, as shown in Figure 5-2. The first task is to draw the board and then to draw the pegs as the players' scores — entered in text boxes — change.

The premise is this: The players play a hand and enter the resulting scores in the text box below their respective names (refer to Figure 5-2). When the score for each hand is entered, the score next to the player's name is updated, and the peg is moved on the board. The next time that same player scores a hand, the peg is moved forward, and the back peg is moved into its place. The inventor of cribbage was paranoid of cheating, and the back peg makes this less likely. If you're unfamiliar with cribbage, you may want to check out the rules at `www.cribbage.org`.

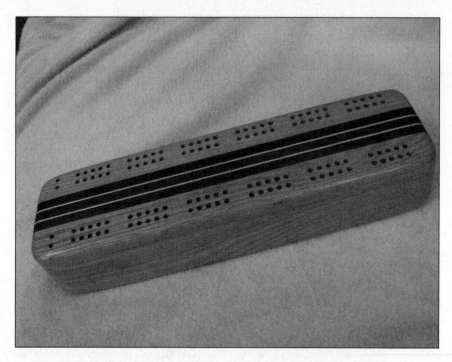

FIGURE 5-1:
A traditional cribbage board.

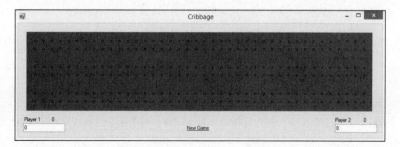

FIGURE 5-2:
The digital cribbage board.

Setting up the project

To begin, create a playing surface. You set up the board shown in Figure 5-2 without drawing the board itself — you see later how to paint it with System. Drawing objects. Your board should look like Figure 5-3 when you're ready to start creating business rules. The various controls, from left to right, are named **Player1Points** (Label), **Player1** (TextBox), **WinMessage** (Label), **StartGame** (LinkLabel), **Player2Points** (Label), and **Player2** (TextBox).

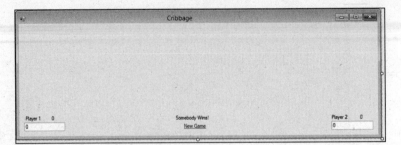

FIGURE 5-3:
The basic board.

Handling the score

The following method handles score changes by calling it from the TextChanged event handlers. The method is purposely generic to make it easier to use the same code for both players.

```
// Fields used to keep track of score.
private int Player1LastTotal = 0;
private int Player2LastTotal = 0;

private void HandleScore(TextBox scoreBox, Label points,
    Label otherPlayer, ref Int32 lastScore)
{
    try
    {
        if (0 > Int32.Parse(scoreBox.Text) |
            Int32.Parse(scoreBox.Text) > 27)
        {
            // Display an error message and ensure the errant
            // score textbox has focus.
            WinMessage.Text = "Score must be between 0 and 27";
            scoreBox.Focus();
        }
        else
        {
            // Clear any error message.
            WinMessage.Text = "";

            // Update the last score.
            lastScore = Int32.Parse(points.Text);

            //Add the score written to the points
            points.Text = (Int32.Parse(points.Text) +
                Int32.Parse(scoreBox.Text)).ToString();
        }
    }
    catch (System.InvalidCastException ext)
    {
```

```
            //Something other than a number
            if (scoreBox.Text.Length > 0)
            {
                WinMessage.Text = "Score must be a number";
            }
        }
        catch (Exception ex)
        {
            //Eek!
            MessageBox.Show("Something went wrong!  " + ex.Message);
        }
        //Check the score
        if (Int32.Parse(points.Text) > 120)
        {
            if (Int32.Parse(points.Text) /
                Int32.Parse(otherPlayer.Text) > 1.5)
            {
                WinMessage.Text = scoreBox.Name.Substring(0,
                    scoreBox.Name.Length - 6) + " Skunked 'em!!!";
            }
            else
            {
                WinMessage.Text = scoreBox.Name.Substring(0,
                    scoreBox.Name.Length - 6) + " Won!!";
            }
            WinMessage.Visible = true;
        }
    }
```

Creating an event connection

Of course, if you have something that's associated with an event, you must have
event handlers. Double-click Player1 and Player2 in turn to create the following
event handlers:

```
private void Player1_TextChanged(object sender, EventArgs e)
{
    // Handle the score.
    HandleScore(Player1, Player1Points, Player2Points,
        ref Player1LastTotal);

    // Update the board.
    Form1.ActiveForm.Invalidate();
}

private void Player2_TextChanged(object sender, EventArgs e)
{
```

```
    // Handle the score.
    HandleScore(Player2, Player2Points, Player1Points,
        ref Player2LastTotal);

    // Update the board.
    Form1.ActiveForm.Invalidate();
}
```

Note that you must pass the private field used to hold the previous player's score by reference. Otherwise, the fields won't update.

In addition, you must call Form1.ActiveForm.Invalidate(). Otherwise, the board won't redraw, which means that you won't see the pins move.

Drawing the board

The application needs to paint right on a form to create the image of the board for the cribbage application. This means gaining access to the Graphics object through the PaintEventArgs object passed to the application during each redraw event. From there, you need to complete these tasks:

>> Paint the board brown using a brush.

>> Draw six rows of little circles using a pen.

>> Fill in the hole if that is the right score.

>> Clean up your supplies.

The following method redraws the board every time it gets called. To make the method purpose more understandable, the code calls it CribbageBoard_Paint().

```
private void CribbageBoard_Paint(object sender, PaintEventArgs e)
{
    // Obtain the graphics object.
    Graphics g = e.Graphics;

    // Create the board
    SolidBrush brownBrush = new SolidBrush(Color.Brown);
    g.FillRectangle(brownBrush, new Rectangle(20, 20, 820, 180));

    //Paint the little holes.
    //There are 244 little holes in the board.
    //Three rows of 40 times two, with the little starts and stops on
    //either end.
    //Let's start with the 240.
```

```
int rows = 0;
int columns = 0;
int scoreBeingDrawn = 0;
Pen blackPen = new Pen(System.Drawing.Color.Black, 1);
SolidBrush blackBrush = new SolidBrush(Color.Black);
SolidBrush redBrush = new SolidBrush(Color.Red);

//There are 6 rows, then, at 24 and 40, 80 and 100, then 140 and 160.
for (rows = 40; rows <= 160; rows += 60)
{
    //There are 40 columns. They are every 20
    for (columns = 40; columns <= 820; columns += 20)
    {
        //Calculate score being drawn
        scoreBeingDrawn = ((columns - 20) / 20) +
            ((((rows + 20) / 60) - 1) * 40);

        //Draw Player1
        //If score being drawn = Player1 fill, otherwise draw
        if (scoreBeingDrawn == Int32.Parse(Player1Points.Text))
        {
            g.FillEllipse(blackBrush, columns - 2, rows - 2, 6, 6);
        }
        else if (scoreBeingDrawn == Player1LastTotal)
        {
            g.FillEllipse(redBrush, columns - 2, rows - 2, 6, 6);
        }
        else
        {
            g.DrawEllipse(blackPen, columns - 2, rows - 2, 4, 4);
        }

        //Draw Player2
        //If score being drawn = Player2 fill, otherwise draw
        if (scoreBeingDrawn == Int32.Parse(Player2Points.Text))
        {
            g.FillEllipse(blackBrush, columns - 2, rows + 16, 6, 6);
        }
        else if (scoreBeingDrawn == Player2LastTotal)
        {
            g.FillEllipse(redBrush, columns - 2, rows + 16, 6, 6);
        }
        else
        {
            g.DrawEllipse(blackPen, columns - 2, rows + 16, 4, 4);
        }
    }
}
```

```
    // Perform the required cleanup.
    g.Dispose();
    brownBrush.Dispose();
    blackPen.Dispose();
}
```

Aside from the math, note the decision making. If the score being drawn is the score in the label, fill in the hole with a red peg. If it's the last score drawn, fill in the hole with a black peg. Otherwise, well, just draw a circle.

REMEMBER

To make the `CribbageBoard_Paint()` event handler work properly, you must associate it with the form. In Design View, select `Form1`. Click the Events button at the top of the Properties window to display the list of events associated with `Form1`. Click the drop-down list box for the `Paint` event and choose the `CribbageBoard_Paint` entry.

Starting a new game

The last thing you need to do is create some method for starting a new game, which is where the `LinkLabel`, `StartGame`, comes into play. The following code sets everything up for a new game:

```
private void StartGame_LinkClicked(object sender,
    LinkLabelLinkClickedEventArgs e)
{
    // Set the scores to zero.
    Player1.Text = "0";
    Player2.Text = "0";
    Player1Points.Text = "0";
    Player2Points.Text = "0";
    Player1LastTotal = 0;
    Player2LastTotal = 0;

    // Reset the text.
    WinMessage.Text = "";
}
```

It's tough to fathom, but this is exactly how large-scale games are written. Admittedly, big graphics engines make many more If-Then decisions, but the premise is the same.

Also, large games use bitmap images sometimes, rather than draw all the time. For the cribbage-scoring application, for example, you could use a bitmap image of a peg rather than fill an ellipse with a black or red brush!

Chapter 6

Programming Dynamically!

*D*ynamic programming* is another one of those buzzwords that really doesn't have a clear definition. At its loosest, it means developing something in such a way that the program makes more decisions about the way it runs while running, rather than when you compile it.

Scripting languages are a great example of this type of programming. When you write something in VBScript, you don't compile it at all — all the decisions are made at runtime. Ruby is another good example: Most of the time, an entire program can just be typed into a command prompt and run right from there.

Some examples are not so good — like VB Classic. Remember the Variant type? You could declare a variable to be Variant, and VB wouldn't decide what it was supposed to be for real until the program ran. In the best of cases, this feature added immense flexibility to the language. In the worst of cases, you got Type Mismatch errors at runtime.

REMEMBER

To give a concrete example, when you declare a variable in a dynamically typed language, you don't have to say what type you are making that variable. The compiler will just figure it out for you. In a static language, such as earlier versions of C#, you do have to say what type you are making that variable. However, starting with C# 3.0, the var keyword lets you leave the decision of which type to use to the compiler.

Microsoft originally promised that dynamic types would never be in C#, but later decided that the feature had to be added. Why? Mostly it's because of the development for Microsoft Office. Office uses COM, the pre-.NET structure for Microsoft applications. Additionally, the WinRT API is not based in managed code and supports JavaScript, one of the original dynamic languages. They probably added dynamic support looking forward to WinRT as well.

COM and WinRT expects that the languages that use it (like VB Classic and C++) will have dynamic types. This made developing for Microsoft Office difficult for C# programmers, which was exactly opposite of what Microsoft wanted to happen. The end result? The dynamic type.

Shifting C# Toward Dynamic Typing

So-called "dynamic languages" are a trend that keeps coming back, like ruffled tux shirts. *Dynamic languages* are languages that allow for loose typing, rather than static. The concept got started in the 1960s with the List Processing (LISP) languge. Dynamic languages came back in the late 1980s for two reasons: network management scripting and the artificial intelligence craze. Thanks to the web, the buzzword is back yet again.

The World Wide Web, for those of you who aren't old enough to remember, was built on View Source and dynamic languages. Microsoft's original web development language, Active Server Pages, was built on VBScript — a dynamic language.

The web is better with a dynamic programming environment, so the trend is probably here to stay this time (until the next big thing, anyway). C# isn't the only language that is adding dynamic language features, and dynamic type isn't the only language feature that has been added to make it more appealing for web programmers. Several dynamic languages have been around for a while, like these:

>> LISP

>> Perl

>> Scheme

>> Smalltalk

>> Visual Basic

Although some of these aren't as popular as they once were, they are still out there and have pushed the trend in the newer languages. You can see this trend in all the new or refurbished languages that have dynamic type systems that have popped up over the last ten years. Many of them have roots in the web, while others are being newly used for the web:

>> Boo

>> Cobra

>> Cold Fusion

>> Groovy

>> JavaScript

>> Newspeak

>> PHP

>> Python

>> Ruby

TECHNICAL STUFF

Some of these languages support multiple coding styles. For example, even though Python supports a dynamic typing system, it can use the object-oriented, imperative, functional programming, and procedural coding styles. It's important to realize that the typing system doesn't necessarily affect the coding style using by a language.

Developers who work in dynamic languages often use them for practically everything except highly structured team-build kinds of environments. Uses include:

>> Data analysis using data science techniques

>> Artificial intelligence

>> Scripting infrastructure for system maintenance

>> Building tests

>> One-use utilities

>> Server farm maintenance

>> Scripting other applications

>> Building websites

>> File maintenance

Dynamic languages are popular for these kinds of tasks for two reasons. First, they provide instant feedback, because you can try a piece of code outside the constraints of the rest of the program you are writing. Second, you can start building your higher-level pieces of code without building the plumbing that makes it work.

For instance, Ruby has a command line interface that you can simply paste a function into, even out of context, and see how it works. There is even a web version at http://tryruby.org/. You can type code right in there, even if there are classes referenced that aren't defined, because Ruby will just take a guess at it.

This moves nicely into the next point, which is that a dynamic language enables you to build a class that refers to a type that you haven't defined elsewhere. For example, you can make a class to schedule an event, without actually having to build the underlying Event type first.

All of this lends itself to a language that is a lot more responsive to change. You can make a logic change in one place and not have to dig through reams of code to fix all the type declarations everywhere. Add this to optional and named parameters (see Chapter 2) and you have a lot less typing to do when you have to change your program.

Other benefits to dynamic languages in general show up as you use them more. For instance, macro languages are usually dynamically typed. If you've tried to build macros in previous versions of Visual Studio, you know what a pain it is to use a static language. Making C# (and VB.NET, for that matter) more dynamic not only makes it a better language for extending Visual Studio but also gives programmers the capability to include the language in the programs they write so that other developers can further extend those applications.

Employing Dynamic Programming Techniques

By now, you must be asking, "What exactly are we talking about here?" Fair question. When you define a new variable, you can use the dynamic keyword, and C# will let you make assumptions about the members of the variable. For example, if you want to declare a new Course object, you do it like this:

```
Course newCourse = new Course();
newCourse.Schedule();
```

This is, of course, assuming that you have a `Course` class defined somewhere else in your program, like this:

```
class Course {
    public void Schedule()
    {
        //Something fancy here
    }
}
```

But what if you don't know what class the new object will be? How do you handle that? You could declare it as an `Object`, because everything derives from `Object`, right? Here's the code:

```
Object newCourse = new Object();
```

Not so fast, my friend, if you make your next line this:

```
newCourse.Schedule();
```

Note the squiggly line appears almost immediately, and you get the famous "object does not contain a definition for `Schedule`. . ." error in the design time Error List. However, you can do this:

```
dynamic newCourse = SomeFunction();
newCourse.Schedule();
```

All this code needs to have is the stub of a function that returns some value, and you are good to go. What if `SomeFunction()` returns a string? Well, you get a run-time error. But it will still compile!

About now you may be thinking: "This is a *good* thing? How!?!" For the time being, you can blame COM. You see, COM was mostly constructed using C++, which has a variant type. In C++, you could declare a variable to be dynamic, like this:

```
VARIANT newCourse;
```

It worked just like the dynamic type, except C# wasn't invented yet. Anyway, because a lot of the objects in COM used `VARIANT` out parameters, it was really tough to handle Interop using .NET. Because Microsoft Office is mostly made of COM objects, and because it isn't going to change any time soon, and because Microsoft wants us all to be Office developers one day, bam, you have the dynamic type.

Say, for instance, that your newCourse is a variant out parameter from a method in a COM class. To get the value, you have to declare it an Object, like this:

```
CourseMarshaller cm = new CourseMarshaller(); //a COM object
int courseId = 4;
Object newCourse;
cm.MakeCourse(courseId, newCourse);
//and now we are back to square one
newCourse.Schedule(); //This causes a 'member not found exception'
```

Line 6 will not compile, even if the Schedule method exists, because you can't assume that newCourse will always come back as a Course object, because it is declared a variant. You're stuck. With a dynamic type, though, you're golden once again, with this code:

```
CourseMarshaller cm = new CourseMarshaller(); //a COM object
int courseId = 4;
dynamic newCourse;
cm.MakeCourse(courseId, newCourse);
newCourse.Schedule(); //This now compiles
```

What happens if newCourse comes back as something that doesn't have a Schedule method? You get a runtime error. But there are try/catch blocks for runtime errors. Nothing will help it compile without the dynamic keyword.

Readers who are long-time Visual Basic programmers, or even newer VB.NET programmers, realize that you can handle this dynamically — and have always been able to — in Visual Basic. Some developers recommend that programmers who work with legacy systems use Visual Basic for their new code, and this is exactly why.

In the interest of language parity, now C# can do it, too. In general, this is good, because many organizations are writing legacy code in VB and new code in C# — and it can get pretty messy in the trenches. This change makes the code base slimmer.

Putting Dynamic to Use

When C# encounters a dynamically typed variable, like the variables you created earlier, it changes everything that variable touches into a *dynamic operation*. This dynamic conversion means that when you use a dynamically typed object in an expression, the entire operation is dynamic.

Classic examples

Here are six examples of how a dynamic operation works. Say you have the dynamic variable `dynamicVariable`. Because the dynamic variable will pass through all six examples, they will all be dispatched dynamically by the C# compiler. Here are those examples, with nods to Daniel Ng.

» `dynamicVariable.someMethod("a", "b", "c");`: The compiler binds the method `someMethod` at runtime, since `dynaVariable` is dynamic. No surprise.

» `dynamicVariable.someProperty = 42;`: The compiler binds the property `someProperty` just like it did in the first method.

» `var newVar = dynamicVariable + 42;`: The compiler looks for any overloaded operators of "+" with a type of `dynamic`. Lacking that, it outputs a dynamic type.

» `int newNumber = dynamicVariable;`: This is an implicit conversion to `int`. The runtime determines whether a conversion to `int` is possible. If not, it throws a type mismatch error.

» `int newNumber = (int) dynamicVariable;`: This is an explicit cast to `int`. The compiler encodes this as a cast — you actually change the type here.

» `Console.WriteLine(dynamicVariable);`: Because there is no overload of `WriteLine` that accepts a dynamic type explicitly, the entire method call is dispatched dynamically.

Making static operations dynamic

If the compiler chooses to make a static operation dynamic — as it did in item 6 in the preceding section — the compiler rebuilds the code on the fly to have it handle the dynamic variable. What does that mean for you? Glad you asked.

Take item 6, `Console.WriteLine(dynamicVariable);`. This piece of code forces the compiler to build intermediary code, which checks for the type of variable at runtime in order to come up with something that is writable to the console. The compiled code first checks whether the input is a static type that it knows. Next, it checks for a type present in the program. Then it will just try a few things that might work. It will fail with an error if it finds nothing.

If this must happen, that's fine. But remember that it is slower than all get-out. This is why `Variant` got such a bad rap in Visual Basic classic. Dynamic is something you don't use until you need it. It puts a tremendous strain on the machine running the program, especially if all variables are dynamic.

Understanding what's happening under the covers

Using dynamic programming techniques doesn't have to be hard. In fact, you can do so with just three functional lines of code by using this simple method:

```
class C
{
    public dynamic MyMethod(dynamic d)
    {
        return d.Foo();
    }
}
```

This is pretty straightforward stuff — a method that accepts a dynamic class and returns the results of the type's Foo method. Not a big deal. Here is the compiled C# code:

```
class C
{
    [return: Dynamic]
    public object MyMethod([Dynamic] object d)
    {
        if (MyMethodo__SiteContainer0.p__Site1 == null)
        {
            MyMethodo__SiteContainer0.p__Site1 =
                CallSite<Func<CallSite, object, object>>
                  .Create(new CSharpCallPayload(
                    CSharpCallFlags.None, "Foo", typeof(object), null,
                    new CSharpArgumentInfo[] {
                    new CSharpArgumentInfo(CSharpArgumentInfoFlags.None,
                null) }));
        }
        return MyMethodo__SiteContainer0.p__Site1
          .Target(MyMethodo__SiteContainer0.p__Site1, d);
    }

    [CompilerGenerated]
    private static class MyMethodo__SiteContainer0
    {
      public static CallSite<Func<CallSite, object, object>> p__Site1;
    }
}
```

Most developers wouldn't want to try to break this code down. Fortunately, they don't have to. That's what compilers are for, right?

Running with the Dynamic Language Runtime

There is more to dynamic languages than just the dynamic typing. You can do some powerful things. Like all power, you have to be careful not to misuse it.

The Dynamic Language Runtime — shown in Figure 6-1 — is a library added to the .NET Framework specifically to provide for adding dynamic languages (like Ruby) to the Visual Studio fold (like IronRuby), or to add dynamic language features to existing static languages (like C# 4.0).

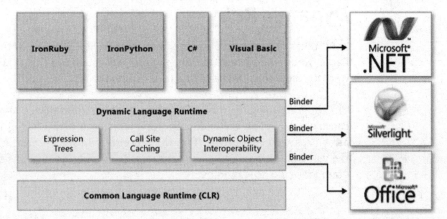

FIGURE 6-1:
The Dynamic
Language
Runtime.

The runtime helps the compiler to construct code in the compiled assembly that will make a lot of choices dynamically. The code block at the end of the preceding section is an example of the simplest kind.

The DLR assisted in the creation of IronRuby, which makes it possible to code in Ruby — the current hot dynamic language — right in Visual Studio. Of course, because the DLR enables C# to take on dynamic language features, much that you can do in Ruby you can now do in C#.

Programming
Dynamically!

Dynamic Ruby

Ruby takes advantage of its dynamic roots in its implementation of the Trabb Pardo-Knuth algorithm. Don't be put off by the name — this is just a straightforward problem that can be solved by computer code.

The program needs to read 11 numbers from an input device — in this case, the console's ReadLine method. It stores them in an array. Then, it processes the array backward — starting from the last entered value — with some function. If the value doesn't exceed some arbitrary threshold, it prints the result. The program looks like this in Ruby:

```
class TPK
  def f( x )
    return Math.sqrt(x.abs) + 5*x **3
  end

  def main
    Array.new(11) { gets.to_i }.reverse.each do |x|
      y = f(x)
      puts "#{x} #{(y>400) ? 'TOO LARGE' : y}"
    end
  end
end
```

This isn't a Ruby book. Nonetheless, this is a good dynamic language to use as an example. Two functions are defined: f and main. Main accepts 11 numbers from the console and then moves them to an integer array (that's what gets.to_i does). For each value in the array, it sets y equal to f(x) and then sees whether it is higher than this arbitrary value. If so, it prints "TOO LARGE"; otherwise, it prints the number.

Why is being dynamic important for this algorithm? It isn't. You could do it all statically typed. The dynamic bit does have an impact, though.

First, f(x) doesn't care what x is. The program assumes that whatever comes in gets changed to an integer at gets.to_i, but the function itself is case agnostic. This is good and bad, because if you do happen to give it a string or some other type, it will fail.

The array itself isn't typed, either. This can have benefits, because it is possible to drop a differently typed value in there if you know you are just going to write it to the screen.

Dynamic C#

Of course, C# now has similar features, right? You should be able to do the same thing! Yes, in fact, you can. Here's the code:

```
static dynamic f(dynamic x)
{
    return (Math.Sqrt(x) + 5.0 * Math.Pow(x, 3.0));
}

static void Main(string[] args)
{
    dynamic[] array = new Array[11];

    for (int i = 0; i < 11; i++)
    {
        array[i] = Console.ReadLine();
    }

    for (int i = 10; i>=0; i--)
    {
        dynamic y = f(array[i]);
        if (y > 400.0)
        {
            Console.WriteLine(string.Format("{0} TOO LARGE", i));
        }else{
```

```
                    Console.WriteLine("{0} : {1}", i, array[1]);
                }
            }

        Console.ReadKey();
    }
```

Line for line, the application does the same thing as the Ruby code, albeit longer. The names are the same to make it easier to follow. Because this example uses for loops to handle the integrators, it made the body of the program quite a bit beefier.

But why use the dynamic type here? Clearly, you could have just used double for this. Use of dynamic just made the program easier to create. Try changing the array to an array of double, like this:

```
Double[] array = new Double[11];
```

Hey, look at that: Now the ReadLine doesn't work. You'll just cast it to a double. Nope, can't do that; you have to use TryParse. You get the picture. Static types are hard to code with. Dynamic types are easier to code with.

What's the other side of this? Well, obviously, if the user enters a string, the program outputs a runtime error, and that's bad. If you statically type everything, you can trap that error much easier and handle it right on user input.

Add to that the reality that C# is making runtime decisions about every single variable throughout the entire run of the program. That's a whole lot of extra processing that you could have avoided if you had just done that static typing.

The take-home here is that using dynamic types makes your programming job much easier and your troubleshooting job much harder. If you are writing a utility script for your own use and don't care if it occasionally crashes with a type mismatch, use dynamic. If you are writing a backup script for a hospital and the lives of thousands are at stake, static types are likely better.

4

A Tour of Visual Studio

Contents at a Glance

Chapter **1**

Getting Started with Visual Studio

You can run much of C# by using a command prompt and cs.exe, but that's not a great way to program. It's unforgiving and slow, and people have trouble remembering the specifics of the language. A better way is to use an Integrated Development Environment (IDE), which is a program that provides a platform for development. An IDE helps to make development easier.

Programmers who are used to starting with a blank screen and a command line often dismiss an IDE as a slow, bogged-down waste of time. However, Visual Studio really does make working with C# faster and more pleasant. It's quick, easy to use, agile, and smart. If you're truly determined to use a command-line interface, consider using a Read, Evaluate, Print, and Loop (REPL) environment such as CShell (http://cshell.net), discussed in the "Using IDE alternatives" sidebar, later in this chapter.

True, you don't have to use an IDE to program, but if you're going to use one, it should be Visual Studio. It was purposely built to write C# code, and it's made to construct Windows programs.

TIP

Other options exist, however. MonoDevelop (http://www.monodevelop.com/) is a tool built for Linux users to write .NET code, but it works in Windows. Sharp-Develop (http://www.icsharpcode.net/) is another IDE that has some awesome potential as a testing platform. When working on the Mac, you might have used Xamarin Studio (http://xamarin.com/studio) in the past. It's now called Visual Studio for the Mac (https://www.visualstudio.com/vs/visual-studio-mac/). These tools are all free.

Of course, you can also get the Visual Studio Community Edition free. All the examples in this book will work with this particular IDE, so you should get the Community Edition get unless you need the advanced features of a paid version of Visual Studio or require one of the other products for some other reason. This chapter introduces you to the various versions of Visual Studio and discusses the C# projects available to you.

Versioning the Versions

Visual Studio has lots of different versions. The reason is its famous licensing problem. If Microsoft just sold the whole package for what it was worth, only the Fortune 50 could afford it, and it would cut out about 99 percent of its audience. If Microsoft makes a lot of different versions and tries to incorporate the features that different groups of people use, it can capture nearly 100 percent of the audience. This chapter discusses the features and benefits of all the major editions.

Community edition

The Community edition is the free version of Visual Studio. It's made for hobbyists, classrooms, and academic research, but many professional programmers use it as their edition of choice for small personal projects, or for working on open source projects. Microsoft also targets this edition to small organizations that have five or fewer developers. So if you work for a small company, you might not need anything more than this edition, which means that C# development will remain free.

Although the Community edition is a little less functional than the Professional edition, you can compile every code example in this book by using the Community edition. It has the power of the .NET Framework, which is also free, and gives you a significant means of learning C#. From a development platform perspective, the Community edition supports everything that all the other editions support, including

USING IDE ALTERNATIVES

One of the complaints about using an IDE is that it's not very interactive. An IDE provides a static environment where you type code, build it, and then run it to test it. Yes, IDE features can point out things like syntax errors, but you really don't get any feedback until you've written a lot of code. Other languages, such as Scala, provide a REPL where feedback is more or less instantaneous. Fortunately, CShell provides you with a REPL for C#. Of course, this approach only works for relatively simple code. If you want to use the REPL for something a bit more complicated, you must provide the code in a script file, but then, you're starting to work in something more akin to the IDE environment again. Consequently, CShell is a great solution for those times when you need to test simple ideas for your C# application quickly, and then move them to your actual application within Visual Studio.

Another approach to the whole issue of static coding environments is the literate programming approach provided by products such as Jupyter Notebook (`http://jupyter.org/`). This product includes a C# plug-in (`https://github.com/jupyter/jupyter/wiki/Jupyter-kernels`) that you can use to write code. *Literate programming* is a report-like technique originally advanced by Donald Knuth to create an environment suitable for scientific research (`https://unidata.github.io/online-python-training/introduction.html`). More importantly, it provides you with the means for creating coding examples that are suitable for group discussions of a much larger project. Unlike CShell, you can write relatively complex coding examples using Jupyter Notebook, but you also lose some of the advantages of using a REPL.

The bottom line is that this book uses an IDE because that's the traditional approach to writing C# code and the approach that you use most of the time when writing applications for any environment. However, you should keep these alternatives in mind when the IDE just won't do the job for you.

>> Windows Desktop

>> Universal Windows Apps

>> Web (ASP.NET)

>> Office 365

>> Business Applications

>> Apache Cordova

>> Azure Stack

>> C++ Cross-Platform Library Development

>> Python

>> Node.js

>> .NET Core

>> Docker Tools

In the past, the various Express and academic editions gave people a taste of what they could do with C#, but tended to move them toward the paid Professional edition. With Visual Studio 2017, Microsoft takes a different route and gives you everything needed to fully experience C#. You even have access to many advanced debugging and diagnostic tools, testing tools, and cross-platform templates. The chart at `https://www.visualstudio.com/vs/compare/` provides a full comparison.

REMEMBER

What the Community edition lacks is enterprise-level support. It's important to note that Microsoft defines an enterprise as an entity having more than 250 PCs or more than $1 million U.S. dollars in annual revenue. If you find that you need enterprise-type support but don't have an enterprise-sized organization, you need the Professional edition. However, for most developers, the Community edition provides everything needed to discover and use the wonders of C#.

Professional edition

Besides designing the Professional edition to work in a larger, enterprise environment, Microsoft endowed the Professional edition with one necessary addition: CodeLens (`https://docs.microsoft.com/en-us/visualstudio/ide/find-code-changes-and-other-history-with-codelens`). This feature is designed to help you look at your code in a detailed manner. Think about it as a sort of magnifying glass for code. You can use CodeLens to perform these sorts of tasks:

>> Find references to your code wherever they might exist.

>> Review the code history and determine how changes might affect your code.

>> Manage the branches in your code.

>> Determine who made code changes.

>> Contact other team members about changes using Lync or Skype.

>> Track linked code reviews and linked bugs.

>> Locate and manage unit tests for your code.

Enterprise edition

There is a huge difference in functionality between the Professional edition and the Enterprise edition. Yes, the Community edition, Professional edition, and Enterprise edition can all create the same kinds of projects, but the tools required to design, build, test, and manage really large projects reside in the Enterprise edition. For example, all the architectural features, such as Architectural Layer Diagrams and Architecture Validation, are part of the Enterprise edition. If you want to validate your design, you need Live Dependency Validation, which is a truly amazing feature described at `https://docs.microsoft.com/en-us/visualstudio/modeling/validate-code-with-layer-diagrams`.

The management features are also designed around the huge project environment. For example, Code Clone (`https://msdn.microsoft.com/Library/a97cd5a6-5ffa-4104-9627-8e59e513654d`) provides the means to detect duplicate code in your project. After all, when a project is huge, multiple developers are apt to come up with the same way to perform specific tasks. Ensuring that you don't have to maintain multiple copies of the same code reduces costs and makes the code easier to manage (not to mention that it eliminates some of the nastier bugs).

You also receive some truly advanced functionality for performing diagnostics and debugging your code. In addition, the Enterprise edition contains additional cross-platform support. However, where the Enterprise edition truly shines is with testing tools. When working with the Community edition or Professional edition, all you get is unit testing. However, the Enterprise edition provides all these other forms of testing:

>> Live Unit Testing

>> Test Case Management

>> Web Load & Performance Testing

>> IntelliTest

>> Microsoft Fakes (Unit Test Isolation)

>> Code Coverage

>> Lab Management

>> Coded UI Testing

>> Manual Testing with Microsoft Test Manager

>> Exploratory Testing with Microsoft Test Manager

>> Fast-forward for Manual Testing with Microsoft Test Manager

MSDN

The Microsoft Developer Network (MSDN) subscription is by far the best way to get Microsoft products. It may seem as though setting up a development environment to develop anything of significance would be impossibly expensive. This is not necessarily the case.

The MSDN subscription is exactly what it sounds like — a subscription to a majority of the Microsoft products that matter. For around $600 a year for a Professional edition subscription, you get access to everything you need. This isn't actually an edition of Visual Studio. (You can learn more about the various subscription costs at `https://www.visualstudio.com/subscriptions/`.)

That $600 sounds like a lot, but think about it this way: Even if you do only one project a year on your own time, your investment will pay off. Considering the fact that Visual Studio alone is half of that, and it gets a revision every two years or so, it's a bargain. Along with Visual Studio Professional, you also get subscriptions to

>> Microsoft Office

>> Windows client platforms

>> Windows server platforms

>> SQL Server

>> Neat middleware like SharePoint and BizTalk

>> Weird bits that you never used before (but will now)

Basically, here's how it works: You go to Amazon or elsewhere and buy an MSDN license code. Then you go to `http://msdn.microsoft.com` and register the code with your Live account. From there, depending on your license level, you can download the software for development use only. The site at `https://www.visualstudio.com/subscriptions/` describes these features in more detail.

Installing Visual Studio

Visual Studio Community edition installs much like any other Windows program. First, assure yourself that your machine can run Visual Studio. Then you run the setup program that you download from the Microsoft site at `https://www.visualstudio.com/vs/community/` and make a few decisions. Then you wait.

Visual Studio is big. It takes a while. The official requirements for Visual Studio are shown in this list:

» **Operating system:**

- Windows 10 version 1507 or higher: Home, Professional, Education, and Enterprise (LTSB and S are not supported)

- Windows Server 2016: Standard and Datacenter

- Windows 8.1 (with Update KB2919355): Core, Professional, and Enterprise

- Windows Server 2012 R2 (with Update KB2919355): Essentials, Standard, Datacenter

- Windows 7 SP1 (with latest Windows Updates): Home Premium, Professional, Enterprise, Ultimate

» **Supported architectures:**

- 32-bit (x86)

- 64-bit (x64)

» **Hardware:**

- 1.8 GhZ or faster processor

- 2GB of RAM (4GB of RAM recommended)

- 10GB of available hard drive space (40GB recommended)

- 5400 RPM drive

- Video card that supports a minimum display resolution of 720p (1280 by 720; higher resolution recommended)

You can run on this configuration, but you may find that some features run slowly and a few don't run at all. Microsoft used WPF to write Visual Studio 2017, which can (with this size of an application) be a resource hog. Here's a more realistic base configuration for Visual Studio:

» 3.4 GHz 64 bit 4-core processor

» 64-bit Windows 10 with 8GB of RAM

» 250GB of available HDD space

» Dual monitors (or a laptop with an external monitor) with one being a touchscreen

Breaking Down the Projects

After you have run the setup program and set your default settings, you just need to start a project and get your fingers dirty. All the project types (except maybe one or two) in the first two minibooks were Console applications, meaning they are meant to be run at the command prompt. Many more projects are available. Notice the main kinds of projects in the Visual Studio New Project dialog box, shown in Figure 1-1. Each of the subfolders shown in the figure contains templates you can use to create various kinds of applications in C#. The following list shows the project types installed as part of Visual Studio Community edition.

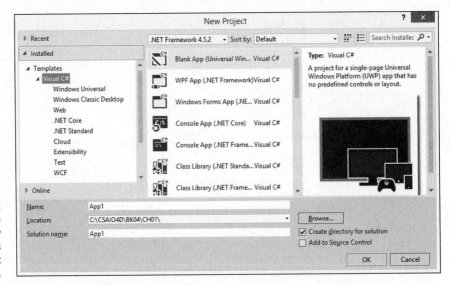

FIGURE 1-1:
The Visual Studio Community edition provides lots of project types.

>> **Windows Universal:** Single-page applications that rely on the Universal Windows Platform (UWP). This app type has no predefined controls or layout.

>> **Windows Classic Desktop:** Rich client applications that compile into .EXEs and run right on your computer. Microsoft Word is a Windows application.

>> **Web projects:** Websites that require a web server to run. (A web server is included with Visual Studio for development purposes.) Microsoft.com is an example of a web application.

>> **.NET Core:** Command-line applications that can run on Windows, Linux, and Mac OS using the features provided by the .NET Core version of the .NET Framework. The .NET Core has significant limits when compared to the .NET

Framework or Xamarin. You can read about Microsoft's recommendations for using .NET Core at http://www.codechannels.com/article/microsoft/when-should-i-use-net-core/.

>> **.NET Standard:** A class library that targets .NET Standard, which is a formal specification that can interact with all the various .NET runtimes. You can read more about .NET Standard at https://docs.microsoft.com/en-us/dotnet/standard/net-standard.

>> **Cloud:** Scalable services that run on Microsoft Azure (https://azure.microsoft.com/). You can create a number of service, web application, job, and mobile application types.

>> **Test:** Unit tests that help you check the functionality of your application using automation.

>> **WCF projects:** Application that rely on the host-independent Windows Communication Foundation (WCF) service class library.

TIP

The default projects that you obtain with any copy of Visual Studio 2017 are the tip of the iceberg. These are the projects that Microsoft assumes that you will likely use most. However, Visual Studio 2017 can support a huge number of other project types that this book doesn't cover. You install them using NuGet (see https://docs.microsoft.com/en-us/nuget/tools/package-manager-ui for details).

Exploring the New Project dialog box

You start all new projects by using the New Project dialog box, shown in Figure 1-1. It's possible to access this dialog box in a number of ways. The most common technique is to choose File ⇨ New ⇨ Project. If you have the Start page displayed, you can open the dialog box by clicking the Create New Project link. When adding a new project to an existing solution, you can also right-click the solution entry in Solution Explorer and choose Add ⇨ New Project.

The left pane of the dialog box is a tree-view selector, similar to the one in Outlook. You have three options — Recent Templates, Installed Templates, and Online Templates. Installed Templates is selected by default. These templates, as Visual Studio calls them, are project types.

The center pane of the dialog box contains a list of project templated in the selected folder. If you click, for example, the Visual C# option in the tree view, all the projects for Visual C# appear in the middle pane. If you click one of the sub-folders, just those project types appear. For example, selecting Windows Classic Desktop displays only the projects that are part of the classic desktop scenario.

The right pane of the dialog box changes to reflect the template you select in the middle pane. The information you see tells you about the project template so that you have some idea of which template to use to meet your needs.

To specify the version of the .NET Framework you would like to develop for, you can use the drop-down list just above the project list that currently says .NET Framework 4.5.2. To change the sorting options, use the Sort By: drop-down list directly to the right. One more step to the right and you can change your view options (icon size in the dialog box).

In the upper-right corner is a search box, which isn't as silly as it sounds given the large number of templates now in Visual Studio. Just below the search box is the description panel, where you can see a text description of the selected project type.

At the bottom are three (or sometimes more) important text boxes:

>> **Name:** The name of this project.

>> **Location:** The path to the project file.

>> **(Optional) Solution:** Determines whether the new project is part of the existing solution or is part of a new solution.

>> **Solution Name:** The name of the solution. Solutions are collections of projects.

Understanding solutions and projects

Visual Studio project files, and the solutions that love them, are a constant topic of interest to Microsoft developers. You work on one solution at a time, with a number of projects within. How you organize your solutions and their projects will make or break you when it comes time to find something.

You can think of solutions as folders that hold projects. They're just folders with special properties. In fact, note the check box in the lower-right corner of Figure 1-1. It's the one labeled Create Directory for Solution. You select this option when you want to add multiple projects to a single solution and want each project to have its own directory within the solution. Keeping projects separate makes it easier to reuse a project in another application.

Projects are where you put the code files for your programs. They store all kinds of things, like references to the .NET Framework, resources like graphics or files, and what file should be used to start the project.

Solutions do the same thing for projects that projects do for files. They keep the projects in a folder and store certain properties. For instance, they store which project should be started when debugging starts.

Neither the project nor the solutions have much to do with a finished program. They are just simple organizational structures for Visual Studio. The installation of the finished program is determined by the setup project.

In reality, the solution is more than a folder. It's a file in a folder that is used by Visual Studio to manage the developer experience. So, inside the folder for the solution is a file describing the projects within and then a bunch of folders containing the projects themselves.

There are files for the projects, too — files that describe the resources and references for the project. They are all XML files that contain text references to the values that you set using Visual Studio. Normally, you don't need to look at the solution or project files. The results of any organization you perform appears in Solution Explorer. Figure 1-2 shows a typical example of a simple application setup.

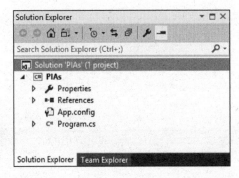

FIGURE 1-2:
Solutions and projects appear in Solution Explorer.

The topmost entry in the list is the solution, PIAs. Note that the entry says that the solution contains just one project. However, a solution can contain as many projects as needed to perform a given task. You add new projects by right-clicking the solution entry and choosing Add⇨New Project from the context menu.

The next entry down is the only project in this solution, also called PIAs. When a solution contains just one project, it isn't uncommon to give the project and the solution the same name. However, when you have multiple projects within a single solution, you usually give each project a unique name.

All the entries that follow are part of the PIAs project. You find project properties, references, configuration information, and source code files. In this case, there is just one source code file, Program.cs, but projects often contain a number of source code files.

Chapter **2**

Using the Interface

I ntegrated Development Environments, or IDEs, are the Swiss army knife of the programmer's toolkit. IDEs provide a mechanism for storing program code, organizing and building it, and looking at finished products with design editors. IDEs make things happen and, in the bargain, cut hours from a task.

Visual Studio is impressive; it is massive. It would be tough to cover all Visual Studio features in a single book, much less a single chapter. In fact, you're unlikely to ever use all the Visual Studio features.

Rather than try to cover everything, this chapter gives you the chance to experience only the features of Visual Studio that you'll realistically use every day. Of course continuing to explore the IDE and discovering new stuff is important — don't just stop with the content of this chapter. It provides only a brief overview of some of the astonishing features in the tool. You can discover more about the IDE at https://docs.microsoft.com/en-us/visualstudio/ide/visual-studio-ide.

Designing in the Designer

One thing that is integrated into an Integrated Development Environment is a way to edit files graphically, sometimes called a Graphic Development Environment or *Designer*. Visual Studio allows you to graphically edit many different types of code bases and provides adjunct tools for the further management of said code bases.

In short, the Designer is the drag-and-drop element of the Visual Studio world. It isn't always the best way to develop a program, but it sure can help sometimes.

REMEMBER

For each major type of project that Visual Studio maintains, there is a Designer. The Designer handles the What You See Is What You Get portion of the experience and usually the behind-the-scenes markup code. In addition to the Designers that Microsoft provides, you can also create your own custom editors and Designers using the material found at https://docs.microsoft.com/en-us/visualstudio/extensibility/creating-custom-editors-and-designers as a starting point. Customer editors and designers enable you to work with application code in new ways and to support languages other than those that Visual Studio supports natively.

The problem is that because of the necessities of the software development world, different designers all work a little differently. A significant difference exists between HTML and XAML, for example, so the web designer and the WPF Designer don't look or act the same. Visual Studio gives you several visual designers to help develop applications, including these commonly used designers:

>> Class Designer

>> Data View

>> Web Forms

>> Windows Forms

>> Windows Presentation Foundation (WPF)

Windows Presentation Foundation (WPF)

Windows Presentation Foundation is covered in some depth in Book 5, but for now you should know that it is the future of Microsoft's Windows development experience. Book 5 talks all about WPF, so you can read more about it there.

The core of the user interface design experience is a language called Extensible Application Markup Language (XAML, pronounced *zammel*), which (unsurprisingly) is an XML-derived domain-specific markup language for the creation of user interfaces. In the Designer, shown in Figure 2-1, the design is in the top frame and the underlying code is in the bottom frame.

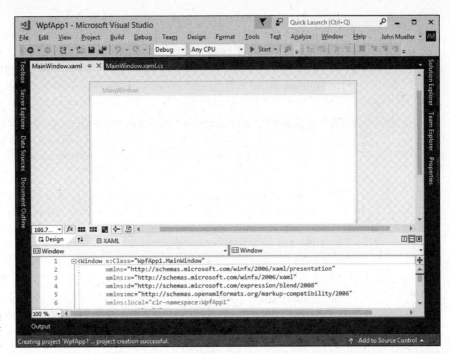

FIGURE 2-1:
The WPF Designer.

You can click the design in the Designer and move things around, if you want, or use the Designer to select things and edit the properties in the Properties panel (covered in the upcoming section "Paneling the Studio"). Additionally, if you change something in the code area, you'll see the change in the design. It's a good system.

There are a few small but significant features in the WPF Designer that should be pointed out. You can see them all in Figure 2-1.

On the left side of the bar at the bottom of the Designer is the Zoom field. The options in this field let you do things like configure the Designer to zoom to fit the current selection. This is invaluable for working on an application that is bigger than your screen, or lightening things just so.

Next to the Zoom field are a series of buttons that make working with the Designer easier. Here are the buttons in order of appearance:

>> **Effects (*fx*):** Toggles user interface effects. Turning the effects off does make the user interface a little less interesting but also conserves processing power for more productive uses.

>> **Show Snap Grid:** Toggles the snap grid. Using the snap grid helps you place controls more accurately and with less effort.

>> **Snapping to Gridlines:** Determines how controls are placed on the form. Using gridline snapping means that controls automatically appear on specific boundaries, which makes placing the controls even easier. However, you also have a little less flexibility in placing controls precisely as you'd like them.

>> **Toggle Artboard Background:** Controls the background shown behind the form you're creating. The default is a gray background like the one shown in Figure 2-1. You can also choose a black background that makes form features pop out better but can also be harder on the eyes.

>> **Snapping to Snaplines:** Controls use of the lines *(snaplines)* that appear when you place controls on the form that show how one control aligns with another. Using snaplines makes it easier for you to align the controls and gives your form a more pleasing appearance. However, snapping to the snaplines can also make it harder to place controls precisely where you want them.

>> **Disable Project Code:** Enables or disables use of XAML code to display form content. Sometimes the XAML that appears in the bottom window in Figure 2-1 has errors in it. You can disable the project code to allow for fixing these errors without crashing the Designer.

At the left side of the dividing line between the Design and XAML frames is a little double-arrow icon. Clicking this icon changes whatever is in the bottom frame to be in the top frame, and vice versa.

On the right side of the same dividing line are three buttons that determine the kind of split you have — a vertical split, a horizontal split (which is the default), or no split (so that the Designer or code editor take the full space). Some people like the code. Some people like the Designer. Some people prefer a mixture of the two. You determine how you want to use the tools.

Windows Forms

The main difference between the Windows Forms Designer and the WPF Designer is the lack of a code panel in Windows Forms. Although there is code backing up Windows Forms, you don't get to edit it directly. The Windows Forms Designer performs this task for you and places the code in a special Designer file, such as `Form1.Designer.cs` for a default project.

The topic of Windows Forms isn't covered in any detail in this book (there are a few projects, such as the network status example in Book 3, Chapter 4 and the image example in Book 3, Chapter 5). Even though it's still an active development platform, most developers are moving to WPF instead, so it pays to spend more time working with an environment that developers use for new projects. WPF performs the same programming duties as Windows Forms but is the newer technology. The Windows Forms Designer is shown in Figure 2-2.

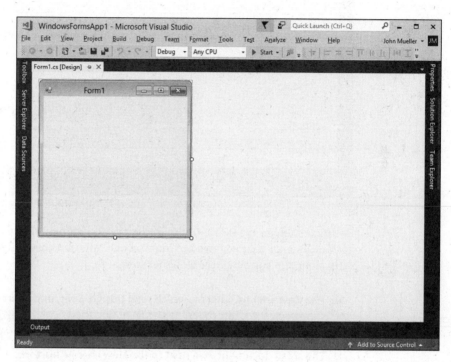

FIGURE 2-2:
The Windows
Forms Designer.

Web Forms

Web programming resembles WPF programming more than it resembles Windows Forms programming, but it's run from a web server and viewed in a browser. (Book 6 is all about web forms.) Because the Designer has a back-end code aspect, you can see a split view, as shown in Figure 2-3.

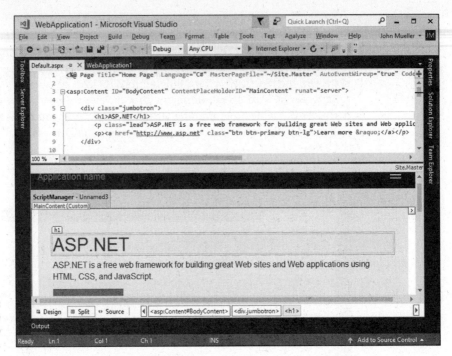

FIGURE 2-3:
Back-end code used with web projects.

Getting around in the HTML Designer is easy. There are two special features in the HTML Designer that you need to know about. You find these features in a menu strip along the bottom of the Designer view:

» **The view change buttons, which read Design, Split, and Source:** Source shows only the HTML code. The Design button shows only the visual designer. Split, unsurprisingly, shows both in two panels, just as the WPF Designer does.

» **The small document tree next to the view change buttons:** You can see where your cursor is in this hierarchal tree in relation to the rest of the HTML document.

Class Designer

You can make a Class Designer from any project. The next example uses the Class Library project, as shown in Figure 2-4.

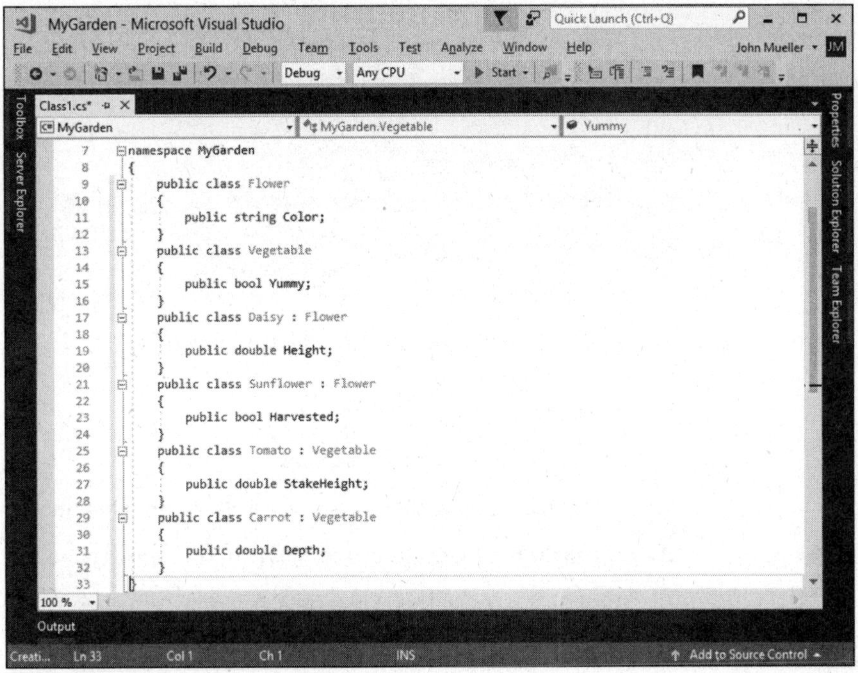

FIGURE 2-4:
A garden, in digital form.

The Class Designer gives you a visual interface into a class library. You can easily see the inheritance, and the members are visible and editable. Here is the class library used for Figure 2-4:

```csharp
namespace MyGarden
{
    public class Flower
    {
        public string Color;
    }
    public class Vegetable
    {
        public bool Yummy;
    }
    public class Daisy : Flower
    {
        public double Height;
    }
    public class Sunflower : Flower
    {
        public bool Harvested;
    }
```

```
    public class Tomato: Vegetable
    {
        public double StakeHeight;
    }
    public class Carrot : Vegetable
    {
        public double Depth;
    }
}
```

To create a class library like this, follow these steps:

1. **Choose File ⇨ New ⇨ Project.**

   You see the New Project dialog box.

2. **Select the Visual C#\Windows Classic Desktop folder in the left pane.**

3. **Highlight the Class Library template in the center pane.**

4. **Type** MyGarden **in the Name field and click OK.**

   Visual Studio creates a new Class Library project for you and displays the code editor with a default class defined. At this point, you can start adding code to the example application.

5. **Replace the default code with a listing of your own.**

   You can use the one in this section, if you want.

6. **Build the class library by pressing Ctrl + Shift + B.**

7. **Save your project.**

You can add methods to your new class as well. Simply press Enter after the `public string Color;` line in the `Flower` class and add a `Water` method by adding the following code:

```
public void Water()
{

}
```

Data View

Data View is usually used with the Server Explorer and is part of an in-studio representation of SQL Management Studio. You can view and edit data tables in SQL Server (and other) database management systems right inside Visual Studio. An example is shown in Figure 2-5; in this case, you see the Show Table Data view of the Address (Person) table of the AdventureWorks2012 database.

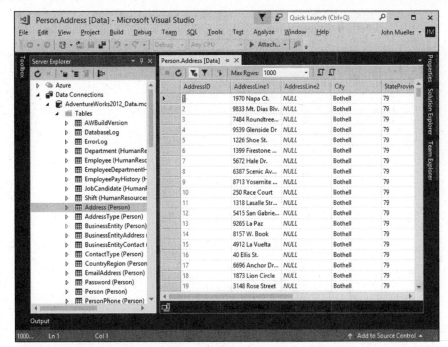

FIGURE 2-5:
When you use
Data View,
who needs SQL
Management
Studio?

There is a remarkable amount of power here, and there just isn't enough space to cover it all. Again, this isn't a database book, so you may want to read the MSDN entries for the Data Connections feature of Server Explorer for more details.

Paneling the Studio

To be as flexible as it needs to, Visual Studio has a large collection of modular windows that are called *panels* (or sometimes panes, depending on whom you talk with). These panels do everything that isn't involved with directly editing a design or code. They manage files, manage objects, show feedback, show properties, do all sorts of stuff.

Visual Studio has more than 30 panels. There isn't room to discuss them all here, so the chapter covers only the five you use most often. The rest you can find on the View or Debug menu.

Solution Explorer

Solution Explorer (see Figure 2-6) manages solutions, projects, and files. Even though solutions consist mostly of files and folders, it is a somewhat more complex operation than it seems at first blush.

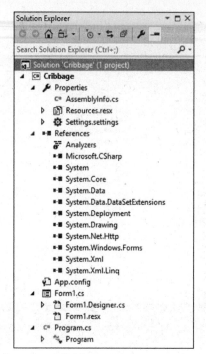

FIGURE 2-6:
The explorer of solutions.

Solutions

For solutions themselves, Solution Explorer provides a number of important tools, including the following:

>> **Solution Management:** Allows you to build, rebuild, or clean a solution. In addition, you can perform analysis that shows how your application runs.

>> **Configuration Manager:** Provides a useful interface for what is basically a settings file in the solution itself. You can specify whether Release or Debug compilation is desired for your build here, if you want all debugging information stored with your file. You can tell the compiler whether you want the software built for 32-bit systems or 64-bit systems too. You can reach Configuration Manager from the Build menu.

>> **Manage NuGet Packages:** Lets you add new packages to your solution to extend the functionality that Visual Studio provides. You can also restore existing packages to the solution as needed.

>> **Project Dependencies:** Shows how your projects are interrelated and describes the way in which your projects depend on each other. It has a tab for the build order, too. When you're getting weird "referenced member not available in object" errors, check here first. Your solution needs to contain more than one project for this command to be available on the Project menu.

» **Calculate Code Metrics:** Makes it possible to determine how fast your application will run and how it uses resources.

» **Add Projects:** Displays dialog boxes that you can use to add new projects to the existing solution.

» **Source Control:** Configures the source control options used to enable more than one party to work on the application design and code.

» **Property Pages:** Determines which project should start on debug and where source files are kept, among other things.

Projects

Projects are the individual compiled units and are divided by type. You can find more about projects in Chapter 1 of this minibook. Solution Explorer brings to projects the capability to add and remove files, make references and services, set up a class diagram, open the representative Windows Explorer folder, and set properties. All this information is saved in the Project file. The project file is just an XML file. There are a few key characteristics of the file:

» It includes a PropertyGroup for each build type. This is because you can set different properties for each type of executable.

» It contains an ItemGroup that has all the references in it, including required Framework versions, and another set of ItemGroups that have the project load details.

» The file includes the import of the project general details and the Target collections. You can actually edit the file manually to make a custom build environment.

You likely won't modify your Project file, but it's important that you know it can be done, and that Microsoft has inline comments. They expect the file to get changed.

Files

Files are a lot less exciting. They are pretty much exactly what you expect. They host the source code of the program being developed. Solution Explorer manages the files in the project basically the way Windows Explorer does. Solution Explorer lists the files and folders and allows them to be opened in the Designer or the code editor.

TIP

Solution Explorer also knows what files to show. If the file isn't in the project, but happens to be sitting in the folder for the project, it won't show in the Explorer. If you can't find a file, try clicking the Show All Files button in the gray button bar at the top of the Explorer. The hidden files will show up grayed out but still won't compile into the project. You can add them to the project if you want.

Properties

The Properties panel (see Figure 2-7) is a simple, flexible tool that allows you to update those endless lists of details about everything in development projects. The panel is basically a window with a two-column-wide data grid. It reads properties in key/value pairs and allows for easy view and edit.

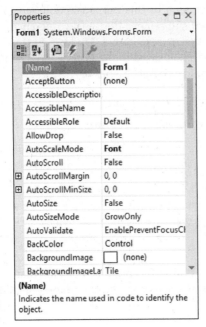

FIGURE 2-7:
Modifying object properties.

You can find details about everything in your application here. If you click nearly anything in Visual Studio and press F4 to bring up the Properties panel (refer to Figure 2-7), you will get properties. Try it with these fun selections:

» Files in Solution Explorer

» Database connections

» A textbox in a WPF project

» An XML tree node

» An item in Class View

If there is any metadata about something, the properties are in the Properties panel. It's a great tool.

The Toolbox

One of the great misunderstood tools is the Toolbox (see Figure 2-8). On the surface, the Toolbox seems so simple. The design-time controls for a given file type are available to drag and drop. Still, there is one important thing you need to remember about the Toolbox: It displays only controls that are appropriate to the file in focus. So if you're running a Windows Form in the Designer, you won't see a database table available to drop. Keep in mind that the Toolbox is context sensitive. It works only when it has a file to work on.

FIGURE 2-8: The Toolbox, with tools.

There is one other interesting property of the Toolbox: It can be used to store text clippings, which can be useful for demonstrations and presentations. It is also handy for storing often-used pieces of code (Book 1, Chapter 1), but snippets (covered in Book 1, Chapter 3) are even better. To do so, follow these steps:

1. **Open a code file.**

   Anything will do, `.cs` file, `.xaml` file, whatever.

2. **Highlight a piece of code.**

3. **Make sure the Toolbox is open and then drag the selected code to the General section of the Textbox.**

   The copied code becomes a tool.

4. **Open up another blank code file.**

5. **Drag the new tool into the code.**

   The copied code now appears in the code file.

Server Explorer

Server Explorer (see Figure 2-9) enables developers to access important services on the local or a remote machine. These could be anything from SharePoint to Microsoft Message Queue (MSMQ) but generally include two types of services:

» Managed services

» Database connections

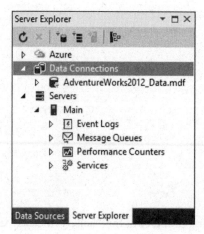

FIGURE 2-9:
Server Explorer.

Managed services

Managed services include services such as Viewer and MSMQ, which you need to look at to test parts of your application. Internet Information Services, for example, is a managed service that shows up in the list. To get a server into Server Explorer, follow these steps:

1. **Right-click Servers.**

2. **Click the Add Server button.**

3. **Type the machine name or IP number of the server you want to add.**

4. **If you want to use different credentials than you used to log in (for a different account, for instance), click Connect Using a Different User Name and enter the new credentials.**

5. **Click OK.**

Play around with the services you see. There are a lot of features in this panel that this book doesn't cover.

Data connections

Above the Services in Figure 2-9 are the data connections. These are data connections that have been made on previous projects, which Visual Studio keeps around in case you need them for any other projects. Although keeping these connections around seems like a bit of a security risk, it sure as heck is convenient.

The goal is to reduce the dependency on SQL Management Console (the old method for managing the database for developers), and it does a darn good job. The key issue is access to the data model (table names and columns) and stored procedures; developing a program without access to the database is tough. In a new connection, these database objects are given default folders:

>> Database diagrams

>> Tables

>> Views

>> Stored Procedures

>> Functions

>> Types

>> Synonyms

>> Assemblies

The key thing you should try is to open a Stored Procedure (you can do this by double-clicking it in the Data Sources panel — which is available in a solution that has data connections). When you do so, you can easily edit SQL code, with indenting and colorization, right in Visual Studio. Use this. It's really neat.

Class View

The last of the five main panels is Class View. As discussed in Books 1 and 2, everything in the .NET Framework is an object. The classes that make up the framework — all derivatives of Object — are viewable in a tree view. The Class View is the home for that tree view (see Figure 2-10).

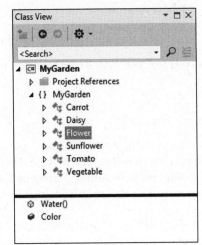

FIGURE 2-10:
A view
with Class.

From the Class View, you can look at all the members of a class and access the inline documentation, which gives you an overview of the framework and custom classes that make up your project.

Coding in the Code Editor

There is a lot to the Code Editor in Visual Studio. This is where you spend most of your time. Code Editor has two primary tools:

>> **The Editor itself:** The first is the screen on which you edit the code — the Code Editor.

>> **Auxiliary windows:** The second are the little auxiliary windows that do a lot of useful things that don't directly relate to the code.

Exercising the Code Editor

The Code Editor is where you edit code. Doesn't matter what type of code; all of it is edited here. Figure 2-4, earlier in the chapter, shows an example of the code editor when used to create a class library. It's a smart tool, however. If you are in XML, it works like an XML editor (such as the lower half of the view in Figure 2-1, shown previously).

You can get to a code file in the Code Editor a few ways. The most common way is to double-click on a source code file in Solution Explorer, and it will open in Code Editor.

If you are viewing something in the Designer, you can get to the code-behind related to the file in question by any of three methods:

>> Click the View Code button in Solution Explorer.

>> Right-click the design surface and select View Code.

>> Double-click a control in the Designer to generate an event for that control and be moved to Code View.

You'll find yourself using all three over time. Note that you can get directly to the code-behind files by clicking the little triangle next to a Designer file and then double-clicking the code files nested within.

Autocompleting with IntelliSense

IntelliSense is Microsoft's autocompletion feature, and it's a prominent part of the Code Editor. You find IntelliSense whether you want to or not. In Code View, click inside a class and press Ctrl+spacebar. Everything you are allowed to type there shows up in a big list.

The nice thing is, IntelliSense is context-sensitive. Type **Console** and press the dot (.). All available members of Console appear. IntelliSense keeps you honest and prevents having to remember the two-million-odd members of the .NET Framework on a day-by-day basis.

IntelliSense helps with method signatures, too. Continue the line you started earlier by adding WriteLine — in other words, type (**Console.WriteLine**) — and then check out the IntelliSense. It will tell you all the overloads for the member in question. Use the up and down arrows to move between them. It's slick.

Outlining

Visual Studio will auto-outline your code for you. Notice the little box with a minus sign (–) next to every namespace, class, and method in the code editor (see Figure 2-4)? Those are close-up sections of the code for readability. It might not seem like much now, but when you have 2,200 lines of code in there, you will be glad.

You can create your own outlining, too. Preceding a section that you want to outline, type **#region** on a new line. After that section, type **#endregion**. This newly defined section — regardless of whether it's at an existing outline point — will get a new outline mark. If a comment is added after a region statement, it will show in the collapsed outline.

Exploring the auxiliary windows

A number of windows affect text input and output in order to solve certain problems. As a group, they don't really have a name, so some developers call them auxiliary windows. Here are a few of them:

>> **The Output window:** You use the Output window regularly for two things:

- *Build logging:* Every time you build, the Output window tracks all the linking and compiling that go on under the sheets and shows any errors that might come up.

  You can use errors listed in the Output window to navigate the code. The buttons in the Output box assist with getting around the code based on the messages in the window.

- *Debug statements:* The second use of the Output window is as a means of seeing debug statements. If you use a Debug.Write statement in your code, the Output window is where it will go. Additionally, if you use Console.Write, but are running a Windows Forms application, for instance, the text will go to the Output window.

>> **The Immediate window:** This window does exactly what one would expect it to do: take action immediately. In debug mode, you can use the Immediate window to send commands to the program as it is running, to change the

state, or evaluate operations. Try the following to see how the Immediate window works:

1. **Open any executable project.**

2. **Put a breakpoint somewhere in the code by clicking in the gray bar running down the side of Code View.**

   A red dot appears.

3. **Choose Debug ⇨ Start Debugging or press F5.**

   The program should stop on the load method.

4. **Select the Immediate window.**

   If you don't see the Immediate window displayed by default, choose Debug ⇨ Windows ⇨ Immediate or press Ctrl+D,I.

5. **Type ? this.**

   See the IntelliSense menu?

6. **Type a . (dot).**

   You see a listing of all the things you can do with the this object at the particular point you're at in the code. The ? command means to print whatever the object contains.

That's what the Immediate window is for. You can do more than print values, too. You can change variable values and modify the execution of your program. It is a powerful part of your debugging toolbox.

» **The Breakpoints window:** If you're still running the last example, you can display the Breakpoints window by pressing Ctrl+D,B. The Breakpoints window appears, and any breakpoints you add will be in it (see Figure 2-11).

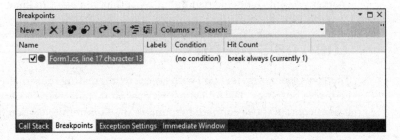

FIGURE 2-11:
The Breakpoints window.

What's cool here is that you can right-click any breakpoint and completely alter the properties of that breakpoint by choosing Settings from the context menu. Try it — the important options are described in this list:

- *Location:* Specifies the location of the line of code that should host the breakpoint. This is convenient if you have filters set and you find you need to shift a line back.

- *Condition:* You can teach the breakpoint to stop at this line only if a certain variable is a specific value.

- *Hit Count:* Stop here only after the *x*th time it is hit.

- *Filter:* It's similar to Condition, except that you can use system values such as MachineName, ProcessName, ProcessId, ThreadName, and ThreadId. It's useful for multiprocessor development, among other things.

- *WhenHit:* You can do more than just stop on a breakpoint — instead, you can do something like print a value to the Output window, or even run a test script.

>> **The Task List window:** While coding, have you ever wanted to tell the developer working after you that something still needs to be done? To make this happen, create a comment and start it with //TODO:. Adding a TODO comment makes it appear as a task in the Task List window (found on the View menu). Clicking the task in the Task List takes you to the line where the task was set, so you don't have to search for it.

Using the Tools of the Trade

Any overview chapter always has topics that just don't fit in any category. This chapter presents a double handful of tools that you want to know about.

The Tools menu

The Tools menu provides you with access to interesting tools that you can use for a variety of purposes. The following list doesn't include every Tools menu entry, but it does contain those commonly found in the Community edition of Visual Studio.

>> **Extensions and Updates:** Displays an Extensions and Updates dialog box where you find new features to add to Visual Studio, plus any Microsoft-supplied updates for the base product.

>> **Connect to Database:** See the "Server Explorer" section, earlier in this chapter.

>> **Connect to Server:** Discussed in the "Server Explorer" section.

>> **SQL Server:** Provides a menu containing tasks that you perform specifically with SQL Server, rather than any other data source.

>> **Web Code Analysis:** Contains a list of entries that help you modify the configuration used when performing web code analysis.

>> **Code Snippets Manager:** You find snippets discussed in Chapter 3 of this minibook.

>> **Choose Toolbox Items:** This tool helps you manage the items in the Toolbox. You can add or remove a variety of components, including .NET, WPF, COM, and Silverlight.

>> **NuGet Package Manager:** Manages Visual Studio Add-ins. Add, remove, enable, and disable.

>> **Node.js Tools:** Helps you configure and use Node.js with Visual Studio.

>> **Create GUID:** Creates a Globally Unique ID (GUID), one of those 25 character codes that are supposed to be unique over the next 2,500 years or something.

>> **WCF Service Configuration Manager:** Provides a graphic interface for the WCF `config` files. Services are covered in Online Chapters 4–7, which you find at `www.dummies.com`, searching this book's title, and locating the Downloads tab on the page that appears.

>> **External Tools:** Enables you to add separate EXE files to the Tools menu, such as Notepad, NUnit, or other tools, that add functionality to Visual Studio.

>> **Import and Export Settings:** Helps you move projects between development tools. You can store your current settings in a file in the `Visual Studio 2012\Settings` directory or change current settings to another batch of settings. You can share settings with other developers.

>> **Customize:** Enables you to alter the look and feel of Visual Studio's menus and toolbars.

>> **Options:** Alters the way Visual Studio works. Options are covered in some depth in Chapter 3 of this minibook. Set Visual Studio up to look and work the way you like.

Building

Previous chapters of this book discuss the basics of building a project. A few other options in the Build menu deserve at least a small explanation, including the following:

>> **Rebuild:** This checks all the references throughout the project before compiling the project. It's useful if your development computer has changed configuration since your last build.

>> **Clean:** This actually deletes not only the EXEs and DLLs created as part of your project (but not your code files), but also all DLLs that were copied into your project by references that were set to that mode.

>> **Batch Build:** This enables you to build release and debug versions (for instance), or 32 and 64 bit (as another example) at the same time.

>> **Configuration Manager:** Use this to set the order and mode in which you build your projects. The most common configurations are DEBUG (for code in progress) and RELEASE (for finished code).

Using the Debugger as an Aid to Learning

You might be surprised to discover how many professional developers learn new techniques, which is by looking at other people's code. It might seem like cheating, but it's actually the smart way to do things because someone else has already done all the hard work. Of course, trying to figure out how a particularly subtle programming technique works could consume days if you just look at the code. It's much easier to determine how the code works when seeing it in action, which is precisely why the debugger is an aid to learning. By running the code and stepping through it a bit at a time, you not only discover new programming techniques but also develop a better sense of precisely how C# works.

The example in this section relies on the cribbage application you first discover in Book 3, Chapter 5. However, the techniques work with any code, and you shouldn't feel the need to work through any particular example. The following sections fill in the details for you.

Stepping through code

The first step in working with the debugger as an aid to learning is to set one or more breakpoints in the code. For example, you might want to see how the Paint() method works for an application. To perform this task, you simply click the gray stripe that runs along the left side of the code editor. The breakpoint appears with a red dot in the left margin and the piece of code highlighted (normally in red as well).

The next step is to start the debugger by pressing F5 or choosing Debug ⇨ Start Debugging. You stop at the first breakpoint that the application encounters, which may not be the first breakpoint you set or the first breakpoint in the code. In fact, it's often revealing to see where you do end up because the location of a breakpoint tells you how the application starts, including what tasks it must perform and in what order it performs them.

Stepping through the code comes next. You see where the instruction pointer moves as the application executes code. You have three options for stepping through code:

>> **Step Into:** Executes the next line of code. When the code is a method call, the instruction pointer goes to that method so that you see the internal workings of that method. Of course, you must have the method's source code in order to see how it works.

>> **Step Over:** Executes the next line of code without entering any method calls. The content of a method call still executes, but you see the result of the method call, rather than how the method call actually works. The method call becomes a black box.

>> **Step Out:** Moves to the next level up and then executes the next line of code. If you have seen what you want to see inside a method call, clicking this button will move out of the method so that you can see the next line of code in the next level of the application (unless you're already at the top level of the application).

Going to a particular code location

When the application is running, you may not want to single step through every line of code. Yes, you want to stop at a certain breakpoint, but then you decide that you don't really want to stay there and execute the code line by line. In this case, you can hover the mouse next to the line of code that you do want to execute next. You see a green right-pointing arrow like the one shown in Figure 2-12.

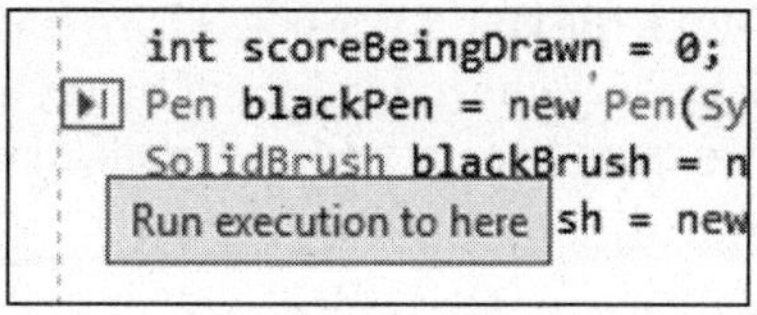

FIGURE 2-12: Executing to a line of code.

When you click the right-pointing arrow, the code from the existing instruction pointer location to the location you point to will execute. You see the results of the execution, but not the individual steps. In some cases, this technique will help you get past problematic pieces of code where timing prevents you from truly seeing how the code executes.

Watching application data

Understanding how data changes over time is an essential part of learning with the debugger. You have access to a number of windows to help you do this. For example, you can include Debug and Trace statements in your code and then view their output in the Output window. To include Debug and Trace statements, you must add using System.Diagnostics; to the top of your application code. Use Debug statements when you want to output values only for debug releases of your application. Use Trace statements when you want to output values for both debug and release versions of your application.

Whenever you execute an application, the Locals window shown in Figure 2-13 contains a list of the local (rather than the global) variables. The local variables are those that are set in the current method and are likely the variables you use most often in well-designed code.

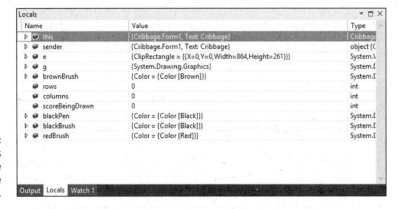

FIGURE 2-13:
Use the Locals window to see local variable values.

The right-pointing arrow next to a variable entry tells you that you can drill down to find more information. In fact, in some situations, you can drill down quite a few levels before you finally reach the end. Some objects are really complex. Viewing the content of objects helps you understand them better and often provides insights into how to better use them to create robust applications.

If a particular variable doesn't appear in the Locals window or you want to view a particular object element in more detail as the code executes, you can use the Watch window, shown in Figure 2-14, instead. You type the variable you want to watch in the window. As the code executes, you see the value change.

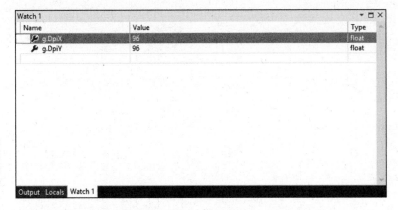

FIGURE 2-14:
Use the Watch window to create custom variable views.

Viewing application internals

Learning to right-click in Visual Studio is a valuable aid in learning. Whenever you see anything that looks interesting, right-click it. The context menu tells you the sorts of things you can do with the object. For example, you might right-click a class and choose one of the detail view entries for it in the context menu. The internal view options you use most are

>> **Peek Definition:** Shows the definition for the requested object in a small window within the current code window. The definition tells you more about the object.

>> **Go To Definition:** Opens the file containing the definition for the requested object. This approach takes you away from your application, but you get more details about the object and its associated objects.

>> **Go To Implementation:** Takes you to the location where the code implements the object, thereby making it usable within the application. A definition describes the object, while an implementation makes it a usable, real object.

>> **Find All References:** Shows every location in the code where the object is used so that you can find every reference to it. Finding where an object is used helps you understand better how to use it for your own needs.

Chapter **3**

Customizing Visual Studio

I n Chapters 1 and 2 of Book 4, you see how to install Visual Studio and make a new project. You also see the bits that the user interface gives you. The fun's over. Now you get to make it work for you.

Visual Studio offers a dizzying array of options for customization. Used poorly, these options have the real potential to make the lives of you and your coworkers miserable. Used correctly, they have the potential to double your productivity.

At its most basic, customization involves setting options to better match your environment, style, and work patterns. These options include everything from your code visibility to source control. The idea is to configure Visual Studio's options to your exact specifications.

The next step is to improve the usability of the application to match your day-to-day operations. One of the best overall ways to accomplish this is to change the button toolbar and the menus to make what you use every day more available. Another great way to do this is to manage or create snippets that automate generation of code.

Finally, you take a short deep dive into the Project and File templates of Visual Studio. Did you know that when you create a new XAML file (for example) or C#

Class file that the contents of that file are controlled by a template and are editable? No? Well, you do now!

All these things put together amount to a rather flexible Integrated Development Environment (IDE). Although the flexibility is nice, the goal is to set a configuration that matches your style. Only you know what that configuration is. This chapter tells you what the software can do and gives you the tools to make the changes.

Setting Options

Choose the Tools⇨Options menu item to open the Options dialog box, which looks like Figure 3-1. (The Environment section may be opened to show its content when you open the dialog box; click the arrow next to the section header to see other entries.) It is generally designed to set Boolean type options like Show This or Provide That or to change paths to resources where Visual Studio will store certain files.

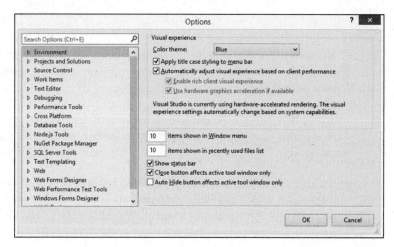

Those details are all well and good, but the goal of this chapter is to introduce the other things that the options provide. The following sections start with adjustments to your environment, describe the remarkable language options, and then explore some neat stuff.

Environment

The Environment section is where you begin in the Options dialog box. Sections here include the font details of code-editing screens, key mappings, and the Really Simple Syndication (RSS) feed settings for the Start page.

The Environment\Font and Colors settings will probably be of interest only when you need them for a presentation or you have a special visual need (such as color blindness or an inability to see small type). Sixteen points is the size of choice for most speakers. There are a number of "code friendly" fonts out there, and this is where you select them.

Defining the Start Page

The *Start Page* is the first page you see when you start Visual Studio. You find this setting in the Environment\Startup page. It consumes an RSS feed from Microsoft with news related to the kind of development you do, as you told Visual Studio when you first installed the software. Often, people change roles, and the RSS feed no longer applies to their work. This is a problem. The At Startup drop-down list box contains these options:

>> **Open Home Page:** You can use any site for your home page. The actual Home Page setting appears on the Environment\Web Browser page, which also contains your Search Page setting. This particular option can open you to potential viruses because any content executes at the same privilege level as the user.

>> **Load Last Loaded Solution:** This option ignores the Start Page completely and gets you right to work. If you want, you can still view the Start Page by choosing File ⇨ Start Page. Use this option if you tend not to view the Start Page content.

>> **Show Open Project Dialog Box:** Use this option when you work on several projects at a time and don't know which project you might start your day working on.

>> **Show New Project Dialog Box:** An experimenter, hobbyist, or student might use this option to get started each day with a new learning experience.

>> **Show Empty Environment:** This option opens Visual Studio without doing anything at all. Use this option when you don't know how you'd like to start your session but find it annoying when Visual Studio tries to make the decision for you.

>> **Start Page:** The default option is to open the Start Page and download developer content from the default start page site.

TIP

The default settings download new content every 60 minutes. The thought might have been that developers need a break, just like everyone else, and the new content would provide an opportunity to do something interesting during the break. Unfortunately, if you happen to have a slower connection, you may actually notice lags in Visual Studio performance during these downloads of content that you're probably not using. You can make Visual Studio more efficient by clearing the Download Content Every option check mark or setting the interval between downloads higher.

Keyboard commands

The most useful settings in the Options dialog box are the Environment\Keyboard settings. This is where you make Visual Studio feel like Emacs (a popular code editor) through the use of keyboard mappings.

TIP

Keyboard mappings are key combinations you set to run commands from the keyboard rather than by clicking your mouse. For example, one commonly used mapping is Ctrl+C, which copies material in the same way that clicking the Edit menu and then clicking Copy does. Many developers feel that using keyboard mapped commands makes the development experience faster and easier.

The keyboard settings essentially enable you to set keyboard commands for any menu selection in Visual Studio. The Apply the Following Additional Keyboard Mapping Scheme drop-down list enables the key mappings to be different, if you happen to like the mappings of other development environments.

Language

The term *language* doesn't mean the Environment\International Settings page settings that enable you to change the display language of Visual Studio if you have additional language packs installed (although that is neat). It refers to the *programming* languages you work in with Visual Studio. The Text Editor section is where you can provide settings for each of these programming languages.

The Text Editor options change the way the Code Editor behaves. All the languages that Visual Studio supports out of the box appear in the tree view under the main heading and allow you to alter general options, tabbing, formatting, sometimes advanced options, and miscellaneous features of the text editor.

For instance, look at Text Editor\C#. To open the C# section, click the right-pointing arrow next to Text Editor and then the right-pointing arrow next to C#. The first view in the Options panel is the General view. Here you can change the default options for statement completion, various behavior settings, and what the Code Editor should display aside from the code. The other panels you can use are

>> **Scroll Bars:** This section contains options for how and when Visual Studio displays scroll bars. You have individual settings for horizontal and vertical scroll bars. All the annotation options also appear on this page.

>> **Tabs:** This section is for people who are obsessive about the tabbing of their source code. The Tabs panel determines how many spaces make up a tab, and whether Visual Studio should insert them automatically.

>> **Advanced:** This section should probably be called *Miscellaneous*. Everything that doesn't fit into other categories is here. In this section, handling comments, interface implementation, and refactoring details all have a check box that basically says, "If you don't like it when Visual Studio does this, click here."

>> **Code Style:** This section has a number of subsections that all define how Visual Studio presents and formats code.

- **General:** Contains all the options for defining how Visual Studio presents this object entries.

- **Formatting:** Formatting in C# is very in-depth. Generally, C# coders are a little persnickety about the look of their code. Visual Studio does a lot of work to help make your code look the way you want it, but you have to tell it what to do. Options for formatting include: General (automatic formatting features); Indentation; Newlines; Spacing; and Wrapping.

- **Naming:** This page contains options for determining when and how Visual Studio alerts you to potential naming issues in your code. For example, there is an option for ensuring that you start all interface names with the letter I. If you create an interface that doesn't have a name that begins with I, the compiler reports it as a Required Style error at the Severity Level you prefer.

>> **IntelliSense:** This section determines how IntelliSense works within the editor. For example, you can determine whether to include completion lists as part of the IntelliSense selections.

Neat stuff

Here's a short list of rarely used features. Right now, they probably won't make a lot of sense, but you will remember them when you need them later.

>> To implement a new source control provider, first install the package (for instance, Turtle for CodePlex's SVN implementation, or Team System) and then go to Source Control in Options to pick the one you want to use.

>> Many people recommend that you store your projects in a short file path, like C:\Projects. You can change where you store projects in the Projects and Solutions section in the options dialog box.

>> Set up automatic Windows Forms data binding in the Designer for custom controls (that you have bought or built) in the Windows Forms Designer / Data UI Customization section of the Options dialog box.

>> You can teach Visual Studio to open a file with a given extension in a certain file editor using the Text Editor / File Extension section of the Options panel.

Using Snippets

Snippets are little bits of precoded logic that are meant to help you remember how to perform some standard code functions in various languages. In VB, for instance, you might not remember how to read from a file, so there is a snippet for that. In C#, you may want to implement a property getter and setter, so you use a shortcut to get the snippet in place.

Using snippets

You can use a snippet in a few different ways, most of which are somewhat slow. The fastest way is through the use of key commands. To use a snippet this way, type its shortcut code and press Tab twice. For instance, try these steps:

1. **Choose File ⇨ New ⇨ Project.**

   You see the New Project dialog box.

2. **Select the Visual C#\Windows Classic Desktop folder in the left pane.**

3. **Highlight the Class Library template in the center pane.**

4. **Type** TestSnippets **in the Name field and click OK.**

   Visual Studio creates a new Class Library project for you and displays the code editor with a default class defined. At this point, you can start adding code to the example application.

5. **In the new class that is created, place the cursor inside the curly braces.**

6. **Type** prop.

7. **Press Tab twice.**

   Your results should look like the ones shown in Figure 3-2.

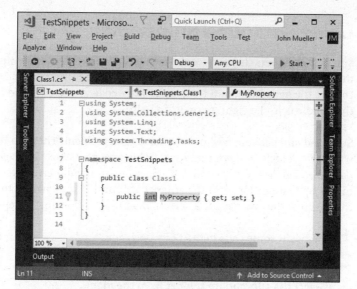

FIGURE 3-2:
The automatically generated property snippet.

See the template that is put into place? Int is highlighted. You can type over it.

8. **Type** string **and press Tab twice.**

   Now MyProperty is highlighted.

9. **Type** FirstName **and press Enter twice.**

   Now you have a finished automatically implemented property. It should look like this:

```
public string FirstName {get; set; }
```

You can get to a snippet in other ways, including this one:

1. **Right-click at the insertion point.**

   You have the option to select Insert Snippet.

2. **Choose Snippet ⇨ Insert Snippet from the context menu.**

   The full list of all the installed snippets appears at the insertion point.

3. **Click an item in the list.**

   The contents of that folder appear. Continue selecting categories (the menu extends to the right) until you have selected the snippet you were looking for.

4. **Double-click the snippet to insert it.**

After they're inserted, populating the variables works just like the shortcut version.

Using surround snippets

Surround snippets are very cool. Have you ever written a few lines of code and then realized that you should probably try to catch errors? You have to add a little code at the beginning, and then add a little code at the end, and then make sure the middle is in the right place. It's a pain.

Surround snippets are designed to solve that problem. They are normal snippets with a bit of logic in them that says, "This part goes above the selection, and this part goes below the selection." If you want to handle errors for a section, you highlight that section, and the snippet will put the try before the selection and the catch at the end. To use a surround snippet, follow these steps:

1. **Highlight some code in the Code Designer.**

2. **Press Ctrl+K,S to open the snippets menu.**

3. **Select the appropriate snippet from the menu.**

   You can choose the snippet that is right for whatever you are coding. Try prop for a property getter and setter. To open submenus, use Tab. To close, use Shift+Tab.

4. **Set the various variables that Visual Studio prompts you with.**

The snippet will appear appropriately above and below the selected text. For instance, if you had this chunk of code:

```
for (int count = 1; count <= 10; count++)
{
    Console.WriteLine(string.Format("The number is {0}.", count));
}
```

and you felt that you needed a try ... catch block around it, you could highlight the code and do the preceding steps. If you select try from the menu, you get this:

```
try
{
    for (int count = 1; count <= 10; count++)
    {
        Console.WriteLine(string.Format("The number is {0}.", count));
    }
}
```

```
catch (Exception)
{
    throw;
}
```

The exception is highlighted in green onscreen. You can tab to that and add the exception type you expect. It's a slick system.

Making snippets

Snippets are XML files that follow a format understood by Visual Studio. They include a Header and Snippet element. The Header includes a title, which is how the snippet is referred to. The Snippet element, where all the work is done, includes a Code element, which has the code to be inserted.

The best way to make a new snippet is to modify an existing one. Snippets can be found in your Visual Studio install directory. If you choose to use the Community edition, you should find them in C:\Program Files (x86)\Microsoft Visual Studio\2017\Community\VC#\Snippets\1033 if you are on a 64-bit operating system (otherwise you can drop the x86). The snippets appear in subfolders, one of which is Visual C#. Right-click the cw.snippet file to open it in Visual Studio. Here's the code:

```xml
<?xml version="1.0" encoding="utf-8" ?>
<CodeSnippets
  xmlns="http://schemas.microsoft.com/VisualStudio/2005/CodeSnippet">
  <CodeSnippet Format="1.0.0">
    <Header>
      <Title>cw</Title>
      <Shortcut>cw</Shortcut>
      <Description>Code snippet for Console.WriteLine</Description>
      <Author>Microsoft Corporation</Author>
      <SnippetTypes>
        <SnippetType>Expansion</SnippetType>
      </SnippetTypes>
    </Header>
    <Snippet>
      <Declarations>
        <Literal Editable="false">
          <ID>SystemConsole</ID>
          <Function>SimpleTypeName(global::System.Console)</Function>
        </Literal>
      </Declarations>
```

```
            <Code
            Language="csharp"><![CDATA[$SystemConsole$.WriteLine($end$);]]>
            </Code>
        </Snippet>
    </CodeSnippet>
</CodeSnippets>
```

This list describes what's in the Header element:

>> **Title:** Shows up on the context menu.

>> **Shortcut:** The key combination you can type for IntelliSense.

>> **Description and Author:** Shows up in the tooltip when you mouse over the snippet in Visual Studio.

>> **SnippetType:** Defines which menus the snippet appears on. The most common types are Expansion and SurroundsWith. *Expansion* means that it inserts the text. *SurroundsWith* means that it's placed above and below the selection.

The Snippet element is where the work is done. In the cw.snippet example, there are two elements in Snippet: Declarations and Code. Declarations declares the variables, and Code is what gets inserted. Within these, the following statements are true:

>> The Literal element describes a variable that will be used in the creation of the snippet.

>> In this case, Function tries to get the simplest version of the System.Console namespace given the current constraints, and ID names it SystemConsole.

>> The Code element specifies the language and then puts the actual code in place.

TIP

If you want to make your own snippet, start with one of the samples provided in the Visual Studio install. You can start from scratch, too. If you want, you can create an XML file and give it a .snippet file extension.

Deploying snippets

To deploy a snippet of your own, use the Code Snippets Manager. The manager is found on the Tools menu and looks like the one shown in Figure 3-3.

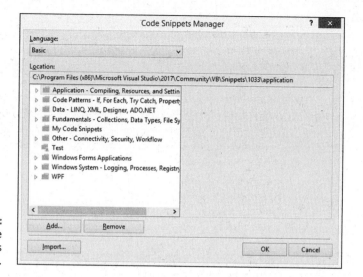

Adding a new snippet this way is fairly simple. After you create your snippets file, click the Import button and select the `.snippet` file. It's placed in the selected folder, so make sure that you have the snippet folder highlighted.

The Add and Remove buttons in the Manager refer to directories, not files. Use them to make new snippet folders. The Search Online feature just searches Visual Studio Help for IntelliSense Code Snippets.

Sharing snippets

Sharing a snippet is a more complicated act than it should be when working with groups. One would think that you could just create a `.snippet` file, send it to the group using something like email, and that would be that. Sending a snippet actually is simple when you want to send it to just one person. However, working in a group situation requires a different process as described in this section.

Group snippet sharing has three components:

>> **The** `.snippet` **file itself:** This topic is discussed in the preceding section.

>> **The** `.vscontent` **file that lists the snippets (even if there is only one):** The `.vscontent` file is one with a listing of snippets in a package. It consists of multiple Content elements that describe the various files in the package. For instance, here is the `.vscontent` file that would be used for the previous `Console.Writeline` example.

```
<VSContent xmlns="http://schemas.microsoft.com/developer/
    vscontent/2010">
    <Content>
        <FileName>cw.snippet</FileName>
        <DisplayName>cw</DisplayName>
        <Description>Console.Writeline</Description>
        <FileContentType>Code Snippet</FileContentType>
        <ContentVersion>3.0</ContentVersion>
        <Attributes>
            <Attribute name="lang" value="csharp"/>
        </Attributes>
    </Content>
</VSContent>
```

This gives you two files in the package — the snippet and the content file. These need to be packaged in a `.vsi` file and then distributed.

>> **The `.vsi` file to package it all together:** The `.vsi` file is a Zip file with a new extension. To make it, zip your folder of snippets with the vscontent file and change the file extension from `.zip` to `.vsi`. Visual Studio users can double-click `.vsi` files to install them. You can also use the command line for more in-depth installs.

Hacking the Project Types

This book recommends that you not start a new project with a blank screen. Click New Project and select a project type in order to get some basic set of code to start with. The `C:\Program Files (x86)\Microsoft Visual Studio\2017\Community\Common7\IDE` folder contains the files that make all the magic project types work.

Hacking project templates

The first, most obvious target for hacking are the project types because they are text based and have a lot of useful information in them. Found in the IDE folder referenced in the preceding paragraph, the ProjectTemplates folder follows the hierarchy of the New Project tree view (see Figure 3-4).

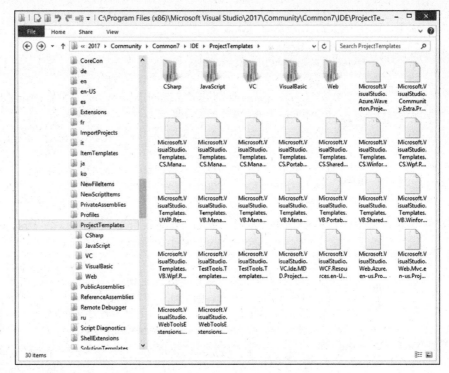

FIGURE 3-4:
A bunch of project-type directories.

This section focuses on the `CSharp` directory tree because this book is about C#. To keep examples to a minimum, open the `Windows/1033` folder to view Windows project types. In a default install, that looks something like this (with each folder representing a project type):

» ClassLibrary

» ConsoleApplication

» EmptyProject

» SharedProject

» WindowsApplication

» WindowsControlLibrary

» WindowsService

» WPFApplication

» WPFBrowserApplication

» WPFControlLibrary

» WPFCustomControl

The ConsoleApplication is the simplest practical project type, and it is a great place to begin creating your own. Open the ConsoleApplication directory and look at the five files it includes:

>> App.config: Contains configuration information in XML format that is used to do things like choose a default .NET Framework version.

>> assemblyinfo.cs: This file goes directly into the project. Take a look at the code; it is the exact code that is in the assemblyinfo file in a project, except there are project-specific variables surrounded by dollar signs. Those are placeholders for the content that will get filled in.

>> consoleapplication.csproj: This is the actual project file; the name will be replaced by the new project-creation process. As with the other included files, there are variable names within the XML of the file.

>> csConsoleApplication.vstemplate: This is the magic file that tells the project-creation process how to build the new project. The important part is the TemplateContent element, which contains the name of the ProjectFile and the ProjectItems that go into the finished product. This is clearly where you would put new files if you needed them.

>> program.cs: This is the default file for the application. This is where you begin when you start coding. Take a look at the code; it should look familiar.

So where does that leave you? You can change the projects. Try these steps:

1. **Copy the** ConsoleApplication **directory from** C:\Program Files (x86)\Microsoft Visual Studio\2017\Community\Common7\IDE\Project Templates\CSharp\Windows\1033.

2. **Paste the directory back into the folder — it should make** ConsoleApplication - Copy.

3. **Drag the new class to your desktop temporarily and rename it** ClassAndConsole.

4. **Open** C:\Program Files (x86)\Microsoft Visual Studio\2017\Community\Common7\IDE\ProjectTemplates\CSharp\Windows\1033\ClassLibrary.

5. **Copy the** class1.cs **file from that folder.**

6. **Paste it into the new** ConsoleAndClass **folder on your desktop.**

7. **Right-click** csConsoleApplication.vstemplate **and select Edit from the menu to open the file in Notepad.**

8. **In the file, change each instance of** ConsoleApplication **to** ConsoleClassApplication.

9. Add the bolded line to the file, in order to reference the new file (some of the longest lines are broken in the book so that they fit; don't break them in the file you create).

```xml
<?xml version="1.0" encoding="utf-8"?>
<VSTemplate Version="3.0.0" Type="Project"
            xmlns="http://schemas.microsoft.com/developer/
               vstemplate/2005">
  <TemplateData>
    <Name Package="{FAE04EC1-301F-11d3-BF4B-00C04F79EFBC}" ID="2320"/>
    <Description Package="{FAE04EC1-301F-11d3-BF4B-00C04F79EFBC}"
       ID="2321"/>
    <Icon Package="{FAE04EC1-301F-11d3-BF4B-00C04F79EFBC}" ID="4548"/>
    <TemplateID>Microsoft.CSharp.ConsoleClassApplication</TemplateID>
    <ProjectType>CSharp</ProjectType>
    <RequiredFrameworkVersion>2.0</RequiredFrameworkVersion>
    <SortOrder>13</SortOrder>
    <NumberOfParentCategoriesToRollUp>2</NumberOfParentCategoriesToRollUp>
    <CreateNewFolder>true</CreateNewFolder>
    <DefaultName>ConsoleApp</DefaultName>
    <ProvideDefaultName>true</ProvideDefaultName>
    <CreateInPlace>false</CreateInPlace>
  </TemplateData>
  <TemplateContent>
    <Project File="ConsoleClassApplication.csproj"
      ReplaceParameters="true">
      <ProjectItem ReplaceParameters="true"
        TargetFileName="Properties\AssemblyInfo.cs">
           AssemblyInfo.cs
      </ProjectItem>
      <ProjectItem ReplaceParameters="true"
        OpenInEditor="true">Program.cs</ProjectItem>
      <ProjectItem ReplaceParameters="true"
        OpenInEditor="true">Class1.cs</ProjectItem>
      <ProjectItem ReplaceParameters="true">App.config</ProjectItem>
    </Project>
  </TemplateContent>
</VSTemplate>
```

10. **Save and close** csConsoleApplication.vstemplate.

11. **Rename** consoleapplication.csproj **to** consoleclassapplication. csproj.

12. Copy the directory file back to the original folder.

13. Close Visual Studio if it is open.

14. **Open the Visual Studio Command Prompt as Administrator.**

(It is in the All Programs folder in the Start Bar, under Visual Studio 2017 ➪ Visual Studio tools.)

15. **Run** `devenv /setup`.

Now, when you open Visual Studio and click New Project, there should be a new project type, called Console And Class. Create a new project based on this type, and it will make you a Console `.cs` file and a class `.cs` file.

Hacking item templates

Items work the same way. Check into `C:\Program Files (x86)\Microsoft Visual Studio\2017\Community\Common7\IDE\ItemTemplates\CSharp` and you'll see the same set of items types that show in the Add New Item dialog box:

- » Code
- » Data
- » General
- » SQL Server
- » Test
- » Web
- » Windows Forms
- » WPF
- » XAML

If you dig into a directory through the Code/1033 folder, you will find more or less the same kinds of things you saw in the project templates in the preceding section. The templates are in directories (and have to stay that way). These files include a `.vstemplate` file that has the details Visual Studio needs. The files that go into the project are in there, too.

Look in the `Code/1033` folder. It contains a `ClassLibrary.` directory that maintains the Class template, if you were to right-click a project name and select Add New Class. Suppose that you want to put the default comment block in here, too. Here's what to do:

1. **Duplicate the Class directory.**

2. **Open the** `class1.cs` **file in Visual Studio.**

3. Add the bold lines to the file.

The file in the project group looks like the following listing. To edit it, you just make a new line before the class declaration and type ///.

```csharp
using System;
using System.Collections.Generic;
$if$ ($targetframeworkversion$ >= 3.5)using System.Linq;
$endif$using System.Text;


namespace $rootnamespace$
{
    /// <summary>
    ///
    /// </summary>
    class $safeitemrootname$
    {
    }
}
```

4. Save the file and close Visual Studio.

5. Put the file back in `C:\Program Files\Microsoft Visual Studio 10.0\Common7\IDE\ItemTemplates\CSharp\Code\1033.`

6. Open Visual Studio and make a new Class project.

7. Right-click the project name and select Add ⇨ Class.

Keep the default name.

Visual Studio makes a new file with the comment block.

5

Windows Development with WPF

Contents at a Glance

Chapter 1

Introducing WPF

WPF, or Windows Presentation Foundation, is a graphical system for rendering user interfaces. It provides great flexibility in how you can lay out and interact with your applications. With Common Language Runtime (CLR) at its core, you can use C# or any other CLR language to communicate with user interface elements and develop application logic. The advantages of WPF for your application are its rich data binding and visualization support and its design flexibility and styling.

WPF enables you to create an application that is more usable to your audience. It gives you the power to design an application that would previously take extremely long development cycles and a calculus genius to implement. Now you can implement difficult things like graphics and animations in as few as three lines of code! This chapter introduces you to key WPF concepts as well as common application patterns used in the software industry today.

Understanding What WPF Can Do

WPF's graphics capabilities make it the perfect choice for data visualization. Take, for instance, the standard drop-down list (or combo box). Its current use is to enable the user to choose a single item from a list of items. For this example, suppose you want the user to select a car model for purchase.

The standard way of displaying this choice is to display a drop-down list of car model names from which users can choose. There is a fundamental usability problem with this common solution: Users are given only a single piece of information from which to base their decision — the text that is used to represent the item in the list.

For the power user (or car fanatic), this may not be an issue, but other users need more than just a model name to make an educated decision on the car they wish to purchase. This is where WPF and its data visualization capabilities come into play.

A template can be provided to define how each item in the drop-down list is rendered. The template can contain any visual element, such as images, labels, text boxes, tooltips, drop shadows, and more!

Figure 1-1 shows a typical display of a combo box. This control has limitations: It can relay to the user only a single piece of information, the text used to represent the car model. Work can be done to display images of the car models in a separate control based on the selection in the list, but this still mandates users to make their selection before seeing exactly what it is they are choosing. In contrast, WPF has the flexibility to display many pieces of information in each combo box item, like a one-stop shop for all the information the user will need to make their decision. (See Figure 1-2 for a WPF combo box.)

FIGURE 1-1:
A typical combo box.

Figure 1-2 shows a sample combo box in WPF. The way the combo box item is rendered is defined using a data template. (Chapter 3 of this minibook covers Data Templates.) Each item in this combo box is rendered to provide the user with a visual cue along with multiple data fields. Displaying all this information enables users to make an educated decision about the choice they are making.

FIGURE 1-2:
Visualizing
data — a WPF
combo box.

Introducing XAML

WPF enables you to build user interfaces declaratively. Extensible Application Markup Language (XAML; pronounced zammel) forms the foundation of WPF. XAML is similar to HTML in the sense that interface elements are defined using a tag-based syntax.

TECHNICAL STUFF

XAML is XML-based, and as such, it must be well formed, meaning all opening tags require closing tags, and all elements and attributes contained in the document must validate strictly against the specified schemas.

By default, when creating a WPF application in Visual Studio 2010 and above, the following schemas are represented in generated XAML files:

» `http://schemas.microsoft.com/winfx/2006/xaml/presentation`: This schema represents the default Windows Presentation Framework namespace.

» `http://schemas.microsoft.com/winfx/2006/xaml`: This schema represents a set of classes that map to CLR objects.

Most CLR objects can be expressed as XAML elements (with the exception of abstract base classes and some other nonabstract base classes used strictly for inheritance purposes in the CLR). XAML elements are mapped to classes; attributes are mapped to properties or events.

At runtime when a XAML element is processed, the default constructor for its underlying class is called, and the object is instantiated; its properties and events are set based on the attribute values specified in XAML. The next section reviews more XAML basics and gets you started on the path of WPF application development.

Introducing WPF

Diving In! Creating Your First WPF Application

Now it's time to get comfortable, so stop for a moment, go grab a caffeinated beverage, sit in a comfortable chair, pull up to your computer, and get ready to go! To create your first project, follow these steps:

1. **Open Visual Studio.**

2. **Choose File ⇨ New ⇨ Project.**

   You see the New Project dialog box.

3. **Select the Visual C#\Windows Classic Desktop folder in the left pane.**

4. **Highlight the WPF App template in the center pane.**

5. **Type** MyFirstWPFApplication **in the Name field.**

   Your dialog box should look like the one shown in Figure 1-3. Note that the project name and the solution name are the same.

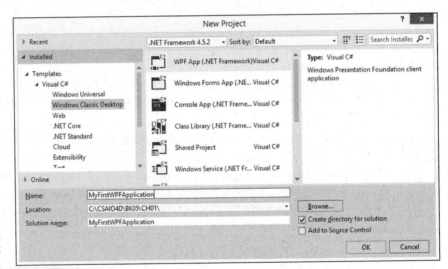

FIGURE 1-3: Creating a project in the New Project dialog box.

6. **Click OK.**

   Visual Studio creates a new WPF project for you and displays both the Designer and the code editor with a default application defined. The WPF Application template creates two XAML files along with their respective code-behind files: App.xaml (App.xaml.cs) and MainWindow.xaml (MainWindow.xaml.cs), as shown in Figure 1-4. At this point, you can start adding code to the example application.

FIGURE 1-4:
WPF Application
solution
structure.

App.xaml represents the entry-point of the application. This is where application-wide (globally scoped) resources and the startup window are defined (see Listing 1-1).

TECHNICAL STUFF

Resources are a keyed collection of reusable objects. Resources can be created and retrieved using both XAML and C#. Resources can be anything — data templates, arrays of strings, or brushes used to color the background of text boxes. Resources are also *scoped*, meaning they can be available to the entire Application (global), to the Window, to the User Control, or even to only a specific control.

LISTING 1-1: **App.xaml**

```
<Application x:Class="MyFirstWPFApplication.App"
             xmlns="http://schemas.microsoft.com/winfx/2006/xaml/presentation"
             xmlns:x="http://schemas.microsoft.com/winfx/2006/xaml"
             xmlns:local="clr-namespace:MyFirstWPFApplication"
             StartupUri="MainWindow.xaml">
    <Application.Resources>

    </Application.Resources>
</Application>
```

Listing 1-1 displays the XAML that was generated by the WPF Application template in Visual Studio. Note that the WPF namespaces are defined. The namespace that represents the CLR objects will be distinguished in the XAML file with the .x prefix.

Introducing WPF

The StartupUri value defines the window that will be displayed after the application is executed. In this case, the MainWindow.xaml window will be displayed.

The x:Class attribute defines the C# code-behind file of this XAML file. If you open App.xaml.cs, you see that its class name is App and it inherits from the Application class (which is the root element of the XAML file).

TECHNICAL STUFF

C# uses namespaces to organize and locate classes. To create objects from a specific namespace, you use the "using" syntax at the top of your class definitions. Similar to C#, XAML also requires you to declare which namespaces are used in the document. Namespaces are typically defined as an attribute within the root element of the document; the root element is the first XML tag in the XAML document. XAML uses XML syntax to define a namespace — "xmlns" means "XML namespace," and it's typically followed by a colon (:) and then an alias. This alias is the shorthand reference to the namespace throughout the XAML document; it's what you use to instantiate an object from a class in that namespace.

For instance, if you want to add the namespace MyTemplates.DataTemplates from the assembly MyTemplates.dll, you could define the namespace as

```
xmlns:myDTs="clr-namespace:MyTemplates.DataTemplates;assembly=MyTemplates.dll"
```

You are then able to instantiate an object from the MyTemplates.DataTemplates namespace as follows:

```
<myDTs:myClass></myDTs:myClass>
```

Declaring an application-scoped resource

To demonstrate the creation and use of a global application-scoped resource, in this section, you create a resource that holds a string used in the application. An application-scoped resource is available to all Windows and user controls defined in the project. Follow these steps:

1. **Add the** System **namespace located in the** mscorlib.dll **assembly.**

    This is where the String class is located.

2. **To do this, add the following namespace to the** App.xaml **root element:**

    ```
    xmlns:sys="clr-namespace:System;assembly=mscorlib"
    ```

    The String class is now available for use throughout the App.xaml document.

3. **Create the resource between the** `Application.Resource` **tags; add the following** `String` **class element:**

```
<sys:String x:Key="Purpose">Hello WPF World!</sys:String>
```

This element instantiates an object of type `String`, initialized to the value `Hello WPF World!`, and keyed off of the key `Purpose`. This resource is now available throughout the `MyFirstWPFApplication` application by requesting the resource "Purpose" (see Listing 1-2).

LISTING 1-2: ## Updated App.xaml with Resource and System Namespace Defined

```
<Application x:Class="MyFirstWPFApplication.App"
             xmlns="http://schemas.microsoft.com/winfx/2006/xaml/presentation"
             xmlns:x="http://schemas.microsoft.com/winfx/2006/xaml"
             xmlns:local="clr-namespace:MyFirstWPFApplication"
             xmlns:sys="clr-namespace:System;assembly=mscorlib"
             StartupUri="MainWindow.xaml">
    <Application.Resources>
        <sys:String x:Key="Purpose">Hello WPF World!</sys:String>
    </Application.Resources>
</Application>
```

TECHNICAL STUFF

You may observe that the `Application.Resource` tag looks kind of odd. `Application.Resources` doesn't define a class as most XAML elements do. It's actually assigning a value to the `Resources` property of its containing `Application` object.

This type of tag is called a *property element*, an XML element that represents a property (or attribute) of an object. Property elements are used when complex objects are assigned to a property of an object that can't be expressed as a simple string value. Property elements must be contained within the tags of the parent element — in this case, within the `Application` tags.

Making the application do something

If you run the application as is, not much happens beyond the display of an empty window. The empty window is the one defined in `MainWindow.xaml`.

REMEMBER

`App.xaml` is the entry point of the WPF application. Within `App.xaml`, the `StartupUri` value defines the window displayed on application startup. In this case, the `StartupUri` value is `MainWindow.xaml`.

Introducing WPF

Add a label to `MainWindow.xaml` that displays the purpose of the String you defined in Resources. Just follow these steps:

1. Open `MainWindow.xaml`.

2. Between the Grid tags, define a grid with a single row and single column by adding the following XAML markup:

```
<Grid.ColumnDefinitions>
    <ColumnDefinition></ColumnDefinition>
</Grid.ColumnDefinitions>
<Grid.RowDefinitions>
    <RowDefinition></RowDefinition>
</Grid.RowDefinitions>
```

Each column and row is defined by the `ColumnDefinition` and `RowDefinition` element contained within the `Grid.ColumnDefinitions` and `Grid.RowDefinitions` properties, respectively. If you want to add more columns, you simply add another `ColumnDefinition` element to the `Grid.ColumnDefinitions` Property Entity. The same goes for adding rows: You add an additional `RowDefinition` element to the `Grid.RowDefinitions` Property Entity.

3. Directly below the `Grid.RowDefinitions` **Property entity, create a label using the following XAML:**

```
<Label x:Name="lblPurpose" Content="{StaticResource Purpose}"
    FontSize="25" Grid.Row="0" Grid.Column="0"/>
```

This markup instantiates a WPF `Label` object accessible to the code-behind file (`MainWindow.xaml.cs`) using the variable `lblPurpose`. The `Content` attribute contains the text that is to be displayed in the label; in this case, you use the Application Resource that you defined in the preceding section by retrieving it using its key value, which is Purpose. The label text is rendered with a font size of 25 units and is to be located in the grid in the first row and first column.

TECHNICAL STUFF

WOW! That line of XAML really packs quite the punch! Here's some of what is going on in there:

» **x:Name:** This attribute assigns a variable name to the object being created by the XAML tag. This enables you to access the object from the code-behind file. In this case, the variable name of the label object being instantiated is `lblPurpose`.

» **Content:** The value assigned to this attribute can be of any type. By default, you can assign it a `string` value, and it will render as you would think a standard label would render. In the WPF reality, `Content` can be composed of anything: a string, an image, an instance of a user control, a text box, and so on. For more info, see Chapter 2 of this minibook.

>> `FontSize`: The size of the font of the label. It is important to note that the size isn't denoted in points; it's expressed in Device Independent Units. WPF gets away from the concepts of pixels and points and moves to a universal sizing strategy. Think of Device Independent Units as more of a ratio than a pixel. For instance, if the containing element of the label were 100 units by 100 units, the label would render as ¼ of that size.

>> `Grid.Row`: Identifies the grid row in which to render the label. Grid row collections are zero based, meaning that the first row is row 0, the second row is row 1, and so on. You should also note that the Label class doesn't contain a property named `Grid`. What you see here is the concept of attached properties. *Attached properties* are a way to assign the context of a current control relative to the properties of an ancestor control. In this case, you assign the label to appear in the first row (row index 0) of its containing grid. Also observe that the label is located within the `Grid` tags; this is how the ancestor `Grid` element is located.

>> `Grid.Column`: Similar to `Grid.Row`, this attached property identifies the grid column in which to render the label. Together with `Grid.Row`, both properties identify the cell where the label is located. In this case, you assign the label to render in the first column of its containing grid. Grid column collections are also zero based.

Go ahead and run your application. You now see Hello World displayed in the label on your Window. Congratulations! You have just created your first WPF application!

Whatever XAML Can Do, C# Can Do Better!

Anything that you can implement using XAML can be implemented in C#. This is not true in reverse; not everything you can do in C# can be done in XAML. C# is the obvious choice for performing business logic tasks with procedural code that can't be expressed in XAML. In the following steps, you create an identical WPF application to the one you created in the preceding section, this time using C# to implement its functionality:

1. **Create a new project by choosing File ➪ New Project.**

2. **Open the Visual C#\Windows Classic Desktop folder.**

3. **Select WPF App.**

4. **Name the application** MyFirstCodeOnlyWPFApplication.

5. **Click OK.**

Visual Studio creates the Solution and Project structure.

6. **Open** App.xaml.cs.

7. **Override the** OnStartup **method to include the creation of the Purpose application resource by adding the following code to the** App **class:**

```
protected override void OnStartup(StartupEventArgs e)
{
    //create and add the Purpose application resource
    string purpose = "Hello WPF World, in C#";
    this.Resources.Add("Purpose", purpose);

    base.OnStartup(e);
}
```

8. **Open** MainWindow.xaml **and give the** Grid **element a name by adding the following attribute:**

```
x:Name="gridLayout"
```

9. **Open** MainWindow.xaml.cs, **and in the default constructor, after the** InitializeComponents **method call, add the following code:**

```
//define grid column and row
this.gridLayout.ColumnDefinitions.Add(new ColumnDefinition());
this.gridLayout.RowDefinitions.Add(new RowDefinition());

//obtain label content from the application resource, Purpose
string purpose = this.TryFindResource("Purpose") as string;
Label lblPurpose = new Label();
lblPurpose.Content = purpose;
lblPurpose.FontSize = 25;

//add label to the grid
this.gridLayout.Children.Add(lblPurpose);

//assign attached property values
Grid.SetColumn(lblPurpose, 0);
Grid.SetRow(lblPurpose, 0);
```

Run the application and observe the resulting product is similar to that obtained in the section "Diving In! Creating Your First WPF Application," earlier in this chapter.

Chapter **2**

Understanding the Basics of WPF

As Chapter 1 of this minibook explains, Windows Presentation Foundation (WPF) not only brings a dramatic shift to the look and feel of Windows applications but also changes the manner of development. The days of dragging and dropping controls from the toolbox onto a form are long gone. Even though you can still drag and drop in WPF, you will find yourself better off and much happier if you work in XAML directly.

What was once difficult is now relatively simple. For example, in traditional Windows applications, when the user changes the size of the form, the controls typically stay huddled in their corner, and a large area of empty canvas is displayed. The only cure for this was a lot of custom code or expensive third-party controls. WPF brings the concept of *flow layout* from the web into the Windows world.

In the GDI/GDI+ world of WinForms, modifying a control's style or building complex looks was a Herculean feat. WPF has completely redefined the control paradigm, giving you, the developer, the freedom to make a control do unimaginable tasks — including playing a video on a button face. However, keep in mind that just because you *can* do something doesn't mean you *should!*

In this chapter, you work with WPF's layout process to control the layout of your application. This chapter also introduces you to the various WPF controls.

Using WPF to Lay Out Your Application

Traditional Windows Forms development deals in absolutes. Position and size for controls are decided at design time and are based on the resolution of the developer's machine. When applications are deployed to users, the form that looked great on the developer's machine could now look very different (and possibly be downright unusable) because of hardware resolution differences.

Instead of depending on screen resolution, WPF measures UI Elements in Device Independent Units (DIUs) that are based on the system DPI. This enables a consistent look between many different hardware configurations.

WPF layout is based on relative values and is adjusted at runtime. When you place controls in a layout container (see the next section), the rendering engine considers the height and width only as "suggested" values. Location is defined in relation to other controls or the container. Actual rendering is a two-step process that starts with measuring all controls (and querying them for their preferred dimensions) and then arranging them accordingly. If controls could speak, the conversation might go something like this:

NEW TECH, NEW TERMS

It seems that every time Microsoft introduces a new technology, developers have to learn a whole new set of terms. WPF is no different! At the root of the change are forms and controls in Windows Forms (WinForms). Here are some of the new terms:

- A *form* in WinForms is referred to as a *window* in WPF.

- Anything placed on a WinForms form is called a *control* (when it has a visual interface) or a *component* (when it doesn't), whereas items placed on a WPF window are referred to as *UIElements*.

- *Panels* are WPF UIElements used for layout.

- A *control* in WPF is a UIElement that can receive focus and respond to user events.

- A Content control in WPF can contain only a single item, which can in turn be other UIElements.

- The WPF Window class is a specialized Content control.

Layout Engine: "Control, how much space would you like to have?"

<This is the Measure Stage>

Control: "I would like 50 DIUs for height, 100 DIUs for width, and a margin of 3 DIUs in the containing Grid cell."

Layout Engine asks all other controls and layout containers.

Layout Engine: "Sorry, you can have only 40 DIUs for height, but I can grant the rest of your requests."

<This is the Arrange Stage>

Arranging Elements with Layout Panels

Designing a window begins with a layout control, or panel. Panels are different than Content controls in that they can hold multiple items, and depending on the panel, a significant amount of plumbing is taken care of for you.

Panels control how UIElements relate to each other and to their containing UIElement and do not dictate absolute positioning. Most application windows require some combination of panels to achieve the required user interface, so it's important to understand them all. WPF ships with six core panels:

- ≫ Stack Panel
- ≫ Wrap Panel
- ≫ Dock Panel
- ≫ Canvas
- ≫ Uniform Grid
- ≫ Grid

The Stack Panel

Stack Panels place UIElements in *stacks*. Items are placed in either a vertical pile (the default), like a stack of DVDs, or a horizontal arrangement, like books on a shelf. It is important to understand that the order items appear in the XAML is the order they appear in the panel — the first UIElement in the XAML appears at the top (vertical) or on the far left (horizontal). Figures 2-1 and 2-2 show the same set of buttons in both orientations. The following code contains the XAML for the Vertical Stack Panel, shown in Figure 2-1.

```xml
<StackPanel Name="pnlStack" Grid.Row="0" Orientation="Vertical">
    <Button Content="A Button"/>
    <Button Content="Another Button"/>
    <TextBlock Text="This is a text block"/>
    <Button Content="Short"/>
    <Button Content="Really Long Button Label"/>
</StackPanel>
```

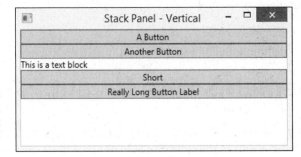

FIGURE 2-1:
Vertical
Stack Panel.

Remember the conversation between the rendering Engine and the Control at the beginning of this chapter? The horizontal layout shown in Figure 2-2 illustrates the clipping that can take place when the sum of the preferred sizes of controls in a container is larger than the container can hold.

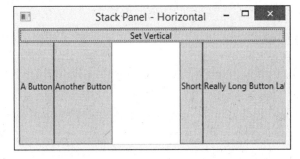

FIGURE 2-2:
Horizontal.

Orientation (as well as all other properties) can be changed at runtime, as illustrated by the following code. The button at the top of the window changes the orientation, the button label, and the window title in the click event. Chapter 4 shows a better way of coding button click events.

```csharp
private void cmdOrientation_Click(object sender, RoutedEventArgs e)
{
    Button button = sender as Button;
    if (button.Content.ToString() == "Set Vertical")
```

```
        {
            pnlStack.Orientation = Orientation.Vertical;
            button.Content = "Set Horizontal";
            Title = "Stack Panel - Vertical";
        }
        else
        {
            pnlStack.Orientation = Orientation.Horizontal;
            button.Content = "Set Vertical";
            Title = "Stack Panel - Horizontal";
        }
    }
```

To access the event handler, you must wire up a control to it. Add the following code to the XAML for the vertical orientation.

```
<StackPanel Name="pnlStack1" Grid.Row="1" Orientation="Vertical">
    <Button x:Name="cmdOrientation" Content="Set Horizontal"
            Click="cmdOrientation_Click"/>
</StackPanel>
```

The use of a second StackPanel allows the cmdOrientation Button to retain its vertical orientation, even when the other controls assume a horizontal orientation. When you plan to change orientation, you need to work with the various controls carefully to obtain the results you want.

The Wrap Panel

The Wrap Panel automatically wraps overflow content onto the next line(s). This is different from how a typical toolbar works, where overflow items are hidden when there isn't enough real estate to show them. Figures 2-3 and 2-4 show the same content controls from the Stack Panel (a mixture of buttons and a text block) in a Wrap Panel. The first window has enough room to show all the UIElements, and the second shows the wrapping of elements because of a lack of room. The initial XAML for the Wrap Panel sample is in the following code.

```
<WrapPanel>
    <Button Content="A Button"/>
    <Button Content="Another Button"/>
    <TextBlock Text="This is a text block"/>
    <Button Content="Short"/>
    <Button Content="Really Long Button Label"/>
</WrapPanel>
```

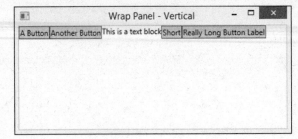

FIGURE 2-3:
Wrap Panel
(wide form).

FIGURE 2-4:
Wrap Panel
(narrow form).

Note that even with the Wrap panel, if the container can't hold the widest item (the last button in the example), some clipping will take place.

The Dock Panel

The Dock Panel uses attached properties (see Chapter 1 of this minibook) to "dock" child UIElements. An important thing to remember is that child elements are docked in XAML order, which means that if you have two items assigned to the left side (through DockPanel.Dock="left"), the first UIElement *as it appears* in the XAML gets the far left wall of the panel, followed by the next item. Here is the code used to create a DockPanel.

```
<DockPanel LastChildFill="True">
    <Button DockPanel.Dock="Left" Content="Far Left"/>
    <Button DockPanel.Dock="Left" Content="Near Left"/>
    <Button DockPanel.Dock="Top" Content="Top"/>
    <Button DockPanel.Dock="Bottom" Content="Bottom"/>
    <Button Content="Fill"/>
    <Button Content="Fill More"/>
</DockPanel>
```

Figure 2-5 shows the output from this example. The Dock Panel also has a setting called LastChildFill. If this is true, the last element in XAML will fill the remaining real estate. Elements (prior to the last XAML element) that do not have a Dock setting specified will default to DockPanel.Dock="Left".

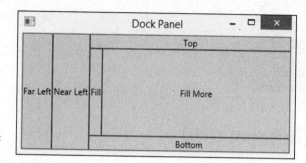

FIGURE 2-5:
Dock Panel.

Canvas

The Canvas is a bit of an anomaly in WPF because it doesn't use flow layout but goes back to fixed position layout rendering. "What?!" you say. "I thought flow layout was the way of the future!" Well, it is . . . most of the time. In some cases, part of your application needs to be laid out the "old way." A graphical application used to design floor plans is a perfect example. Here's the code to create a Canvas.

```xml
<Canvas>
    <Rectangle Canvas.Left="40" Canvas.Top="40" Height="53"
            Name="rectangle1" Stroke="Black" Width="96"
            Fill="#FFE22323"/>
    <Ellipse Canvas.Left="28" Canvas.Top="142" Height="80"
            Name="ellipse1" Stroke="Black" Width="161"
            Fill="#FF0000FA"/>
    <Ellipse Canvas.Left="96" Canvas.Top="14" Height="108"
            Name="ellipse2" Stroke="Black" Width="78" Fill="#FFE5D620"/>
</Canvas>
```

Figure 2-6 shows the output of this example. Items are placed (or drawn) on the canvas relative to any side, and layering is handled through z-order.

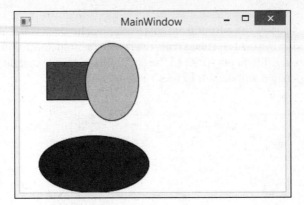

FIGURE 2-6:
Canvas sample.

The Uniform Grid

The Uniform Grid divides the layout area into equally sized cells. The number of rows and columns are defined in the `UniformGrid` XAML tag. As discussed in Chapter 1, cell contents are positioned using the `Grid.Row` and `Grid.Column` attached properties. Note that the rows and columns are zero based. The following code shows how to create a `UniformGrid`:

```
<UniformGrid Rows="2" Columns="2">
    <Border Grid.Row="0" Grid.Column="0" BorderBrush="Black"
            BorderThickness="1" HorizontalAlignment="Stretch"
            VerticalAlignment="Stretch">
        <TextBlock Text="0,0"/>
    </Border>
    <Border Grid.Row="0" Grid.Column="1" BorderBrush="Black"
            BorderThickness="1" HorizontalAlignment="Stretch"
            VerticalAlignment="Stretch">
        <TextBlock Text="0,1"/>
    </Border>
    <Border Grid.Row="1" Grid.Column="0" BorderBrush="Black"
            BorderThickness="1" HorizontalAlignment="Stretch"
            VerticalAlignment="Stretch">
        <TextBlock Text="1,0"/>
    </Border>
    <Border Grid.Row="1" Grid.Column="1" BorderBrush="Black"
            BorderThickness="1" HorizontalAlignment="Stretch"
            VerticalAlignment="Stretch">
        <TextBlock Text="1,1"/>
    </Border>
</UniformGrid>
```

The Uniform Grid shown in Figure 2-7 is not as versatile as the Grid (see the next section), but if you need a very quick checkerboard pattern, it can be an effective panel. To highlight the borders of the cells, the example adds borders. For more on borders, see the section "Exploring Common XAML Controls," later in this chapter.

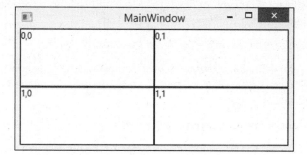

FIGURE 2-7:
Uniform Grid.

The Grid

Chapter 1 of this minibook introduces the Grid, which is the most common starting point to screen design. The Grid is, in fact, the default panel in a Window when you add a new WPF Window to your project.

The Grid divides the layout area with rows (RowDefinitions) and columns (ColumnDefinitions). The difference between the Grid and the Uniform Grid is that the Grid allows for sizing of the cells by defining RowDefinition Height and ColumnDefinition Width. The following code shows how to create definitions for rows and columns by using the Grid.RowDefinitions and Grid.ColumnDefinitions tags.

```
<Grid>
    <Grid.RowDefinitions>
        <RowDefinition Height="2*"/>
        <RowDefinition Height="3*"/>
    </Grid.RowDefinitions>
    <Grid.ColumnDefinitions>
        <ColumnDefinition Width="*"/>
    </Grid.ColumnDefinitions>
</Grid>
```

Sizing rows and columns

There are three GridUnitTypes used for defining heights and widths:

>> Pixel: Fixed size in Device Independent Units.

You define a fixed height or width based on DIUs by specifying a number in the definition. This goes against the Flow Layout grain, but there are certainly valid reasons to do this, such as when a graphic image on a window doesn't scale well (up or down) and needs to be a fixed size. Fixed sizing should be used with caution because it can limit the effectiveness of the user interface. If the content is dynamic or needs to be localized, the controls could clip the content or wind up leaving a lot of wasted space.

» **Auto:** Size is based on the preferred size of the contents.

The Auto definition allows the row or column to determine how large (or small) it can be based on its content. This is decided during the measure stage of the layout process.

» **∗ (asterisk):** Size uses all remaining space.

The Star tells the rendering engine, "Give me all you've got! I'll take it all!" Each star defined gets an equal portion of what's left after all other sizing options have been computed. To achieve proportional sizing, multipliers can be added, as shown in the following code.

```xml
<Grid>
    <Grid.RowDefinitions>
        <RowDefinition Height="2*"/>
        <RowDefinition Height="3*"/>
    </Grid.RowDefinitions>
    <Grid.ColumnDefinitions>
        <ColumnDefinition Width="*"/>
        <ColumnDefinition Width="*"/>
    </Grid.ColumnDefinitions>
    <Border Grid.Row="0" Grid.Column="0" BorderBrush="Black"
            BorderThickness="1" HorizontalAlignment="Stretch"
            VerticalAlignment="Stretch">
        <TextBlock Text="0,0"/>
    </Border>
    <Border Grid.Row="0" Grid.Column="1" BorderBrush="Black"
            BorderThickness="1" HorizontalAlignment="Stretch"
            VerticalAlignment="Stretch">
        <TextBlock Text="0,1"/>
    </Border>
    <Border Grid.Row="1" Grid.Column="0" BorderBrush="Black"
            BorderThickness="1" HorizontalAlignment="Stretch"
            VerticalAlignment="Stretch">
        <TextBlock Text="1,0"/>
    </Border>
```

```
    <Border Grid.Row="1" Grid.Column="1" BorderBrush="Black"
            BorderThickness="1" HorizontalAlignment="Stretch"
            VerticalAlignment="Stretch">
        <TextBlock Text="1,1"/>
    </Border>
</Grid>
```

For example, in Figure 2-8, the first row uses 40 percent (⅖) of the available space and the second row uses the remaining 60 percent (⅗).

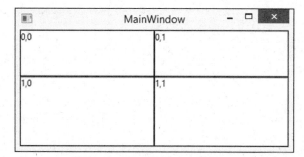

FIGURE 2-8:
Basic Grid with
proportional (*)
row heights.

RowSpan and ColumnSpan

Similar to HTML tables, content in a Grid can span rows or columns by using the Grid.RowSpan and Grid.ColumnSpan attached properties, as shown in the following code:

```
<Grid>
    <Grid.RowDefinitions>
        <RowDefinition Height="2*"/>
        <RowDefinition Height="3*"/>
        <RowDefinition Height="5*"/>
    </Grid.RowDefinitions>
    <Grid.ColumnDefinitions>
        <ColumnDefinition Width="*"/>
        <ColumnDefinition Width="*"/>
    </Grid.ColumnDefinitions>
    <Border Grid.Row="0" Grid.Column="0" Grid.ColumnSpan="2"
            BorderBrush="Black" BorderThickness="1"
            HorizontalAlignment="Stretch" VerticalAlignment="Stretch">
        <TextBlock Text="0,0 - 0,1"/>
```

```
        </Border>
        <Border Grid.Row="1" Grid.Column="0" Grid.RowSpan="2"
                BorderBrush="Black" BorderThickness="1"
                HorizontalAlignment="Stretch" VerticalAlignment="Stretch">
            <TextBlock Text="1,0 - 2,1"/>
        </Border>
        <Border Grid.Row="1" Grid.Column="1" BorderBrush="Black"
                BorderThickness="1" HorizontalAlignment="Stretch"
                VerticalAlignment="Stretch">
            <TextBlock Text="1,1"/>
        </Border>
        <Border Grid.Row="2" Grid.Column="1" BorderBrush="Black"
                BorderThickness="1" HorizontalAlignment="Stretch"
                VerticalAlignment="Stretch">
            <TextBlock Text="2,1"/>
        </Border>
    </Grid>
```

Figure 2-9 shows a grid layout with the border controls spanning both columns in the first row and spanning the next two rows in the first column.

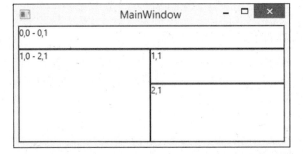

FIGURE 2-9:
Grid with row and column spans.

Horizontal and vertical alignment within parent container's layout slot

You align an element within a container's layout slot by setting the VerticalAlignment and HorizontalAlignment properties. Horizontal settings are Center, Left, Right, and Stretch. Vertical options are Center, Top, Bottom, and Stretch. Stretch specifies the element to fill all available space. Explicit sizing of elements overrides the Stretch setting.

Content alignment within Content controls

The same options can be used for setting the alignment of the content within a Content control by using the HorizontalContentAlignment and VerticalContentAlignment properties in the control.

Margin versus padding

Margins create space around a UIElement and its parent container. Margin values start with the left and rotate clockwise (which is different from CSS, just to keep you on your toes). You can also use some abbreviations. Setting the value as one number makes a uniform margin; setting the value to two numbers (comma separated) sets the left and right margins to the first number and the top and bottom margins to the second.

```
<Button Margin="2,4,2,4" Content="Push Me"/> <!--L,T,R,B-->
<Button Margin="2,4" Content="Push Me"/> <!--LR,TB-->
<Button Margin="2" Content="Push Me"/> <!--LTRB-->
```

Padding increases spacing around UIElements inside a `Block`, `Border`, `Control`, or `TextBlock`. Imagine a picture surrounded by a strip of blue border material, which in turn is inside a frame. Suppose that the picture area (think of it as a container) has a small margin on all sides so that the actual picture is never in contact with the blue border. That's the concept of `Margin`. The blue border itself is extra padding outside the picture area. That's the concept of `Padding`. Think of `Margin` as an inside space and `Padding` as an outside space. This XAML shows something similar: a `TextBlock` and four buttons sitting inside a `StackPanel` with a `Border` around it, using both `Margin` and `Padding`:

```
<Border Background="LightBlue" BorderBrush="Black" BorderThickness="2"
        Padding="15">
   <StackPanel Background="White" HorizontalAlignment="Center"
            VerticalAlignment="Top">
      <TextBlock Margin="10,10" FontSize="18"
               HorizontalAlignment="Center">
         HorizontalAlignment Sample
      </TextBlock>
      <Button HorizontalAlignment="Left">Button 1 (Left)</Button>
      <Button HorizontalAlignment="Right">Button 2 (Right)</Button>
      <Button HorizontalAlignment="Center">Button 3 (Center)</Button>
      <Button HorizontalAlignment="Stretch">Button 4 (Stretch)</Button>
   </StackPanel>
</Border>
```

The `Border` surrounds a light blue area of padding at 15 units. The `TextBlock` inside the white rectangle surrounded by blue shows a narrow `Margin` of 10 on each side as shown in white around the text "Horizontal Alignment Sample." (The Buttons have no margin.) Figure 2-10 shows what you see as output.

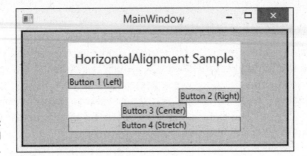

FIGURE 2-10:
Margin and
Padding.

Shared size groups

Most complex windows require multiple panels to achieve the desired user experience. This can introduce erratic windows if the size of the content in one grid is different from that of the other. Figure 2-10 illustrates the problem.

Fortunately, there is a simple solution. By setting the `Grid.IsSharedSizeScope` attached property on the *parent* grid, all the child grids can define `Rows` and `Columns` that subscribe to a `SharedSizeGroup`, and the rendering engine will ensure that they are sized correctly. The following code provides an example that doesn't use shared sizing:

```
<Grid Grid.IsSharedSizeScope="False">
    <Grid.RowDefinitions>
        <RowDefinition Height="Auto"/>
        <RowDefinition Height="Auto"/>
        <RowDefinition Height="Auto"/>
        <RowDefinition Height="Auto"/>
        <RowDefinition Height="Auto"/>
        <RowDefinition Height="Auto"/>
    </Grid.RowDefinitions>
    <Grid Grid.Row="0" Grid.RowSpan="3" Grid.Column="0">
        <Grid.RowDefinitions>
            <RowDefinition Height="Auto"/>
            <RowDefinition Height="Auto"/>
            <RowDefinition Height="Auto"/>
        </Grid.RowDefinitions>
        <Grid.ColumnDefinitions>
            <ColumnDefinition Width="Auto" SharedSizeGroup="Header"/>
            <ColumnDefinition Width="*"/>
        </Grid.ColumnDefinitions>
        <Label  Grid.Row="0" Grid.Column="0" Grid.ColumnSpan="2"
                Content="Zoo Animals"
                HorizontalContentAlignment="Center"/>
        <Label Grid.Row="1" Grid.Column="0" Content="Hippopotamus"
                HorizontalContentAlignment="Stretch"/>
```

```
    <TextBox Grid.Row="1" Grid.Column="1"
            HorizontalAlignment="Stretch" BorderThickness="2"/>
    <Label Grid.Row="2" Grid.Column="0" Content="Giraffe"
            HorizontalContentAlignment="Stretch"/>
    <TextBox Grid.Row="2" Grid.Column="1"
            HorizontalAlignment="Stretch" BorderThickness="2"/>
</Grid>
<Grid Grid.Row="3" Grid.RowSpan="3" Grid.Column="0">
    <Grid.RowDefinitions>
        <RowDefinition Height="Auto"/>
        <RowDefinition Height="Auto"/>
        <RowDefinition Height="Auto"/>
    </Grid.RowDefinitions>
    <Grid.ColumnDefinitions>
        <ColumnDefinition Width="Auto" SharedSizeGroup="Header"/>
        <ColumnDefinition Width="*"/>
    </Grid.ColumnDefinitions>
    <Label   Grid.Row="0" Grid.Column="1" Grid.ColumnSpan="2"
            Content="Pets" HorizontalContentAlignment="Center"/>
    <Label   Grid.Row="1" Grid.Column="0" Content="Cats"
            HorizontalContentAlignment="Left"/>
    <TextBox Grid.Row="1" Grid.Column="1"
            HorizontalAlignment="Stretch" BorderThickness="2"/>
    <Label   Grid.Row="2" Grid.Column="0" Content="Dogs"
            HorizontalContentAlignment="Left"/>
    <TextBox Grid.Row="2" Grid.Column="1"
            HorizontalAlignment="Stretch" BorderThickness="2"/>
    </Grid>
</Grid>
```

Figure 2-11 shows the output of this example. Note that the individual grid elements don't align their content. However, the content is aligned within a particular group.

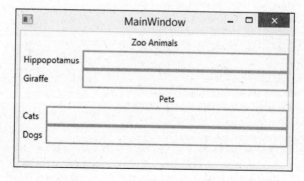

FIGURE 2-11: Multiple grids without shared sizing.

Setting `Grid.IsSharedSizeScope="False"` to `Grid.IsSharedSizeScope="True"` changes the output. Figure 2-12 shows that all the content is now aligned.

Putting it all together with a simple data entry form

For complex data entry forms, the `DataGrid` is the most appropriate form to use. (For more information, see the section "Exploring Common XAML Controls," later in this chapter.) The data entry form in this example uses multiple grids to achieve the desired look. The text boxes are contained in columns with star sizing so that they will grow and shrink with the form. Also notice how the buttons stay in the same relative position as the form size changes. Here is the XAML used to build the window shown in Figures 2-13.

```xaml
<Grid Background="FloralWhite">
    <Grid.RowDefinitions>
        <RowDefinition Height="Auto"/>
        <RowDefinition Height="Auto"/>
        <RowDefinition Height="Auto"/>
        <RowDefinition Height="Auto"/>
        <RowDefinition Height="Auto"/>
        <RowDefinition Height="10"/>
        <RowDefinition Height="Auto"/>
    </Grid.RowDefinitions>
    <Grid.ColumnDefinitions>
        <ColumnDefinition Width="Auto"/>
        <ColumnDefinition Width="Auto"/>
        <ColumnDefinition Width="*"/>
        <ColumnDefinition Width="Auto"/>
    </Grid.ColumnDefinitions>
    <Label  Grid.Row="0" Grid.Column="0" Grid.RowSpan="2" Content="Name"
            HorizontalAlignment="Stretch" HorizontalContentAlignment="Center">
```

```xml
        <Label.LayoutTransform>
            <RotateTransform Angle="-90"/>
        </Label.LayoutTransform>
    </Label>
    <Label Grid.Row="0" Grid.Column="1" Content="First:"
            HorizontalAlignment="Stretch" HorizontalContentAlignment="Right"/>
    <TextBox Grid.Row="0" Grid.Column="2" HorizontalAlignment="Stretch"/>
    <Label Grid.Row="1" Grid.Column="1" Content="Last:"
            HorizontalAlignment="Stretch" HorizontalContentAlignment="Right"/>
    <TextBox Grid.Row="1" Grid.Column="2" HorizontalAlignment="Stretch"/>
    <Label Grid.Row="2" Grid.Column="1" Content="Address:"
            HorizontalAlignment="Stretch" HorizontalContentAlignment="Right"/>
    <TextBox Grid.Row="2" Grid.Column="2" HorizontalAlignment="Stretch"/>
    <Label Grid.Row="3" Grid.Column="1" Content="City:"
            HorizontalAlignment="Stretch" HorizontalContentAlignment="Right"/>
    <TextBox Grid.Row="3" Grid.Column="2" HorizontalAlignment="Stretch"/>
    <Button Grid.Row="3" Grid.Column="3" Content="Lookup" Margin="3,0,3,0"/>
    <Label Grid.Row="4" Grid.Column="1" Content="State:"
            HorizontalAlignment="Stretch" HorizontalContentAlignment="Right"/>
    <Grid Grid.Row="4" Grid.Column="2">
        <Grid.RowDefinitions>
            <RowDefinition Height="*"/>
        </Grid.RowDefinitions>
        <Grid.ColumnDefinitions>
            <ColumnDefinition Width="*"/>
            <ColumnDefinition Width="Auto"/>
            <ColumnDefinition Width="2*"/>
        </Grid.ColumnDefinitions>
        <TextBox Grid.Row="0" Grid.Column="0" HorizontalAlignment="Stretch"/>
        <Label Grid.Row="0" Grid.Column="1" Content="Zip:"
HorizontalAlignment="Right"/>
        <TextBox Grid.Row="0" Grid.Column="2" HorizontalAlignment="Stretch"/>
    </Grid>
    <Grid Grid.Row="6" Grid.Column="0" Grid.ColumnSpan="3">
        <Grid.RowDefinitions>
            <RowDefinition Height="Auto"/>
        </Grid.RowDefinitions>
        <Grid.ColumnDefinitions>
            <ColumnDefinition Width="*"/>
            <ColumnDefinition Width="Auto"/>
            <ColumnDefinition Width="Auto"/>
        </Grid.ColumnDefinitions>
        <Button Grid.Row="0" Grid.Column="1" Content="Save" Margin="3,0"/>
        <Button Grid.Row="0" Grid.Column="2" Content="Close" Margin="3,0"/>
    </Grid>
</Grid>
```

And yes, that's a *lot* of XAML! One of the many great things about WPF is the flexibility to create just about any look and feel you can dream up. But sometimes (well, most of the time), it will take a lot of angle brackets.

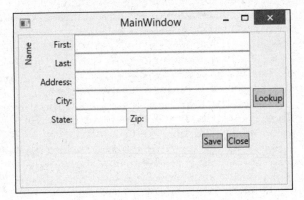

FIGURE 2-13:
Simple data entry form.

In addition to using XAML for layout, you can do all the examples shown exclusively in code. Fixed sizing is specified by assigning a number to the `Width` property of the `ColumnDefinition` or `RowDefinition`. Assigning `Auto` or `*` is more complicated because the `Width` property is of type `GridLength`, as shown in the following code. (You can find additional examples at `http://msdn.microsoft.com/en-us/library/system.windows.gridunittype.aspx`.)

```
//Set to Auto sizing
column1 = new ColumnDefinition();
column1.Width = new GridLength(1, GridUnitType.Auto);
//Set to Star sizing
column2 = new ColumnDefinition();
column2.Width = new GridLength(1, GridUnitType.Star);
```

Panels of honorable mention

In addition to the panels already discussed, there are four additional specialized layout panels. The book doesn't cover them because they're specialized:

>> `TabPanel`: Handles the layout of items on a `TabControl`.

>> `ToolbarPanel`: Handles the layout of items in a `Toolbar`.

>> `ToolbarOverflowPanel`: Handles the layout of the controls that overflow from a `Toolbar`.

» `VirtualizingStackPanel`: Used for large amounts of data binding scenarios. Renders only the visible items in the data collection.

» **InkCanvas:** Canvas panel that accepts digital ink input. Used for scenarios like collection of signatures with Tablet PCs.

Exploring Common XAML Controls

A significant number of controls ship out of the box with Visual Studio 2017 (and more and more vendor-supplied controls are available for free download and purchase). This section covers the more commonly used controls. Many developers prefer to divide the available controls into three categories:

» Display-only controls

» Basic input controls

» List- based controls

All the controls in this section are bindable to data (see Chapter 3 in this minibook) and modifiable through code.

Display-only controls

Four main controls focus on displaying information to the user, as shown in Figure 2-14:

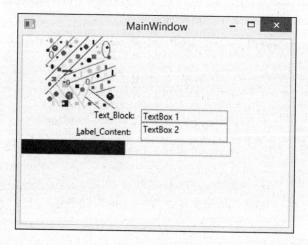

FIGURE 2-14:
Display-only
controls.

» **Image:** The Image control displays images (of type `.bmp`, `.gif`, `.ico`, `.jpg`, `.png`, `.wdp`, and `.tiff`). To preserve the image's aspect ratio, set the `Width` *or* `Height`, but not both. Additionally, the `DecodePixelWidth` should be set to the same size as the `Width`. This will cause the rendering engine to scale the image appropriately, potentially saving a significant amount of memory.

Note, by the way, that you can put images almost anywhere in WPF — for example, how about an image on a button, in a label, or inline in a paragraph of text. And it's quite easy. It's not so fancy here, but you should know about this possibility.

The following code shows the XAML to load an image that shows a fancy-looking bit of color. Only the `Width` is set.

```
<Image Grid.Row="0" Grid.Column="0" Width="100" >
    <Image.Source>
        <BitmapImage UriSource="/Images/Colorblk.gif"/>
    </Image.Source>
</Image>
```

» **TextBlock and Label:** Both the `TextBlock` and the `Label` controls are designed to provide text or other content to the user with a few distinctions. The `TextBlock` control is designed to be the lightweight "little brother" to the label, deriving directly from UIElement.

The `Label` control provides access-modifier capability and also derives from `ContentControl`, which opens up additional possibilities. Placing an underscore (_) before a letter enables the access modifiers. To provide an underscore in the `Label`, use a double underscore. In XAML, because it is essentially XML, the underscore is used because an ampersand would break the XAML. The `Target` attribute specifies the control to receive focus when the access modifier is keyed. You have to use a binding expression, which is covered in Chapter 3 of this minibook.

Both the `TextBlock` and `Label` controls are illustrated in the following code:

```
<TextBlock Grid.Row="1" Grid.Column="0" Margin="5,0"
        HorizontalAlignment="Right" Text="Text_Block:"/>
<TextBox Grid.Row="1" Grid.Column="1" Margin="5,0"
        HorizontalAlignment="Stretch" Text="TextBox 1"/>
<Label Grid.Row="2" Grid.Column="0" Margin="5,0"
        HorizontalAlignment="Stretch"
        HorizontalContentAlignment="Right"
        Content="_Label__Content:"
        Target="{Binding ElementName=SampleTextBox}"/>
```

```
<TextBox Name="SampleTextBox" Grid.Row="2" Grid.Column="1"
         Margin="5,0"
         HorizontalAlignment="Stretch" Text="TextBox 2"/>
```

In the sample, the *L* in the Label content is the access modifier, and the double underscore adds an underscore character to the rendered output.

» ProgressBar: The final display-only control is the progress bar. Although technically a descendant of the RangeBase class, it does not enable user input as the slider does (see the next section). The following code shows a progress bar sample. To have the bar in perpetual motion, set the IsIndeterminate property to True:

```
<ProgressBar Grid.Row="3" Grid.Column="0" Maximum="100"
             Minimum="1" Value="50" IsIndeterminate="False"
             Height="20" Width="300" Grid.ColumnSpan="2"
             Foreground="Blue" Background="White"/>
```

Basic input controls

The workhorses of line of business applications are the basic input controls. You find some of these on every window you create, and they are very straightforward. Figure 2-15 shows all these controls on a single window. Here are the basic input controls:

» TextBox and PasswordBox: The TextBox and PasswordBox both allow for the input of standard text into the window. The PasswordBox obfuscates the characters typed (using either the default system password character or a developer-specified character) and is used for collecting sensitive information. The TextBox exposes its contents through the Text property, the PasswordBox through the Password property.

```
<StackPanel Grid.Row="0">
    <TextBox Text="Some Text"/>
    <PasswordBox PasswordChar="X" Password="Some Text"/>
</StackPanel>
```

» **CheckBox:** Check boxes represent Boolean values through the `IsChecked` property. The `IsChecked` property is nullable, which provides for three-state display (True, False, Unknown). Use a horizontally oriented `StackPanel` to lay CheckBoxes out horizontally, with some margin to separate the boxes:

```xml
<StackPanel Grid.Row="1" Orientation="Horizontal">
    <CheckBox IsChecked="True"
              Content="true" Margin="15,15"/>
    <CheckBox IsChecked="false"
              Content="False" Margin="15,15"/>
    <CheckBox IsChecked="{x:Null}" Content="Null" Margin="15,15"/>
</StackPanel>
```

» **RadioButton:** Radio buttons allow for a single selection within a range of choices. The choices are determined by the `GroupName` property. After one of the radio buttons is selected, the group can be entirely deselected only programmatically.

```xml
<StackPanel Grid.Row="2" Orientation="Horizontal">
    <RadioButton GroupName="RBSample"
                 IsChecked="true"
                 Content="Red" Margin="15,15"/>
    <RadioButton GroupName="RBSample"
                 Content="White" Margin="15,15"/>
    <RadioButton GroupName="RBSample"
                 Content="Blue" Margin="15,15"/>
</StackPanel>
```

» `Slider`: The slider control is a ranged input control. Similar to the `ProgressBar`, the control takes `Minimum`, `Maximum`, and `Interval` values. Additionally, you can specify to show ticks, the location, and the tick frequency. *Ticks?* Those are the value lines that show on sliders.

```xml
<StackPanel Grid.Row="3">
    <Slider Interval="1" Minimum="1" Maximum="10"
            IsSnapToTickEnabled="True"
            TickPlacement="BottomRight"
            TickFrequency="1"/>
</StackPanel>
```

>> DatePicker: The DatePicker control provides a concise method for getting (or displaying) date information by combining a TextBox with a Calendar control. Included in the many options is the capability to select multiple dates for a range of dates.

```
<StackPanel Grid.Row="4">
    <DatePicker/>
</StackPanel>
```

>> Calendar: The difference between the Calendar control and the DatePicker is that the Calendar control is always in full display mode whereas the DatePicker's default look is similar to a text box.

```
<StackPanel Grid.Row="5">
    <Calendar/>
</StackPanel>
```

>> Button: The Button control doesn't really fit in with the other controls in this section because it's more of an action control. Buttons respond to a user's click. To use this control, you begin with the XAML shown here:

```
<StackPanel Grid.Row="6">
    <Button Content="Click Me" Click="Button_Click" Width="60"/>
</StackPanel>
```

However, to make this control work, you must also provide code behind code in the .cs file. The connection between this code and the XAML comes from the Click attribute. Here is the code-behind, which displays only a simple message box in this case.

```
private void Button_Click(object sender, RoutedEventArgs e)
{
    MessageBox.Show("Hello World");
}
```

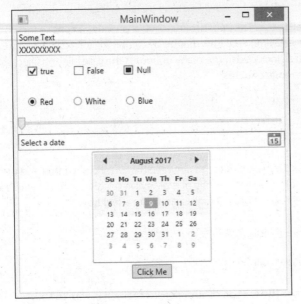

FIGURE 2-15:
All the basic input controls.

List-based controls

The list-based controls (also referred to as `Item` controls) add an incredible amount of flexibility. As discussed in Chapter 1 of this minibook, the list-based controls no longer have to rely on data tricks or other magic to make the content meaningful to the user but can be templated to show greater details about the items contained.

Data binding is covered in great detail in Chapter 3 of this minibook, but the controls don't do anything unless you have something to show. In this case, the examples take an extremely simple approach, the control content is hard coded. However, you do have other options and it's important to know that you do. Here are the list-based controls:

>> ComboBox and ListBox: The ListBox and the ComboBox in the sample below present a group of list items. However, you have other choices, including buttons and menu items. The main difference between the two controls is that the ComboBox displays a single item with a drop-down selector (see Figure 2-16), and the ListBox shows the entire list of items up to the allowed space and then scrolls the rest. The ComboBox can be set up to enable selecting items that are *not* in the list, as well as editing the items in the list.

```
<ComboBox Grid.Column="0" Height="20" Width="100"
        HorizontalAlignment="Stretch" VerticalAlignment="Top">
    <ListBoxItem Content="One"/>
    <ListBoxItem Content="Two"/>
    <ListBoxItem Content="Three"/>
    <ListBoxItem Content="Four"/>
    <ListBoxItem Content="Five"/>
</ComboBox>
<ListBox Grid.Column="1" Height="150" Width="100"
        HorizontalAlignment="Stretch" VerticalAlignment="Top">
    <ListBoxItem Content="One"/>
    <ListBoxItem Content="Two"/>
    <ListBoxItem Content="Three"/>
    <ListBoxItem Content="Four"/>
    <ListBoxItem Content="Five"/>
</ListBox>
```

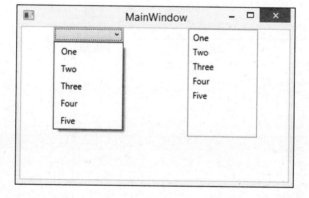

FIGURE 2-16:
The ComboBox
(left) and
ListBox (right).

» TreeView: The TreeView is a hierarchical ItemsControl much like Windows
Explorer. The nodes (or branches) can be expanded or contracted, giving a
nice user interface into any multilevel data. (See Figure 2-17.) The sample uses
hard-coded data, but with a simple hierarchical template, tree views can be
bound just as any other control can.

```
<TreeView Name="myTreeViewEvent" >
    <TreeViewItem Header="Employee1" IsSelected="True">
        <TreeViewItem Header="Jesper Aaberg"/>
        <TreeViewItem Header="Employee Number">
            <TreeViewItem Header="12345"/>
        </TreeViewItem>
```

CHAPTER 2 **Understanding the Basics of WPF**   **677**

```
                <TreeViewItem Header="Work Days">
                    <TreeViewItem Header="Monday"/>
                    <TreeViewItem Header="Tuesday"/>
                    <TreeViewItem Header="Thursday"/>
                </TreeViewItem>
            </TreeViewItem>
            <TreeViewItem Header="Employee2">
                <TreeViewItem Header="Dominik Paiha"/>
                <TreeViewItem Header="Employee Number">
                    <TreeViewItem Header="98765"/>
                </TreeViewItem>
                <TreeViewItem Header="Work Days">
                    <TreeViewItem Header="Tuesday"/>
                    <TreeViewItem Header="Wednesday"/>
                    <TreeViewItem Header="Friday"/>
                </TreeViewItem>
            </TreeViewItem>
        </TreeView>
```

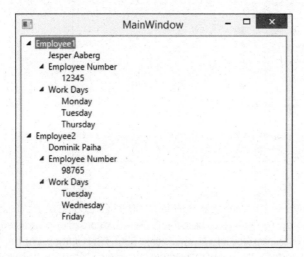

FIGURE 2-17:
The `TreeView`.

» `DataGrid`: Conspicuously absent from the earlier versions of WPF, this control was part of the WPF Toolkit, an *out-of-band* release (one made outside the usual delivery schedule) available from http://www.codeplex.com/ (still a great resource for WPF information). The `DataGrid` has five base columns:

- *DataGridTextColumn:* For Text

- *DataGridCheckBoxColumn:* For Boolean

- *DataGridComboBoxColumn:* For ListItems

- *DataGridHyperlinkColumn:* For displaying Links

- *DataGridTemplateColumn:* For designing custom columns

The DataGrid can be set to AutoGenerate the columns based on the data it is bound to. It then uses reflection to determine the best column type based on the data. Because this control relies on data binding, you see it demonstrated further in Chapter 3.

Chapter **3**

Data Binding in WPF

ata binding allows data from your application objects (the binding source) to be displayed in your user interface elements (the binding target). What this means is that you can bind a Textbox Text property (for example) to the Name property of an instance of your Car class. Depending on the binding mode used when setting up the relationship, changes in the Text property value of the Textbox can automatically update the underlying Name property of your Car object (and vice versa) without requiring any additional code.

It's no mystery these days that most applications deal with data. As a WPF developer, you have full creative reign on how data is presented and how information entered by your user can be validated and used to update your underlying objects. One of WPF's strengths is its rich data binding support. This chapter walks you through the details.

Getting to Know Dependency Properties

Data binding happens when you set up a relationship between a binding source property and binding target property. The binding target object must be a DependencyObject, and the target property must be a DependencyProperty.

Understanding dependency properties is crucial to obtaining a firm grasp on WPF technology. Dependency properties are found in objects that inherit from

DependencyObject. At its root, a dependency property extends the functionality of a regular property that already exists on a CLR object by adding a set of services that is also known as the WPF Property System. (Together, DependencyObject and DependencyProperty make up this property system.) Dependency properties can have their values determined by multiple input sources, meaning that their values can be obtained through a Style or a data binding expression. Dependency properties act like regular properties, but they allow you to set values based on the following:

>> **A default value:** These are predefined on the property.

>> **A calculated expression (similar to CSS expressions in the web world):** This can be a data binding expression or a reference to resources defined in the application.

>> **Data binding:** This actually is built upon the preceding bullet using binding expressions on the binding source object.

>> **Property value inheritance:** Not to be confused with object inheritance, property value inheritance allows values set on parent properties to be propagated down to its children. For instance, if you set FontSize values on the Window element (the root element), child elements such as TextBlock and Label automatically inherit those font property values. You can see another example of this by reviewing the concept of attached properties introduced in Chapter 1 of this minibook.

>> **Styling:** Each style typically contains setters to set one or more property values.

The WPF property system also provides built-in property value change notification and property value validation functionality, which is reviewed in the section "Editing, Evaluating, Converting, and Visualizing Your Data," later in this chapter.

At the end of the day, dependency properties give the developer the capability to set property values directly in XAML as well as in code. The advantage to this is that you can keep your code clean and leave initializing object property values to XAML.

Exploring the Binding Modes

You have full control over how the binding relationship you create behaves. Multiple types of binding modes are available to you in WPF. These include the following:

>> **The OneTime binding mode** is used when you want the source property to only initially set the target property value. Subsequent changes to the source property are not reflected in the target property. Similarly, changes to the target property are not reflected in the source property.

>> **The** OneWay **binding mode** is typically used for read-only behaving properties. In this binding mode, data from the source property sets the initial value of the target property. Subsequent changes to the source property will automatically update the binding target property value. Conversely, any subsequent changes made to the target property value are not reflected in the source property.

>> **The** OneWayToSource **binding mode** is essentially the opposite of the OneWay binding mode. In this binding mode, data from the source property initializes the target property value. Subsequent changes to the source property value will not update the target property. However, updates to the target property value will automatically update the source property value.

>> **The** TwoWay **binding mode** merges the functionality of the OneWay and OneWayToSource binding modes. In this binding mode, the source property value initializes the target property value. Subsequent changes to the source property value update the target property value. Similarly, updates to the target property value will update the source property value.

Investigating the Binding Object

Bindings can be defined using code or XAML. Here you begin with the XAML version. To see how to bind data to your UI elements, you first define a test set of data to work with.

Defining a binding with XAML

Just follow these steps to create a binding with XAML:

1. **Create a new WPF Application project and name it** BindingSample1.

2. **Define a simple** Car **class by adding a new** Class **to your solution named** Car.cs **and code it as follows (note that you don't need any** using **statements in this case):**

```
namespace BindingSample1
{
    public class Car
    {
        private string _make;
```

```
    public string Make
    {
        get { return _make; }
        set { _make = value; }
    }

    private string _model;

    public string Model
    {
        get { return _model; }
        set { _model = value; }
    }

    public Car() { }
    }
}
```

3. In `MainWindow.xaml`, **replace the grid with one that defines a double column and single row grid; then add a label in each grid cell, like this:**

```
<Grid>
    <Grid.ColumnDefinitions>
        <ColumnDefinition></ColumnDefinition>
        <ColumnDefinition></ColumnDefinition>
    </Grid.ColumnDefinitions>
    <Grid.RowDefinitions>
        <RowDefinition></RowDefinition>
    </Grid.RowDefinitions>
    <Label x:Name="lblCarMake" Grid.Row="0" Grid.Column="0"
        Content="{Binding Path=Make, Mode=OneTime}"/>
    <Label x:Name="lblCarModel" Grid.Row="0" Grid.Column="1"
        Content="{Binding Path=Model, Mode=OneTime}"/>
</Grid>
```

Look at the Content dependency property value. The information contained within the curly braces defines the binding for the content to be displayed in the labels. The next section describes what this Binding expression means, but first you need some data to bind to.

4. **Open the** `MainWindow.xaml.cs` **code-behind file and create a method called** `GenerateData` **in the** `MainWindow` **class that instantiates a** Car **object and assigns it to the** DataContext **of the window, like this:**

```
private void GenerateData()
{
    Car car1 = new Car() { Make = "Athlon", Model = "XYZ" };
    this.DataContext = car1;
}
```

TECHNICAL STUFF

DataContext defines the root object relative to which all child elements obtain their values (as long as the DataContext value on the child elements isn't directly set via XAML or code — this property is an example of property value inheritance; its value is obtained from its parent element unless otherwise specified).

5. **Call the** GenerateData() **method in the** MainWindow **constructor method (public MainWindow()), immediately following** InitializeComponents() **call.**

Now, looking back to the XAML file (MainWindow.xaml), the first label lblCarMake will bind to the DataContext's Make property. The value is retrieved from the property specified in the binding's Path component. Similarly, the second label, lblCarModel, will bind to the DataContext's Model property as specified in the binding expression's Path property. Each of these bindings is using a OneTime mode, which means that the label content will be bound only once, regardless of the underlying object property being bound to changes.

TECHNICAL STUFF

The Path component of the XAML Binding expression simply tells the XAML processor to take its value from a specific property of its DataContext. The Path value can also express properties that are nested, such as in the case of nested complex objects. In these cases, you use dot notation to reach the desired property, such as Property.SomeObject.SomeOtherProperty.

6. **Run the application.**

You can see that the labels now display the Make and Model of the Car object that was assigned to the DataContext of the window. (See Figure 3-1.)

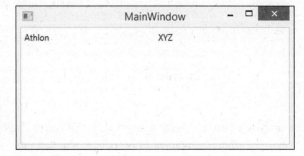

FIGURE 3-1:
Data binding to properties of a DataContext.

Defining a binding with C#

You can also use C# to define bindings. To demonstrate this, remove the Content attribute entirely from both labels in the XAML file. The label markup should now resemble the following:

```
<Label x:Name="lblCarMake" Grid.Row="0" Grid.Column="0"/>
<Label x:Name="lblCarModel" Grid.Row="0" Grid.Column="1"/>
```

Modify the GenerateData() method in MainWindow.xaml.cs to implement the Binding definitions in code. To do this, you must instantiate Binding objects directly. The constructor of the Binding object takes in the string Path value. Use the BindingOperations class to apply the Binding to the Content dependency property of your labels.

TECHNICAL STUFF

BindingOperations is a helper class provided to you by WPF. It has static methods that give you the power to add and clear data binding definitions on application elements.

The following code shows you how to define the Binding objects and assign the binding to the Content of the labels:

```
private void GenerateData()
{
    Car car1 = new Car() { Make = "Athlon", Model = "XYZ" };

    Binding makeBinding = new Binding("Make");
    makeBinding.Mode = BindingMode.OneTime;
    BindingOperations.SetBinding(lblCarMake,
            Label.ContentProperty, makeBinding);

    Binding modelBinding = new Binding("Model");
    modelBinding.Mode = BindingMode.OneTime;
    BindingOperations.SetBinding(lblCarModel,
            Label.ContentProperty, modelBinding);

    this.DataContext = car1;
}
```

Run the application and observe that it runs the same way as when the bindings were defined using XAML.

REMEMBER

Dependency properties are typically defined with the suffix *Property*, but you see them this way only when navigating MSDN documentation and accessing them through code. In XAML, you specify dependency property attributes by dropping the *Property* suffix from the name.

Editing, Validating, Converting, and Visualizing Your Data

In the preceding section, you got a taste of binding syntax and saw data appear on the screen. This section builds on this knowledge and shows you a simple example of updating data, from user interface elements as well as updating the user interface with changes happening to objects behind the scenes. To create an environment in which updates can occur, follow these steps:

1. **Create a new WPF Application project and name it** BindingSample2.

2. **Right-click the solution entry in Solution Explorer and choose Add⇨Existing Item from the context menu.**

   You see the Add Existing Item dialog box.

3. **Highlight the** Car.cs **file located in the** C:\CSAIO4D\BK05\CH03\ BindingSample1\BindingSample1 **folder and click Add.**

   Visual Studio adds the Car class file to your project.

4. **Double-click** Car.cs **in Solution Explorer.**

   You see the file open in the editor.

5. **Change the** BindingSample1 **namespace to** BindingSample2.

   The Car class is now ready for use in this example.

   In this example, you display the make and model of a Car object (the DataContext) in TextBox controls. This enables you to edit the values of the Car properties. You will also use a TwoWay data binding mode so that changes made from the user interface will be reflected in the underlying Car object, and any changes made to the Car object from code-behind will be reflected in the user interface.

6. **Define two buttons, one that shows a message box containing the current value of the** DataContext **and another that forces changes to the** DataContext **through code-behind.**

   In MainWindow.xaml, replace the Grid content with this:

```
<Grid>
    <Grid.ColumnDefinitions>
        <ColumnDefinition></ColumnDefinition>
        <ColumnDefinition></ColumnDefinition>
    </Grid.ColumnDefinitions>
</Grid.ColumnDefinitions>
```

```xaml
<Grid.RowDefinitions>
    <RowDefinition></RowDefinition>
    <RowDefinition></RowDefinition>
</Grid.RowDefinitions>

<StackPanel Orientation="Horizontal" Grid.Row="0"
        Grid.Column="0">
    <Label Content="Make"/>
    <TextBox x:Name="lblCarMake" VerticalAlignment="Top"
        Text="{Binding Path=Make, Mode=TwoWay}"
        Width="200" Height="25"/>
</StackPanel>

<StackPanel Orientation="Horizontal" Grid.Row="0"
        Grid.Column="1" >
    <Label Content="Model"/>
    <TextBox x:Name="lblCarModel" VerticalAlignment="Top"
        Text="{Binding Path=Model, Mode=TwoWay}"
        Width="200" Height="25"/>
</StackPanel>

<Button x:Name="btnShowDataContextValue"
        Click="btnShowDataContextValue_Click"
        Content="Show Current Data Context Value"
        Grid.Row="1" Grid.Column="0"/>

<Button x:Name="btnChangeDataContextValue"
        Click="btnChangeDataContextValue_Click"
        Content="Change Data Context Value with Code-Behind"
        Grid.Row="1" Grid.Column="1"/>
</Grid>
```

7. **In the code-behind file,** `MainWindow.xaml.cs`, **add the following methods:**

```csharp
private void GenerateData()
{
    Car car1 = new Car() { Make = "Athlon", Model = "XYZ" };
    this.DataContext = car1;
}

private void btnShowDataContextValue_Click(object sender,
                                    RoutedEventArgs e)
```

```
{
    Car dc = this.DataContext as Car;
    MessageBox.Show("Car Make: " + dc.Make + "\nCar Model: "
                    + dc.Model);
}

private void btnChangeDataContextValue_Click(object sender,
                                             RoutedEventArgs e)
{
    Car dc = this.DataContext as Car;
    dc.Make = "Changed Make";
    dc.Model = "Changed Model";
}
```

8. **In the constructor for** `MainWindow()`, **add a call to the** `GenerateData()` **method immediately following the** `InitializeComponents()` **call.**

9. **Run this application.**

You see that the values from the `DataContext` display properly in the `TextBox` controls. Feel free to change the values in the `TextBox` controls. For instance, change the `Make` value to `Athlon X`, and the model to ABC. When you finish with your edits, click the Show Current Data Context Value button. The changes you made to the values in the `TextBox` are now reflected in the underlying `DataContext` object. (See Figure 3-2.)

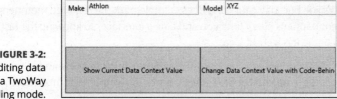

FIGURE 3-2:
Editing data
using a TwoWay
binding mode.

10. **Click OK to get rid of the message box.**

If you look in the `Click` event handler of the Change Data Context Value With Code-Behind button (`btnChangeDataContextValue_Click`), you will note that the `DataContext Car` object properties will be changed to `ChangedMake` and `Changed Model`, respectively.

11. **Click the Change Data Context Value With Code-Behind button.**

Hmmm. Nothing is happening. What's up with that? If you click the Show Current Data Context Value button, you see that the properties have in fact been changed. Because you're using a TwoWay binding, your settings should automatically update your UI, right? Wrong! This is where another feature of WPF, the concept of INotifyPropertyChanged, comes into play.

TECHNICAL STUFF

INotifyPropertyChanged is a simple interface that allows your objects to raise an event that notifies its subscribers (namely your application) that a property value on the object has changed. Client applications subscribe to these events and update the user interface with the new values only when changes occur.

TECHNICAL STUFF

A similar interface exists for collections as well — the INotifyCollection Changed interface. WPF also provides a generic class called Observable Collection<T> that already implements INotifyCollectionChanged for you. When creating an ObservableCollection or your own collection that implements INotifyCollectionChanged, you need to ensure that the objects that will be contained within the collection also implement INotifyPropertyChanged interface.

The INotifyPropertyChanged interface contains a single event that must be implemented. This event is called PropertyChanged, and its parameters are the object that owns the property that has changed (the sender), and the string name of the property that has changed.

12. **Open your** Car **class and add the** using System.ComponentModel; **statement to allow access to** INotifyPropertyChanged.

13. **Type:** **INotifyPropertyChanged after** public class Car **to add the required interface to your class.**

Note that INotifyPropertyChanged has a red underline beneath it. You see this underline because your class doesn't implement the required members. This event happens every time you add a new interface, so knowing the fastest way to handle it is a good idea.

14. **Right-click** INotifyPropertyChanged, **choose Quick Actions and Refactorings from the context menu, and click Implement Interface.**

Visual Studio adds the following code for you:

```
public event PropertyChangedEventHandler PropertyChanged;
```

For the application to be notified of the changes that occur in Car objects, the PropertyChanged event must be fired each time a property value has changed.

15. **To implement this in the** Car **class, create a helper method called** NotifyPropertyChanged **that takes in a string property name and fires the** PropertyChanged **event for the object instance and the name of the property that has changed, like this:**

```
private void NotifyPropertyChanged(string propertyName)
{
    if (PropertyChanged != null)
    {
        this.PropertyChanged(this,
            new PropertyChangedEventArgs(propertyName));
    }
}
```

TECHNICAL STUFF

Checking to see whether PropertyChanged is not null essentially means you're checking to see whether anyone is listening (subscribed) to the Property Changed event.

16. **Modify the** Set **methods in each of the public properties on the** Car **object to call the** NotifyPropertyChanged **helper method each time the property value has changed; edit the public properties, like this:**

```
private string _make;

public string Make
{
    get { return _make; }
    set
    {
        if (_make != value)
        {
            _make = value;
            NotifyPropertyChanged("Make");
        }
    }
}

private string _model;

public string Model
{
    get { return _model; }
    set
    {
        if (_model != value)
        {
            _model = value;
            NotifyPropertyChanged("Model");
        }
    }
}
```

17. **Run the application again.**

Now when you click the Change Data Context Value with Code-Behind button, the changed values get reflected automatically in the TextBox elements. This is due to the combination of the TwoWay binding mode as well as the implementation of INotifyPropertyChanged. (See Figure 3-3.)

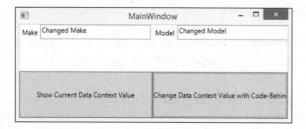

FIGURE 3-3:
Two-way data
binding with
INotify
Property
Changed.

ELEMENT BINDING

In this chapter, you bind Label and TextBox controls to properties of underlying objects. You're not limited to this scenario; you can bind to just about anything from primitive variables to property values gleaned from other UIElements. Element binding in particular has its own component in the Binding expression. For instance, suppose that you have a TextBox and Label control in your window. You'd like to have the Content of the Label automatically update with the changing value of the Text property of the TextBox. The XAML code to accomplish Element Binding between the TextBox and the Label looks similar to

```
<Label x:Name="lblCarMake"
        Content="{Binding ElementName=txtCarMake, Path=Text}"/>
<TextBox x:Name="txtCarMake" Width="200" Height="25"/>
```

The C# code to define this binding looks similar to

```
Binding b = new Binding("Text");
b.ElementName = "txtCarMake";
BindingOperations.SetBinding(lblCarMake, Label.ContentProperty, b);
```

Validating data

It's good practice to validate any input provided to you from the user. People aren't perfect, and some people can be downright malicious. WPF provides a built-in framework for data validation and error notification. It's available to you through the implementation of the IDataErrorInfo interface on your classes. You can add validation to the Car class you already created in BindingSample2 from the preceding section. Just follow these steps to add validation to your Car class:

1. **Open the** Car.cs **file and edit the class to also implement the** IDataErrorInfo **interface, like this:**

```
public class Car : INotifyPropertyChanged, IDataErrorInfo
```

Implementing this interface adds the following methods to the Car class:

```
public string Error => throw new NotImplementedException();

public string this[string columnName] =>
    throw new NotImplementedException();
```

2. **Edit the** Get **method of the** Error **property to return null by modifying the code to look like this:**

```
public string Error => null;
```

Now it's time to add some validation rules to the properties of the Car object. The Car Make and Model properties should enforce the rule that they must always be at least three characters in length. The public string this[string columnName] method is used by the DataBinding engine to validate the properties of the object as they are changed, based on the name of the property (which is what they mean by columnName in the method signature). This method returns any error messages related to the property being edited.

3. **To define and enforce these rules, edit the** public string this[string columnName] **method, like this:**

```
public string this[string columnName]
{
    get
    {
        string retvalue = null;
        if (columnName == "Make")
        {
            if (String.IsNullOrEmpty(this._make)
                || this._make.Length < 3)
```

```
            {
                retvalue = "Car Make must be at least 3 " +
                                "characters in length";
            }
        }


        if (columnName == "Model")
        {
            if (String.IsNullOrEmpty(this._model)
                    || this._model.Length < 3)
            {
                retvalue = "Car Model must be at least 3 " +
                                "characters in length";
            }
        }


        return retvalue;
    }
}
```

In `MainWindow.xaml`, the `Make` and `Model` properties are bound to `TextBox` controls in the user interface.

4. **To enable the text being entered into the TextBoxes to be validated against the constraints defined on the underlying property, edit the binding expressions in each** `TextBox`, **like this:**

```xml
<StackPanel Orientation="Horizontal" Grid.Row="0"
            Grid.Column="0">
    <Label Content="Make"/>
    <TextBox x:Name="txtCarMake"  VerticalAlignment="Top"
        Text="{Binding Path=Make, Mode=TwoWay,
                UpdateSourceTrigger=PropertyChanged,
                ValidatesOnDataErrors=True,
                ValidatesOnExceptions=True}"
        Width="200" Height="25"/>
</StackPanel>


<StackPanel Orientation="Horizontal" Grid.Row="0"
            Grid.Column="1" >
    <Label Content="Model"/>
```

```
    <TextBox x:Name="txtCarModel"  VerticalAlignment="Top"
        Text="{Binding Path=Model, Mode=TwoWay,
                UpdateSourceTrigger=PropertyChanged,
                ValidatesOnDataErrors=True,
                ValidatesOnExceptions=True}"
        Width="200" Height="25"/>
    </StackPanel>
```

UpdateSourceTrigger identifies when the validation calls take place. In this example, validations occur as the text is changing, and UpdateSourceTrigger is fired when the underlying object property fires the PropertyChanged event.

ValidatesOnDataErrors is what enables the IDataErrorInfo validation method to be called on the property.

ValidatesOnExceptions will invalidate the TextBox if the underlying data source throws an exception, such as when, for instance, you have an integer property and the user enters a string. WPF automatically throws the exception that the input string was not in the correct format.

5. **Run the Sample and remove all text from the** Make **and** Model TextBox **controls.**

   You see that the TextBox controls are now rendered in red; as you enter text into the TextBox, as soon as you reach three characters, the red stroke disappears.

   The red stroke is sufficient to indicate that an error has occurred, but it's of little use to the users because they're not informed of the details of the error. A simple way to display the error is to add a tooltip on the TextBox. Do this by adding a Style resource to your window that defines a style that will trigger the tooltip when the data is in an invalid state.

6. **Add the following XAML directly below the Window tag at the top of MainWindow.xaml, like this:**

```
<Window.Resources>
    <Style x:Key="errorAwareTextBox" TargetType="{x:Type TextBox}">
        <Style.Triggers>
            <Trigger Property="Validation.HasError" Value="true">
                <Setter Property="ToolTip"
                Value="{Binding RelativeSource={x:Static RelativeSource.Self},
                Path=(Validation.Errors)[0].ErrorContent}"/>
            </Trigger>
        </Style.Triggers>
    </Style>
</Window.Resources>
```

7. Add a `Style` attribute to your `TextBox` Style, like this:

```
Style="{StaticResource ResourceKey=errorAwareTextBox}"
```

Now when you run the application and remove the text from the TextBox controls, the `TextBox` displays a tooltip with the actual error message. (See Figure 3-4.)

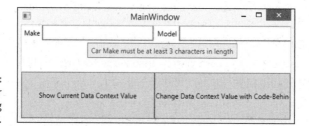

FIGURE 3-4:
Displaying error messages using Styles.

Converting your data

WPF provides you with the capability to create an intuitive user interface. Sometimes this means allowing users to enter data in different formats that make sense to them, giving you the responsibility of translating the user's data entry into a format allowable by your data source. The same is true vice versa; you want to translate data from your data source into a more intuitive form for the user. A popular use-case for this type of conversion is the string representation of a date value, or if you want to display a red or green circle instead of the values True or False. WPF makes converting data easy by providing a simple interface called `IValueConverter` to implement. This interface contains two methods:

» `Convert`: This method obtains values from the data source and molds them to the form to be displayed to the user onscreen.

» `ConvertBack`: This method does the opposite — it takes the value from the user interface and molds it into a form that the data source expects.

Be sure to note that with these methods, you're not held to the same data type as the value being bound. For instance, your data source property being bound can be a Date data type, and the `Convert` method can still return a string value to the user interface.

To demonstrate this feature, create a new WPF application project called `BindingSample3`. This project is a dashboard application that can show the status of servers on the network. In this project, you implement two user controls, `RedX` and `GreenCheck`. You also create a value converter named `BooleanToIconConverter` that converts a Boolean False value to display the RedX control and converts a True value to display the GreenCheck control. These values indicate whether the server is available.

A user control is a collection of reusable XAML. It can be made up of any number of elements and is implemented with the same rules as when you implement a normal Window (for instance, you can have only one root element). You can also define properties (including dependency properties!) on user controls. Follow these steps to create your sample:

1. **Create a new WPF application named** BindingSample3.

2. **Add a new User Control (WPF) to the project; name it** GreenCheck.xaml.

3. **Replace the** Grid **found in** GreenCheck.xaml **with this XAML:**

```
<Canvas x:Name="CheckCanvas" Width="50.4845" Height="49.6377"
        Canvas.Left="0" Canvas.Top="0">

    <Path x:Name="CheckPath" Width="43.4167" Height="45.6667"
        Canvas.Left="0" Canvas.Top="1.3113e-006"
        Stretch="Fill" Fill="#FF006432"
        Data="F1 M 19.0833,45.6667L 43.4167,2.16667L 38,
            1.3113e-006L 19.0833,42.5833L 2.41667,25.3333L 0,
            27.9167L 17.4167,44.25"/>
</Canvas>
```

You're not expected to come up with things like the CheckPath off the top of your head. (The path is what describes how the check mark is drawn.) Various designer tools help you to draw items graphically and export your final graphics in a XAML format. Expression Design (https://www.microsoft.com/download/details.aspx?id=36180) was the tool used to create the user controls in this example.

4. **Add another User Control (WPF) to the project; name it** RedX.xaml.

5. **Replace the** Grid **in the** RedX.xaml **file with this XAML:**

```
<Canvas Width="44.625" Height="45.9394">

    <Path x:Name="Line1Path" Width="44.625" Height="44.375"
        Canvas.Left="0" Canvas.Top="0" Stretch="Fill"
        Fill="#FFDE0909"
        Data="F1 M 0,3.5L 3.5,0L 44.625,41L 42.125,44.375"/>
```

```
<Path x:Name="Line2Path" Width="43.5772" Height="45.3813"
    Canvas.Left="0.201177" Canvas.Top="0.55809"
    Stretch="Fill"
    Fill="#FFDE0909" Data="F1 M 3.7719,45.9394L 0.201177,
        42.5115L 40.353,0.55809L 43.7784,2.98867"/>

</Canvas>
```

6. **Add a new class called** `BooleanToIconConverter.cs`.

7. **Add the following using statement to your class:**

```
using System.Windows.Data;
```

8. **Have the** `BooleanToIconConverter` **implement the** `IValueConverter`
interface.

The code should now contain the `Convert()` and `ConvertBack()` methods.

9. **Modify the** `Convert()` **method so that it looks like this:**

```
public object Convert(object value, Type targetType,
    object parameter, CultureInfo culture)
{
    if (value == null)
    {
        return value;
    }

    if ((bool)value == true)
    {
        return new GreenCheck();
    }
    else
    {
        return new RedX();
    }
}
```

10. **Add a new class called** `ServerStatus.cs`.

11. **Add three properties: the Server name, a Boolean indicator if the server
is up, and a number of currently connected users, as shown here:**

```
public class ServerStatus
{
    public string ServerName { get; set; }
    public bool IsServerUp { get; set; }
```

```
    public int NumberOfConnectedUsers { get; set; }

    public ServerStatus() { }
}
```

12. In `MainWindow.xaml.cs`, **create the** `GenerateData()` **method shown here:**

```
private void GenerateData()
{
    ServerStatus ss = new ServerStatus()
    {
        ServerName = "HeadquartersApplicationServer1",
        NumberOfConnectedUsers = 983,
        IsServerUp = true
    };

    ServerStatus ss2 = new ServerStatus()
    {
        ServerName = "HeadquartersFileServer1",
        NumberOfConnectedUsers = 0,
        IsServerUp = false
    };

    ServerStatus ss3 = new ServerStatus()
    {
        ServerName = "HeadquartersWebServer1",
        NumberOfConnectedUsers = 0,
        IsServerUp = false
    };

    ServerStatus ss4 = new ServerStatus()
    {
        ServerName = "HQDomainControllerServer1",
        NumberOfConnectedUsers = 10235,
        IsServerUp = true
    };

    List<ServerStatus> serverList = new List<ServerStatus>();
    serverList.Add(ss);
    serverList.Add(ss2);
    serverList.Add(ss3);
    serverList.Add(ss4);

    this.DataContext = serverList;
}
```

This code initializes a list of a few ServerStatus objects and makes that list the DataContext of the Window.

13. **Add a call to** GenerateData() **immediately after the call to the** InitializeComponent() **method in the** Window **constructor).**

14. **Save and build your application.**

You do this step so that the user control classes that you've defined are available to your XAML files.

15. **Add the following** Window.Resources **to** MainWindow.xaml **before the** Grid:

```
<<Window.Resources>
    <local:BooleanToIconConverter
        x:Key="BooleanToIconConverter"/>

    <DataTemplate x:Key="ServerTemplate">
        <Border BorderBrush="Blue" Margin="3" Padding="3"
                BorderThickness="2" CornerRadius="5"
                Background="Beige">

            <StackPanel Orientation="Horizontal">

                <Label Content="{Binding
                    Path=IsServerUp,
                    Converter={StaticResource
                        BooleanToIconConverter}}"/>

                <StackPanel Orientation="Vertical"
                        VerticalAlignment="Center">

                    <TextBlock FontSize="25"
                        Foreground="Goldenrod"
                        Text="{Binding Path=ServerName}"/>

                    <TextBlock FontSize="18"
                        Foreground="BlueViolet"
                        Text="{Binding
                            Path=NumberOfConnectedUsers}"/>
                </StackPanel>

            </StackPanel>
        </Border>
    </DataTemplate>

</Window.Resources>
```

16. Add the following code to the Grid in `MainWindow.xaml`:

```xaml
<Grid>
    <Grid.ColumnDefinitions>
        <ColumnDefinition/>
    </Grid.ColumnDefinitions>
    <Grid.RowDefinitions>
        <RowDefinition/>
    </Grid.RowDefinitions>

    <ListBox x:Name="lstServers" Width="490" Height="350"
            ItemsSource="{Binding}" Grid.Row="0" Grid.Column="0"
            ItemTemplate="{StaticResource
                ResourceKey=ServerTemplate}"/>
</Grid>
```

The first thing to note in `MainWindow.xaml` is that the namespace for the local assembly (`BindingSample3`) was added to the `Window` (identified by the namespace definition in the `Window` tag with the prefix `local`). This enables you to instantiate classes that are defined in the current assembly in XAML, such as `BooleanToIconConverter`.

```xaml
<Window x:Class="BindingSample3.MainWindow"
    xmlns="http://schemas.microsoft.com/winfx/2006/xaml/presentation"
    xmlns:x="http://schemas.microsoft.com/winfx/2006/xaml"
    xmlns:d="http://schemas.microsoft.com/expression/blend/2008"
    xmlns:mc="http://schemas.openxmlformats.org/markup-compatibility/2006"
    xmlns:local="clr-namespace:BindingSample3"
    mc:Ignorable="d"
    Title="MainWindow" Height="400" Width="500">
```

In the `Window` resources, you initialize an instance of your `BooleanToIcon Converter`, which is available to you through the local namespace.

```xaml
<local:BooleanToIconConverter x:Key="BooleanToIconConverter"/>
```

The next `Window` resource that is defined is a data template. This data template provides a way to look at the data associated with a server's current status. The data template is defined as follows:

```xaml
<DataTemplate x:Key="ServerTemplate">
    <Border BorderBrush="Blue" Margin="3" Padding="3"
            BorderThickness="2" CornerRadius="5"
            Background="Beige">

        <StackPanel Orientation="Horizontal">
```

```
<Label Content="{Binding
    Path=IsServerUp,
    Converter={StaticResource
        BooleanToIconConverter}}"/>

<StackPanel Orientation="Vertical"
        VerticalAlignment="Center">

    <TextBlock FontSize="25"
        Foreground="Goldenrod"
        Text="{Binding Path=ServerName}"/>

    <TextBlock FontSize="18"
        Foreground="BlueViolet"
        Text="{Binding
            Path=NumberOfConnectedUsers}"/>
    </StackPanel>

    </StackPanel>
    </Border>
</DataTemplate>
```

Chapter 1 of this minibook states that one of the main reasons to adopt WPF as a user interface technology is its data visualization flexibility. Data templates enable you to represent data contained in an object by using any number of XAML elements. The world is your oyster, and you can get as creative as you want to relay application information to your user in the most usable, intuitive fashion by using data templates.

Analyze the `ServerTemplate` data template. This data template represents the display of an instance of a `ServerStatus` object. Look at the `Label` element in the data template.

The `Content` property of the label is bound to the Boolean `IsServerUp` property of the `ServerStatus` object. You'll also notice that there is another component to the binding expression, called `Converter`. This is where the Boolean value (`IsServerUp`) gets passed into the `BooleanToIconConverter` and is rendered as the `RedX` or the `GreenCheck` user control, depending on its value.

The rest of the data template simply outputs the server name of the `ServerStatus` object in yellow and the number of connected users in blue-violet.

Within the Grid on the window, a `ListBox` control is defined that displays a list of servers on the network. Look at the definition of the `ListBox`:

```
<ListBox x:Name="lstServers" Width="490" Height="350"
        ItemsSource="{Binding}" Grid.Row="0" Grid.Column="0"
        ItemTemplate="{StaticResource
            ResourceKey=ServerTemplate}"/>
```

TECHNICAL STUFF

WPF provides a number of controls called ItemsControls that allow you to bind collections of objects to them. Examples of ItemsControls are ListBox and ComboBox (among others). Collections are bound to an ItemsControl through the ItemsSource attribute. A data template can also be applied to each object being bound through the ItemsControl ItemTemplate attribute.

Through Property Value inheritance, the ItemsSource of the ListBox is defaulted to the DataContext of Window. The empty {Binding} element simply states that it will use the current binding of its parent, which uses recursion up the element tree until it reaches a place where a binding is set. Remember that in the GenerateData, you're setting the DataContext binding to the list of Servers to the Window itself, so the ListBox will inherit that list as its ItemSource.

The data template you defined in resources to describe a ServerStatus object renders each object being bound. You see this through the ItemTemplate attribute that uses the StaticResource to point to the ServerTemplate defined in resources. Now when you run the application, you see the ServerStatus data presented in a visually pleasing way! (See Figure 3-5.)

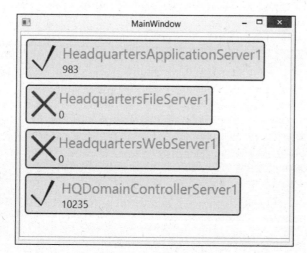

FIGURE 3-5: Rendering a collection of data using a value converter and data templates.

Finding Out More about WPF Data Binding

This chapter is not meant to be inclusive of all functionality possible through WPF's amazing data binding support. Other aspects of WPF data templates worth looking into include these concepts:

>> Using DataTemplateSelector, which is a base class that allows you to render a data template based on some logical condition.

>> Using data templates as a means to provide data adding/editing capabilities to the user.

>> Switching a data template at runtime at the preference of the user. This allows users to switch a data template at will. For instance, in a ListBox, you may display only summary information; however, you can provide a button in your data template that will enable users to switch between the summary template and a more detailed template on demand.

Chapter <u>4</u>

Practical WPF

Even though WPF still supports the direct event handler wire up (for example, through the `OnClick` event), WPF introduces a much better mechanism for responding to user events. It significantly reduces the amount of code you have to write and adds testability to your application. Traditional event handling is all contained in the code-behind for your form, which is extremely difficult to test in an automated fashion.

Software patterns have been around for a long time, first brought to the forefront by the classic tome *Design Patterns: Elements of Reusable Object-Oriented Software* (Addison-Wesley) by Erich Gamma, Richard Helm, Ralph Johnson, and John Vlissides — commonly referred to as the "Gang of Four." Software has evolved, and many new patterns have been developed over the years. One of the most effective user interface patterns developed for WPF is the Model-View-View Model (MVVM) pattern (commonly referred to as ViewModel). Using the ViewModel pattern in your WPF applications will improve software reuse, testability, readability, maintainability, and most of the other "-ilities" as well. (You run across other design patterns throughout this whole book.)

Commanding Attention

The Command Pattern has been around since, well, forever, and you most likely use it every day. Copy and Paste commands are example implementations of the pattern built into Windows and most Windows applications. WPF provides a significant number of built-in commands and also allows for completely customized commands! The following sections provide you with additional information about how commands can work in WPF.

Traditional event handling

Traditional handling of user events (and still supported in WPF) is through an event handler. When the button on the Window is clicked, the code in the event handler (which has to be in the code-behind file) will execute. Here is an example of the WPF for using event handling:

```
<Grid>
    <Grid.RowDefinitions>
        <RowDefinition Height="30"/>
        <RowDefinition Height="30"/>
    </Grid.RowDefinitions>

    <TextBox Name="Message" Grid.Row="0" HorizontalAlignment="Left"
            Width="200" Height="20"/>
    <Button Name="ClickMe" Grid.Row="1" HorizontalAlignment="Center"
            Content="Click Me"  Click="ClickMe_Click"/>
</Grid>
```

REMEMBER

Note how the Button is connected to the code-behind by using the Click event. The mechanism used here is quite simple, but you must perform it for each control individually, making an error likely in some cases. Any change to the code-behind necessitates a change to every location at which the event handler is referenced in the XAML as well. The actual event handler code is equally easy to figure out because it follows the technique used for Windows Forms applications:

```
private void ClickMe_Click(object sender, RoutedEventArgs e)
{
    MessageBox.Show(Message.Text);
}
```

By placing this code in the code-behind event handler, the business logic is now mixed with the user interface code, mixing concerns. To be fair, nothing in the framework *makes* one put the code in the code-behind; it just seems to always end up there. (You can, of course, separate your business logic into classes outside of your code-behind.)

This problem gets compounded when additional UIElements are added to the window that needs to execute the same code. The common fix for this situation is to refactor the code in the original event handler into a separate method and have the event handlers for the related UIElements call the new method. The new method can even be moved into the Business Layer, separating concerns and allowing for testability.

The other issue is one of user experience. Often, menus and buttons need to be actively enabled or disabled based on the condition of the data (or some other condition/user action) in the window.

In this example, the ClickMe button remains enabled all the time because the application doesn't provide any code to enable or disable it based on the content of the Message text box. Realistically, the user interface should disable ClickMe automatically whenever Message is blank. Users tend to click active items repeatedly when given the option, wondering why nothing is happening. The command pattern as implemented in WPF cleanly and easily resolves both issues.

ICommand

ICommand (which is the base interface for all commands discussed here) defines two event handlers and one event, as shown here.

```
bool CanExecute(object parameter);
void Execute(object parameter);
event EventHandler CanExecuteChanged
```

Perhaps the most powerful feature of WPF commands is the capability to determine at runtime whether the bound controls can execute. (See the next section for a detailed discussion.) The following list describes the ICommand elements in more detail.

>> CanExecute is run by the CommandManager whenever focus changes, the PropertyChanged or CollectionChanged events are raised, or on demand through code. If the event handler returns false, all UIElements bound to that command are disabled.

>> Execute contains the code that executes when the user action is processed or the command is executed through code.

>> CanExecuteChanged accesses a mechanism supplied by INotifyCollection Changed and INotifyPropertyChanged that determines when CanExecute is required.

Routed commands

The ICommand interface doesn't provide the entire goodness of commands in WPF. The RoutedCommand class (and its first descendant, RoutedUICommand) takes advantage of event routing to provide additional power.

The CanExecute event handler raises the PreviewCanExecute event, and the Execute event handler raises the PreviewExecuted event. These events are raised just prior to the CanExecute and Execute handlers and bubble up the element tree until an element with the correct command binding is located. This approach is useful to allow the control of commands at a higher level, while the fine-grained elements still control the CanExecute and the Execute event handlers.

Routed commands also expose a collection of InputGestures — keystrokes or other gestures that fire the Execute event handler. You use InputGestures to assign hot-key combinations to commands, such as Ctrl+S for saving.

Using Built-In Commands

WPF provides a number of built-in commands that you can use with little or no code (see the list at https://msdn.microsoft.com/library/system. windows.input.aspx). The most common set used by line of business developers is wrapped up in the ApplicationCommands library. The advantage of using the built-in commands is that all the plumbing is taken care of for you. For example, the CanExecute and Execute event handlers are already implemented. All you have to do is bind them to UIElements through XAML.

TIP

You may end up running the example code several times or have items on the Clipboard from other uses. To ensure that you begin with a clear Clipboard for this example, add the following call after `InitializeComponent();` in the `MainWindow()` constructor:

```
Clipboard.Clear();
```

The sample shown in the following code and Figure 4-1 uses the `Application Commands.Copy` and `ApplicationCommands.Paste` commands to facilitate Clipboard manipulation in your application. As a side note, WPF allows you to abbreviate the built-in commands by dropping the container name (`Application Commands`), so `Copy` and `Paste` are legitimate abbreviations for the command bindings `ApplicationCommands.Copy` and `ApplicationCommands.Paste`.

```xml
<Grid>
    <Grid.RowDefinitions>
        <RowDefinition Height="40"/>
        <RowDefinition Height="30"/>
        <RowDefinition Height="30"/>
    </Grid.RowDefinitions>

    <Menu Grid.Row="0" HorizontalAlignment="Left" Name="menu1">
        <MenuItem Command="Copy">
            <MenuItem.Style>
                <Style TargetType="{x:Type MenuItem}">
                    <Setter Property="Foreground" Value="Black"/>
                    <Style.Triggers>
                        <Trigger Property="IsEnabled" Value="True">
                            <Setter Property="Foreground" Value="Red"/>
                            <Setter Property="FontSize" Value="16"/>
                        </Trigger>
                    </Style.Triggers>
                </Style>
            </MenuItem.Style>
        </MenuItem>

        <MenuItem Command="Paste">
            <MenuItem.Style>
                <Style TargetType="{x:Type MenuItem}">
                    <Setter Property="Foreground" Value="Black"/>
                    <Style.Triggers>
                        <Trigger Property="IsEnabled" Value="True">
                            <Setter Property="Foreground" Value="Red"/>
                            <Setter Property="FontSize" Value="16"/>
                        </Trigger>
                    </Style.Triggers>
                </Style>
```

```
                </MenuItem.Style>
            </MenuItem>
        </Menu>

        <TextBox Grid.Row="1" HorizontalAlignment="Left" Width="200"/>
        <TextBox Grid.Row="2" HorizontalAlignment="Left" Width="200"/>
    </Grid>
```

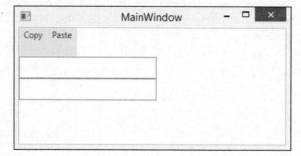

FIGURE 4-1:
Built-in
commands
(with empty
clipboard and no
selections).

TIP

The example contains a bit of trick code that makes it easier to see changes in the UI. Notice how it uses `MenuItem.Style` to change how the menu items appear normally or when they have the focus. Normally, the `Setter` configures `Property="Foreground"` to `Value="Black"`, so you see black lettering. However, `Trigger` watches for `Property="IsEnabled"` to become `True`. When this occurs, the color of the text changes to `Red`. The code also changes the size of the using `Property="FontSize"` and `Value="16"`. Of course, you can use this technique for all sorts of purposes, not only to make UI testing easier.

When the UIElement with focus supports the Clipboard Copy action *and* there are items selected that can be copied to the Clipboard, any elements bound to the Copy command are enabled, as shown in Figure 4-2.

FIGURE 4-2:
Built-in
commands (with
empty clipboard
and text
selection).

When the UIElement with focus supports the Clipboard Paste action *and* there is data in the Clipboard that is supportable by the element with focus, any elements bound to the Paste command are enabled, as shown in Figure 4-3.

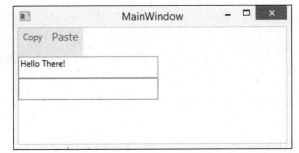

Using Custom Commands

You can use custom commands in all sorts of ways. For example, you might decide to implement the ApplicationCommands.Copy command by using a Button instead of a MenuItem. When you try using just the Command property, as you do with a MenuItem, it doesn't work. You need to create the connectivity that a MenuItem possesses, but a Button doesn't, by using a custom command. The following sections show the simplest method for creating a custom command.

Defining the interface

This example uses two custom buttons, one labeled Copy and another labeled Paste. It also has two text boxes, one to hold the source text and another to hold the destination text. Destination is set for read-only use because the example copies from the source to the destination to keep things simple. You use the buttons as you did the menu items in the previous example. However, the connectivity isn't nearly as automated this time. The following code shows the interface for this example:

```
<Grid>
    <Grid.RowDefinitions>
        <RowDefinition Height="40"/>
        <RowDefinition Height="30"/>
        <RowDefinition Height="30"/>
    </Grid.RowDefinitions>
```

Practical WPF

```
    <StackPanel Grid.Row="0" Orientation="Horizontal"
                HorizontalAlignment="Left">
        <Button Content="Copy" Command="ApplicationCommands.Copy"/>
        <Button Content="Paste" Command="ApplicationCommands.Paste"/>
    </StackPanel>

    <TextBox Name="Source" Grid.Row="1" HorizontalAlignment="Left"
             Width="200"/>
    <TextBox Name="Destination" Grid.Row="2" HorizontalAlignment="Left"
             Width="200" IsReadOnly="True"/>

</Grid>
```

Creating the window binding

To make the example code work, you must create a binding between the controls and the underlying code-behind. You have a number of ways in which to create a binding, and this example shows the most common. In the following code, you define the `Window.CommandBindings` as a series of `CommandBinding` elements. Note that the `Command` attributes here match the `Command` attributes used for the two buttons in the previous section:

```
<Window.CommandBindings>
    <CommandBinding Command="ApplicationCommands.Copy"
                    Executed="CommandBinding_Executed"
                    CanExecute="CommandBinding_CanExecute"/>
    <CommandBinding Command="ApplicationCommands.Paste"
                    Executed="CommandBinding_Executed"
                    CanExecute="CommandBinding_CanExecute"/>
</Window.CommandBindings>
```

When you type certain attribute names, such as Executed, the IDE automatically asks whether you want to create the associated event handler, as shown in Figure 4-4. The temptation is to create a unique event handler for each of the command entries, but this would be a mistake. You want to use a single event handler for everything, as shown in the next section.

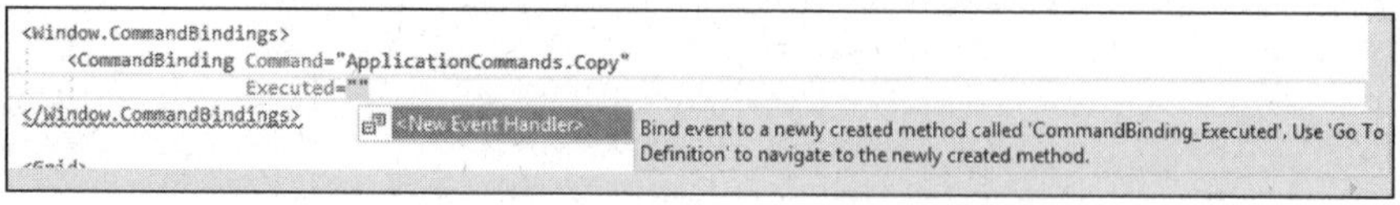

FIGURE 4-4:
Defining an event handler for the command events.

Ensuring that the command can execute

Now that you have controls and binding from the controls to an event handler, you need to create the event-handler code. In this case, you need to determine whether executing the command first is even possible. The buttons will automatically enable or disable as needed based on the value of e.CanExecute in the following code:

```
private void CommandBinding_CanExecute(object sender,
    CanExecuteRoutedEventArgs e)
{
    string Name = ((RoutedCommand)e.Command).Name;

    if (Name == "Copy")
    {
        if (Source == null)
        {
            e.CanExecute = false;
            return;
        }

        if (Source.SelectedText.Length > 0)
            e.CanExecute = true;
        else
            e.CanExecute = false;
    }
    else if (Name == "Paste")
    {
        if (Clipboard.ContainsText() == true)
        {
            e.CanExecute = true;
        }
        else
        {
            e.CanExecute = false;
        }
    }
}
```

REMEMBER

Note that you must convert the incoming e.Command value to a name string as shown in the code so that you can test for a particular command. The command Name is a simple string that contains either Copy or Paste in this case. The values you see depend on how you configure the Command attributes for your application controls.

The determiner for execution differs in each case. The Copy button won't work if the user hasn't selected some text. Likewise, it's not possible to paste text to the destination when the Clipboard lacks data of the correct type. Note that you must use Clipboard.ContainsText() to ensure that the user hasn't copied an image or some other type of data.

Performing the task

Now that you have all the connections defined between the window and the code-behind, you can begin coding the actual task. First you must add the Clipboard. Clear(); call after InitializeComponent(); in the MainWindow() method, as you did for the previous example.

The next step is to handle the Executed event. A single event handler works with both buttons, as shown here:

```
private void CommandBinding_Executed(object sender,
    ExecutedRoutedEventArgs e)
{
    String Name = ((RoutedCommand)e.Command).Name;

    if (Name == "Copy")
    {
        Clipboard.SetText(Source.Text);
    }
    else if (Name == "Paste")
    {
        Destination.Text = Destination.Text + Clipboard.GetText();
    }
}
```

As with the CommandBinding_CanExecute() method in the previous section, this code begins by obtaining the name of the button that the user clicked. It uses this information to select a course of action. The goal is to copy text from Source and place it on Clipboard, or to copy text from Clipboard and place it in Destination.

REMEMBER

You normally wouldn't make the code this simple. The example does so to keep from hiding the workings of the code-behind as it relates to the Window controls. When you first start the application, neither button is activated, as shown in Figure 4-5.

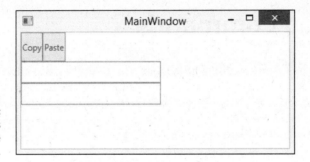

Typing some text and then selecting it enables the Copy button, as shown in
Figure 4-6. Note that the button doesn't become enabled when you type the text;
it's the act of selecting the text that enables it. This is the same action that occurs
when you use menu controls in the previous example.

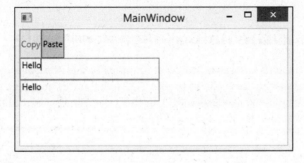

When you click Copy, both the Copy and the Paste buttons are enabled. This action
occurs because the text remains highlighted in the source textbox. When you click
Paste, the Copy button remains enabled. Normally, an application would place the
focus on the pasted location, disabling the Copy button. As previously mentioned,
this example does things simply so that you can see how the connections work.
Clicking in the source text box (so that the text is no longer highlighted) does
disable the Copy button, as shown in Figure 4-7.

Practical WPF

Using Routed Commands

Routed commands require a little more effort, but they also allow you to perform custom actions that ICommand doesn't support. This example does something simple: displays a message box. However, the technique shown works for complex applications as well. The following sections demonstrate how you can use routed commands for both buttons and menus.

Defining the Command class

The center of the exercise is the RoutedUICommand object, cmdSayHello. It provides the resource needed to make the command available. However, to make this object work properly, it must appear within its own class within the RoutedCommands namespace (rather than as part of the MainWindow class).

REMEMBER

To interact with your Command class, you first must create it and then choose Build⇨Rebuild Solution to ensure that the class is visible to XAML. Otherwise, you might find that the XAML you write has blue underlines beneath the various command callouts for no apparent reason. Here is the code used to create the Command class:

```
public static class Command
{
    public static readonly RoutedUICommand cmdSayHello =
        new RoutedUICommand("Say Hello Menu", "DoSayHello",
            typeof(MainWindow));
}
```

WARNING

Note that the Command class and the cmdSayHello field are both static and that cmdSayHello is also readonly. If you don't create your Command class in this manner, WPF will refuse to recognize it. Unfortunately, your application will fail in odd ways, and finding this particular bug can be quite difficult. If you find that your application simply crashes in odd ways, you need to verify that you have created your Command class correctly.

Making the namespace accessible

Modern versions of Visual Studio automatically add the code required to make your namespace accessible as local. The actual entry appears as xmlns:local= "clr-namespace:RoutedCommands" in this case. Here is the full code so that you see where to look for the namespace declaration:

```
<Window x:Class="RoutedCommands.MainWindow"
    xmlns="http://schemas.microsoft.com/winfx/2006/xaml/presentation"
    xmlns:x="http://schemas.microsoft.com/winfx/2006/xaml"
    xmlns:d="http://schemas.microsoft.com/expression/blend/2008"
    xmlns:mc="http://schemas.openxmlformats.org/markup-compatibility/2006"
    xmlns:local="clr-namespace:RoutedCommands"
    mc:Ignorable="d"
    Title="MainWindow" Height="200" Width="400">
```

If you don't have such an entry already in your XAML code, you must create one. Otherwise, your application won't be able to find your custom commands.

Adding the command bindings

As with the `ApplicationCommands` entries used with buttons, you must provide command bindings in order to access your custom commands. The following code shows the command bindings used for this example:

```
<Window.CommandBindings>
    <CommandBinding Command="local:Command.cmdSayHello"
                    CanExecute="CommandBinding_CanExecute"
                    Executed="CommandBinding_Executed"/>
</Window.CommandBindings>
```

REMEMBER

Note how the example code declares the `CommandBinding`. The `CanExecute` and `Executed` entries are much the same as in the previous section. However, the `Command` entry accesses the `local` namespace as `local:Command.cmdSayHello`, where `Command` is the name of the class used to hold the `RoutedUICommand` object and `cmdSayHello` is the name of the object.

Developing a user interface

You can use custom commands with any control that normally supports a click-type event. This example uses both a menu and a button to access the custom command, but you have many other options. The following code creates the application interface, which looks much like the other examples in this chapter:

```
<Grid>
    <Grid.RowDefinitions>
        <RowDefinition Height="40"/>
        <RowDefinition Height="30"/>
        <RowDefinition Height="30"/>
    </Grid.RowDefinitions>
```

```
<Menu Grid.Row="0" HorizontalAlignment="Left" Name="menu1">
    <MenuItem Command="local:Command.cmdSayHello"/>
</Menu>

<TextBox Name="NameStr"  Grid.Row="1" HorizontalAlignment="Left"
        Width="200"/>
<Button Grid.Row="2" Content="Say Hello"
        HorizontalAlignment="Right"
        Command="local:Command.cmdSayHello"/>
</Grid>
```

TIP

Note that the MenuItem element of the Menu control doesn't provide a textual entry for the user to see. On the other hand, the Button does provide this information in the form of the Content property. Even though the MenuItem lacks this information, it still displays Say Hello Menu. This information comes from the RoutedUICommand object declaration. When creating your RoutedUICommand object, it pays to provide a default text definition that works well with menus and then use custom text for other controls as needed.

Developing the custom command code behind

Creating code for your custom command is almost an anticlimax because it works the same as when working with ICommand. You still need to define code for the CanExecute and Executed event handlers, such as the code shown here:

```
private void CommandBinding_CanExecute(object sender,
    CanExecuteRoutedEventArgs e)
{
    if ((NameStr != null) && (NameStr.Text.Length > 0))
        e.CanExecute = true;
    else
        e.CanExecute = false;
}

private void CommandBinding_Executed(object sender,
    ExecutedRoutedEventArgs e)
{
    MessageBox.Show("Hello " + NameStr.Text);
}
```

Obviously, this is a really simple example, but the technique works fine for complex setups as well. Note that you don't need to create different code for menus or buttons (or other controls, for that matter). Everyone uses the same code. Also note that you don't need to perform any special wire-ups to make the application work.

When you first start the application, the menu and button are both disabled, as shown in Figure 4-8. However, when you type text into the text box, both controls become enabled, as shown in Figure 4-9. Clicking either control produces a message box similar to the one shown in Figure 4-10.

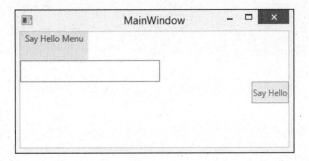

FIGURE 4-8:
The menu and button are disabled on start.

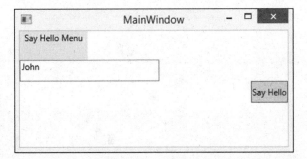

FIGURE 4-9:
Typing a name (or other text) enables both the button and the menu.

FIGURE 4-10.
Clicking either control produces simple output.

REMEMBER

The moment you clear the text, the button and menu item become disabled again, so you know that the CanExecute event handlers works as expected. The main idea to take from this chapter is that WPF provides multiple methods for defining commands that you can use to create robust applications.

6

Web Development with ASP.NET

Contents at a Glance

Chapter **1**

Looking at How ASP.NET Works with C#

At one time, few people knew much about the Internet. However, that has all changed today. Hardly an application appears anywhere that doesn't rely on the Internet in some way. Programmers of all stripes use the web for research and communication. Providers use it for product updates and documentation. It is everywhere.

All the more reason to know how to code in the web environment. The problem is that so many so-called frameworks for development exist that it's nearly impossible to decide which to use with a reasonable methodology. You almost have to draw straws.

If you're working in a Microsoft environment and writing a simple program, it's usually best to use ASP.NET. Why? Sempf's Fourth Law: Simplicity above all. ASP.NET is a straightforward platform for web creation.

ASP.NET has its share of problems, most of which involve writing Google (or some other really big complicated program). You probably aren't writing Google, so don't worry about it. If your site gets famous, you can get some venture capital and rewrite it into some custom framework. For now, just get your site written.

That's what ASP.NET enables you to do — get the job done. With ASP.NET, you can write a good website quickly, one that can be hosted just about anywhere. No one can ask for much more than that. This chapter delves into the details of using ASP.NET with C#.

Breaking Down Web Applications

A web application is a computer program that uses a very light client interface communicating with a server over the Internet in a stateless manner. *Stateless* means that the computer browsing the site and the server providing the site don't maintain a connection. You can see this process at a high level in Figure 1-1.

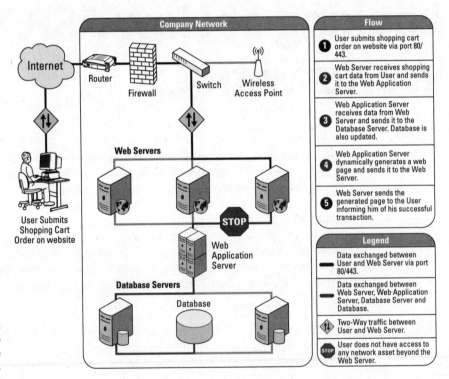

FIGURE 1-1:
The web application process.

The client requests a document from the server, and the server sends the document when it gets around to it. The document, usually a combination of Hypertext Markup Language (HTML), Cascading Style Sheets (CSS), and JavaScript, contains standardized elements, which make up the interface of the application.

Why do you need a web application at all? If you just have a set of documents on the server and the client is just requesting one after another, what's the point of that? Of course, getting a document is a good thing, but where does the application part come in?

The answer is within web applications. Web applications are powerful because the server can construct the document on the fly whenever it receives a request. This server process is what makes web applications work (see Figure 1-2).

The light client interface — called the *web browser* or just the *browser* — provides some important functionality. It handles the user interface and can do things independently of the server.

The server is largely where it's at, though. Because the server can remember things from moment to moment, and because the client is assumed to forget everything from page to page, the server is where the long-running communications all reside.

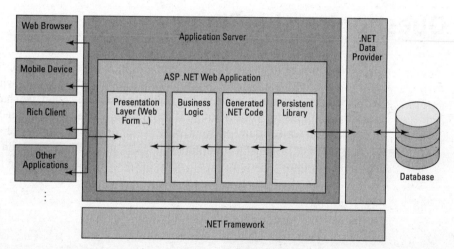

FIGURE 1-2:
ASP.NET
deconstructed.

ASP.NET is a library of controls and processing logic that makes constructing the server side of things much easier. You construct "server pages," but they end up transformed into the documents that the client uses to show you the user interface. ASP.NET is classified as a Web Application Framework, not a programming language.

The programming language, for your purpose, is C#. However, you can code for ASP.NET in any .NET language — it is just another set of tools in the framework.

C# is the language that you use to tell the server how to organize the ASP.NET pieces and send them to the client. The clients will never see any C# code; they won't even know that you coded it in C#.

TECHNICAL STUFF

This gets into the same discussion that the book covers several times regarding the difference between the library and the language. ASP.NET is a library of tools, and that library is language independent. You orchestrate the functionality of the parts of the library using the language.

Web development comes with a few little caveats, however. The client — which doesn't care a whit that you are coding in C# — needs some care and feeding. Web applications have no state, so you need to think a little differently. The client does a lot automatically for you in web development. The server creates some security concerns. Before you dig into the details of using C# with ASP.NET, it's important to take a tour of the details of web development and discover some things you need to keep in mind.

Questioning the Client

When you're writing a Windows Form, WPF, or console application, your platform for the client is a Windows computer (or a Linux or Mac system when using newer .NET functionality). When you're writing a web application, you have no idea what the platform for your client is. It could be a Mac, any one of the Windows operating systems, Linux, Android, iOS, or any of a huge number of other operating systems. It could be a smartphone, a tablet, or a netbook. It could be a television, Blu-ray player, gaming device, or refrigerator (really: see Figure 1-3).

FIGURE 1-3:
Yes, a refrigerator.

The point is that you don't know what you're writing for, so you have a very different development experience for a web browser than you do for a Windows client. You don't know what size the screen is, you don't know what language the machine is set to, you don't know how fast the connection to the Internet is. You know nothing about your client.

You have to question the client. You can't assume much about the browser, so you have to make certain design decisions differently than you usually would.

You can depend on the browser to do some things for you that you might be used to having to do for yourself. The programming details are explained in Chapter 4 of this minibook, but you need to get a good overview now.

First, the client browser has a built-in scripting system called JavaScript, JScript, or possibly ECMAScript (these language dialects are essentially the same but have some differences). Second, the browser can tell you some subset of details about itself, its host machine, and the user that is using it.

Scripting the client

By now you get the idea that communication with the browser occurs via the network, and that the client and browser are disconnected. Although that is true, the client isn't completely out in the fog when it comes to interacting with the user.

You can send a script along with your HTML document. This script references objects on the screen — just as your C# code would — and makes things happen for the user.

Usually this script is in the JavaScript language. Why not C#? Well, C# isn't a scripting language. C# needs to be compiled, and JavaScript isn't compiled. It just sits there, in text, waiting for the browser to run it.

WARNING

The fact that it is in text means that you have to be careful not to put secure information in a script. Right-click any web page in your browser and click View Source to see that page's script code.

A lot of the script that your pages need will be generated by ASP.NET. This book is about C#, not JavaScript, so it focuses on the server features, not the client features. For now, you should just know that "things are happening" on the client side, however.

Getting information back from the client

When a browser makes a request to a server, a lot of useful information about the client gets sent along with the page name that is requested. You can reference this in the backwardly named ServerVariables collection.

This is about as good as learning about the client gets. These details will, however, help you get the most out of your communication with the client. Here are some examples of the values available:

>> AUTH_USER: The logged-in user.

>> REMOTE_USER: The same as AUTH_USER.

>> CONTENT_LENGTH: Size of the request. This is useful if a file is uploaded.

>> HTTP_USER_AGENT: Which browser the client is using.

>> REMOTE_ADDR: The IP number of the client computer.

>> QUERY_STRING: All the stuff after the question mark in the request. Check out the Address bar of a browser in many web applications to see what this term means.

>> ALL_HTTP: Every *header variable* (request details made available to the server) sent by the client.

In total, the header usually contains 63 variables. The most commonly accessed of them are in the System.Web.HttpRequest class. You'll also find the collection of ServerVariables there. You can find out more on getting to that class in Chapter 4 of this minibook. Search MSDN for ServerVariables to get the complete list.

Understanding the weaknesses of the browser

As you can imagine, the browser-as-client model has a few weaknesses. At this point in the book, you should know that the more layers you stack on, the more problems you'll encounter. Not even letting the programmer know what computer the user has is a problem as well. Here are a few of these weaknesses:

>> **Changing window sizes:** The most basic difficulty in using a browser as a client is changing window sizes. In a Windows program, you have at least some control over how large the window is. If it gets too small, you can change it programmatically. In a web application, however, you have very little control over the window size. For all you know, the user could be using a cellphone, right? That's a small window!

Because of this, every form you develop using ASP.NET has to be size-agnostic to the best of your ability. Especially when your form is destined for the public Internet, you just can't make assumptions about the size of the user's screen.

» **Sporadic communication:** When the client wants something from the server, the client requests it from the server. It is the server's responsibility to get the client what it wants and then wait. And wait. And wait some more.

Even if the server wants an acknowledgement from the client, it might never get one. The user might have closed the browser.

Communication from the client to the server is sporadic. Secure transactions are nearly impossible because the server can't be sure that the client will communicate any information in return. Because of the loosely coupled nature of the Internet, you just can't make any assumptions about communication time.

» **Distrusted input:** Browser documents are sent as a package of text and images (and sounds and fonts and Flash movies, if needed) to the client from the server. The requests are sent back to the server from the client in a similar way: textually.

With all this text, you would think that some clients would find a way to fake a request. Oh wait, they have. Lots of them. And it is easy, and free.

Look at Fiddler (`http://www.fiddlertool.com`), a free tool that lets you completely alter the requests sent from a browser (see Figure 1-4). Fiddler gives you the capability to view a request (including the results from a form, even a login form), alter the text directly, and then send it on its merry way.

Security risk? You betcha. You need to distrust every character sent to you from the client. Validate everything in the server code. Chapters 2 and 3 of this minibook discuss this issue.

» **Random implementations:** When you're writing a WPF application in C#, you know that the application will be running on Windows. You might not know which edition, but you have a good idea about how it will work. When you write an ASP.NET system, on the other hand, you know that the client might or might not follow a set of standards, but that's about it. You don't know how the browser will behave.

The more significant impact of this is in positioning, as it turns out. The technology that specified most of the positioning and styling in browsers, called Cascading Style Sheets (CSS), is rife with misimplementation.

That means that not only do you not know how your application will behave out there, but also that it might not look right, either! Yea for the web! Seriously, scripting is another piece of the puzzle that isn't the same across browsers. ECMAScript is another standard, and it is implemented differently by different browser companies.

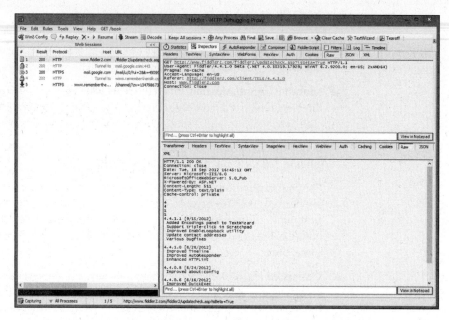

FIGURE 1-4:
Fiddler.

The only way around all this is to test, test, test. If all else fails, take the simplest road. And don't get tremendously picky about a pixel here and there.

Dealing with Web Servers

The other side of this client/server equation is the server. For those of you writing in ASP.NET, the server will be Internet Information Server (IIS) most of the time.

TIP

Other servers also implement ASP.NET in one fashion or another, and you may see them more often because Microsoft is now promoting ASP.NET on other systems. For example, you can see how to configure a Linux system (with Nginx) to use ASP.NET at https://docs.microsoft.com/en-us/aspnet/core/publishing/linuxproduction. In fact, you don't absolutely have to have IIS; you can use other products, such as Apache (see https://wiki.archlinux.org/index.php/ASP.NET_with_Apache for details).

The role of the web server is to accept requests from clients, do whatever processing is required, and then pass back a browser-viewable page. This means that the ASP.NET code you write will be turned into HTML and JavaScript by the web server. You have less control over what is happening than you might think.

Getting a PostBack (Hint: It's not a returned package)

A *PostBack* isn't a returned package from the post office. It is how ASP.NET handles communication between the client and the server so that you don't have to.

The first time users request a page in ASP.NET in a given session, they usually type the URL into the address bar, or click a link like `http://blog.johnmuellerbooks.com`. The next page loaded, however, is a carefully controlled communication with the server, called a PostBack.

A PostBack is a JavaScript function used in place of the built-in POST function to send information about the data on the page back to the server. It looks like this to the client:

```
javascript:WebForm_DoPostBackWithOptions(new WebForm_PostBackOptions(&quot;ctl00
    $cphAdmin$btnSave&quot;, &quot;&quot;, true, &quot;&quot;, &quot;&quot;,
    false, false))
```

Quite a change from a URL, huh? To understand why things work as they do, you need to go back in time.

Looking back to how things used to be

Back in the day, web servers supported GETs and POSTs. What's more, they still support GETs and POSTs.

A GET is a request for a page, using just the URL. You can send data in the URI (after a question mark in the link of text) but that's all you are sending — nothing from the page itself goes back. A GET request looks like this:

```
GET /fiddler2/updatecheck.asp?isBeta=False HTTP/1.1
User-Agent: Fiddler/2.2.4.6 (.NET 2.0.50727.4918; Microsoft Windows NT
    6.1.7100.0)
Pragma: no-cache
Host: www.fiddler2.com
Connection: Close
```

A POST sends values from a form on the page. The form can be invisible, but it has to be there. POSTs are a lot bigger than GETs and have a set format that is hard to navigate at times. Here is an example POST:

```
POST /feedbackAction.asp HTTP/1.1
Accept: application/x-ms-application, image/jpeg, application/xaml+xml, image/
    gif, image/pjpeg, application/x-ms-xbap, application/vnd.ms-excel,
    application/vnd.ms-powerpoint, application/msword,
    application/x-shockwave-flash, */*
Referer: http://www.grovecity.com/feedback.asp
Accept-Language: en-US
User-Agent: Mozilla/4.0 (compatible; MSIE 8.0; Windows NT 6.1; WOW64;
    Trident/4.0; SLCC2; .NET CLR 2.0.50727; .NET CLR 3.5.30729; .NET CLR
    3.0.30729; Media Center PC 6.0; .NET CLR 1.1.4322; InfoPath.2;
    OfficeLiveConnector.1.3; OfficeLivePatch.0.0)
Content-Type: application/x-www-form-urlencoded
Accept-Encoding: gzip, deflate
Host: www.grovecity.com
Content-Length: 69
Connection: Keep-Alive
Pragma: no-cache
Cookie: ASPSESSIONIDAATQCRCA=MJEFOIFACGPONMOBADPIDLKH

user=Bill&email=bill@sempf.net&subject=Test&comment=This+is+a+POST%21
```

All the header variables are there, and then the contents of the form are all linked together at the end of the request.

From the past to the PostBack

Having to handle the header had a lot of problems when it came to the sophisticated web forms that ASP.NET provides, so Microsoft used JavaScript to short-circuit the process. It created a special method that would be on every page that ASP.NET generates. This method formats the information in order to better manage the communication with the server. A PostBack looks like this:

```
POST /admin/Pages/Add_entry.aspx?id=e387aab8-1292-4c75-985f-5f8e5db3089a
    HTTP/1.1
Accept: application/x-ms-application, image/jpeg, application/xaml+xml, image/
    gif, image/pjpeg, application/x-ms-xbap, application/vnd.ms-excel,
    application/vnd.ms-powerpoint, application/msword,
    application/x-shockwave-flash, */*
Referer: http://www.sempf.net/admin/Pages/Add_entry.aspx?id=e387ccb8-1292-4c75-
    985f-5f8e5db3089a
Accept-Language: en-US
```

```
User-Agent: Mozilla/4.0 (compatible; MSIE 7.0; Windows NT 6.1; WOW64;
    Trident/4.0; SLCC2; .NET CLR 2.0.50727; .NET CLR 3.5.30729; .NET CLR
    3.0.30729; Media Center PC 6.0; .NET CLR 1.1.4322; InfoPath.2;
    OfficeLiveConnector.1.3; OfficeLivePatch.0.0)
Content-Type: multipart/form-data; boundary=-----------------------------
    7d922c323b0016
Accept-Encoding: gzip, deflate
Host: www.sempf.net
Content-Length: 9399
Connection: Keep-Alive
Pragma: no-cache


-------------------------------7d922c323b0016
Content-Disposition: form-data; name="__LASTFOCUS"



-------------------------------7d922c323b0016
Content-Disposition: form-data; name="ctl00$cphAdmin$txtTitle"


C# 7.0 at CONDG
-------------------------------7d922c323b0016
Content-Disposition: form-data; name="ctl00$cphAdmin$ddlAuthor"


Admin
-------------------------------7d922c323b0016
Content-Disposition: form-data; name="ctl00$cphAdmin$txtDate"


2017-09-08 22:21
-------------------------------7d922c323b0016
Content-Disposition: form-data; name="ctl00$cphAdmin$txtContent$TinyMCE1$txtCont
    ent"


<p>The sky is blue!</p>
-------------------------------7d922c323b0016
Content-Disposition: form-data; name="ctl00$cphAdmin$txtUploadImage";
    filename=""
Content-Type: application/octet-stream



-------------------------------7d922c323b0016
Content-Disposition: form-data; name="ctl00$cphAdmin$txtUploadFile"; filename=""
Content-Type: application/octet-stream



-------------------------------7d922c323b0016
Content-Disposition: form-data; name="ctl00$cphAdmin$txtSlug"


C-40-at-CONDG
-------------------------------7d922c323b0016
```

Notice the nice layout of the data, with the form field name, and the data and everything all nice to read? Fortunately, you don't have to worry about any of this. ASP.NET gets it for you.

When you create an event handler for an object — a button, for instance — a PostBack will be used for that communication. This is how ASP.NET changes your interface with the server and client. It makes web programming look like Windows programming, at least as far as events are concerned.

It's a matter of state

The other major piece of the puzzle in web server usage is state, which means that the server should know the state of the application at any given time. Web servers don't do a very good job of remembering state because of one of the problems with web browsers: inconsistency of communications. Because the server doesn't know from one minute to the next whether you're going to send anything, it can't depend on getting it.

For this reason, the server tries to remember certain things about your session by putting values in the form that it can use later. The server uses a *ViewState* value for that purpose. The `ViewState` is an encrypted string that the server can use to remember who you are from POST to POST.

Even with these values, maintaining session state has its problems. For instance, in a secure application, you might need to maintain a transaction for a database function. Doing so is nearly impossible in a web application, because you can't be sure that you will get the return acknowledgment. Nearly all the data processing therefore happens on the server. Learn more about data processing in Online Chapter 3, which you can find by going to www.dummies.com, searching this book's title, and locating the Downloads tab on the page that appears.

Chapter 2

Building Web Applications

There is a lot to web development. However, it has gotten easier over the years. At one time, you might need to know upwards of seven languages: SQL, VBScript, XML, Visual Basic, HTML, CSS, and JavaScript. You might have even needed to know C++, which was once required. Fortunately, today you can do much of the required programming using just one language, C#.

With Visual Studio in the mix, things are a little easier than they once were. You have two considerations when you choose Visual Studio to be your tool of choice to build a web application. The first is the tool itself. The second is the way you are going to use the tool, or your *methodology*.

If you've been working with the samples in this book, working in Visual Studio will feel very familiar. There is a Design View for the user interface. The Code Editor works just like the Code Editor in all the other environments. The only caveat is the unusual file types that you'll see occasionally in web applications. You'll get used to those.

The methodology debate — that is, which methodology works better — is harder to get used to because it's a religious war. People will tell you to use one or the other for this reason and that. The point is not to use something only because it is new and shiny. Do the research, try things, and build software that works. In this chapter, you see how to build an application in one methodology, using Visual Studio as your tool.

Working in Visual Studio

You already know the basics of working in Visual Studio in C#; you've been working in Visual Studio all along. Working with Visual Studio in the web world is a little different, but not much. Using Visual Studio to build a web application is a lot like Windows Presentation Foundation (WPF) actually, because web applications have a code element to the Design View — the HTML document, in an ASPX file. Then there is a code element, in an ASPX.CS file.

A lot of other files make web pages work, too. There are images and style sheets and script files. All of them have editors in Visual Studio. None of them have a darn thing to do with C#, though, so this chapter doesn't discuss them much. For more on those files, see the upcoming section, "Recognizing the other file types" or refer to *ASP.NET 3.5 For Dummies* (Wiley) by Ken Cox.

Two project approaches

Visual Studio 2017 Community edition actually offers two approaches to creating a web application. Depending on what you want to accomplish, either approach could work for you.

>> **Standard project:** Creates a standard project, just as you have with desktop applications in previous minibooks. This option has the advantage of offering methods that work on more platforms. However, these projects are most definitely targeted toward applications using the latest Microsoft techniques. This is the option to use if you want to create web applications with complex features, especially if the web application must run on multiple platforms (including Mac OS X and Linux).

>> **Website:** Creates a specific kind of website that you can run and test on your local system. This option has the advantage of providing the look and feel of the projects found in previous versions of Visual Studio. The initial setup for projects of this sort is also easier.

Creating a standard project

The following steps set up a simple site in Visual Studio as a standard project.
You'll use this site to look at all of Visual Studio's cool web features. Then you
can begin looking at more complex sites. Here's all you need to do to set up your
simple site:

1. Choose File⇨New⇨Project.

You see the New Project dialog box.

2. Select the Visual C#\Web folder.

Visual Studio displays the list of projects shown in Figure 2-1:

- **ASP.NET Web Application (.NET Framework):** Creates one of the
standard web applications supported by the Windows platform.

- **ASP.NET Core Web Application (.NET Core):** Supports web applications
on Windows, Mac OS X, and Linux.

- **ASP.NET Core Web Application (.NET Framework):** Creates core-type
applications, but with the advantages of the .NET Framework and only for
the Windows platform.

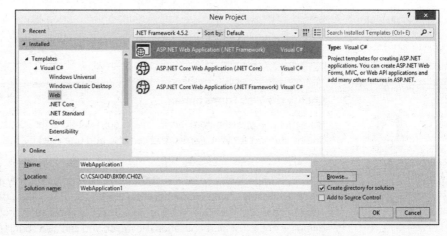

FIGURE 2-1:
The New Project
dialog box
contains options
for various
project types.

3. Type StandardWebApp **in the Name field (or another name of your choice).**

Visual Studio automatically provides the same name in the Solution Name
field. Change the Solution Name field entry if you plan to create multiple
projects in the same solution.

4. **Click OK.**

The wizard displays the New ASP.NET Web Application dialog box shown in Figure 2-2. These projects roughly correspond to the kinds of projects you could create in earlier versions of Visual Studio. For example, if you choose Web Forms, you get a lot of prepopulated content. The Web Forms example has a Default page, along with a Contact and About page, prepopulated. There is already a master page template for the site and configuration and script files in the project.

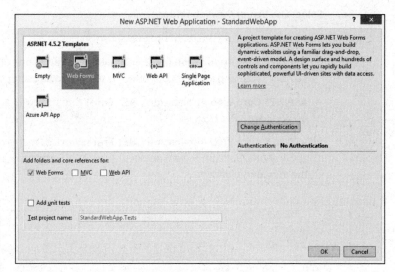

FIGURE 2-2:
Select a project
type to start your
application.

5. **Choose the Web Forms option.**

TIP

Note that the wizard automatically checks some options for you, such as adding support for Web Forms. You can also add unit tests by checking Add Unit Tests.

Security is important, and Microsoft tries to make adding security as easy as is possible. Clicking Change Authentication displays another dialog box where you can choose the kind of authentication that the application should use. The default is not to use authentication. However, you can also configure the application to use individual user accounts, a setup suitable for work or school, or Windows authentication based on a local login.

REMEMBER

To keep things simple, this example doesn't make use of unit testing or authentication support. However, when creating a project application, you likely need to add both.

6. **Click OK.**

Visual Studio makes a project.

Hey, that's it. It runs a lot like all the other projects that you've done, making all the files that you need to make a web project work. To run the project, press F5. When you do so, Visual Studio launches Cassini, the web server that comes with Visual Studio. Your web browser launches, and your project launches.

TIP

This isn't some boring demonstration page. When you run the application, you see links to helpful resources that you can use to build better web applications, as shown in Figure 2-3. Consequently, it pays to spend a little time viewing the sample application.

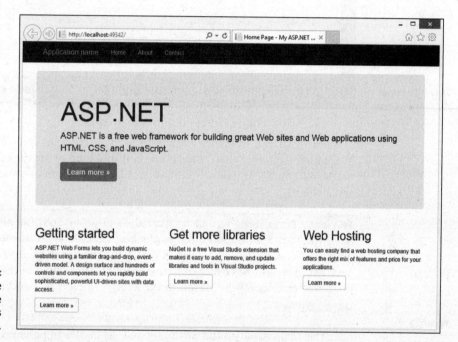

FIGURE 2-3:
Run the sample application to see some resources you can use.

Handling the Form Designer

Visual Studio launches the web project by displaying a helpful page containing an overview of your project. Tabs on the side of this page help you interact with connected services and to publish your project, as shown in Figure 2-4. However, to actually do something with your project, you need to open one of the files and modify it, which is the purpose of this section.

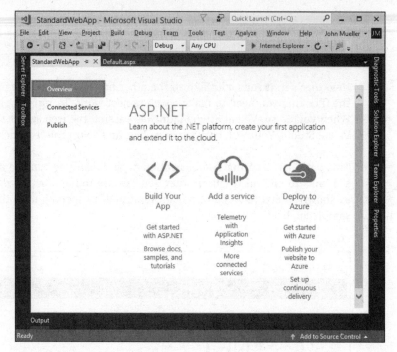

FIGURE 2-4:
The initial page
contains helpful
options for
working with your
project.

The first page you normally work with is Default.aspx. Double-click this file in Solution Explorer. Visual Studio opens it in a kind of source editor that looks much like the XAML editor used for Windows Presentation Foundation (WPF) applications.

To view a Form Designer, click either the Design or Split tab after opening an ASPX file. The Split option often works best because you can see both the page presentation and the HTML used to create the presentation. Delete the standard text that Microsoft has dropped in the MainContent section of the page. Save the project after deleting the HTML in the Source window to see the change in the Design window.

Click the Toolbox tab all the way to the left. Examples in previous minibooks use the toolbox for Windows Forms and other applications. Here it has the controls for web applications. Open the Standard tree view.

The Standard tree view has the main HTML controls that are part of the standard library with an ASP.NET twist. Drag a Label control and a Button control onto the web form. It should look like Figure 2-5.

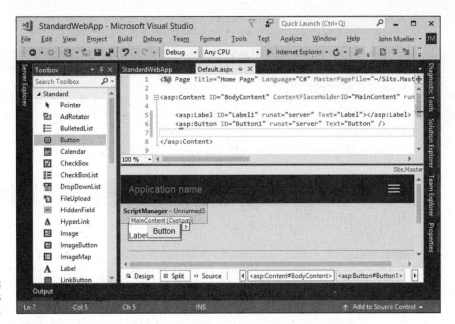

FIGURE 2-5:
Getting started is simple.

Check out the designer source. Here is the code after you remove the original content and add the two controls:

```
<%@ Page Title="Home Page" Language="C#" MasterPageFile="~/Site.Master"
    AutoEventWireup="true" CodeBehind="Default.aspx.cs"
    Inherits="StandardWebApp._Default" %>

<asp:Content ID="BodyContent" ContentPlaceHolderID="MainContent"
    runat="server">

    <asp:Label ID="Label1" runat="server" Text="Label"></asp:Label>
    <asp:Button ID="Button1" runat="server" Text="Button"/>

</asp:Content>
```

The funny-looking code at the top of the page provides a title for your page, tells which language to use for the code behind, provides linkage to a master page for formatting purposes, tells the server to automatically link controls to the code-behind, provides a name for the code behind, and defines the namespace for this application page. Beneath this first tag, you see an <asp:Content> tag that creates the body content for your application — the standard HTML tags, such as <html>, <head>, and <body>. The content provided by the <asp:Content> tag is partially affected by the master page content.

Within the `<asp:Content>` tag are the two control tags: `<asp:Label>` and `<asp:Button>` that you added. To see what these control do, choose Debug⇨Start Without Debugging. You want to start without debugging support to make the generated code a little easier to navigate (you'll be amazed by how much code the server generates). IIS Express launches, your web browser launches, and your new page appears (see Figure 2-6).

FIGURE 2-6:
Your artistic new
web application.

The output looks a lot like the Designer. There are some differences under the hood. Remember that web browsers don't speak ASP.NET; they speak HTML. Your web server must translate the ASP.NET code into something that the web browser can use. To see the generated code, right-click your browser and choose the option for seeing the source, usually View Source, from the context menu. Here is the important part of that translation:

```
<span id="MainContent_Label1">Label</span>
<input type="submit" name="ct100$MainContent$Button1" value="Button"
    id="MainContent_Button1"/>
```

Note that the ASP.NET Label control becomes a `<span>`, and the ASP.NET Button control becomes an `<input>` control. The Designer is simply helping you write markup code. There is no magic here.

**TECHNICAL
STUFF**

After you view your page, you need to close the source view and your browser. In some cases, IIS Express won't shut down automatically. You can see the IIS Express icon in the Windows Notification area. Right-click this icon and choose Exit. You want to shut down IIS Express to ensure that any changes you make to the application actually appear the next time you start it. Otherwise, you may see only the cached version of the previous page.

All the controls that were just added have their default values. To have clean code, you need to intelligently name your controls. Additionally, you may have other values that you need to set on those controls. There might even be things you didn't even know the control could do that you can set.

The trick to doing this is in the Properties panel, introduced in Book 4, Chapter 2. The Properties panel handles the properties of ASP.NET controls just as well as it does anything else. For instance, to rename the controls from the preceding example, follow these steps:

1. **Press F4 to bring up the Properties panel, if necessary.**

2. **In the Designer, click the Label you added.**

   Notice that the Properties panel changes to look like Figure 2-7.

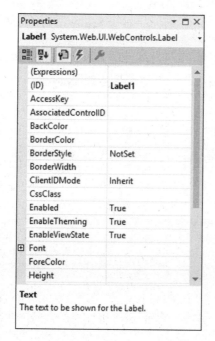

FIGURE 2-7:
Properties look
like this!

3. **Change the Text Property to** This is The Text to Change.

4. **Open the Font tree view by clicking the little plus sign next to the word** *Font*.

5. **Choose Large in the Font\Size drop-down list.**

   See the label change in the Designer?

WARNING

You can also directly type values into the Size property, such as 14 pt. However, this is a truly horrid practice because using exact sizes tends to wreak havoc with the devices that people use today. Best practice is to use a relative size, such as Large, so that the font is automatically adjusted to the context of the device using the application.

6. **Change the (ID) to** TextToChange.

7. **Click the Button in the Designer.**

   The Properties panel changes to show the button's properties.

8. **Change the Text property to** Click Me.

9. **Change the (ID) to** ChangeText.

The Source view automatically changes as you make these changes in the Design View. Here is what you should see now:

```
<%@ Page Title="Home Page" Language="C#" MasterPageFile="~/Site.Master"
    AutoEventWireup="true" CodeBehind="Default.aspx.cs"
    Inherits="StandardWebApp._Default" %>

<asp:Content ID="BodyContent" ContentPlaceHolderID="MainContent"
    runat="server">

    <asp:Label ID="TextToChange" runat="server"
        Text="This is The Text to Change" Font-Size="Large"></asp:Label>
    <asp:Button ID="ChangeText" runat="server" Text="Click Me"/>

</asp:Content>
```

So the management of your code is what the Form Designer does for you. Now, some people don't like Visual Studio messing with their code. Some people don't like to remember all the ins and outs of ASP.NET. It's all up to you; you can use it or not.

This isn't where the magic is, though. This is a C# book, and if you're working in a big shop, your ASP.NET code is probably being written for you anyway. You want to play with the server code.

Coding in the Code Editor

If you go back to the Design View and double-click the Button control that you dragged over, you see the *code-behind*, which is the C# code that makes the form manageable by the server. The code-behind is in a file called Default.aspx.cs, below Default.aspx in its Solution Explorer tree. This code should look like this:

```
using System;
using System.Collections.Generic;
using System.Linq;
using System.Web;
using System.Web.UI;
using System.Web.UI.WebControls;
```

```
namespace StandardWebApp
{
    public partial class _Default : Page
    {
        protected void Page_Load(object sender, EventArgs e)
        {

        }

        protected void ChangeText_Click(object sender, EventArgs e)
        {

        }
    }
}
```

Here are a few things to consider about this code:

>> **This is a partial class.** The rest of this class is built-in web functionality, and it used to appear in this file. Because no one ever needed to edit it, Microsoft took it out.

>> **The class inherits from** System.Web.UI.Page. The Page class provides all the tools you need to keep a collection of the controls in the page together. This is very important for some web applications, but it's a little beyond the scope of this book. Read the documentation for the Page class. It's an important part of ASP.NET.

>> **There is an event handler for** Page.Load. Every ASP.NET page goes through a loading sequence as described in the "Dealing with Web Servers" section of Chapter 1 of this minibook. A load results when the client makes a request or post-back. The Page.Load event handler makes it possible to do pre-setup operations as part of handling the request or post-back.

>> **There is an event handler for the** Button.Click **event.** Double-clicking the control creates this event handler.

Depending on your background, you might find that this feels either very familiar, or very foreign. This is *not* like the classic Active Server Pages days or like modern PHP with inline scripting. Although inline scripting is a way you can code with ASP.NET, it isn't the default way.

If you're a Windows programmer, you'll probably feel very comfortable with web forms. They work in a similar fashion. However, as mentioned in the "Breaking Down Web Applications" section of Chapter 1 of this minibook, there is no real state management on these controls — it is all faked by the ViewState variable in the HTML.

ADDING SOME FUNCTIONALITY USING C#

Start by making the form do something. Code View basically allows the developer to write code that does something useful with the web form. There is already an event handler for the ChangeText.Click event, so use it to change the text of the label. This is a common operation in web applications. The label ID was TextToChange, so you need to add this code:

```
TextToChange.Text = "It has changed!";
```

That was simple. You need to know that this will be the simplest event handler that you will ever write, however. They get harder.

Run the application by choosing Debug⇨Start Without Debugging. Visual Studio will launch IIS Express, and then your browser should launch. Click the Click Me button, and your screen should look like the one in Figure 2-8. When you get done, remember to close the browser and stop IIS Explorer if necessary.

FIGURE 2-8:
Hey, it worked!

USING A LOAD EVENT HANDLER TO ADD EVEN MORE FUNCTIONALITY

Now say the client wants something to happen when the page loads. Pretend that this "something" is dynamic. It won't be dynamic for this example, but it could be.

Because of the nature of ASP.NET, and programming in general for Windows, you can't always code properties in the design time controller — especially for events. Sometimes you need to manually write an event handler to deal with an event. That is what you are going to do — from the Code View out this time. Last time you used the Form Designer. Just follow these steps to write the event handler:

1. **Start by writing an event handler in Code View.**

```
protected void ChangeTheColor(object sender, EventArgs e)
{
    TextToChange.BackColor = System.Drawing.Color.Red;
}
```

TIP

No event arguments are required in C# 5.0 and above, if you aren't planning on using them. If you want the Form Designer to work properly, however, include them.

2. **Change back to Split view and select the** TextToChange **label.**

3. **Open the Properties panel and click the lightning bolt in the button bar at the top.**

   This changes the Properties panel into an Event panel of sorts.

4. **Click the Load event.**

   You should see a little drop-down list.

5. **Pick the** ChangeTheColor **method that you created in Step 1.**

6. **Run the application again.**

   The background color of the label should be set to red.

Recognizing the other file types

At this point, you likely get the idea about the ASPX markup file. There are ASPX files that have markup, and there are ASPX.CS files that have C# code. That's the core of the ASP.NET model.

If you've ever done any web development, you know that there are other files that get used. Lots of other files get used, in fact. Visual Studio has a place for nearly all those other files. Table 2-1 is a breakdown of some of those files, what they are for, and how they are accessed.

TABLE 2-1 **Web Application File Types**

File Type	What It Does	How Visual Studio Handles It
Stylesheets (.css files, usually)	Controls how the page looks. For more on CSS, check out *CSS3 For Dummies*, by John Paul Mueller.	Visual Studio has a fantastic CSS handler.
JavaScript Files	Handles client-side interactivity. For more information about JavaScript, see *HTML5 Programming with JavaScript For Dummies*, by John Paul Mueller (Wiley).	Now that Microsoft supports AJAX, JavaScript (the J in AJAX) is suddenly a lot more important. JavaScript IntelliSense is supported now, as well as real debugging.
Images (GIFs, JPEGs, and PNGs)	Making pretties.	Don't depend on Visual Studio to edit your images. Use Photoshop, or a merged product or suite like Expression Blend.
User Controls (ASCX)	Chapter 4 discusses user controls, but basically they combine the Toolbox controls to do something specific.	Visual Studio provides perfect support, and always has. Visual Studio *wants* you to reuse code, so do it!

Creating a website

You can also create a website by using Visual Studio 2017 Community edition. Many of the same things that you do for a project, you also do for a website, except that the setup differs greatly. Here are the steps for creating a website:

1. **Choose File⇨New⇨Web Site.**

   You see the New Web Site dialog box, shown in Figure 2-9. Note that you can interact with sites on the local drive, an HTTP site, or an FTP site.

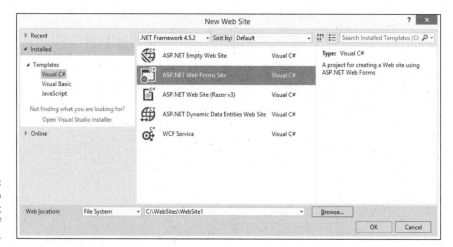

FIGURE 2-9:
The New Web Site dialog box contains a list of website projects.

2. **Choose ASP.NET Web Forms Site.**

   This option creates a Web Forms project similar to the one in the previous section.

3. **Click Browse.**

   You see a Choose Location dialog box.

4. **Locate the source code for this book and create a WebSite folder to hold this project.**

   Your dialog box should appear similar to the one shown in Figure 2-10.

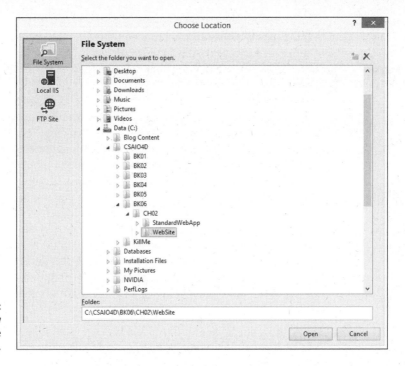

FIGURE 2-10:
Create a new
folder to hold the
project.

5. **Click Open.**

   Visual Studio opens the selected folder and returns you to the New Web Site dialog box.

6. **Click OK.**

   Visual Studio creates a new Web Forms project that looks like the one you worked with in the previous section. The only difference is how you arrived at this point. However, you must remember that you can use this technique to create a website of this sort anywhere: local hard drive, HTTP site, or FTP site.

At this point, you can work with this project by using precisely the same steps you used for the previous Web Forms project. Try it to see for yourself!

Developing with Style

There are a number of different flavors of ASP.NET development. These flavors include inline scripting and regular Web Forms, and also Model-View-Controller (MVC), *n*-tier, three-tier, and forms over data. It's not clear why there are so many patterns for the development of ASP.NET applications, but there are.

REMEMBER

Keep in mind, none of this has much to do with how the application runs. These are just different ways to do the same thing. Each way has pros and cons. Look into them carefully before making your decisions.

You'll find that many of the options here have a lot to do with where to put the code. This falls into the arena of application architecture or software patterns. The following sections translate the ASP.NET patterns into the traditional names as closely as possible, so you can adapt what others say to what you learn here.

REMEMBER

These are just high-level software design principles. Nothing you see here will matter to the end users — they see HTML. Nothing you see here will change the way ASP.NET works. There is still HTML markup with ASP.NET controls, and C# code to manage those controls.

Your style of application will be dictated by several different things. The project type is the first consideration, and your team is second. The following sections discuss a few of the more popular styles and how these variables fit.

Coding behind

The default condition for creating ASP.NET applications is with a code-behind file. Just as you saw in the first example, Visual Studio creates an ASPX file for the markup code and an ASPX.CS file for the C# code. If diagrammed, it would look like Figure 2-11.

FIGURE 2-11:
The structure of a code-behind style project.

There are a few benefits to this, and they are fairly important.

>> **Division of labor:** First, it separates the C# server code from the ASP.NET and HTML template code. Although it doesn't do a perfect job, it's a lot better than scripting languages like Active Server Pages and PHP that have everything merged together. It just makes things easier to keep track of.

>> **Speed and security:** Using this pattern, Microsoft compiles the C# code into a DLL. This is the same approach used for the class library examples in Book 2. Using DLLs makes the application much faster and protects the application somewhat from criminals.

>> **Legacy-based:** This pattern mimics Windows Forms development, going back to Visual Basic 3. It is easy for people to pick up if they already have experience.

Building in n-tier

Going the opposite direction from inline code, many programmers prefer to use a method that used to be called n-tier code, but now it's called a hundred different things. What it boils down to is purposefully dividing the code of the application up into DLLs, instead of just having Visual Studio do it for you.

To show what this approach requires, Figure 2-12 displays a normal code-behind style ASP.NET application. Now, say you put all the data access code — code that talks to the database — in one class project. Then you put all the business logic — math and validation and stuff — in another class project.

FIGURE 2-12:
Structure of
n-tier code.

All the code in the code-behind layer, then, would be stuff that makes the markup work, right? Yup. That's the idea. Layering your application like this makes debugging easier, separates concerns even more, and provides for code reuse. It's also easier to unit test. If you have a cellphone application that uses the same data model, you can use the same database code if you break it out.

Implementing n-tier is simple. Just make a class project for every logical division in your code. Something so simple can sometimes be demanding, however. Determining where to put what and how to hook everything together is nontrivial — but also beyond the scope of this book. Get some of the Wrox Professional ASP. NET titles, such as *Professional C# 6 and .NET Core 1.0* by Christian Nagel (Wiley), to learn more about web application architecture.

Modeling the View Controller

ASP.NET MVC takes the idea of n-tier a step further by formalizing it. The tough decisions mentioned earlier relating to deciding where everything goes are largely made for you in ASP.NET MVC.

In a nutshell, the idea is that your markup goes in the View, your business logic goes in the Controller, and your database connection code goes in the Model. Sounds like n-tier. The differences are mostly theoretical.

The big benefit to MVC over other kinds of web forms apps is that the user inter-face code is much more testable with automated tests. In fact, when you start an ASP.NET MVC project, it asks you to create a test project along with it.

Another difference from n-tier is some formalization to the implementation of MVC. It is a project type, and rather than having to figure out how things hook up, MVC does some of the work for you.

MVC is a big topic that this book can't cover in any detail. If you have a large project for which you need to divide up the work among developers with vary-ing skill sets, it's cool. Read more in a book such as *Professional ASP.NET MVC 5,* by Jon Galloway, Brad Wilson, K. Scott Allen, and David Matson (Wiley) for more information.

Chapter **3**

Controlling Your Development Experience

A SP.NET is a *rendering engine*. It takes preset batches of functionality and renders it into HTML. For instance, ASP.NET can take a database table and a little bit of layout information and make a nice, dynamic HTML table. Rendering engines are a good idea in the web world. With a bunch of different implementations and versions, your rendering engine can produce different user markup out of the same effective code base.

ASP.NET renders code well. You can tell it to make mobile-device markup and text-only markup and rich Internet Explorer markup from the same ASP. NET file, and it will do an okay job. The rendering ability is possible because of *web controls*. Web controls are controls that ASP.NET renders into client-side markup, like HTML, CSS, and JavaScript. Well-programmed controls protect the developer from the implementation details but can still do what is needed to be done when the time comes.

Web controls aren't anything special. Basically, they show something like a pretty text box in the Designer pane of Visual Studio and then emit text — such as an `<input>` tag — when called upon to do so. ASP.NET has a lot of included controls, many other controls are available from third-party providers, and you can even build your own and base them on existing controls. It's a good system.

Showing Stuff to the User

Web surfers want to look at stuff. For them to look at it, you have to show it. Most of the controls in the ASP.NET control library are about showing things to the user.

Although there are a lot of controls, only some of them apply to the subject matter of this book — C#. This doesn't mean you shouldn't use them, but they are more about the HTML and less about the code on the server. So this chapter covers just a few controls. For more, please pick up *ASP.NET 3.5 For Dummies*, by Ken Cox (Wiley).

Labels versus plain old text

The most basic item on an average web page is text. Look at a normal site, such as Microsoft.com. You find a text box, maybe two, and a handful of images as well. Most of what is there is text.

Text comes in a few flavors in ASP.NET. The two this chapter discusses are Label text and, well, *text* text. Label text is text inside a named span that you can change with C# code. Then there is just normal text on the page. This text is static — downloaded to the client just as you typed it. To see how this works, start a new web project. Just follow these steps:

1. **Choose File⇨New⇨Project.**

   You see the New Project dialog box.

2. **Select the Visual C#\Web folder.**

   Visual Studio displays the list of projects.

3. **Higlight the ASP.NET Web Application (.NET Framework) project type.**

4. **Type** WebControls **in the Name field and click OK.**

   The wizard displays the New ASP.NET Web Application dialog box.

5. **Select the Empty template and click OK.**

   The Empty template creates an empty project that you can use to create whatever sort of project you want. You can still add folders and core references used for any of the other template types, as well as add unit tests and security as needed. The Empty template simply gives you the flexibility to decide what your project contains, or whether it contains anything at all when you start it.

Now that you have an empty project, you can see that it doesn't contain much. Solution Explorer contains just the essentials: `AssemblyInfo.cs` (identification and version information for your application), packages.config (a listing of the packages used within the application, such as the targeted .NET Framework version), and `Web.config` (information used to configure the application for various builds). To do anything useful, you must add some files by using the following steps:

1. **Right-click the project entry, WebControls, in Solution Explorer and choose Add⇨Web Form from the context menu.**

   You see a Specify Name for Item dialog box.

2. **Type Text.aspx and click OK.**

3. **Change to Split view.**

   There will be a default `div` that you saw in Chapter 2. However, unlike the Web Form in Chapter 2, this one won't contain any added tags or text.

4. **Press Enter after the opening `<div>` tag and type** This is new text.

   You don't see the text appear in the Design pane. Instead, you see a message saying, "Design View is out of sync with Source View. Click here to synchronize views."

5. **Click the message to perform the required synchronization.**

   Visual Studio displays the text in Design View. Synchronization errors can occur at any time between the two views. In most cases, Visual Studio sees the problem and tells you about it. When you don't see the message appear, saving and building your project will usually solve the problem (unless there is an error in your code, which you must fix before Design View is restored).

6. **On the new line in Design View, drag a Label from the Toolbox.**

   Note how pressing Enter in Design View automatically adds a `<br />` tag to Source view. This tag will appear as output later. Your finished product should look like Figure 3-1.

7. **Double-click elsewhere on the form to get to the code-behind.**

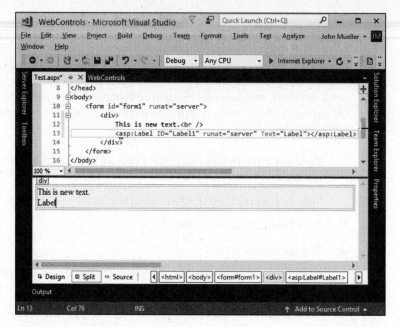

FIGURE 3-1:
There is text, and
there is text.

8. **Change the value of the label in the** Page.Load **event handler by setting the** Text **property.**

The new handler should look like this:

```
using System;

namespace WebControls
{
    public partial class Test : System.Web.UI.Page
    {
        protected void Page_Load(object sender, EventArgs e)
        {
            Label1.Text =
                "This is some text from the codebehind.";
        }
    }
}
```

9. **Choose Debug➪Start Without Debugging to launch the application.**

You'll see that the label text was set by the C# code.

How to decide between labels and text? It's usually easy. Use a label if the text will need to change based on input from the user or the server. Use text if the text is static. A description of an item that is loaded from a database? That's a label. Your CEO's bio? That's text.

Images

Images are next to text in the realm of standard website fare. It's a complex topic because few programmers are graphic artists, and making nice images that fit together and look good is hard. Nonetheless, sometimes you just want to show a picture on a page.

As with text, there are at least two ways you display images. You can use the HTML `<img>` tag, or you can use the ASP.NET `Image` control. Differences? Same as the text: If you need an image that you can manage from the C# side of things, use an image control — a product image, for example. If it is just a static image, like the picture of your CEO, use the HTML tag. Just follow these steps to add an image with ASP.NET's `Image` control:

1. **Add two images to your project by right-clicking the project and choosing Add⇨Existing Item.**

   You can find two images or download some.

2. **Add a new Web Form called** Images.aspx.

3. **Select Split View.**

4. **Press Enter after the `<div>` tag in Source View and drag one of the pictures onto the new line.**

   You see the image appear in Design View.

5. **Press Enter in Design View a few times to make some space.**

6. **Drag an Image control from the Toolbox onto the page where the cursor is sitting.**

   It should appear as a broken image. That's okay.

7. **Double-click elsewhere on the page to get the** Page.Load **event handler and switch to Code View.**

8. **Add the following code to load the second graphic into the Image control:**

```
using System;

namespace WebControls
{
```

```
public partial class Images : System.Web.UI.Page
{
    protected void Page_Load(object sender, EventArgs e)
    {
        Image1.ImageUrl = "Colorblk3.jpg";
    }
}
```

9. **Right-click the** `Images.aspx` **page in the Solution Explorer and select Set as Start Page from the context menu.**

10. **Choose Debug⇨Start Without Debugging to see it run.**

You're probably getting the idea by this point. You can use HTML and set static values, or you can use the ASP.NET controls and set dynamic values. In the examples here, you're obviously just setting "static" dynamic values, but you could be reading from a web service, a database, or even calculating the values. Images can be listed from a directory. Text could be generated and read into a table. The options are endless.

Panels and multiviews

Managing all these text blocks and images can be rough. ASP.NET provides a number of tools that help, including the two following tools:

>> **Panels** are just divs that you can manage in code-behind. As with the text and images you added in the preceding section, panels can be named and controlled in C#. The server will process changes before it sends the HTML to the browser. This helps to break the content into manageable groups.

>> **Multiviews** are essentially containers that hold a lot of panels. You can use them for wizards and tag groupings. They help to manage the panels, which help manage the content. For more information, search MSDN for ASP.NET Multiview.

From the client's perspective, panels and multiviews are effectively the same structure, but they provide developers with a few options. For instance, the multiview shows one view only of itself by default, whereas you have to hide panels that are not in use.

Tables

Tables work like other web controls. In HTML, you have the basic ‹table›, ‹tr›, and ‹td› tags. ASP.NET has a Table control, with TableRows and TableCells. If you add an ASP.NET table, it looks like this:

```
<%@ Page Language="C#" AutoEventWireup="true" CodeBehind="Tables.aspx.cs"
    Inherits="Chapter_3.Tables" %>

<!DOCTYPE html PUBLIC "-//W3C//DTD XHTML 1.0 Transitional//EN"
    "http://www.w3.org/TR/xhtml1/DTD/xhtml1-transitional.dtd">

<html xmlns="http://www.w3.org/1999/xhtml" >
<head runat="server">
    <title></title>
</head>
<body>
    <form id="form1" runat="server">
    <div>

        <asp:Table ID="Table1" runat="server">
            <asp:TableRow runat="server">
                <asp:TableCell runat="server"></asp:TableCell>
                <asp:TableCell runat="server"></asp:TableCell>
                <asp:TableCell runat="server"></asp:TableCell>
            </asp:TableRow>
            <asp:TableRow runat="server">
                <asp:TableCell runat="server"></asp:TableCell>
                <asp:TableCell runat="server"></asp:TableCell>
                <asp:TableCell runat="server"></asp:TableCell>
            </asp:TableRow>
            <asp:TableRow runat="server">
                <asp:TableCell runat="server"></asp:TableCell>
                <asp:TableCell runat="server"></asp:TableCell>
                <asp:TableCell runat="server"></asp:TableCell>
            </asp:TableRow>
        </asp:Table>

    </div>
    </form>
</body>
</html>
```

So what's the point of creating tables this way? Well, you can name those rows and cells and then manage them in the code-behind using C#. At one time, tables were used for two things: layout and tabular data. Layout has been superseded by CSS. Using tables to perform layout tasks will cause you a great deal of woe and won't win you friends with users, either.

For tabular data, tables still work. However, there is a more interesting solution. The GridView (found in the Data section of the Toolbox) is just as functional — and it is bindable. The "Data Binding" section, later in this chapter, discusses the GridView in more detail.

Getting Some Input from the User

Acquiring input from the user is one of the most significant processes that web developers do. Data-active web is all about interactivity. Getting information from a user is job one. You can do a lot of things to get input from the user, but there is a subset of the controls that is generally considered to be *user input.* You'll use those controls a lot.

Using text input controls

The most obvious form of collecting data from a user is the text input boxes, as shown in Figure 3-2. In HTML, there are essentially three defined controls: the standard single line text box, the specialized text box (such as one used for passwords), and the text area. The TextBox ASP.NET control handles all these common and special text box types. A TextMode property tells IIS how to render the control.

FIGURE 3-2:
The three text inputs, all in a row.

TECHNICAL STUFF

The TextMode property values correspond to the HTML5 equivalents, which you set using the type attribute. You can read more about these equivalents at https://www.w3schools.com/tags/tag_input.asp. The supported TextMode property values help you create these kinds of TextBox controls: SingleLine (the default), MultiLine, Password, Color, Date, DateTime, DateTimeLocal, Email, Month, Number, Range, Search, Phone, Time, Url, and Week. Each TextBox control type serves a different purpose in making your application more useful.

To use the TextBox control, drag it into the Designer from the Toolbox. You can change the property of a control instance — the only other significant element — in the ASP.NET markup, the property panel, or the C# code. The properties that you are the most interested in include

>> **ID:** The name that you use to reference the control in the C# code. This needs to be set first, before you can use the control.

>> **TextMode:** This determines the type of text box that gets rendered. ASP.NET actually provides for a wealth of text modes.

>> **MaxLength:** The maximum number of characters that the user can type in the field. Note that this doesn't work when the TextMode is defined as TextArea.

>> **Height and Width:** The size that the text box appears on the page.

>> **CssClass:** The style sheet class that the control will be rendered to use. Must be used in conjunction with a style sheet.

>> **Enabled:** Set if the field can be typed in by the user.

The example in Figure 3-2 relies on three TextBox controls dragged onto the Designer and set each to one of the common TextModes. Here is the resultant ASP. NET markup:

```
<%@ Page Language="C#" AutoEventWireup="true"
    CodeBehind="Textboxes.aspx.cs" Inherits="UsingTextbox.Textboxes" %>


<!DOCTYPE html>

<html xmlns="http://www.w3.org/1999/xhtml">
<head runat="server">
    <title></title>
</head>
<body>
    <form id="form1" runat="server">
        <div>
            1 - The TextBox<br/>
            <asp:TextBox ID="TextBox1"
                runat="server">The TextBox</asp:TextBox>
            <br/>
            <br/>
            2. The TextArea<br/>
            <asp:TextBox ID="TextBox2" runat="server"
                TextMode="MultiLine">The TextArea</asp:TextBox>
            <br/>
            <br/>
```

```
            3. The Password<br/>
            <asp:TextBox ID="TextBox3" runat="server"
                TextMode="Password">The Password</asp:TextBox>
        </div>
    </form>
</body>
</html>
```

Note that even though the third TextBox has a Text property value of The Password, Figure 3-2 shows the resulting text box as blank. The lack of output text makes sense given that no one will have a default password. If you change this third TextBox to some other type, such as SingleLine, you see that the Text property value does indeed show up when you run the example.

To set properties in the C# code, you refer to the ID, as set in the Properties panel. If you use the defaults (don't do this in real code, make real names for controls), configuring the first text box might look something like this:

```
public partial class WebForm1 : System.Web.UI.Page
{
    protected void Page_Load(object sender, EventArgs e)
    {
        TextBox1.MaxLength = 20;
        TextBox1.Height = 22;
        TextBox1.Width = 135;
        TextBox1.Enabled = true;
    }
}
```

Using single-item selection controls

After collecting text, the next most common user-input gathering operation is asking them to choose an item from a list. In HTML, you can do this with check boxes, radio buttons, or drop-down lists (see Figure 3-3). ASP.NET provides for all of these items:

» **The Boolean check box:** This is just one single check box where the answer is Yes or No. This is still considered a single item selection even though there is only one item to select from and is usually used to represent a Boolean or bit in the C# code. It is represented by the CheckBox control.

» **The radio button list:** Radio buttons are nice because they prevent the user from selecting more than one option while seeing all the options. Lists are an interesting beast, because they can be bound to collections. (see the later section called "Data Binding"). This control is RadioButtonList.

>> **The drop-down list:** Represented by the DropDownList control, this type of list allows the user to click to see the list and then click one item, which then closes the list. It can also be bound to a collection.

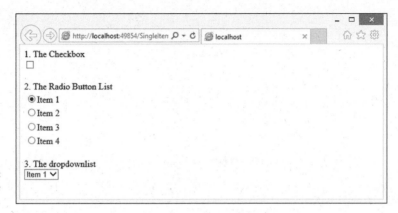

FIGURE 3-3:
The single selectors.

Here is the code for all three. Note that both the DropDownList and the RadioButtonList use the ListItem control to render the list items. In addition, to ensure that the controls appear as users expect them to appear, one of the ListItem entries must have the Selected property set to True.

```
<%@ Page Language="C#" AutoEventWireup="true"
    CodeBehind="SingleItem.aspx.cs" Inherits="ListControls.SingleItem" %>

<!DOCTYPE html>

<html xmlns="http://www.w3.org/1999/xhtml">
<head runat="server">
    <title></title>
</head>
<body>
    <form id="form1" runat="server">
        <div>
            1. The Checkbox<br/>
            <asp:CheckBox ID="CheckBox1" runat="server"/>
            <br/>
            <br/>
            2. The Radio Button List<br/>
            <asp:RadioButtonList ID="RadioButtonList1" runat="server">
                <asp:ListItem Selected="True">Item 1</asp:ListItem>
                <asp:ListItem>Item 2</asp:ListItem>
                <asp:ListItem>Item 3</asp:ListItem>
                <asp:ListItem>Item 4</asp:ListItem>
```

Controlling Your
Development Experience

```
                    </asp:RadioButtonList>
                    <br/>
                    3. The dropdownlist<br/>
                    <asp:DropDownList ID="DropDownList1" runat="server">
                        <asp:ListItem Selected="True">Item 1</asp:ListItem>
                        <asp:ListItem>Item 2</asp:ListItem>
                        <asp:ListItem>Item 3</asp:ListItem>
                        <asp:ListItem>Item 4</asp:ListItem>
                    </asp:DropDownList>
                </div>
            </form>
        </body>
    </html>
```

Using multiple-item selection controls

Sometimes you want the user to be able to choose more than one of the items available in a list. HTML has two controls that handle that: the ListBox and the CheckBox List (see Figure 3-4). ASP.NET replicates these, like this:

» **The** ListBox: This list is a lot like a DropDownList, except that no expansion required — you see the expanded list right away, scroll bar and all. To select more than one item, the user is usually required to hold down the Control or Command key while clicking.

» **The** CheckBoxList: This is exactly what it sounds like: a list of check boxes. It looks just like a radio button list, except with check boxes (see Figure 3-4).

FIGURE 3-4:
Controls
for multiple
selections.

Here is the code for these. As with the DropDownList, the ListItem is used to show the items. If it were databound, the ListItems would not be there — they would just be rendered from the data source at runtime. Note also that because the user isn't expecting to have any particular item chosen (because multiple selections are possible), none of the ListItem entries have the Selected property set to True.

```
<%@ Page Language="C#" AutoEventWireup="true"
    CodeBehind="MultiItem.aspx.cs" Inherits="ListControls.MultiItem" %>

<!DOCTYPE html>

<html xmlns="http://www.w3.org/1999/xhtml">
<head runat="server">
    <title></title>
</head>
<body>
    <form id="form1" runat="server">
        <div>
            1. Checkboxlist<br/>
            <asp:CheckBoxList ID="CheckBoxList1" runat="server">
                <asp:ListItem>Item 1</asp:ListItem>
                <asp:ListItem>Item 2</asp:ListItem>
                <asp:ListItem>Item 3</asp:ListItem>
                <asp:ListItem>Item 4</asp:ListItem>
            </asp:CheckBoxList>
            <br/>
            2. Listbox<br/>
            <asp:ListBox ID="ListBox1" runat="server"
                SelectionMode="Multiple">
                <asp:ListItem>Item 1</asp:ListItem>
                <asp:ListItem>Item 2</asp:ListItem>
                <asp:ListItem>Item 3</asp:ListItem>
                <asp:ListItem>Item 4</asp:ListItem>
            </asp:ListBox>
        </div>
    </form>
</body>
</html>
```

TIP

Note that when using a ListBox control, you must set the SelectionMode property to Multiple. The default mode of operation is to allow only a single item selection. In addition, unlike the CheckboxList, where you can select and deselect items individually, the user must either Shift-click or Ctrl-click to select multiple items in a ListBox control. Clicking a single entry selects only that entry and deselects any other entries that had been selected earlier.

Using other kinds of input controls

ASP.NET provides a number of other input types that are combinations of the above, or are nontraditional inputs. They are all special-use controls, but they need to be in your toolbox so that you can use them when the need arises. They include the following input types:

>> **FileUpload:** The `FileUpload` does exactly what it says. It creates an HTML input of type `File` and makes the form *enctype* (encoding type) into multipart form-data. This allows the web server to accept a long stream of binary data, which you can then capture with a streamreader.

>> **ImageMap:** An `ImageMap` is a relic of a bygone era. Essentially, it allows you to create a pixel map (think of the boundary lines on maps; the lines don't actually exist, but they do help you define regions for reference purposes) on top of images and then assign regions within those maps to URLs or other actions. This control assists you by giving you the framework. You still have to provide the map. Now, usually people use separate images.

>> **Calendar:** The `Calendar` control is just a text box that helps the user format dates properly. It works well. There are a ton of formatting options, too — check them out in the Properties panel.

REMEMBER

There are other input controls, but this and the previous sections list the input controls that you use most often. What you need to remember are the basics — they are visible controls with ASP.NET implementations and HTML output. You can use the Properties panel, the markup, or the C# code to change the properties. And you can bind them to objects in your code —discussed in the "Data Binding" section, later in this chapter.

Submitting input with submit buttons

After you get all this input into a form, you need the user to send it to you. The basic way to do this is through the submit button. Chapter 1 of this minibook discusses the `PostBack` event, and how Microsoft used JavaScript to change the way the posting of forms back to the server works. The submit button is how one does this.

REMEMBER

Let's be clear — *any* control can cause a postback. If you set an event handler for an event in a control, it will cause a postback. You can save changes to the form data at any point after it gets back to the server. You should use the submit button because it is what the user is used to. The ASP.NET default controls have three buttons:

- **»** Button is just what it says — an input of type Button submitted in HTML.

- **»** ImageButton is a button control that has a built-in src property for images.

- **»** LinkButton just shows an HTML anchor and treats it like a button.

Data Binding

Getting the data into a control in a web page isn't enough. You need some way to *persist* (save for reuse) that information after the data is entered. Data binding is the answer. *Data binding* tells a control what member of the underlying class to get its data from. For instance, if you have a collection of Apple objects with a property of Color that you want to show in a text box, you can bind the value Apple.Color to the Text property.

But things get more interesting than that. Say that you want to provide a list of colors and allow the user to select the color of the object in question. You can do that by binding the list of a collection and the selected value to the SelectedItem property of the list control. If you want to show the color itself, you can bind to the FontColor property of a text control.

Setting up your markup for binding

Back in the Active Server Page days, you put all your data on the page by simply printing it there. Sounds simple, but it had a lot of problems. Foremost, your form had to have a lot of knowledge about the data it was showing. This is a bad thing. Anyway, the format for doing it was

```
<%= ThisIsWhatIWantToPrint %>
```

If you needed a list, you looped in the surrounding code. If you needed a method result, you just put the method right in there. What you saw was what you got.

Data binding is the more enlightened form of getting data on the screen. The controls that are built into ASP.NET know how to handle data on their own, as long as that data meets some basic specifics. You create data binding by setting a control property to a member of the underlying class. For a single control, such as a text box, you just set the property in question, like this:

```
<asp:Label ID="Label1" runat="server" Text='<%# BindToThisVariable %>' />
```

To bind to a repeating control, such as a `ListBox`, you set the `DataSource` property. The variables you bind to need to be in the code-behind and be public. If they aren't, you'll get runtime errors. That's also why binding in the code is a good idea (as shown in the next section).

Creating the required mock class

Before you can start performing binding tasks in code, you need a project to perform the task. The following steps get you started:

1. **Create a new project using the steps found in the "Labels versus plain old text" section, earlier in this chapter, and name this project UsingBinding.**

2. **Right-click the project entry in Solution Explorer and choose Add⇨Class.**

    You see the Add New Item dialog box. The wizard automatically selects the Class entry for you.

3. **Type Show and click Add.**

    Visual Studio adds a new class to your project.

4. **Add the following code to your new class:**

    ```csharp
    using System;

    namespace UsingBinding
    {
        public class Show
        {
            public int ID { get; set; }
            public String ShowTitle { get; set; }
            public String EpisodeTitle { get; set; }
            public DateTime ScheduledTime { get; set; }
            public int Channel { get; set; }
        }
    }
    ```

    This class is just for example — it could be a database or a data class or an Entity Framework model.

Adding an existing Web Form

At this point, you have a new project with a kind of data source to use as an example. The following steps provide a quick method of adding a user interface you worked with earlier to the project. You can use this technique when experimenting to keep existing tests intact while moving on to new methods you want to try.

1. **Right-click the project entry in Solution Explorer and choose Add⇨Existing Item.**

   You see the Add Existing Item dialog box.

2. **Highlight the** Test.aspx **file found in the** C:\CSAIO4D\BK06\CH03\ WebControls\WebControls **folder of the downloadable source; then click Add.**

   Visual Studio adds a copy of this existing item to your project so that when you make modifications, they're made to the copy rather than the original. Note that you can choose to add the item as a link, rather than a copy, by using the options found in the drop-down list associated with the Add button. When Visual Studio copies Test.aspx for you, it also copies Test.aspx.cs and Test.aspx.designer.cs, so that you get the complete Web Form, along with its associated code.

3. **Double-click the** Test.aspx.cs **file in Solution Explorer to get to the code-behind.**

   You may have to open the Test.aspx hierarchy to see the Test.aspx.cs file entry.

4. **Delete any code already appears in the** Page_Load.

5. **Change the namespace entry from** WebControls **to** UsingBinding.

   The namespace of the user interface must match the namespace of the underlying class in this case. Of course, you can always import the external namespace instead. This approach is simpler.

6. **Double-click** Test.aspx **in Solution Explorer to open it in Split View and modify the Inherits property, as shown here:**

   ```
   Inherits="UsingBinding.Test"
   ```

   To create a connection between the user interface and its code-behind, the Inherits property value must match the namespace and class of the code-behind.

Creating data binding using markup

Importing the Web Form enables you to use existing code in a new way. The following steps perform the modifications required to demonstrate markup binding.

1. **Add the following code to the** Page_Load **method to create a mock** Show **object.**

```
using System;

namespace UsingBinding
{
    public partial class Test : System.Web.UI.Page
    {
        protected Show show;

        protected void Page_Load(object sender,
            EventArgs e)
        {
            show = new Show { ID = 1, Channel = 5,
                EpisodeTitle = "ASP.NET Databinding",
                ScheduledTime =
                new DateTime(2017, 9, 12, 12, 0, 0),
                ShowTitle = "The C# Show" };
            Page.DataBind();
        }
    }
}
```

REMEMBER

In a real project, you'd get this object from the database or the service layer. To use the resulting object, you must bind it to the page using the Page. DataBind() method as shown.

2. **Modify the** Label Text **property like this:**

```
<asp:Label ID="Label1" runat="server"
    Text="<%# show.EpisodeTitle %>"></asp:Label>
```

3. **Choose Debug➪Start Without Debugging.**

The application starts, and you see the output text of ASP.NET Databinding as expected.

This isn't the interesting way to bind things. It is nice because you can edit the binding without recompiling, but the interesting way is in the C# code. Doing it in the C# code is much more readable and manageable. There are times to use each, but this is a C# book, so the next section shows the C# method.

Data binding using the code-behind

Rather than set a property directly in the markup, you can set it equal to a value in the code-behind. For a repeating control, you can set a DataSource property in the C# code for the control. Then, when you bind the page, it uses that value to load the right value or values from the code-behind. Keep in mind, though, that with the Text property of a Label (for instance), this is just simple data binding. The following sections show how to add a code-behind project to your existing project.

Renaming the existing Test item and adding a new one

You can't add a new item with the same name as an existing item. When creating tests to try new techniques, it's helpful to know how to rename things in Visual Studio. The following steps show how to rename the existing Test item and add a new one.

1. **Right-click** Test.aspx **in Solution Explorer and choose Rename from the context menu.**

   Visual Studio highlights the filename so that you can type a new one.

2. **Type** Test1 **and press Enter.**

   Visual Studio automatically performs all the required renaming for you, including modifying the Inherits property of the Web Form markup.

3. **Right-click** Test **in the** public partial class Test **declaration and choose Rename from the context menu.**

   You see the Rename: Test dialog box, where you can choose what to rename in your code. In this case, all you need to worry about is your code, which is included by default.

4. **Type** Test1 **in place of** Test **for the new class name.**

5. **Click Apply.**

   You may see an error stating that not all references are properly updated. The Inherits property is generally the problem. It must appear as Inherits= "UsingBinding.Test1" in this case.

6. **Choose Debug⇨Start Without Debugging.**

   The application starts, and you see the output text of ASP.NET Databinding as expected.

Now that you have renamed your existing project, you can add a new copy of Test.aspx to use for the code-behind part of the example. The "Adding an existing Web Form" section, earlier in this chapter, tells you how to perform this task. Make sure you set the new Test to be the starting page by right-clicking its entry in Solution Explorer and choosing Set As Start Page from the context menu.

Creating data binding using code-behind

Now that you have a new copy of the test page to use, you can make modifications to use code-behind for data binding. It's then possible to compare Test and Test1 to see the differences in the two techniques.

1. Delete the Text property of the Label control so it appears like this:

```
<asp:Label ID="Label1" runat="server"></asp:Label>
```

2. In the code-behind, set the Text property equal to the property on the control that you want to bind to.

```
public partial class Test : System.Web.UI.Page
{
    protected Show show;

    protected void Page_Load(object sender,
        EventArgs e)
    {
        show = new Show
        {
            ID = 1,
            Channel = 5,
            EpisodeTitle = "Code Behind Databinding",
            ScheduledTime =
            new DateTime(2017, 9, 12, 12, 0, 0),
            ShowTitle = "The C# Show"
        };

        Label1.Text = show.EpisodeTitle;
    }
}
```

Notice that there is no DataBind() method call for the page.

3. Run the application to see the value get set.

This works well, but remember, this is only simple data binding. It's just setting values. Full data binding is for controls with repeating properties.

Using commonly bound controls

Simple data binding gets you started. However, data binding is great for dealing with groups of items, bound to repeating structures in HTML. The typical example of data binding is the `GridView` control. If everything is set up correctly, you have remarkable control over how the grid looks. If things aren't named correctly, you still have the option to show all the data in a default style. To create a databound grid, follow these steps:

1. Add a new Web Form to the project called `Grid.aspx`.

2. Change to Split View.

3. Open the Data section of the Toolbox and drag a GridView onto the design surface.

4. Double-click the design surface to change to Code View.

5. Create a mock collection of Shows by using the following code.

```csharp
protected List<Show> shows = new List<Show>();

protected void Page_Load(object sender, EventArgs e)
{
    shows.Add(new Show { ID = 1, Channel = 5,
        EpisodeTitle = "ASP.NET Databinding", ScheduledTime =
        new DateTime(2017, 9, 12, 12, 0, 0),
        ShowTitle = "The C# Show" });
    shows.Add(new Show { ID = 2, Channel = 5,
        EpisodeTitle = "ASP.NET Styling", ScheduledTime =
        new DateTime(2017, 9, 12, 13, 0, 0),
        ShowTitle = "The C# Show" });
    shows.Add(new Show { ID = 3, Channel = 8,
        EpisodeTitle = "Inheritance", ScheduledTime =
        new DateTime(2017, 9, 16, 9, 0, 0),
        ShowTitle = "Learning C#" });
    shows.Add(new Show { ID = 4, Channel = 8,
        EpisodeTitle = "Partial Classes", ScheduledTime =
        new DateTime(2017, 9, 17, 9, 0, 0),
        ShowTitle = "Learning C#" });
    shows.Add(new Show { ID = 5, Channel = 8,
        EpisodeTitle = "Operator Overloading", ScheduledTime =
        new DateTime(2017, 9, 18, 9, 0, 0),
        ShowTitle = "Learning C#" });
}
```

6. **Add the following** DataSource **property value and the** DataBind() **method call as the last two lines of** Page_Load(), **as shown here.**

```
GridView1.DataSource = shows;
Page.DataBind();
```

7. **Choose Debug⇨Start Without Debugging to see the application run.**

As you can see in Figure 3-5, the columns from the database are all automatically bound to the HTML grid.

ID	ShowTitle	EpisodeTitle	ScheduledTime	Channel
1	The C# Show	ASP.NET Databinding	9/12/2017 12:00:00 PM	5
2	The C# Show	ASP.NET Styling	9/12/2017 1:00:00 PM	5
3	Learning C#	Inheritance	9/16/2017 9:00:00 AM	8
4	Learning C#	Partial Classes	9/17/2017 9:00:00 AM	8
5	Learning C#	Operator Overloading	9/18/2017 9:00:00 AM	8

FIGURE 3-5:
The TV schedule!
Columns here are
bound to the grid.

That's all well and good, but what if you don't want to show the ID or want to put the columns someplace more to your liking? You can do that, too; it just takes a little more effort.

The capability of the GridView to automatically show all columns in a table is handled by a property: AutoGenerateColumns. The first thing you need to do is set that to False. This tells ASP.NET that you're going to set all the columns manually.

Next, you have to tell C# what columns you're using. Perhaps you want to show only two columns — say, Channel and Episode. To do so, you need to define and set up two BoundColumn objects. Then you need to add them to the grid. That's what happens under the hood when you add a datacolumn tag in the markup. Modify the original Page_Load() method call so that it now includes the following code between GridView1.DataSource = shows; and Page.DataBind();.

```
GridView1.DataSource = shows;
GridView1.AutoGenerateColumns = false;

BoundField channelColumn = new BoundField();
channelColumn.DataField = "Channel";
channelColumn.HeaderText = "Channel";
GridView1.Columns.Add(channelColumn);
```

```
BoundField episodeColumn = new BoundField();
episodeColumn.DataField = "EpisodeTitle";
episodeColumn.HeaderText = "Episode";
GridView1.Columns.Add(episodeColumn);

Page.DataBind();
```

When you run the example now, you see only the two columns you expect. You have complete control over the presentation of data using techniques like those shown here.

Styling Your Controls

When you have the data in your controls, you need to get the control looking a certain way. There are a lot of options here. All the controls come with properties that can be set at design time and runtime, or bound to cascading style sheets (CSS).

Being able to style is necessary; being able to manage the styles at runtime with C# is darn near magic. Using a combination of the three methods makes it possible to create dynamic applications that give the user the best experiences.

Setting control properties

By far, the simplest way to set a style on a control is to use the built-in properties. It is straightforward; you know exactly what you're applying a look to; and IntelliSense helps you do so.

Unfortunately, this isn't the best way to do things. Setting control properties incurs a host of problems. If you have more than one control to set up, you have to set the properties on each of them — even if they are the same. The runtime has to handle a lot of extra stuff. Also, it makes your code messy.

Sometimes, though, you need to set a style this way. The best way to see them all is to check out the Properties panel item for the GridView. Set it to Categorized and look at the bottom, as shown in Figure 3-6. If you set properties here, they appear in the markup as in the following example, not the code-behind, but you can at least find the names here:

```
<asp:GridView ID="GridView1" runat="server"
    onselectedindexchanged="GridView1_SelectedIndexChanged">
    <RowStyle BackColor="#FF6666"/>
</asp:GridView>
```

After you get the name of something you want to set, you just set it like any other property:

```
GridView1.RowStyle.BackColor = System.Drawing.Color.Red;
```

The roughest part is discovering what framework element the style will want as a value. The easiest way to determine this is to type the part to the left of the equals sign and then mouse over the property to see how it is declared. BackColor, for instance, requires a System.Drawing.Color element.

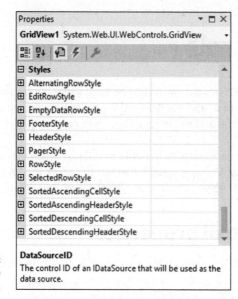

FIGURE 3-6:
Styles in the
Properties panel.

Binding styles with CSS

Because you're in a web application, using cascading style sheets (CSS) seems like a good approach to handle your styles. Nearly every control in ASP.NET has a property — CssClass — that takes advantage of the styles loaded as part of the project. (You can discover more about how CSS works at https://www.w3schools.com/Css/.)

To get started, you need a CSS template. A *CSS template* is a collection of styles that you connect to your markup. The name of a style in the template often matches the name of a markup object, creating a connection between the two. To bind styles with CSS, follow these steps:

1. **Right-click the project in Solution Explorer and select Add⇨New Item.**

   You see the Add New Item dialog box.

2. **Open the Web\Markup folder and highlight Style Sheet.**

3. **Type** Chapter3.css **in the Name field and click Add.**

   Visual Studio automatically opens the style sheet for you and includes a body style.

4. **Add the following style to the style sheet.**

   ```css
   .GridView {
       font-family:French Script MT;
       background-color: lightblue;
   }
   ```

5. **Bind the style sheet to your** Grid.aspx **file by adding the following** <link> **tag entry to the** <head> **element:**

   ```html
   <head runat="server">
       <title></title>
       <link rel="stylesheet" type="text/css" href="Chapter3.css">
   </head>
   ```

6. **Add the** .GridView **class to your** GridView **by adding the** CssClass **property entry shown here:**

   ```html
   <asp:GridView ID="GridView1" runat="server"
       CssClass="GridView"></asp:GridView>
   ```

7. **Choose Debug⇨Start Without Debugging to see the application run.**

   The application now uses a style to display the GridView and associated text. You can also perform this task using the Properties panel. In addition, you can set the style in code-behind by using code such as this:

   ```
   GridView1.CssStyle = "GridViews";
   ```

Making Sure the Site Is Accessible

Everyone has special needs, and those needs change as time progresses. Someone with perfect eyesight in the morning might suffer from tired eyes in the afternoon. Many web users have some sort of special need all the time. Whether the need is intermittent or constant, making your site *accessible* means making it easy for everyone to use.

Microsoft has made a significant investment in accessible web browsing, and you'll be pleased to find that most of the controls make good decisions about accessibility right out of the box. Understanding how to use them for this purpose takes a little effort, however.

TIP

If you're building websites for large enterprises or the government, Section 508 (an amendment to the Rehabilitation Act) makes this very important. Check out *Accessibility for Everybody*, by John Paul Mueller (Apress), and http://www.section508.gov for more information.

Most ASP.NET controls, where applicable, fit a certain feature list for accessibility. The goal is to make coding for accessibility easy for the programmer and functional for the user.

- » Any element that isn't made of text should have an alternate text option. For instance, all image tags support an AlternateText property, which populates the HTML alt tag. Web-to-text readers will "speak" the contents of this tag in place of the image. If you add an image to a web page, Visual Studio even prompts you for the alternate text.

- » Controls don't require the use of style sheets or color dependency. If you want, you can easily strip all style information from a page for simplicity of use by a reader or a low-sight version of the application.

- » All input controls in Getting Input from the User support a TabIndex property, which allows users to tab from control to control. For those not using a mouse, this is optimum.

- » Setting which part of the form has the cursor by default (called *default focus*) is easy in ASP.NET with the DefaultFocus property. Changing it is easy with the SetFocus method.

- » You can give buttons keyboard equivalents by using the AccessKey property.

- » Labels and input controls can be associated, which many web readers depend on.

A feature in Visual Studio called Check Page for Accessibility checks Web Content Accessibility Guidelines (WCAG) and Section 508 errors. If you use this feature, warnings will actually be posted to your build process.

Constructing User Controls

Have you ever been to a site with a three-part U.S. phone number shown as three text boxes? You can usually automatically tab between them, and this structure makes sure that you have exactly the right number of digits in each text box. That's something that you might very well use on every page of many applications, right?

That phone number control consists of things that you already have around you: text box controls, client-side scripting, and validation. All that you need is to put them together.

The technology that you use to combine existing controls in useful ways is called a User Control, or ASCX. ASCX is encapsulated, easy to create, and easier to use. (ASCX is the file extension for the markup files for these controls.)

Making a new phone number User Control

To demonstrate the usefulness of a User Control, this section creates a special control for handling phone numbers. In this incarnation, it is only good for U.S. format, but that's okay. It gets the point across. Just follow these steps to create the PhoneNumber control:

1. **Create a new, empty Web Forms project called CreateUserControl by using the technique you used in the "Labels versus plain old text" section, earlier in this chapter.**

2. **Right-click the project entry in Solution Explorer and choose Add⇨New Item.**

   You see the Add New Item dialog box.

3. **Select the Web Forms User Control item found in the Web\Web Forms folder.**

4. **Type** PhoneNumber.ascx **in the Name field and click Add.**

   Visual Studio adds the new control file to your project.

5. **Switch to Split View.**

6. Drag three TextBox **controls to the Designer, next to one another.**

If you want to get fancy, put hyphens between them. The TextBox controls don't have to appear on the same line for the sake of readability.

7. In the Properties panel, set the MaxLength **for the first two text boxes to 3 and the last one to 4.**

This setting prevents the user from putting too many characters in a field.

8. **Right-click the Designer and select View Code.**

9. **Add the property to the code-behind to allow a page using the control to get to the phone number:**

```
private string _phoneNumber;
public string PhoneNumberValue
{
    get
    {
        _phoneNumber = string.Format("({0}){1}-{2}",
            TextBox1.Text, TextBox2.Text, TextBox3.Text);
        return _phoneNumber;
    }
}
```

So now you have a control — just like the controls in the Toolbox — that accepts a phone number in pieces and formats it nicely. You can play with it in the next section.

Using your new control

You'll love using the PhoneNumber control that you created in the previous section. It really does work just like a Toolbox control. Follow these steps to see how it works:

1. **Right- click the project entry in Solution Explorer and choose Add⇨Web Form from the context menu.**

You see a Specify Name for Item dialog box.

2. **Type UseThePhoneNumber.aspx and click OK.**

3. **Change to Split View.**

   There will be a default `div`, as covered in Chapter 2. However, unlike the Web Form in Chapter 2, this one won't contain any added tags or text.

4. **Drag the PhoneNumber.ascx control right from the Solution Explorer onto the design surface.**

   Ta da! The control shows up the way a plain text box would, but it is just as you formatted it.

5. **Add a** `Label` **and** `Button` **to the Web Form.**

6. **Double-click the button in Design View to create a** `Click` **event handler and add the following code to it:**

   ```
   Label1.Text = PhoneNumber1.PhoneNumberValue;
   ```

7. **Right-click the ASPX page in Solution Explorer and set it as the start page.**

8. **Choose Debug⇨Start Without Debugging to start the application.**

9. **Enter a phone number in the control and click the button.**

   The formatted phone number should appear in the label.

Chapter **4**

Leveraging the .NET Framework

ASP.NET and the .NET Framework are different. ASP.NET has a dependency on the .NET Framework, but it is really defined as the collection of controls that are in Chapter 3 of this minibook, plus others. The .NET Framework brings a different set of tools.

The controls that are in ASP.NET are user-experience focused. They focus on the way the user views the application. The tools that are in the .NET Framework are transport focused — that is, focused on passing information back and forth between client and server. If you look at the System.Web namespace (which is where most of these bits are stored), you'll quickly see that most of the classes within start with "Http." There is a reason for that: HTTP is the transport protocol.

This is important because manipulating the information that goes back and forth between the client and the server is the first and best way to do anything off-trail in a web application. Whenever the default condition of the control, server, or client isn't exactly what you need, the first place you turn is the classes of the System.Web namespace.

Controls in ASP.NET and controls in the .NET Framework overlap quite a bit, but each group is distinct. You should always keep in mind which tools are at your disposal and how best to use them.

Surfing Web Streams

At its core, ASP.NET is about sending and receiving streams of text. The client sends requests in, and the server sends HTML out. Sometimes the application is the client, and sometimes it is the server. Classes in the System.Web namespace handle all these cases.

REMEMBER

Note that these solutions, along with many others within the System.Web namespace, aren't exclusively related to ASP.NET websites. Other applications can sometimes make use of the goodness provided by System.Web, so consider carefully!

Intercepting the request

In a sudden fit of reasonable naming, here's what Microsoft decided to name the object that has all the data from the client request: "Request." That person has since been fired.

There are a few different ways to look at a request, but you're concerned here with the current request, or the context request. Fortunately, this is the default request in the ASP.NET space. You can "intercept" that request with ASP.NET. But we should back up.

Digging up the request data

Every time a user types in a URL or clicks a button in a web page, a request is issued. Requests are processed by the server, and you can access them through the current context.

TECHNICAL STUFF

The *current context* is the object set that ASP.NET gives you just for being there when the request is processed. In short, the class is called HttpRequest, and ASP.NET makes an instance and calls it Request. It is an instance of the HttpRequest class and is the HttpContext.Request property. To create an environment showing a request, set up a project by following these steps:

1. **Create a new, empty ASP.NET Web application by using the steps found in the "Labels versus plain old text" section in Chapter 3 of this minibook and call it PerformRequest.**

    The Empty template creates an empty project that you can use to create whatever sort of project you want.

2. **Right-click the project entry in Solution Explorer and choose Add⇨Web Form from the context menu.**

You see a Specify Name for Item dialog box.

3. **Type** TestRequest **and click OK.**

Visual Studio adds a new Web Form.

4. **Change to Split View.**

There will be a default div that you saw in Chapter 2. However, unlike the Web Form in Chapter 2, this one won't contain any added tags or text.

5. **Drag a button control onto the page in the Designer.**

6. **Double-click the new button to create a** Click **event handler.**

7. **Add the following line of code to the top of the listing:**

```
using System.Diagnostics;
```

8. **Add the following code to** Button1_Click() **to enumerate the Request object.**

```
protected void Button1_Click(object sender, EventArgs e)
{
    foreach (String requestInfo in Request.Form)
    {
        Debug.WriteLine(requestInfo);
    }
}
```

What you're doing here is just looking at the context returned by the request. It is just somewhere for you to put the debugger, really.

9. **Add the following code to** Page_Load() **to see the difference between the original request and the postback.**

```
protected void Page_Load(object sender, EventArgs e)
{
    if (!(Page.IsPostBack))
    {
        foreach (String requestInfo in Request.Form)
        {
            Debug.WriteLine(requestInfo);
        }
    }
}
```

Notice the check for the postback statement.

Leveraging the .NET Framework

10. Put breakpoints next to the two `foreach` statements.

11. Press F5 to run the application.

Before the web application appears, the application breaks on the `foreach` in the `Page_Load()` method. Open the `Request` object in the Autos window and you'll see something like Figure 4-1. Notice that the `ContentLength` is 0 and the `HttpMethod` is GET. This is an initial URL-based request for a page.

Now press F10 until the `Page_Load()` event is over, and Visual Studio returns control to your web browser. Look in the Debug output in the Output window and note that the `Debug.WriteLine()` statement is never called because the `ContentLength` is 0. There is no form because it's an initial request. The `Form` collection (shown in the Autos window in Figure 4-1) is empty. Nothing is there except the basic request information.

Press the button when the browser comes back. Visual Studio breaks again on the other `foreach` statement in the `Button1_Click()` method. View the `Request` object in the Autos window again. All the entries, including Form (shown in Figure 4-2), that have changed appear with red print. There are four items in it, the two hidden fields added by ASP.NET, an event validation, and the button that you added, Button1.

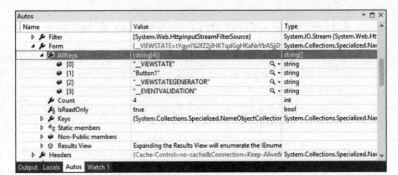

FIGURE 4-2:
The form request.

Look at the HttpMethod property in the Autos window. This is the second type of request: POST. It is in response to a form. This is where a lot useful information can be found.

Using information from requests

The request is a place that you can collect information about the user's needs and use it. Especially on postback (though not just then), there is a lot of information that you can use, including the following:

» **The content of the request.** The type (ContentType) of the request tells you if it has data or just text. You can learn whether it is ISO or Unicode (Content Encoding). You also know how long the request is (ContentLength).

» **The text of the request itself.** For instance, you have all the text of the URL (Url) and the request before this one (UrlReferrer). If you want the query string (the part after the question mark), you can get it with QueryString.

» **Whether the user is logged into a domain** (IsAuthenticated) **and if so, who the user is** (LogonUserIdentity).

» Access to the Cookies **collection** (Cookies).

When you have access to the request, you can make decisions about content. If you need to know about their login information, you have it. Check a cookie — no problem. Confirm the query string. Whatever needs to be done. You get information to the business layer, get what you need back, compose the new page of controls, and then need to modify the response. That's when you need the HttpResponse class.

Altering content sent to clients

ASP.NET and IIS do a good job of setting up markup for a client browser. You can even tell Visual Studio that you are targeting a certain browser (say, in a workgroup environment), and it will tweak the HTML that it sends to the client to make it closer to the exact implementation of the HTML standard that that browser supports.

You sometimes need to change the way the page is rendered on the client. More often, you need to change the way the metadata about the page is handed to the client. An HTML page has a lot more than the values you see on the screen. HttpResponse helps you to manage what you can and can't see.

Sending the user somewhere else

One of the most common uses of the Response object is to send the user somewhere else entirely (called *redirection*). If you look at the request headers and realize (for instance) that the user isn't logged into a Windows domain account (using HttpRequest.IsAuthenticated), you can redirect the user to a login screen:

```
If(!Request.IsAuthenticated){
    Response.Redirect("login.aspx");
}
```

On the other hand, sometimes you need to tell the user that this isn't the right place to be at all. Especially useful if you have to change the structure of your website, RedirectPermanently tells search engine spiders "nope, this isn't here anymore. Go over there and change your index." For instance, say you have a product line that was moved to a whole new URL. You could check the QueryString for the product line statement, and if you find it, redirect the link permanently.

```
If(Request.Querystring("ProductLineId")==4){
    Response.RedirectPermanently("http://newproduct.com")
}
```

Changing the request or response directly

Sometimes you just want to change things directly. Response.Write(), Response.WriteFile(), and Response.WriteSubstitution() all are designed to allow you to do just that. In the old days (before debugging), you had to use Response.Write() to put errors into the HTML that you could view using the View Source command of your browser. If you're using ASP.NET Model-View-Controller (MVC), there is still a place for that.

In today's development, `Response.Write()` is mostly used to do something that you want to do on every page that meets a certain criterion, no matter who coded it. You can add it to the code-behind of the master page and know that the output stream of the site will be altered directly. (You can download Online Chapter 3 by going to www.dummies.com, searching this book's title, and finding the Downloads tab.)

Securing ASP.NET

Book 3, Chapter 1 covers .NET security, and there is a whole book on ASP.NET security that you should read — *Writing Secure Code,* Second Edition (Microsoft Press) by Michael Howard and David LeBlanc. If you want to know about web security in general, check out *Security for Web Developers,* by John Paul Mueller (O'Reilly). This chapter provides an overview of `AspNetHostingPermission` in the `System.Web` namespace.

ASP.NET security is a complex topic. Because visitors to a website are anonymous, bypassing the Windows security system occurs often. That bypassing — called *impersonation* — allows IIS to do things on behalf of the user even if the user isn't really known to Windows. Remember, just because you have entered a username and password doesn't mean that Windows is okay with your credentials.

TECHNICAL STUFF

So ASP.NET websites are run most often with whatever permissions the IIS service is running with. Under normal conditions, this service is a fairly restricted account called Network Service. The fact is, however, that you really have no idea what the permissions will be because a hosting company most likely will be managing that. Your users can have administrative permissions, for all you know.

You can purposefully restrict the permissions of your users in your code. This prevents someone from finding a way through your code logic to call a method you don't want them to be able to call. The general idea is to trust no one. You want to pretend that most people who are going to run your code are the enemy. This strategy isn't any fun, but it's necessary today. There are prebuilt scripts to break into web pages — there doesn't even have to be a real person there to bust in.

TIP

Best practice in creating web applications is to set the configuration element to `High` for sites that you trust. When working with sites that you don't trust as much, such as partner web servers that access code from an external customer, you should set the configuration element attribute to `Medium`. Set the configuration element attribute for everyone else to `Low`, which means that many sites won't run, but it also means that your users will remain safe.

For the record, sites without a permission level set default to Full, which is obviously higher than either of those.

Changing trusts

To change the trust of a class, you want to decorate the class in the ASP.NET application with the hosting permission, like this:

```
using System;
using System.Web;
using System.Security.Permissions;

[AspNetHostingPermission(SecurityAction.Demand, Level=AspNetHostingPermissionLe
    vel.High)]
public class ApplicationClass
{
    //My Code is here.
}
```

So this code uses the High level. The others are None, Minimal, Low, Medium, and Unrestricted. Table 4-1 shows the general breakdown.

ASP.NET Permission Levels

AspNetHostingPermissionLevel	Description
None	Can't get anywhere. Don't ask.
Minimal	The code can execute, but it can't DO anything.
Low	You have read-only access to some restricted information, like the Request itself. Very rough.
Medium	More or less can look at anything — database, network, whatever. No write access.
High	Read/Write for any managed code, but can't run unmanaged (native) code.
Unrestricted	Full run of the box.

Fixing problems

The most common problem with web application security is the use of None or Minimal as a permission level. It's hard to know why Microsoft offers these choices. If you set the class to Minimal, nothing can get to anything. Stick to High for trusted environments, and Medium for shared servers.

Managing Files

The `Forms` collection contains all the data being sent back from the client. That includes any file that is being uploaded, using the multipart-data format. ASP.NET uses a two-part plan to get file data to you. Keep in mind that you can do this manually, but this all goes back to the idea behind the ASP.NET model. Controls on the front end; System.Web stuff on the back end.

Start with the Design View. All the user must do is select a local file, and the browser handles encoding the file and sending it up to the server. The file encoding standard is built into the protocol, as is HTML itself. Follow these steps to set up the upload:

1. **Create a** `FileUpload.aspx` **page in the current project by using the technique in the "Digging up the request data" section, earlier in this chapter.**

2. **Drag a** `FileUpload` **control from the Toolbox onto the design surface.**

3. **Drag a** `Button` **onto the surface.**

   The `Button` on the `FileUpload` control is just for selecting an item on your file system. You still need to postback the form.

   That gives you a good start. The `FileUpload` has a text box and a button that gives you access to the local file system. The `Button` provides a submit function.

   All the magic happens on the back end for this example. The browser handles the file upload for you. The server is your responsibility.

4. **Double-click the submit** `Button` **on the design surface to create a** `Button1_Click()` **event handler.**

5. **Add the following code to the** `Button1_Click()` **event handler:**

```
protected void Button1_Click(object sender, EventArgs e)
{
    String localPath = Server.MapPath("~/UploadedFiles/");

    if (FileUpload1.HasFile)
    {
        try
        {
            FileUpload1.PostedFile.SaveAs(
                localPath + FileUpload1.FileName);
        }
```

```
        catch (Exception ex)
        {
            Response.Write(ex.Message);
        }
    }
}
```

The example begins by creating a place to upload the file on the server. This folder is actually part of your project. To add it, right-click the project entry in Solution Explorer and choose Add⇨New Folder from the context menu. Type **UploadedFiles** as the folder name.

The remainder of the code verifies that there is actually a file to upload, and then attempts to perform the task. The try...catch block will report an error when the attempt fails. Note how you obtain an upload path for the file. The Server.MapPath() method returns the local path for the server, and you add the upload location to this path.

After you create and build your file upload application, you can test it to see whether it really does work. Run the application and exit as usual. In Solution Explorer, right-click the UploadedFiles folder and choose Open Folder in File Explorer. File Explorer opens, and you should see the file that you uploaded.

To build a comprehensive file upload function, you need a little more stringent programming practice, such as checking for the existence of another file with the same name. The idea here, though, is that there is a FileUpload control that gives you significant back-end control.

TIP

While you're here, take a look at the HttpFileCollection, which is the System. Web class that gives the FileUpload control its power. All the properties of the FileUpload control, such as the file's bits, name, and so on, are in the HttpFileCollection. Check it out if you need more fine-grained control than the FileUpload control gives you.

Baking Cookies

Cookies are a bit of data that could contain anything. They're the only thing that a website can directly save on a client machine without the client's direct permission. It still requires indirect permission in the sense that a user can disable cookies, but passively a cookie can be saved without anything asking the user, "Is it okay if I save this?"

Cookies are useful for state management. If you know the ID of the client's shopping cart, for instance, you can save that ID in a cookie, and even if the client goes away for a week and comes back, you still will be able to go back to the business layer and look up the information.

Cookies are stored in a collection — actually a dictionary — of keys and values. If you know what you're looking for, you can query the collection for the value you want; if you don't, you can loop through the collection until you find it.

The Cookies collection is managed using the Request and Response object, based on the HttpRequest and HttpResponse classes covered in the section "Surfing Web Streams," earlier in this chapter.

Coding for client-side storage

To get a cookie, you have to first leave a cookie. In part of the response to a client — say, after logging in — you can tell the platform to save information in the Cookies collection.

REMEMBER

Most cookies are plain text — anyone can read them. Never store something that can be used by someone wearing a proverbial black hat. Create a System.Guid (a globally unique identifier or GUID) and use that to track information. You can persist the GUID somewhere in your back-end data store.

Even better, store information about the session itself and have an understanding that the information will be removed from the database after some time limit. This prevents the impersonation of the user by someone who intercepts the cookie. There are a lot of options, but check out the best practices offered by Microsoft and other organizations before setting up your cookie strategy.

If you want to store information about the session in the cookie and tell the database that your customer is using that session, generate a GUID and save it in both places. You can retrieve the cookie at the next request, compare it to the available GUIDs in the User collection, and find the user in question. The following steps demonstrate how to work with cookies in ASP.NET.

1. **Create a** Cookies.aspx **page in the current project using the technique you used in the "Digging up the request data" section, earlier in this chapter.**

2. **Drag a** TextBox **control from the Toolbox onto the design surface.**

   This control will display the cookie value later.

3. **Set the** TextMode **property of the** TextBox **to** MultiLine **and the** ID **to** CookieValue.

Using a multiline control will make it easier to display the GUID.

4. **Drag a** Button **control from the Toolbox onto the design surface.**

The Button control will cause a postback so that you can obtain the cookie value.

5. **Set the** Text **property of the** Button **to** Get Cookie.

6. **Double-click anywhere on the form to access the code-behind and add the following code to the** Cookies **class:**

```
// The user making the request.
WebUser currentUser = new WebUser();

// A list of users who are working with the application.
List<WebUser> usersInDatabase = new List<WebUser>();

protected void Page_Load(object sender, EventArgs e)
{
    if (!Page.IsPostBack)
    {
        //This is a first request, so set the cookie
        Guid sessionGuid = new Guid();
        currentUser.SessionId = sessionGuid;

        //Tell the database about the new user
        usersInDatabase.Add(currentUser);

        //Set the cookie
        Response.Cookies.Add(
            new HttpCookie(
                "SessionId", sessionGuid.ToString()));
    }
    else
    {
        //The is a postback so we need to get the cookie
        string cookieSession = Request.Cookies.Get(
            "SessionId").Value.ToString();
        Guid sessionGuid = new Guid(cookieSession);

        // Obtain the user information from the database.
        var returningUser =
            from u in usersInDatabase
```

```
          where u.SessionId.ToString() == sessionGuid.ToString()
          select u;


     foreach (var user in returningUser)
     {
         //Better only be one
         currentUser = user;
     }


     // Output the cookie value.
     CookieValue.Text = cookieSession;
   }
}
```

The code consists of two sections: one to save the cookie and the other to get the cookie. The first section occurs automatically when you load the page the first time. The second section is executed after you click the Button on the user interface.

7. **Add the following** WebUser **class below the** Cookies **class:**

```
//This class would be in the library somewhere,
//not actually in this file.
public class WebUser
{
    public Guid SessionId { get; set; }
}
```

The WebUser class simply represents an application user in this case. In most cases, you add more information to the user, such as specifics about user identity. However, in this case, all you really need is a representation of any user.

8. **Run the application.**

The moment the page loads, the application saves the cookie. Of course, you can't see it. Click Get Cookie and now you see the GUID (which should be all zeros) displayed in CookieValue.

How ASP.NET manages cookies for you

A lot of the stuff that you used to store in a cookie is now managed by the ASP. NET engine. Session state, the most common example (discussed earlier in the "Surfing Web Streams" section), is now handled by the ViewState object. You can store information in the ViewState as you would in a variable, and the information is encoded for you and kept in a special field in the markup.

ViewState has its problems, and a lot of people don't like to use it. In fact, many ASP.NET applications in enterprises have turned it off to save bandwidth and prevent poor coding practices. In these cases, a return to cookies is your best bet to maintain a constant communication with the user.

Tracing with TraceContext

The TraceContext class provides all the detailed server processing information about a web page in ASP.NET. It is exposed in the code-behind as the Trace object and allows you to write messages to the trace log and the screen when certain things happen.

The benefit is that the Trace code runs only when you have tracing turned on. This gives programmers the option to leave tracing code in a working application without its impacting the performance or functionality.

This allows you to think about debugging while you code. It's important to assume that your application will break at some point as you build it. Programming is hard, and web programming is harder. Either you or the environment is likely to have a fault at some point. Why not make it easy on yourself later on down the road?

If you decide which parts of the application are most likely to have problems while you code them, you can insert trace messages as you go. It seems like a defeatist attitude, but really it's a realist attitude. Even if a problem is just caused by bad data in two years, you're probably going to spend some time debugging.

TIP

To use tracing, you can alter the @Page statement at the top of each page in the application, or you can alter the Web.config file. Altering the @Page statement is fine if you expect problems only with that page, but realistically, any page can break. If you want to set up the whole site for tracing, just add the following bold code to the Web.Config:

```
<configuration>
  <system.web>
    <trace enabled="true" requestLimit="40" localOnly="false" />
  </system.web>
</configuration>
```

Follow these steps to see tracing in action in the single page scenario:

1. Create a `Tracing.aspx` **page in the current project by using the technique you used in the "Digging up the request data" section, earlier in this chapter.**

2. **Add the** `Trace` **statement to the @page directive of the new Tracing.aspx page.**

```
<%@ Page Language="C#" AutoEventWireup="true"
    CodeBehind="Tracing.aspx.cs"
    Inherits="PerformRequest.Tracing"
    Trace="true" %>
```

3. **In the code-behind, add the following code to the** `Page_Load()` **event handler to fake an exception and catch it and then write to the Trace.**

```
protected void Page_Load(object sender, EventArgs e)
{
    try
    {
        throw new ApplicationException(
            "This is the fake exception.");
    }
    catch (ApplicationException ex)
    {
        Trace.Warn(ex.Message);
    }
}
```

4. **Press F5 to run the application.**

The page will look nothing like you expect. A ton of information is dumped on the page, `Response.Write` style, including the Trace message (check out Figure 4-3). Note that the warning message appears in red type in the Begin Load section of the output.

You don't want to show the user all of this, of course, but if you get word of a problem with the application, wouldn't it be nice to be able to turn on the Trace for the page in question? You could give it a little input and then see how the server processing details respond by using the Trace.

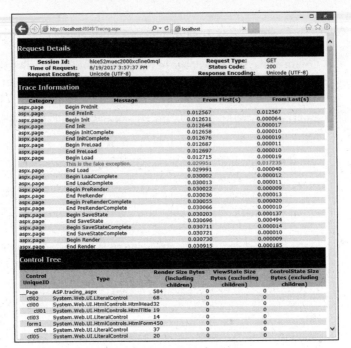

FIGURE 4-3:
An example of
ASP.NET tracing.

The figure shows a browser window at `http://localhost:49549/Tracing.aspx` with the following content:

Request Details

Session Id:	hlce52muec2000xcfine0mql	Request Type:	GET
Time of Request:	8/19/2017 3:57:37 PM	Status Code:	200
Request Encoding:	Unicode (UTF-8)	Response Encoding:	Unicode (UTF-8)

Trace Information

Category	Message	From First(s)	From Last(s)
aspx.page	Begin PreInit		
aspx.page	End PreInit	0.012567	0.012567
aspx.page	Begin Init	0.012631	0.000064
aspx.page	End Init	0.012648	0.000017
aspx.page	Begin InitComplete	0.012658	0.000010
aspx.page	End InitComplete	0.012676	0.000019
aspx.page	Begin PreLoad	0.012687	0.000011
aspx.page	End PreLoad	0.012697	0.000010
aspx.page	Begin Load	0.012715	0.000019
	This is the fake exception.	0.029951	0.017235
aspx.page	End Load	0.029991	0.000040
aspx.page	Begin LoadComplete	0.030002	0.000012
aspx.page	End LoadComplete	0.030013	0.000011
aspx.page	Begin PreRender	0.030022	0.000009
aspx.page	End PreRender	0.030036	0.000013
aspx.page	Begin PreRenderComplete	0.030055	0.000020
aspx.page	End PreRenderComplete	0.030066	0.000010
aspx.page	Begin SaveState	0.030203	0.000137
aspx.page	End SaveState	0.030696	0.000494
aspx.page	Begin SaveStateComplete	0.030711	0.000014
aspx.page	End SaveStateComplete	0.030721	0.000010
aspx.page	Begin Render	0.030730	0.000009
aspx.page	End Render	0.030915	0.000185

Control Tree

Control UniqueID	Type	Render Size Bytes (including children)	ViewState Size Bytes (excluding children)	ControlState Size Bytes (excluding children)
__Page	ASP.tracing_aspx	584	0	0
ctl02	System.Web.UI.LiteralControl	68	0	0
ctl00	System.Web.UI.HtmlControls.HtmlHead	32	0	0
ctl01	System.Web.UI.HtmlControls.HtmlTitle	19	0	0
ctl03	System.Web.UI.LiteralControl	14	0	0
form1	System.Web.UI.HtmlControls.HtmlForm	450	0	0
ctl04	System.Web.UI.LiteralControl	37	0	0
ctl05	System.Web.UI.LiteralControl	20	0	0

Navigating with Site Maps

A *site map* is an XML file that assists web design tools in formulating dynamic navigation. There has been a more interesting use for them recently, however. They are used by search engines for indexing your site better. The site https:// www.bing.com/toolbox/webmaster/ is a Microsoft product that makes your site more available to users of Bing. It uses the site map file to make your site more indexable. Check it out!

Search Engine Optimization (SEO) is a big topic these days, and site maps can make your life a lot easier. Search engines have set up readers that check for the site map and then use it to walk the file structure and make sure that the links to the site are accurate. To make a site map, follow these steps:

1. **Right-click the project and choose Add⇨New Item.**

2. **Select Site Map from the context menu.**

3. **Accept the default name,** Web.sitemap, **by clicking Add.**

4. **Modify the default template code to include all the projects for this chapter, as shown here:**

```xml
< <?xml version="1.0" encoding="utf-8" ?>
<siteMap
  xmlns="http://schemas.microsoft.com/AspNet/SiteMap-File-1.0" >
  <siteMapNode url="Default.aspx" title="Home"
               description="The main page">
    <siteMapNode url="TestRequest.aspx" title="Request"
               description="Coding for the Request"/>
    <siteMapNode url="FileUpload.aspx" title="File Upload"
               description="Upload files to your server"/>
    <siteMapNode url="Cookies.aspx" title="Cookies"
               description="Learn all about Cookies"/>
    <siteMapNode url="Tracing.aspx" title="Tracing"
               description="Configure an app for debugging"/>
  </siteMapNode>
</siteMap>
```

The template file shows you a guideline for adding the navigation of a site. If you have a number of files inside an About section, you make a <siteMap Node> of About; then, inside that (before the closing </sitemapnode>), you add the pages in that section, such as Contact Us or Our Story.

The site map is only part of the picture, though. You need some way to display it. Next you need to create some means of displaying the information, which could be a master page or just a simple Web Form, as used in this chapter.

5. Create a Default.aspx **page in the current project by using the technique you used in the "Digging up the request data" section, earlier in this chapter.**

6. **Add the following code between the opening and closing** <div> **tag to create controls to display the site map, as shown here:**

```xml
<!-- Shows the current path -->
<asp:SiteMapPath ID="SiteMapPath1" Runat="server">
</asp:SiteMapPath>

<!-- Specifies the data source -->
<asp:SiteMapDataSource ID="SiteMapDataSource1" Runat="server"/>

<!-- Displays the map in tree form -->
<asp:TreeView ID="TreeView1" Runat="Server"
    DataSourceID="SiteMapDataSource1">
</asp:TreeView>
```

When you run the example, you see the site map shown in Figure 4-4. Note how the TreeView reflects the hierarchical structure of the Web.sitemap. The Home page acts as an anchor for the entire site. Obviously, you can configure your site map as needed to meet your specific needs.

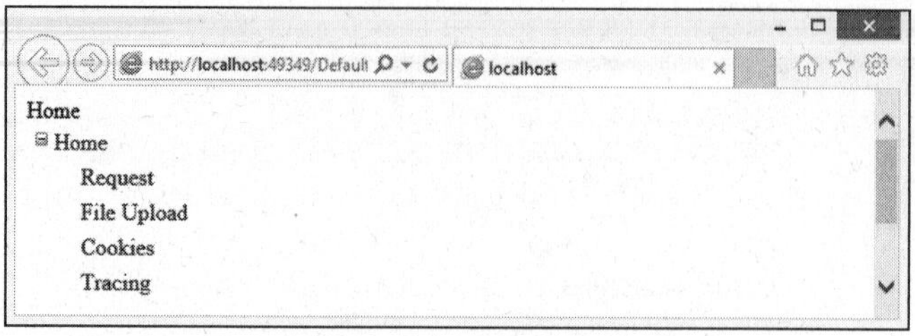

FIGURE 4-4:
The site map
should reflect
the hierarchy of
the content on
your site.

Navigating a site with SiteMap

With the web.sitemap file installed safely in the application, IIS now has a SiteMap collection that includes the XML file you made right there in memory. If you need to figure out what other pages are related to the page the user is viewing, you can do that. Follow these steps:

1. Drag an empty ListBox **control onto the** Default.aspx **page.**

2. Go to Code View.

3. Add the following code to Page_Load() **to loop through the items in the** SiteMap **collection and add items to the** ListBox.

```
protected void Page_Load(object sender, EventArgs e)
{
    // Reference the parent node to keep the object model happy.
    string baseNode = SiteMap.CurrentNode.Title;

    // Check to make sure there are subpages.
    if (SiteMap.CurrentNode.HasChildNodes)
    {
        foreach (SiteMapNode sitemapKids in
            SiteMap.CurrentNode.ChildNodes)
        {
            // Put the node name in the listbox.
            ListBox1.Items.Add(new ListItem(sitemapKids.Title));
        }
    }
}
```

If you get interested, put a debugger in the loop and check out that SiteMap object. It's a nice collection of the pages that have been referenced in the Web.sitemap file. Though this technology won't cure every navigational problem on every site, it is a nice, underused part of System.Web.

Index

Symbols

| operator, 82
|| operator, 83
& operator, 82
&& operator, 82
! operator, 81
^ operator, 82
+ (add) operator, 76
* (asterisk), 75, 76, 376, 662–663
} (closed curly brace), 19
: (colon), 648
{} (curly braces), 324
/ (divide) operator, 76
"" (double quotes), 36
// (double slash), 17
= (equals sign), 24, 82, 274
== (logical comparison), 81
- (minus sign), 16, 76, 376
% (modulo) operator, 76, 155
* (multiply) operator, 75, 76
?? (null coalescing operator), 220–221
|| (OR) operator, 111
+ (plus sign), 16, 376
# (pound sign), 376
[] (square brackets), 121, 161, 281
~ (tilde), 354, 376
/// (triple slash), 17

A

abstract class, 380, 381–383, 408–409
abstraction, 235–237
access control, 240–241, 306–312
access keywords, 446–452, 455–456
AccessControl namespace, 498
accessibility, of websites, 777–778

Accessibility for Everybody (Mueller), 778
accessing
  collections, 157–159, 160–165
  current objects, 290–298
  data foreach container, 159–160
  members of objects, 246
  namespace, 716–717
accessor methods, 307
accessors
  with access levels, 315
  expression-bodied, 326
AccumulateInterest() method, 342
Add button, 633
Add() method, 137, 139, 144, 170, 477–478
Add New Item dialog box, 638
add (+) operator, 76
adding
  command bindings, 717
  constraints, 195–197
  items to sets, 144
  projects, 607
  projects to solutions, 442–443
  structures to arrays, 480–481
  Web Forms, 768–769
addit method, 460
additall method, 464
AddRange() method, 137, 138, 144–145
Address() method, 290
Advanced Encryption Standard (AES), 492
Advanced section (Text Editor), 627
advertising events, 428–429
AES (Advanced Encryption Standard), 492
affected users, 488
alignment, 664
Allen, K. Scott (author)
  Professional ASP.NET MVC 5, 752

Allthis, 574

ALU (Arithmetic Logic Unit), 31

American National Standards Institute (ANSI), 525

American Standard Code for Information Interchange (ASCII), 525

anonymous methods, 426

ANSI (American National Standards Institute), 525

Apache (website), 730

App.config file, 636

Append() method, 74

Application.Resource tag, 649

applications

creating, 646–651

laying out, 654–655

viewing internals, 621

watching data, 620–621

web, 724–726

application-scoped resources, 648–649

App.xaml file, 649

architectures, for Visual Studio, 591

arguments

matching definitions with usage, 270

methods and, 267–275

passing to base class constructor, 347–348

Arithmetic Logic Unit (ALU), 31

arithmetic operators

about, 75

assignment operator, 77–78

increment operator, 78–79

operating orders, 76–77

simple, 75–76

Array class, 120–126, 160

ArrayList class, 178

arrays

adding structures to, 480–481

converting between lists and, 138

defined, 119

fixed-value, 121–122

initializing, 126, 141

Length property, 125–126

loops for each, 126–128

range of, 123

sorting, 128–132

of strings, 62

var for, 132–133

variable-length, 122–125

as operator, 343–344

ASCII (American Standard Code for Information Interchange), 525

AskForStrokes() method, 403

ASP.NET

about, 723–724

questioning clients, 726–730

securing, 789–790

web applications, 724–726

web servers, 730–734

ASP.NET 3.5 For Dummies (Cox), 736, 754

AsReadOnly() method, 405

assemblies, 305, 437–439, 438

assemblyinfo.cs file, 636

assigning

multiple catch blocks, 211–213

types, 85–86

assignment operators, 24, 77–78, 81

asterisk (*), 75, 76, 376, 662–663

asynchronous I/O, 524

At Startup drop-down list, 625–626

authentication

about, 488–489

using Windows login, 489–492

Authentication class, 545

Authorization namespace, 498, 545

Auto, 662

autocompleting, with IntelliSense, 613–614

auxiliary windows, 614–616

Average() method, 276–277

AverageAndDisplay() method, 268–269, 270, 272, 277

B

Balance() method, 311

BankAccount class, 302–305, 318, 333–336, 350–355, 380

BankAccount.Withdraw() method, 364–366

methods *(continued)*

IndexOfAny( ), 56, 67

Init( ), 293, 295, 318, 319, 353

InitBankAccount( ), 304, 318, 336

InitializeComponent( ), 709, 714

InitSavingsAccount( ), 336

InputInterestData( ), 263, 265

InputPositiveDecimal( ), 265

Insert( ), 74

instance, 258, 287–289

InstanceMethod( ), 258, 259

IntersectWith( ), 145–146

IsAllDigits( ), 58–60, 62

IsEmpty( ), 193

IsNullOrEmpty( ), 56

Join( ), 62

LastIndexOf( ), 56

LastIndexOfAny( ), 56

LookUpWordBreak( ), 266

Main( ), 20–21, 65, 151–152, 168–169, 171, 174, 188–189, 194, 205–206, 209–211, 219–220, 258, 263, 268–269, 285, 287, 291, 293, 295, 297–299, 305, 307, 317, 331, 336–337, 350, 353, 358, 367, 370, 400–401, 416, 445, 448–449, 528, 531, 538–539

MainWindow( ), 709

MakeAWithdrawal( ), 367, 370, 371, 372

MakeCalendar, 199

MakeSchedule, 200

Move( ), 407–408, 410

MoveNext( ), 158, 159, 171

MyCalc( ), 466

MyMethod( ), 159, 173

MyOtherObject( ), 322

NameFavorite( ), 377, 378

New, 465

Output( ), 268, 382

OutputBanner( ), 298

OutputInterestTable( ), 263

OutputName( ), 284, 287, 298

overloading, 271–272

overriding, 371–373, 481

Pad( ), 63–65

PadRight( ), 65, 394

Paint( ), 618

passing objects to, 283–285

Path.Combine( ), 531

Pop( ), 157

PositiveIntegers( ), 174

ProcessAmount( ), 342–343

Push( ), 157

Read( ), 249

ReadByte( ), 540–541

ReadChar( ), 540–541

ReadFileToConsole( ), 539

ReadLine( ), 51, 57, 93, 249, 539, 580

RecordShoppingList( ), 390

RedisplayDocument( ), 266

Remove( ), 55, 74

Reparagraph( ), 266

Replace( ), 55, 65–66, 73, 74

Reset( ), 158, 160

Response.Write( ), 788

Response.WriteFile( ), 788

Response.WriteSubstitution( ), 788

returning multiple values using tuples, 279–282

returning values, 275–279

SavingsAccount.Withdraw( ), 364–366

Schedule, 463

SetFirstName( ), 292

SetName( ), 285, 287, 289, 291, 293

signature of, 423

Sin( ), 275

SomeFunction( ), 575

SomeMethod( ), 203, 331, 341, 369

SomeOtherMethod( ), 205, 212–213, 331

Sort( ), 131, 200, 400–401

Split( ), 60–62, 67–68, 541

Start( ), 318

String.Concat( ), 52

String.GetType( ), 43

String.IndexOf( ), 217–218

String.Split( ), 60

structures and, 475

Student.SetName( ), 290–298

structures *(continued)*

  comparing to classes, 470–472

  creating, 472–479

  using as records, 479–481

`Student.SetName()` method, 290–298

style

  about, 749–750

  coding and, 750–751

  controls, 775–777

  n-tier code, 751

stylesheets, 747

subclass, 238

`SubClass` class, 330–331, 346–347, 354

submit buttons, 766–767

submitting input, 766–767

subscribing to events, 429

subscript, 160

substitutable classes, 341

`Substring()` method, 55, 56, 73

`Sum()` method, 299

surround snippets, 630–631

`sw.Close()` method, 531

switch statement, 53–54, 99–101, 224, 230–231

switchboards, running, 99–101

switching case in strings, 53–54

`SymmetricExceptWith()` method, 146

syntax

  collections, 134–135

  iterators, 171–172

`System.Data` namespace, 500–501, 503–513

`System.Drawing` namespace, 560–562, 564–570

`System.Net` namespace, 544–545, 547–557

`System.Security`, 498

T

`<T>`, 135

tables, development experience and, 759–760

`TabPanel`, 670

Tabs section (Text Editor), 627

`TakeANote()` method, 388

`TakeOff()` method, 363

tampering, 487

Target collections, 607

Task List window (Code Editor), 616

tasks

  delegating, 415

  performing, 714–715

Technical Stuff icon, 3

ternary operator, 96

test, 593

`Test()` method, 276

testing

  class libraries, 444–446

  classes, 164–165

`Test.Main()` method, 457

text, 525, 561–562

Text Editor, 626

text input controls, 760–762

`TextBlock` contol, 672–673

`TextBox` control, 673, 692

`TextMode` property, 760, 761

`TextReader` class, 523

`TextWriter` class, 523

`this` keyword, 292–293, 293–296

throwing

  exceptions, 207

  expressions, 220–221

thumbprint security, 486

tilde (~), 354, 376

Tip icon, 3

`ToArray()` method, 138, 477

`ToBankAccountString()` method, 336

`ToBoolean()` method, 58

`ToDouble()` method, 58

`ToFloat()` method, 58

Toggle Artboard Background button (Visual Studio), 600

`ToInt32()` method, 58

`ToLower()` method, 54

`ToNameString()` method, 289, 298

X

Y

About the Author

John Mueller is a freelance author and technical editor. He has writing in his blood, having produced 104 books and more than 600 articles to date. The topics range from networking to artificial intelligence and from database management to heads-down programming. Some of his current works include a book about machine learning, a couple of Python books, and a book about MATLAB. He has also written *AWS For Admins For Dummies*, which provides administrators with a great place to start with AWS, and *AWS For Developers For Dummies*, the counterpart for developers. His technical editing skills have helped more than 70 authors refine the content of their manuscripts. John has always been interested in development and has written about a wide variety of languages, including a highly successful C++ book. Be sure to read John's blog at http://blog.johnmuellerbooks.com/. You can reach John on the Internet at John@JohnMuellerBooks.com.

Dedication

To Rebecca. You're in my heart forever!

Acknowledgments

Thanks to my wife, Rebecca. Even though she is gone now, her spirit is in every book I write, in every word that appears on the page. She believed in me when no one else would.

Russ Mullen deserves thanks for his technical edit of this book. He greatly added to the accuracy and depth of the material you see here. Russ worked exceptionally hard in helping with the research for this book by locating hard-to-find URLs and also offering a lot of suggestions. This was also an especially difficult book because of the changes involved in moving to C# 7.0 and Visual Studio 2017. There were a lot of really tough decisions that Russ helped me make.

Matt Wagner, my agent, deserves credit for helping me get the contract in the first place and taking care of all the details that most authors don't really consider. I always appreciate his assistance. It's good to know that someone wants to help.

Finally, I would like to thank Katie Mohr, Susan Christophersen, and the rest of the editorial and production staff at John Wiley & Sons, Inc. for their unparalleled support of this writing effort.

Publisher's Acknowledgments

Executive Editor: Steve Hayes

Project Manager and Copy Editor: Susan Christophersen

Technical Editor: Russ Mullen

Sr. Editorial Assistant: Cherie Case

Production Editor: Antony Sami

Cover Image: © whiteMocca/Shutterstock

Take dummies with you everywhere you go!

Whether you are excited about e-books, want more from the web, must have your mobile apps, or are swept up in social media, dummies makes everything easier.

Find us online!

dummies.com

dummies
A Wiley Brand

Leverage the power

Dummies is the global leader in the reference category and one of the most trusted and highly regarded brands in the world. No longer just focused on books, customers now have access to the dummies content they need in the format they want. Together we'll craft a solution that engages your customers, stands out from the competition, and helps you meet your goals.

Advertising & Sponsorships

Connect with an engaged audience on a powerful multimedia site, and position your message alongside expert how-to content. Dummies.com is a one-stop shop for free, online information and know-how curated by a team of experts.

- Targeted ads
- Video
- Email Marketing
- Microsites
- Sweepstakes sponsorship

20 MILLION PAGE VIEWS
EVERY SINGLE MONTH

15 MILLION UNIQUE
VISITORS PER MONTH

43% OF ALL VISITORS ACCESS THE SITE
VIA THEIR MOBILE DEVICES

700,000 NEWSLETTER SUBSCRIPTIONS
TO THE INBOXES OF
300,000 UNIQUE INDIVIDUALS EVERY WEEK

# of dummies

Custom Publishing

Reach a global audience in any language by creating a solution that will differentiate you from competitors, amplify your message, and encourage customers to make a buying decision.

- Apps
- Books
- eBooks
- Video
- Audio
- Webinars

Brand Licensing & Content

Leverage the strength of the world's most popular reference brand to reach new audiences and channels of distribution.

For more information, visit dummies.com/biz

...ONAL ENRICHMENT

Staying Sharp

9781119187790
USA $26.00
CAN $31.99
UK £19.99

Facebook

Carolyn Abram

9781119179030
USA $21.99
CAN $25.99
UK £16.99

Guitar

Mark Phillips
Jon Chappell

9781119293354
USA $24.99
CAN $29.99
UK £17.99

Investing

Eric Tyson, MBA

9781119293347
USA $22.99
CAN $27.99
UK £16.99

Beekeeping

9781119310068
USA $22.99
CAN $27.99
UK £16.99

Digital Photography

Julie Adair King

9781119235606
USA $24.99
CAN $29.99
UK £17.99

Meditation

Stephan Bodian

9781119251163
USA $24.99
CAN $29.99
UK £17.99

Pregnancy

9781119235491
USA $26.99
CAN $31.99
UK £19.99

Samsung Galaxy S7

Bill Hughes

9781119279952
USA $24.99
CAN $29.99
UK £17.99

iPhone

Edward C. Baig
Bob "Dr. Mac" LeVitus

9781119283133
USA $24.99
CAN $29.99
UK £17.99

Crocheting

Karen Manthey
Susan Brittain

9781119287117
USA $24.99
CAN $29.99
UK £16.99

Nutrition

Carol Ann Rinzler

9781119130246
USA $22.99
CAN $27.99
UK £16.99

PROFESSIONAL DEVELOPMENT

Windows 10

Andy Rathbone

9781119311041
USA $24.99
CAN $29.99
UK £17.99

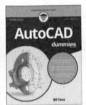

AutoCAD

Bill Fane

9781119255796
USA $39.99
CAN $47.99
UK £27.99

Excel 2016

Greg Harvey, PhD

9781119293439
USA $26.99
CAN $31.99
UK £19.99

QuickBooks 2017

Stephen L. Nelson, MBA, CPA, MS in Taxation

9781119281467
USA $26.99
CAN $31.99
UK £19.99

macOS Sierra

Bob "Dr. Mac" LeVitus

9781119280651
USA $29.99
CAN $35.99
UK £21.99

LinkedIn

Joel Elad, MBAs

9781119251132
USA $24.99
CAN $29.99
UK £17.99

Windows 10

Woody Leonhard

9781119310563
USA $34.00
CAN $41.99
UK £24.99

SharePoint 2016

Rosemarie Withee
Ken Withee

9781119181705
USA $29.99
CAN $35.99
UK £21.99

Fundamental Analysis

Matt Krantz

9781119263593
USA $26.99
CAN $31.99
UK £19.99

Networking

Doug Lowe

9781119257769
USA $29.99
CAN $35.99
UK £21.99

Office 2016

Wallace Wang

9781119293477
USA $26.99
CAN $31.99
UK £19.99

Office 365

Rosemarie Withee
Ken Withee
Jennifer Reed

9781119265313
USA $24.99
CAN $29.99
UK £17.99

Salesforce.com

Liz Kao
Jon Paz

9781119239314
USA $29.99
CAN $35.99
UK £21.99

Coding

Nikhil Abraham

9781119293323
USA $29.99
CAN $35.99
UK £21.99

Learning Made Easy

ACADEMIC

9781119293576
USA $19.99
CAN $23.99
UK £15.99

9781119293637
USA $19.99
CAN $23.99
UK £15.99

9781119293491
USA $19.99
CAN $23.99
UK £15.99

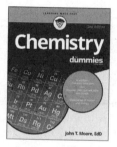

9781119293460
USA $19.99
CAN $23.99
UK £15.99

9781119293590
USA $19.99
CAN $23.99
UK £15.99

9781119215844
USA $26.99
CAN $31.99
UK £19.99

9781119293378
USA $22.99
CAN $27.99
UK £16.99

9781119293521
USA $19.99
CAN $23.99
UK £15.99

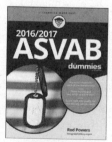

9781119239178
USA $18.99
CAN $22.99
UK £14.99

9781119263883
USA $26.99
CAN $31.99
UK £19.99

Available Everywhere Books Are Sold

dummies.com

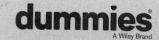

A Wiley Brand

nall books for big imaginations

GETTING STARTED WITH Coding
Get Creative With Code!
Camille McCue, PhD

9781119177173
USA $9.99
CAN $9.99
UK £8.99

MODDING Minecraft™
Build Your Own Minecraft Mods!
Sarah Guthals, PhD
Stephen Foster, PhD
Lindsey Handley, PhD

9781119177272
USA $9.99
CAN $9.99
UK £8.99

MAKING YouTube VIDEOS
Star in Your Own Video!
Nick Willoughby

9781119177241
USA $9.99
CAN $9.99
UK £8.99

DESIGNING Digital Games
Create Games with Scratch™!
Derek Breen

9781119177210
USA $9.99
CAN $9.99
UK £8.99

GETTING STARTED WITH Raspberry Pi®
Program Your Raspberry Pi™!
Richard Wentk

9781119262657
USA $9.99
CAN $9.99
UK £6.99

EXPERIMENTING WITH Science
Think, Test, and Learn!
Camille McCue, PhD

9781119291336
USA $9.99
CAN $9.99
UK £6.99

CREATING Digital Animations
Animate Stories with Scratch™!
Derek Breen

9781119233527
USA $9.99
CAN $9.99
UK £6.99

GETTING STARTED WITH Engineering
Think Like an Engineer!
Camille McCue, PhD

9781119291220
USA $9.99
CAN $9.99
UK £6.99

WRITING Computer Code
Learn the Language of Computers!
Chris Minnick and Eva Holland

9781119177302
USA $9.99
CAN $9.99
UK £8.99

Unleash Their Creativity

dummies.com

dummies®
A Wiley Brand